Memory in Oral Traditions

MEMORY IN ORAL TRADITIONS

The Cognitive Psychology of Epic, Ballads, and Counting-out Rhymes

DAVID C. RUBIN

New York   Oxford
OXFORD UNIVERSITY PRESS
1995

Oxford University Press

Oxford   New York
Athens   Auckland   Bangkok   Bombay
Calcutta   Cape Town   Dar es Salaam   Delhi
Florence   Hong Kong   Istanbul   Karachi
Kuala Lumpur   Madras   Madrid   Melbourne
Mexico City   Nairobi   Paris   Singapore
Taipei   Tokyo   Toronto

and associated companies in
Berlin   Ibadan

Copyright © 1995 by Oxford University Press, Inc.

Published by Oxford University Press, Inc.,
200 Madison Avenue, New York, New York 10016

Oxford is a registered trademark of Oxford University Press

Library of Congress Cataloging-in-Publication Data
Rubin, David C.
Memory in oral traditions :
the cognitive psychology of epic, ballads, and counting-out rhymes /
David C. Rubin.
p.   cm. Includes bibliographical references and index.
ISBN 0-19-508211-7
1. Oral tradition.   2. Memory.
3. Counting-out rhymes—History and criticism.
4. Ballads—North Carolina—History and criticism.
5. Epic literature—History and criticism.   I. Title.
GR67.R83   1995 153.1'33—dc20   94-8997

Page v constitutes an extension of the copyright page.

1 3 5 7 9 8 6 4 2

Printed in the United States of America
on acid-free paper

To
Evelyn, Shira,
and Ariel

PREFACE

I proposed writing this book in 1983, because by then I believed that I understood the phenomenon of gesture sufficiently well to expound upon it at length. No doubt this self-deception served a useful purpose. I doubt now that I would have set out on a project of such vastness if I had known that it would take nearly ten years to finish.

McNeill, 1992, p. 5

Our parents have graciously agreed to take responsibility for any mistakes remaining in the book.

Moulton & Robinson, 1981, p. xvi

In 1977 Leo Treitler invited me to take part in a roundtable, "Transmission and Form in Oral Traditions," at the Twelfth Congress of the International Musicological Society. There I learned how Gregorian chant, jazz, and other forms of music were handed down through memory with continual variation, but without large, systematic changes. Musicologists documented and analyzed their material with great care and skill, but the mechanisms of transmission were not well known. For the most part, musicologists did not know that psychologists knew anything useful about memory, and psychologists did not know that musicologists had exquisitely analyzed an impressive feat of memory. I read further in the interdisciplinary field of oral traditions and found theoretical speculations about narrative structure and imagery that paralleled those in psychology. The mutual ignorance held the promise of double-blind, converging evidence and increased theoretical sophistication. Here was a highly efficient way to increase our understanding both of oral traditions and of human memory. What we knew about memory from the theories and methods of cognitive psychology came mostly from people and situations in which memory performance was not impressive. Here was a case where memory worked extraordinarily well. As soon as I got tenure, I started on the project in earnest. This book is the result.

From this brief history, it follows that this book is an attempt to understand stability and change in oral traditions from the point of view of a cognitive psychologist. The goal is to increase our understanding of both oral traditions and the human memory that supports them. Oral literature is discussed from an empirical framework; that is, I write about what I can measure. Such an approach has limitations, but it provides an interesting addition to much of what has gone before.

The task is ambitious, and therefore much is omitted. Three genres are considered in detail, but little is said about any others. A review of cognitive psychology is provided as it applies to oral traditions, but such a review omits much from the field. A massive integration is attempted, but it is motivated by a phenomenon in search of a theory, not a theory in search of support. Extensive references are given so that scholars can enter disciplines other than their own, but scholars will therefore find their favorite relevant references replaced with unfamiliar ones.

Books that merge many disciplines, each with its own terms and assumptions, can be difficult to read. Therefore, I have tried to simplify the reader's task, often at the cost of elegance. To this end, each chapter begins with an overview and ends with a brief conclusion, much as a textbook might. In addition, I have tried to put many of the points that would be of interest only to a specialist, as well as all statistics and details of unpublished studies, in notes at the end of chapters. Moreover, in my attempt to be intelligible to readers in many disciplines, I have erred on the side of being pedantic. Common terms in one field are often followed by an explanation.

Many people have helped with this book in many ways.

At Duke, Shari Alexander and Hazel Carpenter typed early versions of the text when there still were typewriters and later helped with the word processing. Edna Bissette made editorial improvements. Susan Havrilesky and Susan Dovenbarger drew most of the figures. Kevin Mallory helped with data analysis.

Many Lawrence and Duke University undergraduates took an active role in the project, including Bobbie Brown, who collected the children's counting-out rhyme data, and Erin Cooperrider and David Talbert, who began the study of Beatles' songs with Ira Hyman, Jr. I owe special thanks to Helen Clarke, who helped design and run an experiment to test Duke undergraduates' knowledge of counting-out rhymes and who took part in my first attempts to measure the objective properties of the counting-out rhymes. Numerous other undergraduates worked as paid assistants, collecting, counting, and checking the data presented here.

A generation or two of graduate students at Duke helped change my thinking in various ways, including especially Elise Axelrad, Kelly Braun, Linda Garro, Barbara Houston, Brian Meyer, Kirsten Nielsen, Cheryl Pou, Chris Puto, Caroline Roe, Matt Schulkind, Charles Vance, Wanda Wallace, Maria Watson, and Jenny Zervakis. Their work often finds its way into the citations, but more often than not, they were part of an ongoing discussion that became absorbed, and from their perspective often distorted, in this volume. In some cases, the student's work became a major part of the book. Brian Meyer, who received a Ph.D. in clinical psychology at Duke, had written an undergraduate honors thesis at Harvard under the direction of Albert Lord. I report his undergraduate work, with extensions, in Chapter 2, and our interaction led to the analysis of scripts in Chapter 9. Over the course of the research reported in the book, Wanda Wallace progressed from a graduate student working with another faculty member in my department, to a Ph.D. research associate on the grant funding our research, to a co-principal investigator, to a faculty member in Duke's Fuqua School of Business. We started by collaborating closely and now work independently on many of the same questions. She first introduced me to ballads as a living tradition in North Carolina during a course I was teaching on memory and oral traditions, and her expertise on ballads helped shape our work in that area.

Institutional support has been crucial. Lawrence University, in part because of its small size but more because of its intellectual nature, provided an environment in which interdisciplinary ideas developed naturally. My colleagues at Duke valued and encouraged projects like this one that were a bit out of the traditional. Most of the writing was completed during two sabbaticals. The Medical Research Council: Applied Psychology Unit in Cambridge, England, was an exciting and congenial place to learn and try out ideas. My stay there was made possible with a Raymond McKeen Cattell Fund Sabbatical Award. The Netherlands Institute of Advanced Studies in the Humanities and Social Sciences, through funding from the Royal Netherlands Academy of Arts and Sciences, provided a chance for me to learn more about what was known of oral traditions in the humanities and to try to make myself clear to a range of humanists. Our Orality and Literacy Theme Group, organized by Saskia Kersenboom and Wim Gerritsen, was a lively and stimulating forum. The importance of such supportive homes, and homes away from home, cannot be overstressed. The National Science Foundation, through its Human Cognition and Perception Program headed by Joe Young, has provided funding for this research for the past decade under Grants BNS-8410124 and BNS-9010074. This funding afforded me the luxury of conducting experiments and collecting naturalistic data that otherwise would not have been possible.

Many scholars were generous with their time, providing criticism of chapters in their area of expertise. These include Roger Abrahams, Flemming Andersen, Egbert Bakker, Franz Bauml, Diskin Clay, Herb Crovitz, Wim Gerritsen, Lynn Hasher, Doug Hintzman, Greg Kimble, Albert Lord, Marc Marschark, Makiko Naka, Ulric Neisser, Don Norman, Holger Nygard, Iona Opie, Alan Paivio, Matt Serra, Barbara Herrnstein Smith, Keith Stanley, Brian Sutton-Smith, Kees Vellekoop, and Wanda Wallace. Elise Axelrad and Ian Hunter provided criticism on the entire book informally, and Roger Brown, John Miles Foley, and David Pillemer provided formal reviews through Oxford University Press. Joan Bossert was a most encouraging, energetic, and helpful editor. She, Helen Greenberg and Irene Pavitt transformed my manuscript into a more clearly written book. I owe all these people more than I can acknowledge for replacing my ignorance with their detailed knowledge, for their gentle but hard questions, and for their encouragement. I hope this volume is a partial return on the debt.

Through it all, my family has provided support, and it is to them that I dedicate this book.

April 1994   D. C. R.
Durham, N.C.

CONTENTS

Memory in Oral Traditions

CHAPTER 1

Introduction

Traditions that are carried entirely in human memory without a external mnemonic aids are of obvious relevance to a science that would have something to
say about long-term retention and retrieval. Indeed from a descriptive point of
view, one may consider any corpus of folkloric texts as a "natural experiment"
in memorization conducted on the grandest of scales: with a cast of thousands
performing across periods of centuries.

Vikis-Freibergs, 1984, p. 326

There is one last thing to be said about my research style. It has always started
with a phenomenon and only later become theoretical. . . . I have tended to
pick some mystery and poke it and prod it and turn it all round in an effort to
figure it out. . . . While no one seems to recommend a phenomenon-centered
approach to research, it can be argued that its record is at least as good as that of
theory-centered work.

Brown, 1989, p. 50

This chapter provides the motivation for the book and a guide for its reading. In the
first section, the basic phenomenon is described: oral traditions, which rely on
human memory for storage and oral/aural means for transmission, change little over
long periods, though they do change from telling to telling. The second section is a
brief overview of the assumptions of the study and the topics included. Following
Roger Brown's strategy, which begins this chapter, I take as my "mystery" the
transmission of oral traditions, and I "poke it" and "prod it" with a wide range of
literatures and theories. Like Brown, I start with the phenomenon.

The Phenomenon

The transmission of oral traditions is remarkable to the modern, literate observer.
Songs, stories, and poems are kept in stable form in memory for centuries without
the use of writing, whereas the literate observer has trouble remembering what
happened yesterday without notes. This book examines the mechanisms for this

stability and for change in oral traditions. To begin, examples are provided from the three genres considered in detail in this book: counting-out rhymes, epic, and ballads.

Counting-out rhymes are the most common of the three genres, and the most common of these in English is *Eenie Meenie*. The variant recalled most frequently by Duke undergraduates is

> Eenie, meenie, miney, mo,
> Catch a tiger by the toe.
> If he hollers, let him go.
> Eenie, meenie, miney, mo.

This rhyme in this form has remained stable for over a century. There have been only two systematic changes, though many variants exist now and many existed 100 years ago. One systematic change is the word *hollers*. Until recently it was an American word, but not a British word, and so *hollers* was replaced for a period in the United Kingdom by *squeals*. The second change is that *tiger* is a recent modification of the rhyme; the original word was expunged by social forces occurring outside the genre starting at around the time of World War II. The time course and selection of this substitution are examined in detail in Chapter 10, but for now, what is important to note is that a piece from an oral tradition remained remarkably stable. Moreover, it is difficult to see how writing or other external memory aids could have played a large role in its stability. The piece remained stable in the collective memory of English-speaking children worldwide. If we knew how this happened, we would know a good deal about the genre of counting-out rhymes, about cultural transmission, and about human memory.

Epic poetry, at least the South Slavic epic, for which a large database exists, is not as stable. The plot, the rhythm, the general cast of characters, the formulaic descriptions of characters and places, and other aspects of the genre and the piece remain stable, but the exact words sung do not. Changes in meaning and form are apparent to a literate reader with a written text, but these do not affect the basic organization. For instance, the particular leaders that form an assembly, and the particular way in which a hero arms, disguises, or is shown hospitality can all vary from singing to singing, with the resulting versions being judged to be the same by expert singers. As an example, consider the following translations by Lord (1960, pp. 74–75) of two beginnings of the same epic sung by Petar Vidić, a year and a half apart.[1] The same general meaning is transmitted in the same style in both cases, but many words change:

> Marko Kraljević is drinking wine
> With his old mother,
> And with his true love,
> And with his only sister.
> When Marko had drunk his wine,
> Then Marko brimmed the glass
> To the health of his old mother,
> And his love and his only sister.
> "Expect the sun and the moon,

But me Marko never!''
And his old mother asked him:
"Whither are you going, Marko my only son?''
Marko Kraljević spoke:
"I am going, mother, to the sultan's army
For a period of nine years.''

August 1933

Kraljević Marko arose early
In Prilip in his white tower,
And next him his old mother,
And next the mother his true love,
And next his love his sister Andija.
He toasted them in clear brandy:
"Yesterday a brief letter arrived
From the sultan, illustrious czar.
The sultan summons me to the army,
To serve him for nine years.''

December 1934

Lord presents six variants of the beginning of this epic by the same singer from which the two examples presented are drawn. In the first version given here, the hero is drinking wine; in the second version given here, clear brandy; in two other versions, brandy; in one, nothing; and in another, coffee. In the first version given here, the location of the hero is not stated; in the second version given here and in one other, he is in Prilip in his white tower; in the three other versions, he is in his white tower. What the hero drinks and whether his location is stated to an audience that probably knows where the hero lived are not central to the story. They are details that are added for poetic, rhythmic, or narrative purposes. Like the other differences between the two versions presented, they do not affect the story. After hearing two versions of a long epic with similar differences, even a literate audience with a clear concept of what *verbatim* means to a scholar analyzing the texts might say that they were exactly the same.

Compared with counting-out rhymes and epics, ballads are intermediate in length and stability. As in the epics, the general properties, or constraints, remain stable. In addition, the exact words change more slowly. Here, however, unlike the counting-out rhymes and many of Lord's examples, writing, in the form of broadsides, cannot be ruled out as a stabilizing influence over part of the transmission. Table 11.1 provides several variants of verses of a ballad along with full references, from which were taken the following two relatively stable variants of the same verse recorded more than two centuries apart:

This brown Bride had a little Penknife,
That was both long and sharp,
And betwixt the short Ribs and the long,
Prick'd fair Ellinor to the Heart.

London 1723

The brown girl having a little pen knife,
The blade was keen and sharp,

> Right between fair Ellen's ribs
> She pierced her to the heart.
>
> Wanchese, North Carolina, 1941

Not all ballad verses remain as stable. Here are verses from a different ballad covering about the same period:

> Then spoke the little ship boy
> In the Neather-lands
> Then spoke the little ship boy
> In the Neather-lands
> Master, master what will you give me
> And I will take this false gallaly
> And release the Sweet Trinity
> Sailing in the Low-lands
>
> I'll give thee gold and I'le give thee fee
> In the Neather-lands
> I'll give thee gold and I'le give thee fee
> In the Neather-lands
> And my eldest daughter thy wife shall be
> Sailing in the Low-lands
>
> London, 1680s (Child, 1898, 286A)

> Up steps a little cabin boy, saying, "What'll you give me
> If I will sink her in the saltwater sea,
> As she sails on the lowland lonesome low,
> As she sails on the saltwater sea?"
>
> "I have a house, and I have lands,
> And I have an only daughter, who shall be at your command,
> If you will sink her in the lowland low,
> If you will sink her in the saltwater sea."
>
> Zionville, North Carolina, 1914 (White, 1952, 147A)

In both ballad examples, the same basic ideas and some of the poetic structure remained stable over two centuries. In the first pair of verses, the rhythm and most of the exact words are the same. In the second pair of verses, the alliterative *Low-lands* remained and expanded to the *lowland lonesome low,* though its reference to the Netherlands was lost.

Drawing from the literature on oral traditions as a whole, transmission cannot be viewed as verbatim recall of the fixed texts of literate readers. Remembering a piece from an oral tradition does not require the recall of exact words: recall of the general meaning and form is sufficient. Even *Eenie Meenie* varies on retelling, as is seen in Chapter 10. In particular, Hunter (1984, 1985) has convincingly argued that there are no documented cases of pieces over 50 words long being recalled verbatim in any oral tradition without a parallel written record available to the singers. In fact, the whole concept of verbatim recall requires a record other than human memory; otherwise, it can only mean accurate within the limits of human memory. Variability within limits can aid long-term stability in two ways. First, variability allows a singer to adapt a piece to suit individual habits and needs, and in this way to develop an easier-to-recall variant that would be less likely to disappear from the singer's repertoire than the original. Second, the ability to produce songs with variability instead of in a fixed form allows the singer to alter a piece to suit a particular audience, situation, or change in culture (as described in Chapter 6) without distorting the basic organization. Singers may report that they repeat a piece word for word, but their actions do not support their claim (Goody, 1987; Hunter, 1984, 1985; Lord, 1960). For instance, in spite of South Slavic epic poets' claims of verbatim recall,

> there is nothing in the poet's experience (or even ours if we listen to the same song from several singers and to the same singer telling the same song several times) to give him any idea that a theme can be expressed in only one set of words. Those singers whom he has heard have never reproduced a theme in exactly the same words, and he has no feeling that to do so is necessary or even normal practice. (Lord, 1960, p. 69)

Bartlett (1932) makes a similar point by analogy to another instance where rapid performance is required:

> Suppose I am making a stroke in a quick game, such as tennis or cricket. . . . When I make the stroke I do not, as a matter of fact, produce something absolutely new, and I never merely repeat something old. . . . I may say, I may think that I reproduce exactly a series of text-book movements, but demonstrably I do not; just as, under other circumstances, I may say and think that I reproduce exactly some isolated event which I want to remember, and again demonstrably I do not. (pp. 201–202)

Some rituals, like *Eenie Meenie,* are intended to be recalled verbatim. But even here the evidence is that verbatim recall in an oral culture means no more than accurate within the limits of human memory.

It is not just that verbatim memory is absent. What I claim, and what is more intriguing, is that one specific variant of a song is not being transmitted at all. Rather, what is being transmitted is the theme of the song, its imagery, its poetics, and some specific details. A verbatim text is not being transmitted, but instead an organized set of rules or constraints that are set by the piece and its tradition. In literary terms, this claim makes the structure of the genre central to the production of the piece. In psychological terms, this claim is an argument for schemas that involve imagery and poetics as well as meaning.[2]

In many situations, oral traditions provide a more appropriate model of everyday human behavior than do psychological experiments on memory. At times, people do have to remember what exactly happened on one particular occasion, as in eyewitness testimony. It is much more common, however, to abstract and remember the structure from many similar events, no one of which by itself is the best version. In general, people are better suited for the more common task (Bartlett, 1932; Neisser, 1981; Rubin, 1986).

Nonetheless, there are great differences in stability between oral traditions and most everyday activity. Consider our most common analog. The changes that occur in the transmission of rumors in the laboratory are so great that after a message passes through a handful of people, it is often difficult to see any relation to the original. In the laboratory, the message shortens, details are dropped, and changes in meaning are introduced (Allport & Postman, 1947; Bartlett, 1932). Oral traditions are much more stable. One set of mechanisms can account for both the instability of rumors and the stability of oral traditions when details of the methods of transmission and the nature of the material transmitted are considered, as is done in the first six chapters of this book.

Having provided some indication of the stability of the oral traditions considered in the book, I present a brief list of other properties. Not all properties hold for all traditions, and some properties follow directly from the working definition of an oral tradition as a genre of literature transmitted for long periods of time with minimal use of external memory aids. No one property that I can find is a defining feature, and the differences among genres are so great as to make general statements like these vague. For a given genre, in a given language, in a given culture, at a given time period, much more can be said (Foley, 1990, pp. 3–19). Nonetheless, the list reveals a sense of the phenomenon, and the properties that do not follow from the definition provide hints worth following in uncovering the mystery of the stability of oral traditions.[3] Oral traditions

- Are universal; that is, they appear in all present cultures and past cultures that have been studied.
- Are fixed only within the accuracy of human memory.
- Exist in genres; that is, they appear in restricted, coherent forms.
- Are transmitted in a special social situation, such as a performance or a ritual.
- Are entertaining by modern literate standards, though this is not always their primary traditional function.
- Are considered as special speech, either art or ritual.
- Transmit useful cultural information or increase group cohesion.
- Are poetic, using rhyme, alliteration, assonance, or some repetition of sound pattern.
- Are rhythmic.
- Are sung.
- Are narratives.
- Are high in imagery, both spatial and descriptive.

Understanding the Phenomenon

The Approach

The general approach used throughout is that outlined by Roger Brown in the quote that begins this chapter. As he notes, it is not a common one in psychology. A brief justification and explanation is therefore in order. A form of this approach was once more popular:

> During the years 1900 to 1930, studies of verbal learning were carried out largely by a group of psychologists calling themselves *functionalists*. . . . The guiding idea was to dissect any given task, such as serial verbal learning, into a number of components or constituent skills, and to analyze these experimentally. The concern with empirical description led researchers to avoid the global theories and their associated controversies

that raged in the animal conditioning laboratories; instead verbal learning researchers thought the truth would be revealed by patient empirical analysis of specific learning tasks. (Bower & Hilgard, 1981, pp. 134–135)

The phenomenon-centered approach is among the best ways to advance science. But unlike the functionalism of much of the early verbal learning, it cannot be used without knowledge and application of numerous theories. For the study of oral traditions, much is known in dozens of fields that cannot be applied without theory. In fact, more theory must be known and applied in phenomenon-centered than in theory-driven psychological research because when a phenomenon is chosen for study, the theories that will turn out to be applicable cannot easily be limited. Moreover, because the focus of this research is a particular problem rather than a particular theory, theories are evaluated in ways and under conditions for which they were not initially devised or tested. In this way, flaws in theories that were difficult to see in the paradigms under which they were devised may become obvious.

Support for a similar approach comes from Newell (1973). He argued against the dichotomies that often come with theory-driven research in psychology. He suggested that

an alternative is to focus a series of experimental and theoretical studies around a single complex task, the aim being to demonstrate that one has a sufficient theory of a genuine slab of human behavior. All of the studies would be designed to fit together and add up to a total picture in detail. (p. 303)

This book is a start. For the complex task of transmitting oral traditions, I will describe naturalistic observations, formulate hypotheses to account for them, search the existing literature for tests of these hypotheses, devise new tests, modify the hypotheses as needed, and combine them into a comprehensive model.

The approach outlined is not a replacement for research driven by a single theory or a single laboratory paradigm. However, because of the dominance of such theory-driven research in cognitive psychology, the approach outlined can be both efficient and fruitful when measured in terms of theoretical output. Moreover, it can offer an empirical evaluation of the predictive ability of psychology's knowledge of human memory, an evaluation that turns out to be quite positive.

A Preview

Following Parry and Lord (Lord, 1960, 1991), oral traditions are viewed as human behavior, not as reified texts.[4] Here, in contrast to other works, what is known from cognitive psychology will be central. There has been considerable progress in both the humanities and cognitive psychology, and it seems wise to try to integrate the fields. Moreover, from a psychological and biological perspective, the behavior being studied is not a quaint, nostalgic art form at the margins of a technological society. The transmission of culture is universal and has a large effect on the fitness of the species. Oral traditions play a role in that transmission and should be able to tell us what cognitive resources are available to it.

Oral traditions depend on human memory for their preservation. If a tradition is to survive, it must be stored in one person's memory and be passed to another person who is also capable of storing and retelling it. All this must occur over many generations. That is, the transmission of oral traditions must yield results very different from those obtained by the standard rumor procedure in psychology, or the traditions would have changed radically or died out. Oral traditions must, therefore, have developed forms of organization (i.e., rules, redundancies, constraints) and strategies to decrease the changes that human memory imposes on the more casual transmission of verbal material.

The social nature of the repeated transmission should also produce an art form that is easier to study. As Neisser (1976, pp. 182–186) notes, it is difficult for a psychologist to understand the behavior of an artist, or of any expert, who is more skilled in a particular domain than the psychologist. With oral traditions there is a better chance of understanding because the processes at work are not those of a single creative mind trying to be novel, but of many minds trying to be conservative. In oral traditions idiosyncratic inventions that cannot be appreciated by those who follow will play minor roles in the tradition because they will not endure.[5]

Folklorists have used the analogy of pebbles made smooth by many tellings. The rough edges and odd protrusions are worn down. What is not mentioned in this analogy is that the pebbles do not become perfect spheres. Their shapes say something about the stone from which they were formed and about the tides and stones around them. By looking at the shapes that remain, something can be learned. A Darwinian metaphor may be more appropriate than a geologic one. If a genre (species) is to survive, it must be transmitted (reproduced) successfully. Changes in the environment can change (select for) aspects of the genre. However, if these changes in the genre are too extreme, or if the genre fails to be transmitted at all, the genre will die out (become extinct). Genres that survive the test of time come to be good figures for memory in the gestalt sense (they are well suited for their niche). Many different genres can exist, each providing a solution to survival under different conditions.

From either the geologic or the biological metaphor, it follows that by studying the song, something can be learned about the environment of memory in which it exists, and by studying memory, something can be learned about the song. One cannot, however, assume that human memory was designed to facilitate oral traditions. For some tasks, memory is exceptionally good; for others, it is remarkably poor. It is likely that oral traditions developed to make use of the strengths and avoid the weaknesses of human memory. Each of the next three chapters deals with an area of relative strength.

Oral traditions are systems of multiple constraints. These constraints include the organization of meaning (Chapter 2), imagery (Chapter 3), and patterns of sound (Chapter 4), including the poetic devices of rhyme, alliteration, and assonance, as well as rhythm and music. These constraint systems are easy to separate, have their own sets of rules and regularities, and often have different physiological substrates. There are different ways to categorize the world, but the one used here is far from arbitrary. These constraints lead to stability without fixing the text; they limit the choices of what can be sung in a given context, and they cue memory.

Psychologists and computer scientists have devised several ways to talk about the structure of meaning in text. Technical terms, such as *scripts* (Schank & Ableson, 1977), *story grammars* (Mandler & Johnson, 1977), and *causal chains* (Trabasso & Sperry, 1985), are among the forms of organization discussed in Chapter 2 that can be employed in oral traditions. In addition, simple associations among words and phrases are relevant. In oral traditions, as opposed to the texts usually studied by psychologists, the immediate local context of cues is more important than the overall global structure of the whole piece. Where global structures exist, they can often be analyzed in terms of the local cues they provide. This may be one reason why scripts, which are action sequences that occur in a set order, and causal chains, in which sequential ideas are logically related, are easy to apply. Common scripts in the traditions discussed here include the sequence of concrete actions taken in arming a hero or the hero's horse, assembling an army, joining battle, and wrecking a train. The scripts are at least as well formed and strict as an undergraduate's knowledge of the sequence of events that occurs in going to the dentist's office or a fast-food restaurant (Bower, Black, & Turner, 1979). As most oral traditions are collections of concrete actions, scripts are well suited for their description. Longer sequences can be diagrammed in terms of grammar-like structures, though the rules for these structures need to vary from tradition to tradition.

Visual imagery is perhaps the most powerful and widespread factor in mnemonic systems (Paivio, 1971; Yates, 1966). As Paivio (1971, 1986) notes, imagery is most effective for concrete (versus abstract), parallel-spatial (versus sequential), and dynamic (versus static) processing. Oral traditions predominantly consist of sequences of concrete actions. For epic, Havelock (1978) stresses that rather than employing abstract principles, only concrete examples by active agents are included. Thus Homer has only concrete examples of heroism, wisdom, and justice, not abstract statements. But visual imagery can no longer be viewed as a unitary system. Spatial and descriptive imagery can be distinguished behaviorally and neuropsychologically, and both are important in oral traditions.

Poetics and music add their own unique contribution. When two words in a ballad are linked by rhyme or alliteration, undergraduates have a higher recall for them than when these sound-pattern repetitions are broken (Wallace & Rubin, 1988b). Furthermore, when ballad singers perform the same ballad twice, they are less likely to change such poetically linked words (Wallace & Rubin, 1988a, 1988b). Some genres, such as counting-out rhymes, have nearly all their words related by such sound-pattern repetitions, whereas others, such as Homeric epic, have few. We know from the extensive work by Nelson and McEvoy that rhyme cues function differently than semantic cues (e.g., Nelson, 1981; Nelson & McEvoy, 1979a; Nelson, Schrieber, & McEvoy, 1992). It is as if rhyme cues a whole set, while semantic, or meaning, cues single out the target. Unlike semantic cues, rhyme tends to work best with fast presentation rates, small set size, and strong cue strength, three conditions that tend to be present in oral traditions. Thus rhymes have their own peculiar properties, which have been studied extensively and which are well suited for oral traditions.

The three oral traditions considered in this book are highly rhythmic. Their rhythm functions like other constraints or forms of organization to limit word choice, in this case to words with the correct number of syllables or stress patterns

(Hyman & Rubin, 1990; Kelly & Rubin, 1988). In addition, the rhythm provides a global organization, allowing singers to select, substitute, and add or delete whole rhythmic units (e.g., verses) and still continue. Rhythm also emphasizes certain locations within lines, which facilitates other constraints, such as the placing of rhyme and alliteration on stressed syllables.

Imagery, meaning, and poetic devices provide organization or constraint. Once the properties of each are listed, it is easy to add them together to produce an impressive degree of constraint or organization. However, more powerful and subtle effects are common (Chapter 5). In addition, the specific properties of the various types of organization complement one another. For instance, when imagery is used, the original wording is changed into a nonverbal, atemporal image (Paivio, 1971, 1986). When verbal output is needed, the original words and their ordering need to be generated from that image, resulting in possible changes in wording and in the order of ideas. The new scene described might look the same but be expressed differently. Meaning constraints, however, will help to preserve the temporal order lost by imagery. Even so, in most current psychological theories, words are kept in memory in an abstract form that loses all information about the sound pattern. But this shortcoming is remedied by the poetic devices, which constrain the sound pattern and thus help recover the original words.

The cognitive factors discussed so far have focused on the structure of pieces in oral traditions, but the process of transmission (Chapter 6) also needs to be considered. Songs from oral traditions are highly practiced, and that practice is especially effective because it is spaced over long periods. The same songs are heard from more than one source, and differences are noted implicitly, if not explicitly, before a new version is sung. The songs are reproduced by people who have become experts in the genre, who have heard many similar songs, and who know how to produce songs that follow the regularities of the genre, even if the version they heard was flawed.

Recall of a piece in an oral tradition is serial. It starts at the first word and proceeds sequentially to the end. As discussed in Chapter 7, cues must distinguish the item to be recalled from all others in memory. Each of the various forms of constraint acts in its own way. Having many different kinds of cues makes it much more likely that there will be a unique solution.

The theory developed to integrate these considerations in Chapter 8 is one of cue–item discriminability developed from the interference-theory literature and later studies of cuing.[6] Thus what is sung cues what remains to be sung, and the various cues that unfold as the song is sung help distinguish an item from all others in memory. In this way, a running start aids recall. This local, implicit, word-by-word or phrase-by-phrase cuing, which is the dominant form of cuing in oral traditions, is easiest to discuss as a network of associations, but other formulations are possible.

In summary, the project is as follows: a complex problem that appears tractable and that has theoretical and practical interest has been selected. That problem is the stability of oral traditions. Theories and empirical findings that could aid in understanding the stability of oral traditions are surveyed, and the most promising ones are examined in more detail. Modifications are made in the theories as needed. Simple demonstration experiments are undertaken to ensure that the modified theories work in ideal situations, though more such tests are needed and tests that allow for quantitative estimates of the size and nature of effects should ultimately be added. The review and some simple tests of the existing theories are presented in the early chapters. In particular, Chapter 2 discusses theme and meaning; Chapter 3, imagery; Chapter 4, patterns of sound; and Chapter 5, how these forms of organization combine. These four chapters deal mostly with the structure of the material and processes involved with these structures. The next two chapters deal with more general processes affecting transmission. Chapter 6 examines aspects of the mode of transmission that affect stability, and Chapter 7 summarizes and adapts what is known about recall.[7] An integrated model is then formulated, applied to laboratory studies in Chapter 8, and applied descriptively to observations from three existing oral traditions—epic, counting-out rhymes, and ballads—in Chapters 9, 10, and 11, respectively. To the extent that the model building succeeds, our understanding of oral traditions and of cognitive psychology is increased, but things are learned even when predictions fail. The success and limitations of this strategy are examined as it is applied throughout the book and in Chapter 12. Finally, the Epilogue considers the implications of the differences between oral and written transmission for the differences between written and electronic transmission.

Notes

1. The first example is used again in Chapter 4. The original Serbo-Croatian for both texts is in Lord (1960, pp. 72–73).

2. The difference between transmitting a theme, an image, and a poetic structure, and transmitting a particular instance of that theme, image, and poetic structure, has methodological implications for how memory is studied. In most oral traditions, behavior at one time can be compared with behavior at another time to abstract the organization, but one behavior cannot be judged against another for correctness or accuracy. Ideas such as *the piece or the original version* make little sense in analyzing variants. In contrast, in the psychological literature on recall of text (e.g., Rubin, 1985), a version of a story is presented to people for later recall. Errors and omissions in recall are analyzed to test theories about the underlying structure of the story and its processing. Students of ballads and epic perform similar procedures with their singers; however, they do not consider changes introduced by a second singer in the text of the first singer as errors. In fact, the song of the second singer can be a better rendition of the underlying structure. In both the psychological literature and the oral-tradition literature, inferences about the structure of a piece are made by comparing variants of that piece, but only in the psychological studies is the earlier variant considered correct.

3. For alternative lists, see Ong (1982, pp. 36–57) or Turner (1985, p. 6).

4. For a bibliography of this approach, see Foley (1985) and periodic updates in the journal *Oral Tradition*. Foley (1988) provides a general overview.

5. There are more ambitious books that do discuss the relationship of psychology to literature and art in general (Gardner, 1982; Kreitler & Kreitler, 1972; Lindauer, 1974; Turner, 1985; Winner, 1982). The goal here remains more narrow, concentrating on the interplay of cognitive psychology and oral traditions.

6. The proposed theory is a set of procedures operating on structures. It is developed verbally, but not nearly well enough to be implemented as a computer model. The term *theory* may be pretentious, but it is more accurate than the term *model, hypothesis,* or *approach.*

7. Chapters 1 to 7 serve as a selective review of the principles of cognitive psychology relevant to understanding the transmission of oral traditions. More details are presented than will be applied to the three genres of oral traditions studied here. This is done not only because such details are useful for other genres, but also to provide the reader with more than just the relevant ''facts'' and theory. Series of experiments are often described to give the reader a feeling for the kinds of data accepted as evidence and the kinds of arguments used to support theory. When such reviews become tedious to the novice in the field or pedantic to the expert, they should be skimmed and returned to later as needed.

CHAPTER 2

The Representation
of Themes in Memory

The eye can review, that is, retrospect: the ear and mouth cannot. The com-
poser-reciter works steadily forward, and only forward, and the memory that
repeats the composition works forward also. This means that what we are
tempted to call correspondence or symmetry is really a process of continual
anticipation.

Havelock, 1971, p. 53

In a world of constantly changing environment, literal recall is extraordinarily
unimportant.

Bartlett, 1932, p. 204

The tale's the thing.
Lord, 1960, p. 68

In general, oral traditions tell organized, coherent stories. This chapter explores the
way in which such meaningful structure affects what is remembered. The chapter
begins with examples of themes from epic. It then examines some of the methods
psychologists have used to understand the recall and structure of organized verbal
material. Bruner (1986) claims that "there are two modes of cognitive functioning,
two modes of thought, each providing distinctive ways of ordering experience, of
construction reality. The two (though complementary) are irreducible to one
another" (p. 11). These modes are the narrative and the logical argument. In each
mode there is a different criterion for quality. What makes a good story does not
make a good argument. There is a different criterion for creativity. There is even a
different criterion for the proper use of the word *then,* as in the usage *then they left,*
versus the usage *if x, then y.* Oral traditions demonstrate only the first of these two
modes, and it is this narrative mode that is described here.

Themes in Oral Traditions

A Sample Theme: The Novice Hero in Epic

To provide a concrete example, one theme from epic poetry—the theme of the novice hero's first adventure—is examined in detail (e.g., Bynum, 1968; Lord, 1960, 1976; Meyer, 1980; see Campbell, 1949, for a more general treatment). Like other themes, this one contains and can be contained in other themes.

This theme causes several problems for critics of Homer. The *Odyssey* is about the return of Odysseus after the Trojan War, and yet no sooner does the story begin than there is an interruption in the plot. Odysseus's son, Telemachus, goes on his first adventure, but does nothing to help Odysseus's return. Then after four books, the theme of Odysseus's return begins again, with Athena reminding Zeus and the audience what the story is all about (Lord, 1960).

The theme of Telemachus's first adventure can be divided into the following component themes and attributes, as adapted from Bynum (1968):

1. There is a novice who does not enjoy the privileges of manhood.
2. The novice is of noble ancestry.
3. The novice is an only son.
4. An elder hero, usually the novice's father, is incapacitated.
5. The novice attends an assembly of elders or heroes.
6. The novice is discontented at the assembly.
7. The novice quarrels at the assembly.
8. The novice is asked to restore the authority of the house of the elder hero.
9. The novice temporarily assumes the rights of manhood.
10. The novice consults mentors.
11. The mentors recognize the novice through his appearance.
12. A patron, often female, equips the novice and sends him on a quest.
13. The novice dresses specially.
14. The novice's horse or ship is prepared.
15. The novice is blessed.
16. The novice travels with an escort.
17. The novice is entertained and instructed while traveling.
21. The elder hero or another captive is released, often through no direct action of the novice.

If this list of actions and attributes of characters is really a theme, then it should appear elsewhere in the tradition. There is one other famous example that was probably derived from the epic oral tradition, but of which we have no record until Roman times, when it appears in *Plutarch's Lives* (Langhorne & Langhorne, 1879). The story of Theseus involves all the components mentioned except numbers 1, 5, 6, 7, and 11. The Theseus story contains three additional actions that are common occurrences for novices. Using the same numbering system, they are

18. The novice meets an interdictor or captor of girl(s).
19. The novice destroys the interdictor.
20. The novice weds the girl.

The most surprising evidence for this theme, however, comes from a different oral tradition, culture, and time period.

Bynum (1968) took a sample of nine epic poems describing the first adventure of a novice hero from modern South Slavic epic. The nine poems were collected between 1880 and 1940 and range from 57 to 12,311 verses long, the longest poem being Avdo Medjedović's *The Song of the Wedding of Smailagić Meho* (Lord, 1960, 1976). Each of the 21 components just listed is contained in at least six of the nine epics. With the exception of 1 more component (boasting by other members of the assembly), which is present in the South Slavic but not the Greek epic, no other component exists in more than two songs. Bynum concluded that the two Greek epics agree with the pattern of the nine South Slavic epics as well as would two newly selected South Slavic epics. This is in spite of a difference in location, language, culture, and the passage of more than two millennia. Similar patterns exist in Russian byliny (Bynum, 1968) and Arthurian legend, as well as in other epics and folklore. Thus the theme is quite widespread.

Moreover, the novice theme, as outlined by Bynum (1968) and Lord (1976), extends well beyond oral traditions. Meyer (1980) found a similar pattern in 16 stories by four of the most popular contemporary science-fiction writers—Lloyd Alexander, Robert Heinlein, Frank Herbert, and Ursula Le Guin—as well as in the movie *Star Wars*. There are changes that reflect changes in culture, but the basic pattern of the novice hero remains. Meyer attributed this similarity to the common problems and processes of adolescents' coming of age. From a Freudian, or analytic, perspective there is a break from the parents, an emphasis on the uniqueness of the self, a switch to "narcissistic objects" in the form of a companion or companions, advice and equipment provided by mentors who serve to provide the novice with the values of society, and finally, mature love, followed in traditional societies by marriage.[1]

The theme of a young hero's first adventure thus has a life of its own that transcends any particular singing. In the example just given, the theme was transmitted within a single tradition and was present in many traditions, even though there were changes in components of the theme, including the particular novice, older hero, mentors, sponsors, and form of recognition. The existence of alternative forms of a particular component of a theme is termed *multiformity* by Lord (1960) and is a major factor in the development of the schema theories discussed later in this chapter.

The mystery of why Telemachus plays no role in the return of his father, Odysseus, to Ithaki is solved to the extent that the novice hero often does not succeed in this task. Instead, the novice succeeds in becoming a hero, and the person the novice sets out to rescue returns with or without the novice's help. The modern critic may wonder why Telemachus did not play a more integral part in freeing his father, but the traditional listener would not.

There are many possible answers to the remaining question of why the story of Telemachus is included at all, but the one most relevant to the present discussion is given by Lord (1960). The theme of the young hero consists of themes, such as assembly, arrivals, departures, and disguising, that are used elsewhere in the epic tradition. In addition, the theme as a whole belongs to a family of related themes including return and rescue themes. The story of Telemachus fits the *Odyssey* because, in large part, it parallels and utilizes many of the same components as the story of Odysseus's return to Ithaki. The tale of the son is a preview of the tale of the father. Moreover, these tales are not unique. The returns of Telemachus and Odysseus to Ithaki have a parallel, which is explicitly noted in the *Odyssey,* to the returns of Orestes and Agamemnon to Argos.

The example of the theme of the novice hero demonstrates how themes function to lighten the memory load on the singer and his audience. Once a novice who is an only son and is of noble birth expresses his unhappiness at an assembly of elders because he is not being treated as a man, much of the rest of the plot can be inferred. Similarly, if an older hero at an assembly accepts a task, his arming, journey, and recognition on foreign soil are also predictable and, with certain regular exceptions, are similar to those of the novice. In this way, themes help to constrain and stabilize the tradition.

Other Themes in Epic

Of the three genres of oral traditions considered in this book, epic is used to provide examples of themes. Although examination of the corpus of counting-out rhymes could provide themes or recurring topics such as, of course, counting, the rhymes themselves are too short to benefit from all but the simplest thematic structure. In contrast, ballads have a complex and well-analyzed thematic structure that is best presented in Chapter 11 after other aspects of their structure are considered. Other genres have their own properties, which differ (e.g., Einstein, McDaniel, Owen, & Coté, 1990; McDaniel, Hines, Waddill, & Einstein, 1994), especially if the other constraints of the genre differ.

In a survey including among other epics—the Babylonian *Gilgamesh,* the Greek *Iliad* and *Odyssey,* the Anglo-Saxon *Beowulf,* the French *Song of Roland,* and modern epics in Russian, South Slavic, Albanian, Armenian, Turkish, and Arabian—Bowra (1952) noted several recurring themes of relatively short duration. These themes, or "detailed descriptions of actions which are in themselves trivial" (p. 179), include arrivals, departures, waking, going to bed, dressing, arming, disguising, feasting, sailing, and riding. Each of the themes at this level consists of even more detailed themes and combines to form longer themes such as returning home, stealing a bride, or a novice hero's first adventure.

The themes afford the singer considerable structure and flexibility in composition. For example, the assembly theme, which Bowra includes under feasting, is used seven times in the first two books of the *Iliad* (Lord, 1960). It provides the singer with a good way to introduce a catalog of the major characters, background information, a history of the plot, and a situation in which many people can be measured against one another. Thus in an assembly, a hero can relate his past and thereby motivate his future actions, or the hero can challenge another hero, or the hero can ask for help, a debate can take place that tells the listener everyone's position on an issue, or a letter or messenger can arrive with news or a problem to be solved. No matter which of these devices is used, within a single tradition the major characters, the location of the assembly, and the manner of arrivals and departures are set within limits. In this way, the singer's and listener's tasks are made easier because they have a familiar structure in which to place the tale. Within a theme, one component leads to another, minimizing the need for an initial overall plan or outline to be kept in memory.

Within a particular tradition, a theme has a relatively fixed pattern that can promote stability even when the theme is used in a novel way. For instance, in the Homeric tradition the theme of arriving includes (1) the visitor's being welcomed by his host, (2) the visitor's being washed and fed, (3) the visitor telling who he is and what his ties are to the host, and (4) the visitor's being presented with gifts. The pattern, as Bowra (1952) noted and as discussed in Chapter 9, is maintained even in odd circumstances.

Epic also provides numerous examples where themes preserve the stability of the tradition as a whole, but cause changes in the retelling of individual pieces (Lord, 1960, especially chaps. 4 and 5). Often a singer will expand a theme treated only briefly by another singer or will use his method of arming a hero or delivering a message rather than the one he heard from another singer. The details of a song may change, but not the set of themes organizing the genre. The overall effect is conservative. For instance, omissions can even be corrected:

> If, for one reason or another one of these themes is omitted or expressed only by implication or inadequately in the singing of one man, it will reappear in full bloom in the singing of another who has learned the song from him, but is already aware from other songs of the tensions binding the themes. (Lord, 1960, p. 112)

Additional evidence for themes is provided by the inconsistencies present in epic. Lord (1960) relates the case of a novice hero who goes on his first adventure. The novice is, according to the appropriate theme, wearing armor provided by a patron, in this case his uncle. In a recognition scene, however, he is recognized by the armor he took in single combat from another hero. Recognition by armor won in battle, another common theme in epic, interferes with the appropriate theme for a novice hero, who by definition can have no such armor. Themes that are likely to occur at a given time often do so even when they are inappropriate.

Before we leave the description of themes in epic, two observations attributed to the length of epic poems need to be mentioned. First, epics are long enough that themes can and do exist at many levels, with themes at one level containing themes at a lower level as components. For instance, the theme of the novice hero may contain the theme of assembly as a component, and the theme of assembly itself may contain the theme of the arrival of a messenger. Students of epic distinguish between the different levels (Foley, 1988; Lord, 1960), but following the cognitive psychology literature on schemas, which is reviewed in this chapter, that will not be done here. The concept of theme and schema appear to be used to account for the same observations regardless of whether they include the whole tale or a small portion of it.

The second observation attributed to the length of epic poems is that the structure noticed in a song need not be part of a conscious overall plan that exists at the beginning of the song and usually does not result in an overall plan that is as tightly organized as one from a written work might be (Havelock, 1963; Ong, 1982; but see Stanley, 1993, for an opposing view for Homeric epic). One theme, component, or action can lead to another in a local short-range fashion that does not depend on a long-range plan. Nonetheless, it is a property of the thematic structure of epic (and of the limitations of a listening audience that cannot turn back to see what happened on an earlier page) that the aesthetically pleasing overall thematic structure does exist for epic poems. Epic poems do not contain the single systematic rise and fall in tension that readers might expect in a literate tradition or the sudden unraveling that occurs at the end of a written detective story, in which all details that were previously left unresolved now come to be understood (Ong, 1982, chap.6). Such structure is available only with the use of external memory aids, such as writing, which allow a piece to be reworked before performance and which allow the relationships among the parts of the poem to be "seen" and manipulated in retrospect. Nonetheless, sequential thematic structures do exist and have a large role in guiding the behavior of singers of epic. The description of structures suitable for oral traditions makes up the rest of this and all of the next chapter.

One remaining point should be noted before examining how cognitive psychology has described themes. That is the puzzle of how suspense is built in an oral tradition in which not only the particular song, but also the whole class of songs, always have a known ending. Known endings, however, can be put in doubt in the context of a story, even a highly controlled, minimal, one-paragraph story written by a psychologist. Gerrig (1989) wrote brief stories about well-known events such as "George Washington was elected the first president of the United States" and "the *Titanic* sank when it hit an iceberg." The stories manipulated both suspense and the salience of prior knowledge. To study the role of suspense, half the stories provided information that contradicted the known outcome, such as the fact that Washington wanted to retire after the American Revolution or that the captain of the *Titanic* was not worried when the ship hit the iceberg. To study the effect of stressing prior knowledge, the well-known events appeared explicitly in half the stories. Both of these manipulations had independent effects. People were about 10% slower to verify the well-known events when they appeared immediately after the suspense stories and about 16% faster when the well-known events appeared explicitly in the story. Thus the effect of suspense was present even when the information was read several sentences earlier. The effect also held when the questioning was delayed by 10 minutes, but was not present when the suspense was resolved by providing information consistent with the well-known events in the last sentences of the story. Thus even with simple stories, people can be made to be less certain of known events. Themes that constrain outcomes need not be a problem for the maintenance of suspense.

Schemas

Representation

In trying to understand how themes are represented in oral traditions, humanists often postulate structures that share properties with the regularities they notice in their material. In trying to understand how people abstract and remember the gist of an event or a story, psychologists do much the same, though often in a much more formal manner (Rumelhart & Norman, 1986).[2] The goal of the psychological enterprise is the development of representations that are rich enough to describe the relevant behavior and that lead to models that act in human ways. That is, psychologists try to develop models that find the same things difficult that people do, that make the same errors that people do, that take longer in the same situations that people do, and that produce narratives like the ones people do. A model that attempts to account for some of these or other similar kinds of observations is formulated, and a representation of theme is sought as a major component of that model. The representation consists of both a structure and a process operating on that structure, though here and in most models the process is usually quite simple, leaving the structure to account for the observed behavior (Rubin, 1988a).

Psychologists have been aided in their task by advances in linguistics and computer science. Linguistics has developed models to account for how people understand language. Computer science provides a concrete, mechanical device with which the adequacy of representations can be tested. In addition, the questions that arise when attempts are made to build intelligent machines often lead to advances in the theory of representations. Although linguistics, computer science, and psychology often have different goals and different rules of evidence, their advances, as is demonstrated in this section, inform one another. The forms of representation discussed in this chapter, with the exception of associations considered in isolation, are all special cases of schemas, and so this more general concept will be discussed first.

General Properties of Schemas

The closest concept in the psychological literature to *theme* is *schema*. In 1932, Bartlett defined the term *schema* as follows: " 'Schema' refers to an active organisation of past reactions, or of past experiences, which must always be supposed to be operating in any well-adapted organic response" (p. 201). The implication of this definition is that

> remembering is not the re-excitation of innumerable fixed, lifeless and fragmentary traces. It is an imaginative reconstruction, or construction, built out of the relation of our attitude towards a whole active mass of organised past reactions or experience, and to a little outstanding detail which commonly appears in image or in language form. (Bartlett, 1932, p. 213)

From 1932 until the 1960s, the concept of schema received little attention. By the late 1960s, advances in computer science and in linguistics made it possible for psychologists to envision concrete structures that had some of the properties of a schema, and thus to make the concept of schema operational in ways that allowed for more objective testing. The discussions of scripts, story grammars, associative networks, and parallel distributed processing that follow are such ways. In general, for oral traditions, a schema can be thought of as a singer's or a listener's use of a theme. There are predictions that any version of a schema theory would make, or, alternatively, there are behaviors that would support the notion that a schema is operating. The most important predictions or behaviors for our present purposes are contained in the following list drawn from a general reading of the literature, as well as from specific discussions of schema theory (e.g., Alba & Hasher, 1983; Brewer & Nakamura, 1984; Rubin & Kontis, 1983; Rumelhart, Smolensky, McClelland, & Hinton, 1986; Thorndyke & Yekovich, 1980):

1. If a piece matches a schema, it will be recalled with fewer omissions and changes, both in order and in content, than one that does not.[3]
2. Changes in the recall of a particular piece will make it more like the schema, both in order and in content. If a detail cannot be recalled, a common substitute from the schema will often be used. If a detail in a particular piece does not seem to fit the schema, a more common detail can be substituted in its place.
3. The schema allows the listener to draw inferences about omitted portions of a piece. Thus in singing a piece to a knowledgeable audience, it is possible, and often desirable, to omit parts of the schema that the audience already knows. Such omissions do not indicate that singers forgot that portion or even that the audience was not reminded of it (Foley, 1991, pp. 80–83).
4. The schema allows the listener to appreciate the underlying structure of a piece, including (a) boundaries between the components of a schema and (b) the equivalence of components that play the same role in a schema. If the time required to understand a piece is measured, it will vary as a function of the schema structure, with boundaries between components of the schema taking longer. In addition, substitutions and confusions will be made among functionally equivalent components, even though they may not share obvious surface similarities (i.e., Lord's [1960] term *multiformity*).
5. Aspects of a piece that are more central or important to a schema will be recalled better and responded to more quickly than aspects that are not (Albrecht & O'Brien, 1991).

It should be noted that these five predictions do not depend on the physical properties or similarities of the stimulus per se. Rather, they are a function of the stimulus's role in the schema.

These five properties of schemas have a conservative effect. The conservative effects of schemas, however, do not apply to each individual telling or even to each individual piece, but rather to the genre as a whole. A schema is an abstraction of many individual variants and is therefore not greatly affected by any one variant. Organizations and details that repeat become part of the schema and are better recalled than organizations and details that change (Bower, 1974; Hintzman, 1986;

Thorndyke, 1977; Thorndyke & Hayes-Roth, 1979). If a particular variant is different from most other variants or omits parts that are usually present, then knowledge from the schema can be substituted. This can be done consciously, but it need not be. Moreover, in transmission through many people, as occurs in oral traditions, the effects attributed to schema operate on each retelling and are therefore amplified (Bartlett, 1932; Kintsch & Greene, 1978; also see Chapter 6).[4]

Neisser (1981) presents a real-world example of the properties of schemas providing a conservative effect in his analysis of the discrepancies between John Dean's testimony before the Senate Watergate committee and transcripts of tape recordings that Dean did not know existed at the time of his testimony:

> What his [Dean's] testimony really describes is not the September 15 meeting itself but his fantasy of it: the meeting as it should have been, so to speak. In his mind Nixon *should* have been glad that the indictments stopped with Liddy, Halderman *should* have been telling Nixon what a great job Dean was doing; most of all, praising him *should* have been the first order of business. In addition, Dean *should* have told Nixon that the cover-up might unravel, as it eventually did, instead of telling him it was a great success. By June, this fantasy had become the way Dean remembered the meeting. (p. 10)

In oral traditions, such fantasies, in which what *should* happen actually happens, are the rule, and so there is little reason to distort.

Three examples of attempts by psychologists to capture thematic structure are examined in detail: scripts, story grammars, and associative networks. The three differ on several dimensions. For example, scripts and associative networks function in an inherently sequential fashion, whereas story grammars are global structures that operate on the story as a whole. Also, scripts and associative networks make no distinction between meaning and form, whereas story grammars attempt to separate form (i.e., grammar) from meaning.[5] In addition to these three ways of capturing thematic structure, associations considered in a simple pairwise fashion instead of in associative networks will be included briefly as a more traditional model that has clear applications in oral traditions. Descriptions of thematic structure from outside cognitive psychology are omitted except as they clarify issues, even though they usually are based on the same structuralist assumptions and capture more of the regularity in the genre they were designed to describe than do the more general psychological models. Also omitted from this chapter are several models of sequential text processing that do not result in easy-to-characterize classes of structures (e.g., Gernsbacher, 1990; Just & Carpenter, 1987, 1992; Kintsch & van Dijk, 1978; which Britton & Gulgoz, 1991, have recently applied; St. John, 1992), though more will be made of the sequential approach in Chapter 8.

What all attempts at formalizing schemas have in common is the claim that a person's response to a stimulus is not based on that stimulus alone, but on past stimuli as well—that is, on "a whole active mass of organised past reactions or experience" (Bartlett, 1932, p. 213). In terms of oral traditions, a listener does not hear a song in isolation but in relation to past events, especially but not exclusively the songs heard from that tradition. Under the concept of *immanence,* Foley (1991, 1992) has convincingly argued that the meanings of words and larger units of a song in an oral tradition are not to be understood in terms of the text in which they appear, but in terms of the entire tradition to which that text belongs. The concept of schema makes the same point, but includes literate works and all that people encounter. Oral traditions are just an especially clear place to make the claim.

Scripts

The theme in the three oral traditions considered in this book is carried by series of concrete actions. Although the role and structure of the meaning in the counting-out rhymes are limited, the poetry of the oral traditions discussed here, to use Bowra's (1952) phrase, is "the poetry of action" (p. 48). Havelock (1963, 1978) made a similar point. Concrete actions are used where a more modern, literate genre would use abstract statements. Thus instead of a listing of ships or heroes in some logical, abstract order, there is a scene of arriving ships or heroes. Instead of an abstract, unmotivated occurrence such as a sickness, there is a concrete action taken by a god in response to specific actions taken by people. The sequencing of actions that make up scripts is a good way of describing short, recurring themes such as arrivals, departures, and arming, as noted by Bowra (1952), and is also useful in accounting for the "and next" organization noted in oral traditions (Havelock, 1963, p. 180; Notopoulos, 1949; Ong, 1982). In general, the reliance on action, which is part of the general tendency for oral traditions to contain only material that is easy to image (Chapter 3), makes scripts an especially useful version of schema theory.

Formal Properties of Scripts

"A script is a predetermined, stereotyped sequence of actions that defines a well-known situation" (Schank & Ableson, 1977, p. 41). Scripts were developed in an effort to provide knowledge structures that would allow computers to understand and make appropriate inferences about such trivial, everyday human activities as going to a restaurant or a dentist's office.

Consider the following two very dull narratives:

1. Chris ordered his standard meal. The bill came to more than usual.
2. Cliff paid another visit to the dentist. The magazines were getting boring.

These two sequences of events, which are as common to us as the script of a novice hero is to the audience of an epic poet, allow for several observations. First, in terms of linguistic usage, note that the second sentence of each narrative begins with the definite article, *the*. This implies that the referents of the noun phrases introduced by the word *the* were mentioned before. Ordering a meal and visiting a dentist's office invoke many actions and objects, and these are assumed by listeners to be mentioned, whether or not they are made explicit. Thus ordering a meal implies a bill and visiting a dentist's office implies magazines, just as in epic a novice hero implies a journey.

Second, members of a culture have considerable knowledge about the kinds of routine activities that scripts describe, and they can use this knowledge to make inferences and set expectations. Because we know what conditions enable a restaurant script, we can infer either that Chris was hungry or that it was his usual time to dine. We may be wrong some of the time, but not often. Because we know the activities that constitute the script and their sequence, we can infer that Chris received his meal. Because we know the usual characters and props involved in the restaurant script, after the first sentence we would not be surprised by the presence of *the* waiter or waitress or of *the* fork. We would, however, be surprised in the first script by *the* or even *a* dental hygienist, drill, or magazine.

Third, scripts can be more specific or more general than implied by the two example narratives. On the one hand, the visit to the dentist's office shares most activities with visits to other health-care professionals and so can be considered as a special case of a more general script. On the other hand, there are many kinds of restaurants, each with a somewhat different script. The substitution of a waiter for a waitress, and the change from one related script to another, are ways to formalize the observations that Lord summarized with the term *multiform*. A singer can substitute many different details, actions, or series of actions, as long as they fill the same slot or role in a script. The small amount of change that is needed to vary the whole nature of a script demonstrates the need for an extensive inference system (or alternatively, as discussed under the heading of associative networks, a large set of connected nodes). For instance, if Chris's standard meal was a Whopper or a Big Mac with ketchup and french fries, then people familiar with contemporary North American culture would not expect a waiter, a tablecloth, wine, or a lengthy meal, whereas if the meal were coquilles St-Jacques, they would. Similarly, details of a hero's early actions in an epic can indicate which particular script is being used.

Fourth, scripts were developed for the kind of knowledge people have about stereotyped *causal chains* (Trabasso & Sperry, 1985; Trabasso & van den Broek, 1985). An individual action in a script usually cannot be performed until the actions prior to it have been performed and usually must be performed before actions that follow it. If the script is understood by all members of an audience, each action need not be stated explicitly; nonetheless, the actions enable and are enabled by one another. In oral traditions, this causal linking of events is usually present, and serves to preserve the temporal order of events in the theme and usually the actual order of the presentation of the events in the piece itself (Brewer, 1980, 1985; Havelock, 1963, chap. 10).

Usually scripts are components of larger structures such as stories. Thus, as discussed earlier and in Chapter 9, classicists have long noted short sequences of events that are part of longer stories, sequences that psychologists would call scripts. For example, when arming, different items can be explicitly mentioned or not, depending on the importance of the hero and the battle to follow. However, in Homeric epic, the order of the items mentioned is always tunic, bow and quiver, greaves, corselet, sword, shield, helmet, and spear(s). In oral traditions, such embedding of scripts in nonscript structures is not the only use of scripts. The entire Telemachus example is one script. As demonstrated by the consistent use of the same enabling conditions and actions in the Greek and South Slavic epic traditions, the Telemachus theme is certainly stereotyped enough to acquire script status. In contrast, stories we might tell involving a restaurant or a dentist's office are not. This is because scripts about everyday life are in themselves usually not stories, and the stories of everyday life do not have repetitive enough sequences of actions to be scripts.[6] In oral traditions, where the expectations of novelty are less, scripts can be sufficient to describe whole themes.

Psychological Studies of Scripts

Scripts have been presented as knowledge structures intended to capture some apparent aspects of human behavior in a form specific enough for computer implementation. People's judgments and recalls of scripts and script-based stories serve to test and extend these initial intuitions. Many of the types of experiments reported here for scripts were developed for testing other aspects or versions of schema theory. The effect of organization on recall, therefore, rests on a much larger empirical base than is presented.

A major function of scripts in the real world of undergraduates and in oral traditions is to preserve the order of events. Following the first two predictions of schema theory made at the beginning of this section, if the actions of a script are presented in their normal order as opposed to a scrambled, or partially scrambled, order, then students recall more of the presented material. Moreover, for actions presented in their normal order, the order of recall better approaches the order of presentation. Changes in order observed in the recalls from scrambled presentations tend to be changes toward the normal order (Bellezza & Bower, 1982; Bower, Black, & Turner, 1979).

The order-preserving aspect of scripts can also be observed in tasks that measure the time required to produce a response. Rapidity of response is especially important in oral traditions. Because the songs are rhythmic, they do not afford a singer the luxury of waiting for an appropriate response to come to mind. Undergraduates list more actions from a script in a 20-second period when they are asked to list the actions in their normal sequential order than when they are asked to list them from last to first, or from most to least central to the script, or even in any order they choose. In contrast, when asked to list as many instances as they can from a category, such as furniture or vegetables, undergraduates are faster when allowed to list items in any order; next fastest when asked to first list items that are most central, or prototypical; and slowest when asked to list in terms of size, a dimension chosen for comparison with temporal order. Thus scripts appear to be organized in a way that is not like other kinds of categories. Moreover, the order of output of actions of the scripts when students were allowed to use any order they wanted followed closely the normal sequential order (Barsalou & Sewell, 1985).

In addition to preserving the order of events, scripts should be able to ensure that actions that belong to a script are transmitted even if they are not explicitly stated. Following the third prediction of schema theory made at the beginning of this section, missing actions at a moderate level of specificity can be inferred both from concepts that are more general and from concepts that are more specific than the missing action (Abbott, Black, & Smith, 1985); actions that are typical for a script are often recalled even when not explicitly presented (Bower et al., 1979); and the tendency to infer missing actions increases as the time between the initial presentation of material and its later recall increases (Graesser, Woll, Kowalski, & Smith, 1980). In addition, unstated typical actions are more likely to be recalled if, as often occurs both in the real world and in oral traditions, more than one text using the same general class of scripts is presented (Bower et al., 1979). Effects observed in recall are evident even when students are given a set of actions and asked to judge which ones were actually presented to them. These effects include the erroneous recall of unstated, typical script actions, the increase in such erroneous recall with increases in the time between presentation and recall, and their increase with the presentation of similar scripts (Bower et al., 1979; Graesser et al., 1980; Graesser, Gordon, & Sawyer, 1979).[7]

Following the fourth prediction of schema theory, undergraduates can reliably list actions that compose common scripts (Bower et al., 1979; Graesser et al., 1979). In fact, some children spend time rehearsing scripts of their activities as soon as they can talk (Fivush 1991; Nelson, 1988, 1993). Later, they are quite willing to record them. One of my daughters, at age 6, wrote the following: "wen uo get ap uo mac uor bed then uo et breft then uo brash uor teth then uo get jrest," which in more standard orthography is "When you get up you make your bed, then you eat breakfast, then you brush your teeth, then you get dressed." I commented that it was a nice story, to which she responded that it was not a story; it told her what to do when she got up in the morning. Not only did she classify it as a genre apart from stories, but she used the impersonal *you*, instead of the first person, *I*, and the historical timeless present tense. That is, she was actually working on a general-purpose script.

Finally, following the fifth prediction of schema theory, the time it takes people to decide whether an action belongs to a script depends on how central that action is to the script (Galambos & Rips, 1982), and more central items are recalled better (Graesser, 1978).

The scripts from our culture that have been studied by psychologists are dull sequences, not stories. By themselves, they are the things we learn to omit from conversation because the other person already knows them. It is, therefore, the deviations from these everyday scripts that are more likely to be recalled. In oral traditions this need not be the case. Nonetheless, studies of scripts from our culture are instructive in showing the kind of novelty in a story that is memorable. Bower et al. (1979) found that interruptions were recalled better than script actions, which were recalled better than extraneous statements. Bellezza and Bower (1982) found that normal script actions and script actions containing an atypical object were remembered equally well, and both were recalled better than actions that were atypical.

Thus it appears that, at least with the dull scripts that describe everyday sequences, actions that interrupt the progress of the script are recalled better than actions that advance the script, and both of these types of actions are recalled better than irrelevant actions. Two factors are most likely at work here. First, and not specific to scripts, stimuli that are novel or discrepant with respect to the set of stimuli to be recalled tend to be recalled better (see Rubin & Corbett, 1982, for a review). Second, scripts provide the structure to cue recall. Actions that are unrelated to a script are not cued by the script and are therefore not as often recalled. Actions that interrupt the script are more difficult to overlook in using the script as a cue (Bellezza & Bower, 1982).

Part of the usefulness of scripts derives from the fact that the stereotyped sequence of actions that constitute them is a causal chain (Schank & Ableson, 1977). This aspect of scripts has been studied independently by examining causal chains that were not scripts (e.g., Black & Bern, 1981; Trabasso & Sperry, 1985; Trabasso & van den Broek, 1985; van den Broek, 1990, 1994). A causal connection exists between two events of a story if, when the first event is assumed not to occur, it follows that the second event also does not occur. The degree to which each event was part of a causal chain was measured by two criteria: the number of direct causal connections each event had and whether the event was part of a causal chain that went from the beginning to the end of the story. These two measures predicted ratings of the importance of events in a story, whether the event would appear in a summary (another measure of importance; Rubin, 1978), and whether the event would be recalled. Thus the logical necessity of each action in the causal chain is an easy-to-recall and important aspect of the structure of stories: if part of a causal chain is forgotten, it can and must be constructed from what remains. Initial research stressed the causal relations of the complete causal chain, but recent work has shown that the local structure that develops as a text is processed is also important (van den Broek, 1990, 1994).

Parallels have been drawn between the behavior of undergraduates toward scripts that they know and that of participants in an oral tradition for scripts that they know. Two differences, however, need to be stressed. First, the scripts of an oral tradition are simpler and more regular than the scripts of most real-world events because the choice and sequence of actions in oral traditions are simpler than those in the real world. The results obtained for undergraduates and their real-world scripts should, therefore, be expected to be stronger in oral traditions. Second, in many oral traditions, actions that are part of a script cannot be omitted as easily as they could be in real-world scripts. The telling would not be complete if each action were not mentioned explicitly, even though missing actions could be implied.

Story Grammars

Ballads and epics tell stories. The stories not only entertain (Brewer & Lichtenstein, 1981, 1982), but also help to constrain the choice of words and in this way aid the singer's memory.

Formal Properties of Story Grammars

A story grammar is an attempt to capture the organization present in stories. In form, it is a set of rewrite rules that describes the structure of all stories, regardless of their content, much the same way that rules of syntax attempt to describe the structure of all English sentences without regard to their content. Thus in contrast to a script, which contains information about form and content and which is intended to be applicable to only a specific domain of knowledge, a story grammar contains information about form, but not about content, and is intended to be applicable to stories from all domains of knowledge.

Story grammars are based on transformational generative grammars (Chomsky, 1965). Instead of the rule *SENTENCE goes to NOUN PHRASE plus VERB PHRASE*, a story grammar might have the rule *STORY goes to SETTING plus EPISODE*.

SETTING and *EPISODE* are technical terms, just like *NOUN PHRASE* and *VERB PHRASE*, and have rules on how they are to be treated. For instance, *SETTING* might be rewritten using English words, whereas *EPISODE* might use the rule *EPISODE goes to BEGINNING cause DEVELOPMENT cause ENDING*, leading to the application of still more rewrite rules (e.g., Mandler, 1984).[8]

Psychological Studies of Story Grammars

Story grammars are specific forms of schemas, as are scripts, and therefore should, like scripts, make empirical predictions that are specific forms of the predictions made at the beginning of this section for schema theory. The research on different versions of story grammars has, in fact, confirmed such predictions (e.g., Glenn, 1978; Lakoff, 1972; Mandler & Johnson, 1977; Rumelhart, 1975; Thorndyke, 1977). Following the first three general predictions of schema theory, if the text presented does not follow the rules of a story grammar, either because parts are missing or because the story-grammar order is shuffled or altered in more subtle ways, undergraduates tend to recall the text less well and to alter the order of their recalls from the originally presented order to an order that is closer to one generated by the story grammar. Moreover, additions to the originally presented text made by the undergraduates during recall tend to follow the rules of story grammars (Glenn, 1978; Mandler, 1978, 1984; Mandler & Johnson, 1977; Thorndyke, 1977).

Following the fourth general prediction for schema theory, if undergraduates are asked to divide stories into their components, they tend to use most of the same divisions that a story grammar would (Mandler, 1984). The same effect is present in tasks other than direct judgments. For instance, the reading time for the first sentence of a new component of the story, as determined by a story grammar, is longer than the reading time for other sentences (Haberlandt, 1980; Mandler, 1984). The increased latency is interpreted as the time needed to finish understanding and storing one component and to develop expectations about the next. Following the fifth general prediction for schema theory, aspects of the text that story grammars determine are more central or important tend to be better recalled over a wide range of circumstances (Mandler, 1984; Mandler & Johnson, 1977; Rubin, 1985; Thorndyke, 1977).

Story grammars divide the world of discourse into two parts: stories and nonstories. It is not clear from empirical evidence, however, that this dichotomy is the best division to make. There may be forms of organization and processing shared by all verbal material, forms shared by all coherent text, forms shared only by stories, forms shared only by one genre of an oral tradition, and forms shared only by one subgenre of an oral tradition. In oral traditions, each genre has its own peculiarities; these are what make it a genre. These peculiarities can be cataloged, and casual observation indicates that many of them could be captured with a genre-specific grammar. Thus in Chapter 11, it is argued that the *STORY goes to SETTING plus EPISODE* rule has to be modified for ballads and most other oral traditions because they often lack settings. More restrictive, genre-specific rules could also be added. For example, consider including the rule of threes, which holds for much of Western folklore (Olrik, 1909/1965) and literature: Goldilocks will try three chairs, and the king will have three sons. In story-grammar form, the rule might be

EPISODE ——> ATTEMPT + GOAL
EPISODE ——> ATTEMPT + ATTEMPT + ATTEMPT + GOAL

If there is more than one attempt, there will be three. Other rules might specify character types. Thus either the same or three different people can make the three attempts, but only the protagonist can make the last attempt. If there is more than one person, then they should all be of the same gender and they should go in the order of oldest to youngest (Jacobs, 1959).

Grammars for specific genres would supplement rather than replace scripts. Unlike scripts, grammars written for specific genres could still be content free. That is, they could contain rules that applied to the form, or style, of the story, but not to the semantic content. They would, however, allow rules to be applied only in the context of particular semantic features.

What could a story grammar specifically written for Greek and South Slavic epic add to the script analysis of Telemachus and Theseus given earlier in the chapter? The script analysis provides a series of actions with little overall structure, except that some sequences of actions can be grouped together more strongly than others in a hierarchical fashion (Abbott et al., 1985; Bower et al., 1979; Galambo & Rips, 1982). In contrast, a story grammar provides a hierarchical structure indicating which actions go together and what their relation is to the story as a whole.

For example, several of the sequences listed in the Telemachus story can occur more than once. It is possible to have more than one mentor, to have more than one trip with an escort, or to meet more than one interdictor. A grammar could indicate where such repetitions of episodes could occur and could indicate their location in the hierarchical structure of the story. The grammar could set an upper limit on the number of such repetitions, or could even indicate that if one instance occurred, then a certain number of repetitions were obligatory. For instance, there are 3 repetitions in European fairy tales, as noted earlier, 5 repetitions in certain American Indian tales (Boas, 1925; Hymes, 1976–1977; Jacobs, 1959), though others use 4 repetitions or the more complex case of 5 for males and 4 for females (Jacobs, 1959, pp. 224–228); and 14 repetitions in Greek, Hebrew, and Christian genealogies of the first century (Bikerman, 1952).

The order of the telling of the events in the Telemachus sequence follows the temporal order of the events. That is, the discourse or narrative structure follows the event structure (Brewer, 1985; Brewer & Lichtenstein, 1982). A genre-specific grammar could force this to be the case or could allow rules or transformations that would allow flashbacks to occur in specified places. A grammar could specify the nature of the form, or style, of the tale without specifying its content.

Story grammars are global structures that operate on the story as a whole. Oral traditions work in a serial fashion. What has been sung cues the production and sets the context for understanding what is to be sung next. To apply story grammars and other global structures to the production and comprehension of oral traditions, serial equivalents need to be developed that indicate the likely role of a proposition in the grammar of the emerging story. This is not a criticism unique to story grammars or oral traditions. All oral language is sequential. For instance, transformational grammars for sentences are global structures that operate on sentences as a whole, but people do not wait several seconds until the end of a sentence to begin processing it (Rubin, 1976c). To apply grammars of sentences to speech, sequential heuristics need to be developed (Wanner, 1988). In oral traditions, where the end of a story can be minutes or hours away rather than seconds, the problem is more serious. Moreover, as discussed in this chapter and in Chapter 4, oral language does not afford the possibility of scanning or reading ahead. Such factors combine to produce forms of organization in oral traditions, including thematic organization, that operate in a serial fashion (Chapter 8).

Associations, Associative Networks, and Parallel Distributed Processing

Associations are certainly one of the oldest and most widespread ways of trying to account for the organization of memory. After a brief review of some of the effects that can be understood in terms of associations between two words or ideas, a mathematics is described that gives networks of association-like connections the properties of schemas.

Associations

If I ask for the first word that comes to mind in response to the word *dog,* the answer is usually *cat;* for *table,* it is usually *chair.* Similar pairs of words with varying strengths of association exist in any familiar domain, including oral traditions; in epic, *resourceful* often brings to mind *Odysseus,* and in ballads, *roses* often bring to mind *briars.* A single word bringing to mind another word, or a small set of words, provides a rapid, effortless, and often very useful way to aid recall. Even if the associated words are not recalled explicitly, they are primed and are more available as responses if needed. In oral traditions, repeated pairings of ideas or words are noted as one way the individual words acquire traditional meanings within their genre (Andersen, 1985; Foley, 1991, 1992). In psychology, such organization is clearest if more complex forms of organization, such as scripts and story grammars, are removed. For example, if people are given a list of words in a random order, they tend to recall associated words next to each other by category (Bousfield, 1953; Kausler, 1974). Even if the list has no clear structure, they will impose one (Tulving, 1962).[9]

There are important functions for such local associations in oral traditions. For instance, having the mention of a word increase the probability of the recall of words it is usually sung with increases stability. Such word-to-word cuing is responsible, in part, for the "running start" effect, discussed in detail in Chapter 8, in which a word cannot be recalled without first recalling the words before it. Thus although the type of cuing that simple word-to-word or phrase-to-phrase associations are capable of is limited when compared with the cuing of schemas or networks of associations, it plays an important role in serial recall (Rubin, 1977).

The simplest way of demonstrating associative structure is to ask people to list all the members of a category that they can (Bousfield & Sedgewick, 1944; Gruenewald & Lockhead, 1980; Rubin & Olson, 1980). The list of words output by people can be viewed as a tracing of the path they took through their individual networks of associations. To obtain such tracings, 100 undergraduates were asked to list all the words that they could in 60 seconds that belonged to a category, such as the parts-of-the-body category shown in Figure 2.1. Singular and plural forms of the words were kept separate in order to facilitate comparison with work on rhymes presented in Chapter 4. The most frequent 20 responses in the category were selected for further analysis. Two analyses were performed on these data. First, for each domain, the number of times each of the possible pairs of these 20 words were listed next to each other was counted as a measure of similarity (Rubin & Olson, 1980). A computer program determined the location of the words in Figure 2.1 that best preserved the relative similarity among words. For the second analysis, the number of times each word was followed by another word was used to produce the arrows connecting the words (Rubin, 1990).[10]

Figure 2.1 provides a graphic representation of the kind of associative structure that is available to cue recall. The more often people recall two words immediately adjacent to each other, the closer together these two words appear in Figure 2.1 and the more highly associated they are assumed to be. The singular and plural terms were not combined because they have different rhymes and so might be used differently in an oral tradition. In Figure 2.1 they are separated because a single person would not recall both the singular and plural terms and thus could not recall them

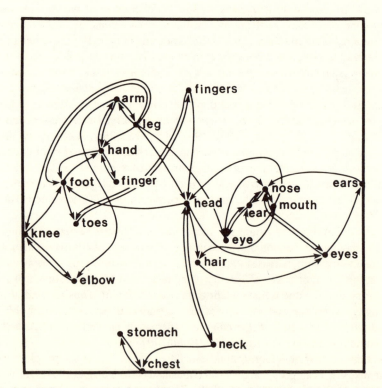

Figure 2.1. A directed network formed from undergraduates' listings of the semantic domain of parts of the body. The locations of the nodes and the arrows were calculated using standard statistical procedures.

next to each other. The arrows indicate the path that associations from any word are likely to take. Figure 2.1 thus provides a description of the data obtained by undergraduates' listings of the parts-of-the-body domain. The distances among the words on the directed paths connecting them indicate what words are likely to follow other words. A similar, but genre-specific, associative structure is assumed to be available to singers and listeners in oral traditions.

Associative Networks

Until recently, associations were considered as operating serially among pairs of items, a rather weak mechanism that was contrasted to often less well-defined but more powerful schemas (Bartlett, 1932; Lashley, 1951). Associations, or more generally excitatory and inhibitory connections among nodes, however, can be considered as operating in large networks (Grossberg, 1980, 1988; McClelland & Rumelhart, 1985; Rumelhart, McClelland, & the PDP Research Group, 1986). Operating in this fashion, connections among nodes of a network are able to account for the major behaviors that schema theory was devised to describe, including the five properties of schemas listed at the beginning of this section, as well as learning prototypes from instances, discriminating among different but overlapping instances, and recognizing a whole from only a subset of its parts.

In order to provide an example that does not require sophisticated simulations, consider how the theme of the novice hero would be learned as simple network of associations. Initially, a collection of nodes sufficient to account for the genre of epic would be assembled. These would include the 21 components listed for the novice hero and a few hundred other components of similar scope from other themes in epic. No connections would exist among the nodes. Figure 2.2(a) shows a small piece of such a network. The network would then be presented with a large number of epics, some containing the novice-hero theme. Each time two components appeared together (or were absent together) in the same telling of an epic, the strength of the connection between their nodes would be made more positive or excitatory. Each time one component appeared but a second did not appear in the same telling of an epic, the strength of the connection between their nodes would be made more negative or inhibitory. In this fashion, each node would develop a record of how often it occurred in the same epic with other nodes.

After many tellings of Homeric epics, each as different from the others as are the South Slavic epics recorded by Parry and Lord (Lord, 1960), the network might look something like Figure 2.2(b). For ease of presentation, the continuous scale of connection strengths is divided into three categories: (1) positive or excitatory, (2) neutral, and (3) negative or inhibitory. Solid or excitatory lines connect nodes that were both present (or both absent) in most tellings, no explicitly drawn lines connect nodes that were both present (or both absent) in about half of the tellings, and dotted or inhibitory lines connect nodes that were both present (or both absent) in less than half of the tellings.

The network has now learned something about the novice-hero theme. Certain nodes are part of a theme that contains the *novice-discontented* node; other nodes are not. The network has also learned about funeral games and other details. It abstracted this information from a collection of instances. Suppose now that just the

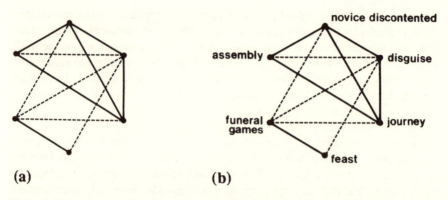

Figure 2.2. (a) Nodes representing components from epics; (b) a hypothetical associative network formed on those nodes by tallying co-occurrences of pairs of components from many epics. A solid line represents a high probability of co-occurrence; a dashed line represents a low probability of co-occurrence; and the absence of a line represents a moderate probability of co-occurrence.

novice-discontented detail is presented to the network, exciting the *novice-discontented* node. Nodes for *assembly* and for *journey* will be highly excited because of their strong, direct connection with the *novice-discontented* node. They will also excite each other through their mutual connection, and will excite the rest of the small cluster of nodes that are involved in the novice-hero theme. Similarly, the *funeral-games* node will be inhibited by its negative connection with the *novice-discontented* node and, in turn, will inhibit the *feast* node, with which it is positively connected, and excite the *disguise* and *journey* nodes, with which it is negatively connected. The history of past occurrences is stored in the network and interacts as an "organised mass," to use Bartlett's (1932, p. 197) term, with the new material presented.

All nodes influence all other nodes in a positive, negative, or neutral fashion, thus requiring considerable calculation to assess the exact effect of presenting the network with just the *novice-discontented* detail. Nonetheless, it can be seen how presenting just one detail can excite nodes related to one theme and inhibit nodes relating to other themes. Presenting several nodes from one theme will produce a stronger effect, but the point to note is that only a subset of the details from a theme have to be presented for all the details to have their nodes excited. Thus, like a schema, a network can recover implicit information.

The example just given demonstrates how a single network (1) can learn a theme or a set of themes from multiple instances, none of which has to contain the complete theme; (2) can discriminate appropriate from inappropriate themes, given a detail or set of details by exciting the nodes of the appropriate theme and inhibiting the nodes of the inappropriate theme; and (3) can recover details of a theme that were not explicitly presented in a manner that might be termed *inference* or, if the rest of the theme were still to be presented, *expectation*. If we add a few reasonable assumptions about how recall might occur, given an input and an extended network containing Figure 2.2(b), it is easy to see how the associative network would make changes in the recall of a piece to make it more like the theme the network has abstracted, and would recall nodes that are central (i.e., most highly connected) in its abstracted theme more than nodes with less excitatory connections in the theme. The network in Figure 2.2(b) as it stands has no knowledge of the order of events, but sequencing is not beyond networks of this kind. If the connections in Figure 2.2(b) were directional, as they are in Figure 2.1, the order as well as the co-occurrence of each pair of components would be noted.

Note that in this discussion two kinds of changes have been distinguished. The first are long-term changes in weights. The second are short-term changes in activation. The activation, which may outlast the presentation of the stimulus, leads to changes in the long-term weights, which, in turn, affect the spread of activation. Keeping track of all this can result in fairly complex mathematics, which is currently being developed.

Parallel Distributed Processing

The simple algorithm just presented provides, in nonmathematical terms, a general idea of how associations among nodes could come to reflect the pattern of combinations of individual stimuli. In the actual mathematical procedure of parallel distributed processing, a more complex calculation often employing feedback is used (McClelland & Rumelhart, 1985; Rumelhart, McClelland, et al., 1986). If feedback were given after each presentation of a stimulus, the output of the network would be compared with what it should have been if the presented pattern were processed correctly. The strengths among the nodes would then be adjusted by a small amount to improve the fit. Iterations with new stimuli would further improve the fit. The feedback procedure, as well as other algorithms that do not require feedback, allow the effects of all nodes on all other nodes to be taken into account in setting the strength between any two nodes, something the simpler co-occurrence model used here for explanation does not do. Thus the mathematics of parallel distributed processes can be more powerful and fundamentally different in the way they set the actual values in a network than the mathematics of associations or co-occurrence tables. Nonetheless, the simplified co-occurrence method used for explanation and the parallel distributed processing approach share the basic idea of a network of connections that is formed and continuously changed by its interactions with the environment. A major difference is that parallel distributed processing methods have actually been demonstrated to work in numerous cases.

The technical details of how the calculations are accomplished are beyond the scope of this chapter; however, descriptions along with examples are available (McClelland & Rumelhart, 1985; McClelland, Rumelhart, & Hinton, 1986; Rumelhart, Smolensky, et al., 1986), as are different approaches using other mathematics on networks (e.g., Grossberg, 1980, 1988). Particular formulations of parallel distributed processing networks appear to be good psychological models. Unresolved issues include distinguishing individual models from one another and from other kinds of models, and handling problems like learning complex sequential orders and not forgetting old sequences when new sequences are learned (Barsalou, 1990; Hintzman, 1990; McCloskey, 1991; McCloskey & Cohen, 1989).

Theme, Schema, and Memory

This chapter has reviewed the concepts developed by students of oral tradition and by students of memory to understand the role of meaning. The convergence of the two approaches, each based on its own database, lends support to both. The schema theories postulated by psychology are intended to describe many of the same phenomena as the more literary theories, though often in a more formal manner. Oral traditions are more constrained than stories in general and should allow for less ambiguous parsing of tales into scripts and story grammars. In most oral traditions, singers attempt to tell a traditional tale in a traditional way. They are creative, but not by trying to break the rules. The set of actors and actions that can be described is also limited. Thus, for instance, although there may be an infinite number of ways to fill the terminal strings of a story grammar (Garnham, 1983), in a single oral tradition the options are limited. Moreover, if memory constrains oral traditions and if schemas are a basic aspect of memory, then oral traditions should allow for clearer examples of schemas than can be obtained in the real world. Freed from many of the constraints of real lives and real dentists' offices, oral traditions should demonstrate structure in a purer form (e.g., Propp, 1928/1968).

Themes, motifs, and *multiformity* are among the terms formulated to describe and understand common aspects of the role of meaning in oral traditions as well as other literature. They have been subjected to empirical test by assessing their ability to account for repetition of meaning without strict repetition of exact wording in large samples of text from numerous genres. *Scripts, story grammars,* and *networks* are among the terms formulated to describe and understand common aspects of the role of meaning in more general contexts. They have been subjected to empirical test in a host of tasks other than textual analysis. The results of both the literary and psychological inquiries support each other and can in part account for stability and change within oral traditions.

By way of a more concrete review, consider the five predictions that were said to be shared by schema theories and that were said to be important to the stability of transmission of oral traditions:

1. A piece matching a schema will be recalled more accurately in order and in content.
2. Changes will make recall more like the schema.
3. Schema-based inferences will be drawn about omitted material.
4. Portions of variants that play the same role in a story will tend to be confused and substituted for each other even if they bear no other obvious resemblance.
5. Aspects of pieces that the schema determines are more important will be better recalled.

These predictions held for the three kinds of schema theories reviewed, and to the extent investigated, they were supported by the empirical observations generated to test each of the theories. Psychologists usually tested their claims by comparing recall with an originally presented correct stimulus and by noting errors. In oral traditions these predictions were supported, more in the actual spirit of schema theory, by comparing variants of a theme, none of which was more correct than any other.

The theories reviewed in this chapter are intended to account for the stability of meaning, but not for the stability of wording. In oral traditions, there is also considerable stability in form and in the exact words. The next two chapters describe additional constraints operating to increase stability. These will work with much of the same freedom as schemas do. In combination, they allow flexibility within a system that maintains stability.

Notes

1. Such analyses of literature are certainly in the Freudian spirit. A similar application of analytic theory to fairy tales (Bettelheim 1976), however, may not be as appropriate to the oral tradition from which the fairy tales were drawn (Darnton, 1984) as is the Meyer (1980) study.

2. From observation of behavior, it is extremely difficult, if not impossible, to infer internal mechanisms. Attempts to separate imagery from propositions in Chapter 3 and classical schema from networks of associations or instances in this chapter are examples. A model of how the nervous system functions requires that the nervous system be examined. A mechanical or computer-based model requires that the internal states of the computer be examined. Otherwise, there is an indeterminacy that cannot be resolved. If one can develop a biological or computer model of a complex behavior—and this is not a easy task if the goal is to account for specific behaviors in a detailed fashion—there is no way to know from observing behavior whether the model follows the same mechanisms as the person. Behaviorists have made this point repeatedly, and cognitive psychologists have slowly come to agree as they try to argue the relative merits of their models (e.g., Watkins, 1990).

Nonetheless, and for good reason, psychologists—and they are not alone among scientists—are fond of mechanisms. Theories are developed in this framework and data collected. It is difficult to discuss what we know without such models. At times, evidence from observing workings inside people's skins is used to supplement claims for such models. Where this is not possible, the inherent ambiguity of the situation must be stressed.

In this chapter, mechanisms for the various forms of schemas are not considered. Behavioral distinctions can be made among scripts, story grammars, and pairwise associations. Different forms of associative networks, however, can mimic these other three, and thus cannot be distinguished in general from them on purely behavioral grounds, though particular instances of them can. We return to this problem in Chapters 7 and 8, where the network metaphor is chosen as a mechanism in presenting a theory of serial recall.

In this chapter, as in much of the literature on which it is based, the structure of the representation is stressed and the processes involved in using the structure are minimized (Rubin, 1988a). Both structure and process are needed for any representation to function (Rumelhart & Norman, 1986), but for ease of exposition, discussion of the process is omitted until Chapters 7 and 8.

For a critique of what is lost with this more mechanistic approach to understanding theme, see Bruner (1990).

3. Items that are distinctive (Hunt & Mitchell, 1982), especially if they are inconsistent, as opposed to irrelevant to a schema, can also be remembered well, though this is more often the case with recognition tasks than in the recall situation of oral traditions (Bellezza & Bower, 1982; Bower et al., 1979; Brewer & Tenpenny, 1993; Graesser et al., 1979, 1980).

4. Some versions of schema theory make additional and stronger claims than those made here (Alba & Hasher, 1983). First, no claim is being made in this chapter about the relative

strength of the meaning and the surface forms of a piece in memory. In fact, in Chapter 4, the organization, or constraints, afforded by poetic structure will be presented in a way that allows one to talk about schemas for poetics. Second, no claim about the effects of schemas on the initial encoding of a piece is being made. In oral traditions, as well as in laboratory recall of text, the major effect of schemas appears to be on recall.

5. An additional difference that will not be used here is that scripts and story grammars use symbolic summary statements to represent the structure they capture, whereas associative networks can use such labeled summary statements as nodes in their networks, but need not.

6. Everyday scripts as studied by cognitive psychologists are dull, lacking in plot structure. This need not be the case in our culture for scripts used in literature. The script of the novice hero in science fiction is an example of a script that is a story. Even the repeated actions of a television hero who triumphs over evil at the same time each week for many years can contain repeated actions that are part of the story plot. Moreover, such television scripts can remain entertaining even when retold verbatim through the magic of reruns.

7. Here and elsewhere in this chapter, the claims made for a particular form of schema, such as a script, a story grammar, or an associative network, have been found with other forms of schemas as well.

8. In general, grammars for sentences benefit from the extensive studies of linguistics. Story grammars do not have a parallel scholarly tradition. Thus the large number of arbitrary decisions that had to be made in formulating a grammar for sentences received "independent motivation" from well-studied properties of language, whereas grammars for stories received much less aid. Another difference between grammars for sentences and grammars for stories is in their terminal strings—that is, those strings that are not rewritten by the grammar. Grammars for languages have a finite number of terminal strings (i.e., words or morphemes), and these strings are identified as belonging to a small set of word classes (e.g., nouns, verbs). Story grammars have an infinite number of terminal strings (i.e., strings that could replace *SETTING* in the example grammar), and these strings do not belong to a small set of classes. This difference makes it impossible to decide the underlying structure of an arbitrarily chosen story with anything like the precision that is possible for an arbitrarily chosen sentence (Garnham, 1983). Nonetheless, adequate parsers might be able to be developed for the more stereotyped stories of individual genres of oral traditions in which the terminal strings are more limited and better defined.

9. Such associations among pairs of words are not schemas. They are included here because they have been used in psychological, as well as almost all other, theories of memory. As will be seen shortly, however, when combined as part of a network of associations, they do take on all the properties of schemas.

10. The symmetrical "next-to" similarity matrix was submitted to a smallest space analysis multidimensional scaling solution (Lingoes, 1973). The asymmetrical "followed" similarity matrix was submitted to a pathfinder scaling algorithm (Schvaneveldt, 1990). The arrows in Figure 2.1 are the set of minimally spanning trees that connect the 20 words. The exact procedure and analysis are provided in Chapter 4, where the structure of semantic categories, such as parts of the body, is compared with rhyme categories, such as all words rhyming with *ee*.

CHAPTER 3

Imagery

> Mental imagery is remarkably able to substitute for actual perception.
> . . . Possibly, rules governing spatial structures and transformations, having
> been incorporated into our perceptual machinery by eons of evolution in a three-
> dimensional world, are now at the service of creative thought.
>
> Shepard, 1978, p. 125

> Imagery is assumed to be specialized for the symbolic representation of concrete
> situations and events, speed and flexibility of transformational thinking (the
> "flights" as compared to the "perchings" of the stream of thought), and parallel
> processing in the visual-spatial sense. The verbal system, on the other hand, is
> presumably characterized by its capacity to deal with abstract problems, con-
> cepts, and relationships, and for processing sequential information.
>
> Paivio, 1971, p. 434

A few examples of the role of imagery in oral traditions should help put into context the academic discussions that follow. The 20-stanza ballad that appears on pages 260 and 261 is typical of oral traditions. The story is told in terms of concrete, imageable actions. The description in each stanza is graphic. In addition, at about every stanza or two, the action shifts to a new location, providing a spatial layout that accompanies the story line. The same observations can be made for epic. Consider the following passage from the *Iliad,* analyzed in Chapter 9, in which Patroclus is killing one of a long series of Trojan warriors. Each of these killings will occur in a slightly different part of the battlefield, and epic as a whole has a clear spatial path that is tied to the story line. If anything, the graphic detail is more than the modern reader might want.

> Next he attacked Thestor son of Enops, who was sitting hunched up in his polished
> chariot. This man had lost his head completely and the reins had slipped from his hands.
> Patroclus came up beside him and struck him on the right side of the jaw, driving his
> spear between the teeth. Then, using his spear as lever, he hoisted him over the chariot-
> rail as a fisherman sitting on a jutting rock pulls a monster fish out of the sea with his line
> and his burnished hook. Thus with the bright spear Patroclus hauled his gaping catch out
> of the car and dropped him on his face, to die as he fell. (Rieu, 1950, p. 303)

Even the counting-out rhymes of children are graphic, to the extent that they have meaning. The following two examples were chosen because they were the most well known among Duke undergraduates after *Eenie Meenie* and *One Potato,* the rhymes that are discussed at length in Chapter 10:

> Engine engine number nine,
> Running on the Chicago line.
> If the train should jump the track
> Do you want your money back?

> My mother and your mother
> Were hanging out clothes
> My mother gave your mother
> A punch in the nose.
> What color was the blood?

For the variants of both rhymes just given, the person on whom the last word falls answers and the answer is spelled out, with each letter counting out one person. For instance, for the second rhyme the answer and counting might be ''Blue. B   L   U   E.''

Imagery is difficult to define. Neither philosophers nor psychologists have come to complete agreement on what imagery is or on what behaviors, if any, would necessarily support the claim that imagery aids memory, though experimental psychologists have come to a consensus on operational definitions. This is not for want of effort (Block, 1981; Kieras, 1978; Kosslyn, 1983; Kosslyn, Pinker, Smith, & Shwartz, 1979; Paivio, 1971, 1986; Richardson, 1980; Rollins, 1989; Rumelhart & Norman, 1986; Tye, 1991).[1] Nonetheless, at a functional level, the concept of imagery allows the explanation of human behavior to be simpler and more complete. For instance, people not trained in the subtleties of philosophy or cognitive psychology can reliably judge the ease with which verbal material can be imaged, and material that people judge easy to image is remembered differently from material that people judge hard to image. Moreover, as is discussed later in this chapter, the neural bases of imagery and language are different, supporting the argument for different systems. For the purposes of this book, imagery is an analog system for representing and manipulating visual and spatial information.[2] Its u e can, but need not, be accompanied by a conscious awareness of having an image.

The concept of imagery discussed in this chapter and the concepts of themes, scripts, story grammars, and associative networks discussed in Chapter 2 are ways of describing the organization and processing of experience. Imagery differs in many respects from the verbal meaning discussed in Chapter 2. In the first main section of this chapter, the unique properties of imagery are described and contrasted with those of verbal meaning. Some of these properties are directly relevant to the transmission of oral traditions; others are not as relevant, but are needed for a full description of imagery. As in the last chapter, I attempt to provide not only the conclusions that cognitive psychologists draw, but also a sense of the evidence and reasoning used to draw those conclusions. For some readers such evidence may become tedious, but it allows the reader to judge the soundness of the arguments used by cognitive psychology and the reasonableness of extending findings beyond the laboratory to oral traditions.

In the first main section that follows, I review evidence (1) that imagery is an analog system that has many similarities to perception and (2) that imagery aids memory for the concrete, (3) the dynamic, and (4) the spatial, in part (5) by providing alternative forms of organization, and (6) specific details. The implications of the neural bases of imagery are then discussed. In the second main section, the role of imagery in oral traditions is considered in light of the psychological data and theory reviewed in the first section.

Imagery and Memory

Imagery Is an Analog System

The term *analog* is used in the psychological literature on imagery in two senses. The first is continuous—that is, analog as opposed to digital or discrete (Kosslyn, 1983). This sense of analog is of little practical use because a continuous image and a fine-grained discrete image are hard to distinguish (Rumelhart & Norman, 1986). The second sense of analog is that imagery and perception of the same object or scene share certain, but not all, properties with each other—that is, analog in the sense of analogy (Rumelhart & Norman, 1986; Shepard, 1978). The properties that are typically shared are the ones that would be present in a picture drawn to represent either the image or the perception of the actual object or scene.

In the remainder of this section, I provide behavioral evidence that imagery shares many properties with perception. The details of the studies will not be used in later discussions of the nature of oral traditions. Rather, the experimental studies provide evidence for viewing imagery as a "picture or movie created in the head" in which size, distance, color, shape, location, and intermediate steps in the movement of objects all function much as they would in perception, and in which the formation of images takes time that can be measured and used to draw inferences about imagery.

Several demonstrations of the analog nature of imagery involve size judgments. Moyer (1973) presented people with the typed names of two animals and asked them to judge which of the two animals was larger. The time to decide was a function of difference in the size of the animals. Thus people acted as if they had an analog, size-preserving, representation of the animals.

Paivio (1975b) extended this study and, using several clever manipulations, made explanations not based on an analog imagery system much less tenable. In one condition, people had to decide which of two objects in the real world was larger. They were presented with either the names or the drawings of the objects. In either case, one of the pair of stimuli was about twice as large as the other, as shown in Figure 3.1. People judged size differences more quickly with the drawings than with the words. For the drawings, but not for the words, they were faster if the member of the pair of stimuli that was drawn larger was also the larger member in the real world. To ensure that there was nothing odd about the drawings themselves, Paivio

Figure 3.1. Sample drawings and words used by Paivio (1975b).

had different people judge the same drawings, but this time they had to decide which object was farther away. Reaction times were now faster if the member of the pair of stimuli that was drawn larger was smaller in the real world. Finally, to ensure that drawings are not responded to more quickly than words in all situations, Paivio had a third group judge which member name of each pair was easier to pronounce and found that the typed stimuli yielded faster reaction times than the drawings.

Assuming that drawings map more directly onto an imagery system and words map more directly onto a verbal system, Paivio's results support the notion that there is an analog imagery system that is faster than the verbal system for imagery-related tasks and slower for verbal tasks. In addition, the size of the drawing interacts with size information stored in the imagery system in a manner consistent with an analog system, whereas the size of the typed words does not interact with size information stored in the imagery or verbal systems. It is difficult to account for this collection of results at a functional level without an analog imagery system.

Shepard (1978) reviewed several lines of evidence that he and his students have used to demonstrate the analog nature of imagery. Unlike the Moyer and Paivio studies, which used judgments of size, Shepard's work depended on the shape or other holistic properties of the imaged objects. Shepard's first line of evidence is that people who were asked to judge the perceptual similarity among the members of various sets of visual stimuli—including the shapes of the states of the United States, colors, and familiar faces—produced statistically indistinguishable judgments when they performed the task with the stimuli present and when they used imagery in the absence of the stimuli. For example, people judged the similarity of familiar colors in the same way whether the colors were present or absent. This means that the structure present in the judgments of actual stimuli (e.g., the color circle for colors) was also present in the judgments based on imagery, and that in the judgment tasks memory, presumably in the form of images, could successfully substitute for real objects.

The second line of evidence involves reaction times to spatially localized probes. People were presented with a 5 × 5 grid either with a letter shaded in or with an empty grid on which to image the letter. A dot was then placed on one or more squares of the grid, as shown in Figure 3.2. The task was to indicate as quickly as possible, by pressing one of two buttons, whether or not a dot was on a real or an imagined shaded square. People were quite accurate and were only about 0.05 second slower when the letter had to be imaged than when it was actually shown. Further support for the analog nature of imagery comes from the detailed analysis of reaction times as a function of the position of the dots. The reaction time to say "yes" was faster for dots falling on the intersections of bars, and the reaction time to say "no" was faster for dots falling farther away from grids containing the imaged letter. In addition, the absolute position of the dot made no difference to the reaction times, indicating that people were not using a strict left-to-right or top-to-bottom search; instead, they scanned the image in whatever order was most useful, much the way people scan an actual display.

The third line of evidence allowed Shepard (1978) to make even stronger claims by defining an *analog process* as one in which intermediate steps in the transformation of an image correspond to intermediate steps in the external world. Thus, for example, the intermediate images present when an image of a letter is rotated from upside down to upright are the same intermediate steps that would be seen if the actual letter were rotated.

Cooper and Shepard (1973) timed how long it took people to judge whether an alphanumeric character was presented normally or in mirror-image form. Any of six characters could appear in any of six orientations. Figure 3.3 presents some sample test characters. Before the test character was presented, a blank (condition B), the letter to be tested shown in an upright orientation (condition L), or the letter to be tested shown in the test orientation (condition O) was displayed for 2 seconds. If the letter was shown in the upright position, it might be followed by an arrow indicating the orientation of the test character. The arrow was presented for either 0.1, 0.4,

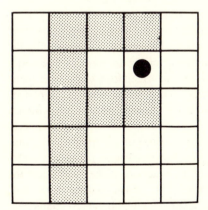
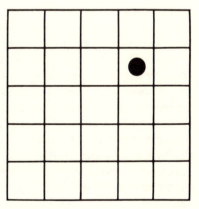

Figure 3.2. Stimuli like those used by Shepard (1978). Undergraduates had to judge whether the dot fell on a real or an imagined letter.

Figure 3.3. Examples of regular and mirror-image characters in various orientations. (After Cooper & Shepard, 1973)

0.7, or 1.0 second before the test character (conditions .1, .4, .7, and 1, respectively).

Of immediate interest is the top plot in Figure 3.4 (condition B). When no advance information was given, the time needed to judge whether or not a character was a mirror image increased as the orientation of the character moved away from upright, reaching a maximum of 1.1 seconds when the character was upside down (i.e., at 180 degrees). It is as if the test character had to be rotated into an upright position. In fact, if the confounded effects of orientation and amount of rotation are separated, the time to rotate the image is a linear function of the degrees of rotation needed. Similar results have been found with complex figures made out of blocks and with outlines of hands (Cooper & Shepard, 1975; Shepard & Metzler, 1971).

The fourth line of evidence is that images formed in preparation for a judgment reduce the time needed to make that judgment. Figure 3.4 demonstrates that this effect can be dramatic. Consider the bottom plot of Figure 3.4 (condition O), in which the test-character letter is shown in non-mirror-image form in the test-character orientation for 2 seconds, followed by a blank screen for 1 second and then the test character. All that is necessary is to keep the letter in mind exactly as it appeared for the 1 second it is not on the screen and then judge whether the test character on the screen is the same as or a mirror reversal of the image in memory. The time taken to perform this task is 0.4 second, regardless of the orientation. Thus the preparatory image greatly reduces the time needed to perform the task.

It is not necessary to give people a drawing of the exact image they will need. In the remaining plots in Figure 3.4, an upright letter was presented and the individual had to rotate an image of the letter into position to compare it with the test character. If an arrow indicating the orientation of the test character was shown for 1 second after the upright letter (condition 1), then people were almost as quick at the task as when the letter was shown in the orientation of the test character. If, however, the orientation arrow was shown for only 0.7 or 0.4 second, there was not enough time to rotate the letter completely into the position of the test character; thus the response times for these conditions (conditions .7 and .4) fall between those for the blank (condition B) and the oriented-letter (condition O) conditions. If the orientation is shown for only 0.1 second, the response times are the same as if just the letter is shown (condition L). That is, 0.1 second is not enough time to begin rotating the image. The results shown in Figure 3.4 offer strong support to the interpretation that people can manipulate images, that such manipulation takes a period of time proportional to the amount of manipulation needed, and that the manipulated images can be used to perform tasks more quickly. Similar results have been noted with other stimuli (Shepard, 1978).

The analog nature of imagery, in which intermediate steps in the transformation of an image correspond to the intermediate steps in the transformation of objects in the external world, is both one of the most fascinating aspects of imagery and one of the most useful for oral traditions. If images can be manipulated, they can serve as structures to organize ongoing activity. The movie is a better model for imagery than the photograph.

Rumelhart and Norman (1986) accentuate this property of imagery when they suggest that images can be considered as "mental models" and "mental simula-

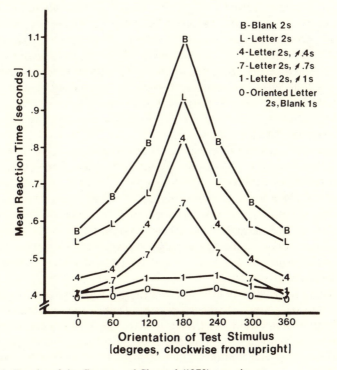

Figure 3.4. Results of the Cooper and Shepard (1973) experiment.

tions.'' Images can be viewed as ways of testing in the mind what would happen if something were done in the external world by transforming the image to correspond to hypothetical changes in the external world. For instance, imagery can be used to evaluate what would happen if a certain move were made in chess or if a piece of furniture were moved to a new location. Similarly, an athlete can improve performance compared with no practice by repeatedly imaging an event—for example, dart throwing (Neisser, 1983). It is therefore not at all unreasonable to consider that imagery, conscious or not, can be used to transform one state to another and serve as a cue for verbal recall along the way.

Imagery appears to be like perception not only in general functioning, as just reviewed, but also in more subtle and detailed properties of the visual system. For instance, imagery appears to have a definite field of view (Kosslyn, 1983; Lockhead & Evans, 1979) and limited acuity (Finke & Kosslyn, 1980). That is, there appears to be an angle outside of which images cannot be seen and a limit to the resolving power of images, much as there is with normal sight. Studies showing detailed parallels between vision and imagery are among the most fascinating, but are also the most difficult to interpret due to methodological difficulties (Finke, 1985).

Imagery Aids Memory

Up to this point, all that has been argued is that imagery is an analog system that shares many properties with visual perception. This argument is important in order to characterize what is meant by imagery and to indicate the kinds of data on which that characterization is based. The remainder of this section provides evidence that imagery is a powerful memory aid (Paivio, 1971, 1986, 1991), with properties that are especially useful for oral traditions. Most of the results presented will be for relatively long-term effects, though imagery is also important in short-term or working memory (Baddeley, 1986) and can even be seen as having most of its effects there rather than in long-term representation (Marschark, Richman, Yuille, & Hunt, 1987). Again, the details of the studies are presented mainly to give a sense of the data on which the arguments are based.

The observation that visual imagery is an aid to memory predates experimental work on imagery by about 2,000 years (Paivio, 1971; Yates, 1966). Almost all the mnemonic systems developed from the time of the ancient Greeks and Romans through the Middle Ages to the present generation of stage mnemonists and authors of books on how to improve memory are based on visual imagery. The oldest recorded system, the method of loci (Bower, 1970a; Cornoldi & De Beni, 1991; Yates, 1966), is still one of the most popular. The way Cicero described it is still the way it is practiced today and is the way I, and several classes of my students, learned it for a classroom demonstration.

In my version, a path of 40 locations, or loci, that passed through the campus of Lawrence University was committed to memory. The easiest way for me to learn and review the 40 locations was to walk the path in my mind, anticipating each location that I would see. This was done in much the same way that I would walk the path in my mind in order to give directions along the path to a stranger. There are several reasons for using a path. First, the path uses the spatial component of imagery to compensate for the lack of sequential information in a single image. If one item is put in each location, there is no sequential recall within an image. Second, the path, as opposed to another kind of list of imageable objects, makes use of the spatial component of imagery in order to reduce the initial time spent learning the technique. Paths are easier to learn than random lists. Third, the path ensures that items are not easily omitted. When several items are put in one image, all may be seen but only some may be reported. With the one-item-per-locus rule, this cannot occur. In many tales from oral traditions, a real or an imaginary path of travel can take advantage of the same spatial ability and can serve the same sequential-cuing function that my 40 locations do.

In order to learn a list of 40 items, each item is paired with a location. An image is formed of the first item interacting in as vivid and unique a way as possible with the first location. As each succeeding item is presented, it is imaged interacting with the next location on the path. As Luria's (1968) mnemonist points out, the items must be imaged in a clearly visible manner. If they are too small, obscured by other details, or even not well lit in the image, they will not be "seen" later. To recall the items in the order presented, the path is walked again, and each location is examined to see what image it contains.

At the beginning of a class, I have 40 students each tell me in turn one item they might purchase from a supermarket. Not being a professional mnemonist, I am quite slow and take 5 to 10 seconds to form a good interactive image of each item and the location at which it happens to fall. After lecturing for a half-hour, I recall the list in the order given, typically without error. I then show the students a set of 40 slides corresponding to the 40 locations on the pathway and describe the interactive image that tied each item to its location. Finally, I show the slides again and ask the students to recall as many items as they can. Even though they made no effort to learn the items, just having the interactive images described to them is sufficient to allow them to average about 37 items correct out of 40. Moreover, even students who claim to have very poor imagery do well. A particularly good image can stay with me from one term to the next, yet a set of 40 new items can be learned immediately after the first set with minimal interference from the first set. The power of the method of loci and its reliance on imagery reported in this anecdote have been demonstrated under more controlled conditions (Bower, 1970a; Rubin 1978). The method works with stories, especially when presented orally (Cornoldi & De Beni, 1991).

The method of loci involves instructions (1) to form integrated images in which the items to be remembered interact with their loci and (2) to use, or transform the material to be learned into, easily imageable items. Both of these factors have been shown to aid memory in controlled laboratory research. First, instructions to produce an image in which the items to be learned are interacting produces superior memory than instructions either to produce an image in which the items are separate or to use various verbal methods such as repetition and association (Begg & Sikich, 1984; Bower, 1970b; Paivio, 1971).[3] Second, when no instructions are given to college undergraduates, it is routinely found that words that are easiest to image are easiest to recall (Paivio, 1969, 1971, 1983a).

Studies comparing numerous properties on their ability to predict the memorability of words report much the same results (Paivio, 1968; Rubin, 1980; Rubin & Friendly, 1986). In the most extensive of these studies (Rubin, 1980), 34 properties of words were used to predict which words would be remembered from several different recall tasks, including the method of loci. In addition to measures of imagery, the set of properties included measures of orthography, frequency, pronunciability, meaningfulness, availability, age of acquisition, goodness, and emotionality. Imagery was uniformly the best predictor of recall.

In both the mnemonic systems developed to aid memory and the controlled laboratory studies of learning, imagery has been found to be a powerful aid to memory. The remainder of this section examines particular ways in which imagery functions to aid memory and how these ways add to its special strengths and weaknesses.

Having argued that imagery is like perception and that it aids memory, we now examine, in turn, the arguments that imagery is (1) dynamic, (2) spatial, (3) a form of organization in the same sense that theme is a form of organization, and (4) specific. Each of these four topics helps define imagery and shows how it could function to increase stability in oral traditions. As in the previous sections, the details of experiments are included mainly as ways of evaluating the evidence for each of these properties. Such details will not be used later to clarify the transmission of particular genres, but the properties will be used.

Imagery Is for the Dynamic

Paivio (1971, pp. 28–33) argues that imagery is especially well suited for transformational thinking—that is, for moving rapidly from one situation to another. Complex images can be changed rapidly into different images and back again, whereas the manipulation of a similar amount of verbal information would take longer. Although plausible, little direct evidence has been obtained for this claim. Nonetheless, many studies support the claim that responses are faster for concrete situations. A brief review of the most relevant studies follows. For instance, people can more rapidly verify that a string of letters is a word if the word is concrete as opposed to abstract (James, 1975); people can more rapidly verify that a sentence makes sense if it is concrete (Holmes & Langford, 1976; Klee & Eysenck, 1973); and people can more rapidly decide that a sentence is true on the basis of general knowledge (Jorgensen & Kintsch, 1973) or on the basis of a recently read passage (Just & Brownell, 1974) if the sentence is concrete.[4]

People are also quicker to detect changes in concrete sentences. Moeser (1974) had undergraduates read a set of 10 sentences, spending as much time as they felt necessary on each sentence to learn it sufficiently well so that later they could decide which of 20 additional sentences were identical to one of the original 10. The undergraduates spent less time reading each of the original 10 sentences and less time deciding that a sentence had been seen before if the sentence was concrete as opposed to abstract.

Effects can also be observed if the instructions instead of the material are varied. Seamon (1972) asked people to rehearse verbally, image separately, or image interacting sets of between one and three nouns. The people were then presented with a noun and asked if it was a member of the set they had just learned. The normal increase in latency to respond as the number of items in the set increased was not found when interactive imagery was used to learn the set of words. This resulted in an overall faster response for the interactive-imagery condition.

Similar effects on the amount of material to be searched have been noted by Paivio (1975a) and by Just and Brownell (1974). Paivio reported studies in which two, three, or four unrelated abstract words, concrete words, or pictures had to be combined into one sentence or one image. For all three kinds of stimuli, as the number of items to be combined increased, the time needed to form a sentence increased much more than the time needed to form an image. In particular, it took about 3.5 seconds for each additional item in the sentence condition and only about 1 second for each additional item in the image condition. In the Just and Brownell study, sentences from longer passages took reliably longer to verify if the passages were abstract than if they were concrete. The increase in the time needed with the increased length of material becomes much more important than the overall time taken if the results with the relatively short laboratory material are to be generalized to the longer material of most traditions.

Most of the tasks that measure reaction time, including those just cited, use visual presentation of stimuli because visual presentation is easier to time and allows a more direct comparison of pictures and words. Because the need to attend to a visual presentation appears to interfere with the formation of images (Garrod & Trabasso, 1973), however, even larger effects of imagery might be expected if auditory presentation, such as is used in oral traditions, were used in the experiments.

Imagery Is for the Spatial, Not the Sequential

Paivio (1971, 1975a, 1975b, 1983a, 1983b, 1986, 1991) amassed considerable data in favor of the view that imagery is better than verbal processing for spatial memory and that verbal processing is better than imagery for sequential memory. Not all the experiments in the literature show this effect, and, as is always the case, no single experiment is without an alternative explanation (Richardson, 1980); but if all the evidence is considered, there is substantial support for this view. Paivio (1975a) provides the following commonsense argument for his position:

> I have often asked people to describe the contents of their living rooms . . . to describe what is on the right as one enters the room, or what is straight ahead, and so on. The answer comes promptly in each case, indicating that the layout of the room is available all at once in memory.
>
> Speech is a temporal sequence in the obvious sense that the acoustic signal and verbal behavior are temporal in nature, but also because the syntax that gives linguistic units their meaning involves sequential structure. . . . Thus, most people can easily recite some familiar poem from the beginning but find it very difficult to recite it backward. Even a forward recitation is awkward if one is asked simply to begin in the middle of the poem. This contrasts with the absence of such constraints in the retrieval of information from the memory image of one's living room. (pp. 148–149)

Of course, the representation of meaning, as described in Chapter 2, need not be as sequential as verbal output, though some of the models described to account for the meaning structures found in oral traditions, in fact, are. Likewise, images can be constructed to preserve sequential information, as is demonstrated by the use of pathways in the method of loci. Mental images, like physical images, do not preserve sequences unless a set search path is specified for the images. Images such as spatial pathways, sequences of photographs, or movies have an inherently sequential nature that is avoided in the experiments that demonstrate a deficit in sequential representation. In oral traditions, however, pathways, often reinforced by the story line, are used to overcome this deficit in maintaining the order of information. Nonetheless, there is a clear, intuitive difference between the spatial nature of images and the sequential nature of verbal behavior that could lead each to have its peculiar strengths and weaknesses in preserving information and could lead to difficulties in translating between the two.

There are numerous studies using a variety of procedures that, for the most part, support Paivio's spatial–sequential distinction (for reviews, see Anderson, 1976; Healy, 1977; Snodgrass, Burns, & Pirone, 1978). Two studies, which use different procedures, are considered here: that of Paivio and Csapo (1969) and that of Healy (1977).

In one of the earliest studies, Paivio and Csapo (1969) compared tasks that required sequential order to be preserved with tasks that did not require sequential order to be preserved. For instance, recall could be required to be in the order of presentation, or recall could be allowed to be given in any order. Pictures, concrete words, or abstract words were presented at either a slow or a fast rate. Paivio and Csapo reasoned that the slow rate should allow time for the pictures to be labeled verbally and thus would increase the chance of their being remembered in the correct sequential order. As expected, the presence of verbal labels increased performance differentially for tasks that required sequential order.

Healy (1977) presented the same four letters to people whose task was to remember either in what spatial position (i.e., far left, left middle, right middle, or far right) or in what sequential order the letters occurred. One of four interference tasks filled the time between the presentation of the four letters and the recall of either their spatial position or their sequential order. All the interference tasks consisted of reading digits that appeared where the letters had appeared. The four interference conditions were:

1. The name of the digit was read aloud.
2. The name of the digit was read silently.
3. The position of the digit was read aloud.
4. The position of the digit was read silently.

If Paivio's prediction is correct, then reading the position of the letter (which involves spatial processing), as opposed to reading the name of the letter (which involves language), should have a greater negative effect on memory for spatial position than it does for temporal order. Similarly, reading aloud (which makes more use of language processing than does reading silently) should have a greater negative effect on sequential order than it does for spatial position. Both of these predictions were confirmed. In addition, as would be expected by Paivio, a detailed analysis of errors showed that phonemic coding was more prevalent in the sequential than in the spatial condition.

The review so far is based on comparisons of spatial and sequential information. There are, however, numerous studies that concentrate on only the spatial component of imagery. For many of these, spatial location need not be visual at all, but could as well be location known by auditory or tactile means. There are a number of spatial effects, including:

1. Spatial location is a cue to recall (Bahrick, 1974; Bellezza, 1983).
2. Attributes of stimuli are easier to associate if paired in consistent locations (Geiselman & Crawley, 1983; Winograd & Church, 1988; also see Rescorla & Cunningham, 1979, for studies with pigeons).
3. Spatial location is an important attribute of memory (Underwood, 1969) or is automatically processed (Hasher & Zacks, 1979).
4. People have good recall for the location of information on a page (Rothkopf, Fisher, & Billington, 1982; Zechmeister & McKillip, 1972).

More directly related to oral traditions are studies in which images of imaginary places are constructed and used to guide memory. When people read, they construct a spatial model for the information needed to understand the text, if one can be made (Johnson-Laird, 1983). Undergraduates who read a passage that described a geographic setting could answer questions about relative locations that were explicitly mentioned in the text. They could also answer questions about relative locations not mentioned explicitly, though it took them slightly longer, leading to the inference that memory both for the text read and for a spatial model constructed from it could be consulted, though the latter was a slower process (Perrig & Kintsch, 1985; Taylor & Tversky, 1992). The spatial information was given in either bird's-eye geographic-survey terms or from the perspective of a traveled route. Under some conditions, people were faster to use the perspective originally read (Perrig & Kintsch, 1985); under other conditions, which included a higher degree of learning, either perspective led to the same behavior on survey or route questions (Taylor & Tversky, 1992). In addition to answering questions about spatial relations, the undergraduates could draw accurate maps after reading the texts and seemed to learn the same information from maps as from the text (Taylor & Tversky, 1992), supporting the idea that a map-like representation was being formed from the text.

Text focuses the reader's or listener's attention on different spatial locations. The simplest demonstration of this is to consider the following sentences from Bower and Morrow (1990):

1. John walked past the car up to the house. The windows were dirty.
2. John walked into the house after passing the car. The windows were dirty.
3. John was walking past the car on his way to the house. The windows were dirty.

In the first pair of sentences, the windows are the house windows. This could be because the word *house* was mentioned last, but sentences 2 and 3 show that this is not the case. In all three sentences, the windows referred to are the windows that are near the protagonist. Morrow (1985) showed this to be the case experimentally using a model of a house, so that the path traveled could be known more clearly. Prepositions and verb aspect, rather than the order of mention, help locate the protagonist.

Once this observation was confirmed experimentally, questions about the spread of attention spatially from the protagonist could be asked. Undergraduates learned the layout of artificial scenes and then read a text about the movements of a protagonist through the remembered layout. At times, instead of another line of text, the names of two objects would appear on the computer screen and the undergraduate would have to indicate from memory whether the objects were located in the same room. If the objects were in the same room as the protagonist, the time needed to answer was less than if the objects were in another room, leading to the conclusion that attention spread not only to the protagonist, but also to the protagonist's immediate surroundings (Morrow, Greenspan, & Bower, 1987).

Using this technique, several questions about spatial attention could be asked. For instance, it was found that the location about which the protagonist was thinking was more important than the location of the protagonist; in addition, locations along the path received attention, even if they were not explicitly mentioned. In fact, unmentioned locations on the path received more attention, as measured by decreased time to answer, than locations explicitly mentioned as having been where the protagonist had just been (Morrow, Bower, & Greenspan, 1989; Wilson, Rinck, McNamara, Bower, & Morrow, 1993).

Undergraduates construct models of the spatial layouts of texts if they are useful to understanding or to tasks required of them. Once such models are learned, they control the speed with which undergraduates will make inferences and answer questions. It is likely, given the importance of spatial information in oral traditions, that audiences and singers also construct relatively stable spatial models of the world described in a genre or piece and use them to understand and to remember.

Imagery Is a Type of Organization

Although imagery can have major effects on the processing of a stimulus taken in isolation, in recall imagery appears to function mainly by providing a form of organization for a set of stimuli that would otherwise be less integrated (but see Marschark, 1985; Marschark & Hunt, 1989; Marschark et al. 1987).

In an early study that tried to elucidate why imagery aided memory, Bower (1970b) had people learn pairs of words (1) by repeating the words aloud, (2) by imaging the objects denoted by the words in separate halves of an imaginary visual field, or (3) by imaging objects denoted by words interacting in an integrative scene. A list of test words was then presented. Half the test words were the left-hand member of the original pairs, and half of the test words were new. For each test word, a decision had to be made on whether the word was seen earlier (i.e., recognition) and, if so, what word had been paired with it (i.e., cued recall).

If imagery functioned by increasing the memorability of individual items, then both the separation- and the interactive-imagery instructions should increase performance on both the recognition and the cued recall tasks when compared with repetition instructions. In contrast, if imagery functioned by organizing items into larger units, then no difference among the three types of instruction would be expected for the recognition task, which does not involve integrated units, and the interactive-imagery instructions should do better in cued recall than the separation-imagery instructions. In fact, the separation-imagery instructions should not be better than repetition because neither of these forms of learning leads to integrated units. The results were completely consistent with the organizational hypothesis, though in other experiments imagery instructions have been shown to aid recognition (Paivio, 1976).

In numerous experiments, Begg (e.g., Begg, 1972; Begg & Sikich, 1984) has demonstrated the importance of imagery in organizing otherwise isolated units. This work has been extended from word pairs to phrases to items and their contexts. Begg and Sikich demonstrated that the same type of integrative imagery that is necessary for imagery to increase the recall of otherwise unrelated pairs of words is necessary for imagery to increase the recall of objects in a context. This finding is important for many oral traditions in which an action is described in the context of background information.

Thus although imagery may have some effects on the processing of isolated stimuli, in recall it appears that the main effect of imagery is to organize stimuli into an integrated whole. But what role does this leave for imagery as we move from lists of minimally organized words and pictures to stimuli, such as prose and poetry, that have the advantage of the types of organizations discussed in Chapter 2? One might expect imagery to play less of a role in determining how much is recalled because other forms of organization exist. Moreover, in cases in which the image formed by the piece and the theme abstracted from the piece contain similar information, the various forms of organization could be similar. Thus, for example, the aspects of a story that might be most important in the theme might also be most important in the images formed by the story. Nonetheless, the special properties of imagery could lead to differences in processing not captured by amount-recalled measures. This is what appears to happen.

Marschark (1985) presented undergraduates with stories that were similar in structure and length, but differed on the degree of imagery they aroused. The sentences of the paragraphs were presented in their normal order or in a random order. The recall of the high- and low-imagery paragraphs did not differ when they were presented in normal order, but twice as much was recalled from the high-imagery paragraphs as from the low-imagery paragraphs when random order was used. Similarly, both the superior recognition (Pezdek & Royer, 1974) and the more rapid reading time (Schwanenflugel & Shoben, 1983) of concrete, as opposed to abstract, sentences disappeared when the sentences were placed in a passage.

A lack of difference in one measure, however, does not imply that the high- and low-imagery passages are processed in the same manner. The use of more subtle measures can still demonstrate differences. For example, Marschark (1979) presented passages similar to those he used in his 1985 paper in their normal order, orally, in a word-by-word fashion. Undergraduates, who were told that they would later have to recall the paragraphs, pressed a button to control when each new word would be presented. Again, there were no differences in the amount of recall. However, an analysis of how much time was spent on each word did produce differences. For high-imagery paragraphs, more time was spent pausing at semantic as opposed to syntactic boundaries, while the reverse was true for low-imagery paragraphs. Moreover, the undergraduates reported using more visual imagery with the high-imagery paragraphs and more rehearsal with the low-imagery paragraphs. Similarly, Marschark and Paivio (1977) found that people both reported using different strategies and made different types of errors with high- compared with low-imagery sentences.

The smaller effect of imagery on the amount of recall from organized material should not be taken to imply that imagery has only a minimal role to play in organized material. Imagery, at least in its spatial sense, pervades our language both directly (Herskovits, 1986) and in metaphor (Lakoff & Johnson, 1980). In English, we even have a special syntactic class of words, prepositions, with the semantic function of noting the relative locations of objects. Combined with verb aspect, prepositions provide the spatial layout and determine which parts of events are most prominent in text (Morrow, 1985). This mapping of language and imagery is a common and important function both in oral traditions and in discourse in general, and one that can occur only in organized material.

Imagery Is Specific

Having demonstrated the effectiveness of imagery as a mnemonic aid, we now consider some studies that account for some of imagery's effectiveness without making use of the visual aspects of imagery. Chase and Ericsson (1981, especially pp. 161–163) provide an explanation of how imagery could aid memory based on the details activated in memory. As an example, they contrast the ease of remembering two sentences differing in concreteness: "Truth is good" and "The cow kicked the ball." In the latter sentence, there are distinctive aspects of the two nouns that could lead to a more elaborate memory if the image formed were detailed enough to include them. For instance, the cow has horns, udders, and black and white spots and is in a specific location, facing in a particular direction. In addition, there are many details that connect the two nouns in their role as *agent* and *object,* including these: the cow is facing the ball, the speed with which the cow's foot hits the ball, and the direction and velocity of the ball relative to the cow. By comparison, the two nouns in "Truth is good" have little that is distinctive when examined individually and little that can provide elaboration of the *subject–predicate* link between them.

A similar argument for why interactive imagery has such a powerful effect is made in an elegant series of experiments by Buggie (1974; also see Hintzman 1993). Buggie presented lists of concrete noun pairs joined either by the single noninteractive relation *next to* or by a series of interactive images such as *flying, kicking,* and *crushing.* Thus one list would begin *horse next to a kite, whale next to a football, beaver next to a piano;* another list would begin *horse flying a kite, whale kicking a football, beaver crushing a piano.* People were told to rate the vividness of the image and then were given a surprise recall test in which one of the words was given as a cue. The standard interactive-imagery effect was observed, with people recalling twice as many items on the interactive lists. Buggie, however, had an additional condition to test whether it was the interactive imagery itself or the specific relationships between noun pairs that made a difference. For lists in this additional condition, the relationships between the two nouns were interactive, but were the same for all noun pairs. Thus people might see a list beginning *horse kicking a kite, whale kicking a football, beaver kicking a piano.* For these lists, the amount of recall was the same as for the noninteractive *next-to* lists.[5] Thus the specific, distinctive relationships, and not the interaction of the imagery, was the cause of increased recall in these experiments. Therefore, in oral traditions, the effects of interactive imagery on recall could be caused by increasing such distinctive, specific relationships.

Another possibility is that it is not imagery that matters for memory, but the availability of a context in which to put the verbal material that has to be learned. The image is effective because it provides a specific context. Thus abstract sentences take longer to read than concrete sentences, but not if they are in the context of a paragraph (Schwanenflugel & Shoben, 1983). In addition, ratings of the ease with which a word makes available a contex account for many of the effects of ratings of imagery (Schwanenflugel, Akin, & Luh, 1992).

There is added evidence that specific words integrate better with one another other to form organized wholes. This integration can be viewed in terms of either a unified image or meaning structure, but in any case, it results in increased memory. If people are given a sentence to remember consisting of a general subject and a specific predicate, such as *The container held the apples,* they remember the predicate more often when cued with the specific term *basket* than when cued with the general term *container* (Anderson et al., 1976; Gumenik, 1979). This is true even though they are not presented with the term *basket* before it is used as a cue for recall and even though, in the great majority of cases when asked to remember the whole sentence, they do recall *container,* and not *basket,* as the subject of the sentence. The most likely explanation of the effect is that specific words are better retrieval cues because they share more with the representation of the rest of the sentence (Gumenik, 1979). In oral traditions where one line often serves to cue the next, such cuing effects are important. Moreover, the observation that the exact cue need not be present at the time of learning, as long as the cue fits the image or context, is important in traditions that allow change over retellings. Specific cues can be effective even if they were not the specific word originally present.

Images in oral traditions are often exaggerated by normal standards. They are of epic proportions. Mnemonics such as the method of loci always use exaggerated or bizarre images. The laboratory evidence in their favor has been mixed, though such images should be better in that they usually involve distinctive relationships. Einstein and McDaniel (1987; Einstein, McDaniel, & Lackey, 1989; McDaniel & Einstein, 1986) have shown that images with common relationships interfere more with other common images and that images with bizarre relationships interfere more with other bizarre images. Thus over long periods of life in which most images are not as exaggerated as those of oral traditions, exaggerated images will be remembered better than common images. In addition, the bizarre images seem to function by strengthening the tie among the items in the image, having their greatest effect on free recall, where one aspect of the image serves to cue the others. In contrast, common images result in better recall of the individual items. Thus bizarre relationships function through their ability to form units (Einstein et al., 1989).

These analyses and experiments argue that much of the role of imagery can be understood through concepts like *context availability, specificity,* and *distinctiveness,* which are used in other contexts (Marschark & Hunt, 1989); thus imagery may not be as special as it seems. Nonetheless, increased context availability, specificity, and distinctiveness in a narrative are difficult to obtain without imagery, so for oral traditions these mechanisms and imagery go together. Increasing the concrete, imageable nature of a story will increase the number of specific details and links among ideas that can cue recall and limit alternative responses.

Specific, concrete details have beneficial effects in addition to improving memory (Medin & Ross, 1989). Concrete details make stories seem more accurate, thoughtful, and believable (Pillemer, 1992). Although there are data to the contrary (Winograd & Neisser, 1992), people act as if memory for details implies that the central points are remembered correctly. For instance, an eyewitness's testimony is more effective if details are included, even if they are irrelevant to the case (Bell & Loftus, 1989), and sensory details make people likely to judge that they did an action rather than just thought about it (Johnson & Raye, 1981). In addition, specific details aid in maintaining emotional balance (Williams & Dritschel, 1988) and, as Pillemer notes, increase the sense of emotionality, intimacy, and immediacy when compared with abstract statements that remove the events described from particular situations. While these features may make a narrative more memorable, they do more. Concrete details that increase the sense that a narrative is accurate should influence tellers not to change it. Concrete details that increase emotionality, intimacy, and immediacy should lead to more frequent tellings.

Specific details are more likely to be mentioned if a speaker has an image; thus a listener is likely to take specific details as a sign that the speaker has an image. Again, specific details are confounded with the image. However, for some of the added functions of the specific, it is reasonable to argue that the image is the driving force. For instance, Brewer (1986) argues that if you report having an image, then you are more likely to consider your memory veridical. In addition, in describing what separates a personal (i.e., autobiographical) memory from a fact about one's life, Brewer takes as the defining characteristic of an autobiographical memory the presence of an accompanying image. You may know numerous details about an event in your life because you were told about them, but unless you can picture yourself at the event, you might know you were there but not consider that you have an autobiographical memory of being there. That is, you may know something without being able to recollect it. In this book imagery is a process, of which we are sometimes aware, that aids memory. In the everyday sense of memory as a recollection, however, an image of which one is aware may be the memory, whereas the words of a song are not a memory at all but just something that one knows or can produce when needed.

When differences between oral and written language are discussed in Chapter 4, *involvement* (Chafe, 1982) will be one of the main characteristics of oral language. This is marked by use of the first person and of dialogue, traits of many oral traditions. These traits are present when one seems to others to be reliving an experience (Pillemer, 1992) or perhaps seeing it in the mind's eye.

The Neural Substrate for Two Systems of Imagery

The most compelling evidence for a separate analog imagery system comes from neuropsychology (see Tippett, 1992, for a recent review). By combining behavioral and physiological measures, it is possible to exclude explanations that are difficult to exclude on the basis of behavioral data alone (Paivio & te Linde, 1982). Instead of asking whether imagery is a different system than language or other representations, we ask whether imagery relies on a different neural substrate. Farah (1988) reviewed evidence that visual imagery in intact, normal adults uses the same parts of the brain as visual perception. Several studies used one of two techniques that indicate which regions of the brain are active: measures of cerebral blood flow and electrical recordings of the brain made from the scalp. When people perform tasks that should involve visual imagery, such as imagining a flashing light or judging from memory whether pine-tree green is darker than grass green, the areas of cortex used in visual perception become more active compared with other areas of the brain. When people perform tasks that should not involve visual imagery, the areas of cortex used in visual perception do not become more active relative to other areas of the brain.

A second observation is that people with brain damage often have the same specific deficits in both visual perception and visual imagery (Farah, 1988). Color is one feature of visual stimuli that has a known separate neuroanatomical basis, and people who lose their color perception due to brain damage often lose their ability to image in color. Another distinction is between objects to the left and to the right of center in the visual field. People with an intact sensory apparatus but with acquired brain damage in one hemisphere of the brain can exhibit a deficit known as *visual neglect*. Objects in one-half of their visual field are ignored: half a plate of food is uneaten or half of the face is unwashed. Imagery follows the same pattern as vision in these people. Only half of an imaged scene that was learned before the injury is reported, with the half reported varying with the half of the image that falls in the neglected visual field (Bisiach & Luzzatti, 1978).

Moreover, these arguments can be extended to separate descriptive (or object) visual imagery from spatial imagery (Farah, Hammond, Levine, & Calvanio, 1988; Watson, 1994). The visual system can be divided neuroanatomically into a system for knowing what an object is and a system for knowing where an object is (Livingstone & Hubel, 1988; Ungerleider & Mishkin, 1982). Damage that affects the perceptual ability of one system, but not of the other, also tends to affect the imagery ability of that system, but not of the other. In order to avoid confusion with other uses of the word *visual*, Ungerleider and Mishkin (1982) use the term *object* to refer to what Farah and others refer to as the *visual* perceptual and imagery system.

The neurophysiological evidence for a functional distinction between a spatial- and an object-perceptual system comes from a wide range of data, though the anatomical basis varies from species to species. In the late 1960s, several researchers, working independently, found that their evidence converged on a distinction between two types of visual mechanisms, one specialized for spatial orientation and the other for identifying visual stimuli (Held, 1968; Ingle, 1967; Schneider, 1967; Trevarthen, 1968). For instance, by assessing the behavioral deficits that followed ablation of different areas, Schneider dissociated the mechanisms for spatial orientation and object identification, localizing these in the superior colliculus and visual cortex of the golden hamster, respectively. The dissociation in the visual system was later confirmed in primates, with the capacities localized in cortical areas (Pohl, 1973; Ungerleider & Mishkin, 1982).[6]

The two perceptual systems underlie different components of imagery. Clinical neuropsychological data demonstrate that either perceptual system can fail separately and that imaging deficits in a patient parallel perceptual deficits (Farah et al., 1988; Levine, Warach, & Farah, 1985). There is also evidence that the contents of the image affect the distribution of activity. For example, mental rotation is correlated with activity in the parietal region (Peronnet & Farah, 1989; Wijers, Otten, Feenstra, Mulder, & Mulder, 1989), while imaging concrete words is associated with activity in the occipital and the posterior or inferior temporal regions (Farah, Weisberg, Monheit, & Peronnet, 1989; Goldenberg, Podreka, Steiner, & Willmes, 1987).

There is also behavioral evidence for the distinction between object and spatial imagery. Garro (1982) examined differences among individuals in their imagery ability by comparing 35 imagery-based tasks and tests. The basic result—that people vary in ability along two different dimensions of imagery: spatial and object—is a reliable finding (Lorenz & Neisser, 1985; Richardson, 1969). Moreover, pencil-and-paper spatial tests predicted individual differences in performance on the spatial tasks. Analyses of a wide range of human and animal behavioral data, as well as epistemological considerations, led Neisser (1987, 1988) to draw a similar distinction in imagery and in perception.

The review of the neural basis of imagery returns us to the issue of definition. We do not really mean spatial versus object imagery; we mean the spatial system in humans that involves some parts of the posterior parietal cortex versus the complex visual-pattern system that involves some parts of the inferior temporal cortex. Exactly which behaviors belong in which system cannot be known until the neuroscience is done adequately, and the neuroscience cannot be done adequately until the functions are known. An iterative process is needed. Consider the problem of sorting the lines of ballads into predominantly spatial and predominantly object categories, the results of which are reported in Chapter 11. Of the following two lines, the first has a large spatial component; the second is more complicated.

> He rode and he rode till he came to the castle;
> He made the knocker to ring.

Is moving the knocker enough movement to be spatial or is it mostly descriptive? Does *implying* that the rider is now at the front door evoke spatial processing? We have some behavioral evidence on the second issue, (Morrow et al., 1989), but we have no detailed definitions. A contributing factor in the difficulty of defining imagery and other aspects of human behavior may be that the definitions are not of abstract systems, but of systems that reflect the products of a messy history of evolution.

Distinguishing spatial from object imagery is made more difficult by the fact that imagery tasks involve both systems to varying degrees. Thus even in Shepard's (1978) highly spatial rotated-characters task, a character has to be compared with its mirror image. For this reason, the review of the imagery literature that preceded this discussion could not easily be divided into two separate reviews, one for each system. This may be one reason that humanists and almost all cognitive psychologists failed to make the distinction and attributed the effects to generalized visual imagery, not mentioning a separate spatial component. Once the distinction is made, however, oral traditions appear to be remarkably spatial.

The neural substrate for imagery was discussed in some detail because it is the clearest case in this book of how knowledge of anatomy and physiology can affect theories of behavior. It is not the only one (Posner, Petersen, Fox, & Raichle, 1988; Roland & Friberg, 1985). We have long known from clinical cases, and recently from brain-mapping techniques, that language has its own neural pathways (Caplan, 1988). There is also recent work on the various forms and components of attention (Posner & Petersen, 1990), music (Joseph, 1988; Peretz & Morais, 1988; Samson & Zatorre, 1991; Zatorre, 1985), and other topics. At a gross level, the divisions found among human abilities match the classical divisions of literary devices used in this book, such as theme, imagery, rhyme, and rhythm. At a detailed level, though, especially in language, theories based on behavior do not always clarify the observed neuropsychology. As brain-scanning techniques and behavioral measures are studied together, the dependence of each on the other will grow.

Imagery in Oral Traditions

Phenomenological Reports

Some singers report using images to construct or remember their songs. This provides one kind of evidence for one use of imagery, as well as some insights into how imagery might function. Paivio (1983b) and Shepard (1978) review some of the more famous cases of phenomenological reports of imagery affecting the creative work of writers and scientists, and less well-known cases certainly occur in everyday thought (Adams, 1974; Arnheim, 1969). Nonetheless, reports of conscious imagery use provide only a weak test of whether imagery functions in oral traditions because imagery can operate without such reports. Moreover, it has long been known that individuals differ greatly in their conscious reports of imagery and that such reports have little to do with performance in many tasks in which imagery is thought to be relevant (Galton, 1883; Richardson, 1969).

The evidence for the conscious use of imagery in oral traditions is scattered, though this may be more a comment about the behavior of folklore collectors than of singers. MacDonald (1978) reports a conversation with Donald Alasdair Johnson, a storyteller in the oral tradition of South Uist. The following quotes are a translation of Johnson's responses to questions about how he remembered the story he had just finished:

> You've got to see it as a picture in front of you or you can't remember it properly. . . . I could see, if I were looking at the wall there, I could see just how they were—how they came in—the people—and how this thing was and that and the other. (p. 15)

Yes, it's easier to tell a story right through, from the beginning, because it's there in front of you to the end, all the way. All you have to do is follow it. . . . It comes to me little by little there—it keeps coming to me as it goes on—as it ought to. . . . There's was no vision ahead but just as you went ahead yourself, and the vision, kept pace with you just as if it were coming upon you, like that. (pp. 18–20)

To Johnson, remembering a story appears to be much like watching a movie. The difference is that Johnson is directing the movie he is watching. It is clear from the transcript that Johnson is using imagery, but it is not clear how he is constructing the images. Although Paivio (1971) has speculated about these types of transformations of images, the closest we have come to them in the laboratory is the image-rotation studies by Shepard, Cooper, and their colleagues, reported in the first section of this chapter.

Oral Traditions Are Concrete, Not Abstract

The genres of epic and ballads consist of concrete, easy-to-image words and ideas. This is also true of counting-out rhymes, to the extent to which this genre contains meaningful words of any kind. It is difficult to find an abstraction in these genres that is not personified or in some other way represented by a concrete person, object, or action.

The observation that oral traditions avoid the abstract, and the theoretical claim that the abstract can enter only when writing is present to lessen the demands on memory, are made convincingly by Havelock (1963, 1978) in his discussions of Homeric epic and the Greek written literature that followed it. Havelock (1963) stresses three properties of the content of oral traditions—the same three he notes that Plato, in the *Republic,* attributes to *opinion* in his arguments against the use of Homeric epic in education. Epic is composed of (1) agents, usually heroes or gods, producing a series of actions, (2) that are particular, specific examples, (3) of a concrete, vivid, easy-to-visualize nature. There are many reasons why epic would consist of such material, but the ones Havelock (1963) and this chapter concentrate on are their role in memory:

Actions and their agents are in fact always easy to visualise. What you cannot visualise is a cause, a principle, a category, a relationship or the like. . . . To be effectively part of the record, they [concepts] have to be represented as agents or as doings particular to their context and sharply visualised. (p. 188)

That is, if concepts in an oral tradition are to be easily remembered, they should be presented in imageable forms. This requires the use of concrete actions and agents performing specific acts that are easy to image.

Epic and ballads, for the most part, consist of a series of actions carried out by agents whose roles and appearances are well known by the singers and listeners. In epic, the agents are usually heroes or gods. Heroes and gods are easy to image: they are "larger than life," attention is paid to the details of their dress and stature, and they each have unique features that make them easy to place and to distinguish in an image. Moreover, the heroes and gods can substitute for abstract concepts that cannot be easily imaged; that is, they each have a characteristic that they personify.

In addition, heroes and gods often symbolize or take the place of a particular group of people that would be difficult to image otherwise. As Havelock notes, having a Pantheon of gods has mnemonic advantages over monotheism. Characters, or character types, in other oral traditions often serve a mnemonic role similar to that of the Greek heroes and gods. Each character has an expected image and an expected role to play that exemplifies some more abstract, not easily imageable concept.

Havelock's (1963) first property is that the actions of epic, and of most oral traditions, are themselves easy to image. They are concrete, often on a grand scale or in some other way notable, and involve familiar, imageable gods and heroes. Havelock notes that the images of the actions cue one another in recall. Thus the image of Zeus throwing thunderbolts can invoke the image of Apollo shooting arrows. But the actions can be, and usually are, organized in more complex patterns, such as the scripts described in Chapter 2. In this way, abstract concepts can be tied to images and images can be organized in coherent, easy-to-recall sequences of narrative. Events that we, as literate critics, might attribute to historical causes, societal problems, or natural disasters can instead be attributed to easier-to-image, and thus easier-to-remember, concrete actions taken by known actors, such as a feud between two heroes or gods. Havelock claims that the lack of abstract thought in oral traditions may be due to the requirement that all knowledge be preserved without the benefit of external memory aids, an issue returned to in the Epilogue.

For example, Havelock (1978) analyzes lists, genealogies, and similar passages. The catalog of ships in the *Iliad* is not in the form of a modern list of those who took part in the Trojan War, but is a series of concrete actions taken by particular heroes set in an overall theme. The rank and relations of each hero are not given in abstract terms, but in the number of imageable men and ships the hero is in the midst of leading. Similarly, the lineage of a hero or god is not given in efficient, abstract kinship terms, but in easy-to-image scenes of procreation.

Oral traditions prefer the concrete to the abstract. Thus epic and most oral traditions do not contain discussions of justice or heroism, but specific, concrete, imageable instances of someone being just or heroic:

> Oral information is likely to be unfriendly to such a statement as "The angles of a triangle are equal to two right angles." If however you said, "The triangle stood firm in battle, astride and poised on its equal legs, fighting resolutely to protect its two right angles against the attack of the enemy," you would be casting Euclid backward into Homeric dress, you would be giving him his preliterate form. However, triangles are not personal agents and Homer was not very interested in them. (Havelock, 1978, p. 42)

Oral Traditions Are Spatial

Humanists have noted that oral traditions contain the concrete rather than the abstract. If imagery is divided into two components, object and spatial, then oral traditions are mostly spatial. There are graphic scenes, but most of the lines involve movement and location rather than description, and much of the description that does exist is in the form of "formulas" or "commonplaces." In Homer, the sea is always wine dark; the dawn, rosy fingered. In ballads, hands are always lily white, the first horse is a milk-white steed, and the second is a dappled bay. It may be no accident that epic heroes are always on the move; invoking a highly developed spatial-memory system increases memorability. If all the actions occurred at one place, more confusion and interference might occur. Moreover, individual images are better for spatial relations than for sequencing, but by using a series of images tied to a path that passes through a known sequence of places, the order of events can be made more stable. Place is an added cue, but a special one that can rely on a highly developed neural system—a system that can work without reducing attention to the other aspects of the stimulus (Hasher & Zacks, 1979).

Because ballad and epic scholars have made little explicit mention of the spatial nature of imagery in oral traditions, less can be said about oral traditions with respect to this aspect of imagery. Nonetheless, casual observation of oral traditions shows spatial layout to be a major component of imagery. For ballads, this will be explored in more detail in Chapter 11, but for now it can be noted that each stanza of a ballad tends to be at one location or point of view and that after each stanza or two, the location tends to change. There are no one-scene epics; travel is the rule. Homeric epic refers to itself as *oimê* (path).[7] The *Odyssey* is an odyssey, with hypothetical maps of travel shown in some editions. Even in the *Iliad,* where large segments occur between Troy and the sea, the location of battles and other events is constantly changing. Because such spatial layout typically follows a known path, order information can be preserved. In contrast, it might be confused if there were one large, simultaneous image.

The Role of Imagery in Oral Traditions

As noted in this chapter, imagery has many strengths as a way of increasing the memorability of an oral tradition. Imagery is one of our most powerful mnemonic aids. It is especially useful where the rapid retrieval of information is important, as it is in singing to a fixed rhythm, and where the spatial layout and interacting components of a scene offer additional forms of organization. Imagery, by its very nature, also seems to be well suited for the rapid transformations and actions of the type that Donald Alasdair Johnson reports imaging and that most oral traditions require.

As a mnemonic device, though, imagery has some definite limitations, only some of which can be corrected in the context of oral traditions. Imagery is not very useful for directly expressing abstract concepts and patterns of thought based on them. This, as Havelock notes, may be one reason why oral traditions tend to lack explicit statements of such concepts. The solution of providing concrete instances to symbolize abstract concepts can result in language that is more memorable, emotional, rich, and interesting than it would be with abstract concepts, but it does not offer a general solution. As Havelock (1963) observes:

> Kantian imperatives and mathematical relationships and analytical statements of any kind are inexpressible and also unthinkable. Equally an epistemology which can choose between the logically (and therefore eternally) true and the logically (and eternally) false is also impossible.[8] (p. 182)

The remaining major limitation of imagery, the loss of sequential order and exact wording, can be corrected within the framework of oral traditions. In an oral tradition, imagery involves the transformation of a sequential verbal input into a spatial image and back to a sequential verbal output. Both the order of events and the exact wording used can easily be lost in the transformation, thereby decreasing the stability of transmission. This would be a major problem if oral traditions did not contain other forms of organization, or constraint, to limit possible changes. Within the realm of imagery itself, the sequential weakness is lessened by placing only a few events at each location and having the locations linked by a path of known sequence. The exact wording weakness is lessened by having only a few descriptive phrases for each situation and by having characters, props, and places that are visually distinctive. These devices, however, are not enough. The meaning constraints outlined in Chapter 2 and the sound-pattern constraints outlined in Chapter 4 combine to provide the information that might be lost in the imagery transformations. Meaning constraints, such as scripts, causal chains, and story grammars, tend to preserve sequential information, and poetic constraints tend to preserve the exact wording. Thus, as opposed to the limitations placed on subject matter by the use of high-imagery language, these weaknesses of imagery are compensated for by other constraints.

Notes

1. To get a flavor of the debate, the reader might start with Block's (1981) book, especially the introduction, which is titled ''What Is the Issue?'' and with Kosslyn et al.'s (1979) paper, which is published along with commentaries by many of the major participants in the debate. Rumelhart and Norman (1986) do an extremely clear job of discussing imagery within the context of mental representations in general. For a more recent book, see Tye (1991). In this chapter, in addition to minimizing philosophical discussions, I have spared the reader the history of the arguments that helped to develop the psychological theories of imagery. Instead, I have tried to portray what now appears to be true. For example, since the time Paivio (1971) pioneered his dual-coding theory, a quote from which begins this chapter, psychologists have learned a great deal about the representation of knowledge and about memory. Knowledge of such topics changes the way imagery is viewed even in the absence of new information about imagery itself. Many of the earlier disagreements therefore are no longer relevant to the task of trying to predict stability.

2. Imagery in sensory modalities other than vision has for the most part been ignored by modern cognitive psychology (but see Reisberg, 1992). The term *imagery* therefore must, for the present, refer to visual and amodal spatial imagery. In principle, however, imagery should include senses other than vision.

3. For another interpretation, see the discussion of Buggie's (1974) experiments later in the chapter.

4. Images take time to form, so for studies of memory for word pairs, rapid presentation rates can minimize the use of imagery. Once the initial time is taken to form an image, rapid changes are possible. In oral traditions, where a new image is formed only once every scene and where scene boundaries coincide with pauses at rhythmic boundaries, the initial time needed is not a problem. Moreover, the images of oral traditions are practiced images within their genre and should be formed more quickly than the novel combinations used in the laboratory. When concrete and abstract stimuli are compared, the results are more uniformly in favor of concrete stimuli. Whatever image can be formed in the time before the response seems to help.

5. One possible artifact is that the relations like *flying, kicking,* and *crushing* were chosen to fit the nouns rather than being randomly assigned. It is unlikely that this artifact, however, could completely explain the results. For instance, in a follow-up experiment, Buggie (1974) had people learn lists of 32 descriptions in which 8 noun pairs were joined by a single "static separation" such as *next to* or *within sight of,* 8 noun pairs were joined by a single "distant active" relation such as *chasing* or *leaping at,* 8 noun pairs were joined by a single "unified" relation such as *painted on* or *shaped like,* and 8 noun pairs were joined by a single "interactive" relation such as *chewing on* or *playing with.* There were no differences in recall or recognition among the four categories.

6. In more technical terms, Ungerleider and Mishkin (1982) argued that primate vision is subserved primarily by the geniculostriate system, and the terms *what* versus *where* were adopted to refer to two cortico-cortical pathways that diverge after primary visual cortex. The dorsal pathway to the posterior parietal cortex is involved in visual-spatial information, whereas the ventral pathway to the inferior temporal cortex is involved in object recognition. Inferior temporal neurons are selective for object attributes such as shape, pattern, color, and texture, and respond to stimuli across large portions of the visual field. In the posterior parietal cortex, visual information is integrated with information from other sensory areas to construct a supramodal spatial representation in which neurons are selective for movement and location. The division in some species may begin in two types of retinal ganglion cells and extend through the lateral geniculate nucleus, where magnocellular and parvocellular layers, differing in their response characteristics, form the basis of the division evident in the higher visual areas (Livingstone & Hubel, 1988; but see Zeki, 1993).

7. I owe this point to John Miles Foley.

8. This criticism may seem like an unfair comparison. Epics are not proofs, and proofs are not epics. But the difference Havelock (1963) notes does exist and is mirrored in Bruner's (1986) difference between narrative and logical argument from the beginning of Chapter 2. Perhaps it should not be termed a limitation any more than it is a limitation of proofs that they lack emotional impact for most readers.

CHAPTER 4

Sound

Sound exists only when it is going out of existence. It is not simply perishable
but essentially evanescent. . . .

Ong, 1982, p. 32

The standard distinction among the terms *meaning, imagery,* and *sound* has been
applied here, in part based on neuropsychological data. Like patterns of meaning
and imagery, patterns of sound are viewed as constraints that cue memories and
restrict choices. In the first section of this chapter, some general properties of sound
that elude the more structural and experimental approaches of cognitive psychology
are considered. The second section, which is of interest mainly to psychologists,
examines the biases against the study of patterns of sound in psychology and provides arguments against them. The final two main sections examine two major forms
of sound pattern: the poetic devices of repetition of sound, including rhyme, alliteration, and assonance, and the timing of sound, as discussed under rhythm and meter.
Some mention of music is included, but, in general, is left to those with greater
expertise (for reviews, see Deutsch, 1982; Dowling & Harwood, 1986; Sloboda,
1985).

Performance

Sound Is Now; Sound Is Social

The evanescent property of sound, as opposed to writing, noted in the epigraph,
required oral traditions to be maintained in human memory, at least until the invention of sound-recording devices. As Havelock (1986), Lord (1960), Ong (1982), and
others have noted, there is no looking back or looking ahead in an oral tradition.
What is available at any time is the present, what is remembered of the past, and
expectations for the future. Fish (1970) makes a similar point for all text, but it is
even stronger here. In oral traditions, one cannot see how long it is to the end of the
chapter (or album), turn to a different page and compare texts, or look back to

answer a question (Alessi, Anderson, & Goetz, 1979; Brown, 1979; Christie & Just, 1976). As discussed in Chapter 2, this evanescence has an effect on the kind of thematic structure that is possible, and it is a determining factor in the theory of serial recall proposed in Chapter 8. It also ensures that transmission is social.

Because sound exists only when it is going out of existence and because sound cannot be heard very far from the speaker, oral transmission is social in a way that written transmission need not be. You are reading this book at a different time and place from where it was written. In fact, it was written in many different places over the course of a decade. In contrast, if you listen to an epic, a ballad, or a counting-out rhyme in an oral tradition, you are in the presence of the singer and, except for a slight lag, what is on the singer's lips is in your ear. The contents of your short-term, or working, memory and the singer's are synchronized. In this technical sense, you and the singer are conscious of the same text at the same time.

In this way, the text comes into being as it is sung, and it comes into being for a group of at least two people. It is possible to sing to oneself on occasion, but for an oral tradition to exist longer than the lifetime of the singer, others must be present as it is sung. Thus a performance produces an embodiment of the text, and if there is no folklorist nearby with a recorder, the text disappears as it is performed.

Performance to—or, better, with—a group ensures an audience to correct, encourage, and shape the piece. Lord (1960) describes these effects on South Slavic epic, Rosenberg (1988) gives graphic descriptions of the effect of congregation response on the quality of spontaneous oral sermons, and other examples are given in Chapter 6. In rituals (Devisch, 1993; Kapferer, 1991), the "audience" response can control the course of the performance. Such feedback, or the anticipation of it, is important to authors of written texts, but not in the direct way it is with an oral performance to a group that can alter and add to what is occurring at the time. For instance, people restricted to overhearing a conversation but not being able to take an active role in it understand less (Schober & Clark, 1989). Not being there (Larsen, 1988), or not being able to affect what is said, makes understanding more difficult in large part because the performance of the speaker is improved by feedback. There are even effects of group participation at the level of prosody; groups read poems with a more regular rhythm than do individuals (Boomsliter, Creel, & Hastings, 1973).

In the group setting and oral performance, rhythm allows a greater degree of synchrony. Havelock (1978) stresses the effects of this rhythm on group cohesion, pleasure, and even a form of hypnosis that focuses attention and improves memory. Empirical tests of his claims are lacking, but his observations are generally convincing. A strong rhythm brings groups together and maintains the song as the controlling influence. Bodily movements synchronize with the song, as discussed in Chapter 5. These effects of rhythm, which are considered later in the chapter, occur more clearly with sound than with writing.

Speech Is Not Writing

Language produced as speech is different from language produced as writing. Part of this difference is due to differences between auditory and visual modalities in perception and memory. For instance, Baddeley (1986, 1990) clarified the extensive literature on short-term, or working, memory by making a basic distinction between two kinds of memory buffers: an auditory phonological store and a visual store. Directly related to the constraints studied in this chapter is the finding that auditorily presented rhythms are reproduced more accurately than visually presented rhythms (Glenberg & Jona, 1991). But differences exist between speech and writing even when the speech is transcribed, and it is these differences on which the rest of this section concentrates.

Oral traditions are special forms of speech, not special forms of writing, and they must be evaluated as such. Some devices in literature that might be attributed solely to an oral-tradition style, or to an imitation of one, are actually products of speech in general, as will be seen here and in Chapters 9 and 11. Some exceptions to rules noted in oral traditions are exceptions only if compared with rules of written grammar, not with rules of spoken grammar. The clearest case of this will be seen in Chapter 9, where Bakker's (1988, 1990) work on Homeric epic is discussed. For now, examples are used to provide a general sense of the range and size of basic differences between speech and writing.

Four samples from books by Albert Lord were chosen for comparison: two oral and two written. These small, in some cases translated, samples were selected to exhibit certain properties. Quantitative estimates of the differences displayed are available elsewhere (for a review, see Chafe & Tannen, 1987; Nielsen, 1992). The samples, however, do provide a flavor of the differences seen in oral traditions that may be due to their oral nature rather than anything about their particular genre.

As two examples of speech, consider the following translation by Lord (1960, p. 74) of the beginning lines of an epic and then his translation of the beginning of a conversation between Nikola Vujnović (referred to as N), Lord and Parry's assistant, and their best singer, Avdo Medjedović (referred to as A) (Lord & Bynum, 1974, p. 58):

> Marko Kraljević is drinking wine
> With his old mother,
> And with his true love,
> And with his only sister.
> When Marko had drunk his wine,
> Then Marko brimmed the glass
> To the health of his old mother,
> And his love and his only sister.
> "Expect the sun and the moon,
> But me Marko never!"
> And his old mother asked him:
> "Whither are you going, Marko my only son?"

N: Now I'll ask you about your songs.
A: All right.
N: From whom did you learn the one about how Sultan Selim captured Bagdad?
A: From that fellow Kasum Rebronja.
N: Where did this Kasum Rebronja come from?
A: From Godusa, from the district of Lozna.

N: Is that a long way from here?

A: It's five hours away.

N: Where did you hear him sing?

A: I heard him here in Bijelo Polje, in a café.

N: What was he doing here?

A: He came here one day on some business at the court, and they got him to sing for them while he was here: "Come on now, give us a song!" He used to sing here in town.

Compare these transcriptions with two written samples. The first is a three-sentence prose summary of a longer section of an epic also by Avdo Medjedović and also from Lord (1960, p. 223). To match the beginning section of the oral samples just given, the first three sentences following the invocation are given. The second written sample is the first two sentences of Lord (1960, p. 3):

> Praise of Bosnia in the time of Sulejman the Magnificent. Thirty-six aghas were sitting and talking in the stone loggia in Kanidza. Mustajbey was at their head with seven standard-bearers; at his right was Hrnja Mujo with four standard-bearers; at his left Durut Ahmetagha with four standard-bearers.

> In the early thirties of this century, when Milman Parry began to write the book from which this one takes its name, what was needed most in Homeric scholarship was a more exact knowledge of the way in which oral epic poets learn and compose their songs. Now in the late fifties of the same century the need is still great; in spite of the number of books about Homer and his poems, about epic poetry in general, and about specific epic traditions in various parts of the world, the student of epic still lacks a precise idea of the actual technique of *poiesis* in its literal meaning.

There are several differences to be noted here that are hallmarks of oral written differences, as described by Chafe and others (Chafe, 1982; Chafe & Danielowicz, 1987; Goody, 1987; Tannen, 1982, 1989), and that occur under controlled conditions in which the people drawn from the same population produce language about the same topic under the same conditions (Nielsen, 1992).

Before a presentation of oral–written differences can be made, units of comparison are needed. For writing, this is simple. Lord punctuated his own sentences. For the oral poetry, each line of the South Slavic epic example can normally be taken as an idea unit. Each exchange in the oral conversation can be taken to be one idea unit, except that (1) some of Avdo's replies may be better divided into two units where Lord placed a comma following the grammatical rules of writing and (2) for the last of Avdo's replies the alternative parsing, which follows, is favored:

A: He came here one day on some business at the court.
   And they got him to sing for them while he was here.
   "Come on now, give us a song!"
   He used to sing here in town.

Chafe argues that the idea unit for speech is not the phrase, clause, or sentence of written grammar, but the intonation unit. The exact intonation pattern of the speech sample was not transcribed by Lord, except as noted by punctuation and as aided by knowledge of the rhythm and melody of the sung epic. Nonetheless, the units used here are close enough for current purposes, though it is likely that if the speech itself were examined, some units would be further divided. The intonation units of speech are shorter and grammatically less complex than the sentences of writing. Complete ideas are expressed in a few words, relying on the past speech and shared context of the speaker and listener. Consider Avdo's replies: "All right"; "From that fellow Kasum Rebronja"; "From Godusa, from the district of Lozna" (which might be parsed as two intonation units if the tape were heard); "It's five hours away." To be complete grammatical sentences by written standards, such intonation units often depend on verbs and other major constituents understood from what was said earlier, but the intonation units are not ambiguous or unclear in context. According to Chafe (1990), each intonation unit corresponds to "the amount of information that can be active at any one time" (p. 88). In terms used by cognitive psychology, each intonation unit corresponds to the contents of working memory. Intonation units and their relation to memory and linguistics will be examined again in Chapter 5 when phrases are considered as basic units of oral traditions.

A major difference between speech and writing, in Chafe's terms, is that speech is fragmented, whereas writing is integrated. That is, speech consists of series of small units strung together, whereas writing puts more information into fewer words by using assorted grammatical devices. The fragmentation of speech when applied to oral traditions is regarded as additive style. Consider the use of the word *and* in speech and writing (Schiffrin, 1987, pp. 128–190). In speech, *and* is often used to mark or introduce a new phrase, without indicating any specific semantic relation between it and what proceeded. Thus *and* is a common first word for lines of ballads, as will be seen in Chapter 11, and was even added to the beginning of lines of manuscripts in the Middle Ages to make the written text easier to read aloud (Gerritsen, 1976). Here *and,* which is a consistent translation for the Serbo-Croatian *I,* begins 4 of the 12 lines taken from the epic, and *but,* which fills a similar role, begins another of the 12 lines. If the alternative parsing of Avdo's reply is used, *and* also starts one of his idea units. *And* is not used to begin any of the written sentences; rather, it is used to join phrases, allowing more information to be placed in the same number of words by allowing redundant words to be deleted. For instance, in the written summary the 36 aghas are both "sitting *and* talking," and in the first sentences of Lord's book, oral-epic poets both "learn *and* compose" their songs. In each case, the subject of the two verbs is mentioned only once.

Another device used to make writing more integrated in English is series of prepositional phrases. Although in English, prepositions are not much more common in writing than in speech, series of prepositional phrases are. In the translations of oral samples, there are several series of prepositional phrases, such as *"from* the district *of* Lozna.*"* Two of these are separated by a comma and may be separate intonation units. In contrast, much of the written sample consists of series of two prepositional phrases that are not separated by commas or other marks of punctuation. In the translations, there are even two cases of three prepositional phrases in a row: *"of* Bosnia *in* the time *of* Sulejman the Magnificent" and *"of* the actual technique *of poiesis in* its literal meaning."[1]

In addition to the fragmentation–integration dimension, Chafe (1982) notes that speech exhibits more *involvement,* whereas writing exhibits more *detachment:* "Speakers interact with their audiences, writers do not" (p. 45). One device that increases involvement is the use of direct quotes. Both oral samples have these, and neither written sample does. The inclusion of such direct dialogue is also common in ballads. Another device to increase involvement is the inclusion of the first person. Both oral samples include *I* or *me,* as well as the second person, *you;* neither written sample does.

Speech and writing differ. The fragmented, additive style of oral traditions is common in speech, but not in written literature. The use of dialogue and the first person found in oral traditions is also common in speech, but not in most written literature. Thus these properties need not be attributed to the special nature of oral traditions, but can be regarded as a product of their oral mode of transmission.

Surface Schemas

Schemas, as discussed in Chapter 2, can exist for surface form as well as for meaning. When patterns of sound exist, they can aid recall.

It may seem odd in a book on oral traditions to argue that patterns of sound, such as rhyme, aid memory, but the literature from and attitudes of cognitive psychologists prove otherwise. Consider the reports of cognitive psychologists who considered memory their primary research interest and who had published at least one paper on the subject (Park, Smith, & Cavanaugh, 1990). Their responses were contrasted to those of psychologists with other specialties and to those of college professors and researchers who were not psychologists. The three groups, each with approximately 60 members, were quite similar in their reports of how frequently they used various techniques to improve their memory performance. All three groups cited lists, organization, rehearsal, telling others to remind them, and the physical placement of objects as their most frequently used techniques and various formal mnemonic devices, such as the method of loci, as their least often used techniques. There was, however, one statistically significant difference among the groups in reported usage. Memory researchers reported using rhyme less often than the other two groups. Memory researchers reported using rhyme as the 18th most frequent technique out of 20, whereas the other groups reported it as their 11th and 12th most frequent technique, respectively.

The main source for the concept of schema for research in human memory is Bartlett (1932). Bartlett's data led many readers to the erroneous conclusion that meaning or gist is the dominant and possibly the only dimension along which organization that aids memory takes place. It is this claim that schemas for surface structure of stimuli do not aid memory that is contested.

The anti-surface-schema claim exists not only in schema theory, but also in aspects of cognitive psychology as diverse as psycholinguistics and verbal learning. It deserves to be examined in some detail because it is clearly at odds with the view taken here and with a large body of existing data from tasks not involving laboratory recall. Consider the claim that schemas can and usually do exist for the form, as well as for the meaning, of stimuli. That is, consider the claim that we are sensitive to patterns of sound and other surface features and that we use them to aid recall where possible. Support for the claim is so widespread that it is unnecessary to present it to anyone who is not trained in psychology. Perhaps the clearest evidence comes from parody. The observation that parodies exist for as diverse a set of stimuli as magazines, Bach concerti, and political leaders indicates not only that some people are sensitive enough to patterns in surface structure to abstract and reproduce them with minor changes, but also that most people can recognize such similarities in form when they are presented.

Evidence also exists from more controlled observation and experimentation. The demonstrations of the gestalt psychologists show that surface visual features with no inherent meaning beyond their form can lead to organization in perception and memory (Kohler, 1974). Research on social register shows that people know and can produce surface forms that differ in their intonation, syntax, and vocabulary when talking to different audiences (Brown, 1986). Linguistic research on phonetics clearly shows the rule-bound nature that all speakers and listeners of a language know (e.g., Chomsky & Halle, 1968). There is even memory research that shows the effects of surface organization. People familiar with a literary style, such as legal or biblical writing, make reconstructive errors consistent with that style (Brewer & Hay, 1984). People cluster rhyming words together when recalling lists (Bousfield & Wicklund, 1969). Learning words using a strategy that focuses on rhyme interferes with similar learning, but not with learning that focuses on any of a host of other aspects of the stimuli (Bird & Campbell, 1982). Undergraduates' knowledge of coins (Rubin & Kontis, 1983) and of the form of words belonging to certain semantic categories (Rubin, Stolzfus, & Wall, 1991) includes organized surface information.

From this evidence, it is clear that schemas for the surface form of stimuli exist. Moreover, limited evidence exists that such schemas can aid memory. Given the observation that people can use the form of stimuli in various ways, is it really true that cognitive psychologists have argued that form cannot be the basis for schemas and therefore cannot have much effect on memory? Bartlett initially led in this direction by arguing for the importance of meaning in organizing the stimuli he used. Others read him to imply that form was not important.

Recent research has done little to change the position. In a review of modern schema theory, Alba and Hasher (1983) took as one of the four basic processes common to schema theory that of ''abstraction—a process that stores the meaning of a message without reference to the original syntactic and lexical content'' (p. 203). Along the way, students of verbal learning also accepted the assumption that surface forms and attention to surface details led to less durable memory (e.g., Craik & Lockhart, 1972), though there have been convincing counterarguments (Jacoby & Brooks, 1984; Kolers & Roediger, 1984; Morris, Bransford, & Franks, 1977). Even recent work on expertise has assumed that surface structure is unimportant and that expertise brings with it a switch to organization along more meaningful lines (Rubin, Wallace, & Houston, 1993; Chapter 7). This may be true for some areas of expertise, but it need not be true for playing music or singing in a genre (see Chapter 11 for a demonstration). Most surprising is the acceptance of the anti-surface-schema view by psycholinguistics (e.g., Sachs, 1967; Wanner, 1968). Linguistics has outlined many rule-bound and subtle patterns in the phonetic and intonational patterns of speech that were studied by psychologists, yet psychologists argue that such patterns add little to memory.

If there is evidence that people routinely use surface-structure information in an organized fashion, how is it that the unlikely claim that surface structure does not aid recall maintains its popularity? Several factors contribute to the confusion. First, Bartlett (1932) argued for an "effort after meaning" (p. 227), but the word *meaning* is ambiguous. In a general sense, it denotes whatever is important or structured in stimuli. In a specific and technical sense, it denotes gist as opposed to form, semantics as opposed to syntax and phonetics, or underlying propositional structure as opposed to surface structure. The general sense includes all forms of organization; the specific technical sense does not. This chapter and book argue that the first sense is the correct one for schema theory, that people take advantage of whatever forms of organization they can find in performing tasks. The problem is that the ambiguity of the word *meaning* allows psychologists to test one sense and intend another.

The second factor in the omission of surface organization in memory research is that the most important form of organization for Bartlett's task, and for most of the ones that followed it, is gist (i.e. *meaning* in the specific, technical sense). This is because the recall procedure allows about half of a passage to be recalled, uses stimuli without any poetics, and does not break the cultural expectation that only the gist of a passage is important. In this way, the procedure provides subjects with implicit instructions to recall the gist but not the form. Gist becomes the most salient form of organization in the particular recall tasks used, and so it is erroneously taken to be the only form of organization that can be used in any recall task. When the surface form is important, it can be recalled (Rubin 1977). When surface structure organizes the stimulus or restricts possible responses, it aids memory (Bower & Bolton, 1969).

The third factor is that because verbatim recall is rare, surface features are assumed to be unimportant. It is true that verbatim recall is rare, but this does not mean that surface structure is at fault any more than is gist. Verbatim recall relies either on many trials (Ebbinghaus, 1885/1964) or on a special interest (Keenan, MacWhinney, & Mayhew, 1977; Kintsch & Bates, 1977) to master unorganized stimuli, or on stimuli, such as songs and poems, that are highly organized in terms of both gist and surface organization. Where surface organization is great but meaning is not, recall is organized with respect to surface structure not gist. Thus many popular songs learned by adults (Hyman & Rubin, 1990) and prayers and patriotic songs learned by children have errors in recall that preserve more of the surface organization, including the poetics and rhythmic structure, than the gist. A lack of verbatim recall is no more evidence against surface schemas than it is against the role of gist.

To summarize, schemas exist for surface form as well as for meaning, though such schemas are ignored or denied by most theories. Evidence is presented in this chapter and in the ones that follow that such schemas aid memory.[2]

Rhyme, Alliteration, and Assonance

The Repetition of Parts of Words

The repetition of sounds is widely used as a poetic device in oral traditions and literate poetry. When the last stressed vowel of a word and all sounds that follow it repeat, the poetic device is called *rhyme*. When the initial consonant cluster of a word repeats, the poetic device is called *alliteration*. When a stressed vowel of a word repeats, the poetic device is called *assonance*. Definitions such as these and actual usage vary among authorities, genres, and historical periods (Lanz, 1931; Zwicky, 1976). Other poetic devices have been used and are part of the literary critics' categories. Thus the symmetrical measure to rhyme (i.e., all sounds up to and including the first stressed vowel) and the symmetrical measure to alliteration (i.e., the final consonant cluster) could be used (Leech, 1969). For present purposes, all that is important is that a pattern of repeating sounds functions in a genre at levels above chance (Skinner, 1939, 1942). Differences among the various devices are discussed as appropriate. Because most research on sound repetition has involved rhyme and because the definition of rhyme varies from study to study, for the remainder of the chapter the word *rhyme* will be used both as the general term for all the poetic devices of sound repetition and as the specific term for referring to word endings.

Having noted this conceptual equivalence among the patterns of sound repetition, we must also note that all locations of words are not equally effective mnemonic devices. In a variety of tasks, the beginnings of words are more salient than the ends, and the ends are more salient than the middles. Horowitz, White, and Atwood (1968) had undergraduates learn lists of either six-letter or nine-letter words. The undergraduates were then shown the first, middle, or last third of the word as a cue and had to recall the remainder of the word. For the word *minute,* either *mi_____,* __*nu*__, or ____*te* was the cue, and for *beautiful* either *bea_____,* ___*uti*___, or _____*ful* was the cue. Overall, the first, middle, and last position cues were effective 89%, 68%, and 72% of the time, respectively. In addition to the accuracy of the responses, the time taken to make a response was recorded. The length of time it took people to recall a word followed the same pattern as the amount-recalled data, with people being quicker for positions in which they recalled more. The mean latencies to recall were 1.7, 3.3, and 2.7 seconds for the three positions, respectively. The same pattern of results held for less common words (Horowitz, Chilian, & Dunnigan, 1969). Similar results were obtained from different laboratories for paired-associate learning in which the to-be-learned pairs of three-letter consonant-vowel-consonant (CVC) words matched on the first, middle, or last letter. The first words from pairs that matched in their first letters were consistently better cues for the second words of pairs than were words that matched in their middle or last letters (D'Amato & Diamond, 1979; Nelson & Garland, 1969). The paired-associate learning experiments model recall cued by the repetition of sound patterns in oral traditions.

Brown and Knight (1990) did not have people learn lists; rather, they investigated people's ability to recall words they already knew. Undergraduates were given a definition, such as *the unit of measure for a 6-foot depth of water*. If they failed to recall the word, a letter cue, like the cues used by Horowitz et al. (1969), was given. Averaged over two experiments, these first, middle, and last letter cues were effective 33%, 15%, and 23% of the time, respectively. This experiment models the situation in oral traditions in which the original word is not known, but the general meaning and part of the sound pattern are provided by the context. This could occur where memory failed or where a line changed in meaning or rhyme, causing the line that followed it to be created to fit the new constraints.

The Brown and Knight findings are consistent with studies of the *tip-of-the-tongue phenomenon* (Brown & McNeill, 1966). People given the definition of a word on the edge of their vocabulary can find themselves in a state where they know that they know the word, but cannot recall it. When a word is on the tip of their tongue, they can often recall the first and last letters or phonemes (and often the number of syllables and stress pattern) (Brown & McNeill, 1966; Rubin, 1975). Thus the beginnings and ends of words play a special role in the way people access words.

Before examining possible explanations for these position effects, one detail needs to be noted. First letters are more effective in cuing recall than last letters in most of the experimental literature. This does not mean that alliteration is more effective than rhyme. Alliteration is for the initial consonant or consonant cluster, but rhyme involves everything after and including the last stressed vowel. A fairer comparison between alliteration and rhyme would be between the first letter and the last two letters combined. Alliteration is roughly as effective as rhyme, though first-letter cues are more effective than last-letter cues.[3]

First letters and endings are more effective than the middle of words in a variety of tasks that model aspects of the transmission in oral traditions. Three explanations exist for this finding. The most common one (e.g., Horowitz et al., 1968; Lima, 1993) is that the letters of the beginning and endings of words are more evenly distributed and thus carry more information in the technical information-theory sense (Shannon & Weaver, 1949). This explanation is based on constraints limiting choices; the more information transmitted, the fewer the choices left. The claim, however, is usually based on people's ability to predict letters and not on objective frequency counts, and the two are not the same (Rubin, 1976a, 1976b, 1976c). The subjective estimates share some of the same behaviors that are trying to be predicted. In general, however, the information explanation does not seem able to predict the data.[4]

The second explanation is based on perceptual clarity (e.g., Bruner & O'Dowd, 1958). Letters at the beginning and end of words are clearer because there is no other letter next to them on one side. This explanation finds strong support in visual perception, where words are, by convention, separated by blank spaces, which does not occur regularly in speech or in oral traditions. The explanation may be of value in oral traditions, however, where the words that carry alliteration or rhymes are more likely to be stressed or to occur at the beginning or end of intonation units, respectively, and thus have pauses adjacent to the sound repetition.

The third explanation is based on the sequential production and perception of language (Marslen-Wilson & Tyler, 1980; Rubin, 1975). It is similar to the theory of serial recall of verse proposed in Chapter 8. In order to speak fluently, it helps to know the first letter(s), number of syllables, approximate length in phonemes, and, to a lesser extent, ending of a word well ahead of its being uttered, so that the position of the mouth and the breath can be set. The pronunciations of the ending of the word preceding the word in question and the beginning of the word following the word in question depend on the beginning and ending sounds of the word. Under this explanation, the hypothesized privileged access to a word's beginning, ending, and length needed for normal speech production is adapted for use in cuing recall in laboratory recall tasks and in oral traditions. The internal sounds of a word are also needed, but could be part of a more local motor, word-internal structure not as easily accessible for planning and recall. This privileged access also results in the beginning sound, the end sound, and the length of a word being known when the sound of the middle is not in the tip-of-the-tongue phenomenon.

Rhyme Limits Choices and Cues Memory

The repetition of a sound is an aid to memory. When a sound repeats, the first occurrence of the sound limits the choices for the second occurrence and provides a strong cue for it. The repetition is emphasized if it occurs in a specified place, such as alliteration in the example given in the next paragraph; in Old English occurring between one or both of the two stressed syllables of the first half of a line and the first stressed syllable of the second half of that line (Fry, 1967); or in the first word of most lines in songs by the Beatles (Hyman & Rubin, 1990; Chapter 8). The most common occurrence of repetition of sound in modern English is, of course, rhyme. The function of limiting choices and cuing recall is common to all types of constraints used in oral traditions, and will be discussed in more detail in Chapter 5 and included in a theory of serial recall in Chapter 8. Here it is considered briefly, before the unique properties of rhyme are discussed.[5]

Consider the first 10 lines from the existing 104 lines of an archaic Irish legal poem from the seventh century (Binchy, 1971, p. 158). The poetic device used is alliteration, and it is used in a clever way. The last word of each line alliterates with the first word of the next line, helping to tie the piece together. The pattern is common in Irish texts of the period, many of which have probable origins in oral traditions (see Watkins, 1963, for more examples). The pattern makes omissions and changes in the order of lines more difficult.[6]

Ma be rí rofesser	If thou be a king thou shouldst know
recht flatho,	the prerogative of a ruler,
fothuth iar miad,	refection according to rank,
mesbada slóg	contentions of hostings,
sabaid cuirmthige,	sticks [quarrels] in the ale-house,
cuir mescae;	contracts made in drunkenness;
mess tíre,	valuation of lands,
tomus forrag,	measurement by poles;
forberta díri	augmentations of a penalty,
díthle mesraid;	larceny of tree-fruit;

This function of reducing options was clarified in an elegant series of experiments by Bower and Bolton (1969). Undergraduates learned a list of 36 paired associates. The stimulus member of each pair of consonant-vowel-consonant (CVC) words was presented, and the undergraduates' task was to guess or remember the response member of the pair. Following their response, the full pair was shown. After all 36 pairs of the list were shown, the procedure was repeated for a total of nine learning trials. Half of the 36 pairs rhymed, and half were unrelated. Words from the rhyming pairs were always in red, whereas the unrelated words were in black in order to let the undergraduates know whether or not to give a rhyming response to the stimulus member of the pair. On all nine trials, the rhyming words were better remembered. Overall, the rhyming words were correct 66% of the time and the unrelated words, 46%.

Different undergraduates performed the same task, but this time, instead of half the pairs of the list being rhyming pairs (i.e., pairs in which only the first letter of the CVC word differed), half of the pairs differed in only the last letter. Thus instead of comparing rhyming pairs with unrelated pairs, pairs that shared both alliteration and assonance were compared with unrelated pairs. As with the rhyming pairs, on all nine trials the related words were remembered better, with the related words being correct 60% of the time and the unrelated words, 40%. Thus another pattern of sound repetition that reduced choices functioned as well as rhyme.

In the next task, the recall test of the paired-associate procedure was replaced with a multiple-choice test. Instead of having to respond with the correct response member when shown the stimulus member of the pair, the undergraduates had to choose from among a set of five possible responses. For rhyming pairs, the correct choice and the four incorrect choices all rhymed. For the unrelated pairs, none rhymed. In this way, the ability of rhyme to limit choices was removed. For both the rhyming and the unrelated cases there were always five choices, and knowing that the desired response rhymed was of no help when faced with five choices that all rhymed. Thus there should have been no choice-limiting advantage of rhyming, and there was no difference in recall.[7] Thus the main effect of rhyme in the experimental procedure tested was to limit choices.

D'Amato and Diamond (1979) followed a similar procedure using lists of pairs of CVC words. There were four groups, each of which saw a different kind of list. For each group, the pairs of words matched (1) no letters, (2) the first two letters, (3) the first and last letters, or (4) the last two letters. As expected from the Bower and Bolton (1969) results, lists with matching letters had more words recalled on the 12 trials of paired-associate learning than on the list with no matching letters. Recall was one and one-half to two times better than that of the no-matching-letters group. Following this was a free-recall task in which the undergraduates were asked to recall all the pairs, without any additional cues. For this task, there were no differences among the groups, even though there were large differences in cued recall on the paired-associate task. In the paired-associate task, where the first member of the pair was given as a cue, associations between the words of the pairs could cue memory and limit choices, thereby increasing the recall of the second member of the pair. In the free-recall task, there was an association between the words of each pair, but no associations that tied the pairs to the list as a whole. Thus there was nothing that could be used to cue memory or limit choices, and free recall of the list of pairs did not benefit.

This study is consistent with Bower and Bolton's and adds a point that is important for memory in oral traditions. Rhyme among words in a song will aid recall, but only after the first member of the rhyming set has been sung and is available to cue recall of the later members. Having many rhyming words in the last two lines of a song will not aid their recall until the last two lines are reached; other mechanisms are needed to ensure that the singer gets that far. This observation is central to the theory of serial recall developed in Chapter 8.

Bower and Bolton's final experiment has added implications for oral traditions. The same basic procedure was used, but now one-third of the pairs rhymed, one-third were unrelated, and one-third were interfering pairs that were unrelated as presented but that would rhyme if they were rearranged. For example, *pin* was paired with *hat* and *cat* was paired with *fin*. There was no color difference to let the undergraduates know which stimulus words came from rhyming, unrelated, or interfering pairs. For all trials, rhyme pairs were easier than unrelated pairs, which were easier than interfering pairs. For all three kinds of pairs, words not on the list intruded, but the undergraduates had an especially difficult time with the interfering pairs because there was a tendency to re-pair them with other words from the list in order to repair the rhymes. When only the unrelated and interfering pairs were included in a list learned by different undergraduates, a list in which no mention was made of rhyme, the interfering effect disappeared. Thus expecting rhymes led people to remember them too often.

Similar effects are noted when variants of a piece in an oral tradition are examined. In experimental situations, when some of the rhyme and alliteration is removed from a piece to be learned, it often reappears in recalls (Wallace & Rubin, 1988b; Chapter 11). Even errors in undergraduates' recall of Beatles' songs preserve rhyme and alliteration by introducing new rhymes instead of the ones in the original song (Hyman & Rubin, 1990; Chapter 8). Thus the cuing and choice-limiting functions of rhymes help to maintain the organization of the list and the songs, though they may lead to rhyme-preserving changes.

Rhyme Cues Widely, Meaning Narrowly

From the studies reviewed, rhymes, like other forms of constraint including theme and imagery, can cue recall and limit choices. Rhyme, in addition, has its own peculiar properties, and we turn to these next. The most complete studies on the effects of rhyme on memory are the products of the Nelson and McEvoy laboratory (e.g., McEvoy & Nelson, 1990; Nelson & Borden, 1977; Nelson & McEvoy, 1979a, 1979b; Nelson, McEvoy, & Casanueva, 1982; Nelson, Wheeler, Borden, & Brooks, 1974; for reviews, see Nelson, 1981; Nelson, Schreiber, & McEvoy, 1992). Unlike many research programs, which perform a handful of experiments on a topic, hundreds of experiments with enough overlap in procedure to be comparable have been completed. For this reason, the remainder of this section is one of the most difficult in the book for those not familiar with experimental psychology. It provides a sense of the strengths and limitations of the extensive and varied database on which conclusions are drawn. The three main points are as follows. First, in laboratory recall experiments, alliteration and rhyme cues function only if attention is drawn to them, whereas semantic cues always function. In contrast, in oral traditions, attention is always drawn to the genre-specific forms of sound repetition. Second, semantic cues draw attention to one particular meaning or aspect of a word, whereas rhyme cues do not. Semantic cues therefore cue more narrowly than rhyme cues. Third, words in rhyme categories are unstructured, except that each word has a link to the rhyme sound that defines its category. The second and third points lead to rhyme cues being more useful in accessing alternatives.

Because of the extensive number of manipulations, several distinctions must be kept in mind. In the basic experiment, undergraduates are shown a list of *target words* to learn, one word at a time, and later are asked to recall them. At learning, *context words* can be paired with the target words. The target word *red* might be presented alone or may be paired with a *sensory*-context word, a *semantic*-context word, or an unrelated-context word. For *red,* the sensory-context word might be a first letter/alliterative cue, a rhyme cue, or an ending cue that may have the same spelling but a different sound. The semantic-context word might be an association, like *brick,* or a category name, like *color.* Independent of what context words occur at learning, the same types of words can be given at recall, but now they are called *cues.* These cues can be either the same words used as context words at learning or *extralist* words that were not part of the original learning list. Thus *red* might occur in a list of words to be learned, either alone or paired with a sensory-, a semantic-, or an unrelated-context word; and at recall, *red* might be cued by nothing more than a request to remember all the words in the list, by the same context word it was paired with at learning, or by a new different (i.e., extralist) word of the same or different type as the one with which it was originally paired.

The cues, context words, or target words can be independently varied along two dimensions: *strength* and *set size.* Strength is the probability that one word will bring another word to mind. For instance, *color* is a strong cue for *red* because *red* will often be the first word that comes to mind when *color* is mentioned, whereas *color* is a weak cue for *faded.* Set size is the number of words in a category. For instance, some rhyme categories, such as *ed,* and semantic categories, such as *colors,* have many members, whereas others, such as the rhyme category *eg* and the semantic category *seasons,* have only a few.

A general summary of many of the results can be made by distinguishing four classes of experiments. In the first class, (1) no context words are used, (2) cue strength and cue set size are varied, and (3) target set size is controlled. Strong cue to target links produce higher recalls than weak links, cues with small set sizes produce higher recalls than those with large set sizes, and there is no difference in amount of recall between sensory and semantic cues once strength and set size are controlled.[8] In the second class, as in the first class, (1) no context words are used, but (2) the target set size varies, while (3) the cue strength and set size are controlled. Here there is lack of symmetry between sensory and semantic measures. The semantic set size of a target word has an effect when either a semantic or a sensory cue is used; however, the sensory set size of a target word has an effect only when a sensory cue is used

Nelson (Nelson, 1981; Nelson et al., 1992) interprets the difference between the first and second classes of experiments as follows. If attention is not brought to the sensory dimension of the target word, its sensory set size does not matter. In contrast, given the habits and expectations of the people taking part in the experiments, the semantic dimension is always salient, even if no cue or a sensory cue is used. Thus when a sensory cue is used at recall, as in the first class of experiments, attention is drawn to the sensory dimension, and the sensory strength and set size of both the cue and the target have an effect. When a semantic cue is used at recall, attention is not drawn to the sensory dimension, and the sensory strength and set size of the target do not have an effect.[9]

The sensory-strength and set-size properties of the target word fail to be important in the experiments unless attention is drawn to them. This deficiency in sensory or surface forms in the experimental context has already been discussed in this chapter. Once people realize that sensory organization or constraints matter, however, sensory cues can be used and are effective as semantic cues.

For the third and fourth classes of experiments, either semantic- or sensory-context words are presented at learning. In the third class, (1) semantic-context words are used at learning, (2) the cue strength and set size of these context words are varied, (3) either the context words or extralist words are used as cues, and (4) if extralist words are used as cues, they are either sensory or semantic. In the third class of experiments, in which semantic-context words are used, the effects of semantic strength and set size of both cues and targets are eliminated or are greatly reduced, compared with the no-context conditions of the first two classes of experiments, and there is no sensory-set-size effect of the target. The fourth class is identical to the third, except that sensory-context words are used instead of semantic-context words at learning. Here there is an effect of the semantic and sensory strength and set size of the targets.

Nelson interprets this collection of replicable but nonintuitive findings by making two plausible theoretical statements that contrast sensory and semantic cues. The first, stated as a summary of the first two classes, is that in order for sensory cues to function, attention needs to be drawn to them, whereas semantic cues always function. The same conclusion is made by Ozier (1978) based on alliterative cues used in a different paradigm. The second theoretical statement is that semantic cues draw attention to one particular meaning or aspect of a word. In contrast, sensory cues do not, but activate the set of related sensory cues as a whole. Under this interpretation, the reason semantic-context words eliminate or greatly decrease semantic target set-size and strength effects is that the semantic set size is reduced and the strengths are changed by the context words. Returning to the example of the target word *red,* a semantic cue of *brick* or of *apple,* when combined with *red,* activates different aspects of *red;* brick red and apple red are different reds. The strength and set-size values collected without any context words are no longer valid. In contrast, the alliterative cue *r* or the rhyme cue *ed* makes no such change in the target word or in its sensory or semantic set sizes or strengths.

Independent evidence that sensory activation exists over short periods comes from studies in which words prime other words within their rhyme category, reducing the time taken to respond. For instance, people are faster to judge that a string of letters presented visually is a word if it is preceded by a word that rhymes with it than if it is preceded by a word that does not (Meyer, Schvaneveldt, & Ruddy, 1975). The effect persists even when the first word is presented auditorily, indicating that sound organization, and not just graphemic or graphemic/phonemic correspondence, is at work (Hillinger, 1980). By having people name or categorize either pictures or words, it is possible to show that if the sound of the word was accessed either by naming (as opposed to categorizing) or by viewing a written word (as opposed to the corresponding picture), then priming of rhyme sound occurs (Lupker & Williams, 1989). Thus priming or activation of a rhyme category by using a member of the rhyme category occurs, at least over the short periods of time measured in the experiments, though such priming need not increase memory.

Research on semantic cuing also provides evidence consistent with Nelson's findings in that specific aspects or senses of the meaning of a word are effective primes. By less than 0.5 second after a prime, associates of the appropriate sense of a word will be primed more than associates of inappropriate senses. Thus after the sentence *The townspeople were amazed to find that all the buildings had collapsed except the mint,* which ends with the ambiguous word *mint, money* will be judged to be a word more quickly than *candy.* In less than 1 second, inferred words such as *earthquake* will be judged to be words more quickly than unrelated words (Kintsch, 1988). Similar effects are found for different senses of unambiguous words, such as *gold* being valuable and *gold* being a particular color (Tabossi, 1988). These effects also occur with older adults, but the irrelevant inferences and associates are more likely to interfere (Hamm & Hasher, 1992; Stolzfus, 1992).

The experimental manipulations clarify the way sensory and semantic context and cues function, but they contain no-context situations never found in oral traditions. Oral traditions always have a semantic context, so specific meanings of words are always selected. Oral traditions always have an organized sensory context, which draws attention to particular sound constraints and thereby removes the deficiency of unnoticed sensory properties noted in the laboratory. In the context-rich organization of oral traditions, semantic contexts and cues select particular aspects of the meaning of a word. This selection can make semantic cues very effective at retrieving the word with which they were originally paired, but the problem is that if a cue does not retrieve the original word, it will not be especially effective at retrieving alternatives. If the semantic cue is not the one that was present in the learning context, it may not benefit and may be hurt by the original semantic context. In contrast, sensory cues, such as rhyme and alliteration, do not focus on a particular meaning or sound of a word. They therefore may not be as effective at cuing a particular word in a set or one aspect of that word, but if that word is not found, they will be effective at cuing the set of alternatives. Thus semantic context and cues focus on the exact target, whereas sensory context and cues arouse a whole set of alternatives.

These results suggest different structures for semantic and sensory domains. Psychologists know a great deal about the structure of semantic categories (Deese, 1965; Fillenbaum & Rapoport, 1971; Friendly, 1977, 1979; Gruenewald & Lockhead, 1980; Meyer & Schvaneveldt, 1975; Rosch, 1975; Rubin & Olson, 1980), but much less about the structure of rhyme categories, though rhyme is central to the understanding of retrieval in many domains. Based on cuing effects reviewed, Nelson (1981) suggested that words in rhyme categories are unstructured, except that each word has a link to the rhyme sound that defines its category. Figure 4.1 is a hypothetical network of the *air* rhyme category based on Nelson's (1981) representation of a rhyme category; the individual words do not link to one another, and the strength of a word's membership is given by the length of its links to the central rhyme node. In contrast, semantic categories such as *animals* and *parts of the body* (Figure 2.1) are highly structured and show many links among the items, as well as a

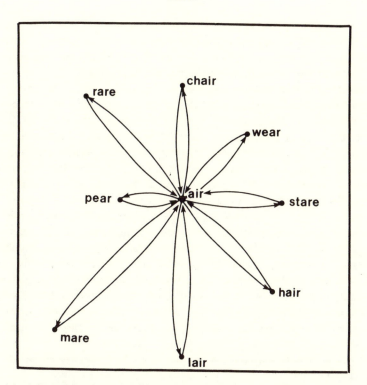

Figure 4.1. A hypothetical network for the rhyme category *air*. (Based on Nelson, 1981)

link to the central concept. Thus if people were asked to recall all the members of a semantic category, they could go from item to item, listing related items next to each other in rapid bursts. For *animals,* such a listing might be *dog, cat, . . . lion, tiger, bear, . . . cow, horse, sheep, . . .* For the rhyme category *air,* no such structure is assumed, and so the order of different people, or the same person on many occasions, would be different and no structure would result. Alternatively, some strategy could be adapted to produce an ordering of rhyming words.

To test this idea, 100 Duke University undergraduates were asked to list all the words they could in 60 seconds that had the rhyme sounds of *air, ear, ed,* and *ee,* as well as all the words they could list that belonged to the semantic categories *animals, beverages, furniture,* and *parts of the body* (Rubin, 1990). All responses were compiled, with different responses being combined under the same word only if they were different spellings of the same word. Singular and plural words were not combined because they have different rhymes. Thus *eye* and *eyes* were scored as separate responses. The 20 most frequent words in each category were selected for statistical analysis. For each category, the number of times any of these 20 words was emitted in succession was counted as a measure of similarity (Rubin & Olson, 1980).

The *parts-of-the-body* category was provided as an example in Figure 2.1. The location of the points was determined by a smallest space analysis multidimensional scaling solution (Lingoes, 1973), which tries to preserve the relative similarities among the items in the distances in the plot. This domain can be divided into a head cluster on the right, a limb cluster on the left, and a torso cluster at the center bottom. *Eyes* and *ears* do not appear immediately next to *eye* and *ear* because nobody ever said *"eye, eyes"* or *"ear, ears."* They are, however, close to each other because these words were often said next to *nose* and *mouth*. The network of arrows, which indicates which words were emitted most often after other words, comes from a Pathfinder analysis (Schvaneveldt, 1990). The network divides into three major areas: the head, the extremities, and the body. The recall does not traverse the body in an orderly fashion based on location; rather, analogy is the key. The pairs *fingers* and *toes, elbow* and *knee, arm* and *leg,* and *hand* and *foot* are all connected. Thus this semantic domain and the others are clearly structured along semantic dimensions (for details, see Rubin, 1990; Rubin & Olson, 1980).

Figure 4.2 presents the nodes that consist of a single letter followed by the rhyme sound *air*. A U was chosen to place the points to make the figure clearer. In this figure and in figures for all four rhyme categories tested, there is a clear alphabetical organization. Most of the cycles and jumps over nodes are caused by homonyms. Words near the end of the alphabet often link back to the first alphabetical word of the category (e.g., *wear* to *bear*). This probably results from recalls in which the alphabetical search started from the last of a series of easy-to-access words rather than from the beginning of the alphabet. It appears that no clear organization was

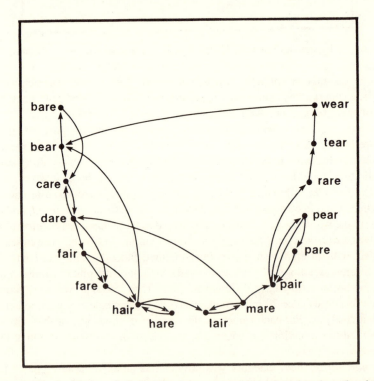

Figure 4.2. The Pathfinder solution of the rhyme category *air* plotted to show the alphabetical organization of the words formed by a single letter followed by the *air* rhyme ending.

available in long-term memory, and a search strategy of using the alphabet to cue words was used. This is a common strategy when trying to think of people's names or other blocked words (Gruneberg, 1978), and it is especially effective for rhyme categories. All a person has to do is combine each letter of the alphabet in turn with the rhyme ending and decide if a word resulted. Thus it appears that constructive techniques are used even for common rhyme categories.

Thus Nelson's (1981) hypothesis based on cuing data is supported. Undergraduates have an interpretable, stable structure for all semantic categories tested, but seem to have no such structure for the rhyme domains. Rather, they produce rhyme categories when needed, using an alphabetic strategy with additional searches for homonyms and any semantic structure that exist, such as *we, he, me,* and *she* in the *ee* category.[10]

Other differences between sensory and semantic cues indicate that sensory cues play a unique role in oral traditions. In no-context conditions, which are never present in oral traditions, rhyme cues present at recall lose their effectiveness faster than semantic cues as the time between learning and recall increases (Nelson & McEvoy, 1979a). In rhyme-context conditions, however, a 1-day delay does not reduce rhyme-set-size effects. In contrast, there are substantial losses in semantic-set-size effects for much shorter delays in which people switch attention to other tasks (Nelson et al., 1992). Thus once rhyme organization is apparent at learning, it can have an even longer-term effect than meaning.[11]

Rhyme Works Quickly

Another difference between sensory and semantic cues involves the effects of the rate of presentation, with rhyme having an advantage at quicker rates of presentation corresponding to those used in oral traditions. Images take longer for people to form and use than semantic associations (Chapter 3), and the evidence shows that rhyme functions more quickly than semantic associations. Whether words (or word pairs) are presented at a rate at which they can just be pronounced (about 1.5 seconds each) or at half that rate, rhymes are just as effective as cues. In contrast, recall increases substantially for semantic cues at the slower rate. This rate-of-presentation effect holds whether the cues were present as context words or not (Nelson & McEvoy, 1979b, Table 1; Nelson et al., 1974, Table 1), producing a situation in which rhyme cues equal in strength and set size to semantic cues are more effective than semantic cues at fast but not slow presentation rates. Later work demonstrated that slower rates can reduce rhyme-set-size effects while giving semantic cues and imagery more time to function (McEvoy & Nelson, 1990).

Theme, imagery and rhyme all function differently from one another, and, as will be seen in Chapters 5 and 8, these differences provide oral traditions with flexible mechanisms for stability. In this set of constraints, rhyme has definite advantages. Rhyme functions well at the rapid rates of presentation and recall common in oral traditions. Rhyme also casts a wider net than semantic cues. Rhyme categories are relatively unstructured, and rhyme-context words present at learning do not interact with their target words, as do semantic cues. Thus rhyme cues can be more effective than semantic cues if they are similar, but not identical, to the ones present at learning. As verbatim recall is not the rule in all oral traditions, this property is useful.

Rhyme in Text

The studies reviewed all concerned lists of words. There are some studies with children, however, comparing rhyming and nonrhyming versions of text. For instance, in a study by Johnson and Hayes (1987), 4-year-olds were read one of two versions of a passage. The passage was in verse form, with four lines to a stanza. For half the children, the last words of lines 2 and 4 of each stanza rhymed; for the other half, the lines were rearranged to break the rhyme pattern. The first two lines of each stanza were read to a child who then recalled them, followed by the second two lines and a recall, and finally, by all four lines of the stanza and a recall. Half the children were asked to recall the passage verbatim, and half in their own words. For the children who were asked for verbatim recall, the rhymed version produced more words recalled correctly and more words recalled in the correct order. For the children who were asked for paraphrased recall, the rhymed version produced fewer ideas recalled correctly, though this effect was not statistically reliable for all stanzas. Thus rhyming helped with verbatim recall and with recall in the original order, as would be needed in most oral traditions, but not with paraphrased recall.

This result is consistent with other studies of children's recall of prose and verse. For instance, Sheingold and Foundas (1978) found that rhymed versions led to better ordering of pictures describing the story, but not to better answering of questions from the story. Hays, Chemelski, and Palmer (1982) found that paraphrased recall was worse for rhyming versions of a verse, except for those words specifically involved in rhymes. This local effect of rhyme is common in oral traditions, as is seen in Chapter 8 and 11. In fact, the benefit of rhyme in the verbatim-recall condition of Johnson and Hayes (1987) may have been due, in part, to their having children recall in individual stanzas and pairs of lines.

On the Aesthetics of Rhyme

This section on rhyme should not be ended without mentioning the long controversy in literary criticism over the usefulness of rhyme as a literary device (Lanz, 1931; Wesling, 1980).[12] Here this controversy is secondary because rhyme limits choices and cues recall, thereby increasing the stability of genres of oral traditions that employ it. But once writing, with its perfect memory, replaces oral transmission, this mnemonic function is not needed and rhyme must be justified on aesthetic grounds.

The issue of aesthetics in written forms should not be cast onto oral traditions, where rhyme serves a mnemonic function, but it should not be ignored either. Aesthetically pleasing songs will be sung more often and therefore remembered better. There is, however, a problem with using this aesthetics as an explanation for improved recall. Judgments of what is aesthetically pleasing are less well understood than the recall tasks they explain. Such judgments are conditioned by culture, exposure (Zajonc, 1968), and a host of other factors (Smith, 1985) that, at present, make aesthetics a poor explanatory principle. One could even take a Darwinian perspective and say that rhyme is pleasing because it increases the memorability of useful information and therefore the probability of survival of those using it (Havelock, 1978), much in the way that food is hypothesized to be pleasing to animals well adapted to survive. The presence of rhyme-like patterns in the songs of whales (Guinee & Payne, 1988) is consistent with this perspective and can limit theoretical speculation.[13] Again, however, little is gained, at present, by being able to predict the details of when and how rhyme functions in oral traditions by assuming that rhyme increases the fitness of those who use it.

One difference in aesthetics between oral traditions and literary practice should also be made explicit. Wesling (1980) asks, "How did we come to a state of affairs at which a poet wants every rhyme to be his own invention, inscaped and selved?" (p. 38). He cites Wallace Stevens as saying, "In the 'June Book' I made 'breeze' rhyme with 'trees,' and have never forgiven myself. It is a correct rhyme, of course—but unpardonably 'expected.'" The oral poet has no need for "every rhyme to be his own invention." It is fine to use rhymes that are "expected." Memorability, not novelty, is important if an oral tradition is to survive, and expected rhymes are more likely to be reproduced.

Meter and Rhythm

The discussion of meter is spread throughout this book. Much of the study of the effects of rhythm on memory involves the use of intonation-unit length segments. These are reported in Chapter 5, where the role of the phrase as a unit in oral traditions is considered. Another important aspect of meter is its ability to organize an entire piece. How this organization aids memory is a central theme of the theory of serial recall proposed in Chapter 8. The particular meters of epics, counting-out rhymes, and ballads and how they affect memory are investigated in detail in Chapters 9, 10, and 11.[14] This section provides only a general overview.

The first function of rhythm is that of a constraint, like others, cuing and limiting the choice of both words and larger units to those with the correct rhythmic pattern (e.g., the correct number of syllables and stress pattern in English). For instance, in Homeric epic, which has a strict rhythmic constraint, words three or more syllables long typically can appear in only one or two specific locations in a line (see Foley, 1990, for a recent discussion). This placement depends only on the pattern of long and short syllables in the word, not on other considerations such as meaning (O'Neill, 1942). Sensitivity to stress patterns is not limited to oral traditions or poetic genres. American undergraduates without special training are sensitive to the stress pattern of English words. Although most two-syllable English words are trochaic (i.e., stressed–unstressed; Cutler & Carter, 1987; Cutler & Norris, 1988), two-syllable verbs have an iambic (i.e., unstressed–stressed) stress pattern more often than two-syllable nouns (Kelly & Bock, 1988). Undergraduates are more likely to read the nonsense word *mernak as mer nak'* when it appears in a sentence as a verb than as a noun. Attention to such constraints develops early and could be a major aid to language learning. By the age of 9 months, infants listen longer to two-syllable words with the more common stressed–unstressed pattern (Jusczyk, Cutler, & Redanz, 1993), and evidence for the bases of voluntary rhythmic behavior is present from birth (Thelen, 1981) and is often timed to adult speech (Condon & Sander, 1974). Thus attention to and implicit knowledge of prosody and rhythm in oral traditions should be expected.

Memory for units larger than the word also benefits from rhythmic constraints, especially units approximately the length of the intonation unit discussed earlier in the chapter. Memory studies using such phrase-length units are discussed in Chapter 5, and their functioning in oral traditions is discussed in Chapter 9. Such units correspond in length to the formulas of oral traditions and to the capacity of working memory.

Rhythm also has additional integrative roles (Devisch, 1993, pp. 259–264). For instance, a second function of rhythm is that it situates a performance in time, providing an organizing principle that allows all aspects of the performance to be integrated. Within one person, rhythm helps the coordination of the verbal component with body movements and music. Within groups, rhythm helps the coordination of the actions of all the people. Moreover, when a group performs together, rhythm is more regular (Boomsliter et al., 1973).

A third function of rhythm is to emphasize certain locations within lines, thereby facilitating other constraints. The meter of a piece draws attention to certain times and creates the expectancy that something important will occur then (Jones & Boltz, 1989; Jones, Kidd, & Wetzel, 1981). Thus the effects of rhyme in text and song can be increased by rhythm. For instance, in Chapters 10 and 11, it will be shown that the poetic devices of rhyme and alliteration are more likely to be placed on stressed than on unstressed syllables. Another example in counting-out rhymes is that a final unstressed syllable of a line with trochaic feet (i.e., strong–weak) will often be omitted from the text, but will remain as a rest in musical transcription. Another mechanism commonly used to accomplish the goal of putting stress on the last word of a line in a counting-out rhyme that otherwise has trochaic feet is to invert the last foot from trochaic to iambic (i.e., weak–strong). These techniques, which are discussed in more detail in Chapter 10, allow the last word of the line, which rhymes, to fall on a stressed syllable. It also allows the last word of the counting-out rhyme, which determines who is chosen, to fall on a stressed syllable. Similar mechanisms are noted in ballads in Chapter 11.

Fourth, rhythm provides an organized hierarchy of rhythmic units. Thus in English, syllables form feet, which form lines, which form stanzas. These rhythmic units typically coincide with meaning units in oral traditions (Bakker, 1990; Lord, 1960). This hierarchy of meaningful, rhythmic units allows singers to select, substitute, add, or delete whole rhythmic units while producing a coherent piece. Thus a ballad singer can delete a whole stanza without disrupting the music or poetics in any way. The only requirement for successful deletion is that the stanza contribute meaning that is not necessary for the story or that can be inferred from the remaining stanzas. Similarly, whole stanzas can be added to embellish a point without altering the music or poetics of other stanzas.

Fifth, rhythmic units, at all levels of the rhythmic hierarchy, create slots or gaps that need to be filled; they do not allow for the omission of part of a rhythmic unit. This produces a demand to recall something rhythmically appropriate to fill a gap a fraction of a unit long. Whereas the previous functions can be seen as leading to stability by increasing constraints, this one increases variability. In an evolutionary analogy, it would be a force for mutation because new material must be created and added to the tradition. The added material must fit the metrical scheme and other constraints. One way to add is to borrow or adapt something that occurs in the same relative metrical location elsewhere in the piece or in another piece with the same meter. Such movement is seen in oral traditions, as well as in the psychological laboratory (e.g., Ryan, 1969a).

Sixth, rhythm depends more on the genre than on the particular piece, and even when it depends on the particular piece, it is set after very little of the piece is sung. The meter for every line of an epic, or every stanza of a ballad, is the same. Once the first metrical unit is sung, the meter is set for the whole piece. That is, unlike the other forms of constraint studied, the rhythmic organization of a piece is fixed very early in its singing. For this reason, rhythm is less sensitive to the cues provided by a running start and thus can function in its absence. If the cues needed to recall the next part of a piece are lacking, the meter is still known, often making it possible to start again at another rhythmic unit. Stated another way, rhythm provides markers at the beginning of each metrical unit that allow serial position within a piece also to act as a salient cue.

Meter affects memory for units at many levels of analysis, from the word to the stanza, in varied but understandable ways. The mechanisms at the various levels need not be the same; rhythm may be heard differently at the level of the word than at the level of the stanza. Nonetheless, the various ways in which meter operates produce similar effects, making meter one of the most pervasive and important forms of constraint in oral traditions.

Rhythm is an important constraint in oral traditions and in literature in general. Like the constraints of alliteration and rhyme discussed earlier in this chapter, and of gist and imagery discussed in other chapters, rhythm is not peculiar to literature.[15] Rather, rhythm is a general property of language that has been adapted for use in oral traditions. The assignment of stress to syllables is central to the study of language and often relies on poetry for examples and clarifications (e.g., Dresher & Lahiri, 1991; Kelly & Bock, 1988; Keyser, 1969). A common theme in this endeavor is that English favors a pattern of alternating strong and weak syllables—that is, a rhythm. Moreover, the application of this and related rules can affect the stress assigned to at least some words, changing the nominal stress pattern given in a dictionary (for various positions, see Hayes, 1984, 1988; Keyser, 1969; Kiparsky, 1975; Liberman & Prince, 1977; Takezawa, 1981). The pervasiveness of rhythm can be seen in oral traditions (Hymes, 1976–1977), everyday speech (Lenneberg, 1967; Scollon, 1982; Tannen, 1989), and social interaction (Condon, 1982) not considered as poetic or rhythmical by the casual observer. Thus the meters of oral traditions, along with the other constraints studied, cannot be viewed as special mechanisms, but as extensions of existing forms of linguistic and cognitive constraints, extensions that vary with the specific properties of each language and genre.

As with rhyme, the aesthetic function of rhythm should at least be mentioned. The arguments put forth here all assume an oral tradition that relies on human memory. When writing enters and the survival of the tradition no longer depends on memory, the functions of rhythm can change. Its mnemonic function is reduced. In addition, as private reading replaces public performance, rhythm's function of group cohesion is also reduced. Finally, as music is removed from the oral performance, the rhythms of the words must stand on their own without musical support (Smith, 1968; Stewart, 1925).

Sound Patterns

Meaning, imagery, and sound have been considered as the three main classes of constraints in oral traditions. All three provide forms of organization that cue recall and limit choices, and all three accomplish this in different ways. Repeating patterns of sound in the form of rhyme and alliteration cue memory more broadly and in less time than either imagery or meaning. The temporal patterns of sound in the form of rhythm organize whole songs in relatively simple ways, while they restrict the individual words and phrases that can appear. Although psychologists have not concentrated their efforts on the effects of sound patterns, strong evidence exists for their role in recall and in the stable transmission of oral traditions.

Notes

1. Series of prepositions are a mark of English writing, not South Slavic writing. In the original South Slavic, the same series of noun phrases that are characteristic of writing exist, but they are marked with inflections for the genitive (possessive) case instead of prepositions for the genitive case.

2. A demonstration of the use of surface form in an organized, schema-like fashion is theoretically important because of its implications for the distinction between schema theory and other models of cognition. The abstraction of meaning was formerly thought to be the main distinction between schema theory and theories based on associations or on the storage of unorganized instances. However, it has been shown mathematically that both models that store information as networks of associations (McClelland & Rumelhart, 1985; Rumelhart, McClelland, & the PDP Research Group, 1986) and multiple-trace models that store individual experiences as an unstructured list of feature vectors (Hintzman, 1986) can produce the meaning abstraction that is the hallmark of schema theory. Data showing abstraction based on meaning have always been consistent with schema theory, but over the past several years they have also become consistent with schema theory's rivals—theories based on instances and theories based on associations. Thus data demonstrating meaning abstraction no longer discriminate among the theories they were collected to discriminate among.

Only schema theory is committed to abstraction that is based solely on meaning, not on surface form. Demonstrations of the use of organizations other than meaning therefore require the modification of schema theory to remove this last empirical distinction. Once this modification is made, there is no data to distinguish schema theory from recent instance or associative theories.

3. In the Nelson and Garland (1969) paired-associate study, the number of errors in learning the paired associates was counted. For the first, middle, and last letters of the response CVC words, the average number of errors for each condition was 12, 20, and 17.

When the stimulus and response CVC matched on the last two letters, producing a rhyme, there was an average of only 7 errors. In a different paradigm in which similarity among words produces interference rather than benefit, Nelson and Rowe (1969) found that, averaged over two experiments, matches of the first, middle, and last letters of three-letter, mostly CVC, words produced 57, 36, and 46 errors, whereas matches of the middle plus last letters produced 53 errors. For the Brown and Knight (1990) study, which had first, middle, and last letter cues effective 33%, 15%, and 23% of the time, the last two letters combined were effective 32% of the time.

4. In two of the studies cited, actual frequency counts were made. For three-letter, mostly CVC, words the information explanation is supported (Nelson & Garland, 1969). This is because there are fewer vowels than consonants in English, so knowing which vowel is present transmits less information than knowing which consonant is present. For the longer six- and nine-letter words, the claim is not supported (Horowitz et al., 1968). The average frequencies of the bigrams of the six-letter words and the trigrams of the nine-letter words are 583, 546, and 1628 for the first, middle, and final thirds of the words, respectively. Thus unlike the recall data, the middle and first thirds are equally informative and the last third is much less so. That is, because the endings are much more frequent, they can be guessed more easily without any help and thus carry less information. These figures are supported by an analysis of a sample of 1 million words of text (Rubin, 1978). For this sample, the five letters *e, s, d, t,* and *n* together ended 62% of the words of running text, whereas the most frequent five initial letters, *t, a, o, s,* and *i,* together accounted for 49% of the words. Moreover, the clusters *ed, er, ing,* and *on* each ended about 3% of the words. Thus, except for very short words, endings carry less information than other parts of the word and cannot be better cues because of their high information content. The possibility remains that the middle could contain less information if sequential probabilities are considered, since the middle can be predicted from both the beginning and the end, but this is not enough to salvage the information explanation.

5. In addition, the placement of alliteration or rhyme in a specific location also reinforces the meter by demarcating specific places in the line, often its beginning or end.

6. The use of this pattern was made clear to me by Doris Edel.

7. For the first experiment there was an advantage of rhyme of 67% versus 56%, but on replication with more items that advantage disappeared, with 67% and 68% correct, respectively.

8. These results and those that follow hold for a wide range of subject populations, rates of presentation, retention intervals, and a whole host of other factors. For instance, in reporting these set-size effects, Nelson et al. (1992) review results from 144 experimental contrasts.

9. The attention need not be noted consciously, but it can involve implicit, unnoticed changes in processing.

10. Constructions of ad hoc semantic categories such as *things to take on a camping trip* have been noted by Barsalou (1983, 1987), but these categories are structured.

11. This comparison is between different conditions and needs more study, but it does show that the effects of rhyme need not fade as quickly as is often claimed.

12. Dana Wynne is responsible for drawing my attention to this problem.

13. For evidence of "cultural" transmission of songs in birds, see Payne, Payne, and Doehlert (1988).

14. Rhythm plays a dominant role in other genres of oral tradition. For the importance of rhythm in the learning and delivery of folk sermons, see Rosenberg (1988, especially pp. 63–64, 106–107).

15. Evidence for the prevalence of alliteration and rhyme in nonpoetic language is provided in the next chapter, where concord morphology within phrases is discussed.

CHAPTER 5

Combining Constraints

The stream of thought flows on; but most of its segments fall into the bottomless abyss of oblivion. Of some, no memory survives the instant of their passage. Of others, it is confined to a few moments, hours, or days. Others, again leave vestiges which are indestructible, and by means of which they may be recalled as long as life endures. Can we explain these differences? . . . The "secret of a good memory" is thus the secret of forming diverse and multiple associations with every fact we care to retain.

James, 1890, Vol. 1, pp. 643, 662

A system, economy or constitution . . . is a one or whole made up of several parts; but yet, that the several parts even considered as a whole do not complete the idea, unless in the notion of a whole you include the relations and respects which those parts have to each other. Every work both of nature and art is a system.

Butler, 1726; in Humphrey, 1933, p. 9

The earlier chapters demonstrate that oral traditions have many forms or organizations or constraints. Here it is argued that oral traditions are stable, in large part, because of the combination of these constraints. There are few options that can simultaneously fit the constraints of a theme, an image, and the multiple forms of sound patterns. Combined constraints produce effects much larger than those of the individual factors by decreasing the memory load and increasing the number of cues to recall.

This chapter considers the problem of how the factors isolated by the division of academics into disciplines, and then even further by the careful efforts and analyses of scholars, can be integrated to increase our understanding of oral traditions. After providing examples of the power of multiple constraints, we consider their role in oral traditions in more detail. Next, three general approaches are examined that put together what scholarship has taken apart. All make contributions, but none offers a complete solution. A fourth approach, building a psychological theory of the processes that combines the constraints in a process that a singer could use, is postponed until Chapter 8. The second major section of the chapter examines the phrase as a unit of analysis. This is done not only because the phrase is a level at which many constraints combine, but also because the phrase is the closest linguistic and psychological unit to the formula that has been central to debates on the nature of oral traditions. The final major section examines individual combinations that play a major role in oral traditions.

Combining Constraints

The Power and Uses of Multiple Constraints

Before beginning theoretical discussions, a few examples are given. Consider the letters in Figure 5.1. Although the ink blot covers part of each letter, the letters are easily recognizable as forming a word. The three letters could have easily been letters that do not form a word, as shown in Figure 5.2. The letters are indeterminate without the word, and the word cannot be known without the letters; but if knowledge of the possible letters and knowledge of the possible words are taken together, there is only one word that is a solution. Moreover, the phenomenon is reported as one of direct perceptual recognition rather than conscious decision making. Thus visual constraints on what letters or words could exist behind a partial screen and linguistic constraints on what words exist in the language combine to limit possible choices.

The second example comes from a popular report on the archeology of classic times. The trireme, an Athenian war ship with sails and oars, was used to ram enemy ships. It was a wonder of its time. No examples exist, but there are descriptions of its use and general appearance. In building a full-sized, working model of the trireme, Coates, one of the designers, is reported as saying,

> Hydrostatics, fluid mechanics, physiology and properties of materials fix this very lightly built ship within very tight limits. Change any factor very much and the results of the calculations tell you the thing will not be able to withstand ramming the enemy or cannot achieve the necessary speed and maneuverability. (*Boston Globe,* August 22, 1988, p. 31)

Figure 5.1. Letters covered with an inkblot. (After McClelland, Rumelhart, & Hinton, 1986)

A different design, with three people to an oar instead of one person to each of three vertically arranged oars, could work, but with the basic design set, the details of the design are fixed. In mathematical terms, there are widely separated local minima. The multiple constraints listed by the designer and others combine to limit the choices, though each constraint taken in isolation would not. That is, if we did not know from records that the trireme could travel 184 nautical miles in a day, that it had to be able to fit within the columns found in the ruins of its storage shed, and that it destroyed enemy ships by ramming them, then more solutions would exist. The constraints, including those from physics, and the physiology of rowers reduce the design alternatives.

An example more directly related to oral traditions than the previous two is that of cuing words with combined rhyme and meaning cues (Rubin & Wallace, 1989). The sound pattern and the meaning of a word are distinct properties in that one seldom tells anything about the other (Brown, 1958; Taylor & Taylor, 1965). That is, one distinguishing feature of language is that sound is arbitrarily assigned to meaning (Hockett, 1963). Although sound and meaning are independent in this sense, they combine to limit choice in the laboratory as well as in oral traditions.

To show the limiting effect of combination, data from an existing study were supplemented. Fisher and Craik (1977) found a set of 54 target words that could be cued with either a rhyming word or a semantic associate. Rubin and Wallace (1989) then gave 35 Duke undergraduates a list of the 54 double cues formed by combining Fisher and Craik's rhyme and associative meaning cues. The first column was labeled "brought to mind by," the second column was labeled "rhymes with," and the third column contained blanks. For the word shown in Figure 5.1, *red,* an associative cue might be *color* and a rhyme cue might be *bed.* A rhyme cue or a meaning cue would produce the target word only 6% of the time when used individually, but 86% of the time when used together. Each individual constraint was weak, but combined they were powerful.

A second study was undertaken using the same procedures for all conditions (Rubin & Wallace, 1989). Target words were found that were cued by a rhyme and also by a semantic category cue two or more times per 100 tries in existing norms. In this way, idiosyncratic responses were eliminated and the target words could be assumed to be reasonable responses to their cues even if they were not generated by the Duke undergraduate who produced the new norms. Tape recordings of the cue lists contained only the rhyme sound presented twice for the rhyme cue (e.g., *ed, ed*), only the category name for the meaning cue (e.g., *a color*), or the repeated rhyme sound followed by the category name for the dual cue (e.g., *ed, ed, a color*). The tapes allowed 10 seconds for subjects to respond with a word that fit each cue. Data were scored until 50 valid responses were obtained for each cue. For the 110 target words obtained, the rhyme cue produced the target words 19% of the time; the meaning cue, 14%; and the dual cue, 97%. In spite of differences in the materials, procedures, and people tested, the two studies produced the same basic finding. Again, two weak single cues combined to produce a strong dual cue.

Set size is the number of different responses a group of subjects gives to a cue (Nelson, 1981). For the study just reported, the set size is the number of different words that were given out of 50 responses. For the rhyme cues, the average set size was 11 (range, 3 to 25). For the meaning cues, the average set size was 12 (range, 3 to 30). For the dual cues, the average set size was 1.3 (range, 1 to 3). Thus in the two single-cue conditions, an average of 11 unique words out of 50 responses was given for each cue, with a minimum of 3 and a maximum of 30 unique words out of 50 responses; by contrast, in the dual-cue condition, most cues produced the identical response for all 50 subjects, with a maximum of only 3 different words out of 50 responses. Moreover, this maximum set size of 3 for the dual cues was achieved for only 6 out of the 110 dual cues. Thus for dual cues, the set of responses is greatly reduced and the probability of a response being the target is greatly increased.

To assess the generality of this set-size effect, two existing norms were reanalyzed for rhyme and meaning category overlap. This analysis of the existing norms is more representative of dual cuing by rhyme and meaning than is the set-size analysis just reported. In that analysis, words were included in the sample only if they belonged to *both* a rhyme and a meaning category. Here words were sampled without regard to this property. Responses that subjects had given in the norms to a sample of rhyme cues and a sample of meaning cues were examined in order to see how many responses were present in both a rhyme and a meaning category.

McEvoy and Nelson's (1980) norms of rhyme endings and McEvoy and Nelson's (1982) norms of semantic categories contain responses from approximately 175 undergraduates who were asked to list the first instance that came to mind for categories such as words that end with the sound *ed* or that are a *color*. In order to include categories of different sizes, 15 small, 15 medium, and 15 large rhyme categories and 15 small, 15 medium, and 15 large meaning categories were chosen. On average, the small categories each contained about 5 different exemplars, the medium categories about 14, and the large about 28. When these arbitrary rhyme and meaning categories were paired, the same word or words were found in both categories in about 3% of the cases (see Rubin & Wallace, 1989, for details).

Of equal importance to the small number of rhyme and meaning categories that shared words is the set size of the particular category pairings that shared words. In all 38 cases where there were words cued by both rhyme and meaning cues, the set size was one, indicating that each double cue uniquely determined which word would be selected. The pairing of 97% of the rhyme and meaning categories yielded no words from the norms that belonged to both sets, and in the 3% of the cases in

Figure 5.2. Letters from Figure 5.1 with the inkblot removed.

which such a word did exist, it was the only word. Again, the dual-cue condition severely constrains the available responses, so the remaining responses, if any, are much more likely to occur.

The results of the various analyses of cuing words with their rhyme and meaning categories can be summarized as follows. In approximately 97% of the arbitrarily selected rhyme and meaning categories, there was no word in one category that fit into the other category. For over 2% of arbitrarily selected rhyme and meaning categories, based on the set-size analyses of both sets of data reviewed, there was only one word that belonged to both categories. For less than 1% of arbitrarily selected rhyme and meaning categories based on both sets of data reviewed, there was more than one word that fit both the rhyme and the meaning constraint. If you are looking for a word to end a line that has a particular rhyme and a particular meaning, chances are that it does not exist; but if it does exist, chances are that it is the only solution. One reason that rhyme is such a common poetic device in English may be its ability to provide limited search sets when combined with a meaning constraint.

The occluded word, the Athenian trireme, and the combination of rhyme and meaning cues are three examples of the uses and power of multiple constraints. Others are common. Whether diagnosing a disease, locating a malfunction in a car or computer, or solving the mystery in a detective novel, people try to make many observations under different conditions. Each observation could result from many different causes, but the combination of observations can have fewer causes and perhaps only one cause. People even make use of combined constraints in a systematic way when answering questions from short stories (Graesser, Lang, & Roberts, 1991). More powerful examples of combined constraints are presented in the chapters on individual oral traditions. There it will be argued that multiple constraints increase the stability of transmission by limiting choices and by cuing the recall of words and phrases that will either be the same as those used on earlier occasions or, if not, at least other good solutions to the requirements of the genre.

The Problem for Oral Traditions

Many properties contribute to the stability of oral traditions. The roles of meaning, spatial and object imagery, rhyme, alliteration, and rhythm were reviewed in Chapters 2, 3, and 4. Each property provides its own forms of organization or constraint. Most have their own neural substrates. But in oral traditions, they do not work alone. A combination of the various constraints is needed. The forms of organization add to produce an impressive total degree of organization. Yet, as was just shown, more than additive effects are found. Two cues, one meaning cue (Chapter 2) and one rhyme cue (Chapter 4) each succeeded in producing a target 6% of the time when used individually, but 86% of the time when used together.

Besides interacting to limit choices, the specific properties of the various forms of organization complement one another. For instance, descriptive or object imagery (Chapter 3) leads to a transformation of the original verbal stimulus into a nonverbal, atemporal representation (Paivio 1971, 1986). When verbal output is needed, the original words and the order of presentation will not be available for retrieval and will be generated from the image, resulting in changes in the wording and order of ideas. Spatial imagery and meaning constraints (Chapter 2), however, function to preserve the temporal order lost by object imagery. Even so, in most models of the internal representation of meaning, words are translated to and from a more abstract representation that contains none of the sound pattern, allowing for the possibility of translation errors. This remaining lack is remedied by poetics (Chapter 4), which preserve the sound pattern. Moreover, we know from studies of cuing with associative and meaning cues that meaning and rhyme cues differ in other complementary ways (Nelson, 1981; Nelson, Schreiber, & McEvoy, 1992). For instance, meaning cues tend to elicit the exact word that was present earlier, but rhyme cues make all members of a rhyme category more likely to be output, filling in when the word used on previous recitations cannot be recalled or no longer fits. Little will be said about music, but an active literature on the combination of rhythm and melody exists that in many ways parallels the claims made here for words (Boltz, 1991; Boltz & Jones, 1986; Dowling, Lung, & Herrbold, 1987; Jones, 1987).

The combination of constraints has been described as a static property of complete texts. In Chapter 8 a theory that produces pieces in their sequential order is considered. There the order of involvement of the various constraints is different from that in the preceding paragraph, with rhythm entering first as an overall organizing device known at the beginning of a piece, and with meaning, imagery, and repetition of sound pattern operating only locally and acting later in the process.

Three Theoretical Approaches to Combining Constraints

The laboratory is the ideal place to tease apart effects, and psychology has done this well. However, without guidance from other sources, the number of possible combinations makes the laboratory a tedious place to put back together many isolated effects to examine how they interact. Instead of examining all possible interactions, ones that are important to oral traditions are studied. The problem of how to examine even a limited number of combinations, however, is complex, so three theoretical approaches are discussed next. More detailed models suggested for perception (Garner, 1978; Lockhead, 1972, 1992), information integration (Massaro & Friedman, 1990), and memory (Horowitz & Manelis, 1972; Jones, 1976, 1987; Rubin & Wallace, 1989) are omitted.

Systems Theory

The most general formulation of interactive factors is systems theory. The quotation from Butler that begins this chapter is a good description of a system, as is von Bertalanffy's "complex of interacting elements" (1968, p. 42) or Simon's description of a complex system as "a large number of parts that interact in a nonsimple way" (1962, p. 468). The lack of a strict definition is appropriate for this approach at a general level. Systems theory has its own journals, technical terms, and issues; rigorous mathematical definitions are available for specific uses when needed.

Systems theory is often viewed as a broadening of scientific method (Sinnott, 1989) that is often contrasted to the more traditional cause-and-effect approach. For instance, in the last chapter of McBurney's (1983) text on methods in experimental psychology the following rationale for systems theory is given: "Traditional psychological theories are not intended to deal with situations in which the dependent variable can affect the independent variable via a feedback mechanism. . . . These more weighty problems can be handled by a type of theory called systems theory'' (pp. 253–254). Systems theory, in its general form, does handle feedback, but it also does more (von Bertalanffy, 1968, pp. 43–44). Nonetheless, it need not alter the basic scientific approach. As Simon (1962) notes, ''In the face of complexity, an in-principle reductionist may be at the same time a pragmatic holist'' (p. 468). In fact, all science, and probably all intellectual activity, uses the more commonsense aspects of systems theory without using the label. For instance, the world is always divided into domains (i.e., systems or, more accurately, partial systems) that can be studied to a fair level of completeness without concern for what is outside them.

As a concrete example, consider a person as a system. First, the person is a system (actually, a partial system) made up of other systems, such as the nervous and digestive systems. Each of these systems is made up of systems, such as the brain or stomach, which in turn are made up of systems, reducing eventually to the individual cell and continuing through molecules, atoms, and subatomic particles. Similarly, the person is embedded in a system, such as the family, which itself is embedded. Second, each of the systems at each level interacts. Thus the nervous and digestive systems are separate to an extent, but influence each other. Third, at each level of these embedded systems are properties that would be difficult to deduce from knowledge of other levels. This is true of the example of a person, the person's nervous system, brain, and so forth at all levels mentioned. It even holds for fascinating examples where groups of animals act as systems with properties usually applied only to single animals (Franks, 1989; Seeley, 1989). Fourth, the person has a boundary, usually taken as the skin, which defines what is inside and what is outside the system. Fifth, the system is defined by its organization, not necessarily by its contents. Thus the molecules making up the person change over time, though the basic organization does not. That is, at the molecular level, you are a changing product of what you eat, though at the person level the organization need not change. Sixth, the person, as a system, tries to maintain itself. Not all systems have this property, but most living systems do have such an ''urge for survival.'' In general, if the system is disturbed it may return to a new stable state, often not far from its initial state. Seventh, the system, especially a living system, reduces entropy within its boundary without becoming rigid or fixed. A person is and remains far from a random collection of molecules as long as the person is alive, yet change and reorganization need to be possible. A rigid system could not adapt and thus would be more likely to be destroyed (Sinnott, 1989).

A person is a good example of a system because, from many theoretical perspectives, the person has these and other systemic properties. Consider a more speculative example: a song or piece from an oral tradition, such as an epic, a counting-out rhyme, or a ballad, as are analyzed in depth in the chapters that follow.

First, the song is a system made up of systems. Here the song was analyzed into systems of constraints, each considered in its own chapter. Each of these systems can be considered as being made up of systems, such as the spatial and object systems of imagery or the rhyme and alliteration of patterns of sound repetitions.

Similarly, the song is embedded in a system, the genre, which itself is embedded in the class of all oral traditions, and so forth. Second, each of the systems at each level interacts. This is the problem of the current chapter. Third, at each level of these embedded systems are properties that would be difficult to deduce from knowledge of other levels. Several of these properties at the level of the song itself will be discussed later in this chapter. Fourth, the song has a boundary, which defines what is inside and what is outside the system. Variants of one song are within the possible manifestations of the systems, but different songs are not. If the song changed too much, it would either become a different song or die out. Fifth, the system is defined by its organization, not necessarily its contents. Thus the particular words making up the song change over time, though the basic organization does not. This property will be stressed in Chapters 9, 10, and 11 on the individual genres. Sixth, the song maintains itself. Oral traditions contain songs that have survived as systems within boundaries for long periods. Although one cannot posit an intentional "urge for survival," there is a tendency for songs (as well as genres) to maintain themselves or change slowly, which has been described as *self-correction* or *homeostasis* (Ong, 1982). By definition, songs and genres that do not have this property could not be part of an oral tradition for any length of time. Seventh, the system reduces entropy within its boundary without becoming fixed. A song in an oral tradition is and remains far from a random collection of words or tones as long as it exists as a song, yet the song does not become fixed. The song will adapt to changes in the genre and to changes from the outside culture or risk no longer being sung. Thus, for example, ballads and epics lost much of their mention of supernatural forces over time as the cultures in which their genres were embedded changed, yet they maintained much of the story originally motivated by the supernatural forces.

Systems theory has many strengths. At a general level, the approach is correct; people and songs are systems. In fact, there seems no other way to view the example of the person. The properties of systems outlined for the person and the song provide a perspective and raise questions that might not otherwise have been considered. A new set of concepts and vocabulary becomes available. In the areas of biology, thermodynamics, and other fields, these concepts are assumed, but they are not commonly used in cognitive psychology. The most general weakness of the systems theory approach, however, is that it does little to answer questions in a detailed fashion. Rather, specific mechanisms are needed, and these usually must come from outside systems theory.

In particular, for the problem of how to combine constraints, the second property of systems listed, systems theory suggests that the interacting constraints be viewed as systems, but says little about exactly how they should be combined other than that each subsystem needs to maintain its boundaries and organization in the process. The sixth property of systems listed was that many systems maintain themselves, and if disturbed, may return to a new stable state, often not far from their initial state. This property is true for an animal, a song, and a buffered chemical solution, but the mechanisms used have little in common. Nonetheless, noting that a system maintains itself leads one to look for places where the system might remain stable (i.e., local minima), for ways of describing and testing the kinds of displacement and equilibrium that might occur, and for the means used to maintain stability.

Similarly, other useful perspectives fit well with systems theory. At a global, theoretical level, systems theory brings the concept of good form and the entire approach of gestalt psychology to bear (Kohler, 1974). The ideas that the whole is different from the sum of its parts and that certain figures are good figures for memory have received considerable attention in psychology, and much is known about the general properties of good figures in perception.

Systems theory also fits well with debates about the degree of modularity in human cognition. Human cognition can be viewed as one general-purpose ability, or it can be viewed as a collection of communicating but separate modules, each with its own particular properties (Fodor, 1983). The several classes of constraints discussed have been viewed as systems or modules at the behavioral level of description rather than as arbitrary manifestations of a general ability. Systems theory provides a formalism for such separate but interacting modules.

At the physiological level, most of these constraints have identifiable separate neural substrates, and some (such as spatial and narrative) have separate plausible evolutionary histories. In both the neural substrates and the evolutionary histories, the constraints appear as interacting systems. The general view held by most students of the brain is that new functions evolve from older ones, leaving the brain as a collection of leftover parts cannibalized for new purposes rather than as a planned, organized whole. The constraints that have been considered for oral traditions are reasonable candidates for such a collection of spare parts rather than arbitrary aspects of descriptions of genres. They may be the better part of a small set available to aid memory, and their interactions could be clarified by systems theory.

Systems theory also draws attention to assumptions that should be made explicit. For instance, systems theory can be used to examine the usefulness of the idea, common especially in older studies of oral traditions, that the song or genre has a life of its own and can be studied in terms that might predict its ability to survive. Systems theory provides a clean way of acknowledging and giving a place to aspects of oral traditions that are not being studied here, such as changes in culture and language, by explicitly stating that they are external to the system. In this way, areas of ignorance are identified.

Systems theory emphasizes that the level of analysis is arbitrary but important. One could choose either the piece or the genre and decide what are the next levels of systems up and down from the level of analysis. More than one hierarchical system is possible, and each would emphasize different things. Here the piece has constraints as subsystems, but it could just as well have phrases and then words down to distinctive features. Moreover, although systems theory is being used here simultaneously to incorporate several constraints as mechanisms that increase stability, equilibrium states and changes between them do not require knowledge of the mechanisms involved.

Having each constraint function as a somewhat isolated system contributes to stability in that changes in one system need not affect other systems. Consider language as a system fairly isolated from the referents of its words. The arbitrariness of the way the name or sound of words is related to the referent of words provides language as a system with great conservative force (Hawkes, 1977). Relations within language determine terms, and these relations are difficult to alter without making many changes at once. Language, then, does not have to change drastically when referents in the world change. This is also true of a genre or piece considered as a system.

In summary, systems theory provides a perspective that raises or emphasizes worthwhile questions. It provides a language and a set of concepts, but it provides little in the way of detailed guidance. Here, these must come from the study of oral literature and cognitive psychology.

Information Theory

Information theory is a mathematical formulation in which information in a technical sense is a measure of how unlikely it is that an event will occur. More information is transmitted if an unlikely event occurs than if a likely event occurs. Although related to the colloquial use of the term, the quantifiable formulation of information is what is important here.[1] The concept of information as a technical measure was important in the early development of cognitive psychology (Neisser, 1967) in that it provided information as a concrete object to study, replacing concepts such as energy transfer and drawing attention away from the mechanisms involved in the transfer. In order to determine the information transmitted, the entire set of possible events and how each decreases our uncertainty about what will occur needs to be measured. When this measure is applied to oral traditions, the power of multiple constraints to decrease uncertainty becomes clear. In the rhyme–meaning dual-cue example given earlier in the chapter, knowing both the rhyme and the meaning cue decreases uncertainty much more than might have been suspected from the information in each cue alone because the dual cue limited choices much more than either single cue alone.

Information theory makes it clear that the probability of events given two cues depends on the combined distribution of possible targets to the two cues and cannot be reduced to the effectiveness of each cue taken alone. For instance, in the rhyme–meaning dual-cue example, there were target words such as *ghost, steel,* and *year* that were cued an average 3% of the time with their individual cues and 100% of the time with their dual cues. In contrast, there were words such as *cat, dog,* and *sad* that were cued an average 27% of the time with their individual cues and 74% of the time with their dual cues. The difference between the first set of words, with nearly 0% single cuing and 100% dual cuing, and the second set of words, with more moderate single and dual cuing, is that in the first case, though the individual cues were weak, together they limited choice to only one word, whereas in the second set there was always more than one word cued by the double cue. For instance, *ghost* is the only mythical being that rhymes with *post,* whereas both *cat* and *rat* are four-footed animals rhyming with *hat* (Rubin & Wallace, 1989).

As the previous example shows, information theory emphasizes that the complete set of alternatives always needs to be consulted. Thus in determining how stable part of a piece will be, not only the quality of a particular alternative, but also the set of possible alternatives that may be present in the language or the genre, needs to be considered. This idea of competition among alternatives, which is missing from most theories of text memory, is especially important in material with a regular rhythmic structure. A whole line of an epic or a whole stanza of a ballad can be omitted, but not a half-line or half-stanza. The rhythmic line and stanza structure of the pieces do not allow omissions of less than a complete rhythmic unit. Thus in text, omissions are common, whereas in rhythmic and sung pieces, alternatives need to be found to complete the rhythmic and melodic structures. If an alternative exists it may be incorporated, though it is recognized as a change.

The problem in applying information theory to actual oral traditions is that we often do not know the distribution of all possible words and phrases that can be substituted or recalled and still fill the existing multiple constraints. In addition, information theory deals only with choice among alternatives and not with the particular properties of the constraints.

Parallel Distributed Processing

Parallel distributed processing is a recently developed, general mathematical approach that provides the most promising way simultaneously to combine the effects of multiple constraints in a rigorous fashion (Grossberg, 1988; McClelland & Rumelhart 1985; Rumelhart, McClelland, & the PDP Research Group, 1986). The basic approach, which was described in Chapter 2 and which will be the basis for the theory proposed in Chapter 8, uses a network of connected nodes.[2] As a mathematical or modeling technique, it is useful or not, rather than true or not. Specific models or architectures can be tested against data, but there are many alternative algorithms, and at present the relation among them has not been specified. One of the main advantages of parallel distributed processing is its success with simultaneous multiple constraints (McClelland, Rumelhart, & Hinton, 1986). For instance, Figures 5.1 and 5.2 are drawn from this approach. Its main disadvantage is that a successful model, at present, often contains many assumptions, as well as a matrix of association strengths or weights that is difficult to interpret. For both the assumptions used to build the model and the weights it produces, it is usually not possible to know which aspects are central to the explanation and which are arbitrary and peripheral (see McCloskey, 1991, for a more sophisticated analysis). Nonetheless, a mathematics that can account for complex human behaviors has real advantages over the kind of narrative model given in this book (Hintzman, 1991).

Considerable space has been used in trying to place the theoretical and empirical findings of multiple constraints in a broader context. Systems theory, information theory, and parallel distributed processing have been investigated. All three add useful insights at the level of clarifying theoretical issues and suggesting hypothetical mechanisms, and all three have affected this book. At the global level, such modeling is informative, in part because it demonstrates the varied mechanisms that can work and in part because it clarifies and demystifies theoretical issues. At a detailed level, we still lack the knowledge to make strong predictions or limitations on theory from this general level. Similarly, recent advances in cognitive neuroscience, which place imagery, meaning, and music in different brain locations, have affected the way we view their interaction. At present, the most efficient approach remains to provide quantitative descriptions of the various interactions, to formulate specific hypotheses that can account for them, and to test these hypotheses. Such hypotheses are then combined into more comprehensive models when possible. In

Chapter 8, this is done by hypothesizing processes that progress word by word through the piece to be recalled.

Constraints at the Level of the Phrase

Systems theory makes it clear that there is no ideal level at which to study a complex organization, but rather many embedded levels. In oral traditions, Lord (1960) concentrated on six levels: the formula, which in this chapter corresponds most closely to the phrase; the rhythmic line; the theme; the piece as a whole; the story pattern; and the genre. When genres other than epic and the broader linguistic and psychological considerations are included, at least two levels have to be added: the word[3] and the stanza, with its repeating melody. At each of these levels, constraints combine to limit choices for recall and increase stability. An example at the word level from the first section of this chapter is how rhyme and meaning combine.

Phrases are examined here in detail for several reasons. Phrases are usually the lowest level at which the meaning, musical, and poetic components come together in oral traditions. They are a basic level of analysis in language, in general, and in oral traditions, in particular. They are also a unit of production in music (Sloboda, 1977). Phrases are often the level at which the rules of the language or genre can be stated most easily. In oral traditions, phrases serve the same linguistic function they serve in the language in which they are sung, but they do more because of the special requirements of remembering and performing songs. In oral traditions, a phrase is often a formula, and thus the phrase is the level at which the theoretical debates on formulaic theory in oral traditions, which are discussed in Chapter 9, take place. In Homeric epic, the phrase often fills a half-line. In South Slavic epic, it can also fill a whole line. In either case, the phrase often coincides with a rhythmic unit of the genre.

In the final section of this chapter, other levels will be considered in more detail.

The Rhythmic Phrase as a Basic Unit in Memory

The simplest way to examine the role of phrases in memory is to examine phrase-length groupings of unrelated items, later adding the syntactic and meaning components. Ryan (1969a) presented a tape-recorded list of nine randomly selected digits to people and asked them to recall them in order as soon as the list was completed.[4] In one condition, the items were presented every 0.55 second, for a total time of 5 seconds for the list. In another condition the items were presented every 0.45 second, with an added 0.45 second, after the third and sixth items, again for a total time for 5 seconds for the list. This movement of time changed the list from one of nine digits to one of three phrases each of three digits.

Because there were only nine items on the list and these were drawn from among 10 digits, there were few omissions, so Ryan scored errors caused by putting the digits in the wrong position. The temporal grouping produced a large decrease in errors. The temporal grouping produced only 26% as many errors as the ungrouped lists. Moreover, the errors occurred in different places. For the ungrouped lists, there was an increase in the likelihood of an error from position 1 to position 8, with a drop for position 9. For the temporally grouped lists, there were almost no errors at positions 3, 6, and 9, the positions followed by a pause. When a number was recalled in a wrong position in the ungrouped list, it was next to its correct position 61% of the time; two away, 23%; three away, 11%; and four away, 5%. For the temporally grouped list, it was next to its correct position 56% of the time; two away, 9%; three away, 32%; and four away, 1%. Thus there was a tendency in the temporally grouped list to place items three positions away in the same position in which they occurred in a phrase, but in an adjacent phrase (also see Robinson, 1977).

As discussed in Chapter 2, organization helps memory. Even the organization of grouping unrelated items helps, so Ryan wanted to show that the pauses that caused the phrase-like, rhythmic grouping were special. To examine this, she used three other conditions. In one, "pips" were placed after the third and sixth items to signal grouping, in a second there were instructions to group each list into groups of three, and in a third both pips and instructions were used. Compared with the ungrouped condition, the pips produced 83% as many errors; the instructions, 75%; and their combination, 67%—all a large distance from the reduction to 26% produced by the brief pauses. Thus although any form of organization might help, adding a rhythmic, phrase-like structure has a larger effect.[5]

Ryan then performed several other experiments to probe the finding. Ryan (1969a) found that regular groupings of threes were more effective than other divisions of nine items into three groups, with divisions that put one, two, six, and seven items into a group being the worst. Grouping into units of three is also nearly optimal in studies of expertise in long-term memory (Chase & Ericsson, 1981; Staszewski, 1990). Also, the length of the pause and the speed at which the list was presented had very little effect (Ryan, 1969b). In an ungrouped presentation in which letters, as opposed to numbers, were presented every 1.10 seconds or every 0.55 second, people who had 10 seconds to learn a list of nine consonants scored the same as people who had 5 seconds per list. Inserting pauses reduced the error rate to 78% of what it was without the temporal grouping, a value near that of the the pips and instructions manipulations of Ryan's previous study. The effect of pauses was the same for the two rates of presentation, even though for the 10-second condition the entire added 5 seconds were divided between the two pauses. Thus it appears that a large amount of time is not needed for the effect, just enough to indicate the groups—a result confirmed for nonrandom series in long-term memory in a different domain (Restle, 1972).

Ryan does not speculate on the difference between the reduction to a 26% error rate with digits and a 78% error rate with consonants, but it seems to point to a difference raised later in the literature between pauses as recoding and rehearsal points that allow larger units or chunks to be formed and the simpler effect of just isolating or marking a group (Frick, 1989; Laughery & Spector, 1972). For digits, it is likely that during a series of 40 lists, people learn to change groups of three numbers such as *seven, nine, three* into reorganized units or chunks such as *seven hundred ninety-three*, producing a large combined effect of chunking and of isolating the group. This reorganization into larger units is harder to do consistently with random series of consonants such as *K, W, P.* Thus there are several effects of rhythmic grouping in phrases, but just demarcating sets of items into groups is enough to have an effect (Frick, 1989).[6]

The Ryan studies used random orders of digits and consonants. This allowed the study of grouping effects in isolation from their interactions with other constraints, though in experiments with digits the use of habitual conceptual and linguistic categories of hundreds, tens, and units was present. Bower and Springston (1970) introduced both meaning and sound constraints in one experiment, stressing the recoding and chunking function of rhythmic pauses. This addition of constraints is closer to the situation in language and in oral traditions, where the pauses mark meaningful syntactic phrases. Undergraduates were presented with tape-recorded lists of 12 individual letters grouped by pauses and intonations into four phrases of 3 letters each. Some lists were made of sequences that were meaningful to the undergraduate, such as *FBI PHD TWA IBM.* These were compared with the same lists, but with the pattern broken by moving the last letter to the first position, transforming the list into *MFB IPH DTW AIB.* Other lists consisted of pronounceable nonsense syllables such as *DAT BEC JAX PEL.* Moving the last letter to the first position produced more difficult-to-pronounce lists—in this example, *LDA TBE CJA XPE.* Thus all lists had the same letters in the same order, with pauses in the same places; the difference was that for half the lists, the last letter was moved to the first position. For both the meaningful and the pronounceable lists, recall dropped about 25% with the last-letter shift. In other experiments, it was shown that the original lists read without pauses had recalls at an intermediate level and that the same finding held with sequences of 4, 3, 3, 2 instead of 3, 3, 3, 3 if appropriate lists such as *YMCA DMZ FBI TV* were used.

Other experiments from about the same period also showed the positive effects of phrase units on recall. For instance, O'Connell, Turner, and Onuska (1968) replaced the syllables in real sentences with nonsense syllables, but kept the two function words *the* and *a* and the morphological endings *y, ed, est,* and *s.* This would change "A little boy lifted with effort the biggest wooden block" to "*A* ha-key kex re-cil*ed* ou di-son *the* koo-t*est* pa-va deeb*s.*" Undergraduates heard strings with both the syntactic cue words *the* and *a* and the morphological endings, just the morphological endings, or neither. The strings were read either in a monotone or in normal intonation. Recall was better with increased grammatical structure, but only if the strings were read with intonation. Thus the intonation pattern combined with the syntactic cues produced an effect on recall that neither had alone.

In another study, Suci (1967) had undergraduates learn a 48-word story and then, 1 week later, learn the story again after it had been broken into units and presented with the units in random order. The units were formed either by breaking the story at the nine longest pauses used by the individual in recalling the story during the initial learning or by selecting breaks halfway between the nine longest pauses. When the pause units used by the individual were maintained, the randomized story was learned in half the trials compared with when the between-pause units were used. Thus Suci showed that much of what the undergraduates had learned was within phrase connections.

The Rhythmic Phrase as a Basic Unit in Language and Oral Traditions

The Privilege of Occurrence of Phrases[7]
The sentence "All the horsemen mounted their horses" (Lord, 1960, p. 51) can be divided into a noun phrase and a verb phrase. In normal language, the order of the sentence could be changed while preserving the individual phrases, and each phrase could be replaced by a single word, the pronoun "they" for the noun phrase "All the horsemen" and the proverb "did" for the verb phrase "mounted their horses." Thus the following sentences are possible paraphrases or questions based on the original sentence, though the music and poetics would prohibit such changes in an oral tradition: "They mounted their horses." "All the horsemen did." "Did they?" "They did." To the speaker of English, two cues to phrase structure based on the privilege of occurrence of phrases are found in the ways sentences can be transformed. One is the way other words, especially pronouns and proverbs, can be substituted for whole phrases. The other is the way phrases move as units, remaining the same under transformations (or changing in a few set ways, such as by the auxiliary verbs in questions or by the addition of *were* and *by* in the passive).

  In epic and other oral traditions, such phrases are often the repeated epithets, or formulas, that are used when a given meaning and sound pattern requirement are needed (see Chapter 9 for a fuller discussion). Because phrases with similar meanings are used in similar ways in a genre, their distribution, or privilege of occurrence, notes them as being of the same kind. Thus "horse," "white horse," "winged white horse," and "bedouin mare" will occur as object of a verb meaning "to mount," combining to form a verb phrase (Lord, 1960, pp. 46–52). Similarly "Zeus of the counsels," "Zeus the cloud gatherer," and "the father of gods and men" are all noun phrases with the same referent; the choice among them is decided by the number of syllables needed to complete a line (Lattimore, 1951, p. 39).

  Thus the repeated epithets or formulas of oral traditions tend to fill the linguistic role of meaningful phrases and stay together as a unit with one idea, as do the phrases in a natural language. This is one reason they can be used so productively.

Meter, Intonation Units, and the Prosody of Phrases
The use of music and meter in oral traditions is widespread. The equivalent in language is prosody, "a complex of supersegmental features, including lexical stress, phrase and compound stress, sentence accent, utterance rhythm and utterance intonation" (Cutler & Swinney, 1987). Prosody serves to mark phrases in several ways. In the sentence "All the horsemen mounted their horses," there would be a change in pitch and rhythm at the boundary between "horsemen" and "mounted" (Cooper & Paccia-Cooper, 1980; Morgan, Meier, & Newport, 1987), much as pause length was used to mark the phrases of digits, consonants, and words learned in the psychological laboratories. In addition, the change (usually lowering) of pitch, the lengthening of the final syllable, and any additional pausing would all help accent and strengthen the perception of a rhyme at the end of a phrase and therefore at the end of a line, making this an especially good place for a rhyme.

  In spoken as opposed to written language, the intonation pattern of phrases plays a more central role. Unlike writing, speech does not come in sentences. Rather, it is segmented into intonation units. According to Chafe and Danielewicz (1987),

> The prototypical intonation unit has the following properties: (1) it is spoken with a single, coherent intonation contour, (2) it is followed by a pause, and (3) it is likely to be a single clause. Although . . . others are no more than a prepositional phrase, or even just a noun phrase, or syntactic fragment of some other kind. (p. 95)[8]

Moreover, the combination of these intonation units into narrative is accomplished without the complex syntactic structures of literate prose, such as relative clauses, and strings of prepositional phrases. Chafe and Danielewicz's description of the combination of intonation units mirrors descriptions of the additive style of oral traditions (Lord, 1960; Ong, 1982) and is consistent with the prosody of phrases.

If intonation units are a basic unit of speech, it is little wonder that they make their way into oral traditions and are combined in the same additive fashion. The most sophisticated application of the idea that the syntactic structure of oral traditions is based on that of speech, and not that of the writing on which we usually base our syntax, is Bakker's (1990, 1993b) analysis of Homeric epic, which is considered in Chapter 9. For now, it is important to note that the emphasis being placed on pauses and phrases has support from linguistic studies of the transmission of oral information that are not part of the special language of oral traditions.

Intonation enhances the segmentation of speech into phrase units. It can even override the normal hierarchy of segmentation. One definition of a unit, consistent with the idea of a system from systems theory, is that it resists being broken or divided. If clicks are played while a sentence is being read, they tend not to be heard as breaking up phrases; rather, they tend to be heard as occurring in the breaks between units, though they actually occurred within the units (see Fodor, Bever, & Garrett, 1974, for a review). That is, clicks tend to migrate toward the divisions between units. Geers (1978) used this phenomenon to measure the ability of intonation to alter the strength of units. A trained phonetician read sentences either with a normal intonation, which stressed the major break in the sentence, or with an intonation pattern stressing a minor break. The following sentence is an example with a | indicating the major break between two clauses and a | indicating the minor break that was stressed—here, a break between a verb and the noun phrase that is part of the verb phrase. The click locations are shown by the numbers on the line below the sentence, which indicate how far the clicks were placed from the break. For each presentation of a sentence, only one click location was used.

I don't know | how he put on | my shoes.
−2 −1 0 1 2 −2 −1 0 1 2

In both intonation patterns, clicks migrated to both boundaries, indicating that syntactic cues were sufficient to define the units. The intonation pattern, however, could make either location the better one in attracting clicks, implying that for each reading, the units surrounding the stressed location were the stronger ones. The effect even worked with sighted and deaf adults who saw a videotape of the speaker with no sound, and who had to indicate the position of a flash of light instead of a click while lip-reading. The intonation pattern did not work to displace clicks in either reading when the syllables in the sentences were replaced with the letters of the alphabet, so that the example just given would become *A B C | D E F G | H I.* Thus the multiple constraint of the intonation, and the meaning and syntax of the sentence, combined to produce an effect that the intonation alone could not produce in this situation.

Like changes in intonation, the use of music and meter in oral traditions serves to make phrase boundaries clearer. One aspect of this in oral traditions is that the end of a meaningful phrase and the end of a rhythmic unit tend to coincide, whereas in literate poetry a meaningful phrase often runs past the end of one rhythmic line to the next. The low frequency of such enjambement in oral traditions is a basic observation of formulaic theory, as discussed in Chapter 9. It is also an aid to memory, as seen in the Bower and Springston (1970) study, in which meaningful phrases like *IBM* were easier to remember if they were set off by pauses (also see Gernsbacher, 1990).

In speech, there is a tension between placing pauses at phrase breaks in order to accentuate the units of language and placing them in a regular manner to establish a set rhythm, a tension that is exaggerated by the more regular meter of poetry. Grosjean, Grosjean, and Lane (1979) studied this combined determination of pauses in reading prose. They found that the length of pauses that undergraduates put between words in sentences they read corresponded to how important the breaks were in linguistic terms. Thus the longest pauses usually occur between the noun phrase and the verb phrase of a sentence, whereas the shortest pauses occur between words in the same phrase, such as an adjective and the noun it modified. Linguistic theory predicted the length of the breaks that undergraduates used in reading the written sentences, but there were exceptions. If the noun phrase was much shorter than the verb phrase, people tended to put the longest pause closer to the middle of the sentence at another reasonable division. By combining linguistic theory with the rhythmic constraint that the units should be of close to equal length, it was possible to predict pause length quite accurately. The model worked well even with data collected in American Sign Language. In oral traditions, the tension between pausing between linguistic units versus pausing at regular intervals is accentuated by the rhythm of poetry. The choice of words and word order must minimize the discrepancy, producing an added constraint.

Alliteration and Rhyme as a Result of Concord in Phrases
Concord morphology is a linguistic device, not used in English, that also serves to mark phrase boundaries. In concord morphology, inflectional markings (i.e., prefixes and suffixes) are applied to most or all words in a phrase. For instance, in some forms of concord morphology, nouns and the adjectives modifying them have the same endings to mark case, number, tense, or other grammatical categories. Consider the following two sentences taken from Morgan et al. (1987). From Latin, where the *us* ending is used for the nominative case and the *um* ending is used for the accusative case, comes the gem "The good son saw that good master," or *"Filius bonus vidit illum bonum dominum."* From the Spanish, where the *os* ending is used for masculine plural and the *as* ending is used for feminine plural, we get "The rich boys are buying some small apples" or "Los muchach*os* ric*os* compran un*as* man-

zan*as* pequeñ*as.*'' Although there are different functions in the different languages for adding the endings, in each case the endings mark the phrases as units. In other languages, such as Swahili, the added syllable would come at the beginning of each word; it can even come at both the beginning and the end, as in Hebrew. Concord morphology is not always a reliable cue to phrase structure, but often it is.

Although English does not use concord morphology in normal language, oral traditions do use techniques to make words that share some structural relation share the same initial or final sound. Rhyme and alliteration are two of our major poetic devices. Both work best when the words related are next to each other (Cermak & Youtz, 1976), and thus usually in the same phrase, or are in the same place rhythmically, such as the first words of alliterating lines or the last words of rhyming lines. Although it is possible to consider rhyme and alliteration as arbitrarily chosen devices used to make a more pleasing pattern of sounds, the use of concord morphology in other languages makes their choice for English poetry, in general, and for the unification of phrases in oral traditions, in particular, appear much less arbitrary. It is a minor paradox that rhyme and alliteration seem more common in the poetry of languages that do not have concord morphology. This is probably because rhyme and alliteration are easier to note as special poetic devices when there is no competition from rhyme and alliteration that are part of the normal syntax of the language.

The Rhythmic Phrase as a Basic Unit in Language Learning

Consider a young child faced with the task of learning the mother tongue, an adult starting to learn a second language, or anyone learning an oral tradition. Learning to parse the language into phrases is important not only because it provides units that can be used initially as idioms and later in a productive fashion, but also because it makes the task of learning the regularities in language much easier (Gleitman, Gleitman, Landau, & Wanner, 1988). In learning a language, one hears a finite input from which the linguists' rules of the language, or some equivalent formulation, must be induced. The problem is that the finite input underdetermines the rules of the language (Chomsky, 1965). Much of the structure of language is based on phrases: either occurring within noun, verb, prepositional, and other phrases, or occurring among the phrases considered as wholes. That is, the rules with which linguists describe language use phrases as an important level. Not including this level would make the rules much more complicated. Thus drawing the learner's attention to phrase boundaries should make the learner's task easier.

When a foreign language is first heard, it is difficult to isolate words and phrases. As the learner gains experience, words and phrases start to separate themselves from the stream of sound. Meanings and permitted usages can then be assigned to these units, even if they do not correspond to the word units of written language. To aid in this process, people use a special kind of speech, or register, when talking to foreigners, the elderly, or young children (Brown, 1973). These speech registers use prosody and other techniques to accentuate the phrase structure and individual words of the language, making the initial parsing much easier to do (Gleitman & Wanner, 1982; Gleitman et al., 1988). Children who are learning language pay attention to such speech in situations where they ignore normal adult speech. Moreover, for such speech registers, children orient themselves to speech that has been interrupted at clause boundaries rather than between clauses (Nelson, Hirsh-Pasek, Jusczyk, & Cassidy, 1989).

Oral traditions also clearly mark their phrase boundaries, as just outlined, thereby separating the phrases and making them easier to detect and recombine (with any needed modifications) in new situations. Whether the primary function of this marking is to make the structure of an oral tradition easier to learn and appreciate is an open question, but it has this added benefit.

Several studies have investigated the role of phrase-boundary marking in the learning of artificial languages. For instance. Morgan et al. (1987) had people learn simple artificial grammars and tested their knowledge with a battery of tests of grammatical knowledge. In several experiments, marking the phrases produced by the artificial grammar improved learning. The improvement came whether the phrases were indicated with prosody, with imitation function words represented by the vowels *a, e, i, o,* and *u,* or with imitation concord morphology inflections such as the endings *ra, ri, ro, ru,* and *rira.* Moreover, when phrases that did not correspond to the rules of the language were consistently marked, they were recognized as phrases more easily, but the learning of the rules of the artificial language did not benefit.

Thus when people learn real and artificial languages, they are helped by marked phrases. The implication is that the regular rhythmic and phrase structures of oral traditions also make them easier to learn. This improvement in learning is accomplished not only by emphasizing repeating segments, but also by making the rules of the genre easier to learn.

Specific Combinations

This section lists many specific combinations of constraints. Some of these are included because of the central role they play in oral traditions. Others, especially those at the end of the section, are included as examples of the large number of possible subtle combinations. They show that even in everyday language, choices are more limited than might be expected from casual observation.

Combining the Constraints of Meaning and Sound Pattern

This section is brief because much of its contents have been covered earlier in the chapter or will be covered when formulaic theory is discussed in Chapter 9. However, the combination of meaning and sound pattern is too important to pass over without mention. Meaning and sound pattern are, for the most part, paired arbitrarily in language (Rubin, Stolzfus, & Wall, 1991). Once a vocabulary of words is set in which sounds are designated to correspond to meanings, their arbitrary relation provides for two independent systems that can be combined to severely limit choices. The example of combining rhyme and meaning, discussed earlier, is a good example. The rhyme ending of a word tells little about its meaning, but once a category of rhyme ending and a category of meaning are fixed, the set of words that can fit both constraints is very small. Similar interactions occur at various levels in speech perception (Salasoo & Pisoni, 1985) and speech production (Dell & Reich, 1981).

Another kind of interaction occurs in which the units of sound and the units of meaning are made to coincide, drawing emphasis to the structure in each. For instance, maintaining the match between meaningful sets of letters and the rhythmic pauses between them in the Bower and Springston (1970) study greatly facilitated recall. Similarly, as will be discussed at length in Chapter 9, ideas or events as units of meaning tend to correspond to the rhythmic units of lines or stanzas in oral traditions.

The most important interaction of sound and meaning in oral traditions is the formula, which is discussed at length in Chapter 9. Phrases are used to convey an idea, with the phrase being used whenever it fits the rhythmic pattern of the line. Homeric epic is composed of a strict meter of long ($-$) and short ($\smile$) syllables. Lattimore (1951) notes that the phrase *brilliant Odysseus* is used when $-\ \smile\ \smile\ |\ -\ -$ is needed to finish a line, *resourceful Odysseus* when $\smile\ \smile\ |\ -\ \smile\ \smile\ |\ -\ -$ is needed to finish a line, and *long-suffering brilliant Odysseus* when $\smile\ |\ -\ -\ |\ -\ \smile\ \smile\ |\ -\ -$ is needed to finish a line. For the same three metrical contexts we would have *glorious Hektor, Hektor of the shining helmet,* and *tall Hektor of the shining helmet,* or *Zeus of the counsels* (or *Zeus of the wide brow*), *Zeus the cloud-gatherer,* and *the father of gods and men.* The epithet must fit the rhythmic constraint.

All these combinations of sound pattern and meaning help to make oral traditions more memorable and stable in transmission than everyday speech, which relies more heavily on meaning alone.

Combining the Constraints of Words and Music

The words and the music of a song form a unit in which each supports the other. Linguistic stress and musical meter, which have independent effects on the duration of sung syllables, tend to coincide in literate genres of music (Palmer & Kelly, 1992) and in oral traditions (Wallace & Rubin, 1991). If people are asked to recall the words of a familiar song, such as their national anthem, they remember more if the music is played than if it is not, but even no music is better than the wrong music (Rubin, 1977). This agrees with the reports of singers in an oral tradition (Lord, 1960, p. 99). Moreover, it is the fit of the music and the words that helps at the local level; it is very difficult to recall one line when the music to the next line is playing. Similarly, Wallace (1994) reports that when several stanzas are learned to the same melody, they are learned more easily than when they are spoken without the music, even if the spoken version maintains the rhythm.

In a series of experiments, Serafine, Crowder, and Repp (1984) and Serafine, Davidson, Crowder, and Repp (1986) studied the interaction of music and words using recognition memory. Undergraduates heard excerpts from a series of unfamiliar songs and then had to judge whether either the words or the melody of each of a second set of songs was from the first set. The second set of songs consisted of some old songs from the first set, some entirely new songs, some songs made by carefully combining old words with old melodies but not the ones with which they were originally heard, old words combined with new melodies, and new words combined with old melodies. The undergraduates were better at recognizing the words and the melody when each was paired the same way they were in the original learning. In fact, their recognition was almost at a chance level when they had to recognize a melody when it was paired with new words. The authors were not surprised, noting that most people do not recognize *Baa, Baa, Black Sheep* and *Twinkle, Twinkle, Little Star* as having the same melody, or *Merrily We Roll Along* and *Mary Had a Little Lamb*.

To try to understand this interaction of combined constraints of words and melody, the experimental conditions were varied. Using different singings of the songs for the recognition test ensured that the undergraduates would not recognize the songs from the particular sounds of one recording. Using nonsense words instead of the actual lyrics ensured that it was not a case of the meaning or mood of the words influencing the perception of the melody. Introducing choices in the recognition test in which the melody was hummed with no words, and in which the words were read with no melody, excluded the possibility that it was not the original pairing that was helping, but the new pairings that were interfering. Although each of these factors could play a role, the effect existed even when each factor was removed, showing that more than one of these factors was causing the effect.

The authors speculated that the increased recognition may come from subtle effects that words and melody have on each other. For instance, the particular consonants and stress pattern used in the words might affect the attack, stress, or other aspects of the melody. Similarly patterns of pitch, loudness, and stress in the melody could affect the pronunciation of the words. Because a new context subtly changes the words and melody, recognizing the words or melody as basically the same becomes more difficult.

To test these speculations Crowder, Serafine, and Repp (1990) performed an experiment slightly more complex than the previous ones. The same basic recognition experiment was used. They needed similar-sounding but not identical words to test if the sounds of the words in the previous experiment made submelodic changes in the melody, changes that would not occur with similar-sounding words. To do this, they changed the consonants of the songs they had used earlier to similar-sounding consonants. For instance, the phonemes corresponding to the letters *b, d,* and *g* (or *n, m, l* or *p, t, k*) were interchanged so that the line *Cobbler, cobbler make my shoe* in a song might change to either *Poggret, poggret nate nie foo* or *Toddwen, toddwen lape lie thoo*. In this way, each of the songs used in the previous studies became two songs with similar-sounding nonsense lyrics. In the experiment, people never heard the original meaningful songs. They heard one of the derived nonsense songs in the first set of songs and then, in the second set, had to judge whether they had heard the melody before, when another nonsense song derived from either the same original meaningful song or a different meaningful original song was sung. People recognized a melody better if it was matched with nonsense words derived from the same meaningful song than if it was matched with nonsense words derived from a different meaningful song.

Combined with the earlier findings, this experiment suggests that the nonsense words changed the melody. A melody was easier to recognize when paired with nonsense words that sounded similar to rather than different from the nonsense words originally sung with the melody. Thus the words sung changed the physical melody in subtle ways, and this accounts for part of the effect of combined constraints. In a later experiment, it was shown that associations that do not physically alter melody also have an effect, so changes in melody are not the whole story.

In oral traditions, unlike laboratory experiments, there is a long time for changes to occur, so especially good fits can form between lyrics and music. Moreover, the changes are less subtle than the submelodic ones used in the laboratory, making the laboratory studies an underestimate of what can occur in oral traditions. In oral traditions, the words and melody can provide especially good cues for each other because any changes in one will decrease the fit with the other.

Boswell and Reaver (1962) list many ways in which words can change to fit the melody of oral-tradition folk songs. Syllables can be inserted to fit the text to the melody. A four-line text can have its fifth line repeated to fit a five-phrase melody. When a four-line text is changed from common meter (lines of 4, 3,4, and 3 feet) to long meter (lines of 4, 4, 4, and 4 feet), meters that are commonly used in oral-tradition ballads, the new second and fourth lines need a metrical foot that is often filled by repeating the last word of those lines. Similarly, the addition of meaningless syllables like *O* at the end of some lines can be seen as required by fitting the words of a common-meter song to a long-meter melody. The scansion given to the words changes with the melody, producing the common "wrenched accent" of ballads. As is discussed in Chapter 11, Stewart (1925) even has argued that ballads have their own peculiar meter, the dipodic foot, which can exist in oral traditions only if there is music against which to mark the accents. A melody with a refrain or chorus will require a whole new stanza of words to be composed.

Among the ways a melody can change to fit the words in a folk song, Boswell and Reaver (1962) list the following:

> The use of two eighth notes in place of a quarter note. . . . Change in pitch of a note or notes, change in length more accurately to fit another word . . . grace notes (ornaments), . . . A 4/4 measure may be used at the end of a line of verse in a song in 3/4. . . . Substitute trochaic feet will readily move the measure bar over a beat to the left. A two syllable word will induce syncopation and cause the pitch of the note on its second syllable to be identical with that on its first syllable. (pp. 191–192)

Whether the words or the melody change most is determined by the "strength" of the melody, according to Boswell and Reaver. They claim that "strong" melodies, such as Serafine et al.'s (1986) example of *Twinkle, Twinkle, Little Star*, which are used for more than one set of words and often exist as music apart from words, resist alteration by the words. But "strong" words—that is, those with highly organized structures or good figures in the gestalt sense—also could be a factor. In any case, the combined constraints of two forms of organization, or systems, one for the words and one for the melody, increase stability in both. Once the words and melody change to fit each other, most changes in words and melody produce worse fits. Thus the words and melody each acquire especially effective cues to the retrieval of the other in that they better cue the original than any alternatives it may have.

The previous discussion was restricted to singing. If a musical instrument is added, as is common in epic and recently in ballad, then added interactions are possible. The "finger memory" of a hand playing a guitar, lyre, or gusle can help fix tones sung even in performances without the musical instrument (Wallace & Rubin, 1988b; Chapter 11). This is a special form of the interaction of motor movement and language.

Combining the Constraints of Motor Movements and Language

Language is commonly viewed as an abstract reasoning system relatively independent of the body producing it. In the terms used in this chapter, it is a separate system. The sample of studies that follow show that the interplay of speech and motor activity is more integrated than is often thought. First, consider the role of gesture in interpreting language. Klatzky, Pellegrino, McCloskey, and Doherty (1989) had undergraduates judge whether statements about actions were sensible (e.g., "crumple a newspaper" versus "crumple a window"). Before making judgments, the undergraduates learned to make four gestures: pinch, poke, clench, and palm extended. If the judgment was preceded by an informative prime for a gesture (e.g., "clench" before "crumple a newspaper"), the judgments were made more quickly than if no prime was given. This occurred even when the gestures were learned to and indicated by an iconic symbol (e.g., $> > > >$ for clench, $| | | |$ for palm, $>$ for pinch, and $|$ for poke) instead of a word, but not when the undergraduates were trained to give a verbal label to the symbols but no gesture. These last two conditions ensured that the gesture and not just the verbal label produced the effect.

Klatzky et al. showed that gestures help in interpreting the meaning of sets of words. Horbury and Guttentag (1992) demonstrated that gestures help in finding a word, given its meaning. Undergraduates were given a definition of a rare word and asked to think of the word that had the definition. They thought of the word more often when they were free to gesture than when their hands grasped a bar. In a related study, Morrel-Samuels and Krauss (1992) had undergraduates describe photographs. They found that gestures lasted longer and preceded words by a longer period for rarer words and phrases. When Horbury and Guttentag's undergraduates were later asked to recall as many as possible of the words they had defined, those whose hands were free did better than those whose hands grasped the bar, though everyone was free to move their hands at the later recall and though the comparisons were made relative to the words originally defined. Thus hand movements aided both the retrieval of words, given their meanings, and the words' later recall.

The effect of movement on later recall shown by Horbury and Guttentag occurs in situations other than following word retrieval. Saltz (1988) had groups of adults with average ages of approximately 30, 40, 50, 60, and 70 years learn sentences. Some people learned the sentences without any motor movements, others acted out the sentences as they learned them, and still others enacted them both at learning and at recall. Whether the people attempted to act out the sentences at recall made no difference, but motor enactment at learning increased recall by 165%. Moreover, there was a greater effect with increased age (Nyberg, Nilsson, & Backman, 1992; Zimmer, 1991). Saltz and Donnenwerth-Nolan (1981) tried to ensure that the motor activity could not be attributed to visual imagery accompanying the motor enactment. Following learning with either visual imagery or motor enactment, people recalled what they had learned with a visual-, a motor-, or a verbal-interference task. The visual-interference task interfered with information learned with visual imagery but not with motor enactment, and the motor-interference task interfered with information learned with motor enactment but not with visual imagery. Thus the motor enactment appears to be caused by the motor actions, not by any accompanying visual imagery. Saltz (1988) then repeated part of this study using covert instead of actual motoric enactment (i.e., motoric imagery) and found similar results, showing that mental practice of motor actions provided benefits similar to those of actual enactment.

The previous studies showed how motor activity aided comprehension, lexical access, and recall. The next study shows how language and motor activity regulate each other. Chang and Hammond (1987) had men repeat the syllable "stak" while repeatedly flexing a finger. There were three conditions. In one, the men asked maintain a constant amplitude in the loudness of the speech and the finger movements; in the second, they were asked to alternate loud and soft syllables while keeping finger movements at the same amplitude; and in the third, they were asked to alternate small and large finger movements and keep the loudness of each syllable the same. In all three conditions, the men kept the speech and the movement in synchrony, one syllable for each movement cycle, though this was not requested. All variations in amplitude were compared with those from the constant-loudness, constant-movement condition. Finger-movement variation increased 198% when the instructions were to alternate finger movement and 58% when they were to keep finger movement constant but alternate loudness. Loudness variation increased 72% when the instructions were to alternate loudness and 36% when they were to keep loudness constant but alternate finger movement. Thus varying the speech system drives the motor system, and varying the motor system drives the speech system to synchronous and amplitude-linked behavior.

Moreover, this entrainment of speech and motor movement occurred with both the left and right hands for right-handed men. In many tasks, interference occurs only if the same neural structures are involved. If the simple repetition of a single-syllable task does not activate both cerebral hemispheres, then the entrainment appears to occur across hemispheres. Assumptions about neural location aside, interference is assumed to occur if two tasks use overlapping processing, as in the Saltz experiments just reported or in the arguments about separate imagery systems in Chapter 3. In the tasks of Chang and Hammond, then, one functional system controls the timing and amplitude of both the speech and motor outputs.[9] In general, one role of rhythm may be to coordinate such actions.

In addition to the experimental effects reviewed, motor movements, in the form of gestures, can be shown to be part of everyday utterances, integrated in subtle ways into their syntactic and semantic structures. McNeill (1987, 1992) observes that gestures and speech are synchronized, often coinciding, but when they do not coincide they still follow a tight, regular coordination, with the gesture beginning before speech. Moreover, McNeill notes that there is only one gesture per clause, though systems such as American Sign Language exist in which more than one gesture per clause is possible. Each gesture–clause unit corresponds to a single image in McNeill's system. Finally, McNeill notes situations in which gestures are used to provide information not given by speech, thereby simplifying the speech. For instance, in one example, a gesture of removing a glove from a hand and placing it in a pocket occurred simultaneously with the phrase ''by hiding the glove'' in the sentence ''And he seeks to protect her by hiding the glove and not telling any of the other detectives about this'' (McNeill, 1987, p. 21). Consistent with the Horbury and Guttentag experiment, when speech is made more difficult, gestures increase, and they increase in places where speech would produce the most errors. Thus speech and gesture are two aspects of communication that coincide temporally, that express the same underlying images, and that can compensate for each other.

McNeill (1987) also argues that gestures are fundamentally different from speech in two ways. First, gestures are iconic rather than arbitrary. The meaning and sight of a gesture need to be related because we do not have a complete, socially agreed-on system of gestures, whereas the meaning and sound of words are linked in an arbitrary way, with different sounds transmitting similar meanings in different languages. Second, gestures are holistic and cannot be divided the way phrases can be divided into words, morphemes, and phonemes. These differences allow McNeill to use gestures as a window through which to view speech production. For our purposes, they show a motor system different from but highly integrated with the speech system: a motor system that can easily be adapted for use in oral traditions either as gestures, much like those accompanying everyday speech, or in more stereotyped, formal systems (Kersenboom, 1991).

Oral traditions are rhythmic, with the rhythm providing the context for the speech. This can be just a matter of how many syllables there are in a line or stanza and where the accented syllables fall, but from the studies reviewed, it can be more. Motor movements of gesture and those accompanying the rhythm of music are integrated with speech in the several ways experimentally tested and naturalistically observed. Casual observation of recalls from oral traditions is consistent with these findings. Ask someone to recall the words to a jump-rope rhyme or a childhood clapping game, and chances are that you will observe hand movements from the activity before any verbal recall starts. Moreover, those movements will become synchronized with the verbal recall. Ask that the hands be folded, and verbal recall will suffer. The same observation can be made for musicians in oral or literate traditions trying to recall a tune using ''finger memory.'' A literate, educated concept of memory for linguistic material is that it is separate and abstract; observations from oral traditions, experimental psychology, and psycholinguistics do not support this view. The interaction of these two systems is a multiple constraint that can limit changes in recall.

Combining the Constraints of Different Meanings of a Word

Once the primary meaning of a word is set, not all synonyms are appropriate substitutes, even if they have the same number of syllables, stress pattern, and other properties of the original word. Synonyms do not carry all the connotations of the original. Psychologists often study memory for words, sentences, and stories in isolation where changes in surface form do not have the implications for meaning that they can have in larger contexts (Bates, Masling, & Kintsch, 1978). For instance, actors starting to learn a script often report not trying to memorize the words verbatim, but rather paying attention to the exact wording in order to understand their character (Noice, 1991, 1992, 1993). The actor's initial auditions and rehearsals are often with script in hand. The exact words of the script provide the actor with information about the character that is needed to develop a proper interpretation. The actor not only searches for the kind of meaning in the text that psychologists often study, as described in Chapter 2, but also searches for the underlying motives and personality of a character that would make the character believable even in situations outside the text. This kind of study and the mastery of the character helps lead to verbatim recall, even though the purpose is to achieve understanding: the character could say only the exact words in the original script; a paraphrase would be out of character. Thus the complex of constraints on the meaning of the text and the nature of the character speaking a line restrict word choice.

Similar evidence comes from the observation that jokes, insults, and other utterances of high interactional content are often recognized verbatim from distracters differing only in word order or synonym substitution. This can occur even after the passage of days with no suspicion of a test (Bates et al., 1978; Keenan, MacWhinney, and Mayhew, 1977; Kintsch & Bates 1977). Such utterances are often more distinctive and emotional than the surrounding discourse, but they also often have meanings on several levels, so that a synonym that has the equivalent meaning at one level has a less than equivalent meaning at other levels. For instance, whether a proper name, a pronoun, or a role (e.g., her father) is used to refer to a character in a particular line in a television soap opera does not affect which character is referred to, but it does change the pragmatic value. Referring to someone by role rather than by name stresses different information (Bates et al., 1978). Such differences in the sense or implications of words can limit substitutions and thereby increase stability.

Combining the Constraints of Case Frames, Meaning, and Syntax

Another major limitation on word choice, and therefore on recall, is the way in which a word affects the word order and the choice of other words in its sentence. English can be considered as having case structure, though it does not mark most cases explicitly with an inflection, as do Latin and other languages (Fillmore, 1968).[10] Consider the following sentences. Those marked with an * are not permissible to most speakers. Those marked with an x, if acceptable, leave a sense of something not being told and change who dies.

    1a. John killed Fred with arsenic.

    1b. John murdered Fred with arsenic.

* 1c. John died Fred with arsenic.

    1d. John caused Fred to die by giving him arsenic.

    2a. Arsenic killed Fred.

* 2b. Arsenic murdered Fred.

* 2c. Arsenic died Fred.

2d. Arsenic caused Fred to die.

x 3a. Fred killed.

x 3b. Fred murdered.

3c. Fred died.

4a. Fred killed himself.

? 4b. Fred murdered himself.

* 4c. Fred died himself.

In sentence 1a, *John* is the agent (the animate perceived instigator), *Fred* is dative (the animate being affected), and *arsenic* is the instrument (the inanimate force or object causally involved in the action). These case roles do not change when the syntactic structure does. Thus *arsenic* is still the instrument in sentence 2a, even though it is now the subject of the sentence. The words *kill, murder,* and *die* have closely related meanings, but different case frames. *Kill* must have a dative case and either an agent or an instrument or both. *Murder* differs in that it must have both a dative and an agent, and can have an optional instrument. *Die* takes only the dative.

A less gruesome set of examples could be generated from *see, show,* and *look,* three words with a similar base meaning, but different case frames. *See* requires an object and a dative, *look* requires an object and an agent, and *show* requires an object, a dative, and an agent. The differences in the case frames add to the multiple constraints to produce stability in recall. Although the words may be considered as synonyms, their different case frames mean that changing from one word to another often can be accomplished only by changing the structure of the entire sentence. Such changes often disrupt the rhythm and end rhyme of a piece. The interaction of case frames, meaning, and syntax thereby increases the likelihood of verbatim recall. There are even effects that span sentences (Tanenhaus & Carlson, 1989). Cases that are expected to be filled but that are left unspecified, as in the dative cases in sentences 3a and 3b, allow easy ties to the unspecified noun in nearby sentences. After sentence 1a, a sentence beginning *"The* victim" would be more reasonable than a sentence beginning *"A* victim" because the dative case was stated or implied. However, a sentence beginning *"The* victim" is almost expected after 3a and 3b because the dative case was left empty (also see Singer, 1980).

Sequential Interactions: A Bias to Repeat Words and Syntax

There are many subtle mechanisms that produce conservative behaviors and thereby constrain recall. Although not constraints in the same sense as theme, imagery, and sound pattern, they combine with such constraints to limit variability. For instance, without trying, people increase the frequency of, or mimic, words that they have just heard.[11] Kubovy (1977) asked people to give either "the first digit that comes to mind" or "the first one-digit number that comes to mind." When the word *one* was mentioned in the question, it was given as a response 18% of the time, compared with 2% when it was not. Similarly, people were asked for either "the first four-digit number" or "the first number between 1,000 and 9,999" that comes to mind. The first digit of the response was one 52% of the time when the word *one* was mentioned in the question and 24% when it was not. In contrast, the first digit of the response was four 27% of the time when the word *four* was mentioned in the question and 4% when it was not. The effect does not seem to be a conscious mimicking. When a more obvious use of a number is made, such as by adding to the end of the request for "the first number between 0 and 9" the phrase "excluding fractions and only using whole numbers like, 1" there is a much smaller increase from 2% without the added phrase to 5% with it.

There also is a strong tendency for people to mimic syntactic forms that have recently been produced. For instance, Levelt and Kelter (1982) called shopkeepers in Nijmegen and asked them either "What time does your shop close?" or "*At* what time does your shop close?" The answers corresponded to the form of the question in that they included the word *at* when it was part of the question and excluded the word *at* when it was not 60% of the time, whereas 50% would be expected by chance. The experiment was repeated in the laboratory with a sample set of sentences using four other prepositions with a 73% correspondence, compared with 50% by chance.[12] The effect was not simply one of trying to mimic a short question (i.e., without the preposition) with a short answer or a long question (i.e., with the preposition) with a long answer. If this were the case, then the answers to the short question could have been shortened by leaving out the verb (e.g., "Five o' clock" instead of "We close at five o' clock"), but this was not done more often in answers to the short questions than to the long questions. If the shopkeepers were asked the same questions, except that these were followed by another sentence (e.g., "*At* what time does your shop close, since I have to come into the town especially to see you?"), the correspondence effect disappeared. However in the laboratory, having people listen to another question between hearing and answering the one from the experiment did not remove the effect, though it decreased the correspondence from 73% to 58% in one study (Levelt & Kelter, 1982, Experiment 1 versus Experiment 2) and from 70% to 60% in another (Levelt & Kelter, 1982, Experiment 5).

People who rehearsed a six-digit number while the question was being read to them did not show a decrease in the correspondence effect (75% correspondence without rehearsal versus 73% with it), demonstrating that the effect does not rely on working memory. Moreover, people judged sequences of questions and answers that both used or both did not use the same preposition as more natural than sets of questions and answers in which only one member of the pair had a preposition. Levelt and Kelter (1982) speculated that one reason for their correspondence effect is that reusing surface forms just heard is easier than generating speech each time from a semantic base. In oral traditions, where poetic as well as semantic constraints exist, there is even more reason to favor repetition of form.

Children also increase their use of passive sentences after an adult models such sentences (Whitehurst, Ironsmith, & Goldfein, 1974). Passive sentences such as "The *ball* was hit *by* the boy" include the words *was* and *by*, which simple sentences such as "The boy hit the ball" do not. As with the Levelt and Kelter study, these words, rather than the syntactic form itself, could be causing the effect. However, the lexical and syntactic factors can be unconfounded by using sentences like the following four from Bock (1989):

1a. The secretary is taking her boss a cake.

2a. The secretary is baking her boss a cake.

1b. The secretary is taking a cake *to* her boss.

2b. The secretary is baking a cake *for* her boss.

Sentences 1a and 2a both end with two objects. Sentences 1b and 2b transmit the same information, but end with an object followed by a prepositional phrase. Because the two prepositions are different, the lexical and syntactic effects can be separated. We already know that particular words, like *one* and *four,* increase in frequency when primed by previous use. Bock's work establishes that there are also purely syntactic effects.

Bock (1986, 1989) had people read a priming sentence, like one of the four just listed, and then describe a picture containing new actors and objects. The pictures could be adequately described either with two objects or with one object and a prepositional phrase beginning with *to.* For example, the picture could be described as either "The girl is handing the boy the paintbrush" or "The girl is handing the paintbrush *to* the boy." Whether the priming sentence used *to,* as in sentence 2a, or *for,* as in sentence 2b, had no effect, demonstrating that the particular lexical entry played no role in the experiments. The syntactic form, however, had a large effect. In a series of three experiments (Bock, 1986, Experiment 1; Bock, 1989, Experiments 1 and 2), priming with either the two-object or the object–prepositional-phrase sentences increased by about 50% the likelihood of the same syntactic form being used to describe the pictures.

To decide whether the effect was caused by changes in the syntax or in the underlying conceptual or grammatical-case structure, Bock and Loebell (1990) contrasted sentences such as 3a, 3b, and 3c:

3a. The wealthy widow gave an old Mercedes to the church.

3b. The wealthy widow drove an old Mercedes to the church.

3c. The wealthy widow sold the church an old Mercedes.

Sentence 3c is the control or neutral prime. Sentences 3a and 3b both have the same syntactic structure of subject, verb, direct object, and prepositional phrase. However in 3a, the church is the beneficiary of the action, whereas in 3b, it is the location or locative case. These sentences preceded the pictures described earlier. If syntactic form is important, both 3a and 3b should prime the prepositional-phrase form. If the conceptual idea or case form of beneficiary is needed, only 3a should prime the prepositional-phrase form. In fact, sentences like both 3a and 3b increased the frequency of prepositional-phrase sentences by about 34%, compared with sentences like 3c. Syntactic form mattered; the conceptual or case structure did not.

A final consideration was that the sound pattern accompanying the syntactic form, and not the syntactic form itself, might be at work. Therefore, Bock and Loebell (1990) used sentences like 4a, 4b, and 4c, which all have the same number of syllables and stress pattern, with 4a and 4b also having the same function words in the same position. The sentences differ in syntactic structure, with 4a ending with an object and a prepositional phrase, 4b ending with an object that includes an infinitive, and 4c being a control sentence that ends with two objects. Again, syntactic structure is important. Sentences like 4b and 4c did not differ, but sentences like 4a were followed by 42% more prepositional-phrase sentences.

4a. Susan brought a book to Stella.
4b. Susan brought a book to study.
4c. Susan brought the student a book.

Thus if either a song in an oral tradition or a genre as a whole uses a syntactic form frequently, there is a mechanism to reinforce that form's frequency. Moreover, if the same syntactic mimicry that occurs with overt production occurs for listening or singing along silently, then a person learning the song or genre would be primed to repeat the frequent syntactic forms even if the specific words were not repeated. In this way, syntactic constraints could be learned without conscious effort.

Discussion

The multiple constraints outlined in this chapter should be of help to all singers of oral traditions, but they should be especially helpful to older singers, and older singers are held to be the best in most oral traditions. Stine and Wingfield (1990), in their review of the literature on qualitative age differences in discourse processing, note that older adults benefit more than young adults from the types of constraints present in oral traditions, possibly to compensate for deficits in the older adults' encoding of new information. In particular, older adults benefit more from normal variations in stress, intonation, and timing; from appropriate syntactic and semantic context at the level of the sentence; and from a standard narrative structure in which one episode follows another, as opposed to being interleaved or randomly scrambled with it. In most cases, the recall of older adults is nearly equivalent to that of young adults when there is support by intonation, syntax, or semantics, but it is considerably inferior when these supports are removed.

Multiple constraints decrease choices and increase cues, thereby increasing stability in transmission. But this does not occur without cost. Each constraint cannot be optimized if a combination of constraints needs to be met. The best word or phrase to express a meaning may not be used because it has the wrong number of syllables or rhyme. The best rhythmic or rhyme solution may not be used because it has the wrong meaning. In genres such as epic in which characters appear in many songs and each song can be hours long, what is not said explicitly in one context can be assumed from what is stated elsewhere. But this is not possible for all information in epics and cannot occur as easily in other genres.

Consider the ballads to be discussed in detail in Chapter 11. Ballads are composed in stanzas, each usually four lines long, with a total of 14 or 16 stressed syllables per stanza. Following the principle discussed earlier in this chapter, the metrical unit and the unit of meaning coincide. Each stanza transmits one complete idea and usually one complete image. The limit of 14 or 16 stressed syllables leaves little room for phrases like "he said" and "she replied," and they are rare. A singer cannot tell who said something in one verse and what was said or the second half of what was said in the next. In contrast, epic has a line rather than a stanza structure, allowing such introductions of dialogue to be added as lines. As will be discussed in Chapter 9, when combined with the name of the person speaking and an epithet, full lines such as "Then in answer again spoke brilliant swift-footed Achilleus" (*Iliad*, Book I, line 121; Lattimore, 1951, p. 62) are common. However, in ballads, the constraints of expressing an idea within the boundaries of a small metrical unit limit explicit statements of who is speaking. This constraint can cause ambiguities, and different resolutions of these ambiguities lead to changes in transmission.

Similarly, because oral traditions are easy to image, many difficult-to-image internal states, motives, and feelings of characters are left unexpressed. Epic can use added lines of easy-to-image similes to describe internal states, but again, this is not possible in all situations or genres, still leaving ambiguities that lead to change. Attempts of singers to disambiguate and motivate actions appear to be a major force for change in medieval Dutch ballads (Gerritsen, personal communication, December 1991). If the tale could be told without the added constraints of metrical structure and imagery, such ambiguity would be easier to minimize.

Thus while multiple constraints increase stability in oral traditions, they are not a perfect solution. They introduce their own genre-specific problems and beauty. Because multiple constraints encourage the same solutions repeatedly in a genre, the solutions come to take on meanings from their various contexts, as described in Chapter 2. What is not mentioned in one situation is immanent because of the collection of uses in the tradition as a whole. Change, as well as stability, in oral transmission is therefore due in large part to the combination of constraints.

On a more general level, if multiple constraints are as prevalent and as powerful in oral traditions as claimed here, recall may involve much less of a thought process and much more of a pattern-recognition device. Instead of analyzing a situation and deciding on the best alternatives, singers need only recognize a situation and respond appropriately. As will be noted in Chapter 7, this is the same conclusion that Chase and Simon (1973) suggested for expert chess players and that Norman (1988) suggested for most everyday expertise. What is being claimed here for oral traditions has more general application. Such a use of multiple constraints to change analysis to recognition is a reason Plato gave for wanting to ban from his republic poets who were versed in the oral tradition of Homeric epic. Poets were not likely to analyze a situation carefully, but to respond with a verse that fit the constraints of the situation in much the same way that they would find a phrase to complete a line. This characterization of the poets is close to the view put forth in this chapter. All stimuli in oral traditions and in the world cannot be adequately described by a combination of carefully analyzed parts or features. Rather, they must be considered as wholes and in relation to other stimuli.

Notes

1. Information is defined as $-\log(p_i)$, where p_i is the probability that an event, i, will occur. The average information in a set of events is the sum of $-p_i * \log (p_i)$.

2. As discussed in Chapters 2 and 7, there exist other mathematical formulations that produce results like those of parallel distributed processing and that could be substituted in much of the discussion that follows.

3. Here and throughout the book, for the sake of clarity and to be consistent with the psychological literature, the term *word* is used to mean a word as entered in a dictionary. This may not always be the best choice for oral traditions. When singers in several genres of epic talk about words, they often mean lines or half-lines (Foley, 1990, pp. 44–50, 137–155, 219). Moreover, words from an oral tradition carry with them all the special meanings that accrue to them through use in their tradition (Foley, 1991, 1992).

4. This is an immediate-memory test, in contrast to the long-term-memory task of remembering a piece in oral traditions. It can be used to investigate the nature of processing as it is occurring and still in consciousness. Long-term-memory tasks cited later in this section support the conclusion drawn from this immediate-memory test.

5. The only statistically significant differences were between the temporally grouped lists and the ungrouped lists and between the temporally grouped lists and the pip lists.

6. This interpretation comes from studies by Bower and Winzenz (1969) and by Laughery and Spector (1972). The former study used digits, and the latter provides contrast by using consonants. These two studies involved long-term as well as the immediate, short-term memory of the Ryan (1969a, 1969b) studies, extending the results.

7. The remainder of this section follows the outline of the introduction of Morgan et al. (1987), though it uses different evidence.

8. In much of the data that follows, evidence was collected for the clause instead of, or in addition to, the phrase. Both units are important, and the clause, which contains all the components of a sentence, often produces stronger effects. This section concentrates on the phrase because it more closely matches the formula of Homeric epic described in Chapter 9 and the additive style of oral traditions in general.

9. Inhoff and Bisiacchi (1990, Experiment 3) found similar results for the timing of finger movements, but also found an asymmetry with respect to the speed of finger movements, so interference is related to which hand is used for at least one measure not involving the coordination of speech and motor movement. For a review of the related literature, see Inhoff and Bisiacchi (1990).

10. A more current and sophisticated view would be in terms of thematic relation (Jackendoff, 1987; Tanenhaus & Carlson, 1989; Wilkins, 1988), but case grammar is sufficient for the current arguments and is familiar to those who know a language that explicitly marks cases.

11. In Chapter 7, a cue–item-discriminability model is proposed. In such a model, as well as in any of a class of associative models, the excitation of a node corresponding to a word or a syntactic form can be made to decay slowly. In this way, the word or syntactic form corresponding to the node is more likely to be output not only when initially excited, but also for a period after excitation.

12. All examples are translations from the Dutch.

CHAPTER 6

The Transmission of Oral Traditions

Acquisition of semipermanent knowledge typically involves repeated exposure to information, with losses of information during intervals between exposures. Continued maintenance of knowledge depends on periodic access.

Bahrick, 1979, p. 296

All of the methods so far described deal with factors influencing individual observers. They help to show what occurs when a person makes use of some new material which he meets, assimilating it and later reproducing it in his own characteristic manner. Already it is clear, however, that several of the factors influencing the individual observer are social in origin and character.

Bartlett, 1932, p. 118

The changes that occur when a passage is transmitted from person to person are much greater in psychology experiments than they are in oral traditions. For instance, Bartlett (1932) had one person read a brief passage, wait between a quarter- and a half-hour, and then write down what was remembered. The recall of the first person was given to a second person, who performed the same task. The procedure continued until about a dozen people had in turn read and recalled a handed-down version of the passage. Bartlett summarized the extensive studies he performed using this procedure as follows: "In every single case, except that of the cumulative stories, the final result, after comparatively few reproductions, would hardly ever be connected with the original by any person who had no access to some intermediate versions" (p. 171). Bartlett is not alone in his findings (e.g., Allport & Postman, 1947), and they are robust enough to make for classroom demonstrations and party games.

The same general laws should apply to both transmission in an oral tradition and transmission in Bartlett's experiments.[1] In fact, Bartlett's experiments were explicit attempts to study the more easily controllable aspects of the normal oral transmission of stories (Bartlett, 1920a, 1920b, 1932). General laws, however, require a description of the specific material transmitted and specific conditions of transmission to be applied. For example, in Bartlett's studies, the *cumulative stories,* which showed greater stability, were highly structured sequences of events in which each action depended on the preceding actions, a device used in oral traditions. This chapter turns from the nature of the material being transmitted to the nature of the transmission itself.

For a genre of oral tradition to continue, pieces from the genre must be (1) retained within individuals so that they can be retold, (2) spread among individuals, and (3) handed down from older to younger individuals. Each of these three aspects of the transmission of oral traditions is the topic of a main section of this chapter. The ways in which these aspects of transmission occur in the oral traditions of counting-out rhymes, ballads, and epics are shown to have clear implications for the survival of these genres in memory.

Effects of Transmission on the Recall of an Individual

Learning and Overlearning

How does the degree of learning affect later retention? Over a wide range of initial learning from no learning to twice as many repetitions as are needed to just learn a list, and over a range of retention intervals up to 2 weeks, the more times a list is learned, the better retention will be.

Ebbinghaus (1885/1964) learned lists of nonsense syllables in eight degrees of learning from no learning to twice the number of trials needed to just master the list. On the trials that occurred after learning the list, Ebbinghaus tried to maintain the same attitude of *attentive repetition* that he had before the list was mastered. The next day, he relearned each list until the first time he could recall it without error. From these data, he computed the amount of time saved in learning a list the second time caused by learning the list the first time. The same result held no matter whether he repeated the list 0, 8, 16, 24, 32, 42, 53, or 64 times on the first day. Each three trials on the first day saved Ebbinghaus one trial on the second day. Learning a shorter list to four times the number of trials needed to just master it produced less of an effect, indicating that there are limits to the amount of overlearning that is efficient during a single session.

Krueger (1929) provided people with just enough, one and a half times, or two times the number of trials they needed to master lists. The lists were then relearned 1, 2, 4, 7, 14, or 28 days later. His results are presented in Figure 6.1. Krueger's results are comparable to Ebbinghaus's for the 1-day retention interval. For longer intervals, the lists learned just enough for mastery show little savings, and the lists initially overlearned to one and a half or two times the number of trials needed for mastery show relatively little difference from each other. Thus for longer intervals, some overlearning is very efficient, but there are diminishing returns. Slamecka and McElree (1983) found parallel curves similar to those of Figure 6.1 for degrees of initial learning up to just mastering the lists with a host of materials, including categorized lists and lists of sentences scored for gist instead of exact wording, as did Gilbert (1957) for two degrees of overlearning of a prose passage.

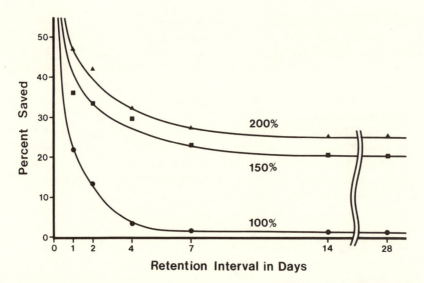

Figure 6.1. Krueger's (1929) classic study of overlearning. The percentages are the number of learning trials, with 100% being just enough trials to master the list and 150% and 200% being one and a half and twice that number, respectively.

Consider the difference between the degree of overlearning in oral traditions and the degree of learning in Bartlett's rumor procedure. Little verbal material is repeated more often than a ballad singer repeats a favorite ballad or than a child repeats the counting-out rhyme of *Eenie Meenie*. The twice-the-number-of-trials-needed-to-just-learn overlearning used by Ebbinghaus and Krueger, though it gave Ebbinghaus a headache, is child's play in comparison. In contrast, the pieces passed on in Bartlett's procedure were read only twice. Once a piece became short enough so that it could be learned to a criterion of one perfect recall in less than the two repetitions allowed, overlearning could occur and transmission became much more stable. Until then, as Bartlett noted, what was transmitted changed greatly.

Spaced Practice

In the overlearning experiments reported, all practice occurred during the same session. Spacing the practice over a longer interval, however, is even more effective. In addition, the limit to the amount of overlearning that is possible in a single session can be overcome by spacing the overlearning across many sessions. For example, Ebbinghaus took fewer trials to learn the same list on each of 4 successive days. In particular, on the 4 successive days he took 18, 12, 8, and 6 repetitions. In contrast, he had to greatly overlearn a comparable list, repeating it 68 times in 1 day, to be able to relearn it in 7 trials on the next day. Thus 18 + 12 + 8, or 38, trials spaced over 3 days were as effective as 68 trials massed on 1 day. Moreover, whereas all the 68 massed trials occurred 1 day prior to the critical test, almost half the 38 spaced trials occurred 3 days before the test. Perkins (1914), using a similar procedure, found an even larger effect. Two weeks after the last learning trial, people recalled 79% of the syllables seen once on each of 16 successive days as opposed to 9% of the syllables seen eight times on each of 2 successive days. Thus spacing is effective enough to overcome the loss of strength caused by the time it involves. In fact, part of the effectiveness of spaced practice may depend on such loss (Cuddy & Jacoby, 1982). In general, spaced practice can greatly aid (e.g., Glenberg & Lehmann, 1980; Landauer & Ainslie, 1975) and a lack of spacing can greatly hinder (Osborne, 1902) retention over long intervals.

Glenberg and Lehmann (1980) found that spacing tends to be most effective when the time between spacing approximates the time between the last presentation and the test. Words were presented at two learning sessions. The learning sessions were either 2 minutes or 1 week apart and were followed by a recall test either 2 minutes or 1 week after the second session. For the recall test 2 minutes after learning, 42% of the words were recalled if the spacing between the learning lists was 2 minutes, but only 24% of the words were recalled if the spacing between the learning lists was 1 week. However, for the recall test 1-week after learning, 6% of the words were recalled if the spacing between learning lists was 2 minutes, but 14% if the spacing was 1 week.

Landauer and Ainslie (1975) present a consistent and even more dramatic result. One year after completing a postgraduate course, students retook the final exam. Some students took an additional final exam either 6 weeks or 6 months after the course. Students who took an additional final at 6 months showed no loss at 1 year for the final they had taken at the end of the course. Students who took an additional final at 6 weeks were indistinguishable at 1 year from those who had taken no additional final and showed a loss of about 0.7 of a standard deviation from the final they had taken at the end of the course. That is, a student whose score was at the middle of the class would drop to the 23rd percentile if his or her 1-year-later final were used.

Although spacing is important for retention over long intervals, several hedges must be noted. First, spacing and retention intervals of less than a few minutes have attracted most of the theoretical attention. In such studies, the main effects of spacing can be between adjacent sequentially presented items and items spaced one or two items apart. The effects of spacing can be much smaller for such intervals (Underwood, 1961),[2] and the mechanisms at work may not be the same. Second, spaced practice has been considered from many different perspectives (Hintzman, 1974) and appears to be due to multiple mechanisms (Greene, 1989; Smith & Rothkopf, 1984). Thus although spacing is one of the most consistently studied phenomena in cognitive psychology (Bruce & Bahrick, 1992; Dempster, 1988; Ruch, 1928), none of the current theories can account for all the data. Therefore, without either advances in theory or the accumulation of parametric variations, it is difficult to predict the optimal schedule of practice or the size of the effect in novel situations, though such optimization work has been undertaken in specific situations (Atkinson, 1972). Third, most studies concern the learning of lists of isolated items; those by Landauer and Ainslie (1975) and those discussed in the next section, by Bahrick, are exceptions. As discussed in the next chapter under the topic of expertise, oral traditions are productive systems, not isolated lists. Thus overlearning and spaced practice need to be considered as skill mastery as well as item storage, making some of the comparisons more complex. Nonetheless, it is clear that for long retention intervals spaced practice is important, and that the repeated singing, in oral traditions, of pieces at spaced intervals aids in their recall.

Bahrick's Studies of Long-term Retention

Bahrick and his colleagues (Bahrick, 1979, 1983, 1984; Bahrick, Bahrick, Bahrick, & Bahrick, 1993; Bahrick, Bahrick, & Wittlinger, 1975; Bahrick & Phelps, 1987) have provided the most complete studies on retention over a lifetime. They used two methods. First, they used laboratory studies in which the same person is tested at several intervals ranging from no delay to delays as long as 8 years. Second, they used naturalistic studies in which different people are each tested at one interval, which may be up to 50 years after the initial learning. The variables most often examined are the two just reviewed: the degree of initial learning, or overlearning, and the spacing of various forms of practice. Let us start with a laboratory study.

Bahrick (1979) and Bahrick and Phelps (1987) had undergraduates learn 50 English–Spanish word pairs over a course of six sessions. On the first trial of the first session, all 50 pairs were presented. Next, the 50 English words were presented alone, and each undergraduate had to respond orally with the corresponding Spanish word. On the second trial of the first session, only those words that the undergraduate missed on the first trial were presented and tested again. This continued for as many trials as were needed for all words to be learned. Using this procedure, at the end of the first session each undergraduate made one, and only one, correct response to each of the 50 English words.

The second through sixth sessions continued in the same way, except that there was no initial presentation of the 50 word pairs; rather, these sessions started with a test consisting of the 50 English words. By the end of the six sessions, each subject had responded correctly to each English word exactly six times and had been presented with each English–Spanish pair as often as was needed for this to be accomplished. In the extreme case in which an undergraduate learned a pair on the first trial of the first session and then succeeded in getting it correct on the first trial of the remaining five sessions, the pair would have been presented only once. This procedure involves an equal overlearning of five correct responses for all words, as defined by the number of correct responses after the first correct response, and no overlearning, as defined by the re-presentation of pairs that were already learned (i.e., once a pair was learned, it was no longer presented).

The main variable of interest in this study was the spacing of practice. All six sessions occurred immediately after one another during the same day, on successive days, or spaced 30 days apart. The left half of Figure 6.2 shows the percentage of words recalled correctly on the first trial of each session.[3] The near-zero recall on the first trial of the first session represents the undergraduates' knowledge before the experiment began and was estimated from a control group. As one would expect, the most rapid learning was found for the group that had all its sessions massed on the same day because it would forget the least between the last trial of one session and the first trial of the next session. Nonetheless, undergraduates manage to learn fairly well even with 30 days between sessions.

The right half of Figure 6.2 shows the percentage of words recalled correctly 30

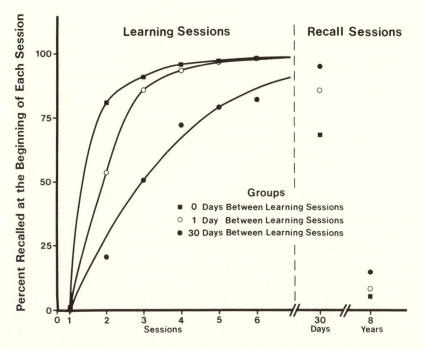

Figure 6.2. Learning and later recall of English–Spanish word pairs. (From Bahrick, 1979; Bahrick & Phelps, 1987)

days and 8 years after the sixth learning session. As expected from the discussion of spaced practice, though the longer intersession interval led to slower learning, it resulted in better long-term recall, with the effect holding even after 8 years (also see Bahrick et al., 1993).

A second observation of interest is that words that were learned easily were recalled better 8 years later. Words that initially took one to two presentations were recalled 16% of the time, words that took three to six presentations were recalled 7% of the time, and words that took seven or more presentations were recalled 3% of the time. This result occurred in spite of the fact that all words were recalled correctly the same number of times (i.e., once in each of the six training sessions) and in spite of the fact that words that were easier to learn were presented less often. In oral traditions, whole pieces are presented, so that the easy-to-learn parts are presented as often as the difficult ones. Thus the easy parts are overlearned compared with the difficult ones, which could increase the differential between easy- and difficult-to-learn portions.

The second method Bahrick and his colleagues have used to study long-term memory has been to examine something most people learn at the same age and see how much is remembered by people of different ages. In this way, recall for the geographic map of a college and its surrounds (Bahrick, 1979, 1983), the names and faces of high-school classmates (Bahrick et al., 1975), or Spanish learned in school (Bahrick, 1984) can be examined immediately after learning and up to 50 years later.

In this approach, experimental control is greatly reduced because the learning and the retention intervals all take place outside laboratory control. The natural variation in relevant variables is therefore included in a correlational analysis. Let us continue with the Spanish-vocabulary example.

Figure 6.3 shows how much different groups recall of their vocabulary words and idioms compared with a group of students just completing their studies.[4] There is rapid forgetting immediately following the courses, but then the forgetting appears to stop, and for about 25 years people recall nearly the same amount. Bahrick refers to this phenomenon as *permastore,* not to imply a fixed nature or high accuracy, but to indicate that little, if anything, is lost after the first half-dozen years or so. Similar functions exist for grammatical rules, reading comprehension, and other measures. In all cases, the material remembered was interrelated, was learned with spacing over a long period, and was in large part overlearned. In addition, measures of the degree of learning and overlearning, such as the grades obtained and the number of courses taken, had large effects that lasted over the 50-year period.

The effects of spaced practice after high school and college were not large because the people Bahrick studied had little exposure to Spanish after their formal schooling, reporting an average of only 1 hour per year of speaking, listening, or reading. Thus the results shown in Figure 6.3 are for the material learned or overlearned over an extended period and then rarely used until the recall test, much like a singer who, for many years or decades, had not sung a particular song or sung any song in a once practiced genre. Where exposure is greater, such as visits by alumni to their college campus, the effects of a little practice spaced at long intervals are substantial. In fact,

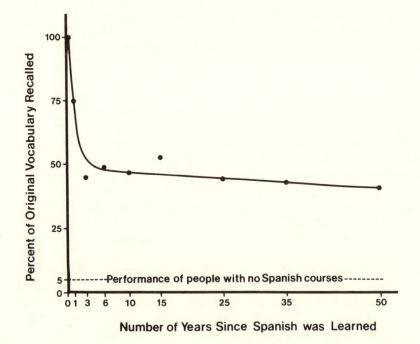

Figure 6.3. Recall of Spanish vocabulary words learned in school. (From Bahrick, 1984)

from his data, Bahrick calculated that it would take about twelve 1-day visits per year or four 5-day visits per year of spaced practice to maintain alumni's knowledge of street names and relative locations at the level of their senior year learning.

Recall Aids Recall

From the earliest scientific studies of memory, it has been known that *recitation*, the technical term for the mixing of test trials with study trials, aids learning. The size of the effect is substantial in organized material and is even larger in lists of unrelated material, especially once a little initial learning has taken place (Gates, 1917; Thompson, Wenger, & Bartling, 1978). There are many reasons to include recitations—that is, attempts to recall a piece both before and after it is mastered:

> Recitation furnishes an immediate goal to work for and is more stimulating than continued reading of the lesson. . . . recitation forces the learner to utilize what he has already learned, to depend upon himself instead of on the book. He discovers what he already knows and what he has still to master. (Woodworth, 1938, p. 210)

Some of the advantages of recitation proposed by Woodworth remain speculation; others can be studied experimentally (Thompson et al., 1978). Bahrick, in the work just reviewed, notes that one reason delayed rehearsal may improve recall is that it acts like a recitation test, allowing the subject to remove rehearsal strategies that are unsuccessful at the eventual recall period. Thus part of the effectiveness of spaced practice and the lack of effectiveness of immediate repetition, or "maintenance rehearsal," in short-term memory may be due to Woodworth's proposed evaluation mechanism of recitation. This is consistent with what we know about the increase in accuracy of people's ability to judge whether or not they will recall an item as the time between the learning and the judgment increases (Dunlosky & Nelson, 1992).

Each performance of a piece in an oral tradition is a recitation. Each time a singer sings or anticipates the lines of another singer, the advantages of recitation are present.

Motivation

Motivation is an integral part of studies of animal learning, but has received much less attention in studies of human memory (Weiner, 1966). Nonetheless, it is obvious that the interest aroused by participating in an oral tradition far exceeds that aroused by participating in an experiment on the learning of lists of nonsense syllables or the passages used by Bartlett, and that this increased interest should help increase the amount learned. One area of motivation, that of increased motivation resulting from the choice of the material to be learned, has direct applications to oral traditions and has received special attention in the psychological literature.

Perlmutter, Monty, and their associates (e.g., Monty, Geller, Savage, & Perlmutter, 1979; Perlmutter & Monty, 1977; Perlmutter, Monty, & Kimble, 1971; also see Langer, 1983) have shown that giving a person a choice of which materials to learn improves performance. Initially this was thought to be largely because people would choose material idiosyncratically suited to them. The differences in material chosen are most likely a factor in oral traditions, as is seen in the section "Conduits"; however, it is not the only factor. In laboratory learning, the effect appears even if the material learned is the same. For instance, the effect of choice is not diminished by having people choose only a small portion of what they will learn. Moreover, it is the perception of a choice, rather than the actual choice itself, that matters (Monty et al., 1979).

In oral traditions, singers typically choose their pieces within the limits of the genre and its social contexts. In rumor experiments, they do not. Choice is therefore offered as one motivational factor about which some detailed information is known. There are other motivational factors that play important roles. If oral traditions once did serve to transmit information that was important to the survival of the singers and listeners (Havelock, 1978), then from a Darwinian perspective some of these motivational factors might be quite strong (Staddon, 1981).

Transmission Among People

Bartlett's Laboratory Studies of Transmission

Bartlett developed two methods of studying distortions in recall. In the *method of repeated reproduction,* one person hears a story and recalls it several times. In the *method of serial reproduction,* one person hears a story and recalls it once, with the recall being the story the next person hears. Psychologists have used both methods to study distortions, assuming that the methods were much the same except that serial reproduction produced distortions more rapidly. However, from the perspective of a psychologist studying oral traditions, the two methods are very different. Repeated recalls from the same person can repeatedly access what remains of the original memory. Different contexts, types of memory tests, or cues can produce different recalls without necessarily indicating a systematic change in the memory (Alba & Hasher, 1983) or a trend in distortions, though there will be a strong tendency for the same distortions to occur repeatedly if the recall conditions do not change (Bartlett, 1932; Cofer, 1941). In contrast, when the recall of one person is the initial stimulus for that of another, the first person's recall is all that is transmitted of the original; there is no chance for a new context to recover information that was known by the first person, but was not told. The recall of the second person will be a product of the recall of the first person, the biases or style of the second person, and the conditions of the second person's recall. Thus what was not selected for the first recall will be lost, and what was selected for the first recall will not only be a source of information, but also help shape the expectations and biases of the second person.

This analysis of differences between the methods of serial and repeated reproduction suggests two separate sources of variation in oral traditions: transmission between people and memory within people. The method of serial reproduction is affected by both; the method of repeated reproduction is affected only by memory within a person.[5] Thus "new button gold" instead of "new beaten gold" for the cage of a parrot in a ballad is more likely an error in transmission than an error in memory within a singer; if the singer understood the concept of beaten gold when the song was first heard, it is unlikely that this error would occur later through changes in what was remembered. A singer may forget, but is unlikely to show a lack of appreciation of a constraint that was once known. This lack of appreciation is most likely to be one of meaning, not sound, making the transmission errors more likely to preserve sound. For children's counting-out rhymes, such lack of understanding may be more common and acceptable to the users of the tradition, providing one of many possible reasons for children's stressing sound over meaning.

Bartlett (1932) studied the serial reproduction of folk tales, descriptive passages, and argumentative passages that were not oral traditions for his subjects. Of his two methods, serial reproduction provides the better experimental analog of transmission in oral traditions, though the lack of nets and conduits, which are discussed in the next two sections, accentuate changes. From this work, he made six basic observations (pp. 172–176).

Two observations highlight differences between Bartlett's material and oral traditions. First, radical changes occurred. Second, the recalls became shorter. Bartlett's materials and procedures lacked the features proposed to increase stability in oral traditions, so changes should be expected. Moreover, without the poetics and music to define the duration of lines, verses, and performances, omissions were an easy change to make.

The remaining four observations demonstrate that serial oral transmission transforms a range of materials to make them more like those found in oral traditions. First, in Bartlett's materials, the titles of passages and proper names were quickly lost. In oral traditions, if there ever were titles, then they have been lost, and where proper names are mentioned once, as they were in most of Bartlett's materials, they do change. However, in oral traditions, most names and characters repeat within and among the songs of a genre, making the loss of names that are mentioned only once less of a problem. Second, there is a bias toward the concrete. According to Bartlett, "Every general opinion, every argument, every piece of reasoning and every deduction, is speedily transformed and then omitted" (p. 172). The one exception is the tendency for folk tales to acquire a moral, which Bartlett attributes to group convention. Third, there is a loss of individual characteristics:

> All stories tend to be shorn of their individualising features . . . the arguments tend to be reduced to bald expression of conventional opinion. . . . Where the opinions expressed are individual they appear to tend to pass over into opposed conventional views; where the epithets are original they tend to become current commonplace terms. (p. 173)

Fourth, the material is "rationalised" and made coherent to a "form which an ordinary member of a given social group will accept with a minimum of questioning" (p. 175). It is hard to imagine a view more consistent with that found by studying oral traditions than these four points. The changes noted by Bartlett transform his sample of material to the high-imagery, formulaic, conventional, scripted material of oral traditions.

Thus the conclusions Bartlett drew from careful examination of serial recall of material outside a living oral tradition support what would be expected from the views put forth here. Where differences in the materials and processes of transmission lead us to expect greater changes in recall, they are found. Moreover, the changes in recall transform the material Bartlett presented to make it more like that found in an oral tradition.

Conduits

In Bartlett's experimental procedure, randomly selected people wrote their recalls on pieces of paper, which were read by other randomly selected people. Transmission in oral traditions, and in much everyday activity (e.g., Brown & Reingen, 1987), is much more complex and much more conducive to stable transmission.

Folklorists, especially von Sydow (1948/1965) and Degh and Vazsonyi (1975), stress that not all people normally can or will transmit a particular genre. For each genre, a person could be an active bearer, a passive bearer (i.e., someone who listens, but does not perform), or no bearer at all (von Sydow, 1948/1965). The person who tells jokes may not pass rumors or sing ballads. Even within a genre, singers have clear preferences for the particular kinds of songs sung. A ballad singer might hear countless songs about one topic, but still prefer to sing about another.

People who are not active or passive bearers of a genre—that is, people who do not form a part of the genre's normal conduit—will not transmit pieces from that genre as well as people who are, even if they are highly motivated and otherwise have good memories. Conduits may not be terribly important for many types of laboratory memory tasks, but transmitting pieces of a genre is a skill that, due to exposure, interest, or ability, only some people develop.

Bartlett (1932) provides an example of the differences in interest that help to make up a conduit. Hearing reports of the remarkable verbatim memory of the Swazi, Bartlett tried several of his standard recall experiments with material he thought would be appropriate. He reported that as a group the Swazi were no better or worse than other people he tested. Bartlett then conducted a test of the memory of a Swazi herdsman about the cattle purchased by the settler for whom he worked. To quote Bartlett:

> Most Swazi culture revolves around the possession and care of cattle. Cattle are the centre of many of the most persistent and important social customs. . . . An animal may stray and get mixed up with other herds. It may be away for a very long time. However long the interval, if the owner comes with a description of the missing beast, his word is almost never questioned, and he is peaceably allowed to drive the animal back. (pp. 249–250)

The herdsman came to Bartlett with a sealed book listing the nine purchases of cattle the settler had made a year earlier. A sample entry read, "From Gampoka Likindsa, one young white bull, with small red spots, for one pound" (p. 250). The herdsman had been present at the sales but did not take part, except for driving the cattle back to the main farm, and had not seen the cattle since the sale. The herdsman recalled the list rapidly, with no noticeable hesitation, interest, or excitement. Much like a singer in the traditions described in this book, "he seemed to be reciting a well-known exercise and in no way reconstructing the deals on the basis of a few definitely remembered details" (p. 250). The herdsman made two minor errors: the 1 pound, 10 shilling purchase price of one ox was remembered as 2 pounds, and the color of one heifer described in the book as red was recalled as black.

The effects of conduits are amplified because oral traditions involve many individuals:

> Every storytelling event is a social experience. . . . In every storytelling event, the participants operate in accordance with a specific set of status relationships. . . . The storyteller's duties are to formulate, encode, and transmit a message in accordance with socially prescribed rules with which he and the other participants in the storytelling event are familiar. (Georges, 1969, pp. 317–318)

From this social viewpoint, it is easy to see why conduits are so important. Transmission will suffer if all people involved in the transmission process are not operating under the same set of rules and assumptions. An established conduit will transmit a piece with less change than a group of people who are unfamiliar with the genre.

Chains and Nets

In the laboratory, it has been customary to pass a piece from one person to the next with no individual seeing more than one version of the piece. Although psychologists have experimentally studied other patterns of the flow of information, the effects on memory have not been their main interest (Collins & Raven, 1969; Shaw, 1964). In oral traditions, it would be unusual for this pattern to occur. Many versions of the same piece are heard, often from different people (Fine, 1979). Figure 6.4 provides a graphic representation of the difference. Both panels contain three variants of a piece, variants A, B, and C, each of which is transmitted by a series of five people. Figure 6.4(a) represents three instances of the form of transmission that Bartlett (1932) used. Figure 6.4(b) represents a simplified version of the form of transmission that is more common in oral traditions. I will call these *chains* and *nets*, respectively.

In the real world, the net pattern of transmission is much more complex than is

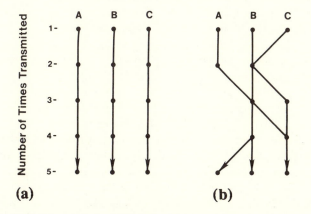

Figure 6.4. A simplified schematic of the difference between the (a) chain transmission used in psychology experiments and the (b) net transmission used in oral traditions and rumors.

shown in Figure 6.4(b), with some lines dying out and others branching dozens of times or looping back onto singers earlier in the net. If the figure were drawn in its full complexity for a single individual, the chain would have a single line leading in and a single line leading out. In contrast, for a single individual, the net would have an indefinite number of lines leading in and out, each at a different time, with the possibility of some listeners arriving after some singings had already taken place and with the possibility of hearing a song from or singing a song to another person more than once. That is, the difference between chains and nets is that in a chain an individual hears only one version and transmits it to only one other person, whereas in a net individuals can hear and combine many versions before passing on their own version any number of times to any number of people.

The main advantage of a net over a chain is that if the version transmitted by one singer omits parts or introduces changes that are outside the tradition, then other versions can be substituted for these lapses. All that is necessary is that the singer performing the synthesis understands the tradition well enough to choose. Multiple versions from many sources serve another purpose. They allow a listener to learn the range of acceptable variation (Lashley & Wade, 1946) and to discern aspects of a piece that are due to the particular style of one singer. Although the distinction between chains and nets need not involve the conduits discussed in the preceding section, in oral traditions nets would use conduits amplifying the differences with laboratory studies of randomly assigned chains of subjects.

The differences between chains and nets have been stressed in the folklore literature. The following translation from Anderson is by Degh and Vazsonyi (1975):

> In 1923 I have laid down the following Law of Self Correction: ''the extraordinary stability of folk narratives is explained by the fact that (1) every narrator had heard the respective *Marchen* (or *Schwank,* legend, and so on), from his predecessor, as a rule not once but several times; (2) that, as a rule, he has heard it not only from one single person but from a whole group of persons (and in different versions).'' (p. 225)

Goldstein (1967) offers a naturalistic experiment that demonstrates the advantage of even a very simple net in an oral tradition. Goldstein collected stories from Lucy Stewart, age 58, in Aberdeenshire, Scotland. She reported hearing one story, *The Brewer and the Devil,* multiple times, but only from her mother. While collecting stories from Lucy Stewart's sister, Goldstein collected a fuller, more integrated, and quite different version of the story. Lucy Stewart's sister also reported hearing the story only from her mother, and reported never telling the story in Lucy Stewart's presence. Goldstein collected an additional version from each sister to ensure that the versions he initially recorded were stable. Then he had Lucy Stewart's sister tell her version at a family gathering that Lucy Stewart attended.

Over the next 6 months, Goldstein collected more versions of the story from Lucy Stewart. They all included the story line and many of the details of her sister's version. When asked about the change, Lucy Stewart responded that she had thought she had the story right, but after hearing her sister's version, she realized that her sister's was just like their mother's. Whether the combined version was more accurate is not known, but both Lucy Stewart and Goldstein thought it was a better tale, and thus one less likely to be altered by further inputs.[6]

An approximation to the increase in stability found with nets in actual oral traditions has been observed with college undergraduates in the laboratory using stimuli that are not part of an oral tradition. Kalat (1985) had his students transmit tape-recorded stories using either a chain in which each student heard the previous version of the story twice or a very simple net in which each student heard the previous two versions of the story once. The expected results were obtained, with the net being more stable than the chain.

Feedback

One aspect of oral as opposed to written communication is the presence of an audience that lets the speaker know if a message is being understood or is having the correct emotional impact. More formally,

> every storytelling event is a communicative event. . . . The codes utilized to encode the message of every storytelling event are linguistic, paralinguistic, and kinesic. . . . The transmission and reception of the message of every storytelling event generates continuous perceptual responses that are interpreted by the encoder and decoder as feedback. (Georges, 1969, p. 317)

There are many examples of a singer altering the length, style, and content of a piece to suit an audience's response (e.g., Basgoz, 1975; Lord, 1960). Moreover, an audience knowledgeable in a tradition is a strong conservative force that keeps the singer within traditional bounds by voicing its approval, by offering alternative versions it thinks are preferred, or even by providing corrections. As Finnegan (1977) pointed out, the degree of feedback varies greatly from tradition to tradition and from situation to situation. There may be no feedback during the songs a shepherd sings to his flock, and tremendous feedback during work songs or Gregorian chants (Treitler, 1974) sung in unison or during other group recitals (Hunter, 1979).

The feedback received by a singer can affect the quality of the performance and often the amount of remuneration the singer receives. In the case of the preachers described by Rosenberg (1970, 1988), the elicitation of feedback in many ways is the purpose of the sermon. The sermons are composed orally, using rhythmic timing, set themes, and formulas. The following is a description of the middle of a typical sermon preached not far from my university office:

> About one third of the way into his sermon the prose has verged into a very rhythmical delivery, punctuated into periods (more or less regular) by a sharp utterance which I suppose might be called a vehement grunt. . . . Within the rhythmical framework, the rises and falls eventually build to a climax when he lapses into a sort of chant, still with the same punctuation, but with a recognizable tonic (tonal center). Some of the congregation (who respond ad libitum throughout) here lapse into hummimg along with him. (Letter by A. Jabbour, cited in Rosenberg, 1970, p. 5)

Rosenberg (1978) described the feedback:

> The responses of the congregation aid the preacher's timing; they punctuate his lines. . . . The congregation sings, hums, yells, and joins in the service as it chooses, and almost always its tone and timing is musically correct. The quality of the congrega-

tion seems to have a great effect upon the sermon, influencing the preacher's timing, his involvement in the service, and sometimes even the length of his performance. A sermon of this type often fails or succeeds according to how well the preacher can stimulate the congregation's rhythm by his own chanting. Clearly, chanting builds up the emotions of the audience as no other means can, and it is at such moments of emotional intensity that the Spirit of God is said to be most noticeable. Such is the avowed purpose of the sermon. (p. 5)

Transmission Across Generations: Learning to Be a Singer

An oral tradition must be handed down from generation to generation in order to survive. New, younger singers must learn the traditions. This process is examined in four genres: the three considered throughout the book and a fourth especially well-studied case.[7] The discussion is guided by two assumptions. First, genres of oral traditions can be considered as poetic languages, or *overlay systems* (Zwicky, 1986), or rule-bound registers of speech (Foley, 1992). Second, learning such poetic languages is similar in many ways to learning first languages (Foley, 1990; Lord, 1960; Rubin, 1988). These two assumptions are made both to stress the creative, rule-bound nature of oral traditions and to bring to bear on the study of the learning of oral traditions our understanding of first-language learning.

Support for the claim that parallels exist between learning to be a singer in an oral tradition and learning a first language are numerous. Properties present in both first and poetic languages and their learning include the following:

1. Structure is learned that can be expressed as generative rules, or schemas. This allows the production of novel instances that are clearly members of the language.
2. The language learned can help preserve and transmit cultural knowledge (Havelock, 1978; Ong, 1967, 1982).
3. Speaking in and listening to the language learned appears to be inherently entertaining or reinforcing in that individuals often engage in such behavior without other obvious external reward (Staddon, 1981).
4. The process of learning and what is learned are not available to introspection. That is, the rules formulated by the scholar are followed, but they cannot be stated by the native speakers. This is true for the music as well as the words that accompany it (Krumhansl & Keil, 1982).
5. Most learning occurs without special training beyond the availability of a model, or models, who can be observed producing clear instances of the language. This does not imply that learning is effortless and occurs without practice (Weir, 1962).
6. First-language learning is present in all societies. The poetic language of oral traditions may have also been present in all societies before literacy (Havelock, 1978). Poetic language is, at a minimum, extremely widespread (Finnegan, 1977), and claims exist that music, a common component of the poetic language of oral traditions, is a universal (e.g., Serafine, 1983).

Poetic languages differ from first languages in that they are usually just a subset of first languages created by added constraints (Zwicky, 1976), though they often preserve vocabulary and syntax from an earlier time. Nonetheless, the point is that the added constraints are learned and used much like the rest of a first language.

Learning the Genre of Counting-out Rhymes

The learning of the genre of counting-out rhymes is different from, and harder to study than, other oral traditions. It is different in two important ways. First, the total number of rhymes learned by an individual is much smaller than the number of pieces learned in other traditions. Second, although, as in most other traditions, the oldest singer of counting-out rhymes is usually considered the most knowledgeable, the oldest singer is a child. The learning process is hard to study because the limited repertory leads to rapid learning and makes it more difficult to argue that for a particular individual a rule-governed genre is learned, as opposed to a collection of pieces. Moreover, introspections from young singers and their even younger students about the subtleties of instruction are difficult to obtain. Little, therefore, can be said about the learning, as opposed to use, of counting-out rhymes, though it is clear that children already know the basics of the language and narrative structure (Fivush 1991; Nelson, 1988, 1993) of their culture when they begin learning counting-out rhymes. Nonetheless, Chapter 10 provides evidence that a rule-governed genre has been mastered.

Learning to Sing South Slavic Epic Poetry

Besides the musical accompaniment, the singer of epic needs to learn (1) the names of people and places; (2) formulas about these names and such things as heroes and horses; (3) themes for activities such as arming, battles, council meetings, weddings, and heroes in disguise returning home after long absences; and (4) the higher-level themes that are the story lines of the poems. The structure of the poems tells us that the singer must know how to combine these components of the scholar's analysis in ways that appear rule-bound. In doing this, a special language for a genre is mastered.

Avdo Medjedović was the best singer recorded by Lord and Parry. An example of his learning a new song provides insights into what it is that the poetic-language learner must learn about his genre (Lord, 1960; Lord & Bynum, 1974). A singer sang a song of 2,294 lines that Avdo Medjedović had never heard before. When the song was finished, Avdo Medjedović was asked if he could sing the same song. He did, only now the song was 6,313 lines long. The basic story line remained the same, but, to use Lord's description, "the song lengthened, the ornamentation and richness accumulated, and the human touches of character, touches that distinguish Avdo Medjedović from other singers, imparted a depth of feeling that had been missing" (p. 78). Avdo Medjedović's song retold the same story in his own words, much as subjects in a psychology experiment would retell a story from a genre with which they were familiar, but Avdo Medjedović's own words were poetic language and his story was a song of high artistic quality. Although the particular words changed, the words added were all traditional; and so the stability of the tradition, if not the stability of the words of a particular telling of a story, was ensured.

Several aspects of this feat are of interest. First, the song was composed without preparation and sung at great speed. There was no time for preparation before the 6,313 lines were sung, and once the song began, the rhythm allowed little time for Avdo Medjedović to stop and collect his thoughts. Such a feat implies a well-organized memory and the equivalent of an efficient set of rules for production. Second, the song expanded yet remained traditional in style, demonstrating that more than a particular song was being recalled. Rather, rules or parts drawn from other songs were being used. Third, although Avdo Medjedović was creative by any standards, he was not trying to create a novel song; he believed that he was telling a true story just the way he had heard it, though perhaps a little better. To do otherwise would be to distort history.

In describing this example, Lord noted an error that gives insight into Avdo Medjedović's store of scripts. In the original song, the messenger asks to be paid, providing a chance for the singer to demonstrate the hero's poverty and generosity. Avdo Medjedović's script for someone's receiving a letter, a script that is used often in South Slavic heroic poetry, consists of the letter's being opened and read and then the head of the assembly asking the reader about the letter's contents, but nothing about a request for payment. Avdo Medjedović, using this script, forgot about the messenger's request for payment and had to return to it later when it became apparent from the story that something was missing.

This example provides an indication of the regularities that the poetic-language learner must master. Like the child, however, the poetic-language learner cannot state the rules followed.

If this is what a singer must know, when does he start and how is he taught? Most of the singers Lord and Parry interviewed began actively trying to learn the tradition in their early adolescence. It is a male tradition, and many performances were in coffeehouses open only to men. (See Bartok & Lord, 1951, for genres sung by women.) The young singers, like the child, are given little special instruction. The most active instruction is having a song repeated. It is not known whether the language to be learned is presented more simply or slowly for beginners, as is often done for children learning a first language.

Lord (1960) postulates the existence of three stages in the learning of poetic language. In the first stage, the novice listens, becoming familiar with the tradition. In the second stage, the novice sings, but without a critical audience. In the terms of the first section of this chapter, the novice starts to use recitation. Following the optimal procedure found in the experimental literature, recitation is delayed until some degree of initial learning has taken place through just listening. In this second stage, the act of singing forces the novice to fit his ideas into the fixed, rhythmic pattern of the song. In a sense, the novice is continually testing his own knowledge. In Lord's (1960) words:

> He is like a child learning words, or anyone learning a language without a school method; except that the language here being learned is the special language of po-

etry. . . . He had no definite program of study, of course, no sense of learning this or that formula or set of formulas. It is a process of imitation and of assimilation through listening and much practice on one's own. (pp. 22–24)

This second stage ends, and the third stage begins when the singer can sing a song for a critical audience. There is still much to learn. The set of formulas, scripts, and songs increases. The skills of singing, playing, and ornamenting improve. Although there are cohort effects, for Parry and Lord the older singers are generally the best.

The learning of two singers provides brief case studies. Avdo Medjedović, mentioned in the previous example, was Lord and Parry's most skilled singer. He was an illiterate butcher who started singing when he was 15. His father, a singer, encouraged him and was his first teacher. Later he learned from whomever he could (Lord & Bynum, 1974). Avdo Medjedović produced 78,000 lines of recorded epic poetry. The longest song was 13,000 lines, or approximately 16 hours of singing time. These 78,000 lines, however, are only for the 9 different epic songs that were recorded. Avdo Medjedović reported a repertory of 58 epics. Thus it could be calculated that he knew a total of about 500,000 lines, or 600 hours of epics, compared with 27,000 lines in the *Iliad* and *Odyssey* combined. However, such a calculation would take numbers too seriously. As the example of learning a new song shows, Avdo Medjedović could create lines and even large segments of epic at will. Thus the number of lines that he could have produced was limited only by how much he sang in much the way that the number of different sentences an adult can produce is limited only by how much that adult says.

Sulejman Makic, an illiterate woodcutter and farmer, was 50 years old when he talked with Parry (Parry & Lord, 1954). Sulejman Makic reported a repertory of about 30 songs, 1 for each day of Ramadan, and possibly a few more. When Sulejman Makic was 15, a singer stayed in his house for a year. Sulejman Makic said, "He sang and I listened, until I learned. . . . Yes, he used to instruct me. He would sing it through to me once, and I would sit beside him. Then he would go back and sing it through again, and I would learn it" (pp. 263–264).

Sulejman Makic's report of how he would learn a new song provides an example of the constructive process at work, even though any construction was denied by the singer. When asked if he could learn a new song he heard just once, Sulejman Makic replied, "Yes, I could sing it for you right away the next day" (pp. 265–266). When asked about the delay, he replied:

It would stay in my mind. Then I would sing it right away from memory. . . . It has to come to one. One has to think . . . how it goes, and then little by little it comes to him, so that he won't leave anything out. It would be possible right then and there, but one couldn't sing it like that all the way through right away. (p. 266)

When asked if he would sing exactly the same song he had heard, he said that he would, and that he would neither add nor omit anything. "I would sing it just as I heard, whatever was worthwhile; what's the good of adding things that didn't happen. One must sing what one heard and exactly as it happened" (p. 266). Verbatim recall was never observed by Parry or Lord in any of their singers (also see Hunter, 1984, 1985). Sulejman Makic, however, was not bragging. If one does not read, then "exactly the same" is a judgment based on memory, not a verbatim, text-based criterion. Although the singer is using poetic language in a productive fashion, he will not admit it. If put to the test, Sulejman Makic's performance might have been much like that of Avdo Medjedović—exactly the same, but three times as long as the original.

The learning of South Slavic epic makes obvious several similarities among first-language learning and poetic-language learning. In both cases of language learning, the learners do not have much insight into either the units and rules being learned or the processes underlying the learning. The learners listen; the learners learn. The language learners do not receive much in the way of specialized instruction. The language learners, nonetheless, learn complex, rule-bound systems that can be used with little effort.

The lack of ability of singers to distinguish among variants of the same song may seem a bit odd to readers, but it is consistent with controlled laboratory studies. Bransford and Franks (1971) constructed four complex ideas, each of which contained four simple ideas. For example, one of their four complex ideas was "The rock which rolled down the mountain crushed the tiny hut at the edge of the woods." It contained the four simple ideas (1) "The rock rolled down the mountain," (2) "The rock crushed the hut," (3) "The hut was tiny," and (4) "The hut was at the edge of the woods." From this sample, a total of 48 sentences can be constructed that are one, two, three, and four simple ideas long. One group was read 24 of these 48 sentences, and another group was read the remaining 24 sentences. In order to ensure that people paid attention to the sentences in a meaningful manner, after each sentence was read, there was a brief delay followed by an elliptical question about the sentence, such as "Where?" or "Did what?" Both groups were then read all 48 sentences, and were asked to indicate if they had heard each sentence before and how confident they were of their judgment on a 5-point scale from 1, "very low," to 5, "very high." These ratings were multiplied by $+1$ if the person answered that the exact sentence had been heard before and by -1 if the person answered that it had not been heard before. Thus a $+5$ would mean a very high confidence rating that a sentence had been heard earlier, and a -1 would mean a very low confidence rating that a sentence had not been heard earlier. Because the sentences that were heard by one group were not heard by the other, differences could not be due to the sentences themselves.

Figure 6.5 shows the average ratings for both groups combined for their old and new sentences as a function of sentence length. There are two basic findings. First, people could not tell sentences they had heard from ones they had not heard, except for sentences that were only one simple idea long. Second, the number of simple ideas in a sentence had a large effect; people were much more confident that they had heard the longer sentences, whether they had heard them or not. For instance, four-idea sentences were judged, on the average, with high confidence of having been heard earlier, whether or not they actually were, whereas one-idea sentences were judged, on the average, to have not been heard with low confidence if they had not been heard earlier and with very low confidence if they had been.

If such results extended to oral traditions, this would mean that if the basic ideas of a song were known, people might not know exactly in which form or exactly which ideas were presented, but they might still be quite confident that the ideas had

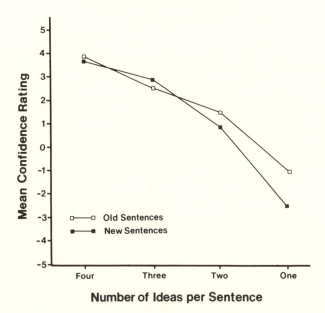

Figure 6.5. Confidence judgments of recognition for sentences of various lengths. (From Bransford & Franks, 1971)

been presented as a unified whole and therefore that the song just heard had not changed at all from the last time they heard it. This might help explain Avdo Medjedović's and Sulejman Makic's confidence that they sang exactly the same song they had heard.

Learning to Sing North Carolina Ballads

Like the data on epic, all our data to date on learning to sing ballads come from self-report.[8] The ballad singers questioned learned to sing at various ages, but generally singing is learned early, perhaps simultaneously with first-language learning. Not surprisingly, then, the main first model is usually a family member, though most of the songs a singer knows as an adult may have been learned from another model. The singers usually reported not being corrected if they made a mistake or, at most, hearing a statement like "This is the way I learned it." The singers also reported not practicing per se; unlike the situation of epic singers, the singing itself is their only practice.

Singers reported that an accomplished singer could learn a new song after hearing it a few times. According to one singer, the reason for this was that an accomplished singer would know most of a new song even before it was heard. Verbatim learning of a new song was expected, though some singers admitted that they change songs freely. The expectation of verbatim learning is consistent with the commonly held view among singers that most songs are about true stories and real people their older relatives knew. Such beliefs occur even with songs whose story line dates back hundreds of years. Supporting the singers' emphasis on verbatim learning is the observation by one singer that she recalled learning words that at the time had no meaning to her, but were just part of the song.

Caedmon's Poetic-Language Learning

Although Caedmon was not a singer in one of the three oral traditions considered in detail elsewhere in this book, he provides the most famous case of an individual learning a poetic language. Caedmon was an illiterate cowherd who was employed at the monastery at Whitby around A.D. 680. Bede (731/1969) provides the description of how Caedmon learned to sing. The relevant parts of the story follow.

It was the custom at feasts that a harp would be passed around and everyone would take turns singing. Although well advanced in age, Caedmon would leave when the harp approached rather than remain and sing. On one such occasion, he went to the stable to mind the animals and to sleep. In his dream, Caedmon was asked to sing about creation, which miraculously he immediately did, singing verses he had never heard. In the morning, he reported his dream and was brought before the abbess and some learned men. There he recited the song he had composed. Caedmon was then read a sacred passage and asked to construct a song from it. Caedmon returned the next morning and repeated the passage in excellent verse. At the abbess's request, Caedmon took monastic vows and was taught sacred history. He learned all he could by listening, "ruminating over it like some clean animal chewing the cud" (Bede, ·731/1969, p. 419), and produced excellent verse.

Several observations are clear from the story. First, an oral tradition of singing to the harp existed in Whitby around 670, and all men were expected to be able to take part in it. Second, Caedmon often heard songs, though he did not sing in public. Third, Caedmon's singing of sacred material was so unusual and of such high quality as to be considered a miracle worthy of note in church history. Fourth, Caedmon's process of composition consisted of listening to a sacred story, often translated into Old English from the Latin, ruminating, and then singing; Caedmon could not write and so had to keep his text in mind while composing.

Bede warned his reader that the translation of verse, including his own translation of *Caedmon's Hymn,* is impossible without changing the original. Old English versions of *Caedmon's Hymn,* however, do exist and provide some further insights into Caedmon's technique of composition. Magoun (1955) found that 15 of the 18 verses of *Caedmon's Hymn* occur verbatim or, with minor changes, elsewhere in 30,000 lines of the existing Anglo-Saxon poetic corpus. Fry (1975), in a contrasting analysis, noted that all the half-lines exist in the same corpus if one looks not for verbatim occurrences, but for productive formulas in which different words with the same general meaning and poetic properties (here, meter and alliteration) can be substituted for each other.

The story of *Caedmon's Hymn* is an especially interesting case of learning poetic language, not only because of its antiquity and because it is the only Anglo-Saxon poem that we know was orally composed from evidence external to the poem itself (Fry, 1975), but also because we know the singer composed by rule, not by rote memorization. Caedmon sang a hymn he had never heard before. In fact, he sang in a genre of poetry, sacred poetry sung in traditional Anglo-Saxon style, that was itself novel.

There are some obvious parallels between Caedmon's learning of poetic language and Lord's description of how singers of epic learn. First, there is a period in which the singer listens, but does not perform. For Caedmon, this period was longer than is usual for the singers of epic. Caedmon's embarrassment at not being able to sing at the feast indicated that this period was also longer than was common among Caedmon's peers. The second period of practice without a critical audience was either not present or not recorded for Caedmon, except for a single instance in a dream. The slow development was worthwhile. When Caedmon first entered the third stage of true performance, he was already an expert.

The story, and the content of the little that remains of Caedmon's singing, tell us what Caedmon was learning in his first two stages. He was learning themes from the Christian tradition and poetic language from an Anglo-Saxon oral tradition. The Anglo-Saxon poetic language was from an oral tradition because oral transmission was all that existed for Caedmon (Fry, 1975, 1980). Combining these two traditions was made easier for Caedmon because formulas for heroes and gods in the Anglo-Saxon tradition were often well suited for the figures in the Christian tradition (Fry, 1975).

It is not clear that Caedmon could ever compose extemporaneously without ruminating; however, this skill should not be expected. Caedmon was combining the content of one tradition with the language of another, so he was at a disadvantage compared with epic singers for whom certain formulas fall naturally into place in certain thematic contexts. Moreover, even some of Parry and Lord's better singers, such as Sulejman Makic, liked to sleep before returning to sing a new song for the first time. It is clear, however, that both the content and the language were stored without the use of external memory aids such as writing, and that the songs produced, if not composed extemporaneously, were stored in memory until they could be sung to learned men. Caedmon's mastery of Anglo-Saxon poetic language, however, was sufficient to allow him, without the aid of writing, to produce sacred poems with such speed and virtuosity as to have the feat labeled miraculous by the abbess, her learned men, and the Venerable Bede.

Transmitting Traditions

Chapters 2, 3, 4, and 5 were concerned with properties of the text of oral traditions. In contrast, this chapter dealt with how the text is transmitted. Studies of laboratory learning of verbal material, of modes of transmission in oral traditions, and of how novice singers learn a tradition were reviewed in turn. Both the structure and the transmission of the text add to the stability of oral traditions in understandable ways, and both point to the importance of learning the general organization, constraints, or rules of a genre as opposed to the rote learning of a collection of instances without the ability to extend them to new situations.

The study of learning conducted in psychology laboratories since the turn of the century has pointed to several conditions of learning that increase memory for verbal material. These same conditions of overlearning, spaced practice, and recitation are normal consequences of the transmission of an oral tradition. Other aspects of the laboratory study of learning, including motivation and the learning of rules, are also applicable to understanding the stability of oral traditions. In general, the laboratory research is consistent with what would be expected if the conditions of transmission of oral tradition tended to maximize their memorability.

The experimental laboratory has not been as helpful to the study of the social aspects of transmission that appear to be important from naturalistic observation of oral traditions. Nonetheless, enough data exist from such observation and from experimentation outside the laboratory to demonstrate some of the effects of conduits, nets, and social feedback on transmission. The paths along which information travels in oral traditions are much more complex than those that have been used to simulate transmission in the laboratory, and this complexity leads to greater stability of transmission than would be expected from laboratory research. Better simulation experiments, however, are possible and could help clarify the roles of conduits, nets, and social feedback in the stability of transmission.

Although experimental and cognitive psychologists have not, until recently, used much effort trying to understand how systems as complex as oral traditions are learned and maintained, students of language development have. If learning to sing in an oral tradition is considered as a special case of learning to speak a language, then many of the remarkable achievements of the singer become less surprising, and many of the more difficult-to-study problems become analogs of ones that have already received considerable attention.

The eclectic review in this chapter provides a beginning to our understanding of cultural transmission in general.[9] Much more is now known than was known when Bartlett began his investigations of this topic, and, perhaps of greater importance, methods and theory now exist to uncover much of what needs to be added. Singers not only learn to sing new songs, but also learn how to learn and retain more efficiently all new songs belonging to a genre, a topic discussed in the next chapter.

Notes

1. Here, as elsewhere in the book when discussing basic processes, I am ignoring differences in the material learned in psychological experiments and the material learned in oral traditions. That is, along with Ebbinghaus, I am assuming that general laws of learning exist for verbal material and that these laws can be studied using highly controlled material. I know of no evidence to the contrary. As demonstrated in this book, powerful factors do come into play with the highly organized material of oral traditions that are not prominent in lists of isolated items. This observation, Bartlett (1932) not withstanding, however, does not contradict Ebbinghaus's assumption, although it does make the application of the general laws to specific situations more difficult (Landauer, 1989; Rubin, 1985). Nonetheless, most of the results reported in the first section were found with materials and learning situations very different from those of oral traditions. Moreover, the various factors were usually studied in isolation, though they may modify one anothers' effects. For these reasons, only effects that appear to be both robust and substantial have been mentioned.

Differences in the measures of retrieval used can make a difference in the conclusions drawn from actual data (Bahrick, 1965; Rubin, 1985; Slamecka & McElree, 1983; Underwood, 1964), but, such differences are mentioned only where relevant. If similar results were obtained using several different measures, as in spacing effects at long time intervals, the results of the different measures are all presented.

In general, the simplest approach to reporting empirical findings is used in the first section. Currently debated issues that do not bear directly on transmission in oral traditions are avoided. The historical problem of the inadequacy of the concept of *strength* and the concept of *a single trace*, however, needs to be mentioned in order to do justice to what is known about memory. It is convenient to present the first section in terms of the strength of a single memory trace. In general, however, memory cannot be viewed as measured in terms of the strength of a trace because the recall obtained depends on the type of retrieval task given and the match between that retrieval task and the type of learning originally done (Tulving & Thomson, 1973). For instance, recall and recognition tasks can produce very different results when used to retrieve a trace of the same strength. The idea that there is a single trace is also problematic. When a piece is learned on two occasions, logically there could be one combined trace, one separate trace for each presentation, or one combined trace and two separate traces. Different experimental situations favor theories that take different positions on what is stored (Crowder, 1976). In practice, these problems are addressed when a theory is proposed later in the book, with different retrieval tasks being considered as different retrieval cues to a fixed memory, and storage in memory requiring explicit assumptions about multiple versus single traces.

2. In Chapter 7, it is argued that one problem with theoretical discussions in interference theory is that at times the researchers mixed their units. They measured at the level of the list, while their theories were at the level of the individual item. Underwood may have had a similar problem in his work on spacing in that he also measured at the level of lists, whereas spacing effects at short intervals are found between items. I owe this point to Thomas Nelson.

3. Figure 6.2 combines findings from the Bahrick (1979) and the Bahrick and Phelps (1987) papers, ignoring the complications that occur because some people had only three, not six, sessions.

4. Figure 6.3 was calculated from Table 6, VSEREC, VESREC, and IDREC, which means Spanish–English, English–Spanish, and Idiom recall. No recognition was used.

5. For a partial experimental separation of these factors in recall of Beatles' songs, see Hyman and Rubin (1990).

6. For another example, see MacDonald (1978, pp. 25–26n.5).

7. An earlier version of this section appears in Rubin (1988b). As with all aspects of oral traditions, the genres considered here do not cover the full range of genres available. Finnegan (1977) discusses the learning of numerous other oral traditions, including some that have formal training. Rosenberg (1988, especially pp. 30–31, 105–109) discusses the development of folk preachers. Each genre taken as a whole is a stable solution to the problem of transmission without the use of external memory aids.

8. The section on learning North Carolina ballads is based on collecting done by Wanda T. Wallace.

9. For a more complete discussion, see Tomasello, Kruger, and Ratner (1993) on cultural learning and the 35 pages of "open peer commentary" that follow their article.

CHAPTER 7

Basic Observations
on Remembering

The psychologists who have spent a century studying esoteric forms of memory in the laboratory are not really uninterested in its more ordinary manifestations, and have always hoped that their work would have wide applicability sooner or later. Their preference for artificial tasks has a rational basis: one can control variables and manipulate conditions more easily in the lab than in natural settings.

Neisser, 1978, p. 13

The first topic considered is forgetting and the ways to reduce it. A review of studies from classic psychological literature on interference theory from the 1960s shows that, with proper cuing, that which first appeared lost can be recovered. The concept of cue–item discriminability is proposed to put these findings into a framework that can be used in a theory of memory in oral traditions. Simply put, a word is likely to be recalled if, on the basis of the cues available at the time, it can be discriminated from all else in memory. The second topic investigates what aspects of lists and prose are remembered. Although changes are noted in how much is remembered with changes in retention interval, motivation, the people remembering, and other factors, the relative frequencies or probabilities of recall of the various parts of a list or text are not affected by these factors, greatly simplifying the task of generalizing from the laboratory to oral traditions. Moreover, as long as the cues available at recall do not change, the same words and phrases of a song from an oral tradition will remain most likely to be recalled under a variety of different performance conditions. The third topic returns to the importance of cuing, as noted in studies of interference, and looks at cuing as a function of retention interval. The effects of multiple constraints, reviewed in Chapter 5, are again shown to be of great importance. Finally, the fourth topic looks briefly at what is known about memory expertise and its role in learning oral traditions. Memory is often considered as a storehouse, but for oral traditions a better metaphor is that of a well-practiced skill dependent on extensive experience.

Throughout this review, there is a need to establish basic observations about human memory, including some that exist only in reanalysis of data collected for other purposes. The emphasis differs from that found in most reviews of cognitive psychology in three ways. First, results are stressed in relation to their application to oral traditions. Second, recall as a function of retention interval is much more important here because the time scale of oral traditions exceeds by several orders of magnitude that of most studies in cognitive psychology. Third, because findings, as well as theories, need to be extended beyond the laboratory in which they were tested, the potential generality of findings is stressed (Mook, 1989).

This chapter may be difficult for those without some background in cognitive psychology. I suggest that such readers reread this introduction and then skip to the next chapter, returning to this chapter after finishing the book if they want to learn the historical basis and empirical support for the claims made later. For those with a background in cognitive psychology, this chapter is more important; it organizes standard findings in a novel and sometimes counterintuitive way that may challenge their existing views.

The Causes of Forgetting

The ability to recall something just learned decreases quickly at first and then more slowly, appearing to level off with time. In mathematical terms, a power function provides a reasonable fit to many data sets, including those of Krueger (1929) and Bahrick, discussed in Chapter 6 (Anderson & Schooler, 1991; Rubin, 1982; Wixted & Ebbesen, 1991). But clearly, time does not cause the drop in recall (McGeoch, 1932), and analyses based on time alone provide no help in showing how the loss is minimized in oral traditions.[1] Rather than time, changes in the environment and intervening activity have been examined as the causes of forgetting. Changes in the environment are modeled in the laboratory by changes in cuing and context; intervening activity is modeled by the learning of different material. Psychologists have studied these effects using interference theory. The basic premise of interference theory, supported by many experimental studies, is that learning material similar to the target material causes interference. Interference theory was the most intensive, unified, and sophisticated attempt to understand human memory before the development of the computer-based models of cognitive psychology in the 1970s. Interference theory focuses on the causes of forgetting and thus still provides most of the data on this subject in human memory. As research progressed, interference theory became increasingly complex; one of my colleagues attributed its decreased importance to the fact that most psychologists could no longer understand it without great effort (Kimble, personal communication, October 1982).[2] All that is offered here is enough of a primer to allow the basic results to be synthesized and applied to oral traditions.[3]

Activity that reduces recall is termed *interference*. Interference that occurs before an item is learned is *proactive interference*. Interference that occurs between the time an item is learned and when it is recalled is *retroactive interference*. Initially, retroactive interference received most of the attention. Retroactive interference is measured as the difference in amount recalled between a baseline and an experimental condition. The baseline condition consists of learning a target list, waiting for a period that does not involve learning or involves the learning of material unrelated to the target list, and then remembering the target list. The experimental condition is identical to the baseline, except that the waiting period is filled with learning material related to the target list.

Proactive interference has a similar definition, but involves material that is presented before the target list is learned. It was introduced as a major cause of forgetting by Underwood (1957). Underwood noted that in many experiments only 25% of the items, usually nonsense syllables, were recalled 1 day after they were learned. Because all lists were learned until one perfect recitation occurred, this meant that 75% of the items were forgotten in 1 day. Because there was no experimental retroactive interference, a retroactive-interference explanation would mean that activity outside the experiment was the cause. Underwood found this unlikely because similar losses were found for shorter times and because "even if we agree with some educators that much of what we teach our students in college is nonsense, it does not seem to be the kind of learning that would interfere with nonsense syllables" (pp. 50–51). He noted that recall of a list decreased with the number of lists learned before it and postulated proactive interference as the cause. To test this further, he reanalyzed data from 14 published studies in which lists were learned to one perfect recitation, using massed practice and then recalled 1 day later. The studies included paired-associate learning and serial recall; they used a variety of list lengths and presentation rates; and they used a variety of materials, including geometric forms, nonsense syllables, and words. Nonetheless, as Figure 7.1 shows, the effects of proactive interference are consistent and large. With no previous list, 75% is remembered 1 day later; with 20 previously learned lists, 75% is forgotten.[4]

Two types of studies demonstrate that material suffering from interference is not lost and show how it can be recovered. The first type is release-from-proactive-

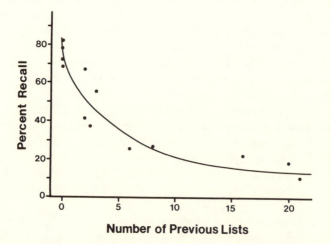

Figure 7.1. Recall of lists 1 day after they were learned to one perfect recitation as a function of the number of previous lists learned. (Redrawn from Underwood, 1957)

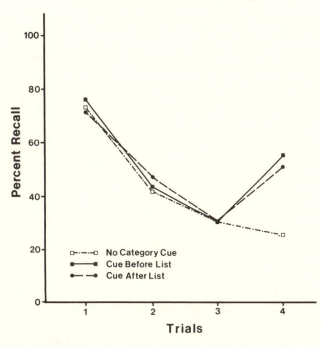

Figure 7.2. Recall as a function of the type and timing of category cues used to demonstrate the role of cuing in release from proactive inhibition. (Redrawn from Gardiner, Craik, & Birtwistle, 1972)

interference studies; the second type is cue-dependent forgetting in retroactive-interference studies.

In release-from-proactive-interference studies, several lists drawn from the same category are presented, with the usual proactive-interference decrease in recall with each list. Next, a list from a new category is presented and recall is as good as it was on the first list, demonstrating a release from proactive interference (Wickens, 1970). In these studies, a single presentation is often used instead of learning to one perfect recall, but the logic is the same. By noting when release occurs, such studies offer a way to determine empirically what is the "same category."

The technique also can be used to demonstrate that material that suffers from proactive interference is not lost, but can be recovered. Gardiner, Craik, and Birtwistle (1972) presented people with three lists from the same category and subcategory, and then with a fourth list that was from the same category, but from a subcategory that was not perceptibly different from the previous three lists. For example, people were told that their lists would contain flowers and were shown three lists of wild flowers followed by one list of garden flowers. One group was told nothing more, and in interviews after the experiment they reported not noticing the change. As shown in Figure 7.2, this group showed the standard proactive-interference effects for all four lists. Another group was told, before receiving the last list, that it contained a new subcategory (e.g., garden flowers) and demonstrated the standard release from proactive inhibition. The remaining group was also told that the last list contained a new subcategory, but not until after they had finished viewing the list. They also showed a release from proactive interference, demonstrating that the items were not lost, but could be recovered with appropriate cuing.

The cue-dependent-forgetting study is similar to the Gardiner et al. study just presented, except that it involves retroactive inhibition. People were presented with between one and six lists, recalling each after it was presented (Tulving & Psotka, 1971). Each list consisted of four common items from each of six categories, with items from the same category presented together to emphasize the category structure. Thus a person might have seen four common flowers, followed by four common fruits, four common metals, and so on for six categories. Following this, everyone was asked to recall all the words on all the lists. The percentage of words recalled from the first list decreased as the number of intervening lists increased, as expected with retroactive inhibition. When only one list was learned, approximately 70% of its words were recalled. When four, five, or six lists were learned, approximately 30% of the first list was recalled. For all cases, the same average number of words was recalled from each category. Retroactive inhibition affected only the number of different categories from which words were recalled. A second recall of all words was then attempted with a small gain, but still with a marked retroactive-inhibition effect. Finally, a third recall of all words was attempted, but this time all the category names were listed. For this cued recall, the percentage of recalled words from each list returned to the level it was at immediately after that list was learned, and all retroactive inhibition disappeared.

Both the release-from-proactive-interference and the cue-dependent-forgetting-retroactive-interference studies demonstrate that items that cannot be recalled are not lost and that they can be recovered with the proper cue. In both cases, cues that discriminated items by indicating which categories had to be recalled removed interference effects.

How can these and other results from interference theory be summarized to allow them to be applied to the study of oral traditions? Interference theory evolved from one set of hypotheses and findings to the next in a progressive fashion that left a complex history of ideas. Ideas that had merit were abandoned because they could not explain all the data that were created as tests within the theoretical framework of their time. When one stands back from the fray, with the full benefit of work that has progressed since then, it is possible to modify some early ideas to account for much of the data. Years of experiments have shown that the unit of measure and the theoretical unit must be the same; items and lists cannot be mixed arbitrarily. Also, all items in memory need to be considered, regardless of whether they are the target items (i.e., the to-be-remembered items), the interfering items from the experiment, or the interfering items from the world outside the experiment. Not only do items internal and external to the experiment interfere with the target item, but the target item interferes with the rest of memory.

A parallel distributed processing network model, like the one described in Chapter 2, can be use to apply the findings of interference theory to oral traditions. Memory cues are the inputs; the cues increase or decrease the activity of nodes representing items depending on weights determined by past associations; and the node or nodes with the highest activity for a given set of cues outputs its item. The weights between nodes are increased when items occur together and are decreased when items do not appear together. It is necessary to add to this model a way to code the relative time of learning, an encoding of the context or environment in which learning takes place, and a base of preexperimental associations among items. The main work in such a network-activation model is done by cue–item discriminability—that is, how easily a given cue isolates an item.[5]

It is common to separate organization from distinctiveness in memory research (Hunt & Einstein, 1981; Hunt & McDaniel, 1993), but here they are combined. The mechanism is how easily a set of cues accesses (finds, excites, resonates with) particular items. The way in which a cue works might be viewed as either through organization or through distinctiveness, but, in fact, it is through the match of the cues and the item.[6]

How would such a theory account for the interference-theory results presented so far? The similarity of the target and other items leads to both proactive and retroactive interference because it spreads activity over many items. The temporal cue excites all items from about the same time in a graded fashion, as does the similarity among the target and interfering items. Thus there may be no one item with a clear superiority. If the times, the items, or another feature of the cue–item match distinguished the target from other items, then interference would be less. This explains how the category cues reduced interference in the release-from-proactive-interference and the cue-dependent-forgetting studies. Category cues add activation only to the relevant set of target items, thereby increasing their chance of being the most active items.

In the account put forth in the next chapter for oral traditions, cue–item discriminability functions to reduce interference. As a piece is recalled, each word sung helps discriminate the next words to be sung from among all other words in memory. In oral traditions, this discrimination is not primarily temporal or category based, as it is in laboratory experiments, but is based on meaningful associations, theme, imagery, rhythm, rhyme, and alliteration, as discussed in Chapters 2, 3, and 4, and on their various interactions, as discussed in Chapter 5.

The remainder of this section on the causes of forgetting extends the model to account for classic findings in interference theory, demonstrating their application to oral traditions. For psychologists, this provides a way of summarizing and integrating a large number of experimental findings, though it may be difficult for those with different backgrounds.

The first experiment considered focuses on a classic temporal effect. The length of the period of unfilled time between learning and recall leads to greater proactive inhibition. According to the network-activity model, a long wait after a set of learning trials increases proactive interference because the time between items, or lists of items, becomes less of a discriminating cue. If two lists are learned in 5 minutes each, then a test on the second list 5 minutes after it was learned can use temporal cues to distinguish it from the earlier list. The ratio of 10 minutes to 5 minutes is 2.00. A day later, the temporal cues should be much less effective. The ratio of 24 hours, 10 minutes to 24 hours, 5 minutes is 1.003, which is too close to 1.00 to be of much use in distinguishing items. This same explanation has been used to account for proactive inhibition at much shorter times and can be used for the course of forgetting in general (Baddeley, 1976; Glenberg & Swanson, 1986; Neath & Crowder, 1990; Turvey, Brick, & Osborn, 1970). With the passage of time, events cannot be separated and, in colloquial terms, become a blur. This interpretation is consistent with measures of distinctiveness based on the logarithmic transformation of temporal and order scales (Helson, 1964; Johnson, 1991; Murdock, 1960).

There are several other classic effects that produced problems for theories in the history of interference theory, which are handled by cue–item discriminability in a natural way. Many standard effects in interference theory that have led to theoretical debates hinge on the relationship of the item to the list of which it is a part. When items are presented together repeatedly, they form units, much as was argued in the formation of themes from events in Chapter 2. In terms of the network-activation model, the way this happens is that items appearing together build up increased positive associative weights with one another, so that if any one of the items is later cued and so receives activity, it will activate the other items that have appeared with it. As the list becomes better learned, these positive weights, or associations, among items will strengthen, as will the negative weights among possible competing responses that have not appeared together because they are not part of the same list.

As a concrete example, consider the learning of pairs of words in a standard paired-associate procedure. In standard terminology, the first list learned contains A–B pairs. These are all presented one at a time, and then each A word is presented one at a time and the appropriate B word has to be provided. This is repeated until all the A–B pairs are known for one perfect recitation of the whole list. According to the model, what happens during the learning of the first list is that associative weights are strengthened between the members of each A–B pair. In addition, weaker weights are established among all the A and B words because they are presented near each other in time and in the same context, though not at the exact same time. When a particular A word is presented, its B word gets the most activity and is recalled, but all A and B words receive some activity.

Next, another list is learned. It is possible to measure both the proactive inhibition of the first list on the learning of the second and the retroactive inhibition of the second list on the later recall of the first. Consider the retroactive-inhibition case where the second list contains A–D pairs; that is, the same stimulus words are used again, but this time with new response words. According to the model, the new A–D associations are developed, though more slowly because the old A–B associations have existing weights that compete. With each A–D trial, the strength of the particular A–D weights increases. By definition, once the A–D list is fully learned, there will be stronger associations from the A words to the D words than from the A words to the B words, so when an A word is given as a cue, it will activate the appropriate D word. During the course of learning, this will not always be the case. Sometimes the B word will get more activity, and the B word will be recalled as an intrusion in the A–D list that is supposed to be recalled. Sometimes no word will receive sufficient activity to be recalled, perhaps because the particular A–B association is still stronger than the A–D association, but the associations among all members of the A–D list are stronger than the associations among all members of the A–B list and therefore suppress the activity of the particular A–B pair.

According to the model, over the course of learning of the A–D list, if an attempt is made to recall the A–B list, there should be a steady increase in the amount of retroactive interference. This is because, with increased learning, the A–D associations are consistently becoming stronger than the A–B associations. Thus when the cue A is given, relatively more of its activation goes to the D than to the B member, making the temporal and other cues that could recover the B member less likely to be stronger than the cues to D. From the model, intrusions of the D members into the recall of the A–B list should first increase as the A–D list is learned, but then they should decrease as the A–D list becomes overlearned. This decrease occurs because, with increased learning, the associations among all the words of the A–D list become stronger and thus more easily discriminable from those of the A–B list. The temporal cue to recall the first (i.e., the A–B) list is sufficient to inhibit activity of the later A–D items once they form a strong interrelated unit that is activated as a whole. Thus the increased strength between the A–D pairs and among all the A and D words serves to decrease both the A–B recall and the A–D intrusions. In fact, this is what happened in a study that served to demonstrate that overt response competition could not account for retroactive inhibition (Melton & Irwin, 1940).

A–B, A–D experiments produce considerable retroactive interference, but even A–B, C–D experiments, in which the interfering list has no words from the earlier lists, produce some retroactive interference when compared with a rest period. This is because the C–D list shares with the A–B list all associations to the room, experimenter, general time period, and other contextual factors (McGovern, 1964). However, if a multiple-choice test is given in which the incorrect answers, or foils, are all drawn from the B members, retroactive inhibition disappears (Postman & Stark, 1969). According to the model, this would occur because the multiple choices would act as cues and increase the activity of all words in the A–B list, but not of any words in the C–D list. Thus the retroactive interference of the C–D list would be removed because its activity would now be relatively lower than that of the A–B list. If, however, the foils were chosen from the D as well as from the B members, the multiple-choice format should still show retroactive inhibition because both lists would be activated, and it does (Anderson & Watts, 1971). For the same reason, the model predicts correctly that retroactive inhibition would occur in multiple-choice tests where the two lists use the same words, but pair them in different ways (i.e., an A–B, A–B$_r$ condition), though this result made trouble for some theories of the time (Postman & Stark, 1969).

A situation analogous to the A–B, A–D experiments exists throughout oral traditions. Different sets of words are learned to the same melody. Different characters appear in similar themes and settings. Different pieces in a genre use the same poetic form. In such situations, intrusions and effects on the ease of learning from A–B to A–D and from A–D to A–B are expected to the extent that there are no other disambiguating cues. Unlike the verbatim learning of randomly arranged nonsense syllables, however, in oral traditions the intrusions are not necessarily a problem because they often fit the constraints of the genre. In addition, the effects on the ease of learning can be facilitative rather than interfering if there exists enough similarity in the structure of the ''lists.''

It is possible, using the A–B, A–D experiment described earlier, to examine the role of distributed versus spaced practice on proactive interference. This is important in general because in oral traditions and in everyday life proactive interference has a large opportunity to reduce recall and because, unlike most laboratory learning, most learning in oral traditions and everyday life is spaced or distributed over time. In an experiment in which the A–B list was learned for 12, 32, 48, or 80 trials that were either massed on 1 day or spaced over 4 days, it was found that distributed practice produced much less proactive interference on the A–D list than did massed practice (Underwood & Ekstrand, 1966). The model explains the result in terms of the discriminability of the temporal distribution of events. This can be considered in two ways. First, the spaced learning over 4 days produces an A–B list with no clear temporal cues, but the once learned A–D list does have a clear temporal marker and can thus be differentiated from the A–B list. In contrast, when both the A–B and A–D lists are learned on 1 day, temporal differentiation is more difficult. Second, for the massed practice, all A–B and A–D learning occurred in the same session, making it difficult to distinguish the lists temporally 1 day later. In contrast, for the spaced practice, three of the four sessions for the A–B learning occurred on different days than for the A–D learning, allowing easy temporal differentiation.[7] From the perspective of the model and given these data, it is not surprising that spaced, overlearned associations that occurred outside the laboratory are not affected by the learning of experimental pairs (Slamecka, 1966).[8]

Like all previous attempts to account for the complex set of findings of interference theory with a simple, unified set of processes, this attempt is bound to fail. For the moment, however, it is my best effort at summarizing what is known about forgetting. Although quantitative predictions require both an implemented model and a detailed analysis of the experimental procedures and material, the verbal model at least serves as a good rule of thumb that can account for most of the data in a general way.[9]

Oral traditions must contend with the same processes of memory as other material, so their structure and mode of transmission must offer ways around the limitations documented in the laboratory. There are several obvious differences between laboratory learning and the transmission of oral traditions. First, laboratory learning is massed learning. The learning of material is crammed into a 1-hour session for most experiments, with tests of retention often occurring a day later. In contrast, learning in oral traditions is spaced over long periods of time. In Chapter 6, spaced practice was shown to be one of the most important factors in improving long-term retention. In the interference literature, material learned using spaced learning produces less proactive and retroactive interference in other lists and suffers less proactive and retroactive interference itself than does material learned using only massed practice (Keppel, 1964; Underwood & Ekstrand, 1966).

A second difference between learning in the laboratory and oral traditions is the degree of overlearning. Like spaced practice, overlearning was shown in Chapter 6 to be important to long-term retention, an effect also shown in the interference literature. In fact, it is the overlearning of items learned early in a list that makes the criterion of one perfect recital of the whole list problematic for certain theoretical conclusions. For instance, Warr (1964) performed a study of proactive interference of paired associates in which the criterion of one perfect recitation was often reached on the 13th or 14th trial. Items that were learned on these last trials were recalled about 40% of the time a day later, whereas items that were learned on the first two trials, giving them 13 or 14 trials of overlearning, were remembered nearly perfectly. Of course, these latter items were easier to learn in the first place, but the results are still impressive. In oral traditions, overlearning commonly occurs to a much greater extent than it does in the laboratory. A favorite song can be sung hundreds of times. What overlearning does, according to the model developed to explain laboratory interference, is to make the song into a unit, easy to cue as a whole and resistant to interference from other units. This chunking of items into wholes is a way to look at the organization of memory and a way to look at the building of larger units in expertise.

A third difference, possibly the most important, is that unlike laboratory learning, oral traditions use many forms of organization to make items more discriminable. Laboratory studies of interference use lists of nonsense syllables or words that usually are assigned randomly to lists. In contrast, if the contents of oral traditions are viewed as lists of words, they are lists organized by meaning, imagery, rhythm, and poetic devices, which provide extra cues to recall, thereby altering the results observed with less organized lists (Myers, O'Brien, Balota, & Toyofuku, 1984). Before a song is begun, these cues are known, to the extent that they hold for the whole genre. Once the song is begun, each word output provides cues for later words, limiting the meaning, image, and rhyme scheme that can follow. Not only does the multiple cuing increase the cue–item activity, but it provides some redundancy, so that even if some cues are missing, the same item is likely to be recalled. Such organizational cues do not prevent all failures in recall. In fact, they can produce a change from the original word by cuing a word that was not in the original variant of a song strongly enough. The new word is recalled, though the original word is also cued. Such "interference" could result in intrusions of words, formulas, lines, verses, characters, props, and even themes from other songs. Such intrusions do occur when cues facilitate them. If such intrusions, or building of songs from a vocabulary of larger units, occur regularly in a tradition, they will prevent the formation of fixed songs expected through overlearning while maintaining what appear to be organized rules.

The role of spaced practice, overlearning, and multiple cues noted in oral traditions is clearly compatible with the cue–item-discriminability-network-activity model that has been used in this section to summarize the interference literature. Thus the same basic processes that were found to operate in the laboratory with interference-theory studies may be operating in oral traditions, with the differences in material and processes limiting decreases in recall.

What Is Remembered?

Having examined the causes of losses in remembering, we now turn to the question of exactly which items are remembered. Assume that a list, a story, a poem, or a piece from an oral tradition is learned. We need to ask not only about the amount recalled later, but also about what aspects will be remembered. Following the point drawn from the history of interference theory, the units of analysis should be the units measured. Formal analysis of this problem exists for lists and prose (Rubin, 1974, 1978, 1980; Rubin & Friendly, 1986), and the results are much the same for both kinds of material (Rubin, 1985).

Assume that a list of words, a story, or a poem is given to many people, and the ease of recalling each unit (i.e., each word or each proposition or each line) is expressed as the proportion of people who remember that unit. It is an empirical observation that the rank order of units from most to least likely to be remembered is constant over a wide range of conditions.

Let us start with changes in the length of the retention interval. It is expected that much more will be recalled after 10 minutes than after 1 month; however, the units that will be recalled most often by people tested after 10 minutes and the units that will be recalled most often by different people tested after 1 month will be the same units. That is, if someone did poorly and recalled only 50% after 10 minutes, and if someone else did well and recalled 50% after 1 month, you could not tell their recalls apart on the basis of which units they recalled. In particular, Rubin (1978) had groups of 16 undergraduates read and recall a passage after no delay, 10 minutes, 1 week, or 1 month, at which times they recalled 70%, 60%, 54%, and 43%, respectively. Exactly which units each of the 64 (i.e., 16 × 4) individuals recalled was predicted from the number of units he or she recalled and either the rank order of units from most to least likely to be recalled from his or her particular retention-interval group or the rank order from the four groups combined. The predictions were correct 80% percent of the time when the individual retention-interval-group means were used and 79% of the time when the combined rank order was used.

This is an important finding because it means that in making predictions about what will be remembered, the amount of time that passes between encoding and recall will affect how much is remembered, but not the relative likelihood of which particular units will be remembered. This finding is counter to the intuitions and interpretations of many psychologists who expected one kind of unit or another to drop out differentially with the passage of time. With a few exceptions, which will soon be considered, it is nevertheless consistent with their data (Rubin, 1978, 1985). It is true, for instance, that details will be forgotten first, but only to the extent that they were less likely to be recalled in the first place.

The fixed-rank-order hypothesis, as applied to retention intervals, has considerable empirical support. Rubin (1985) reviewed and reanalyzed a dozen prose-recall studies from different laboratories with retention intervals varying from immediate recall to 3 months. The units that were most likely to be recalled at one interval were most likely to be recalled at another; only the total amount of recall varied.[10]

Perhaps the most interesting finding came from a theory rather than from the data itself. Kintsch and van Dijk (1978) proposed a model that is successful in predicting which units are recalled. The model has three parameters that are fit from the data. The parameter that is used for the most important units changed only slightly across the immediate, 1-month, and 3-month retention intervals. The other two parameters that are determined by the less important units changed by about a factor of 5. Kintsch and van Dijk interpreted this as indicating that the retention interval differentially affected both important and unimportant units. The interpretation from the fixed-rank-order hypothesis is that the units that were important, and thus well recalled immediately after presentation, were also well remembered after a 3-month delay, so the parameter connected to them did not change much. In contrast, the unimportant units were forgotten over these periods, so the parameter connected with them changed. If this latter interpretation is correct, then the units remembered from Kintsch and van Dijk's immediate, 1-month, and 3-month data should correlate highly, and they do, with an average correlation of .90. More surprising, the probability of recall values for the units that were predicted by the model correlated an average of .99 for the same intervals (Rubin, 1985). That is, although the model could be interpreted as requiring differential decay rates, it could be more parsimoniously interpreted as having a fixed rank order of the probability of recall of units at all intervals.

The age of the people recalling stories, at least from second graders to 60-year-olds, presents a picture similar to that presented by retention-interval studies, according to a reanalysis of 12 studies (Rubin, 1985; Stine & Wingfield, 1990).[11] Similarly, a reanalysis of 10 studies that compared people differing along dimensions other than age supports the notion that the same rank order of units from most to least likely to be recalled will be remembered from stories by most people, even when there are large differences in the amount recalled. In these studies, schizophrenics, Korsakoff amnesiacs, memory-impaired elderly, language-impaired individuals, people with different reading and verbal-ability levels, and people with different literacy levels were compared with appropriate control groups.[12] Further work with persons with Alzheimer's disease, multi-infarct dementia, closed-head injury, metabolic disorders, and affective disorders produced similar results (Schultz, Schmitt, Logue, & Rubin, 1986).

There was a miscellaneous collection of other factors in recall studies that also had little effect on the rank order from most to least likely to be recalled. These factors included rate of presentation, whether the undergraduates intended to learn the story or not, how motivated they were to learn, whether they were expecting a recall or recognition test of remembering, and whether the story was presented as a movie or in text form.[13] Some of these factors, such as rate of presentation and motivation and intention to learn, have obvious applications for the transmission of oral traditions.

The point of this lengthy list of differences in people and conditions that do not affect the rank order from most to least likely to be recalled is to stress that recall results can be generalized. Thus if we can understand what is remembered under one set of circumstances, we are well on our way to understanding what is recalled under a wide range of circumstances. The implication is that if singers remember half as much as they might, it makes no difference whether it is because they have not sung the song for a long time, because they are beginning to become senile, or because they are less motivated; they will sing the same parts of the song. Certain factors, like retention and aging, do not have strong effects on the quality of recall, only on the quantity. In mathematical terms, this means that the function determining the probability of recall of each item can be divided into two factors. The factor that determines the overall amount of recall is affected by retention interval, motivation to learn, age, and clinical syndrome. The factor that determines the probability of recall of an item relative to other items is not affected by these variables. Psychologists are slow to appreciate such regularities in their theoretical endeavors. Differences produce easier tests of theories (Rubin, 1989). But in applying laboratory and naturalistic findings to novel situations, such observations of regularity are crucial to constructing general theories.

There are several factors that do have marked effects on the rank order of items from most to least likely to be recalled. These factors mark the limits of generalizability and indicate where changes in what is remembered are likely to occur in the transmission of oral traditions. Among the retention-interval studies reviewed by Rubin (1985), there were two studies in which the fixed-rank-order hypothesis failed (Graesser, Woll, Kowalski, & Smith, 1980; Smith & Graesser, 1981). In both of these studies, the passages were based on scripts of the kind discussed in Chapter 2. The passages contained details that were from the dominant script of the passage, such as "Jack sat down at the table" in a restaurant script, and statements that were not from the dominant script, such as "Jack put a pen in his pocket." Over time, the details that were related to the script were better remembered than those that were not. In addition, more script-related than script-irrelevant details that were not part of the original story intruded into the recalls. Similar effects could easily occur in oral traditions, with variations introduced that fit not only the script and other theme-related constraints, but also the poetics and music organization. From these results, it would be expected that if details that are not part of the constraints of the genre are introduced, they will be lost more quickly. These apparent contradictions to the fixed-rank-order hypothesis are another application of Jost's second law (1897). Two kinds of knowledge were presented in the passages: information learned long ago and new information about irrelevant details. Because the script-related details were learned earlier than the script-irrelevant details, Jost's law can be applied. Given equal strength immediately after learning, the older script-relevant details will show less loss over time.

Other studies that produce results inconsistent with the fixed-rank-order hypothesis involve differences in the knowledge or perspective of the person recalling the story. A person instructed to read a description of a house from the perspective of a home buyer remembers different things than a person reading the same passage from the perspective of a burglar (Grabe, 1979; Pichert & Anderson, 1977). Moving a paragraph from one place in a long story where it is central to the overall content to another place where it is peripheral also produces results inconsistent with the fixed-rank-order hypothesis (Meyer, 1977). Large shifts like these are not likely to occur for people familiar with an oral tradition, but when a piece is transmitted across cultures or to people outside the tradition, such changes in what is recalled are likely.

Recall for lists of unorganized words functions in much the same way as does recall for prose, except that the lack of thematic constraint leads individuals to differ more on the particular words they recall (Rubin, 1989). Nonetheless, although there are fewer studies to analyze for lists, the fixed-rank-order hypothesis holds over a wide range of recall tasks, including free recall of lists at a 5 second per word presentation rate, with undergraduates rehearsing any way they liked or, in another condition, rehearsing only the word being presented; a 1 second per word presentation rate of a much longer list; surprise recall after rating the words for orthographic distinctiveness or emotionality; surprise free recall of either the stimulus or the response words after paired-associate learning; and surprise free recall after a lexical-decision task. As with prose, there are some tasks with lists for which the fixed-rank-order hypothesis does not hold. People remember different words with tasks depending heavily on imagery, as opposed to the tasks just considered. An example of an imagery task is the recall of words learned using the method of loci, in which an image for each word is integrated into a different imagined geographic location (Bower, 1970a; Yates, 1966). Moreover, we can say how those words differ. The rank order of most to least likely to be recalled is the same as the rank order of ease of forming an image ratings made by other undergraduates (Rubin, 1980, 1985).[14]

For both prose and lists, the nature of the retrieval task affects which units are recalled (Rubin, 1978, 1985). The studies reviewed involved free recall—that is, recall in which people were asked to recall the last story or list they remembered with no additional cues. If people are given cues, such as in paired-associate learning or stories in which every fifth word is missing, the rank order of units from most to least likely to be recalled is different from what it would be for free recall, and varies as a function of the details of the task and the cues. Recognition tasks, in which the correct word is presented and needs only to be judged as familiar or not, or else is selected from among a few alternatives, also produce different rank orders.

A cue–item-discriminability model was formulated to summarize the findings of interference theory so that they could be applied to the study of oral traditions. If it is assumed that only changes in processing that result in changes in cue–item discriminability produce violations of the fixed-rank-order hypothesis, then the cue–item-discriminability model is consistent with the findings summarized using the fixed-rank-order hypothesis. For the recall studies just reviewed, it makes sense that cue–item discriminability would be stable under most manipulations. The exceptions are also reasonable. For instance, changing the perspective of a reader from that of a home buyer to that of a burglar is likely to change the cues the reader uses in recall. Similarly, having the experimenter provide added cues to recall should change the cue–item discriminability, especially in the cases where some of the words of the story were used as prompts in a fill-in-the-blanks response format, or where the words themselves were used as cues in a recognition task in which the person had to indicate whether or not the word appeared in the story or list.

Given the robust nature of the fixed-rank-order hypothesis in free recall, we can ask what leads a unit to be easy to recall—that is, what leads to cue–item discriminability. For both prose and lists recalled under most conditions, there is not just one factor that predicts the rank order from most to least likely to be recalled, but many factors, each accounting for some variance. For prose, measures of each unit's contribution to theme and imagery, the two main constraints outlined in this book that apply to prose, as well as measures of the serial position of the unit in the story, and measures of the degree to which each unit was connected to other units in the story, all predicted recall (Rubin, 1978). For lists, a consistent set of predictors occurred for three data sets reanalyzed by Rubin and Friendly (1986): (1) 214 undergraduates who recalled the same 125 words using the collection of free-recall tasks listed earlier; (2) a collection of multiple-trial free-recall tasks that used a set of 925 words performed in Friendly's laboratory in York University, Ontario (Rubin & Friendly, 1986); and (3) a standard free-recall task using 900 of the 925 words that

Friendly used taken from a laboratory at Vanderbilt (Christian, Bickley, Tarka, & Clayton, 1978). For all three sets of data from the three different laboratories, the same three predictors of ease of recall emerged: imagery, availability, and emotionality. Over the three samples, imagery and availability make nearly equal contributions, with the contribution of availability being slightly larger in the two studies based on more words. Emotionality makes a consistent but generally smaller contribution.[15] Given the differences in procedures and subjects, these results provide a strong basis for theorizing.

The independent contribution of imagery in both prose and lists is expected from the discussions in Chapter 3, as is the contribution of theme in prose from the discussions in Chapter 2. The recall of emotional words, especially in lists of unorganized and otherwise dull lists, is clear, though occasionally forgotten by cognitive psychologists whose theories, as discussed briefly in Chapter 6, have tended to omit the motivational factors of earlier behaviorists. The surprise is the success of the availability variable.

The availability, or associative frequency, of a word is calculated by counting how many times the word is given as a response to a large set of stimulus words. People are given a large sample of words, one at a time, and asked to respond with the first word that comes to mind; the more often a word comes to mind, the higher its availability. Thus the availability of a word can be seen as an indicator of the likelihood of that word being cued averaged over all likely word cues (Rubin, 1980, 1983). The effects of cuing noted in the review of interference theory were usually implicit—that is, without awareness or conscious effort. Implicit cuing will also be seen as the main form of cuing in the theory of serial recall for oral traditions proposed in this chapter. Availability, as a measure based on the first word that comes to mind, is the closest measure to the average implicit association or implicit verbal response (Underwood, 1965) for an isolated word. In terms of cue–item discriminability, high-availability words are more likely to receive activation from other words in and prior to the list just learned and from self-cuing.[16]

If this analysis of availability is correct, several observations should follow, and they do. The increased cuing over a range of words makes high-availability words easier to recall in free-recall tasks, as previously shown. This same argument predicts that high-availability words used as the word to be recalled, or response member, make recall in paired-associate learning easier. In contrast, the availability of the cue, or stimulus member, is not a main predictor of how easy a pair will be to learn; the number of associations given to the stimulus member, rather than the number leading to it, predicts ease of learning. Because high-availability words have more associations leading to them, they are judged as more familiar or frequent even when objective frequency is controlled. This, in turn, makes high-availability words more attractive foils in recognition tasks. That is, when people are given a set of words and asked which ones they have seen before in an experiment, they more often falsely recognize high-availability words as being present. In contrast, high-availability words are harder to recognize because their raised familiarity produces a more difficult background against which to make a judgment of whether they were present in the experiment or just present in daily life outside the experiment (e.g., it is easier to judge that the word *cobblestone* as opposed to the word *chair* did not appear in the last 10 pages). These predictions hold even when other confounding factors are controlled (Rubin, 1983). Thus words that are given as associations to many different words show the properties that would be expected of them, supporting the self-cuing hypothesis.

Cuing as a Key to Remembering

Both the review of interference theory and the role of availability in predicting which words are recalled from random lists support the importance of cuing to recall. We store much more than we can retrieve at any given time without help (Bjork & Bjork, 1992). Here studies from other laboratory approaches to cuing are reviewed, and the time course of the effectiveness of cuing is examined. In oral traditions, individual cues are made more salient by the repeated use of similar cues throughout a genre and by the experience, or expertise, that follows. Cuing in an oral tradition should therefore have even larger effects.

The free recall of lists is by design a situation with minimal cuing. People are cued only by the request to recall the last list or lists they saw, and the lists themselves are typically made of randomly assigned and ordered items. This situation is an extreme case of what Watkins (Watkins, 1979, 1990; Watkins & Watkins, 1975) termed *cue overload*. There is only one cue for all the items in the list. Each cue defines many items, so cue–item discriminability is low. Thus if any search or retrieval process is assumed, it must be based on self-generated cues or cues from other items in the list. In terms of the model put forth to summarize the interference-theory data, cue–item discriminability from the situation is minimal. In this context, the success of availability as a predictor of recall in situations where other cuing is minimal is an argument for the role of cuing. When few cues are present, people provide cues for themselves, in part using associations among words in the list, and the average of their attempts leads availability to be important.

The problem of cue overload is more general than list-learning experiments. For instance, requests to list all the different kinds of animals one knows (Bousfield & Sedgewick 1944; Gruenewald & Lockhead, 1980; Rubin & Olson, 1980) or all the events that can be remembered from one's life (Crovitz, Schiffman, & Apter, 1991; Galton, 1879) result in an output that is less than one can produce with more detailed cuing.

If lists and other laboratory situations produce cue overload, then oral traditions produce "cue underload." Multiple redundant cues are given for each word to be recalled. Given the laboratory situation of free recall as a base of what occurs with minimal cuing, we can examine what happens as cues are added. With more cues, more should be recalled (Johnson, 1982; King & Anderson, 1976). Consider the following experiment by Earhard (1967) as an example of increased cuing.

Students learned lists of 24 nouns. The lists were divided into 2, 3, 4, 6, 8, 12, or 24 groups of equal size. All the words in each group began with the same letter, and this unique way of designating a particular group of words later served as a cue for recall. Thus the letters used for each list cued 12, 8, 6, 4, 3, 2, or 1 word. After each of 20 learning trials on which the words were presented one at a time in a different random order, the students were prompted with a letter and asked to recall all the words that began with it. Recall averaged 88% when there was 1 target word per first-letter cue, 84% when there were 2 target words per cue, 78% for 3, 75% for 4, 69% for 6, 67% for 8, and 63% for 12. Thus there was a decrease in the effectiveness of the cues as the number of targets per cue increased. Recall averaged 69% for the uncued recall of a list with 24 words each beginning with a different letter, or for a list in which all 24 words began with the same letter. This was the level of first-letter cued recall with 6 target words per cue. The cued-recall levels for 8 and 12 target words per cue were less than for the free recall, indicating that the students' own organization with no first-letter cues was better than a letter-by-letter organization with more than 6 target words per cue.

Bahrick (1969) provides a parametric investigation of the role of the strength of cues in prompting recall. By testing over 2,000 undergraduates, he found 20 target words that had cue words that would produce them as associates at five different levels of probability. For instance, the target word *blue* was given as an associate with a probability of .03 by *velvet*, .10 by *gray*, .28 by *green*, .58 by *azure*, and .66 by *sky*. The average probability of a cue cuing its target is the bottom curve in Figure 7.3. Bahrick then made each target word the response word in a paired-associate-learning task. Continuing with the example, *blue* became the response word to the unrelated stimulus word *time*. Trials proceeded until a moderate level of learning was achieved, and recall was tested either immediately or at 2 hours, 2 days, or 2 weeks. If an undergraduate did not recall a target-word response when given the stimulus member of the pair as a cue (e.g., recalling *blue* when presented with the unrelated word *time*), an added cue from one of the five levels of cuing was given (e.g., *gray*). The probability of recalling one of these initially unrecalled words, when provided with an association as a cue at each of the five strength levels, is the middle curve in Figure 7.3. The combined probability of recalling the target word with the stimulus member of the pair as a cue, and if that failed with an added associative cue, is the top curve in Figure 7.3. The figure demonstrates that the likelihood of a word's bringing another word to mind is related in an orderly, almost linear, fashion to its effectiveness as a cue in recall studies and shows that the effect can be strong[17]

In oral traditions, there are often many cues at work, and even weak cues can combine to produce strong effects. Solso and Biersdorff (1975) provide a quantitative example of the way in which multiple cues of the type used in oral traditions combine to aid retrieval. Undergraduates were presented sequentially with no cue, a single cue, a double cue composed of two single cues, or a triple cue. For each target word, the single cues were a semantic associate, as Bahrick had used, a rhyming word, or the word's first letter (i.e., an alliteration cue). Thus for the target word *pin,* the single cue was *has a meaning related to needle, rhymes with inn,* or *begins with p.* All three single cues, all six combinations of the double cues, and the triple cue were used equally often. After each cue, the undergraduates were asked to respond with a target word that was selected before the experiment began. Half the undergraduates had been shown a list of the 20 target words that were being cued and were asked to recall them; the other half were not shown the list of target words and were asked to guess the words given the cues.

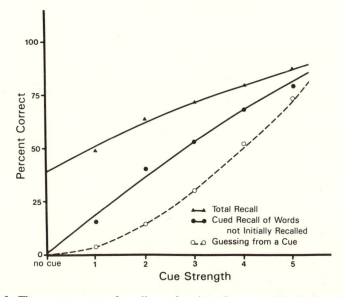

Figure 7.3. Three components of recall as a function of cue strength: (1) guessing, or the ability of a cue to produce the target word without the target word being shown earlier; (2) cuing of words not recalled without cues; and (3) total recall, which shows the level of recall with no cuing as its left most point. (Data from Bahrick, 1969)

Figure 7.4 shows the effect of cuing on the percentage of correct responses. For both the undergraduates who saw the list of target words and those who did not, a single cue was not much better than no cue at all, but the double and triple cues led to much a higher level of correct responding. In contrast, repeated opportunities to respond without additional cues had little effect. Thus the combination of meaning, rhyming, and alliteration cues greatly improves the recall of previously seen material and the guessing of novel material. As discussed in Chapter 5, the effect of combining cues is striking. The increment of the various cues to recall resembles that shown in Figure 7.3, with the difference between responding with the target word when it was seen versus when it was not seen earlier diminishing as the probability of a correct response approaches 100%.[18]

Since Bahrick's results have been supported with a study more easily applied to oral traditions, Bahrick's study can be used to make a further point. Because four different retention intervals were used, Figure 7.3 can be replotted as a function of retention interval averaged over cue strength. Figure 7.5 plots four curves as a function of time. The curve that drops to the lowest level is the forgetting of the response member when only the stimulus member is given as a cue. This curve shows the rapid loss of the ability of the stimulus member of the paired associate to cue the response member without an added associative cue. The relatively straight solid curve is the level of effectiveness of cues for words that were not recalled without cues. This curve shows that there is little loss with time in the cuing ability of preexperimental associations. The top curve is the combined probability of recalling the target word with the stimulus member of the pair as a cue and, if that failed,

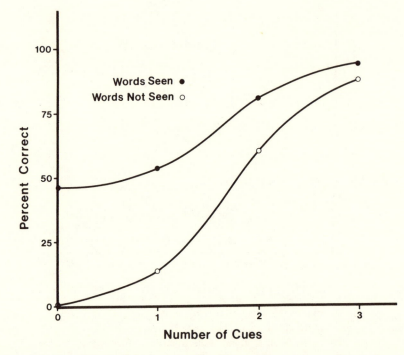

Figure 7.4. The effect of combining cues. Recalling words seen or guessing words not seen with one cue is not much greater than with no cues, yet the combination of two or three such weak cues is effective. (Data from Solso & Biersdorff, 1975)

with an added associative cue. This combined-recall curve is calculated as the sum of the probability of a word being recalled without an added associative cue plus the probability that if it is not recalled without a cue, it will be recalled with a cue. The combined recall shows less loss with time than unaided recall. The horizontal, straight, dotted line is the probability of the cues yielding the target-word responses if those words were not presented in the learning experiment, which is assumed not to change over the course of the experiment.

Figure 7.5 contrasts the newly formed association between the stimulus word and the target-response member (e.g., between *time* and *blue*) to the much older association between the associative cues and the target (e.g., between *gray* and *blue*). The slow loss in the effectiveness of cuing with associates demonstrates one of Bahrick's main points: something remains of memory for paired associates that is not seen in the all-or-none recall-without-added-associative-cuing task. In terms of the cue–item-discriminability model, the stimulus member of the paired associate, when given alone, loses its ability over time to discriminate the response member, but when existing long-term associative cues are added, they often combine to provide enough discrimination.

To make the time course clearer, Bahrick's data have been extrapolated beyond 2 weeks. Assume, Figure 7.5 does, that recall without added associative cuing goes to nearly zero in 2 years. Also assume, as the figure does, that the ability of the associative cues to cue target words that were not presented in the paired-associate task remains constant. That is, given the spaced practice and overlearning that continue to add to the associations' strength through normal language use, their strength should not drop at all over the course of the experiment. Thus we have a floor for recall without cuing at zero and a floor for recall with cuing at the cuing without a previous learning level of 35% correct. From the data, it is clear that the ability of the associative cues to aid recall does not drop as quickly as the strength of the stimulus member alone, and if the graphic extrapolation were correct, this associative-cuing factor would lead to recall of over 40% at 2 years when the contribution of recall without added cuing had disappeared.

One implication for oral traditions is that existing associations, which are part of the culture, language, or genre, and which benefited from overlearning and spaced practice, will show the effects of time less than associations that are tied to only a newly learned piece. A similar conclusion was drawn earlier in the chapter for the recall of script-related versus script-unrelated recall of text (Graesser et al., 1980; Smith & Graesser, 1981). When the newly learned associations are practiced over time, they too will become part of the genre and will be less subject to loss. As in Figure 7.5, this effect goes beyond guessing to involve memory that could not be observed without the aid of the added cuing. Bahrick (1970) provides a model for this added contribution of established associations that holds that the associations generate potential responses. Based on what is already activated in memory, there is a recognition of the correct response from among these potential responses. In oral traditions, the correct response is often not needed, but only a response that fits the constraints of the piece and the genre. Therefore, a judgment of goodness of fit could often be made instead of one of recognition. This kind of judgment would allow such

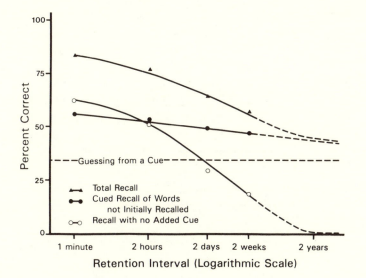

Figure 7.5. A replotting of Figure 7.3, with retention interval replacing cue strength on the horizontal axis.

established associations to play the important role of fitting a new piece into the genre, and would blur the distinction between tasks that require judgments of recognition and those that do not (Jacoby & Hollingshead, 1990).

One additional series of experiments on cuing needs to be reviewed. Mantyla (1986) had undergraduates list either one or three properties or descriptions for 168 words on each of 3 consecutive days. At the end of the third day, they were given a surprise recall task for half the 504 words and asked if they would like to return in a week for another experiment. On return, they were asked to recall the remaining words. The procedure produces immediate, 1-day, 2-day, and 1-week retention intervals. The cuing conditions were the person's own single properties as cues, the person's own sets of triple properties as triple cues, someone else's single cues, or someone else's triple cues. Other undergraduates were given just the single or triple cues and asked to guess the words. The results are shown in Figure 7.6.

There are several important findings from this study. First, even without the intent to learn a list of 504 words, people did quite well, recalling over 90% correct at no delay with their own triple cues. Second, one's own cues are better than someone else's, suggesting that in oral traditions, if the words used most often as cues are not standardized within a genre, then there will be a force for increasing individual differences among singers. Such idiolects exist in oral traditions, substituting the individual singer's use of particular constraint-satisfaction solutions for those of other singers (see Foley, 1990, pp. 288–324, for an example). Third, as with the Solso and Biersdorff (1975) study, three cues are better than one. Fourth, and most important for long-term retention, recall with three cues shows little decline from 1 day to 1 week, whereas recall with one cue shows a drop. If this finding holds, it indicates that, counter to the fixed-rank-order hypothesis discussed earlier in the chapter, multiple cues retain their effectiveness over time more than do single cues.

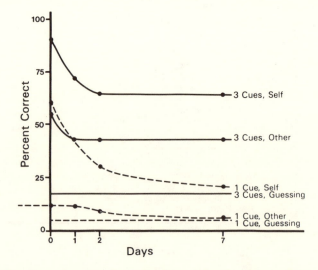

Figure 7.6. Recall as a function of retention interval for six cuing conditions. (Data from Mantyla, 1986)

In terms of the model, the cue–item discriminability of the three cues loses less with time than does that of the single cues.

Two artifacts can easily be ruled out; a third is more difficult. First, the result cannot be due to the fact that three cues are better than one. If the curve of three cues from another person is compared with the curve of one self-generated cue, both are at roughly the same level at 0 and 1 day, but differ at 2 days and 1 week. Second, the result cannot be due to the fact that recall can be cued if any of the three cues of the triple cue remain. A curve based on this hypothesis would decrease with time more rapidly than those shown in Figure 7.6. Third, the major effect on the initial level of recall, and therefore also the overall amount of recall in these studies, is not the number of cues, but whether they are self-generated or not. The leveling due to the number of cues did not lead to a statistically significant interaction and could be an artifact of some interaction with the more powerful self-versus-other factor. More detailed analyses, however, indicate that this is not the case. Given the wide range of conditions over which the fixed-rank-order hypothesis holds in free recall, this exception in cued recall is noteworthy and may offer a way to increase long-term retention.[19]

In a further study (Mantyla & Nilsson, 1988), undergraduates generated properties as before or else were asked to generate properties that they would be likely to generate again if the task were repeated. The purpose of this manipulation was to see if the reason for the cue's loss of effectiveness with time was that people had changed over the period and would not use the same cue at the time of retrieval that they had provided unknowingly for themselves at encoding. In three experiments, the drop in retention was several times greater with the standard instructions than with the modified ones. This may explain why self-generated cues showed a greater loss than other-generated cues in the original Mantyla (1986) study. For self-generated cues compared with other-generated cues, the person generating the cues would have a state of mind more similar to that of the person recalling at short retention intervals, but one that would change more rapidly over time. That is, all people may change the cues they would have used over the course of a week, but the change should not cause as large a systematic difference in the effectiveness of the cues chosen by other people. For current purposes, the added instructions resulted in the undergraduates choosing cues more like the genre-specific, stereotypical cues used in oral traditions. Thus multiple stereotypical cues, like those used in oral traditions, appear most effective for longer retention intervals.

The most general implication from this section and the section on the causes of forgetting is that cuing, especially as it adds to cue–item discriminability, plays a crucial role in remembering. Loss of cue–item discriminability is the cause of forgetting, and reinstatement of cue–item discriminability by the addition of cues is the way to recover the forgotten.

Expertise in Remembering[20]

Cue–item discriminability can increase recall only if ties exist between cues and items to be recalled. Many of these ties come from general experience and the language in which a piece is sung; others are genre-specific. The way in which singers come to appreciate and use the genre-specific cues needs to be considered. Chapter 6 reviewed observations on the ways singers come to be experts in several genres. Here a brief review of the psychological literature on expertise is given. It is possible to couch the findings of research on memory expertise in terms of the cuing framework used here (Bellezza & Buck, 1988). Expertise becomes the accumulation of cue–item associations that facilitate performance.

Research on human memory, including most of the research reviewed in this chapter, has concentrated on experiments in which people enter the laboratory, learn something, are tested once, and never return. How this experience changes them for future studies is ignored or viewed as a nuisance variable. Thus the development of their memory skills is ignored. In 1949, Harlow stressed the need to understand not only learning to perform isolated tasks, but also learning how to learn related sets of tasks. Harlow clearly demonstrated that with practice, monkeys and people improved in their ability to solve new problems, but he was hampered in his attempts to uncover the mechanisms of such learning to learn by a lack of some of the theoretical and methodological sophistication we have since gained.

One way to examine the acquisition of expertise of the kind needed for oral traditions is to look at rule learning in the laboratory, because much of what is learned from a piece in an oral tradition is not a set of items but a skill. Psychologists study *learning how to* as well as *learning that*, but little of this study of learning how to involves verbal material. In learning a piece from an oral tradition, singers learn not only words, but also knowledge about the rules, or constraints, of the genre. It is this learning of rules or *learning how to learn* that Harlow (1949) found lacking in the psychology of his day. The problem is still in need of attention, but the increase in our knowledge of mental representation, such as was described in Chapters 2, 3, and 4, makes progress more likely. For now, an example of the long-term retention of rules is given.

Allen and Reber (1980) exposed students for approximately a half-hour to letter strings generated by two artificial grammars. The rules of the grammars were never explicitly given. From the knowledge gained from the examples, a decision had to be made about which test strings followed the rules of the grammars. Overall, 78% of the choices were correct compared with a chance performance level of 50%. Two years later, the test was again given to the unsuspecting students. The mean correct score was 67%, and letter strings that had more than one letter incorrect were identified 80% of the time. The participants could not state the rules that they had formulated 2 years earlier to help them decide which strings were grammatical. They just had a feeling about which strings were right. In addition, the conditions of initial learning still had an effect 2 years later. People who were initially biased to pay attention to the details of the letter strings did better on strings that they had learned than they did on other rule-generated strings that they had not previously learned. In contrast, people who were initially biased to draw inferences showed no difference between strings that were previously learned and strings that were not. Similar conclusions have been found using different procedures (e.g., Stadler, 1993).

If the results of such experiments generalize to other domains, memory for implicit knowledge abstracted from a set of instances should be quite stable. It would not be surprising to find that the inferred, usually unstated, rules of an oral tradition are retained much better than knowledge of individual words, and that, as noted in Chapters 2, 3, 4, and 5, much of what has to be retained to sing a piece is just such rules.

One reason constraints, as opposed to fixed isolated instances, are important in oral traditions is that large numbers of similar songs and variants of songs are heard. Such variability within limits can even encourage the abstraction of patterns at recall in computer models that store only individual instances (Hintzman, 1986). When memory is studied in the laboratory, identical stimuli are usually presented repeatedly, whereas in oral traditions and in the world in general, the stimuli are variants; that is, they vary in a constrained fashion. This leads laboratory studies of memory to focus on accuracy, whereas in oral tradition and in the world in general, as Bartlett (1932) notes, the abstraction and use of regularities, not verbatim recall, are usually what are important. The development of expertise almost always involves variability in stimuli.

Psychologists have studied laboratory learning that occurs with stimuli that change within limits, but usually not to study memory per se. The artificial-grammar study just presented is an example. From such studies we know that people can abstract prototypes, or central members of a set, in that they recall and judge the prototype as a member of a set even if it was not presented (Bransford & Franks, 1971; Posner & Keele, 1968). They make such an abstraction either implicitly or explicitly (Broadbent, FitzGerald, & Broadbent, 1986; Porter, 1991). The range of stimuli judged as similar is dependent on the variability of the set of stimuli presented, on properties of the judging organism (Lashley & Wade, 1946), and on knowledge outside the set of stimuli being presented (Rubin & Kontis, 1983).

In addition to such studies of the laboratory learning of related stimuli, there is a small but long history in mainstream memory research of the study of memory expertise as its own phenomenon (Ericsson, 1985). Five general observations of this research effort that are relevant to oral traditions follow.

First, memory expertise is an everyday result of routine cognitive processes (e.g., James, 1890; Neisser, 1982). Everyone is a memory expert in many areas. We are in awe of memory expertise only when it occurs for unusual tasks and domains, ignoring the more common occurrences. As Harlow (1949) notes, expertise is part of the normal course of development. Thus the memory feats of oral poets, though impressive, may be no more amazing than those of a chess master, a mental calculator, or an expert in any field of knowledge such as cognitive psychology, folklore, classics, automobile repair, or baseball statistics.

Second, memory expertise is limited to specific tasks and genres (e.g., Glaser & Chi, 1988). Expertise is a specific set of skills, not a general ability to remember all materials or perform all memory tasks. Although people vary in their general interests and abilities in ways that contribute to expertise (Ackerman, 1987; Holding, 1985; Hunter, 1990; Luria, 1968), the largest component of expertise is due to specific skills, not general faculties (see Singley & Anderson, 1989, for a review). Thus a large digit span does not imply a large consonant span (Chase & Ericsson, 1981), and the ability to recall the location of pieces from a chess game (Chase & Simon, 1973) or cards from a bridge hand (Engle & Bukstel, 1978) does not imply a large digit span or even a good memory for randomly arranged chess pieces or playing cards. Reports on singers in oral traditions, though not systematic, bear this out. Singers excel at their genres, but not necessarily at other cognitive or memory tasks. If expertise can be modeled by the development of a network of problem-to-solution or cue-to-item associations, then this specificity is consistent with the cue–item-discriminability model proposed earlier in the chapter.

Third, memory expertise in a domain requires a great deal of knowledge, though the knowledge need not be stated explicitly or used in tasks different from those usually performed (Smith, 1990). Moreover, the knowledge must be able to be organized in a way that allows for rapid use in the expert task. In particular, expertise involves the ability to grasp organized, domain-specific stimuli quickly. A chess expert can remember a board seen for only seconds (Chase & Simon, 1973). For oral traditions, the speed needs to be sufficient to allow for the use of the organization present in complex auditory stimuli presented in real time. Performances must proceed to the rhythm of the piece.

Fourth, using their knowledge, memory experts organize the stimuli presented to them to a greater extent and in different ways than do novices. This is often summarized to mean that experts find meaningful patterns, whereas novices do not. But for oral traditions, *meaningful* must be taken to mean task appropriate (Morris, Bransford, & Franks, 1977) and stimulus appropriate (Rubin, 1985) rather than deep or semantic. That is, it is common in the expertise literature to find that with increasing expertise, there is less reliance on surface forms (Chi, Feltovich, & Glaser, 1981; Dee-Lucas & Larkin, 1988; Schoenfeld & Herrmann, 1982; Smith, 1990). But in oral traditions, surface organization is important. Using these surface characteristics is as task appropriate for an expert in an oral tradition as is using an abstract theme. Thus expert singers must know about all the constraints of their genre.

Fifth, memory expertise requires practice, but formal teaching is not needed. People can acquire the skills through trial-and-error attempts, and in most of the cases studied, this is the method used. This is important because, as detailed in Chapter 6, in most oral traditions there is no formal training beyond repetition.

Multiple Cues, Multiple Constraints

This chapter began by arguing that the ease of recall of items depends on cue–item discriminability: the target of recall has to be discriminated from all else in memory, either on its own or with the aid of cues present in the environment or generated in the act of recalling. Time is a good cue for recent targets, but not for those in a past mixed with similar targets. Other cues are needed to isolate the target from the camouflage. A review of what target items are remembered from a set of target items simplified the task of generalizing to oral traditions by showing that the same items were likely to be recalled under different conditions. This review again supported the importance of overall cuing in the form of availability.

A more careful look at cues supported their central role in recall. Consistent with Chapter 5, multiple cues produced high probabilities of recall and, on the basis of an analysis of one study, appeared to suffer much less loss with time than did individual cues. Figures 7.3 to 7.6, among other functions, contrasted guessing with recall. Guessing on the basis of cues can often be successful, but recalling with those same cues is better. The increased cue–item discriminability caused by pairing the cues and items during learning lasts longer than would be observable if the cues were not present. In oral traditions where the cues are more salient and where expertise increases the efficiency of the cues, even larger effects are expected.

Notes

1. In animals, the passage of time is accompanied by activity and environmental change. One can try to separate time from these factors in the laboratory, for instance, by lowering the body temperature of a cold-blooded animal to decrease its activity. However, such manipulations remove the confounding of two factors by introducing an additional confounding factor; time and activity are separated, but instead, a new body-cooled state of the animal is confounded with decreased activity. Studies using sleep to decrease activity in humans develop similar problems by introducing a sleep state and circadian rhythms as factors. Nonetheless, it is clear that different activities that fill the same amount of time have different effects on memory.

2. There are also other reasons. In part, the experiments as a set failed to produce a set of principles that could be generalized reliably to new experiments. Once a set of results was explained with a set of principles, a new clever experiment was designed that produced results that should have fit but did not. If the solution offered here is correct, this is because the theoretical constructs then available were not adequate for the task. Interference theory assumed that memory was an associative network, but it could not build such a network in any detail. Instead, concepts like spontaneous recovery and unlearning were used to describe and explain phenomena at a global level. But the details of the experiments turned out to be important. An associative network with 100 or more nodes is a complex system to monitor and has behaviors that are difficult to predict without some idea of how such associative networks operate. At the time interference theory was being developed, the computer modeling and mathematical procedure to do this was not available.

3. For texts providing more detailed reviews leading up to and including interference theory see Baddeley (1976), Crowder (1976), Kausler (1974), Kintsch (1970), and McGeoch (1942).

4. A criticism leveled against this analysis is that with an increased number of lists per experiment, people became experts at learning lists and spent less time at it. Because each list was learned perfectly, the longer it took to learn the last item learned, the more the first items learned benefited from overlearning. With more lists in an experiment, the learning rate improved, less time was spent learning each list, and the average degree of overlearning per item was less. Thus if the number of trials or the average amount of overlearning per item, instead of the criterion of one perfect recital of the list as a whole, was used as a measure, the lists in the studies Underwood (1957) cited could not be considered equally learned, and his case would be overstated (Warr, 1964). This dilemma of which measure of learning to use, and several other problems, arise in part because the unit of measure is different from the unit of learning. Here the number of items recalled is measured, but the list is learned to one perfect recall. Nonetheless, proactive interference can be demonstrated when this factor is controlled and remains a powerful effect (Baddeley, 1976, 1990; Keppel, Postman, & Zavortink, 1968).

5. This mechanism is being used for explanatory convenience, in part because interference

theory itself assumes associations among words as a model of memory, though ultimately it may not be the best representation. Models could be built using discrete-instance storage without discrete-instance retrieval (Hintzman, 1986), with networks that do not have discrete nodes corresponding to the items, or with reference to only external events (Skinner, 1974; Watkins, 1990). It is difficult, often impossible, to distinguish among such classes of models, as opposed to particular models from each class (Barsalou, 1990; Hintzman, 1986; Rubin, Wallace, & Houston, 1993). The choice, however, is not entirely arbitrary. In parallel distributed processing networks, material is lost in that it is written over by new learning, whereas in instance models it is never truly lost unless a separate forgetting mechanism is added. Given the difficulty many network models have in accounting for relearning material that has undergone retroactive interference (McCloskey & Cohen, 1989), instance models or network models that show less permanent retroactive interference (Grossberg, 1980, 1988; Nigrin, 1993) need to be used.

6. There is competition among items in the network-activity model in that the relative activity at nodes is compared, though not specifically response competition or response-set competition as it was defined in the interference literature. Here the discriminability of an item, or items, given a set of cues determines what item, or items, will be recalled. In contrast, interference-theory competition theories were usually framed as response competitions, but experiments demonstrated that this could not be true in the sense of responses already found in memory competing, often consciously, for a chance to be uttered. There are many studies in which subjects learned two lists and then were asked to recall one list or the other, or both lists, or one list with the other list provided as an additional cue (i.e., modified modified free recall or modified modified modified free recall). From these experiments, it is clear that the failure to recall does not always lie with the person being unable to decide consciously which of two responses is correct. This is because providing people with the opportunity to respond with more than one item or providing the wrong item to make a conscious choice of the correct one easier does not remove all the interference. Rather, it appears that having many related items in memory lessens the chance of the correct one, or any one, being found. Because of such studies, as well as from phenomenological reports, it is necessary to assume that not all decisions are made consciously after a set of possible items is found. Yet at times, such conscious decisions are made. Whether such conscious decisions result when there is enough cuing to exceed some threshold of retrieval for more than one item or through another mechanism is not clear. However, it is clear that not all interference occurs at this conscious level. Moreover, it appears that questions of exactly where in the process competition occurs and where consciousness enters have not speedily advanced empirical prediction.

7. The number of trials of learning for the A–B list had no effect on interference for spaced learning and no linear effect for massed learning. This would be a problem for the model, except that the authors argue that there is little or no interference from the spaced learning, so the lack of a change with learning is a floor effect. Moreover, there is little effect of the number of trial of A–B learning on the recall of the massed A–B pairs taken immediately after interference was measured, so there may not have been a difference in their learning.

8. As discussed in Chapter 6, there is no simple explanation of why distributed practice aids recall as much as it does. It is therefore likely that factors outside the model, such as fatigue at the time of learning under massed practice, may also be needed to be considered here.

9. The major limitation of the theory is the lack of full implementation in quantitative terms. With words, it is too easy to miss implications of the theory and to gloss over problems (Hintzman, 1991). Psychologists have been fooled before—for instance, by not examining what associations and the storage of exemplars could really do. An implementation using a

network or an instance model is possible, and models that exhibit some of the aspects of the proposed verbal theory exist (e.g., Eich, 1982; Hintzman, 1968, 1986; Kintsch, 1988; Lewandowsky & Murdock, 1989; Mensink & Raaijmakers, 1988).

10. For the six studies reporting correlations, the average correlation calculated over the units among recall intervals was .81. For the six studies using analysis of variance, the retention interval accounted for 16% of the variance; the units, 20%; and their interaction, which represents the degree to which the relative recall of units changes across conditions, only 1%.

11. Twelve studies were found in the literature that used analysis of variance. On the average, age accounted for 6% of the variance; the units accounted for 32%; and their interaction, which represents the degree to which the relative recall of units changes across conditions, accounted for only 1%. In fact, the statistical analyses are a bit embarrassing. All 12 unit main effects, which have the same error terms as the interactions, were significant at the .001 level. The median F was 87, with a range of 16 to 794! Yet only half the interactions were significant at the .05 level. It is as if people were using great statistical power to find an interaction that is often just not there.

12. An average of 11% of the variance was accounted for by the subject population, 21% by the units, and 3% by the interaction. The 3% figure is inflated by several studies in which floor effects caused the interaction.

13. For these seven experiments, the manipulations accounted for 4% of the variance; the units, 25%; and their interaction, only 1%.

14. Just rating the imagery of words in a list is not sufficient to produce this effect (Rubin, 1985).

15. The beta weights for the imagery, availability, and emotionality for the Rubin sample are .36, .32, and .36, respectively. For the Rubin and Friendly (1986) and Christian et al. (1978) data sets, analyses combining the variance accounted for by the imagery and concreteness measures into one measure of imagery and combining the variance accounted for by two measures of availability yields beta weights of .25, .31, and .15 for imagery, availability, and emotionality, respectively, for Rubin and Friendly's data and .28, .35, and .16 for Christian et al.'s.

16. Because of the experimental and cultural context in which people provide their associations, availability depends highly on meaningful ties, though in other contexts a similar index could be made for words of a given image, rhyme, rhythmic pattern, or other constraint.

17. The near zero level of guessing, with no previous knowledge of the target words and no cues in Figures 7.3 and 7.4, is based on the expected probability of guessing randomly selected, high-frequency words and not on any data.

18. Data from Solso and Biersdorff's (1975) Experiments 1 and 2 were averaged to produce Figure 7.1 because the minor differences in procedure did not affect the results.

19. The probability of getting the target if at least one of the equally strong cues is effective is $1 - q^3$, where q is 1 minus the probability of a single cue being effective. Using the probabilities for single self-cues at the four retention intervals, the equation predicts recall levels of 94%, 81%, 66%, and 50%, respectively.

The fixed-rank-order hypothesis was established for the free recall, a situation with no cuing beyond the request to recall the last list or story. In the studies reported, if the cues are kept the same, there is no evidence that the fixed-rank-order hypothesis is wrong. Nonetheless, there is evidence of differential retention of items cued by single and multiple cues when those items were equally easy to recall at an earlier time. This is a noteworthy finding.

The problem with sorting out the effects of one versus three cues and self versus other cues in the Mantyla (1986) studies is that the factors are confounded with recall level. Only the two middle curves of Figure 7.6 have the same initial level of learning, so only these can be directly compared. More detailed analyses, however, indicate that the one-cue versus three-cue factor is probably the important one. When plotted on log–log paper, which is appropriate assuming a power function, the slopes over the 1-day, 2-day, and 7-day periods for the three-self-cue, three-other-cue, and three-self-cue from an earlier experiment using a similar procedure are − .05, .00, and − .13, whereas the slopes from the same one-cue conditions are − .36, − .30, and − .28. Although fitting straight lines to three points is not optimal, there appears to be a difference in the slopes at the longer intervals, depending on the number of cues, but not on the self–other factor.

20. Much of this section is drawn from Rubin et al. (1993).

CHAPTER 8

A Theory of Remembering for Oral Traditions

Reminders provide a good example of the relative tradeoffs between the roles of internal versus external knowledge. Knowledge in the world is accessible. It is self reminding. . . . Knowledge in the mind is ephemeral: here now, gone later. We can't count on something being present in mind at any particular time, unless it is triggered by some external event. . . . Out of sight, out of mind.
                                                                    Norman, 1988, p. 80

If we have forgotten the next part of a piece of music we are playing or poem we are reciting, we go back for a running start, not because the music or poem has been stored as a unit of memory, so that one part helps us find the other part, but because the extra stimulation we generate in the running start is sufficient to evoke the forgotten passage.
                                                                    Skinner, 1974, p. 110

If you want to get ahead, get a theory.
Karmiloff-Smith & Inhelder, 1974–1975

Oral traditions, like all oral language, are sequential. One word follows another as the physical effects of the first word are lost. As the song advances, each word uttered changes the situation for the singer, providing new cues for recall and limiting choices. The first two quotes that start this chapter acknowledge this observation from two different theoretical perspectives. Following the advice in the third quote, the findings about the structure of oral traditions are integrated with those on the processes of remembering in order to produce a theory of serial recall in oral traditions.

With the previous chapters as background, a theory of memory in oral traditions is proposed. The theory is based on the idea of cue–item discriminability developed from the interference-theory literature and later studies of cuing. Pieces from oral traditions are recalled serially, from beginning to end. What is recalled early in the piece can be used to cue later recall; the "running start" provides "extra stimulation" or "reminders," increasing cue–item discriminability. Recall experiments are examined to clarify this process theory and to examine the role that various constraints play in the time course of recall.

The Theory

The book to this point has reviewed and summarized many basic findings from cognitive psychology and oral traditions. In this section, a theory is proposed to integrate these findings. The theory accounts for both the naturalistic and the more controlled experimental data by viewing recall in oral traditions as serial recall guided by multiple constraints. The general constraints, such as the use of four-line verses with lines 2 and 4 rhyming in ballads, are set by the genre when the song is chosen. The particular constraints, such as the specific rhyme sound, unfold as the song is sung, providing cues for the remaining recall. The various constraints, such as imagery, theme, rhyme, alliteration, rhythm, and music, contribute in the ways reviewed. Both the general and specific constraints add to cue–item discriminability, increasing the amount recalled and restricting the kinds of errors or variations made.

The process being put forth follows. Recall in oral traditions is serial. It starts at the first word, or perhaps a rhythm or melody, and proceeds sequentially. Even for lists of random words, or words from a small number of different categories, people often prefer to recall items in the order in which they were presented even when they need not do so (Mandler, 1969; Postman, 1972). For lists of random words, however, such serial learning results in marked serial-position effects, with words at the beginning and end of the list being recalled much better than words in the middle (Johnson, 1991; Lewandowsky & Murdock, 1989). To overcome these effects, other forms of constraint are needed. As noted in the earlier chapters, they are present in oral traditions. These constraints serve both to limit choices and to increase the chances of uniquely cuing the target (Jones, 1976, 1983; Rubin & Wallace, 1989). At the beginning of the song, genre-specific (i.e., schematic) constraints are known and are useful as cues. Each word, as it is sung, provides additional cues that are specific to the song the way it is being sung this time. Using the serial-recall cue–item-discriminability model developed to summarize the interference-theory findings, these additional cues serve to distinguish the words or phrases needed to complete the song from all others in memory. Temporal or serial-position cues play a definite role in recall, but by themselves, they cannot discriminate items on long lists like those of oral traditions. Even on short lists, they are not accurate enough to serve as effective cues except near the ends of the lists (Glenberg & Swanson, 1986; Johnson, 1991; Jones, 1976; Neath & Crowder, 1990). The genre- and song-specific cuing is often implicit. That is, the cuing can operate without the singer's conscious awareness of the use of the cues. These implicit cues "activate" and help "discriminate" the responses that follow. The time course of such activation depends on the particular constraint, though little is known of such timing outside the constraint of meaning.

The individual properties of theme and associative meaning discussed in Chapter 2, of spatial and object imagery discussed in Chapter 3, of rhythm and the poetic devices of rhyme, alliteration, and assonance discussed in Chapter 4, and their interaction as discussed in Chapter 5 come into play as the piece is sung, varying according to the extent and manner in which they are present in the genre and the piece. The general properties of each constraint as limits to choices and as cues to recall have been presented, emphasizing that the nature of each contribution is different. Thus, for instance, rhyme is expected to cue more broadly than associative meaning, and the thematic structure will help to organize events sequentially. At very short time intervals, in short lists, constraints such as the ones considered in Chapters 2 through 4 can disrupt order information. However, at longer intervals this does not seem to occur (Nairne, 1990; Nairne & Neumann, 1993), and in longer passages where order is not just among a few easy to isolate items, constraints can help order information by distinguishing where in the longer list the related items occur.

The local, implicit, word-by-word or phrase-by-phrase cuing is the dominant form in oral traditions, whereas more global organization is present in many other kinds of materials and tasks, including the recall of texts most commonly studied in the psychological laboratory. The poetic devices of rhyme, alliteration, and assonance work locally within lines and between nearby lines. Meaning and imagery also appear to function mostly in a local, serial fashion to limit choices and to increase the discriminability of items in memory. Of all the constraints discussed earlier in the book, rhythm is the most effective globally because the specific rhythm being used in the line or stanza being sung is usually the same specific rhythm that is used in all lines or stanzas. The local organization is the global organization. Because the same rhythm repeats, it does not provide much discriminability by itself. However, rhythm does combine with and accentuate other constraints to increase discriminability, and it does change the organization from one long list into a hierarchy of sublists that can benefit more from the discriminability of serial position. Rhythm also provides a framework so that when recall fails locally, it can begin again more easily at another rhythmic location by using the rhythm alone or the rhythm with other cues.

As an example, consider a singer familiar with the genre starting to sing a particular ballad. The singer knows implicitly, and sometimes even explicitly, that the ballad will have four lines to every stanza, with four iambic feet on each line, with lines 2 and 4 rhyming, and so forth. Once the first stanza is completed, the local imagery and theme up to that point will cue and constrain the imagery and theme of the second stanza. More general and global associations to the main characters and type of ballad, as well as foreshadowing of events to come that are given by specific formulas, may also function. The model of cue–item discriminability put forth earlier in the chapter can be applied here, but in serial fashion, with each word output changing the cuing for words yet to be recalled. Once the first few words of the second stanza are sung, an alliteration at the beginning of the first line will cue its alliterative pair later in the line. Once the end of the second line is sung, the rhyme sound at the end of the fourth line will be set. By the time the second stanza is completed, most of the direct cuing effects of the singing of the first stanza will be lost, though many of the constraints set remain effective through the singing of the later stanzas. Although a rhyme between the last words of lines 2 and 4 of stanza 17 is expected by the singer after singing the first stanza, the particular rhyming words or even the rhyming sound are not yet known.

As a second example, consider applying the theory to the variant of *Eenie Meenie* given in Chapter 1. As the recall begins, the entire sound pattern of the word *eenie* will cue the word *meenie,* in which it is embedded. *Meenie* will cue *miney* through rhyme and *miney* and *mo* through alliteration. Once *mo* is recited, completing the first line, the meter of the piece is set, as is the *mo, toe, go, mo* end-rhyme pattern. The word *catch* begins a short stretch of narrative and syntactic structure, and possibly an imagined scene in which thematic, syntactic, and imagery cuing can take place. For a short piece like this, the serial nature of the unfolding of the cuing may not be necessary, but it is for longer pieces.

Kintsch (1988) presents an example of an implementation of a model consistent with the one proposed here. Many alternatives are first considered, but the constraints of the situation act over time to aid in the choice of the most likely alternative. The model has even been applied to the counting-out rhymes discussed in Chapter 10 (Kintsch, 1994). There is general support for the idea that many alternatives are available for a fraction of a second and then reduced by constraints (e.g., Kintsch, 1988; Schwanenflugel & LaCount, 1988; Schwanenflugel & Shoben, 1985; but see Stolzfus, Hasher, & Zacks, 1992; Tabossi, 1988). Moreover, the more constraints present, the fewer alternatives are activated (Schwanenflugel & LaCount, 1988). Detailed analyses of the role of each constraint as it operates in real time need to be developed in future research. For instance, empirical comparisons of the time courses of all the various constraints are not available, though activation-like processes do exist in rhyme (Hillinger, 1980; Meyer, Schvaneveldt, & Ruddy, 1974) and in syntactic form (Bock, 1986, 1989; Bock & Loebell, 1990; Levelt & Kelter, 1982), as well as in the studies of meaning just cited. In addition, although there are theories of thematic structure of text, many need to be adapted from a static theory of overall structure to a serial, sequential theory of performance. Thus the general outline of a theory based on what is known about cuing in general will be given rather than a detailed one based on parametric studies.

It follows from such a process that a pair of lines or words that are linked together by theme, rhyme, or alliteration will not necessarily be recalled more often than other pairs of words. However, if the first member of the pair is recalled, then the second will almost certainly follow. Moreover, without some form of organization or constraint, there can be little cuing except for specific item-to-item or location associations learned for the particular piece. Not only does this make a piece without organization difficult to remember, but if the serial recall fails at some point, it will be hard to start again at another point in the piece. If there is a strong global organization, such as rhythmic units that repeat throughout the piece or a local organization that spans several words, phrases, or lines, then these organizations can be used to start recall again at a new point after a gap. Such organization decreases the marked primacy, or increased recall of the early items in a list, noted in the serial recall of unorganized lists.

The process of remembering just outlined looks much like the process of composition. In fact, no distinction is made in the basic way cuing and item selection works. Songs with highly constrained choices will be more stable than those with fewer constraints; the words from previously sung variants will have fewer alternatives, and those alternatives will be more likely to be cued again. In creating a new song about a new topic, clearly dominant items discriminated by cues probably will not be present in memory, and therefore no dominant items will be recalled. When a singer uses the process outlined here, some words will just flow, but at times there will be no item discriminated by the cues available in the time allowed by the rhythmic constraints of the song, and singing will stop. Conscious effort or a longer time for unconscious search will be needed, perhaps long enough for the singer to "sleep on it." Thus in the theory of serial recall for oral traditions put forth, the creation of novel patterns occurs when existing patterns are not cued. In traditions where innovation rather than stability is valued, a modification is required. A premium must be put on solutions that are not repetitions. In addition, the constraints must be weak enough to allow variation. Nonetheless, to the extent that stability is desired, creativity that leads to novel changes is a failure of memory.

Applying the Theory to Serial Recall Outside Oral Traditions

The general approach in this section is to start with the simplest, least organized situation and then to add forms of constraint, examining their effects on recall. In this way the theory can be examined, first using relatively simple material, with new factors added as successive passages are considered. Instead of using artificial stimuli for this purpose, existing studies of serial recall of text are used. Two sets of examples of serial recall outside oral traditions are given: "sacred" poems and texts that American undergraduates are likely to have once learned, such as the Gettysburg Address; and songs by the Beatles. They were chosen because they provide a scale of increasing constraint and because, unlike oral traditions, there is a generally accepted correct version of the stimulus text against which recalls can be scored. In this way, the theory outlined could be initially tested against existing recall data.

The first set of examples is the recall of culturally important material such as Psalm 23 and the Preamble to the Constitution of the United States, for which there is an implicit demand characteristic to recall the material accurately or not at all (Rubin, 1977). Each of the 50 columns in Figure 8.1 show the recall of 1 of 50 undergraduates, who recalled at least one word of the Preamble. Each row represents recall for one word. A dark line in a column means that the word labeling the row was recalled. The columns are ordered so that the data from the undergraduate who recalled the most are in the leftmost column and the data from the undergraduate who recalled the least are in the rightmost column. The rows are in the order in which the words appear normally in each text.

The first observation to note is the regularity of the data. Figure 8.1 gives the recalls of 50 individuals for 52 words, not the averages of recalls from groups of individuals or groups of words. There was no control over the learning or practice of the material or over the length or contents of the retention interval. Yet the figure is remarkably orderly. People who recall about the same amount recall the same words. If the number of words a person recalls and the rank ordering of words from most to least likely for the group from which the person was drawn is known, exactly

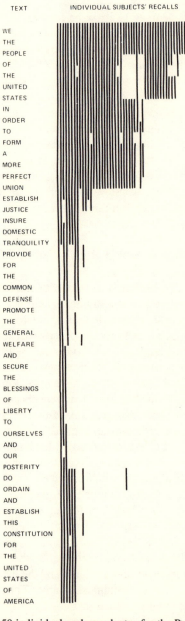

Figure 8.1. The recall of 50 individual undergraduates for the Preamble to the Constitution. (From Rubin, 1977)

which words that person recalled can be predicted with an accuracy of 95% for Figure 8.1.

Because the conditions of learning and retention varied, there must be something in the material, in the process used to recall it, or in the general cultural attitudes to it that makes different people behave the same way. In 1977, I put emphasis on the "sacred" nature of the material that made it different from the stories usually studied by psychologists. This difference could account for the lack of synonyms and other changes in the texts, but not for all the other regularities that fall out naturally once serial recall is considered. The serial nature of recall also offers an additional reason for the verbatim recall once any premium is placed on recalling some of the same words. If a synonym is recalled instead of the original word, the synonym will not possesses all the associations unique to the original word, and may not possess all the other rhythmic and sound-pattern properties of the original word. Thus the synonym will not be as good a cue, and recall will be more likely to end. Recall can proceed on a proposition-by-proposition level, but not if exact words, rhythm, or other nonthematic constraints are to be easily preserved. Translating from an abstract proposition to words of a fixed, rhythmic form is not easy.

Detailed examination of the 50 recalls provides a sense of the processes being used. The undergraduates recalling the Preamble started at the beginning and, with a few exceptions, went as far as they could and then stopped. The five people represented by the five rightmost columns of Figure 8.1 recalled the least of the Preamble. They all recalled the first 3 words and stopped. Another group recalled the first 7 words and stopped, and another the first 14. The stopping points are informative. They can be seen as normal places to take a breath, as intonation units of spoken English (Chafe, 1990; Chafe & Danielowicz, 1987), or as phrases and sentences of written English (Aaronson & Scarborough, 1977). On occasion, whole intonation units or phrases are omitted. For instance, several people recalled 6 of the first 10 words, leaving out the phrase "of the United States." If people do start recalling after a gap, they do so at a natural break. For instance, the undergraduates who began again at the end of the Preamble did so at the beginning of the last sentence. In quantitative terms, we can define a stopping point as two or more words correctly recalled followed by two or more omissions, and a starting point as two or more words omitted followed by two or more words correctly recalled; and we can have people judge the normal place to pause for a breath (Johnson, 1970). For the Preamble, 94% of the stopping and starting points fall on the breath pauses, though only 39% would be expected by chance.[1]

Once people missed a few words of the Preamble, they rarely continued their recall: five people recalled the first 3 words and stopped, nine people recalled the first 7 words and stopped; and nine other people recalled the first 15 words and stopped. For the Preamble, people start at the beginning, and the only cues they have with which to recall the next part are the local associations from what they have already said. There is no clear repeating rhythm, overall theme, or other global structure. Predictions of exactly which words each undergraduate recalled in each condition were made by assuming that if *n* words were recalled, they were the first *n* words in order starting from the beginning. These predictions were correct 93% of the time, almost as high as from the group rank order of most to least likely to be recalled.

When American undergraduates recall the Gettysburg Address, they also tend to start at the beginning and go as far as they can, remembering from the beginning that there were 87 years from the founding of the country to the speech, while forgetting from the end "that government of the people, by the people, for the people, shall not perish from the earth." Although this observation poses problems for explanations based on recall of the most important items, it is consistent with the primacy expected from serial recall of a passage without added cues. If cues are added, however, the cuing of later items only by a chaining of the words and phrases leading up to them is broken, and more can be remembered from the end of the piece. The overall meaning also could act as a cue, but this does not appear to be available. As with oral traditions, storage in serial fashion is often not conducive to understanding. Although many Americans can directly recall anecdotes about the conditions under which the Preamble, Gettysburg Address, or national anthem was originally written or delivered, they cannot provide a summary of the pieces themselves without first recalling them in order and then analyzing their own recalls, a point that will be returned to later when the distinction between implicit and explicit memory is discussed.

Three cuing conditions were paired with the request for the recall of the Gettysburg Address: (1) no additional cues, (2) all content words (Fries, 1952) replaced by blanks of uniform length so that the passage would begin "_____ and _____ _____ _____ our _____ _____ _____ on this _____ a _____ _____," and (3) the same format with the first letter of words added, making it "F_____ and s_____ y_____ a_____ our f_____ b_____ f_____ on this c_____ a n_____ n_____." The first letter cue is an attempt to mimic the effects of alliterative cues common in counting-out rhymes, ballads, and other oral traditions. Here initial letters are given directly instead of having the initial sound of one word cue the initial sound of another nearby word. Undergraduates recalled 8%, 11%, and 26% with the three cuing conditions, respectively. Thus the function words with blanks added little, and most of the effect can be attributed to the first-letter, alliteration-like cuing.[2] Moreover, primacy decreases; that is, words from later in the piece are more likely to be recalled. Predictions of exactly which words each undergraduate recalled in each condition were made by assuming that if n words were recalled, they were the first n words in order starting from the beginning. For the three cuing conditions the predictions were correct 97%, 94%, and 79% of the time. Because the percentage of words recalled varied, changing the accuracy of the predictions that would be made if the data were random, a better measure for comparison is the Index of Consistency (Green, 1956), which equals (prediction − chance)/(100 − chance). For the three cuing conditions, the Index of Consistency is 79%, 68%, and 36%. Again, the first letter, and not the function words with blanks, produced most of the effect.

For the list-like structure of the Preamble and for the Gettysburg Address, the serial-recall cue–item-discriminability theory describes the behavior. People start at the beginning, with each word or phrase serving as a cue to increase the cue–item discriminability of what follows. Once such cuing stops, and especially if the next phrase cannot be cued, there is no way to carry on. Additional cues, such as the alliteration-like-first letter cues, increase cue–item discriminability and allow the serial-cuing process to begin at a new point. In serial recall, the presentation or recall of a word aids the recall of the next word, but other words can hinder recall.[3]

In oral traditions, arguments about the rapid time course of singing (Lashley, 1951) and the planning needed to coordinate breathing and the other articulatory movements needed in singing (Lenneberg, 1967) make it impossible for singers to wait to hear their own words before starting to sing the next word. The running start cannot always be cuing from overt behavior, but must include planning for production if the chaining concept is to fit the physiological limits of the timing of production for adjacent words.

As considered in Chapter 2, the internal mechanisms hypothesized in the construction of a theory are difficult or impossible to determine uniquely from behavior, so no commitment is made to any particular formulation here. If a functioning theory were to be constructed for a particular genre, mechanisms would have to be specified, even if they were not the only possible ones. However, for purposes of exposition and continuity, the cue–item network-activation model is used.[4]

Alliteration differs in one crucial way from the first-letter cues used with the Gettysburg Address. According to the serial-recall theory, alliteration can increase the cue–item discriminability of a word only after the nearby previous alliterating word has been reached, whereas the first-letter cues were given together at the beginning of the cuing. For this reason, alliteration would not be expected to have such a large effect in cuing, except locally, and this is the case. In Chapter 11, evidence is presented that rhyme and alliteration have a large role in determining whether rhyming or alliterating words are recalled and whether their recall is verbatim or with a synonym, but that these repetitions of sound patterns have a small effect on the recall of the piece as a whole. The same point is made later in this chapter with data from the recall of Beatles' songs. There is, however, a cue that does work throughout a piece to provide cuing without the need of recently recalled words. That cue is rhythm.

As discussed in Chapter 4, in oral traditions rhythm is often set by the genre rather than by the particular piece, and even when it depends on the particular piece, it is set after very little of the piece is sung. Thus after a very short running start, the rhythm is determined and can provide cues throughout the piece. The meter of the first line or stanza, therefore, is the meter for all lines or stanzas of the song. In this way, rhythm is a local specific cue that functions as a global cue, helping to overcome the marked primacy effects noted in the free recall of the Preamble and the Gettysburg Address. With the help of rhythmic cues, which provide structure to the whole piece even though individual words may not be known, serial recall can progress, providing additional words with specific cues to improve local cue–item discriminability. In terms of classical verbal-learning theory, without rhythm and other global forms of organization, only associative chaining of words or phrases could be important in a long piece. Rhythm provides markers that allow serial position within a piece to also act as a salient cue.[5]

Rhythm is a constraint, like others, limiting word choice and making words with the correct number of syllables or stress pattern more discriminable. But rhythm also has additional integrative roles. Rhythm provides an organizing principle that allows all aspects of the performance to be integrated. This includes the timing of different individuals' behaviors (Condon, 1982), as well as the timing of the verbal component with the body movements and music within one individual (Handel, 1989, chap. 11). A related role of rhythm is to emphasize certain locations within lines facilitating other constraints—for example, by emphasizing rhyme and alliteration that are placed on stressed syllables. Rhythm also provides an organized hierarchy of rhythmic units; for example, syllables form feet, which form lines, which form stanzas, and these rhythmic units typically coincide with meaning units in oral traditions (Bakker, 1990; Lord, 1960; Parry, 1928/1971a, 1928/1971b). This hierarchy of meaningful, rhythmic units allows singers to select, substitute, add, or delete whole rhythmic units while producing a coherent piece. Moreover, these rhythmic units, at all levels of the rhythmic hierarchy, create gaps that need to be filled. They do not allow the omission of part of a rhythmic unit; only certain whole rhythmic units, such as those at the level where melody repeats (e.g., the line of epic or the stanza of ballads), can be omitted. The demand to recall something rhythmically appropriate encourages something to be produced even when cue–item discriminability is low. In this way, rhythm functions to increase variation as well as stability. In all these functions, rhythm is a local constraint that is the same throughout a piece and therefore acts as a global constraint known before a particular part of the piece is reached.

One way to look at rhythm is to examine a piece with a strong rhythmic structure. Figure 8.2 presents data in the same form as Figure 8.1, but for Psalm 23.[6] The psalm shows the same pattern as the Preamble, except that not all the undergraduates started with the first words, and they were more likely to start again at the beginning of a new sentence or intonation unit after they stopped. In terms of the serial-recall theory, there are more genre cues for the Psalm 23, due to its poetic structure, than for the single-sentence prose Preamble, with its long, embedded list of goals. The pieces, however, differ along many dimensions, so within-piece comparisons are easier to analyze.

A more direct way to emphasize rhythmic cuing is to use music. American undergraduates were asked to recall their national anthem while incorrect music (*Stars and Stripes Forever*), no music, or the correct music was playing. The music had the expected effect on the amount of recall, with 35%, 40%, and 65% recalled in the three conditions, respectively. The correct music also succeeded in reducing the strict serial-recall primacy effect, with the Index of Consistency values for the primacy prediction for the three conditions being 45%, 57%, and −.02%, respectively. Thus primacy was a good predictor of recall in the incorrect-music and no-music conditions, though not as good as it was with the list-like Preamble. However, when the correct music was added, it provided a cue that allowed people to begin again at major metrical units, and primacy failed to predict which words they would recall beyond chance levels.

In terms of the theory put forth here, the additional cues increase cue–item discriminability and thus recall. Once a piece is begun, the running start provides cues that work locally on the next words to be recalled. If recall stops, however, there is often little to cue the remaining text. For most stories in our culture, the

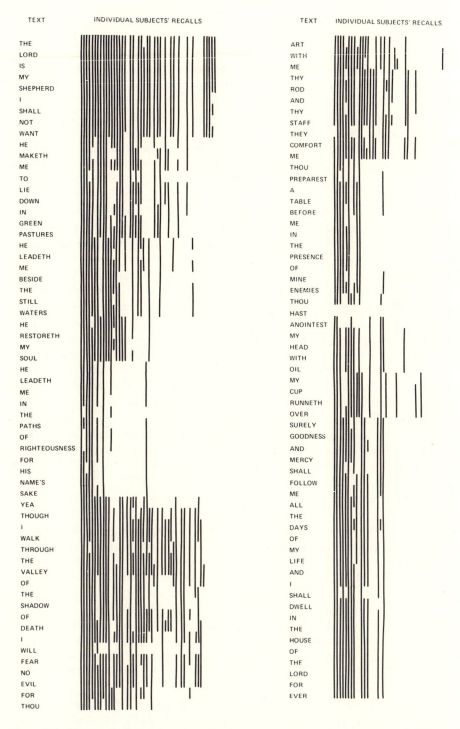

Figure 8.2. The recall of 50 individual undergraduates for Psalm 23. (From Rubin, 1977)

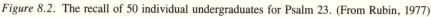

185

theme can serve as a cue to the recall of later parts of a story, but for the poetic material of oral traditions, theme appears of less use. As discussed in Chapter 2, global thematic organization in oral traditions appears to operate through local connections (Ong, 1982). For instance, in Chapter 11, ballads are shown to have to have sophisticated thematic organizations, but these can be argued to depend more on local sequential associations than on an initial plan (Lord, 1991b). Different types of cues provide a way to proceed past a gap in memory to new sections by increasing cue–item discriminability. Examples of such cues include a melodic or rhythmic structure, or cues added throughout the piece in the first-letter cuing in the Gettysburg Address experiment. These cues are needed not only to aid memory, but also if a piece is to be shortened, expanded, or altered during performance.

The second set of examples is songs by the Beatles (Hyman & Rubin, 1990). Although not an oral tradition, they are a genre, or subgenre, with many properties found in oral traditions, and they were known by many of the undergraduates tested between 1983 and 1985. The analyses presented are for 25 songs from the corpus of over 200 songs.

Each line was assigned a value on each of the following variables: the percentage of undergraduates who remembered the line as part of an attempt to recall the whole song, given its title and first line; ratings of how central each line was to the total image of the song, the total meaning of the song, and the ease with which each line aroused an emotion; the number of times the line repeated (repetition); the order of the line in the song and within its verse (primacy); whether the line shared content words with the title; the number of other lines whose last word rhymed with the last word of the line; the number of other lines whose first word alliterated with the first word of the line; and measures of rhyme, alliteration, and assonance within each line, as well as within each verse. Rhythm and music are among the most obvious constraints of the genre and, as just argued, one of the most important for recall. They are omitted here as predictors because they were relatively constant throughout each song and therefore could not be used to make differential predictions about which lines of a song would be recalled.

Of these variables, only three were of value in predicting recall: primacy, repetition, and whether the line shared content words with the title. This finding is consistent with the serial-recall cue–item-discriminability theory if the people who produced the recalls did not have an overall theme or image of the songs. The first predictor, primacy, would be expected from serial recall if no other cues were operating, though its role was probably reduced from what it would have been without the rhythmic cues. The second predictor, the number of times a line repeated in the song, may work simply because repeated lines were heard more often and thus were learned better. In addition, some repeating lines are part of a chorus that starts its own rhythmic unit, as did the starting points in Psalm 23. The third predictor was whether lines shared content words with the title, which was the cue given for recall of the song. Shared words provide strong cue–item discriminability that does not depend on sequential recall.

Nonetheless, at the time the analysis was first done, before the serial-recall theory was formulated, we were puzzled about why the normally important variables of meaning, imagery, and emotion, and the poetic sound patterns that are an integral part of the genre, were not more important. The student ratings of meaning, imagery, and emotion were reliable and moderately high. The poetic sound patterns were frequent within lines and verses, as were the poetic links among lines: even with repeated lines excluded and with a stricter definition of rhyme than the Beatles used (Zwicky, 1976), most of the last words of lines rhymed with other lines and most of the first words of lines alliterated with other lines. In the context of the theory and the earlier results, these findings are understandable. Although the songs have meaning, few have a narrative structure or an image that the undergraduates could use to guide recall; the meaning occurred at the local level of a line or phrase in most songs. Thus in most songs, meaning, image, and emotion could not act as a way to escape from a strict sequential progression, and functioned much as poetic sound patterns of rhyme and alliteration do. Once a line was reached, its meaning, image, emotional content, rhyme, and alliteration could function to cue nearby lines and make certain words and phrases more discriminable, but such constraints could not be used to escape from primacy. This finding is not unique to Beatles' songs. A similar conclusion is drawn for a different type of recall study of ballads in Chapter 11.

To test the ideas of sequential cuing in serial recall, the data from the published Beatles study were reanalyzed. Each of the 25 songs was recalled by 38 students. To accomplish this formidable task, twice that number of students were used, each recalling approximately half the songs. Tables were made for each song, much like Figures 8.1 and 8.2, but here, following the scoring presented in the published paper, the units of the tables were lines rather than words. As with Figures 8.1 and 8.2, the tables were searched for starting points in recall defined by two or more unrecalled units followed by two or more recalled units, as well as for stopping points in recall defined by two or more recalled units followed by two or more unrecalled units. If the basic ideas being argued here are correct, these starting and stopping points should occur more frequently where there is no interline organization.

The first analysis taken was to divide the breaks between lines into those that occurred within a verse and those that occurred between verses. Starting and stopping points fell on 10.5% of the possible opportunities between verses versus 2.5% of the possible opportunities within verses. Thus the students were almost four times as likely to start or stop recalling at a verse break.[7]

The second analysis paralleled the first, but examined the role of end rhyme. The analysis was restricted to breaks within verse, where most end rhyme occurs, to avoid confounding rhyme effects with the powerful verse effect just noted. The within-verse breaks were divided into those that fell between and those that did not fall between end rhymes. End rhymes were restricted to those that were either on adjacent lines or one line apart. Thus in rhyme schemes such as *abbc,* the one break between the *b*'s is within a rhyme. In rhyme schemes such as *abcb,* the two breaks between the *b*'s are within a rhyme. From the verse analysis, we know that 2.5% of the possible opportunities within verses are starting or stopping points in the students' recalls. Within rhyme, this figure is 2.0% and between rhymes it is 3.0%, indicating that the students were 50% more likely to start or stop recalling where no rhyme linked the lines.[8]

If the serial-recall theory is correct, then in addition to the quantitative measures of which lines were recalled, the qualitative errors made by the undergraduates in places where they had enough cuing to produce some response should be informative. In particular, they should follow the cuing of the various properties of the genre, even though the properties did not make the lines more memorable. This was overwhelmingly the case. Instead of statistics to support this claim, a few favorite examples are offered.[9] The original line is given, with the original words that were changed in brackets and the words recalled by an undergraduate in parentheses:

> And you know you [should be glad] (can't be sad)
>
> If you say you love me [too] (true)
>
> I sit and [meanwhile] (lean right) back
>
> To help with good Rocky's [revival] (survival)
>
> Wonder how you manage to [feed the rest] (be caressed)

The substitutions preserve the rhythm, the local meaning in that they make sense in their context, and the poetic sound-pattern. For instance, when the last word of a line is changed, there is a strong tendency to preserve its rhyme or substitute another one. Some changes are impressive. There is probably no better word in the meaning, rhythmic, and sound pattern context to replace *revival* than *survival*. Following the line "Baby at your breast," an undergraduate's replacement of *feed the rest* with *be caressed* is ingenious.

Such errors occurred, but infrequently in the recalls reported earlier. For instance, the only consistent error in the recall of the Gettysburg Address was the substituting of *forefather* for *father* in the first sentence of the speech, an error that follows not only gist, alliteration, and the King James style Lincoln used (Havelock, 1978), but also the repetition of the *four* sound of *Four score and seven years ago our fathers brought forth*. Repetitions of words occur throughout the Gettysburg Address and serve to integrate the speech (Wills, 1992, pp. 171–173), perhaps increasing the salience of the repetition of the *four* sound.

Although the theory is presented in the context of memory research, as the error generation indicates, it can easily be viewed as a theory for the production or composition of a piece in an oral tradition in the sense that Lord (1960) discusses. In oral traditions, the errors noted would not be errors but variation, and the mechanism outlined to account for both the accurate recall and the errors could instead be used to account for variability in performances and for the generation of new pieces.

The Serial Recovery of Theme

Two major constraints, each the topic of an earlier chapter, were mentioned only in passing in the examples. This omission is due to the materials used in the studies presented here. None of the passages or data sets used had a narrative structure perceived clearly enough by the undergraduates to produce recalls nonsequentially, though meaning and imagery did appear to operate at a local level. This cannot be the case for expert singers in all oral traditions. For many oral traditions, the overall theme of a piece enters as a major cuing device. The omissions and changes noted by

Lord (1960) and in Chapter 9 for epic, as well as in Chapter 11 for ballads, involve narrative structures to be considered. As reviewed in Chapter 3, imagery and theme often merge in narrative, with the scene, action, and location becoming an integral part of a tale. For at least one storyteller reported in Chapter 3, the image he saw consciously cued the line he was about to sing. In the earlier chapters, the general properties of theme and imagery were outlined, and theme and imagery will be applied in the chapters that follow on individual genres. Both are important cuing devices, with theme and spatial imagery providing the clearest claim as devices used to maintain the sequence of events and with descriptive imagery increasing cue–item discriminability as each scene emerges. In serial recall, these properties provide for the more complex, often hierarchical, organization needed to account for stability and change in oral traditions.

It is the case in many oral traditions that although theme and imagery may guide recall, they are not cues that are strong enough to function on their own to retrieve material associated with a given theme or image. It is hoped that after finishing the book, the reader will be able to retrieve information to the question "What do we know about the role of rhyme in oral traditions?" without reciting the book from the beginning. That is, human memory is usually "content addressable" in that the content of some aspect of knowledge can be used to retrieve other knowledge about the topic. This kind of retrieval was not possible for some examples used in this chapter. Thus it was claimed that most undergraduates could not give the meaning of the Preamble without first recalling it serially, starting at the beginning. In these cases, it is possible that the meaning was never known. Even in oral traditions where theme plays a clear role, however, it may not be organized in global as opposed to local serial fashion, and even where global organization exists, it may not be a strong enough cue to discriminate items without the help of other cues present in a running start.

Two hedges must be noted. First, some pieces from oral traditions are difficult to summarize even when they are written out in full, the meaning being implicitly tied to the whole genre rather than explicitly to the words sung (Foley, 1990, chap. 1). It is possible, however, that this resistance to summarization is a result of the piece's having been formulated under and for oral presentation. That is, the ability to summarize is a form of expertise (Brown & Day, 1983) that may be better developed for written text. Second, Shakespearean repertory actors who have nearly perfect recall of a fixed, written corpus can access locations in their own parts with the cue of a single word from those parts (Oliver & Ericsson, 1986). It is not clear what causes this difference from other observations, but it may be the actors' need to be able to pick up a part after a distraction or their overlearning of a fixed written text. Regardless of the reason, not all recall that is usually performed serially must always be performed serially.

Serial recall without the ability to access individual items directly can exist even for a written list without any thematic organization if the list is learned to a song or using some other technique that imposes rhythmic chunking on the material (e.g., Chase & Ericsson, 1981; Staszewski, 1990). For instance, in English, children learn the alphabet to the tune of *Twinkle, Twinkle, Little Star*. The song has phrase boundaries between the letters *g* and *h*, *k* and *l*, *p* and *q*, and *v* and *w*. Even though an adult knows the alphabet well enough to search for and sort arbitrary letters, under-graduates with numerous hours of library experience still use the sequential song phrases in their search process rather than accessing the letters directly. Thus it takes them much longer to say what letters come before *h, l, q,* and *w* than before *g, k, p,* and *v,* and much longer to say what letters come after *g, k, p,* and *v* than after *h, l, q,* and *w.* The undergraduates behave as if they have to retrieve the musical phrase that contains the needed letter and then search within that phrase. Jumping over phrase boundaries takes extra time (Klahr, Chase, & Lovelace, 1983).

In oral traditions, a running start is often needed to access a section of a piece and its meaning. For instance, I once saw a singer who was performing a ballad ask the group to join in on the chorus. He tried to play the chorus, but could not. He then sang his way through the first verse to get to the chorus, commenting that he would know it when it came around. Similarly, Halpern and Foley (1978) report asking one of their singers of healing charms for clarification of a passage: "In order to retrieve that small section, she had to go back and start from the beginning" (p. 908). A third case of needing a running start in an oral tradition comes from Bruce Kapferer's attempts to obtain information from exorcists in Sri Lanka:

> I have always had trouble collecting extensive myth material. My method is usually to sit down with specialists and ask them to give me myth narratives of such and such a demon. Numbers of specialists will give this information in narrative form, highly variable and always lacking the details. But some of my informants insisted that I should seek out *mantra karaya* (mantra makers). These specialists compose different verse forms such as mantra, which are mixed language forms, or *kavi,* which are usually in vernacular but archaic. These verse forms have a defined metrical pattern.
>
> So I would approach a specialist, ask for the myth of a particular demon (always an origin myth), and they would respond. "Well, the exact details are in such and such kavi, stotra, etc. I will sing it and you tell me when the demon you want has his name mentioned. Then I will go slow so that you can put it onto your tape recorder."
>
> And this is how I proceeded. The myth information was effectively stored in song and then the "file" is opened and the data flow. (Personal communication, November 1991)

The serial-recall cue–item-discriminability process, then, requires the cues that appear only as the song is sung. The running start is needed, and the information is available only when it comes around. This is not to say that theme and imagery do not play roles in the cuing of the global organization, only that their roles are not strong enough to allow them to act as random access indices on their own.

The issue raised by this example, of what can be recalled consciously, at will, and what comes unbidden or in the course of some activity other than an attempt at recollection, is of theoretical interest to cognitive psychologists (for reviews, see Johnson & Hasher, 1987; Richardson-Klavehn & Bjork, 1988; Roediger, 1990; Schacter, 1987; Tulving, 1985; Tulving & Schacter, 1990). Terms including *explicit, direct, intentional,* and *declarative* are used to describe tasks or measures in which people consciously recollect their past. An example of explicit memory is the recall or recognition of a list at the request of an experimenter. This is the most common use of the word *memory,* but it is probably not the most common use of memory. In contrast, terms including *implicit, indirect, incidental,* and *procedural* are used to describe tasks or measures that do not explicitly mention a past event. Examples of measures of implicit memory include the ease with which words come to mind that were on a list of words that the person is unaware of having seen earlier or any other task in which past experiences affect current behavior without a recollection of those experiences. It is the kind of memory that is often spared in amnesia.

Oral traditions, as the examples indicate, involve a mix of the two. The cuing outlined in this chapter proceeds in most cases without conscious awareness or direct attempts to bring it about, yet it is often part of a conscious, willful act to sing a song. It results in knowledge being sung out loud and available to the consciousness of the singer and others. Recent work finds this combination of explicit and implicit memory necessary to predict a host of memory tasks (Nelson, Schreiber, & McEvoy, 1992). For oral traditions, verbatim recall is not produced and conscious, direct comparison with exactly what was sung the previous time is not needed. The act of singing, once begun, could thus function mostly by implicit cuing (Jacoby & Hollingshead, 1990). This could explain, in part, why laboratory recall tasks, which rely on conscious retrieval of isolated items, do not benefit as much from nonsemantic cues as does skilled singing in an oral tradition where nonsemantic cues greatly restrict the choices (Graf & Mandler, 1984).

The distinction between explicit and implicit memory can also be used to clarify one use of oral traditions. Implicit memory is *knowing how*. It shows the effects of past experience, but not in an intentional, declarative way. It is demonstrated by doing and therefore requires a situation in which the known behavior can be executed. In contrast, explicit memory is *knowing that*. It is a conscious, declarative recitation, explanation, or communication. It can occur in a situation where the behavior can be talked about but not executed. Moreover, both kinds of knowledge can vary independently for the same problem (Berry & Broadbent, 1984; Broadbent, FitzGerald, & Broadbent, 1986; Porter, 1991; Rubin, Wallace, & Houston, 1993). Implicit memory is involved in the act of singing a piece in an oral tradition, but the information transmitted by an oral tradition to a listener is the conscious, explicit, declarative knowledge that the events described in the song occurred. Thus oral traditions can transfer the implicit information necessary to sing a song into a song containing explicit information.

In terms of cultural transmission, implicit memory can survive for events that can be performed frequently enough at one period to allow for mastery by one person and frequently enough thereafter to allow opportunities for observation and modeling by others. Thus routines of daily life can remain available to implicit memory, without the use of explicit memory. Explicit, but not implicit, memory can survive where opportunities for execution are less frequent, but opportunities to talk about the behavior are available. Explicit memory is also useful to educate people about events before they can be observed. Cultural knowledge that can be codified in terms of language can be transformed from knowledge that exists only as implicit memory to knowledge that exists as explicit memory. Storage and transmission of such knowledge in a nonliterate culture is often the task of oral traditions.

Rhythmic singing increases the stability of a piece in a culture that relies on human memory for the preservation of verbal material. This benefit aside, it appears that Plato was right: the reliance on implicit serial cuing means that the songs of oral poets are difficult to analyze until they are written.[10]

A theory was proposed for recall in oral traditions. Recall starts with the first word of the song and proceeds in a linear fashion. Words sung are cues for words yet to be sung. If words are to be recalled, they must be discriminated from other words in memory. The general constraints of the genre and piece, especially rhythm, act as cues from the start, with the singing filling in other cues as it progresses. A piece fitting the constraints of the genre results, not necessarily a verbatim reproduction of a piece produced earlier. Where the constraints are strong, they will limit variation without the help of particular cue–item associations formed when a piece was heard. Where only one variant has been heard, especially when it has been heard repeatedly using spaced practice, individual cue–item associations will be more important and will further decrease variation. This process, after the initial, often conscious decision to sing a song has been made, can go on without conscious intervention, using what has been called implicit or indirect memory. The serial-recall method, however, means that knowledge in oral traditions is not routinely accessed without the cues provided by a running start and often cannot be accessed without them. Thus questions about the contents of a piece can often be answered only after the piece is sung.

Notes

1. For details of the analysis, see Rubin (1977); $p < .001$.

2. $F(2,50) = 77.17$. No control group was found that had not heard the Gettysburg Address, but it is unlikely that the cues would have helped such a group much.

3. Giving randomly selected words from a list as cues in free recall lowers the probability of recall of the remaining words of the list (Slamecka, 1968, 1969), in part because the given words compete with the target words at retrieval (Roediger, Stellon, & Tulving, 1977) and in part because individuals' preferred patterns of organization are disrupted (Basden, Basden, & Galloway, 1977). These results are from lists of words that can be recalled in any order. In serial recall, the order of recall is fixed, and words from a list as cues can help instead of hurt recall (Matt Serra, personal communication, December 1993).

4. This provides the opportunity to join the modeling world by reducing the cue–item-discriminability-network-activation-serial-recall theory to its acronym, CIDNASR. Actual models that progress in a serial fashion exist and are successful at the tasks set for them (Kintsch, 1988; Lewandowsky & Murdock, 1989; St. John, 1992), the Lewandowsky and Murdock model accounting for many laboratory serial-learning data using chaining. In addition, serial, constraint-driven models of comprehension exist and can guide the general approach used here (e.g., Gernsbacher, 1990; Just & Carpenter, 1987, 1992). However, because they concentrate on comprehension and use only the constraints of theme, syntax, and visual form, they are of little direct guidance to the task of serial recall in oral traditions.

5. Meaning and imagery, when added later in this section, will require more complex and more recent theories from verbal learning and cognitive psychology, such as hierarchical structures and sequencing of higher-level nodes, rather than the sequencing of only the words or phrases sung. For a more complete review of the extensive literature on serial learning, especially its philosophical and historical development, see the chapters on serial learning in the texts by Crowder (1976) and Kausler (1974). For a comprehensive serial approach to comprehension, see Gernsbacher (1990).

6. There are many translations of Psalm 23, so some commonly omitted single words, such as the "will" of "I will fear no evil" or the "they" of "Thy rod and Thy staff they

comfort me,'' may be due to the version learned, as well as to the omission of a word that is not critical to the meaning or rhythm of the piece. Verbatim recall was scored, though a word was scored as correct if it was used in any of several versions we consulted.

7. Lines that were sung repeatedly in a song could be scored only once because it was often not clear which occurrence was being recalled. This omission of later repetitions produced lines that appear adjacent in the tables, but were separated by repeating lines such as a chorus. In all analyses reported here, to avoid inflating the results, only breaks between lines that are sung adjacently were considered. In addition, starting and stopping points at the beginning and end of each song could not be measured because these points were defined as being bounded by on both sides by two lines.

There were 395 breaks, 71 between verses and 324 within verses. The number of starting and stopping points per break was divided by the number of possible starting and stopping points (i.e., 38) and multiplied by 100 to calculate the percentages. The difference between the 10.5% and 2.5% figures is reliable, as measured by a matched t-test on the differences between the proportion of starting and stopping points within and between verse breaks [$t(75) = 9.83$].

8. There were 156 breaks between rhymes and 168 that were not. Using the same analysis as with verses, $t(75) = 3.22$. There was no difference between adjacent and one-apart rhymes, with 1.97% and 1.98% falling on each.

9. For a full report, see Hyman and Rubin (1990).

10. This issue is considered again in the Epilogue.

CHAPTER 9

Epic and Formulaic Theory

Don't mix your genres.
Albert Lord, personal communication, August 1983

Must we give reasons for making numerical comparisons in this study of Homeric style? To those who object that a study of style ought not to be a problem in statistics we can reply that the use of figures is our only means of verifying with precision what would otherwise remain a vague impression.
Parry, 1928/1971b, p. 37

This chapter reviews the work on Homeric and South Slavic epic that led to the development of oral-formulaic theory. Homeric epic is one genre. It provides insights into the workings of oral traditions, but care must be taken not to generalize its multiple-constraint solutions to other genres. Homeric epic is an unusual genre in that it has only two major forms of organization or constraint: meter and theme. This has allowed an elegant formulaic system to develop, one that is not equaled in genres with additional constraints and a less strict meter. The process of transmission of Homeric epic can be generalized to new genres, however, if and only if the constraints of the new genres are considered.

The Greek hexameter is the key to understanding the function of the repeated phrases called *formulas,* and so it is presented in some detail. Both formulaic and psychological theories predict that the units of meaning will coincide with the units of meter, reducing the frequency of *enjambement* (the running of a syntactically complete unit of meaning such as a phrase, clause, or sentence past the end of one line and onto the next). Following Bakker (1990, 1993b), however, Homeric diction is viewed as a special form of normal speech, rather than as a special genre of written literature, resulting in even less enjambement than is usually noted. Before examining data collected from the living tradition of South Slavic epic, the other main constraint, theme, is examined. Several themes in Homeric epic are considered as scripts. Finally, a brief review of Parry and Lord's work on South Slavic epic is used to support the general view of oral transmission being argued here.

Homeric Epic and Formulaic Theory

The two Homeric epics, the *Iliad* and the *Odyssey,* together consist of about 27,000 lines. They are the written remains of a more extensive ancient Greek oral tradition of epic. The variants we have are based on a time when Greek literature was first recorded, though at that time epic traditions had existed in written form in other civilizations for more than a millennium.

On the Limitations of the Homeric Corpus

Homeric scholars try to understand Homeric texts. Cognitive psychologists try to understand cognition. In this section, I try to see what each can tell the other. In many ways, it is a fool's errand. The *Iliad* and the *Odyssey* are texts, not behaviors of a known single person or group. Using round numbers to avoid historical debates, the Homeric epics were first recorded over two and a half millennia ago (see Stanley, 1993, pp. 279–293 for a detailed, scholarly discussion). Except for fragments, papyri, and citations in other works, the first transcription and almost every transcription or copy of a transcription that followed for about a millennium and a half are lost. Worse still, there are few variants to compare, and the ones that do exist do not usually make their way into the debate on oral formulaic theory. Thus we have little record of the changes that took place in the first 1,500 years of written transmission that followed any purely oral transmission (Davison, 1962; Foley, 1990, pp. 20–31; Kirk, 1962). We have little solid evidence external to the texts about their performance or about their transfer to writing, though argument from analogy with living tradition is possible (e.g., Bowra, 1952; Lord, 1960, 1991a). The culture described in the epics must be inferred from texts and artifacts rather than from observation. The language is dead. It is a historical accident of the strength of Homeric scholarship, aided by the complex metrical constraints of the genre, that Homeric epic played a central role in the development of the study of oral traditions.

Yet Homer cannot be avoided. From Plato on, literary criticism has accumulated, producing one of the world's largest efforts to understand a poetic corpus. Milman Parry and Albert Lord, working on Homer, increased interest in the study of oral literature in many disciplines, and this book is part of that increased interest.

There is another reason to include Homeric epic here. The problem of what can be inferred from a text about the processes that produced it is a classic one, and one shared by biblical, medieval, and other researchers. Homeric epics are an interesting test because, as noted, they the limiting case: a single written text with few variants, no autograph, and large gaps in their history of written transmission.

In this and all situations, there are good and bad questions. Many questions that have been put to the existing data are unanswerable. In this collection are the following few, to which any reader of the literature on Homeric epic can add more: Did the poet compose, remember, and then later recall the epics, or did the poet compose the epics on the spot? Was the poet also the scribe who first recorded the epics? In the time before writing, were the epics, or parts of them, memorized by people who could not compose? There are aspects of the epics that favor different interpretations, and there is evidence from observations of living traditions (Lord, 1960, 1991a), but what is there in the texts that could settle such questions?

One reason many of these questions cannot be answered is that the mind that writes is not very different from the mind that does not. It has an added tool of writing at its disposal, but it can still work without it.[1] We can say that certain texts must have been transmitted through writing because they have no form of organization that could preserve them through oral transmission. A text like the *Iliad* or the *Odyssey* is not in this category, but that does not mean that its recall was not on occasion aided by writing or conscious memorization. A brilliant, literate poet or even a talented novice could produce parodies that mimic some constraints of an oral genre. With experience, both could even observe regularities in the genre that they could not explicitly state (see Chapter 11 for an example). Similarly, some changes in a text could be attributed with little ambiguity to scribal errors if the scribe were unfamiliar with the piece and genre. However, if the scribe were also a singer of the oral tradition being recorded, or even a passive receiver of that tradition, scribal errors could resemble errors from oral transmission.

A second reason many of the questions asked cannot be answered is that memorization by people is not modeled well by a tape recorder or copying machine. Nonetheless, it is these models of human memory that are implicitly contrasted to creative composition in many of the unanswerable questions. Verbatim memorization of long texts in cultures without writing has never been documented (Hunter, 1984, 1985; Chapter 7). Even in our own literate culture, people make errors in recall that make the recalled piece more like the cultural norm (Bartlett, 1932; Rubin & Kontis, 1983; Chapters 2 and 7). Thus the type of memorization often envisioned in contrasting oral and written literature is a myth in oral traditions, and the memorization, if any, that does occur can, over time, produce results that look more like oral composition.

Nonetheless, Homeric epic sets the stage for the study of living epics. Moreover, because of careful and extensive scholarship, the search for the cognitive processes and multiple constraints operating in the Homeric epics can provide insights, even if it cannot provide answers to all the questions researchers ask.

Formulaic Theory

This book is an attempt by a psychologist to understand oral traditions as human behavior rather than as literary texts. Formulaic theory can be seen as a similar, earlier attempt by scholars whose training was in the genre they studied rather than in human cognition. There are good reviews of the trials and progress of formulaic theory (Bakker, 1988; Edwards, 1986; Foley, 1988; Lord, 1986). Instead of a complete, balanced, historic approach, the enduring and less controversial empirical observations that are the basis of formulaic theory are stressed here.

Oral-formulaic theory was developed for epic, especially Homeric and South Slavic epic, and in this chapter only these epic traditions are considered. Different genres provide different solutions to the problems of oral transmission, and, as Finnegan (1977) and Foley (1988, 1992) have shown, indiscriminately applying a theory that was developed for epic to all genres of oral traditions fails. Instead, if oral-formulaic theory were to be extended, basic principles extracted from the particular ones noted for epic would have to be applied with care and adaptation to other genres. The alternative strategy used in this book is to apply principles taken from cognitive psychology to several genres. For epic, these principles need to account for the same data as oral-formulaic theory does, and to be useful, they need to provide new insights, in either this or other genres.

The view that oral traditions and all other genres are a special form of language has been presented in Chapters 4, 5, and 6. Here, support for the genre of epic comes from the work by Bakker (1990, 1993a, 1993b). Composition in epic is seen as a form of special speech—speech restricted by constraints of its genre, especially meter.

To begin, let us start with the early work of Milman Parry on the observation and formulation of regularities in the behaviors recorded as the *Iliad* and the *Odyssey*. Such regularities have a strong appeal to some psychologists (Rubin, 1989) and classicists. The interpretation of the regularities has been a difficult problem, but the regularities themselves are straightforward and have remained largely unchallenged (see, however, Austin, 1975; Shive, 1987). Parry noted that certain noun phrases consisting of a noun and one or more modifying words, called *noun–epithet formulas,* were used regularly in a given metrical context to refer to a given character. Moreover, there was usually only one such noun–epithet formula appropriate to each person in each metrical context. The discovery of this economy of noun–epithet formulas is remarkable. Later, Parry (1930) extended his findings from noun–epithet formulas to formulaic diction as a whole, creating some theoretical problems (Bakker, 1988; Visser, 1988), but for now, the description of what is least controversial is given.

Greek Hexameter

To understand Parry's findings, the basics of the meter must be appreciated.[2] First, Homeric meter is one of quantity, not stress or accent, as in modern English verse. Thus the basic distinction is between short and long syllables. Homeric epic prosody is based on the line; there is no evidence for stanzas. Each line has six feet; there are no incomplete lines. The first five feet are either dactyls (i.e., long, short, short, or – ⌣ ⌣) or spondees (– –). The last foot is always disyllabic, either – – or – ⌣.[3] Another way to say this is that, except for the last foot, the line is dactylic, but one long syllable can be substituted for two short syllables, changing a dactylic foot (– ⌣ ⌣) into a spondee (– –). However, the change from a dactyl to a spondee must not be done so often as to break the basic dactylic meter. Perhaps for this reason, the fifth foot is almost always a dactyl, so that the line does not in principle end with two spondees. The line thus can be written

$$– \underline{⌣ ⌣} \quad – \underline{⌣ ⌣} \quad – \underline{⌣ ⌣} \quad – \underline{⌣ ⌣} \quad – ⌣ ⌣ \quad – \underline{⌣}$$

where the symbol ⌣ ⌣ indicates either two short syllables or one long one.

This line is too long to be a single phrase or intonation unit. It is closer to two or even three phrases in length and is split at a *caesura.* This creates two, or occasionally three (Bakker, 1990, 1993b), phrase units of the length and syntactic struc-

ture discussed in Chapter 5.[4] The location of the caesura is not at the break between
the third and fourth feet, as might be expected from the simple grouping principles
put forth in Chapter 5, but at the locations marked with a | in the line that follows.
Bowra (1962a) attributes this to two reasons. The first reason is to avoid making the
line seem to end before it really does by having a stop at the end of a foot. The
second reason is to avoid having the end of each foot coincide with the end of a
word.[5] This provides more unity to the line rather than stressing the individual feet.
The two locations for caesuras occur about equally often, accounting for most of the
major syntactic breaks in Homeric lines. The first caesura location is called the
masculine (penthemimeral) caesura; the second, the *feminine (trochaic)* caesura.

$$- \underset{\smile\smile}{} \quad - \underset{\smile\smile}{} \quad -\,|\,\underset{=}{}\,|\,\underset{=}{} \quad - \underset{\smile\smile}{} \quad - \smile\smile \quad - \underset{\smile}{}$$

Secondary locations for breaks in the line occur as indicated by a |.[6]

$$- \underset{\smile\smile}{} \quad -\,|\,\underset{\smile\smile}{} \quad -\,|\,\underset{\smile}{}\,|\,\underset{\smile}{} \quad -\,|\,\underset{\smile\smile}{}\,| \quad - \smile\smile \quad - \underset{\smile}{}$$

The ordering of short and long syllables, and the preferred locations for breaks in
this complex metrical structure, make the fitting of words and phrases difficult.
Many words from the language cannot be used at all unless changed by the use
of a dialect or other means. For instance, words consisting of or containing a
− ∪ − or a ∪ ∪ ∪ syllable structure, though part of the language, cannot be used in
Homeric epic. Even words that do fit cannot go anywhere. The word *Agamemnon*
has a ∪ ∪ − − pattern in the nominative case and a ∪ ∪ − ∪ ∪ pattern in the
genitive case. Each of these forms fills a good portion of the line. In theory, ignoring
the caesuras and secondary breaks, *Agamemnon* in the nominative case could go in
any of the places shown below the metrical line, but in no others. The second
placement listed, however, should be excluded because it would prohibit a word
break at either caesura:

$$- \underset{\smile\smile}{} -\,|\,\underset{\smile\smile}{} \quad -\,|\,\underset{\smile}{}\,|\,\underset{\smile}{} \quad -\,|\,\underset{\smile\smile}{}\,| \quad - \smile\smile \qquad - \underset{\smile}{}$$
$$\underset{\smile\smile - -}{}$$
$$\underset{\smile \quad \smile - -}{}$$
$$\underset{\smile\smile \quad - -}{}$$
$$\underset{\smile\smile \qquad - -}{}$$

In the genitive case, *Agamemnon* could go in any of the places just shown for the
nominative except the last, which would be short one short vowel, and it could go in
the one additional place shown:

$$- \underset{\smile\smile}{} \quad -\,|\,\underset{\smile\smile}{} \quad -\,|\,\underset{\smile}{}\,|\,\underset{\smile}{} \quad -\,|\,\underset{\smile\smile}{}\,|\,- \smile \smile \quad - \underset{\smile}{}$$
$$\underset{\smile\smile - \smile\smile}{}$$

If we want the word *Agamemnon* to begin or end at a caesura or secondary break,
or at the beginning or end of the line, so that the phrase containing *Agamemnon* also
will begin or end in a preferred location, the nominative *Agamemnon* could go in
only two places:

$$- \underset{\smile\smile}{} \quad -\,|\,\underset{\smile\smile}{} \quad -\,|\,\underset{\smile}{}\,|\,\underset{\smile}{} \quad -\,|\,\underset{\smile\smile}{}\,|\,- \smile \smile \quad - \underset{\smile}{}$$
$$|\,\smile \smile \qquad - - \qquad \smile \smile \qquad - -$$

The genitive *Agamemnon* could also go in only two places:

$$- \smile \smile \quad - | \smile \smile \quad - | \smile | \smile \quad - | \smile \smile | \quad - \smile \smile \quad - \smile$$
$$| \smile \smile \quad - \smile \smile$$
$$| \smile \smile \quad - \smile \smile$$

An attraction of working with the Homeric epics is the extensive body of existing analysis. For instance, in 1942, O'Neill examined the first 1,000 nonrepeating lines of the *Iliad* and the *Odyssey,* as well as samples of other Greek hexameter, some of literate poets, noting the position of words with different long- and short-vowel patterns. He reported that words with the metrical word type of the nominative *Agamemnon,* ⌣ ⌣ ‒ ‒, begin at the masculine caesura 2% of the time, end at the end of the line 98% of the time, and occur only once anywhere else in the 2,000 lines of the Homeric epics analyzed (Table 16, p. 145).[7] That is, words with the metrical word type of the nominative *Agamemnon* occur almost exclusively in the second position shown, rarely in the first, and nowhere else, though if the restriction of beginning and ending at a boundary were relaxed, then they could appear elsewhere. Moreover, in this example and in general, what is true of the Homeric epics is true of other Greek hexameter, including that of literate poets. The metrical word type of the genitive *Agamemnon,* ⌣ ⌣ ‒ ⌣ ⌣ , occurs in the first position shown 66% of the time, occurs at the second 33% of the time, and occurs elsewhere only once in 2,000 lines (Table 18, p. 145), though again, if the restriction of beginning or ending at a break were relaxed, it could appear elsewhere.

In general, O'Neill (1942) finds that except for short words with the patterns ⌣, ‒, and ⌣ ⌣, almost all metrical word types occur in only a few of the locations that are possible in principle, based only on the basic meter of the line. That is, in addition to the restrictions placed on word location by the metrical pattern of the line itself, other restrictions, unspecified by O'Neill, further limit the location of words. Most metrical word types occur in two locations for the vast majority of their occurrences, some in one location, only a few in three locations, and only one in more than three (O'Neill, 1942, p. 114). These are the distributions of word types with given patterns of long and short vowels, not of individual words, so the cause is the metrical word type or something correlated with the metrical word type. It is not caused by the meaning of particular words. The name Agamemnon does not occur where it does in the line because Agamemnon is a hero or a king, but because of the pattern of short and long vowels in his name. For the name Agamemnon, it was suggested here that the restriction unspecified by O'Neill is the need to begin or end at a major division of the line to facilitate composition in phrases. If that restriction is the cause of O'Neill's observation, it appears to function not only for the name Agamemnon, but for all words with the metrical word type of the word *Agamemnon,* and not only in Homeric epic, but also in other Greek hexameter, including that of literate poets.[8]

Epithets

A poet must not only satisfy the metrical constraints of individual words, but also must fill the entire line. Thus, for example, any metrical space remaining on either side of *Agamemnon* must be used. To solve this problem, Homeric epic has epithets that suit both the personality of the character and the metrical holes left by the presence of the character's name in the line. The noun–epithet combinations are phrases that fill the time from one end of a line to one of the standard breaks in a line, or occasionally between two of the breaks. Thus to fill the time from the second of the secondary breaks to the end of the line when a nominative *Agamemnon* is required, there is *ruler Agamemnon,* whereas for the time between the feminine caesura and the end of the line, there is *ruler of men Agamemnon* (Parry, 1928/1971b, p. 39). For the genitive *Agamemnon* between the masculine caesura and the end of the line, there is *of Agamemnon son of Atreus* (Parry, 1928/1971b, p. 57). Moreover, these are the only noun–epithet combinations of these lengths for *Agamemnon* in the nominative and genitive case. For a given character, in a given case, in a given place in the line, there is often only one epithet that is ever added. Parry's clear statement of this system of epithets, with its startling economy, launched vast amounts of scholarship on formulaic theory and oral composition (e.g., Foley, 1985, 1988, 1990; Haymes, 1973).

As an example, let us examine epithets for the most frequently occurring character in the *Odyssey,* Odysseus, first in the nominative case. To fill the time from the last of the three secondary divisions to the end of the line, he is *brilliant (dios) Odysseus* 60 times and *noble (esthlos) Odysseus* 3 times.[9] The less frequent epithet begins with a vowel. Because Homeric verse and other Greek verse that followed tried to maintain phonetic continuity and avoid hiatus (i.e., putting a word that ends with a vowel before a word that begins with a vowel), the less frequent epithet cannot always be substituted for the more frequent. Between the second of the three secondary divisions and the end of the line, Odysseus is *resourceful Odysseus* 81 times and *city sacker (ptoliporthos) Odysseus* 4 times. The less frequent epithet begins with two consonants, which, if the preceding word ends in a short vowel, has the effect of changing the short vowel into a long vowel and thus changing its metrical pattern, allowing words that would not otherwise fit to be used in a line. Thus the two epithets for the same character and location are not always interchangeable. From the feminine caesura to the end of the line, Odysseus is *long-suffering brilliant Odysseus* 38 times. From the beginning of the line to the masculine caesura, Odysseus is *born of Zeus Odysseus* 4 times. In the genitive case, Odysseus is *of divine Odysseus* 27 times between the feminine caesura and the end of the line, and *of Laertes' son Odysseus* 12 times between the masculine caesura and the end of the line. For Odysseus in these locations, these alternatives exhaust the possibilities observed.

Overall, the degree of economy in the epithet system described by Parry is high.[10] Parry examined the 11 most frequently occurring heroes and gods in the nominative case in the four most important metrical locations (Parry, 1928/1971b, pp. 39–40). He found 55 noun–epithet combinations. Of these, he reports that 46 are unique in meaning and meter and that these 46 account for 723 occurrences in the *Iliad* and the *Odyssey.* On closer examination, because of initial vowels and double consonants, there are only two cases in which one noun–epithet pair can always substitute for another: *king Apollo son of Zeus* and *king Apollo who strikes from afar,* and *Cow-eyed queen Hera* and *white armed goddess Hera.* For other aspects of the epics, such as formulas for ships (Alexanderson, 1970), there is economy, though it is not as great as Parry found for the major heroes and gods. Economy need not be present in all epic genres as Parry's (1928/1971b) analysis of the later-written heroic hexameter of Apollonius (in Greek) and Virgil (in Latin) shows. Moreover, if the metrical constraints are not as strict as they are in Greek hexameter, an economic system of formulas is not as necessary and more variants in formula would be expected and are found (Bowra, 1952, pp. 236–238)

Economy is especially important because even a literate poet using the meter of Greek hexameter would benefit from having noun–epithet formulas to meet the meaning and rhythmic constraints. Thus formulas are not necessarily a sign of traditional oral composition. Parry argues, though, that poets not tied to a tradition that provided formulas would produce their own and would have little reason to stop with one per multiple constraint. Economy requires a unified tradition, a unity the Homeric epics have. When in an observable, living tradition epics from singers from different local traditions are combined, economy is much less than it is within a single singer (Lord, 1960, pp. 53, 144).

The economy of the system occasionally creates situations in which the epithet that fits the local rhythmic constraint may not fit the local meaning, though some mismatches are more likely caused by a habitual pattern being followed rather than by a lack of metrical alternatives (Combellack, 1965). With only one epithet to choose from for a given metrical constraint, jarring combinations occasionally occur. Nonetheless, for the main characters, the epithets remain consistent with their enduring characteristics. They are personality traits. Their repeated use gives them meanings that extend beyond any one occurrence by evoking other occurrences (Foley, 1991, 1992; see Andersen, 1985, for a similar phenomenon in ballads). Laughing Aphrodite can occur in a line where she is in tears because she is by nature happy, and swift-footed Achilles can appear in a line where he is seated because he is by nature swift. For less frequently mentioned characters, meaning on occasion seems sacrificed for meter, an observation we will see again in Chapter 11. The one-eyed monster Polyphemus gets the epithets *god-like* and *great-hearted;* the herdsman Philoetius gets the epithet *leader of men* (Bowra, 1962b). In contrast, Austin (1975) notes that the use of epithets is often sensitive to the meaning context in subtle ways, and if the available epithets are not appropriate, the poet uses a line structure that requires no epithets (also see Edwards, 1966). This situation is not unique to systems using formulas. Whenever multiple constraints need to be satisfied, solutions can occur that are less than optimal for each constraint considered individually. For most of the Homeric examples, other epithets or solutions could have been used to avoid the mismatch of meanings noted by the critic reading Homer if the poet had the time and desire to do so. But much that would be inconsistent in a written text is accepted in oral performance (Combellack, 1965).

Several points should be noted. First, when all the names of the major heroes and gods used in the *Iliad* and the *Odyssey* are considered, a sophisticated, interrelated system of meaning and meter emerges, a fact Parry uses to argue for the traditional origin of the system.[11] Second, exceptions to the system are rare. Any line-internal editing of the text that has come down to us was done by people who followed the system; therefore, for the kinds of arguments made here, the influences of literary editing are not serious.[12] Third, an epithet allows the character to be used in a certain metrical context, not a certain meaning context, though as Austin notes, changes can be made in the line to select from or eliminate epithets. Fourth, there is usually just one epithet to use in a particular location for a particular character, sometimes two. Because there are so many metrical contexts to fill, the stock of epithets is large, but not much larger than it has to be. Fifth, some epithets are used for only one character; others fit more than one. So, only Odysseus is *brilliant long-suffering,* but both Odysseus and Achilles, who have names with the same metrical pattern in the nominative case, share the epithet *brilliant* (or *divine*) and share it with 30 other heroes of varying status (Parry, 1928/1971b, pp. 84–85, 146–147). The metrical pattern of *brilliant long-suffering* could also be used with Achilles, but its meaning is saved for Odysseus, though it is used to describe him in the *Iliad* before he begins his long odyssey of suffering. Similarly, the names Menelaos and Diomedes have the same metrical pattern and the same epithet, *of the great war cry,* though here it is possible that the meaning was initially attached to their characters because of the metrical pattern of their names.

Taken together, these observations reveal a system that would allow a singer to meet the meaning and rhythmic constraints of the genre. The observations are used by Parry to support a theory of oral composition, but as discussed in Chapter 8, they also could support a theory of memory and of retrieval cuing. Since the theme requires a given character to perform an action that fills a portion of the line, if an epithet exists for that character that helps fill the remainder of the line, it will be cued by the constraints.

There has been concern that this mode of composition reduces the poet to a child playing with building blocks, an impression that readers and literary critics do not obtain from the texts. The concern is misguided (Smith, 1978, pp. 57–64). In the strongest extension of oral–formulaic theory, noun–epithet pairs can be viewed as the words with which the Homeric poet composes. Using this metaphor, the vocabulary of the modern poet is larger, perhaps because the works of the modern poet can be handed down outside human memory. Neither modern poets using words nor Homeric poets using noun–epithet phrases, no matter how creative, can greatly increase their respective vocabularies of words or noun–epithet phrases, though both can make occasional changes and additions. Nonetheless, neither needs to be viewed as a child playing with blocks.

Formula

The noun–epithet formulas are not the only combinations noted by Parry that fit both a meaning and a metrical constraint. These noun–epithet pairs are one type of the more general term *formula,* which Parry (1928/1971b) defined as "an expression regularly used, under the same metrical conditions, to express an essential idea" (p. 13), where *an essential idea* might be "when day broke," "he went," "said to him," or "Odysseus" (Parry, 1928/1971b, p. 14). From the examples and text, this early definition is clear enough when it is applied to the genre for which it was developed. Consider the following phrases that begin lines in the *Iliad* and the *Odyssey* that are completed by the subject phrase *brilliant long-suffering Odysseus* (*polútlas dîos Odyusseu's*) (Parry, 1928/1971b, p. 11). To indicate the rhythmic pattern, a transliteration is given in which long vowels are indicated by a ^ and the syllables stressed by the meter are underlined.[13]

And him, he answered	*ton d' êmeibet' epeita*
And in his turn he spoke to him	*ton d' aute proseeipe*
But he was pondering	*autar ho mermêrixe*
Seeing her, he rejoiced	*tên men idôn gêthêse*
So he spoke and he rejoiced	*hôs phato gêthêsen de*
So he spoke and he shuddered	*hôs phato rîgêsen de*
So he spoke and he smiled	*hôs phato meidêsen de*

Moreover, if we take one of these ways to begin a line, *And him, he answered,* we find that it begins not only a line ending with *brilliant long-suffering Odysseus,* but with all of the following (Parry, 1928/1971b, p. 10):

aged horseman Nestor	*gerênios ippota Nestôr*
cow-eyed queen Hera	*boôpis potnia Hêrê*
swift-footed brilliant Achilles	*podarkes dîos Akhilleus*
Menelaos of the loud war cry	*boên agathos Menelâos*
old Priam looking like a god	*gerôn Priamos theoeidês*
owl-eyed goddess Athena	*theâ glaukôpis Athêna*
Poseidon the earth shaker	*Poseidâôn enosikhthôn*
very thoughtful Penelope	*periphrôn Pênelopeia*

In all, throughout the *Iliad* and the *Odyssey,* there are at least 40 subject phrases made up of a noun and one or two epithet words that fill the same metrical form as *brilliant long-suffering Odysseus*—that is, phrases that begin with a single consonant and fill the line from the feminine caesura to the end. Throughout the corpus, there are 25 predicate phrases that precede *brilliant long-suffering Odysseus,* phrases that fill the time until the feminine caesura and end in a short vowel. If the meaning of any of the 40 × 25, or 1,000, combinations were needed, it would be available in a form that would fit the metrics of the line, though only a few of the combinations account for most of the usage and these often occur in combinations that form whole lines (Austin, 1975).[14]

Noun–epithet formulas are only one way to meet the dual metrical and meaning constraints. Visser (1988) examined all 60 cases in the *Iliad* in which the metrical unit of a single complete line expressed the meaning "X killed Y." Because the killing is described briefly, the victim is always a minor character. All such lines, by the definition of selection, had to have a killer, a victim, and a verb meaning "to kill." In addition, they all had a conjunction that set off and joined the line to the previous discourse of the text of a hero killing many victims. None of the lines, according to Visser, had noun–epithet formulas to fill out the meter. Rather, they depended on verbs and conjunctions of different metrical length. Moreover, when the verbs and conjunctions were examined as a function of their metrical pattern of long and short syllables and whether they began or ended with a consonant or vowel, there was economy. For instance, the shortest verb was *take* (*hel'*), in the sense of to take someone's life, which has the metrical form ⌣. It is the only verb used with this metrical pattern. There are two forms of the verb *take* with the metrical form ⌣ ⌣, one ending with a consonant (*helen*) and the other with a vowel (*hele*). The list progresses in length to two forms of *loosed the knees of* that have the metrical form ⌣ ⌣ – ⌣ ⌣ – ⌣. One ends with a consonant (*hupo gounat' elusen*), and the other ends with a vowel (*hupo gounat' eluse*). The hexameter of the literate poet Quintus, from Smyrna, does not show economy in this way. In addition, as with noun–epithet formulas, the selection of verbs does not depend in any obvious way Visser could find on the meaning context, only on the metrical context. In short, the same analysis that was made for the noun–epithet formulas can be made, at least for the example tried, for verb forms and conjunctions.

A different way of composing within the constraints of the meter is by changing the metrical pattern of long and short syllables of the words used. There are many ways to do this. A few are given in their simplest form to provide the reader with a sense of the constraints and flexibility, even though a more complete description of the metrical principles is beyond the scope of this work. Homeric Greek has words with identical meanings and syntactic function that exist in more than one form. Both the main hero of the *Iliad,* Achilles, and the main hero of the *Odyssey,* Odysseus, have names with the same metrical word type of ⌣ – – in the nominative. Both heroes have an alternative form of their name with a single consonant (e.g., Odyseus versus Odysseus). The single as opposed to the double consonant marks the change in the vowel from long to short, making the metrical word type ⌣ ⌣ –. This opens a new pattern of possible locations for the name within a line. For some verbs, like *take* and *loosen* in Visser's example, it is possible to add the optional "mobile nu" Ionian ending. The /n/ sound at the end of the word can do more than prevent a hiatus (i.e., a word ending with a vowel followed by a word beginning with a vowel); it can also produce a double consonant, lengthening the vowel that precedes it from short to long. Some vowels can be removed, which is how the verb *take* gets to be ⌣ as well as ⌣ ⌣.

Another possibility is that characters need not always be called by their proper names. Agamemnon is a long name, which was shown to be limited in its possible locations in a line. But Agamemnon is also Atreus's son, which in the nominative has the different pattern of – ⌣ ⌣ – ⌣ and can occur at the end of a line. It also can be used with a noun–epithet formula, *hero Atreus's son,* which has the pattern – ⌣ ⌣ – ⌣ ⌣ – and can occur at the beginning of a line.[15]

Finally, it is possible to add optional phrases. For instance, many people are killed with a spear in the *Iliad.* For the idea "with a spear," there is an economical set of nine phrases varying in metrical length from – ⌣ to – ⌣ ⌣ – ⌣ ⌣ – ⌣. Thus the weapon can be implied or unspecified, taking none of the line, or it can fill a variety of metrical space as needed. As with other formulas, there are different shades of meaning among the phrases that the poet can use, but the phrases all carry the same basic idea that a spear was used (Bakker & Fabbricotti, 1991).

Thus the poet has many means available to meet the combined metrical and meaning constraints, including noun–epithet and other formulas discussed by Parry, verb-formula systems, substitute names, and changing short syllables to long syllables for the two main characters and using the mobile Ionian nu.

Hiatus and Enjambement

Besides formulas, Parry integrated two main structural features of Homeric epic into his theory: hiatus and enjambement. In ancient Greek poetry and prose, including Homer, hiatus was avoided (Parry, 1928/1971a). That is, words ending in a vowel were not followed by words beginning with a vowel. Such combinations were avoided just as, in modern English, we would avoid using an *a* before a word beginning with a vowel by instead using an *an*. In Homer, hiatus is rare enough to indicate that it was not desired. However, it does occur much more frequently than in literate poetry and frequently enough to have suggested a change in the pronunciation of Greek to nineteenth-century scholars (see Parry, 1934, for a perspective from his theory). Parry notes that most instances of hiatus occur where two formulas meet. Parry explains this as the inability of a poet composing rapidly to meet all constraints; hiatus is allowed to ease the meeting of the meaning and rhythmic constraints. More troublesome are the few cases where hiatus occurs within a formula. Parry carefully traces these to changes that occurred in adapting an existing formula to a new form or to the pronunciation changes in Greek over time.

Enjambement has received more attention than hiatus in the work that followed Parry's, perhaps because, unlike hiatus, enjambement can be easily applied to other languages and traditions. Enjambement occurs when the meaning structure and the metrical structure do not coincide (see Higbie, 1990, for a more complete discussion). In Parry's work, this is defined as a case when a sentence does not end at the end of a line, but runs into the next one. The psychological studies reviewed in Chapter 5 show that memory works best when pauses occur after meaningful units rather than within them. From this, it would be expected that enjambement should be rare in oral traditions.

Parry (1929) notes two kinds of enjambement: unperiodic and necessary. Unperiodic enjambement occurs where the end of a phrase corresponds to the end of a line, but the sentence continues onto the next line with added phrases. This should not cause any problem from a psychological perspective because the end of the line still corresponds to a phrase. It also causes Parry little trouble, being seen as part of the additive, or paratactic, or bead-stringing style of epic poetry, described by Aristotle and stressed by Notopoulos (1949) and Ong (1982) as a property of oral traditions. It is a style in which a sentence "is not a thought whose parts are closely bound together; it contains several ideas which have been added to one another, and which could not be foreseen, were not even looked for, until each one was told" (Parry, 1929, p. 202). Necessary enjambement occurs where the end of a line falls "at the end of a word group where there is not yet a whole thought, or . . . in the middle of a word group" (Parry, 1929, p. 203). Necessary enjambement should be rare in oral traditions from either Parry's or the psychological standpoint. To check this prediction, Parry compared Homeric epic with the later literate dactylic hexameter of Apollonius and Virgil, as he had done for measures of the economy of formula. For a sample Homeric epic, there is no enjambement for 47% of the lines, unperiodic enjambement for 26%, and necessary enjambement for 27%. For the literate Latin, the figures are 37%, 14%, and 49%, respectively.

Although these figures support Parry's argument, they are not as impressive as they could be (Dukat, 1991). To show this, Parry's use of the grammatical concept of sentence taken from studies of the syntax of writing must be abandoned and replaced with those from the syntax of speech (Bakker, 1990, 1993b).

Speech does not occur in the same form as a written sentence. Speech, like oral traditions, is now known to be much more of an additive, bead-stringing process (Chafe & Danielowicz, 1987; Nielsen, 1992; Tannen, 1987, 1989; Chapter 4). That is, speech has many properties that Parry attributed to Homeric style. Speech is not uttered as "a thought whose parts are closely bound together; it contains several ideas which have been added to one another, and which could not be foreseen, were not even looked for, until each one was told." For instance, in one study Duke undergraduates, who are an unusually literate group, described what a foreigner would have to know to understand basketball, a subject the undergraduates know well (Nielsen, 1992). Written descriptions consisted of sentences; oral descriptions usually did not. Rather, as might be expected (e.g., Chafe & Danielowicz, 1987; Tannen, 1989), their speech consisted of phrase-like intonation units, as discussed in Chapters 4 and 5, given in an additive style.

Because Homeric epic is poetry sung with a strong meter, intonation units should begin and end at the breaks in the metrical line, and this they appear to do. Consider the following two translations from the *Iliad* (Book XVI, lines 401–410) used by Bakker (1993b) to show that Homeric style is best considered as a genre of special speech rather than a genre of writing. The first is an elegant translation by Rieu. The second is Bakker's division into intonation units. For Bakker's translation, the ends of lines are marked by a ||, the two caesuras by a |, and the three secondary breaks by a |. The first translation *reads* better. The second is more like speech and preserves the bead-stringing, additive style of Homer. Bakker's translation is also closer to Bakker's word-for-word translation, which follows the first two translations.

Rieu's (1950, p. 303) prose translation is:

> Next he attacked Thestor son of Enops, who was sitting hunched up in his polished chariot. This man had lost his head completely and the reins had slipped from his hands. Patroclus came up beside him and struck him on the right side of the jaw, driving his spear between the teeth. Then, using his spear as lever, he hoisted him over the chariot-rail as a fisherman sitting on a jutting rock pulls a monster fish out of the sea with his line and his burnished hook. Thus with the bright spear Patroclus hauled his gaping catch out of the car and dropped him on his face, to die as he fell. (p. 303)

Bakker's (1993b) division into intonation units follows. Angled brackets are used to enclose words that are not explicitly mentioned in the Greek but are understood, often from the form of another word:

> And then he ⟨took⟩ Thestor, |
> the son of Enops, ||
> charging for the second time, |
> he in ⟨his⟩ well-polished chariot, ||
> ⟨he⟩ sat crouching: |
> for ⟨he⟩ was knocked out of ⟨his⟩ wits, |
> and from ⟨his⟩ hands, ||

the reins ⟨they⟩ had slipped, |
and he hit ⟨him⟩ from nearby, ||
on ⟨his⟩ right jaw, |
and ⟨he⟩ pierced right through his teeth, ||
and ⟨he⟩ dragged ⟨him⟩ by the spear, |
over the chariot-rail, |
just as a man, ||
sitting on a jutting rock, |
⟨drags⟩ a struggling fish, ||
out of the sea onto the land, |
with linen and shining bronze; ||
so ⟨he⟩ dragged ⟨him⟩ out of the chariot, |
gaping, |
with ⟨his⟩ shining spear, ||
and ⟨he⟩ let ⟨him⟩ fall on ⟨his⟩ mouth, |
and as ⟨he⟩ fell ⟨his⟩ spirit left him. ||

A word-for-word translation was supplied by Bakker (personal communication, June 1992). Hyphens are used to join several English words corresponding to single Greek words. The symbol "prt." is used to represent a particle in Greek that cannot easily be translated.

and he Thestor
of-Enops son
second time rushing
he prt. well-polished in chariot
he-sat crouching
out for he was knocked wits
out and prt. from-hands
reins they-had-sprung
he and with spear he-thrust nearby
jaw right
through and of him pierced teeth
he-hauled and by spear taking
over chariot-rail
like when some man
stone on jutting sitting
holy fish
out sea to land
with linen and shining bronze
like that he-hauled out chariot
gaping
with-spear shining
down and prt. on mouth he-left
falling and him he-left spirit

Several properties of the phrase, or intonation-unit, transcription are important. First, the intonation units correspond to the metrical breaks. Second, the intonation-unit translation is hard to read, and requires a reading with prosody and perhaps even with gesture to disambiguate the characters. Part of this problem is a result of the loss of syntactic markers in translation from Greek to English, but not all. In contrast, the Rieu translation would not pass as speech, but the intonation-unit translation could. Third, many pronouns are understood. In Homeric Greek, both *"he* sat" and *"sat"* are possible translations of the same verb. These pronouns result in *dislocations* of the topic to the *left* or *right*. Similar dislocations occur in spontaneous conversation. Consider the following examples of left and right dislocations: "The professor who called yesterday, he called back." "He called back, the professor who called yesterday." Such dislocations would easily be edited out of even an informal letter, but they are common in speech. Moreover, they could not be edited out of Homer without changing the style and meter.[16]

Returning to the question of enjambement, by switching from the sentence to the intonation unit and from the line to the classically defined metrical units of a line, all unperiodic enjambement is eliminated: an intonation unit—that is, a unit of meaning—ending at a metrical break is not enjambement in any real sense. Necessary enjambement is also reduced, making the occurrences that remain all the more important (Bakker, 1990, 1993b). Throughout the translation into intonation units, pronouns that are understood are indicated in angled brackets. Homeric Greek does not always express such pronouns. Thus "He in his well-polished chariot sat crouching" and "He in his well-polished chariot, *he* sat crouching" are two translations of the same phrase. The understood pronouns were needed in order to break the text into intonation units. They are not needed in Homeric Greek because inflectional endings indicate that the subject of "sat" is the third-person-singular past tense. If their presence is allowed, much of the necessary enjambement disappears. Breaking "He in his well-polished chariot || sat crouching" at a line, as indicated, is necessary enjambement, but breaking "He in his well-polished chariot || he sat crouching" is not (see Bakker, 1990, for examples of classical cases of necessary enjambement). Thus what was a single phrase split at the end of a line becomes a dislocated topic in one phrase and a line with its comment in the next.

Formulas Are the Result of Combining Constraints

Homeric epics contain sophisticated patterns of words of particular metrical form. It is hard to imagine that oral poets would consciously design these forms as limits on their freedom to choose and place words. Rather, the patterns, by all evidence, are the result of a need to meet both meaning and metrical constraints, metrical constraints that are among the most complex in oral or written literature. Phrases of useful metrical and meaning combinations are often used, but these formulas are not the poet's only way to meet the dual constraints. Word choice of single words is another. The dual constraints mean that, at times, either the meter or the meaning receives a solution less optimal than it could have if there were only one constraint. A point that has been troublesome to some Homeric scholars and that also would be to psychologists is that, in these cases, the local meaning is at times sacrificed instead of the meter.

Here Homeric epic has been viewed as a case of a solution to a multiple-constraint problem, a solution that critics, readers, and listeners have found produced some of the most pleasing poetry. There can be little controversy that the poet met these two constraints and met them well, and that formulas are a useful technique in the solution.

Definitions and debates about formulas abound (Andersen, 1985; Bauml, 1984–1985, 1987; Foley, 1976, 1988, 1990; Kiparsky, 1976; Miller, 1987; Nagler, 1967; Nagy, 1976; Rosenberg, 1988; Russo, 1963, 1976). From the perspective taken here, the difficulty in definition is to be expected. Formulas are a symptom of multiple-constraint satisfaction. When the same multiple constraints repeat in a genre, the same, or very similar, solutions will repeat. These repeating solutions are noted as formulas. Rather than being the building blocks of an oral tradition, which were neatly decided on as a system when the oral tradition was begun, they are the history of past solutions to subtle and varied multiple constraints (Chapter 5; but see Nagy, 1974), solutions that are different for each genre. In this view, economy is the tendency to use existing multiple-constraint solutions rather than devising new ones. When alternatives exist, as they seem to do sometimes in Homeric epic, the reason for economy may be to keep the set of formulas small in order to make composition, recall, or understanding easy, or it could be for other stylistic reasons. In this light, Parry's claim is reasonable: a nontraditional poet who had to find solutions because there were no existing traditional ones would not be prone to economy. It would take considerable effort to check all earlier occurrences in a work to ensure economy.

In Homeric epic, formulas are the product of combining metrical and meaning constraints, though formulas with pleasing sound patterns may be favored over those without (Stanford, 1969). In contrast, in counting-out rhymes—which are much shorter than epic, more stable than the epic genres for which we have multiple variants, and rely more on sound pattern than does Homeric epic—formulas play no role. Nonetheless, by any definition, counting-out rhymes are a living oral tradition. Ballads have formulas by various definitions (see Andersen, 1985, for a review) and have long been noted to have repeated formula-like phrases called *commonplaces*. In ballads, however, the metrical and meaning constraints are not the only important ones. Melody, alliteration, line-internal and end rhyme, and other constraints play a role. Thus a formula that ends line 2 or 4 of a stanza might be determined by rhyme and alliteration as well as meter and meaning. Moreover, ballads differ from epic along other dimensions, being shorter and showing less variation than epic genres for which we have multiple variants. Ballad formulas, by any definition, do not produce the tight system that Parry found for Homeric epic. Ballad formulas do have a stronger extranarrative function of foreshadowing the remaining ballad action (Andersen, 1985).

Thus all genres of oral traditions have multiple constraints. Sometimes these lead to strict formulaic systems, as noted by Parry for Homeric epic; sometimes no formulas result, as in counting-out rhymes; and sometimes a formulaic system different from Homeric epic results. The combination of strong metrical and meaning constraints in the absence of other strong constraints produces a system such as Parry's that can be analyzed solely in terms of meter and meaning. Having only two constraints favors a system with more pronounced economy. Even in epic, if the metrical constraints are weaker, as in Russian epic, the formulaic system will not be as well developed and will have less economy (Bowra, 1952, pp. 236–238). Similarly, if alliteration and assonance play a role, as in South Slavic epic, then the formulaic system will not show economy unless these added constraints are used to define the contexts in which a formula can occur (Lord, 1960).[17] Adding alliteration and assonance as constraints means that many more formulas are needed to meet the added situations that arise. That is, there are many fewer combinations of meaning and meter than of meaning, meter, alliteration and assonance. Even within different genres of epic, different solutions to the problem of stability exist (Smith, 1977).

Formulas are not the deciding factor in determining whether a genre is an oral tradition; the ability to be transmitted through human memory and oral performance is. For many but not all oral traditions, this ability depends on formulas.

The singer is not concerned with definitions of formulas. For the singer of epic, Lord's (1960) description of the usefulness of formulas is apt. A stock of flexible formulas allows the singer to group or chunk several words in order to compose in units of half-lines rather than individual words. For many pairings of the constraints of meter and meaning, a phrase-length unit exists, perhaps with minor adaptations, as an already formed solution, and it will be cued and used. Phrase-length, half-line units are a good solution for epic, but they need not be for all genres. For instance, ballad singers need to compose in stanzas, not lines. Thus for ballads, although phrase-length commonplaces are a help, longer formulas that are stanza or half-stanza length also are useful. As is seen in Chapter 11 and in Andersen (1985), such "formulas" exist.

Scripts and Themes in Homeric Epic

The next level up from formulas in the organization of Homeric epic are the shorter versions of what Lord (1960) calls *themes* and what cognitive psychologists call *scripts* (Minchin, 1992). Scripts, as discussed in Chapter 2, are fixed sequences of actions in our normal experience, such as those performed in going to a restaurant or a doctor's office. Epics contain many such sequences of actions that occur in a fixed order. Such sequences are well known to their audience and need not contain any plot or suspense, though lengthy scripts can be inserted to increase a period of suspense. Descriptions of routine actions such as going to a restaurant and arming a hero are potentially boring, and in modern stories they would be the assumed and often unstated background information from which some deviation would occur. As Bowra (1952) notes, in a chapter on themes titled "The Mechanics of Narrative": "No reader of heroic epic can fail to notice that it abounds in detailed descriptions of actions which are in themselves trivial, and would be omitted by a novelist or narrative-poet working in modern conditions" (p. 179). In epic, they are a way of organizing a story for easier recall and performance for the singer and the audience.

Here the *Iliad* and the *Odyssey* were searched for several such scripts that have been identified by classical scholars (Arend, 1933; Armstrong, 1958; Bowra, 1952, pp. 179–214; Edwards, 1992; Fenik, 1968; Foley, 1990, pp. 240–277; Lord, 1960, pp. 68–98; Reece, 1993), as well as one that defines the behavior of a single character, Penelope (Lord, 1960, pp. 172–173). The goal was to see whether the same actions repeat and whether they repeat in the same order.[18]

The procedure follows. All the scenes in the *Iliad* and the *Odyssey* for one of a few common topics, such as arming, were listed. The scenes were broken down into simple actions or props. Scenes containing only one item and items in only one scene were removed because the order for single items cannot be wrong. Thus arming scenes containing only one item, such as "weapons," "armor," or "arming," and items that appeared in only one scene, such as "girt body," "take off dress," and "sandals," were excluded. All the remaining items were placed in the order in which they most often appear. Next, the scenes were ordered by how many events they contain. The order of scenes with equal numbers of events was chosen to put similar patterns together. With this form of tabular presentation, the patterns are easier to see.[19] Table 9.1 provides an example.

The arming scenes, like many scripts that follow, are used for dramatic effect. The length of the arming scene can indicate the importance of the battle that follows it. How does the poet adjust the length of the scene? Different items could be eliminated or added, depending on the meaning needed, but if a script is being used, the order should be the same. The order in which items appear in the arming scenes listed in Table 9.1 is regular, with only one exception, noted by the o in the fifth column from the left. The regularity indicates that there is one system for both Homeric epics.[20]

Besides regularity in the order in which items are produced, there is a similarity in the way in which items are used. There are four cases of six items being used. These are given in the first four columns. These are the four major arming scenes of the *Iliad* (Armstrong, 1958; Lord, 1960, pp. 89–91), which share verbatim many lines. In all four, the same six items are used. These four scenes have been studied in detail in the literature on Homer; what is added here is that the order used for shorter scenes is the same as for the longer scenes.

Similarly, when four items are mentioned, as in the next four columns of Table 9.1, the same items tend to be mentioned, but here some curiosities occur. In the fourth column, Dolon takes a hide instead of a shield. There are three other cases of hides being used, all indicated by an *h* in the table. A hide and a shield are never both used, and whichever is used is mentioned in the same location in the script. All three mentions of the hide occur in the *Iliad,* Book X. There are two possible reasons for this. First, the actions of Book X occur at night, when shields might reflect light. Second, Book X has been suspected of being an interpolation from antiquity. In either case, from the script given in Table 9.1, it is apparent that Book X uses a script for arming like that in the rest of the *Iliad,* but one that differs in one detail.[21] The order in which the shield appears is constant even when Athene arms in the *Iliad,* Book V, and her shield is the Aegis of Zeus. As with scripts used in daily life, there appears to be an underlying pattern, with some slots in the pattern having optional choices. The case of the bow and quiver in the sixth and seventh columns deserves attention. Both are marked with an *r* because the bow and quiver are removed, with the removal coming in the same position in which they are put on in the other cases, though in general, disarming does not follow the order or reverse order of arming (Janko, 1992, p. 412). These two patterns are for two different characters and epics, Teukros in the *Iliad* and Odysseus in the *Odyssey.*

When three or fewer items are mentioned, the order is followed but the items

Table 9.1 Arming Scenes

Item	I III 330–338 Paris	I XI 15–44 Agamemnon	I XVI 130–139 Patroklos	I XIX 369–391 Archilles	I X 333–335 Dolon	I XV 478–482 Teukros	O XXII 122–125 Odysseus	I V 733–747 Athene	I X 21–24 Agamemnon
Tunic								x	x
Bow and quiver					x	r	r		
Greaves	x	x	x	x					
Corselet	x	x	x	x					
Sword	x	x	x	x					
Shield/hide	x	x	x	x	h	x	x	x	h
Helmet	x	x	x	x	x	x	x	x	
Armor									
Spear(s)	x	x	x	x	x	x	x	x	x
Sum	6	6	6	6	4	4	4	4	3

Note: In Tables 9.1, 9.3, and 9.4, *I* indicates that the scene is from the *Iliad*, and *O* indicates that it is from the *Odyssey*. The book and line numbers and the names of the characters, gods, and guests, respectively, are also given. An x indicates that the order shown follows the order given by the listing of items from top to bottom in the table; and o indicates that the order shown is different from the order in the text.

For this table only, a bow and quiver is sometimes just a bow; r indicates that the bow and quiver were removed; h indicates that an animal hide, not a shield, was put on.

vary. A possible exception is the last four columns of the table, which could be considered to consist of two patterns.

The order of arming is stable, as are the items used. Some lines repeat in more than one arming scene. Nonetheless, Armstrong (1958) notes that the arming scenes are not set pieces fit into the poem. Each arming scene is different from the others and is adapted to its context in the epics in sophisticated ways. Thus much in the way knowledge of the actions involved in going to a restaurant or a doctor's office can serve as the background of expectations from which a story can be formed, so the scripts of Homeric epic can serve as the background of expectations from which deviations can be noted.

The bathing scenes shown in Table 9.2 are included in the order in which they appear in the *Iliad* and the *Odyssey*. They are an example of a short, frequent pattern. The script lacks repeating items beyond the minimum, though the role played by the bathing scenes can be studied in detail for other purposes (Foley, 1990, pp. 248–257). There is no sense in reordering the scenes or items because the real-world constraint of having to wash before anointing and having to anoint before dressing, combined with the short sequence of at most three items, fixes this pattern. In all the other scenes examined, such real-world constraints play some role, but not enough to account for the whole pattern, as they do here.

The sacrificing scenes listed in Table 9.3 are regular, with sequences of several lines appearing in more than one place (e.g., *Iliad* [I, 456–463], which is part of the first column, and *Odyssey* [III, 460–466], which is part of the second column). From Table 9.3, it can be seen that there are few exceptions to the order of appearance of items and that if a similar number of items are included, they tend to be the same items. Even the exceptions to the order of appearance have some order. The scattering of barley occurs out of its most common order in two columns, both of which are from the *Odyssey,* Book XIV. Similarly, prayer occurs in a nonstandard location in

I	I	I	I	I	I	O	O	O	I	O
X	XIV	X	X	VIII	X	X	XX	XXI	XIII	XII
254–259	370–373	29–31	260–265	387–391	177–178	261–262	125–127	432–434	241–241	229–230
Diomedes	Poseidon	Menelaos	Odysseus	Athene	Diomedes	Odysseus	Telemachos	Telemachos	Idomeneus	Odysseus
				x						
			x			x				
x			x			o	x	x		
x	x	h			h					
x	x	x	x							
									x	x
	x	x		x	x		x	x	x	x
3	3	3	3	2	2	2	2	2	2	2

Table 9.2 Bathing Scenes

Book	Lines	Character	Bathe	Anoint	Dress
Iliad					
V	905–905	Ares	x		x
X	576–577	Odysseus & Diomedes	x	x	
XIV	170–185	Hera	x	x	x
XVIII	350–353	Patroklos's body	x	x	x
Odyssey					
III	464–469	Telemachos	x	x	x
IV	48–50	Telemachos	x	x	x
IV	252–253	Odysseus	x	x	x
IV	759–759	Penelope	x		x
V	264–264	Odysseus	x		x
VI	96–96	Nausikaa	x	x	
VI	227–228	Odysseus	x	x	x
VIII	64–366	Aphrodite	x	x	x
VIII	454–454	Odysseus	x	x	x
X	358–365	Odysseus	x	x	x
X	449–451	Odysseus's men	x	x	x
XVII	58–58	Penelope	x		x
XVII	87–90	Telemachos	x	x	x
XIX	505–505	Odysseus	x	x	
XXIII	142–142	Odysseus	x		x
XXIII	154–155	Odysseus	x	x	x
XXIV	365–367	Laertes	x	x	x

Table 9.3. Sacrificing Scenes

Item	I I 447–474 Apollo	O III 430–473 Athene	I II 402–438 Zeus	O XII 356–397 Gods	O XIV 420–456 Gods	I VII 314–322 Zeus	O XIV 74–104 Zeus	O VIII 59–74 Zeus	I IX 220–222 Gods
Sacrifice							x	x	x
Dedicate victims			x			x			
Hecatomb	x								
Name god	x	x	x	x	x	x			x
Scatter barley	x	x	x	x	o		o		
Burn hairs		x			x				
Prayer	x	x	x	o	x				
Slaughter victims	x	x	x	x	x				
Skinning	x		x	x		x		x	
Cut meat	x	x	x	x		x	x		
Wrap in fat	x	x	x	x	x				
Double-fold	x	x	x	x					
Shreds of flesh	x	x	x	x					
Cleft stick	x	x	x						
Pour wine	x	x		x					
Burn thighs	x	x	x	x					
Taste vitals	x	x	x	x					
Cut into pieces	x	x	x	x	x				
Spitted	x	x	x	x	x	x	x		
Roasted	x	x	x	o	x	x	x		x
Take off pieces	x	x	x		x	x			x
Feast or eat	x	x	x	x	x	x	x	x	x
Drink	x	x	x		o		x	x	
Singing	x							x	
Sum	21	19	18	16	12	8	7	5	5

Note: There are two senses of the term *sacrifice:* a religious rite and butchering. Only the former can be a long sequence of items; thus only the former appears in the table.

two cases. Whether this is coincidence or an indication that certain items can move, whereas others are fixed in order, cannot be decided with the simple mechanical description used here without a larger sample.

Sacrifice is included as the first item mentioned in Table 9.3, as well as being the label for the script. It is included as one item because it is mentioned as such, but it is a summary statement for many other unspecified events. For this reason, columns that have sacrifice mentioned as an item tend to have fewer other items and thus appear to the right of the table.

As with the case of the shield in the arming scenes, there are also options here. In the first column, provisions are lacking for a proper sacrifice, leaves are used for barley and water is used for wine, yet the replacements occur in their usual place in the sequence.

The poet explicitly states some of the sequencing of guest hosting shown in Table 9.4, as indicated by Odysseus's statement to Telemachos before the slaughter of the suitors (*Odyssey* XXI, 428–430):

O	O	O	O	I	O	O	I	I	I
XIII	XX	III	XI	XI	IX	XV	VIII	XI	I
24–28	250–255	5–9	24–36	726–729	551–553	222–222	548	706	315
Zeus	Zeus	Poseidon	Dead	Gods	Zeus	Athene	Zeus	Gods	Apollo
x	x	x		x	x	x	x	x	
									x
x		x	x	x	x	x	x	x	x
			x						
			x			o			
			x						
x		x			x				
		o							
	x								
x	o			x					
	x								
x									
5	4	4	4	3	3	3	2	2	2

> Now is the time for their dinner to be served the Achians in the daylight, then follow with other entertainment, the dance and the lyre; for these things come at the end of the feasting. (Lattimore, 1965, p. 320)

The hosting of guests (Reece, 1993) is more complex because some, but not all, actions can repeat. For instance, a person can be offered gifts many times, but can accept them only once. To represent this, x, y, and z are used as the first, second, and third passes through a sequence. The order of the columns is by the maximum number of x's, y's, or z's in a column.

In Table 9.4, the sixth column on page 217 is an example of how not to host guests, yet it follows the same pattern. Odysseus and his crew find the cave of the Cyclops, Polyphemos. They make a sacrifice and eat some of Polyphemos's cheese. Polyphemos arrives to find his guests. Polyphemos immediately asks questions of Odysseus, including who he is and from where he comes, instead of serving him food first, breaking a pattern of politeness, which also would have broken a pattern of the script had Odysseus and his men not helped themselves to the cheese first. Odysseus answers some questions, but does not tell who he is. In Table 9.4, this ends the column with x's. Instead of offering Odysseus and his crew food, he eats

Table 9.4. Guest Hosting

Item	O I 118–370 Athene	O VII 145–345 Odysseus	O IV 25–624 Telemachos	O X 333–572 Odysseus	O XVI 14–134 Telemachos	I IX 192–622 Three	O XV 75–153 Telemachos	I XXIV 476–691 Priam	O VIII–IX 449–36 Odysseus	O VI 148–351 Odysseus	O V 195–235 Odysseus
Entertain											
Recognition			y								
Stand	x					x		x			
Request		x						x		x	
Kiss/take hand	x	x			x						
Welcome	x		o		x	x					
Offer	x		x	xy			x		o	x	
Relieve spear	o				x						
Bathe			x	x					x	x	
Dress			x	x					x	x	
Seated	x	x	x	x	x	x		x	x	x	x
Sacrifice						x					
Water	x	x	xy	x			x				
Wash	x	x	xy	x			x				
Food/feast	x	x	xy	y	x	x	x	x	x	x	x
Drink/wine	x	x	xy	y	x	x	x	x	x	x	x
Singer/song	x								x		
Dance	x										
Question	x	x	x	x	x			x	x		x
Response	x	x	x	x	x			x	x		x
Sleep		x	y	o		o					x
Hospitality											
Gift offered	x		y	y	x	x	o				
Gift refused	x		y			x					
Gift accepted			y	y			o				
Gift of travel							x				x
Sum	16	10	20	14	9	9	8	8	8	7	7
Max. of x, y, z	16	10	10	9	9	9	8	8	8	7	7

Note: An x, y, or z represents the first, second, and third occurrences of a repeated action. An o indicates an order different from the table, and its column indicates whether the o is replacing an x, y, or z. *Entertain* and *hospitality* are general summary terms for many items and thus tend to occur in shorter scenes. The three guests in the *Iliad*, Book IX, are Aias, Phoinix, and Odysseus.

two crew members, drinks some milk, and sleeps, ending the column with *y*'s. The next evening, the Cyclops eats two more men, drinks wine given to him by Odysseus, and now, after food and drink, in proper order, asks Odysseus who he is. Odysseus answers his ungracious host at the appropriate place in the script, but with the trick name Nobody (Outis). Next comes the only inversion in order. Instead of sleeping, Polyphemos gives Odysseus his gift: Odysseus is told that he will be eaten last. This inversion is needed because when Polyphemos sleeps, Odysseus and his crew blind Polyphemos's one eye.

Table 9.5 is different from the others in that it is an attempt to show something about a particular character. Penelope is Odysseus's wife. She appears in the *Odyssey,* not the *Iliad.* Her actions are constrained, but her resolve is strong. Two appearances are not listed because they include only one action (*Odyssey* XVI, 328–341; XX, 387–389).

O	O	O	O	O	O	O	O	O	O	O
XIV	XVII	III	V	VIII	IX	X	XV	IV	XXIV	XV
45–359	336–476	34–370	76–147	61–448	231–470	13–23	261–286	532–535	271–279	186–188
Odysseus	Odysseus	Telemachos	Hermes	Odysseus	Odysseus	Odysseus	Theoklymonos	Agamemnon	Odysseus	Telemachos
						x			x	
			x					x		
	o						x			
	x									
x	x	o						x		
							x			
							x			
x		x	x							
x					x					
		y								
		y								
x	x	x	x	x	xyz		x			
x		xy	x	x	yz					
	x			xy						
				xy						
x	x	x	o		x z	x				
x	x	x	x		x z	x				
		y			yo					x
								x	x	
			x		z					
			x							
		y				x		x		
7	7	12	6	8	13	4	4	3	3	2
7	7	7	6	6	6	4	4	3	3	2

This table is the least precise of the set because it is often used as a frame for other actions and conversations, and thus often fills most or all of a book. This makes it difficult to decide which actions are part of the script itself and which are part of embedded scenes. The following general pattern of actions from which a subset is used, however, is clear. Penelope starts from her room; descends to her place near the pillar of the house accompanied by her two attendants; asks a question or gives an order; is lied to or reproached and is told to leave, often by someone she trusts, including her son and husband; and returns to her room. She is often sad, and there is usually mention of her two attendants, but the place of their mention is more variable than that of other events. Thus the actions of a character can be made into a script of stable events, much as was done for the theme of the novice hero in Chapter 2. Here, however, the script repeats many times within the same story instead of defining the story.

Some patterns, like the arming, sacrificing, and hosting sequences shown, have a set of ordered events, but others, like dressing, burial, and eating, could not easily

Table 9.5 Penelope

Item	XVIII 158–303	XXI 0–358	I 328–364	IV 675–767	XIX 53–604	XVI 409–451	XVII 36–60	XXIII 0–365	XVII 492–589	XVII 96–166
Athene puts in mind	x	x								
Descends from her room	y	x	x		x		x	x		
Two attendants	oy	o	x			x				
Stands at pillar	y	x	x			x				x
Veil	y	x	x			x				
Asks				x	x		x			
Converses	xo		x	x	xy			oy	x	x
Sad/tears		o	x	x	x		o			x
Gives order	x	x	x	x		x		o	x	
Reproached/lied to		x	x		1	1	x	x	x	
Changes plan				x					x	
Leaves for her room	y	x	x	o	y	x				
Sleeps	x	x	x		y	x		y		
Bathes				x			x			
Dresses				x			x			
Prays				x			x			
Sum	11	10	10	9	8	7	7	5	4	3

Note: All scenes are in the *Odyssey*. The 1 in the line *reproached/lied to* indicates *lied to*.

be put into tables like those used here. Nonetheless, it seems that arming and dressing, sacrificing and burial, or guest hosting and eating are similar kinds of sequences. Why is this the case? One could argue post hoc that arming is important for a story about battles but dressing is not. One also could argue post hoc that all we are looking at is temporal order, and that for some activities this is not important; instead, other forms of organization are used to aid memory. Neither argument is satisfying, but at present no good argument is available.

Dueling is an example for which there is no clear script. A duel was defined as an exchange of fighting. That is, both people had to fight. One person killing a person or a series of people who did not attempt to strike back (Visser, 1988) was not considered a duel. No clear patterns were found using this method (Fenik, 1968). This may be because all duels involve at least one major character and differences in them are required by the story line. There are, however, regularities. The fighters tend to alternate strikes. Divine interference, which is common, tends to shorten the duel by about one exchange, so that duels with and without divine interference take about as long. There is never a pair fighting a pair, though occasionally two versus one occurs. The order of weapons tends to be spear or arrow (but never both from the same person), stone, and sword.[22] The sword is the last weapon because it always kills, except in the case when it is used against Paris and breaks right before divine intervention.

The use of formulas was claimed to aid recall, performance, and understanding, but at the cost of less than optimal satisfaction of the constraints of the particular situation. This led to occasional usage that would be considered flawed by modern literate standards. The same holds for themes. Scripts involve set actions, and these can occur even when they are either not appropriate or not motivated by the local context. Lord (1960) provides examples from South Slavic epic. But, as with formulas, there are advantages. For Homeric epic, the example of the Cyclops is a case where events occur that one cannot understand from the immediate context but that are made meaningful by a traditional pattern described here as a *hosting script*.

A clear case of inconsistency is given by Combellack (1965). Patroklos, after much heroism, is attacked by Apollo, who strikes him and removes his armor. Without his armor, Patroklos is hit by a spear by one person and then killed by Hektor (*Iliad* XVI, 786–822). The armor is special: it was Achilles's, it was divinely made for Achilles's father, and Patroklos put it on in one of the four major arming scenes of the *Iliad*. Its removal by a god before the death of Patroklos is unusual. The person who kills a warrior usually strips the armor as spoils. The intervention of a god, the removal of the armor before death, and the armor itself are all special, making this scene worthy of note. Nonetheless, the usual pattern is for the person who kills a warrior to strip the armor, and so we find that Hektor reports that he stripped the armor from Achilles when he killed him (XVII, 186–187), and shortly after even Zeus reports that Hektor stripped the armor from Patroklos (198–208). Similar lines attributing the stripping of the armor to Hektor appear later in the epic (Combellack, 1965). Examples such as this can be seen as errors, though they need not be (Foley, 1990, 1991). For current purposes, they are examples of the schematic recall reviewed in Chapter 2; the usual pattern of a script triumphs over the exceptional action.

Epics also contain longer themes, which are not scripts but which are stories with plots and suspense. The theme of the novice hero proving himself, which was described in Chapter 2, is an example. Similarly the theme of absence–devastation–return can be seen as organizing both the *Iliad* and the *Odyssey* (Lord, 1960, p. 186). Epics contain many related themes at this larger plot level, including themes of rescue and return. Like the theme of the novice hero, these contain many actions and events that are expected to occur in a fixed order by a traditional audience, but that are not needed for a causal chain of events by a modern reader unfamiliar with the tradition (Lord, 1960).

A Living Epic

This section provides a brief summary of observations on the living epic tradition used to test most fully the oral-formulaic theory. A fuller description is provided by Lord (1960, 1976, 1991a). Because no original research or data collection was done here with this genre, only enough is given to argue, by reports of direct observations, that epics can be transmitted orally and that when they are, the process works much as expected from views put forth in this book.

Chapter 2 reviews studies of themes in epics, especially the South Slavic studies of Parry and Lord. In that chapter, it is argued that all epics share some themes; that in each genre, themes provide a major constraint; and that the themes can be embedded in each other, offering many levels of organization. In oral traditions that have songs the length of epics, this hierarchical, embedded structure is needed if the overall structure is not to become a long list. Themes contribute greatly to the stability and flexibility of an epic. If details of a particular epic are omitted by one singer, they can be added by another singer who does not know that epic, but who knows the themes of the epic genre. Thus if the details of arming a hero are omitted by one singer, they are not lost from transmission because another singer who sings the same epic can replace them with similar details. This has a cost, as we have seen in the example of Patroklos's armor, in that inconsistencies are created by conflicts between themes and exceptions to the theme.

Chapter 6 reviews the process by which a person becomes a singer of South Slavic epic. The process is an example of the learning of expertise discussed in Chapter 7. Chapter 6 also gives examples of the abilities of mature singers with this expertise. Learning to sing is in many ways like learning a first language. There is little formal instruction, just some possible slowing and repetition of the presentation of the epics to be learned.

Parry and Lord studied South Slavic epic in the hope of supporting a theory of oral composition and transmission derived from analyses of the Homeric epics. They made use of existing collections and collected from singers in Yugoslavia in the 1930s, before there was widespread literacy in the rural areas. Lord collected again in the 1950s and 1960s. Lord reports that their singers came from a cross section of the rural population of Yugoslavia, were often illiterate, and had a strong interest in singing.

Most of the epics that Parry and Lord collected were not of Homeric length, but were hundreds and occasionally thousands of lines long, though a few instances, to be examined later, were. The songs were usually sung and accompanied by the singer himself on a stringed instrument, the gusle. The meter is different from that of Homeric epic, but is complex, with many of the same kinds of restrictions on specific locations in the line (Foley, 1990; Jakobson, 1952; Lord, 1960, pp. 38–41, 282–283). Within a line there is rhyme, alliteration, and assonance. The details of these constraints vary with the region and with the singer.

Parry and Lord conducted many of the experiments that a psychologist might do first. They will be reported briefly here, and some will be repeated with modifications for the genres of counting-out rhymes and ballads in the chapters that follow.

In the first set of experiments, Parry and Lord observed approximately 70 cases in which the same singer produced the same epic more than once (Lord, 1960, pp. 113–119, 288). This is important because it allows the variability within one person to be assessed. From collections of epics, we know that the same basic story is told in many ways by different singers in different regions. To understand the process of transmission, it is important to know how much of this variability occurs within one person and how much is due to transmission of different variants. In the extreme case, two different modes of transmission are possible. At one extreme, each singer would produce a nearly verbatim version of his unique variant at each performance. At the other extreme, there would be one basic epic, and it would be impossible to sort transcriptions of the variants into those done by one singer and those done by another. Different models of recall would be needed for the two extremes; however, without collecting multiple variants from individual singers, it is impossible to know about stability within, as opposed to between, singers.

Parry and Lord varied the interval between singing from immediate repetition to 17 years, collecting as many as six variants of an epic from a single singer. Several observations resulted. First, the basic story is stable, even over the longest periods. However, this does not fix the performances; there is great variation if change is measured at the level of the individual words sung. Second, one major change is in the length of the epic, a change that is produced by expanding or contracting individual themes. Third, the order of presentation of major events is not constant unless this is required by the story. Epic often (by Stanley's [1993] account, constantly) uses a ring structure in which a series of questions is answered or a series of problems is solved in the order opposite to that in which they were posed (see Chapter 11 for a more detailed discussion). Lord attributes the tendency to recall events in one order in one singing and in the reverse order in another to the use of ring structures, which contain both an order and its reverse. Fourth, there is a tendency to substitute one form of a theme for another. Thus a hero has to be armed or recognized for the overall story or theme of the epic to function, but the particular arming or recognition changes among those appropriate for a hero of the type used. Fifth, consistent with the results reviewed in Chapter 7, the length of time does not affect the kinds of changes made. Sixth, individual singers have styles, strengths, and weaknesses that they maintain.

Overall, there are multiple constraints of meaning and form that ensure that the basic story is told in a poetically and musically sound way, but these constraints do not fix the text as much as they do for the genres to be considered in the next two chapters. This makes the process of composition seem an apt description of transmission here, whereas the process of remembering seems apt for the genres with less change. Nonetheless, it is argued that for the three genres considered, singers use the same processes of memory in the way outlined in Chapter 8. For South Slavic epic, the absence of tight multiple constraints that limit choices and the length of the songs result in more changes from one singing to the next than in the more constrained and shorter genres of counting-out rhymes and ballad. One limitation to these conclusions is that Lord stresses the analysis of the themes in his reports, often at the expense of the melodic, metrical, and poetic devices used by the singer, making an argument based on multiple constraints more difficult from Lord's analyses.

A second set of experiments was included in part because the course of transmission is difficult to follow from studying existing collections (Lord, 1960, pp. 102–113). The researcher is never sure from what source or sources a song was learned. To solve this problem, Parry and Lord had a "teacher" sing an epic that the "student" did not know and then tested the student on what was learned. This provides a measure of how faithfully one singer reproduces the song of another. The analysis of differences provides clues to the processes used in learning a new song. If generalizations to the way in which a tradition functions are to be drawn from such experiments, it is important that they not be far from the way transmission usually occurs, and Parry and Lord tried to ensure that this was the case. Expert singers reported that they would learn a new song after hearing it once, and they did.

The changes between singers were, of course, greater than the changes within singers from singing to singing. Singers have individual styles, and the song produced by one singer had to be adapted to the style of another (Foley, 1990, pp. 158–200, 278–328). In addition to the changes that occurred within one singer's ways of producing a theme were changes that occurred because one singer's ways of producing a theme were either not known or not acceptable to another singer. This occurred in transmission among singers who did not know one another, in transmission from father to son, and in transmission from a version read from a song book to an illiterate singer. The last case is important because it shows that the singer did not assume that the written word, which could have been repeated verbatim, needed to be learned verbatim. As with the within-singer experiments, the general constraints of the genre played an important role. New epics were not learned as isolated exemplars, but as combinations of themes that were already known by the singer.

A third set of experiments studied the generation of new songs by epic singers. These are a limited set and are flawed because, as Lord (1960) notes, the themes of the generated songs were not from the tradition, handicapping the singers.[23] Nonetheless, they provide useful information about what the singers can do when recall of a single existing model is not possible. Two generated songs are reported. The first was a request to compose a song about how songs were collected from the singer. The singer responded immediately with a 26-line song (Lord, 1960, pp. 286–288). The second case was *The Song of Milman Parry* (Lord, 1960, pp. 272–275), written and presented to Parry by the singer. It contains a traditional opening and closing, and makes use of traditional travel themes, as the following lines show:

Dear God, praise to Thee for all!
What I shall sing is the straight truth.

(1–2)

Then he said to his companion:
"It is beautiful here, here shall we sit,
And drink our fill of cool wine."
There he spent one day,
But the next day he arose early,
And he left the city of Mostar,

(77–82)

He was there for three white days.
When the fourth day dawned,
Professor Milman arose early,
Before daylight and white dawn.
He leaped to his light feet,
Left the city of Nevesinje,

(99–104)

Honor also to him who begot you!

(149)

As will be seen in Chapter 11, when expert ballad singers, or even students just learning ballads, are given a traditional topic from their genre, they do remarkably well at generating new ballads that follow the constraints of their genre. This argues for their ability to compose within the constraints of their genre.

A final set of observations is especially important. Lord (1960, 1991) is careful to distinguish between epics sung for the entertainment of an audience and epics sung for recording, especially those sung for recording by a scribe. A long-standing problem is that of where and when epics the length of the *Iliad* and the *Odyssey* were performed. Lord's solution is that they were not performed within the oral tradition. The texts were recorded by a scribe over a long period, and the processes produced epics different from those sung to an audience. In performances for audiences, people leave and enter as they will, talk to other people in the audience, and may even interrupt if they arrive with news. Moreover, the singer must finish his song in an evening. In performances for recording, there is a small, attentive audience that is willing and even eager to record an epic that takes many days to sing.

Our texts of the *Iliad* and the *Odyssey* were written, or we would not have them now. Lord argues that they must have been dictated to a scribe because a Homer literate enough to record them would not have been a traditional poet. But even if Homer sang and wrote the epics, there would be no audience to encourage or distract him, and there would be no time limit. In either case, the rate of singing would be slower than if the epics were sung to an audience. Writing is much slower than speech. Thus the *Iliad* and the *Odyssey* are not the result of performances before audiences. From his observations of South Slavic epic, Lord argues that compared with epics performed before audiences, the *Iliad* and the *Odyssey* are much longer, may have more metrical or other irregularities due to pausing after each line or half-line to allow the scribe to work, and may show more effects of planning because of these and other pauses. Writing also allows the singer to look back, or have the scribe look back, so that all the advantages of a permanent record can be used. As is argued in the Epilogue, from the history of the slow development of the uses of writing, it is unlikely that the ability to review what was sung was used much in its early applications to literature.

The two epics Parry and Lord recorded that are of Homeric length were both from their most skilled singer, Avdo Medjedović (Lord, 1956, 1960; Lord & Bynum, 1974). A less skilled singer would not have enough material to produce work of such length or quality. The longest epic was dictated. The dictation was taken by a skilled scribe, so that lines that were not heard well or were garbled in performance could be requested again. The second longest epic was recorded, not dictated, so the singing was not slowed after each line, though the singer could stop as needed and did not need to finish a song at the end of each day. The longest song, *Osmanberg Delibegovic and Pavicevic Luka,* was recorded over 3 or 4 days, followed by a break of 10 days because the singer lost his voice, and then completed in another 3 or 4 more days. The second longest song, *The Wedding of Meho, Son of Smail* (Lord & Bynum, 1974), was recorded over 8 days, with nearly 2,000 lines sung on most days. Together these two songs contain 25,654 lines, nearly the 27,000 of the two Homeric epics. Thus the best singer who could be found under ideal conditions could dictate epics of length and structure similar to the *Iliad* and the *Odyssey,* though this singer had probably never produced an epic even one-fifth as long under the more common performance conditions experienced before the collectors came. By analogy, the same would be true for Homeric epic.

Limitations

Homeric epic is the source of oral-formulaic theory. Its strong metrical and thematic organization in the absence of other strong constraints yields an elegant solution to multiple-constraint satisfaction. Homeric epic is probably the most widely analyzed and criticized corpus of poetry. However, although remnants may remain (Sifakis, 1992), it is a dead tradition lacking in multiple variants. The search for an analogous, living tradition led to the increased study of South Slavic epic singers, the best of whom could sing epics of Homeric length. This removed many objections to the theory that Parry had proposed and provided insights into how oral composition works. Although South Slavic epic serves these functions well, the lack of work on integrating its multiple constraints and the fact that it too seems to be a dying tradition limits its usefulness to the ideas put forth here. Although epic exists in other places as a living tradition (Foley, 1990), to pursue these ideas further, we turn to two very different genres.

Notes

1. For a full argument, see the Epilogue.
2. For a more detailed discussion of the meter, see Bowra (1962a), Foley (1990, pp. 68–84), and O'Neill (1942).

3. The last foot of many meters is different from the rest, perhaps for the sake of closure (Smith, 1968) or for what Foley (1990) terms *right justification*. In counting-out rhymes, the last syllable of a trochaic line is often dropped—for instance, *Ee' nie, mee' nie, mi' nie, mo'* versus *Ee' nie, mee' nie, mi' nie, mo' nie*. In Chapter 11, a similar phenomenon will be discussed in contrasting long and common meter. For epic, counting-out rhymes, and ballads, changing the pattern of the line helps to separate one line from the next. In addition, for counting-out rhymes and ballads, but not for epic, the change in the regular pattern of the meter in the last foot stresses the last syllable, thus putting stress on the syllable that carries the end rhyme.

4. For an argument for four shorter units, see Porter (1951).

5. The break between the third and fourth feet coincides with a break between words in only 22% of the lines in a sample of 1,000 lines from the *Iliad* and 1,000 from the *Odyssey* (Porter, 1951, Table XVI).

6. Other secondary locations are also possible. For a brief review of this ongoing issue, see Foley (1990, pp. 64–84).

7. This discussion simplifies a complex area of Homeric scholarship for which Bakker (1988), Edwards (1986), and Foley (1990) provide bibliographies and brief reviews. In addition to the location of preferred breaks shown in the line, there are bridges where breaks in words and phrases are not supposed to occur. These breaks and bridges are a way of stating the same observations that O'Neill (1942) made in summary form. They are not an explanation. To begin to be an explanation, the location of the breaks and bridges needs to be motivated. Here this was done in terms of producing phrase-length units and, following the Homeric literature, placing those units so as to maintain the unity of the line.

8. For a more recent analysis of this problem, see Foley (1990, pp. 52–157).

9. The Greek is given in English letters only where the pronunciation, spelling, or rhythm is important to the understanding of the point being made.

10. Parry (1928/1971b) choose his examples well. The economy seems highest and the system of formulas clearest for the noun epithets.

11. For an exception that supports the rule, see Sale (1989).

12. For a history of the transmission of Homer in writing, see Davison (1962), Kirk (1962), and Powell (1991).

13. Greek melodic word accent, which often differs from syllable length and rhythmic stress, is not needed for the arguments made here and is ignored.

14. There may be more than 25 predicate phrases of this form because Parry (1928/1971b) notes only those occurring with *brilliant long-suffering Odysseus*. Similarly, there may be more than 40 subject phrases of this metrical form because all the noun phrases found with the new predicate phrases would need to be searched. Thus the values given may underestimate the possibilities of the corpus.

15. Atreus has two sons. The other is Menelaos. So these options can be used for two characters and are ambiguous out of context.

16. I find such dislocations in my electronic mail, an informal written medium in which editing can be difficult and is not expected by the reader.

17. For a comparison of formulas in several epic traditions, see Bowra (1952, pp. 215–253).

18. The search for scripts was a joint effort with Brian Meyer. The ordering of the scripts was checked by Maria Venakides. This attempt to add to the great accumulation of knowledge on Homeric epic by psychologists who cannot translate the word *Odysseus* without a dictionary is fair revenge for the numerous scholars who have invented theories of what memory can and cannot do in order to support their theories of the composition of epic. The analyses offered here, however, would no doubt benefit from the efforts of a classicist armed with a

CD-ROM. For an example, see Reece (1993), which I found too late to incorporate into the chapter.

19. The technique is an adaptation of Guttman scaling with the ordering of items left unchanged, as in Figures 8.1 and 8.2. Usually the order of occurrence is not presented, only whether the item occurred (Kenny & Rubin, 1977).

20. The one inconsistency in order indicates that the pattern was not always followed. It is not an error in the epic. The claim of a fixed-order script is mine, not the poets'.

21. I owe the first interpretation to Keith Stanley and the second to Egbert Bakker.

22. Odysseus, who, at the end of the *Odyssey,* puts an arrow through 10 ax heads and first slaughters the suitors with arrows, never uses an arrow in the *Iliad,* only a spear. His bow is waiting at home for him as a test.

23. For praise poems for Albert Lord and Alain Renoir within the Xhosa tradition, see Opland (1988, 1992).

CHAPTER 10

Counting-out Rhymes

A child tells off with his finger one word of the rhyme for each of the group, and
he on whom the last word falls is "out." This process of exclusion is continued
until one only is left who has the usually unpleasant duty of leading in the sport.
All European nations possess such rhymes, and apply them in a like manner.
These have the common peculiarity of having very little sense, being often mere
jargons of unmeaning sounds.

Newell, 1903, pp. 194–195

No matter how uncouth schoolchildren may outwardly appear, they remain
tradition's warmest friends. . . . They are respecters, even venerators, of cus-
toms; and in their self-contained community their basic lore and language seems
scarcely to alter from generation to generation.

Opie & Opie, 1959, p. 2

The genre of counting-out rhymes is a children's oral tradition defined by function,
not form. Counting-out rhymes are sayings used to decide which child will have the
most desirable, or undesirable, role in an activity. The two instances of this genre
that are remembered by the greatest number of Duke undergraduates are

> Eenie, meenie, miney, mo,
> Catch a tiger by the toe.
> If he hollers, let him go.
> Eenie, meenie, miney, mo.

and

> One potato, two potato,
> Three potato, four.
> Five potato, six potato,
> Seven potato, more.

As a genre to be studied, counting-out rhymes have many advantages. First, they
are a true oral tradition, with little contamination by non-oral transmission. Although
books containing counting-out rhymes exist, they are hardly ever used by the chil-

dren who are the primary transmitters of the tradition. Second, counting-out rhymes are one of the few traditions that can still be studied in a large proportion of the general population. Third, counting-out rhymes are widespread across cultures and languages (Bolton, 1888; Opie & Opie, 1969), suggesting that they are not just odd artifacts and allowing for cross-cultural comparisons (e.g., Burling, 1966). Fourth, the genre has been well documented for the past century. Collections exist to allow the observation of diversity, relative popularity, and change over time. Fifth, because counting-out rhymes are defined by function, not form or content, regularities found in the genre are not part of the definition used to select the rhymes. Thus any regularities of form or content noted in the genre are empirical findings. This would not be the case, for instance, in finding that epic poems are long or ballads are sung.

Two major features distinguish counting-out rhymes from the epic poems and ballads considered in Chapters 9 and 11. First, children are the primary users of this tradition. Thus aspects of the process of transmission may differ solely because children differ from adults (e.g., Piaget, 1965). Second, the rhymes serve the immediate, practical function of choosing people. Thus any changes in transmission might be considered cheating by the audience.

The stability of counting-out rhymes, like that of other oral traditions, benefits from many aspects of the process of transmission. For instance, in order to check the honesty of the person who is counting, attention must be paid to the exact words and rhythm being chanted. Moreover, the numerous intermittent repetitions of the rhymes by different members of a group ensure overlearning, spaced practice, and test trials interspersed with study trials, as described in Chapter 6. Little can be added to our understanding of such performance factors, however, without a detailed record of the everyday usage of the genre, a task not undertaken here. Instead, this chapter concentrates on the properties of the rhymes themselves that lead to stability.

Counting-out rhymes were selected for study not only because of the advantages and distinguishing features listed in the preceding paragraphs, but also because they differ from the more often studied genres of epic and ballad. Counting-out rhymes provide a contrast and thus increase the database, forcing theories formulated for the more widely studied oral traditions to be examined. The achievement of stability in transmission in the three genres studied differs in detail, but not in the general processes outlined. For all three, the multiple constraints reviewed in the earlier chapters limit choices and cue recall.

The chapter is divided into three sections. The first section describes the properties of counting-out rhymes and asks two basic questions. First, what types of constraint, or organization, are present in the rhymes themselves that could lead to stability in transmission? Second, are there enough similarities among different rhymes to claim that this genre, which is defined in terms of function, has a specific form?

The second section considers how recall is affected by the properties noted in the first section. If these properties are constraining recall, as described in Chapters 2, 3, 4, and 5, then variation in recall should occur at points of minimal constraint and should not violate the constraints that do exist. This idea is tested using versions of *Eenie Meenie* and *One Potato* that were collected both from the folklore literature and directly from adults and children. In addition, if rhymes are constructed at each telling from a general knowledge of the properties and some specific details, as claimed in Chapters 1 and 8, then variation in two recalls obtained from the same individual should respect the constraints. But, if the rhymes are recalled as a whole, without regard to internal structure, then a lack of variation, or variation that does not appear to follow the constraints, would be more likely.

The third section examines change over the 150-year documented history of the genre. If the constraints found to affect recall over the short term are the key to understanding stability in an oral tradition, then such constraints should be able to account for stability and change in counting-out rhymes over the last century. Changes in versions of *Eenie Meenie* and *One Potato,* changes in their popularity and in the popularity of one other rhyme, and changes in the properties of the rhymes that were used at various time periods are investigated.

Properties of Counting-out Rhymes

Properties of Two Common Rhymes

Consider the more obvious constraints present in *Eenie Meenie* and *One Potato.* Words that are part of a clear meaning or imagery organization are in capital letters. Sound patterns that repeat, including word repetition, rhyme, alliteration, and assonance, are underlined:

> Eenie meenie miney mo,
> CATCH A TIGER BY THE TOE.
> IF HE HOLLERS, LET HIM GO.
> Eenie meenie miney mo.

> ONE POTATO, TWO POTATO,
> THREE POTATO, FOUR.
> FIVE POTATO, SIX POTATO,
> SEVEN POTATO, MORE.

Although the complexity of the structures described in Chapter 2 is not needed here, meaning constraints are present. In *Eenie Meenie,* the middle two lines tell a coherent story. Any change in these lines would have to result in another story to preserve this organization. In *One Potato,* the whole rhyme is a sequence. Changes that could preserve this organization include counting a different object and shortening or lengthening the sequence. The meaning constraints are not very hard to meet until they are combined with the poetic constraints. The constraints, even at this basic level of description, are strong enough to allow a computer-network activation model to discover that the rhyme is highly organized (Kintsch, 1994).

The poetic devices described in Chapter 4 appear to play a stronger role than do the meaning constraints. Most of the words in the two rhymes contain a repeated sound pattern, usually word repetition, rhyme, or alliteration. All the words not involved in the meaning are involved in one of these poetic devices. The last word of each line of both rhymes either rhymes with or repeats the last word of another line. Alliterating words are close to each other. In addition to the repeating sound patterns, both rhymes contain four lines with four beats to the line, a pattern common in children's literature in general (Burling, 1966), and in counting-out rhymes, in particular. The beats are emphasized because they mark the gesture of pointing and are thereby an integral part of the counting-out function of the rhymes.

More subtle poetics also exist. For instance, the first line of *Eenie Meenie* contains vowels that progress from front to back (as in the *fee, fi, fo* of *fee, fi, fo, fum* or in *ee, eye, ee, eye, oh* of *Old McDonald Had a Farm*). Therefore *meenie, miney, mo* sounds better than *miney, meenie, mo*, and the order is unlikely to change. In addition, the first word, *eenie*, is part of the second word, *meenie*. This is a sophisticated poetic device discussed by Jakobson (1960) in relation to the political slogan *I like Ike*, used by Eisenhower in his presidential campaign. Together these first two words of the first line have four repetitions of the sound *ee*. It could even be argued that the /m/ sound is used because it is the easiest consonant for a child to make.

Changing words without reducing the amount and quality of the poetic devices is not easy. Changing words while maintaining both the meaning and the poetic devices is even more difficult. To be convinced of this, it is only necessary to try to find, for each word in the two rhymes, a word that fits as well as the original. Consider the first line of *Eenie Meenie* again. It has only sound pattern, not meaning, but sound pattern is enough. As noted, *eenie* is part of *meenie*, and there is a front-to-back vowel progression for the middle vowels. *Meenie, miney,* and *mo* alliterate. *Eenie, meenie,* and *miney* rhyme with a sound that repeats as the first vowel of *eenie* and *meenie. Mo* rhymes with *toe* and *go*. The remaining sound, /n/, repeats in the same location in three words. The whole line repeats as the last line, where the one single-syllable word, *mo*, coincides with the person who is chosen. This change from the two-syllable pattern adds to the closure of the piece (Smith, 1968) and emphasizes the end and the rhyme scheme by putting a stress on the last word. Thus there is not a phoneme or even a distinctive feature that can change without breaking some pattern. The whole line can change—for instance, to the Scottish version *Eena, deena, dina, do*, noted later in the chapter—but any single change reduces a sound-pattern repetition. The multiple constraints outlined in Chapter 5 are at work here, resulting in many sounds being overdetermined. Thus a change from the /o/ of *mo* would break the front-to-back vowel progression and the end-rhyme pattern, and a change from *mo* to a two-syllable word would take the stress off the rhyme sound.

Properties of a Sample of Counting-out Rhymes

What properties of the counting-out rhymes could encourage stability? Are the properties noted in *Eenie Meenie* and *One Potato* typical of the whole genre? To investigate such questions in a quantitative fashion, a sample of rhymes is examined.

Abrahams and Rankin's *Counting-out Rhymes: A Dictionary* (1980) was used to provide a list of the 24 most popular rhymes and a random sample of 24 rare rhymes.[1] The popular rhymes account for most of the actual usage of the genre. An analogy to evolution suggests that their popularity, or fitness, is an indication of their quality. The rare rhymes provide a test of whether rhymes noted only once in the folklore literature have properties similar to those of the common rhymes—that is, a test of whether the entire genre can be defined by form as well as function.

The Measures

Separate measures of the proportions of words involved in word repetition, rhyme, alliteration, and assonance were formed.[2] An overall measure of poetic devices was formed by dividing the number of words involved in any of these poetic devices by the number of words in the rhyme. The proportion of lines in each rhyme containing last words that rhyme with the last word of another line was also calculated. Means for these measures and the ones that follow are listed in Table 10.1.

Rhythmic structure is important in guiding children's actions in behaviors such as counting out (Ziven, 1976), and the most common rhythmic structure in children's verse of all kinds is four lines with four beats to the line (Burling, 1966). The proportion of lines with four beats was therefore calculated.[3]

If sound patterns are to have their greatest poetic impact, they should occur on beats. Two measures were formed to see if the counting-out rhymes observed this principle. Calculations were made of the proportions of words involved in the poetic devices of word repetition, rhyme, alliteration, and assonance that fell on beats and the proportions of words not involved in these poetic devices that fell on beats. Three common and five rare rhymes were excluded from the measure because all their words were involved in poetic devices, making the calculation of the proportion of words not involved in poetic devices impossible.

One additional measure of repeated sound patterns was formulated based on the idea that a major purpose of poetics in oral traditions is to provide a form of redundancy to lessen the memory load of the reciter. Five undergraduates were asked to judge the extent to which the sound pattern of a line could be predicted by the sound pattern of the line or lines that preceded it. The scale went from 1 (not at all) to 4 (about half) to 7 (completely). The ratings of the individual lines were averaged to provide one value for each counting-out rhyme. There was good agreement among the five judges on the ratings.[4]

Table 10.1. Properties of Counting-out Rhymes

Property	Mean Value		
	Common	Rare	*T*-test
Citations	28.71	1.00	9.91
Lines per rhyme	4.56	4.04	.80
Words per rhyme	21.42	16.96	1.27
Word repetition*	.19	.14	1.30
Rhyme*	.24	.21	.78
Alliteration*	.25	.21	1.10
Assonance*	.25	.26	.29
End rhyme*	.79	.63	1.76
Overall poetics*	.87	.82	.92
Four-beat lines*	.83	.60	2.05
Rated poetics	4.33	3.72	2.07
Poetic words on beats*	.90	.79	2.53
Nonpoetic words on beats*	.61	.68	.57
Meaningful words*	.79	.77	.24
Rated meaning	2.87	2.79	.21
Rated imagery	2.96	3.16	.59

Note: Properties ending in * are proportions.

Two measures of meaning and one measure of imagery were included. The first measure of meaning was simply the proportion of words in each rhyme that made use of a conventional meaning.[5] The second measure of meaning and the measure of imagery paralleled the subjective measure of poetic redundancy. The same five undergraduates who judged poetic redundancy judged the extent to which preceding lines allowed the prediction of the meaning and imagery of each line. As with the poetics measure, the rating scales went from 1 (not at all) to 7 (completely). Again, agreement among the judges was high.[6]

Evidence for a Genre
Table 10.1 contains the average values of the properties described for the samples of 24 common and 24 rare counting-out rhymes. In order to provide a descriptive statistic of the differences between the samples that is sensitive not only to the average differences but also to the distribution of values in the two samples, a *t*-test is also included for each measure.

The general patterns of values of the common and rare rhymes are similar. The rare rhymes sample a collection that spans more than a century throughout the English-speaking world. The similarity of these rhymes to the common rhymes in their use of nonsense words, meaning, imagery, and poetic devices, and in their length and verse structure, argues that the genre defined by its function has a common form. The rare rhymes were invented or adapted as counting-out rhymes by children who must have imposed the restriction that the rhymes share formal charac- teristics with the more common counting-out rhymes or with other children's litera- ture that they knew. The common and rare rhymes, however, do differ in more subtle ways. The difference in the proportions of poetic and nonpoetic words that fell on beats in the common rhymes is much greater than it is in the rare rhymes.

Three possible reasons for the common form of the genre seem reasonable. First, the common function of counting out means that the rhymes must have a clear, unambiguous rhythm that counts a fixed number of beats. Any possibility of the person's chanting to change the number of beats could lead to cheating. The short length of the rhyme and the multiple constraints observed would make it difficult to make such changes, with the multiple constraints minimizing possible variability, especially variability in stressed words. The strong rhythm could support a number of added constraints either in meaning or in sound pattern. However, if the rhythm and the added constraints are going to work together to limit choices, as outlined in Chapter 5, stressed syllables corresponding to repetitions of sound pattern are easier to find and to hear than stressed syllables corresponding to the most meaningful words. Thus the requirement of a strong, clear rhythm with a fixed number of beats may favor short rhymes, with poetic devices for the additional constraints needed to limit variability. Second, the rhyme is a ritual, a magic procedure to select a child, so nonsense words do not seem more out of place than they do in any hocus-pocus. Third, once a form is established for one rhyme, other rhymes are likely to follow. That is, for any collection perceived as a genre, imitation and parody are likely to occur.

Although the reasons for the particular form of the genre are speculative, the existence of the common form is not. This a well-supported empirical observation.

Moreover, the benefits of a common form are not speculative. Knowing a rhyme or rhymes in the genre makes other rhymes easier to learn and remember because they share general constraints.

In order for there to be a functioning genre of counting-out rhymes, individual users, and not just an individual analyzing the genre, need to know more than one rhyme. To demonstrate this, 88 Duke undergraduates filled out questionnaires. On the first page, they were asked to record any "sayings you used to decide which child would be 'it' or would be left out of a game" and were given the first line of either *Eenie Meenie* or *One Potato* as an example and a prompt. On the following pages were a list of the first lines of 23 of the sample of 48 common and rare counting-out rhymes as prompts, with a request to complete them. Thus counting the *Eenie Meenie* or *One Potato* prompt, which appeared on the first page, 24 rhymes were prompted. Next, the remaining 24 rhymes appeared in full, with a request to rate how familiar they were and how many times they were used. There were two versions of the form so that each of the 48 rhymes appeared once, with its first line as a prompt and once in full to be rated. Undergraduates recalled an average of 1.6 rhymes without a prompt, recalled an additional 1.2 rhymes with prompts, and indicated using 2.3 rhymes they had not recalled. Combining these figures indicates a knowledge of 5.1 rhymes. This is a low estimate because the undergraduates were relying on memory of their childhood and because they may have used rhymes not included as prompts. The most commonly known rhymes were *Eenie Meenie* (99% of the undergraduates), *One Potato* (94%), *Engine Engine Number Nine* (Abrahams & Rankin, 1980, 161) (72%), and *My Mother and Your Mother Were Hanging Out Clothes* (Abrahams & Rankin, 1980, 375) (51%).[7]

An alternative to all this speculation about a genre is that the regularities noted here are true for all English-language children's rhymes, changing the scope of what needs to be explained and perhaps removing the need for explaining genre-, as opposed to age-specific, regularities. Casual observation indicates that this alternative cannot account for all the regularities documented, but following this alternative in detail is an undertaking beyond the scope of this book.

A Detailed Analysis of Rhythm
In order to examine the rhythmic pattern in more detail, Kelly and Rubin (1988) selected a different sample of rhymes from the Abrahams and Rankin (1980) dictionary. As noted, the most common pattern in the sample of 24 common and 24 rare counting-out rhymes was four beats per line. Assuming that each beat was from a two-syllable foot leads to lines eight syllables long. All 433 of the eight-syllable lines in the dictionary were therefore selected. A pattern of stressed and unstressed syllables was assigned by assuming that all single-syllable nouns, verbs, adverbs, and adjectives were stressed and that all other single-syllable words were not. A standard dictionary was used to assign stress to multiple-syllable words. Nonsense words were assigned stress out of the context of their rhyme. That is, the pattern of eight stressed and unstressed syllables was assigned based only on the stresses of the individual words, without consulting the scansion of their line in any way.[8] Maintaining the two-syllables-per-foot assumption, the feet were divided in iambic (unstressed followed by stressed, or ᵛ –), trochaic (– ᵛ), spondaic (– –), and

pyrrhic ($\smile$ $\smile$) feet. Lines with more iambic than trochaic feet were assumed to have an underlying iambic pattern. Lines with more trochaic than iambic feet were assumed to have an underlying trochaic pattern. This mechanical system resulted in 246 trochaic lines, 157 iambic lines, and 30 lines that had an equal number of iambic or trochaic feet. Although far from subtle itself, this objective system of classification allows questions to be asked about subtle patterns without having to worry that the results were biased because the scansion was influenced by experimenter expectations, but the method is not without problems (e.g., Leech, 1969, pp. 113–114).

The application of linguistic theory to formal literary verse (e.g., Chomsky & Halle, 1968; Kiparsky, 1975, 1977) led to several findings, which Kelly and Rubin (1988) investigated in counting-out rhymes. The two adjacent single-syllable words *black bird* are treated in traditional scansion, and in the system used here to assign stress patterns to the lines, as two stressed syllables. However, according to Chomsky & Halle (1968), stronger stress should fall on the second word (i.e., the "nuclear stress rule" would place stress on the rightmost member of the pair). Literary verse follows this pattern (Kiparsky, 1975, 1977). Of the 93 cases of two adjacent stressed syllables falling in lines that were labeled either iambic or trochaic, 61% followed the unstressed–stressed pattern. In contrast, for the compound word *blackbird,* the stress should fall on the first rather than the second syllable. All 7 compound words in the sample had their two syllables fall correctly on stressed followed by unstressed syllables according to the scansion of their lines.

In literary verse, it is more common for the first foot of an iambic line to be trochaic than it is for the first foot of a trochaic line to be iambic (Newton, 1975). Extrapolating this finding to the last foot of a line, there appears to be a tendency to move stressed syllables to the extremes of a line, as if to set the line off from other lines. Thus an iambic line, which starts with an unstressed syllable, is more likely to have its first foot inverted, whereas a trochaic line, which ends with an unstressed syllable, is more likely to have its last foot inverted. Table 10.2 shows this effect for the sample of counting-out rhymes. There is further support for these findings. Thirteen lines in the sample of 433 eight-syllable lines had an equal number of iambic and trochaic feet, with two feet of one kind followed by two feet of another. Of these 13 lines, 12 consisted of two trochaic feet followed by two iambic; that is, 12 started and ended with stressed syllables. Similarly pyrrhic feet ($\smile$ $\smile$) were more likely to occupy the first foot of an iambic line than a trochaic line (40% versus 13%), but were more likely to occupy the last foot of a trochaic line (38% versus 23%). Pyrrhic feet at the beginning or ending of a line cannot set the line off with a stress, but they do not remove an underlying stress when they are first in an iambic line or last in a trochaic line.

Eenie Meenie was not included in these analyses because the version printed in the dictionary had seven rather than eight syllables per line; nonetheless, it supports the

Table 10.2. Position of Inverted Feet

	First Foot	Middle Feet	Last Foot
Iambic ($\smile$ $-$)	21	14	3
Trochaic ($-$ $\smile$)	4	6	82

tendency for lines to begin and end on a stressed syllable. All the 353 lines of *Eenie Meenie* found in the variants cited in the dictionary were examined using the same procedure as was done for the eight-syllable lines, and 94% were trochaic. The eight-syllable trochaic lines end on a weak beat, but in *Eenie Meenie* 93% of the lines are seven syllables long and all these lines end on a strong beat. The line *Eenie, meenie, miney, mo,* unlike the line *Eenie, meenie, miney, monie,* begins and ends on a strong beat. In fact, all but 2 of the 166 collected first and last nonsense lines had a ‒ ‿ ‒ ‿ ‒ ‿ ‒ rhythmic pattern, a pattern that places the end rhyme on a stressed syllable.

Kelly and Bock (1988) argued that stress is a continuum, even though it is often dichotomized into stressed and unstressed. To show this, they took the first 150 single-syllable words of each of 10 grammatical categories in Shakespeare's sonnets and in Milton's *Paradise Lost* and asked how often they fell on a stressed position in the underlying iambic verse. Supporting their position, they found a gradual change across grammatical categories in the proportion of words falling on stressed positions, as shown in Table 10.3. The same analysis carried out for all single-syllable words in the 433 eight-syllable lines produced remarkably similar results.[9] Thus Milton, Shakespeare, and children are equally likely to put a particular part of speech in a stressed position.

Other similarities between counting-out rhymes and literary verse were also noted, such as more pyrrhic than spondaic feet, the tendency for two-syllable words that violate the underlying stress pattern to fall within and not across foot boundaries, and more violations of iambic than trochaic meter (Kelly & Rubin, 1988). It is unlikely that the literate poets were aware that they observed these regularities and even less likely that the children did. Both groups, however, have similar ears when it comes to their rhythmic preferences.

The subtleties of these regularities in the rhythmic pattern add to the more obvious constraints noted earlier. Not only do counting-out rhymes have easy-to-document patterns, such as four beats per line and end rhyme, but in the one case where such constraints were examined in detail, there were also sophisticated patterns. The complex, interrelated organization of easy-to-state patterns demonstrated in most of

Table 10.3. Proportion of Each Grammatical Category That Falls
on a Stressed Position

Grammatical Category	Formal Verse	Counting-out Rhymes
Nouns	.94	.88
Verbs	.76	.80
Adverbs	.71	.79
Adjectives	.61	.61
Modal auxiliaries	.41	.45
Auxiliaries/copulas	.40	.37
Pronouns	.34	.30
Prepositions	.32	.41
Conjunctions/complementizers	.14	.19
Articles	.11	.09

this chapter is probably an underestimate of what would be present if more detailed analyses were possible.

Comparisons of Rhyme and Reason

Table 10.1 shows the extensive use of poetic devices in counting-out rhymes: 71% of the lines share end rhyme, 72% of the lines have four beats, and 84% of the words are involved in rhyme, alliteration, assonance, or word repetition. This high degree of poetic structure fosters stability in that substituting a synonym for a word usually results in a less integrated sound structure. Moreover, there are interrelationships among the measures. Words involved in poetic devices are more likely to fall on beats than are words not involved in poetic devices. Substituting a word that changes either the rhythm or the repetition of sound patterns would upset this interrelation.

The rhymes contain considerable poetics, but little in the way of integrated meaning or imagery.[10] Four-fifths of the words are involved in the repetition of a sound pattern, but one-fifth of the words have no meaning at all to the children using them. Poetic devices are not as important in all situations. For instance, laboratory studies of children's use and appreciation of poetics do not suggest the extent of poetics observed in counting-out rhymes (Hayes, Chemelski, & Palmer, 1982; Jusczyk, 1977).

In summary, it appears (1) that there exists a poetic form that describes the genre of counting-out rhymes, (2) that repeated sound patterns, and not meaning or imagery, are most prevalent in this form, and (3) that the poetics are sophisticated and pervasive enough to severely constrain word choice.[11]

Recall

If the properties outlined up to now in this chapter determine the recall of counting-out rhymes, it should be possible to predict where and with what frequency changes occur in recall. This, however, is too ambitious a prediction because it requires that the set of all possible alternatives be enumerated and rated with respect to the extent to which they fit the constraints. Instead, the prediction is that the changes that occur will follow the constraints outlined. This is a strong prediction and one that can be tested. It implies a sensitivity to the regularities of the genre as expressed in the individual rhymes.

Once a change is observed, it is easy to see if it fits the constraint hypothesis. For instance, from what has been noted earlier, if one initial consonant in the first line of *Eenie Meenie* is changed, three would have to change. Thus *Eenie, feenie, finey, fo* would be permitted but not *Eenie, meenie, finey, mo*. It is not necessary to catch a *tiger;* any two-syllable, animate object with toes will do, though some are better poetically than others and therefore should be more frequent. If a *monkey* is caught, it could *chatter* instead of *holler,* though a *tiger* could not. The complete middle two lines could be replaced by a new story line if the rhythm, end rhyme, and some internal poetics were maintained. The set of possible middle two lines cannot be listed, but once suggested, they can be examined to see the extent to which they fit. To test these predictions, a wide variety of data are used, including published collections, recalls from adults no longer actively in the tradition, and recalls from children. Each sample has its own strengths and weaknesses, but together they provide a consistent picture.

Published Versions of Two Common Rhymes

Recalls of counting-out rhymes collected by folklorists offer an initial sample for study. A library search of the citations listed in Abrahams and Rankin's (1980) dictionary produced 82 versions of *Eenie Meenie* and 36 versions of *One Potato*. Initial examination of these recalls indicated that little variation exists among the versions of each rhyme and that the variation that does exist could easily be described by comparing each recall with the version of the rhymes listed at the beginning of this chapter. The following differences are ignored because they appear to rely more on the conventions of reporting than on actual performance: (1) spelling; (2) whether the last line in *Eenie Meenie,* which is a repeat of the first line, is listed explicitly; and (3) whether there are added lines after either rhyme is completed. Added lines are often rhymes that are used by themselves. Examples include *My mother told me to pick the very best one and you are not it* and *O-U-T spells out and out you must go.*

Eenie Meenie
In order to make all 82 versions into the standard version, a total of 291 words had to be changed (approximately 3.5 words per version). Such changes to an arbitrary standard version are not corrections, but are an objective way to describe the kind and extent of variation that exists. This method is possible only because there are modal versions around which there is little deviation. Thus this method would not prove useful for the analysis of epics that Lord (1960) listed in parallel columns in his book and compared verbally because there are too many differences among them to summarize easily.

The changes are classified into five categories. Following each category is the percentage of the 291 changed words that the classification accounts for:

1. Replacing most of the first and/or last lines   41%
2. Replacing most of the story line   13%
3. Changes in the word *hollers*   9%
4. Miscellaneous changes   12%
5. Changes in the word *tiger*   25%

The most popular changes in the first category were *Eena, deena, dina, do* and *Eena, meena, mina, mo.* Almost all the versions containing these changes were recorded before 1910. Most were recorded outside the United States. Although different from *Eenie, meenie, miney, mo,* the alternative first lines maintained the poetic structure.

The second category was due entirely to four versions. The changes are changing lines 3 and 4 to *Why did you let him go? / Cos he bit my finger so* and *If he hollers daddy-o, / Play it cool and let him go;* changing what is normally line 2 to *Mary had a little lamb;* and changing what is normally line 3 to *Be sure you don't let the nigger go.* The versions that produced the last two changes also used a jumbled line order. Instead of the nonsense lines being lines 1 and 4, they were lines 2 and 4 and lines 1 and 3 in the two versions, respectively. Although different from the standard version, these alternatives maintain the meaning constraint of making sense and usually the sound-pattern constraints of four beats per line and the *o* end-rhyme scheme. The first two categories demonstrate the difficulty of changing most single words in the rhyme without changing most of a line.

The third category consisted of 14 instances of *squeals,* 5 of *holler,* 2 of *screams,* and 1 each of *cries, quarrels, chatters,* and *roars.* The most popular of these alternatives, *squeals,* has less alliteration and one less syllable than *hollers.* This weakening of the poetic structure appears to be because the word *hollers* was not in universal usage in the English language. All 14 versions using *squeals* come from either Great Britain or New Zealand.

The fourth category consisted of 10 versions that used *his* instead of *the;* 8 that used *when* instead of *if;* 3 that used *the* instead of *a;* 2 that used *thumb, send him hum* (i.e., home), and *mum* instead of *toe, let him go,* and *mo;* and 6 other changes that occurred in only one version. The changes preserve meaning and, for the most part, occur in function words that have minimal constraints.

The fifth category is, in many ways, the most interesting. A total of 56 *niggers,* 9 *tigers* (the object caught in the standard version), 3 *neighbors,* 2 *monkeys,* and 1 each of the following were caught by the toe: *baby, beatnik, beggar, feller, lamb, lion, lizard, pig, robber, rooster, schmoo,* and a blank space. As described in the section "Historical Changes in Counting-out Rhythms," the variation in what is caught is recent. Cultural changes made *nigger* unacceptable, producing a naturally occurring test of the effects of meaning and poetic constraints on recall and on the generation of new alternatives.

If *nigger* was not an acceptable word, what could replace it? Unless a whole line or two changed, an animate object with toes was required by the meaning constraint. In all cases, if hooves and claws count as toes to children, the constraint was met. Poetic considerations further reduced the possible substitutions. All but three responses were two-syllable words. The substituted word could be better poetically than the original, though less emotional, if it had rhyme, alliteration, or assonance. Two of the three most popular substitutes, *tiger* and *monkey,* account for 44% of the substitutions. *Tiger* alliterates with *toe,* and *monkey* both alliterates with *meenie, miney,* and *mo* and rhymes with *eenie, meenie,* and *miney.* Thus the sound and meaning constraints described earlier do function in recall and even in the selection of new words. This maintenance of constraints provides a strong indication that the rhymes are recalled with regard to their internal structure and the regularities of their genre.

One Potato

A total of 85 words would have to change to make all 36 versions into the standard version (approximately 2.5 words per version). The changes were classified into four categories. Following each type is the percentage of the 85 changed words that the classification accounts for:

1. Making the word *potato* plural   46%
2. Other changes in the word *potato*   42%
3. Changes in the word *more*   7%
4. Miscellaneous changes   5%

The first category is the largest, but many of the plural *potatoes* may be a function of editorial style rather than of actual usage. The changes in the second category were due to *spud(s)*, *tate*, or *a penny*. The third category consisted of two instances of *or* and one each of *lore*, *nor*, *o'er*, and *raw*. Thus the changes in the first three categories do not alter the meaning or poetic constraints. The fourth category was needed to account for the following single version:

> One potato, two potatoes,
> Three potatoes, or,
> Four potatoes, five potatoes,
> Six potatoes, nor.

In summary, the variation noted in *Eenie Meenie* and *One Potato* in a sample of rhymes compiled from folklore sources was analyzed. The sample spanned much of the English-speaking world for a period of more than a century. The results are clear. There was little variation in the rhyme, and any that did exist followed the constraints noted. Given the lack of control over the data collection and the range of informants, the results are impressive. If all the variants are searched, there are instances of constraints not followed, but these are rare and appear as nonce occurrences that are recorded once but do not become part of the tradition. The exception to this observation is the single-syllable word *squeals*, which disappears from the rhyme when the two-syllable American word *hollers* enters the language of the people who used the poorer rhythmic solution. The question remains of why this genre uses the particular constraints that it does, but it is clear that, used together, the constraints function as expected to limit variation and thus to stabilize transmission.

Recall of Two Common Rhymes by Four Samples of People

Collections of counting-out rhymes report variants of rhymes without an indication of their relative frequency. Because each variant is listed only once, independent of how often it was observed, differences rather than stability are emphasized. To assess how much variation there really is in individual rhymes, four samples of people recalled the two rhymes that pilot work indicated most people would know: *Eenie Meenie* and *One Potato*.

Procedures

Data were collected in 1979 and 1980 from 111 Duke undergraduates (mean age, 19; range, 17 to 22), 39 members of the North Carolina Cognition Group (mean age, 27; range, 21 to 55), and 26 students at the Duke School for Children (mean age, 6; range, 5 to 9). Ten years later, in 1990, 200 Duke undergraduates (mean age, 18;

range, 17 to 22) provided recalls. The adults were tested in large groups. Each adult was given a sheet of paper containing the first two words of each rhyme and asked to complete the rhyme. On the back of the sheet were questions asking when and where they had learned each rhyme and when they had last used each rhyme. The children were tested orally, one at a time. They were told that children often use rhymes to choose sides, and that we wanted to know if they used and knew the rhymes that began with certain words. As with the adults, the first two words of each rhyme were used as cues.

Eenie Meenie

All of the 111 Duke undergraduates tested in 1979 and 1980 recalled at least a part of *Eenie Meenie*. They reported learning the rhymes in 24 different states and 5 different countries. Their average estimate of when they learned the rhymes was age 5, and they reported last using the rhymes an average of 5 years ago (range, 1 day ago to 17 years ago). In order to transform all 111 versions to the standard version, a total of 125 words had to be changed (approximately 1 word per version, compared with 3.5 words in the more diverse folklore sample just analyzed). The same five-category analysis employed with the rhymes found in Abrahams and Rankin's (1980) dictionary was used, with the following results:

1. Replacing most of the first and/or last line   0%
2. Replacing most of the story line   28%
3. Changes in the word *hollers*   3%
4. Miscellaneous changes   38%
5. Changes in the word *tiger*   31%

There were no changes in the first category. A combination of a more restricted geographic and temporal range, the use of the initial two words of the rhyme as a cue, and the stabilizing of the rhyme over time probably account for this consistency.

There was considerable variability in the second category. The set of half-line changes were *if you catch it, if you got him, if he bites you, if the farmer, if you ever, let me know,* and two versions with *don't let go.* The set of changes of a whole line or more were *let him play and he'll be out another day, cause your mommy told you so,* and *make him pay fifty dollars every day.* The standard version of *Eenie Meenie* with the last change, though occurring only once in this sample, is widespread and is treated as its own rhyme (number 134) in Abrahams and Rankin's dictionary.

The third category contains one instance of each of the following: *chatters, halloo, hollows,* and *blows.*

The fourth category, except for 3 instances of *tail* instead of *toe,* 2 instances of *caught* instead of *catch,* and 2 instances of *and* added after *toe,* involves only pronouns. Instead of *the,* undergraduates recalled *his* 21 times and *its* 9 times. Instead of *him,* undergraduates recalled *it* 4 times, *them* 1 time, and a blank space 1 time. Instead of *he, it* was recalled 5 times.

A total of 73 *tigers,* 10 *monkeys,* 10 *rabbits,* 4 *niggers,* 3 blank spaces, 2 *fellows,* 2 *piggies,* and 1 each of the following were caught by the toe: *blackbird, bunny, buyer, chicken, doggie, froggie,* and *wiffer waffer.* In all cases it appears, assuming that hooves and claws count as toes to children, an animate object with toes was caught. In every case but one, a two-syllable word was caught, though it required a *piggie, doggie,* and *froggie* to be caught instead of a *pig, dog,* and *frog.* If the objects caught are considered as substitutes for the original word *nigger,* two of the three most popular substitutes, *tiger* and *monkey,* which account for 80% of all substitutions, increase the amount of repetition in sound pattern.

Thus the relatively few variations that did occur were small and tended to preserve the poetic and meaning constraints of the rhyme. The sound made was appropriate for the particular person or animal caught and was usually two syllables long. The most commonly changed words, except for *tiger,* were small function words, such as *the,* which have synonyms and few poetic constraints. The alternative phrases for lines 3 and 4 preserved the general meaning constraint as well as the poetic constraints of four beats to the line and end rhyme.

One Potato

Two of the 111 students recalled nothing, and 8 had the same beginning as the standard version but did not complete the rhyme. All 8 of the partial recalls ended at the word *four,* which is at the end of a line and a rest (Rubin, 1977). Not counting these omissions, a total of 65 words (approximately 0.5 word per version versus 2.5 in the folklore sample) needed to be changed in the following categories:

1. Making the word *potato* plural   28%
2. Other changes in the word *potato*   3%
3. Changes in the word *more*   51%
4. Miscellaneous changes   18%

Overall, there were few changes. The second category is due entirely to 2 students' changing the last *potato* to a *tater.* The last word of the rhyme, which is noted in the third category, was recalled as *more* (the word in the standard version) by 71 students, *or* by 26 students, *ore* by 4 students, and *nor* by 1 student. The frequency of *or* is much greater than in the Abrahams and Rankin dictionary sample. All changes in the fourth category, except for those of 1 student, were the result of using a word from the standard version in a different location. These changes consisted of *more* after *two potato, more* instead of *four,* and *seven or more* instead of *seven potato, more,* and two instances of *potato* after *four.* Again, variation in recall follows the sound and meaning constraints.

Nature Provides a Test

For both rhymes, similar results were obtained from the other three groups. The only noticeable difference was in what was caught by the toe. The variation in what was caught by the toe, which was caused by pressures from outside the counting-out tradition, is greater with the older group, but less with the children. It is as if a perturbation occurred in the system and over time the system settled into a new, stable form: a form that was the best alternative poetically given the meaning constraints. In particular, the North Carolina Cognition Group caught 15 *tigers,* 15 *niggers,* 3 blank spaces, 3 *persons,* and 1 each of the following: *baby, fellow, froggie, monkey, piggie,* and *spider,* with some members reporting more than one response.[12] The 200 undergraduates tested in 1990 caught 162 *tigers*, 10 *rabbits*, 6 *spiders*, 5 *piggies*, 4 *monkeys*, and 1 each of the following: *fella, lion, tigger,* and *piggy,* followed by a *nigger* in parentheses. Nine undergraduates did not recall any of the lines containing the word. All 25 children who produced the rhyme without excessive prompting caught a *tiger.*

The average dates of learning of the rhymes by the North Carolina Cognition Group, the 111 undergraduates tested in 1979 and 1980, the 200 undergraduates tested in 1990, and the children are 1953, 1965, 1976, and 1978, respectively. Assuming that a single blank space where the word in question should be was included to avoid using *nigger* but that a missing line did not, the percentage of *niggers* caught by these groups is 40%, 6%, 0.5%, and 0%, respectively. If we exclude *nigger,* assuming that it is being replaced in the tradition, the percentage of the remaining responses that *tiger* accounts for in the three groups is 56%, 70%, 84%, and 100%. Thus *tiger,* the one common, two-syllable, animate object with legs, that alliterates with *toe,* was chosen.

Compared with the analysis of rhymes cited in Abrahams and Rankin's dictionary, the recalls collected showed much less variation. This is because of a more restricted temporal and geographic sample and because, unlike reporting variants in a collection, no effort was made to search for unusual versions or to avoid repeating the same version many times. Moreover, particular differences between the published rhymes that Abrahams and Rankin cite and the recall data suggest editing or scribal errors. For example, it would not be surprising to find that some of the plural forms of *potato* and some of the animals caught by toe were editorial alterations. Despite these differences, the two analyses yield similar results.

There was less of a range in the geographic and historical period of the people tested in the present analysis, but there was still no control over how and when the individuals tested learned the rhymes, or in factors involved in transmission, such as spaced practice and overlearning. These variables can affect the amount and accuracy of recall. Nonetheless, as in the previous analysis, there was little variation, and any that did exist followed the constraints noted. This indicates that the constraints are operating under a range of conditions of transmission.

Stability Within Each Person

An experiment was conducted in 1985 to measure the stability within individuals by obtaining recalls from the same people at two different times. Such a measure can be used to help draw inferences about transmission. In particular, with only one recall from each individual, the following two extreme causes of variation are indistinguishable. The variation observed among individuals could be a result of each individual's repeatedly reproducing one perfectly memorized, but perhaps unique, version, or it could be a result of each individual's generating a new version on each particular occasion by using the same constraints and details as all other individuals. That is, the variation could be due to changes in *repeated reproduction* within one person or changes in *serial reproduction* across people (Bartlett, 1932; Chapter 6). Collecting two versions of a piece from the same person at different times can help separate these possibilities of between-versus within-person variation (e.g., Lord 1960).

A class of undergraduates and high-school students enrolled in the Duke summer school were asked to complete the children's rhymes that begin *Eenie, meenie* and *One potato* and then to recall as much as they could of the Preamble to the Constitution (Rubin, 1977), the head and tail of a nickel and dime (Rubin & Kontis, 1983), and the dial of a telephone. The recalls following the counting-out rhymes were included to draw after-class discussion and attention away from the rhymes. One week later, the same students were asked to fill out forms identical to those used by the 111 undergraduates just discussed. The average age of the 26 students was 18 (range, 16 to 22).

The first versions of the rhymes were similar to those from the previous four groups. For *Eenie Meenie,* 18 students recalled exactly the same rhyme twice, 3 students on one occasion recalled part of their other recall, and 5 students produced rhymes that differed. Of these 5 students, 2 differed between *tiger* and *monkey;* 1 changed *screams* to *hollers;* 1 changed the three pronouns *its, it,* and *it* to *his, he,* and *him;* and 1 changed *holler* to *squeak, his* to *its,* and *him* to *it.* For *One Potato,* 17 students recalled exactly the same rhyme twice, 7 students on one occasion recalled part of their other recall, 1 student recalled nothing either time, and 1 student changed *more* to *or.*

These results mimic those of the one-recall-per-person studies. First, there is little variation. Second, *Eenie Meenie* shows more variation than *One Potato.* Third, the variation that occurs does so in the same places within a single person, as it does among people. Although it is clearly the case that two recalls from the same person are more similar than two recalls from different people, there is variation within a single person over a brief time. The kind of variation occurring within people supports the view that the recalls are constructed from partial information of the exact wording aided by knowledge of the sound and meaning constraints.

Review of the Recall Studies

There are several aspects of the data worth reviewing. Although variation has been emphasized in analyzing the recall process, the lack of change in what is recalled, both among and within individuals, should not be ignored. Compared with adult traditions such as ballads and epic poetry, counting-out rhymes show much less variation. This is even more noteworthy because, unlike with most traditions, the data obtained from adults involve not only the variation due to changes within the tradition, but also any variation introduced by changes over time once the individual is no longer an active user of the tradition. For example, the recall of a 50-year-old from the North Carolina Cognition Group is influenced by factors involved in the tradition and by 40 years of relative disuse.

The variations that do occur, in almost every case, follow constraints of the individual rhymes and the genre in general. This generalization applies to variations published in the folklore literature, collected from adults, and collected from children, as well as to variation between two tellings by the same person. Combined, these data provide strong evidence that the properties documented in the first section have a major role in recall and therefore in the transmission of the genre. Perhaps the strongest evidence for the role of constraints comes from the substitutions in what was caught in *Eenie Meenie.* Here a change was introduced into a stable version of a rhyme, and the perturbations that followed resulted in new alternatives, which not only followed the constraints present, but also maximized them.

Recall in Context

Data were collected here just as a psychologist would ask for recall of any text: by asking people to write what they could remember. When these rhymes are put to their use in counting out, the context of recall is quite different. Comparisons with the folklore-literature data indicate that what is recalled in the act of counting out does not appear to differ from what is recalled individually on demand, but examining the counting-out context provides an indication of why rhythm is a central constraint and why the rhymes are used at all.

Counting-out rhymes are a group process, a ritual, a speech act that makes someone "it." Children assemble in a circle. Everyone in the circle becomes part of the group. No one can leave except as the counting dictates. A ritual with a prescribed procedure and incantation of magic-sounding words, such as *eenie* and *meenie,* is chanted by a leader. The ritual shares much with ritual incantations of the adult world (e.g., Kapferer, 1991). For the participants, the ritual chooses fairly and by chance from among the group (Van Peer, 1988). All members of the group must synchronize their movements to produce a combined rhythm that verifies the leader's count. The act of counting out produces the rhyme, with one line cuing the next, as described in Chapter 7. The third line of the rhyme cannot be recited or paraphrased until the lines before it are spoken. In the group setting, the group is the context that produces or embodies the rhyme.

This chapter analyzes the verbal aspects of counting-out rhymes because they are the ones that lend themselves to the methods and theories of cognitive psychology and to the methods of recording most frequently used in the folklore literature. There is a danger, however, of making the rhymes too linguistic and too little social, emotional, musical, and motoric—that is, too cognitive and too little group- and body-centered. Memory is often thought of as abstract traces in the mind, but with counting-out rhymes, as noted in Chapter 4, it is clear that the socially guided rhythm of body movement and gesture is an integral part of transmission and memory. In a literal, as opposed to a metaphorical, sense, and as outlined in Chapter 7, a counting-out rhyme exists only in its performance, and that performance is as much motoric as it is verbal.

Rhythm is the structural measure that most directly reflects the social, bodily, and motor aspects of the ritual of counting out. It integrates the motoric elements of pointing, gesturing, and changing eye gaze with the verbal elements of the rhyme. Each beat is important to the outcome. The rhythm occurs as part of the meaningful movements that indicate on whom each beat falls. All members of the group must therefore tacitly agree on the number and placement of beats. Rhythm is the constraint that synchronizes the group's counting and thereby unifies the group's judgment of a proper selection. If counting-out rhymes are to promote group harmony while they select a person for an unpleasant task, the rhythm must be clear and unambiguous because the counting must be.

As noted in the section "Properties of Counting-out Rhymes," the central role of rhythm and counting in the genre's function may shape its form. The short length of the rhymes helps ensure their ability to serve as fair counting devices. There would be more chance for errors and for deliberate manipulation in longer rhymes. Shorter rhymes might allow the children to count ahead easily enough to predetermine the outcome (see Van Peer, 1988, for remedies to this strategy). The genre must allow little or no change in the number of stressed syllables used to mark the count, and this requires multiple, redundant constraints. Although many constraints could serve to limit change, not all constraints are equally effective when combined with a strong rhythmic structure. It is easier to integrate repetitions of sound pattern with rhythmic structure than it is to integrate meaning or imagery. That is, it is easier to produce an effective counting-out rhyme by placing rhyming and alliterating sounds on stressed syllables than it is by placing the most meaningful words on stressed syllables. Thus the requirement of a strong rhythm with a fixed number of beats may favor short rhymes with poetic devices for the additional constraints needed to limit variability. The ritualistic nature of counting out might also encourage the use of the nonsense words used in the rhymes, a common occurrence in magic in our culture.

Historical Changes in Counting-out Rhymes

Counting-out rhymes have been recorded for the past 150 years or so, but not much longer. Their history before this period is, for the most part, speculation based on similarities across languages (Bickerton, 1982; Bolton, 1888), with ancient charms (Grendon, 1909), and with early base-5 counting systems (Bolton, 1888). Although many current games can be clearly shown to be similar to games played centuries and even millennia ago (Newell, 1903; Opie & Opie, 1951, 1959, 1969), the texts of counting-out rhymes have a much more limited history. Whether this is because such rhymes were not used in earlier times, or because they were used but not recorded, is not clear. What is clear is that counting-out rhymes are now used throughout much of the world, that the rhymes are virtually the same throughout the English-speaking world, and that certain phrases from the rhymes and many whole rhymes cross language boundaries with little change (Bolton, 1888; Newell, 1903; Opie & Opie, 1951, 1959, 1969; Sutton-Smith, 1959). For instance, according to my colleagues in the Netherlands, where much of this book was written, the most common counting-out rhyme begins *Iene, miene, mutten.*

Records of counting-out rhymes from the past 150 years provide a sensitive test of the ideas found in this book. In an oral tradition, transmission over long time periods is the result of many retellings. Changes in the retellings of counting-out rhymes are handed down, to be changed again as new children entering the tradition learn and use the rhymes. In this way, the effects of memory should be amplified over long time periods.

Changes in the Contents of Two Common Rhymes

The 82 versions of *Eenie Meenie* and the 36 versions of *One Potato* drawn from Abrahams and Rankin's (1980) dictionary and analyzed in the second section of this chapter were reanalyzed here. From their earliest citations until their latest, only two systematic changes could be noted in the content of either of these two rhymes:

1. The first line of *Eenie Meenie* has fewer variants as time passes.
2. That which was caught by the toe changes.

Based on Abrahams and Rankin's dictionary, up to 1939, 84% of the rhymes used *nigger;* in the 1940s and 1950s, 62% did; and in the 1960s and 1970s, 37% did. This trend agrees with the changes noted in the recall data, though the values are a bit higher. Other counting-out rhymes beginning with *Eenie, meenie, miney, mo* follow roughly the same course of popularity as *Eenie Meenie,* except for one rhyme (Abrahams & Rankin, 1980, 136), which consists totally of nonsense words. Relative to *Eenie Meenie,* this nonsense rhyme has a decrease in citations over time, especially after 1940. If all rhymes beginning with *Eenie, meenie, miney, mo* were taken to be the sample, this loss in the popularity of nonsense words over time would be a third systematic change over time. Similar reductions in the use of nonsense words in other rhymes are discussed in the last part of this section.

Another way to look for changes in counting-out rhymes over time is to compare the set of recalls examined in this chapter with a set collected much earlier. This compares changes in both the standard version and the range of its variants. If the earliest extensive collection of counting-out rhymes (Bolton, 1888) is examined, only minor differences are noted. Bolton did not list *One Potato,* but Bolton's list of *Eenie Meenie* rhymes in which someone is caught includes rhymes that substitute *squeals* and *screams* for *hollers; when* for *if;* and *Eena, deena, dina, do, Enee, menee, tipsy, toe,* and *Eny, meny, miny, o* for *Eenie, meenie, miney, mo;* as well as rhymes that *make him pay, / Twenty dollars every day,* and a rhyme that uses a *mum, thumb, send him hum* (home) rhyme scheme. Some of these variants (such as *make him pay . . .*) have survived, while others (such as those involving the first line) have not. The slightly greater variety in Bolton's collection could be due to three factors: (1) its more extensive geographic spread; (2) the nature of collections that tend to amass large samples of rhymes but list each variant only once, without an indication of how often it was observed; and (3) the fact that Bolton was collecting closer in time to when *Eenie Meenie* first became popular and thus when it may have had greater variability. In any case, the variants listed do maintain the general constraints of the rhyme and the genre.

Using both a comparison across all versions published in the folklore literature and a detailed analysis of two samples of *Eenie Meenie* collected 90 years apart, there were no trends that violated the constraints of the two rhymes. This observation is all the more impressive if one considers the number of generations that are being considered. Abrahams and Rankin (1980) estimated that children use the rhymes between the ages of 6 and 11. Opie and Opie (1959) reported that "in most schools there is a wholly new generation of children every six years" (p. 8). By either estimate, *Eenie Meenie* has been stable for almost 20 generations. Thus the multiple constraints shown to operate in recall appear to function over historical time.[13]

Changes in the Popularity of Three Common Rhymes

If the content of specific rhymes does not show marked change, is the oral tradition of counting-out rhymes fixed? Some of the historical data just reviewed indicate that this is not so. Rather, it appears that whole rhymes, such as *Eenie Meenie,* may enter the tradition, reach a stable form, and persist for some time. Surely this means that other rhymes must decrease in use. After demonstrating this change in popularity for three rhymes, possible explanations for the shifts in popularity will be explored using the properties of the rhymes.

Plotting the Changes

The best approximation that can be offered to the relative frequency of use of rhymes over time is the ratio of the number of times a rhyme was cited in a folklore collection or other source in a given period to the total number of citations to all rhymes in that period.[14] Abrahams and Rankin's dictionary lists citations to approximately 2,000 instances of 1 of its 582 rhymes being collected. Over 98% of these instances come from citations between 1840 and 1979. This interval was divided into seven 20-year periods, and the number of citations in each period was recorded to all rhymes combined and to *Eenie Meenie* and *One Potato.*[15] To provide a contrast to the two counting-out rhymes that are now the most popular, the rhyme in Abrahams and Rankin's dictionary that has more citations than any rhyme except *Eenie Meenie* was also included. The version of the rhyme listed in the dictionary is as follows:

> Onery, twoery, tickery, teven
> Alabone, crackabone, ten and eleven.
> Pin, pam, musky dam.
> Tweedleum, twadleum, twenty-one.

Figure 10.1 presents the percentage of total citations collected accounted for by each of the three rhymes of interest. It is clear from the figure that, over time, the rhymes vary in popularity. The value not shown in the figure for *Onery Twoery* for the 1840–1859 period is 14.3%. Two earlier 20-year periods, 1800–1819 and 1820–1839, were not included in the figure because they had so few citations. Neither *Eenie Meenie* nor *One Potato* had any citations during these periods, but *Onery Twoery* accounted for 3 of the 12 and 5 of the 14 total citations for these periods, respectively. Thus the decline in popularity in *Onery Twoery* is even more marked than the figure shows.[16]

Evidence Supporting the Plot

From the frequency data, it appears that *Onery Twoery* was probably once the most popular of all counting-out rhymes, but it has suffered a marked decline in use. In contrast, *Eenie Meenie* and *One Potato* have grown in use over the past 150 years to become the most popular. This conclusion is supported by an examination of some

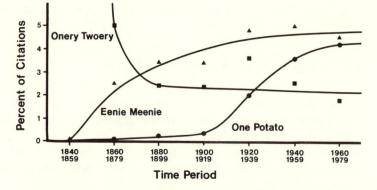

Figure 10.1. The change in popularity of three common rhymes over 140 years.

of the larger counting-out-rhyme collections. In 1883, Newell (1903) listed several versions of *Onery Twoery,* but no version of *Eenie Meenie* or *One Potato.* By 1888, although *One Potato* was not among the hundreds of rhymes Bolton listed, *Eenie Meenie* was listed as "the favorite with American children, actually reported from nearly every State in the Union" (p. 105). Similarly, Monroe (1904) reported that, in 1899, 91% of a sample of 2,050 western Massachusetts elementary-school children listed among the rhymes they used "the unmeaning and inelegant" (p. 47) *Eenie Meenie.* The difference between Newell, on the one hand, and Bolton and Monroe, on the other, was probably not in the date of collection, but that Newell was "obliged to depend chiefly on the reminiscence of grown persons" (p. xv), adding decades to the difference in when the rhymes were learned. Thus in agreement with Figure 10.1, *Eenie Meenie* appears to have gained popularity in the 20 to 50 years before 1888. By 1969, Opie and Opie listed *Eenie Meenie* first among "The Most-Used Dips" (pp. 35–36) and began their section "Counting Fists or Feet" with *One Potato* (p. 54). Sutton-Smith's (1959) extensive study of counting-out rhymes in New Zealand also agrees with Figure 10.1, though he noted that *Eenie Meenie* appeared to be losing popularity.

The study used to argue that individuals know several rhymes further supports the change in popularity shown in Figure 10.1. Of the 48 rhymes used in the first section, *Eenie Meenie* and *One Potato* were the most often recalled: 91% of the undergraduates recalled *Eenie Meenie* without a cue, and 98% completed the rhyme when cued with the first line. The corresponding values for *One Potato* are 63% and 91%. No undergraduate recalled *Onery Twoery* under either condition. Ratings of familiarity provide a more sensitive measure at low levels of recall because the entire rhyme is given and only a judgment of recognition is needed. On a scale of 1 (never heard it before) to 7 (it is the most familiar of these sayings), *Eenie Meenie, One Potato,* and *Onery Twoery* had mean ratings of 6.89, 6.64, and 1.16, respectively. Thus for Duke undergraduates, it appears that *Eenie Meenie* and *One Potato* have reached near-universal use, while *Onery Twoery* has nearly vanished. This finding mirrors what Opie and Opie (1969) found by direct observation of children in the British Isles who learned the rhymes a little before the students Clarke tested.

Discussion

The multiple constraints described in this chapter and shown to affect recall, as expected, restrict changes within rhymes over long time periods. The constraints appear to be so great that an individual rhyme cannot change much over time. The popularity of individual rhymes, like that of individual games (Sutton-Smith, 1953; Sutton-Smith & Rosenberg, 1961), however, clearly does change. In 150 years, one of the most popular rhymes disappeared from the genre and apparently nonexistent rhymes became the most popular. The genre of counting-out rhymes does change over time, in small degree by changes within individual rhymes, but mostly by changes in the rhymes used. From the three rhymes described so far in the chapter, however, it is not possible to know if memory is a factor in the changes in popularity. For this, a more detailed analysis of the properties of rhymes that are popular at different time periods is needed.

Changes in the Properties of Two Samples of Rhymes

The Trends

What could account for the change in popularity of instances of an oral tradition? Analyses of two samples of rhymes were used to try to answer this question. The samples were the 24 rare and 24 common rhymes described earlier in the chapter. The date provided in Abrahams and Rankin's (1980) dictionary was used as an index of when each rare rhyme was popular. These dates ranged from 1888 to 1969, with a mean of 1931. No single date was available for each of the 24 common rhymes. Instead, rhymes were classified into three groups, depending on whether they were increasing ($+1$), approximately constant (0), or decreasing (-1) in popularity.[17]

Table 10.4 presents the correlations of the properties listed in Table 10.1 with the 3-point scale of the common rhymes and with the date of citation of the rare rhymes. Three properties clearly change over time: the number of word repetitions and the number of meaningful words increase, and the number of rhymes decreases.[18] Alliteration, assonance, and overall poetics follow rhyme, a variable with which they correlate (see n. 11); and, reasonably enough, rated meaning and imagery follow the number of meaningful words.

Why the Trends?

An interpretation of these results is that over time the rhymes are becoming more meaningful. Because nonsense words are selected only for sound, rather than for both sound and meaning, the increase in meaningful words and the resulting decrease in nonsense words result in less poetics. In addition, the dual constraints of sound and meaning on meaningful words reduce the set of available words to fill each place in a rhyme and thereby increase the amount of repetition of the same word over the amount that would occur if only sound constraints were present.

What caused this trend in properties? The memory perspective of this book suggests two possible explanations. The first explanation is that rhymes with the dual constraints of meaning and sound are increasing at the expense of those rhymes that possess only sound constraints because rhymes with dual constraints are easier

Table 10.4. Changes over Time in the Properties of Counting-out Rhymes

Property	Correlations*	
	Common 24	Rare 24
Lines per rhyme	.02	−.15
Words per rhyme	.03	−.04
Word repetition	.53	.25
Rhyme	−.63	−.52
Alliteration	−.51	−.52
Assonance	−.44	−.33
End rhyme	.21	−.06
Overall poetics	−.26	−.32
Four-beat lines	.33	.02
Rated poetics	.55	−.13
Meaningful words	.33	.20
Rated meaning	.64	.19
Rated imagery	.63	.23

Note: Positive correlations imply an increase in the property over time. For a sample size of 24, correlations of .40 or above are significant at the .05 level.

to learn and recall (i.e., to transmit). Although the sound constraint alone is enough to keep a rhyme stable, it may not be enough to keep a rhyme popular in competition with rhymes having both sound and meaning constraints. This explanation is consistent with both the data and the theory presented in this book, but it is no more than speculation. Unless one is willing to argue that counting-out rhymes came into being about 150 years ago, and thus were not well formed at the beginning of the period studied here, the explanation begs the question of why nonsense rhymes existed in the first place.

The second explanation of the change in properties is that the rhymes are getting simpler over time. The main effect of this is a decrease in the complex poetic structure of the rhyme, which, in turn, encourages the increase in meaning and in simpler poetic structure, such as word repetition. Such a decrease in poetic complexity could be due to a decrease in the ages of the children using the tradition. Such a decrease has been noted by Sutton-Smith (1953, 1959). The correlations in Table 10.4 do not initially seem to offer strong support for this claim in that there is no marked shortening of the rhymes over time. Nonetheless, the failure to find shortening of the rhymes could be due to the four-line, four-beats-per-line structure of the genre and to the rhymes' function of counting out.

In summary, the rhymes that are popular at different times have different properties; the trend is toward rhymes with fewer nonsense words and less poetics; and although a multiple-constraint theory can account for the recall data, at present no satisfactory account of the observed drift exists.

Rhyme, Not Reason

What can be drawn from this study of counting-out rhymes? Although the rhymes themselves show some variation at any particular time, they are remarkably stable over time. The largest change they show is in relative popularity, not in the form or content of individual rhymes. The conservative nature of the children who use the rhymes, the rhymes' function of choosing people, and a host of learning principles, such as overlearning and spaced practice, conspire to slow change in the individual rhymes. The properties of the once-cited rhymes, the variation that does exist in the individual rhymes, the repeated recalls of individuals, and the substitutions for what is caught in *Eenie Meenie* indicate, however, that more than rote memorization or general principles of transmission are at work. The constraints of the genre and the piece determine the particular changes that take place.

The genre of counting-out rhymes is different from the other two genres considered here, not only in the age of the people transmitting it and in its style, but also in its having less variability in transmission. Yet, with respect to meaning, counting-out rhymes are less constrained. Most traditions rely on interactions of the sound and meaning constraints to slow change in transmission (Havelock, 1978). In places, such as the first line of *Eenie Meenie,* the counting-out rhymes rely only on their sound. This would seem to be a serious flaw if stability was desired. But as noted in Chapter 5, having multiple constraints means compromising on one constraint to accommodate another. It is rare to find lines containing meaning that can rival the meaningless first line of *Eenie Meenie,* in which not one distinctive feature can be changed without breaking a sound pattern.

Formulas have been conspicuously absent in this chapter. Unless one stretches the definition of a formula, none seem to appear in the tradition. This is not a blow to the spirit of the oral-formulaic theory or to the idea that there are many genres that can be better understood by examining them as oral traditions. Stability in oral traditions is achieved by the use of multiple constraints. In Homeric epic, formulas are a useful solution to multiple-constraint satisfaction because there are only two important constraints—meaning and meter—and the same meaning often needs to be expressed in the same metrical context. In counting-out rhymes, with less reliance on meaning and more on sound-pattern repetition, and with fewer repeating multiple-constraint-satisfaction problems, formulas are not as useful. Each genre is a different solution to the problem of stability.

Although the genre of counting-out rhymes lacks formulas, it provides compelling evidence for the oral-formulaic approach in general and for the role of multiple constraints in particular. Counting-out rhymes would be close to the top of the list of situations in which rote memorization would be expected. Children, who object to even one word of their favorite story being read differently, are the transmitters of a genre of near-magical formulas that decide the fate of peers. If a syllable is changed, the outcome differs. In fact, in this situation, a tape recorder would not seem a bad model of human memory to the casual observer. However, closer examination reveals little evidence for rote memory. Rather, there appear to be multiple constraints, with variation within those constraints. Bartlett's (1932) wonderful phrase "effort after meaning" (p. 227) applies even to counting-out rhymes. For *meaning,* one has to read *organization.* Patterns of sound, even more than patterns of meaning, organize counting-out rhymes.

Thus genres with short pieces can maintain stability without the use of formulas, but not because they are memorized in a rote fashion and reworked (see Holoka,

1976, for an alternative view). Formulaic systems are a method of multiple-constraint satisfaction that is most applicable in genres consisting of numerous long pieces and few constraints. In such genres, the same patterns of multiple constraints occur many times in different places, so that using the same solution to those constraints (i.e., the same formula) repeatedly is possible. This is not the case for counting-out rhyme, a genre that for a single singer consists of a few short pieces with many constraints.

Before concluding, it is important to note that there are other genres of oral traditions that consist of short pieces with clear patterns of rhyme, alliteration, and rhythm, but without clear meanings. Moreover, many of these genres are not for children. Rituals performed by adults are often accompanied by strings of seemingly meaningless words (i.e., by "hocus pocus"). These include Anglo-Saxon charms (Grendon, 1909) and South Slavic healing charms (Halpern & Foley, 1978), both of which have poetic structures similar to the ones discussed here. The Anglo-Saxon charms were an adult genre, and the healing charms, though often learned by young girls, could be used only after menopause.

Why are counting-out rhymes so stable? Because the children who use them are sensitive to the constraints of the genre, as expressed in the individual pieces, and once the constraints are followed, there is little that can vary.

Notes

1. The Abrahams and Rankin (1980) dictionary is a listing of all citations to counting-out rhymes found in an extensive search of the literature. The citations are categorized into distinct rhymes in a reasonable and consistent fashion, and one that is blind to the purposes of this book. Of the 582 different rhymes listed, the 30 most frequently collected rhymes were selected. Six rhymes were removed from this sample, either because they were also nursery rhymes now transmitted outside an oral tradition or because they were similar to a more popular rhyme that was included. The remaining 24 rhymes had between 16 and 66 citations in Abrahams and Rankin's dictionary. In addition, 24 rhymes were randomly selected from among the approximately 350 rhymes that had only 1 citation. The variant of the rhyme listed in Abrahams and Rankin's dictionary was used in all analyses.

2. To minimize the role of chance repetitions of sound patterns (Skinner, 1939, 1942), quantitative measures of the individual poetic devices of word repetition, rhyme, alliteration, and assonance were formulated in the following way. The first time a sound pattern occurred, it was not counted; only repetitions of a sound pattern were counted. Moreover, each repetition of a sound pattern was counted in only one poetic measure. In particular, an entire word was considered as counted in the word-repetition measure; thus no part of that word was counted again in the rhyme, alliteration, or assonance measures. A last syllable counted in the rhyme measure was not counted in the alliteration or assonance measures. A first phoneme counted in the alliteration measure was not counted in the assonance measure. This conservative method slightly underestimates the amount of poetics present, but it ensures that each sound pattern is counted only once. In order to provide a proportion that would allow comparisons across rhymes of different lengths, the word-repetition, rhyme, alliteration, and assonance counts were each divided by the maximum value they could have (i.e., the number of words in the rhyme minus 1).

3. In order to see this pattern most clearly, Burling (1966) noted that beats must be allowed to fall on rests. Although our conventional writing system ignores rests, beats on rests are

explicitly marked in music, and their presence in verse can easily be heard by trying to recite a verse without including the appropriate rests. The following rhyme from the sample used here provides an example. Syllables with beats are underlined. Note that the rhyme reads more naturally if the pause between the last word of line 1 and the first word of line 2, which contains no rest, is shorter than the pause between the last word of line 2 and the first word of line 3, which contains a rest. A similar structure will be noted for ballads in the next chapter.

> Acker, backer, soda cracker,
> Acker, backer, boo. REST
> Acker, backer, soda cracker,
> Out goes you. REST

4. Cronbach's alpha = .80 (Cronbach, 1951).

5. Consider the *Acker, backer* rhyme used in note 3 as an example. The word *backer* was not counted as having meaning because it did not appear to make use of any of its dictionary senses. But the word *boo* was interpreted, with some uncertainty, as a meaningful word intended to scare people. Thus 8 of the 14 words of the *Acker, backer* rhyme had meaning, giving the rhyme a value of 8/14, or .57. Strings of letters that were not clearly words were looked up in a dictionary, and effects of dialects were considered. There were few difficult decisions, and these were made with consideration of what a child using the rhyme at the time and place that the rhyme was collected would be likely to know.

6. Cronbach's alphas = .86 and .81, respectively.

7. The third and fourth most frequent rhymes were given in full as examples on the top of page 40. The data were collected by Helen Clarke in 1981. Recall was scored as correct if we could unambiguously match the recalled rhyme with 1 of the 48 rhymes from the sample, or if two or more undergraduates recalled a rhyme not among the 48. The 2 most often recalled rhymes not in the sample of 48 rhymes were *My mother told me to pick the best one and you are not it* (similar to Abrahams & Rankin, 1980, 379 and 380), which was recalled without a prompt by 9% of the undergraduates, and *Bubble gum, bubble gum in a dish. / How many pieces do you wish?* (similar to Abrahams & Rankin 67), recalled by 8%. The first of these rhymes is often used as an added ending, but here it was reported as a separate rhyme by most of the undergraduates. One rhyme (Abrahams & Rankin 415) was not included in the scoring of past use because it may have been recognized from its occurrence in a Beatles' song.

8. For details, see Kelly and Rubin (1988).

9. The correlation between the two columns of Table 10.2 is .98.

10. Examining the ratings, all five judges indicated that they thought they could predict the sound pattern better than they could predict the meaning or imagery of the next line. Means for the three judgments were 4.03, 2.86, and 3.06, respectively. The meaning and imagery ratings did not differ statistically ($t(4) = 0.44$), but the sound-pattern rating did differ from the average of the other two ratings ($t(4) = 3.21$). Moreover, what separated the common from the rare rhymes in terms of the ratings was poetics. All five of the judges rated the common rhymes as having more predictable poetics ($t(4) = 5.33$), whereas only three rated the meaning and two rated the imagery as more predictable ($t(4) = 0.46$, and 1.63, respectively; both p's not significant).

11. Correlations among all the measures listed in Table 10.1 were computed over all the 48 rhymes in the sample. Two findings are of note. First, rated meaning and rated imagery appear to be the same empirical variable. The correlation between the two variables is .90, which approximates their reliabilities. Second, rhyme, alliteration, and assonance correlate highly with one another, with correlations in the .6 range. No other poetic variables, except for the overall poetics measure, which is based in large part on rhyme, alliteration, and assonance, correlated this highly with one another. These three variables seem to form a group that does

not include the end-rhyme measure and the other poetic variables. A factor analysis supported this conclusion. These three variables should not be expected to correlate with one another for spurious reasons because, in the way in which they were measured here, they are in competition, in that sound patterns involved in one measure cannot be involved in another measure. In fact, this appeared to happen with the word-repetition measure, which correlated negatively with rhyme, alliteration, and assonance in the .4 range. Rhyme, alliteration, and assonance might be expected to correlate negatively with the proportion of meaningful words because nonsense words tend to have only poetics to guide their selection. This was the case, with correlations in the .5 range. However, even when the proportion of meaningful words is partialed out, the correlations between rhyme alliteration and assonance remain in the .5 range.

The correlational analysis is theoretically flawed because the sample of 48 rhymes on which it is based is composed of two different samples, one of common rhymes and the other of rare rhymes. The results reported, however, hold for each of these two subsamples of 24 rhymes considered separately. These subsamples are appropriate for correlational analyses: one is a nearly exhaustive sample of the most common rhymes, and the other is a random sample of rare rhymes.

12. The members of the North Carolina Cognition Group reported learning the rhyme between 1929 and 1964, with an average date of learning of 1953. It is interesting to note the discomfort of those asked to recall accurately a rhyme they learned in childhood. Of the 18 members who used a blank or the term *nigger,* 14 included additional, unsolicited comments ranging from drawing a line through the word to asides such as "Sorry, but this is the way I heard it. *My* kids haven't learned it this way."

13. Folklore and literary analyses add understanding to what can be deduced from existing versions. Opie and Opie (1951) provide references, and Bolton (1888) provides examples to support the claim that the first, and therefore last, line of *Eenie Meenie* is older and more widespread across languages than the rest of the rhyme (but see Bickerton, 1982, for an opposing view based on a Creole origin for this rhyme). Potter (1949) goes as far as suggesting that the line comes from the Druids' choosing human sacrifices, who would leave for the Isle of Mona by way of the Menai Strait. Others have noted that the first line, as well as the beginnings of several other counting-out rhymes, bears a fair resemblance to older base-5 Anglo-Cymric or shepherd's score counting schemes (Bolton, 1888; Opie & Opie, 1969; Potter, 1949). My personal favorite is Kipling's (1923) theory that "Eenee, Meenee, Mainee, and Mo / Were the First Big Four of the Long Ago" (p. 279).

In contrast to the documented age and highly likely Old World source of the first line, "the word nigger is common in American folk-lore but is unknown in any English traditional rhyme or proverb" (Opie & Opie, 1951, p. 156). Potter (1949) suggested that the middle two lines entered the tradition when English-speaking children in Canada or New England tried to imitate the French rhyme *Meeny, meeny, miney, mo, / Cache ton poing derriere ton dos . . .* (p. 339) (i.e., Hide your fist behind your back). This, unlike Bickerton's (1982) theory, provides a location that is consistent with the rhyme's earliest popularity. Whether Potter's suggestion is true or not, it appears that the first and last lines came from the United Kingdom and that the middle two lines were added in North America. The complete rhyme then spread from North America to the rest of the English-speaking world, where it rapidly grew in popularity, displacing other older rhymes.

14. Several limitations exist in this use of Abrahams and Rankin's (1980) dictionary, but none seriously affect the basic conclusions to be drawn. The first and major limitation is in the definition of an individual rhyme. Changes over time that are so great that compilations such as Abrahams and Rankin's dictionary list the changed versions as different rhymes will not be noted by the quantitative methods used here. The reported qualitative analysis of the corpus of

rhymes beginning with *Eenie, meenie* was used to minimize this problem. The second limitation is in the original collecting. Some collections are from adults observing children at play; others are from the recalls of adults. This difference does not appear to introduce much change, if the recall data collected here are an indication, but it does introduce some indeterminacy in the dating. The third limitation is that the frequency of citations in collections is not equivalent to the frequency of use. Common rhymes are underreported because they are typically listed only once in a collection, though they may be observed many times. Rare rhymes may be overreported because they are especially worthy of note in a collection. Thus the 5% level of *Eenie Meenie* and *One Potato* in Figure 10.1 for recent years severely underestimates the proportion of times these rhymes were used by children in counting out. Nonetheless, it is likely that the rank ordering of citation frequency is a good index for the rank ordering of actual use. This is especially true if many small collections are combined as was done here.

15. Citations were dated using the following rules. (a) Only dates listed in brackets in Abrahams and Rankin's (1980) dictionary were considered. (b) Only the date on which a rhyme was recorded, not the date on which the report was published, was included if both dates were listed. If, however, a phrase such as "current since" was used, it was assumed that the rhyme was collected at both the earlier date and the date of publication, and so both dates were included. (c) When a range of dates, such as "the 1880s," was given, the middle of that range was used. Using these rules, the earliest documented citations in Abrahams and Rankin's dictionary to *Eenie Meenie, One Potato,* and *Onery Twoery* are 1870, 1885, and 1810, respectively.

Together, two large collections, Bolton (1888) and Opie and Opie (1969), contribute 346 citations to Abrahams and Rankin's dictionary. Although the three rhymes of interest may have been observed many times while compiling the Bolton (1888) and Opie and Opie (1969) collections, each of these collections can add only one citation to the three rhymes. This is because once a rhyme is collected, the number of times it is collected is not recorded. In this way, the relation between popularity and citation frequency is distorted by these large counts. For this reason, the Bolton (1888) and the Opie and Opie (1969) collections, which are much larger than any of the others, were excluded from the computations that led to Figure 10.1.

16. Chi-square tests were performed using the most recent five 20-year periods shown in Figure 10.1 and a sixth period consisting of the earliest two periods shown in the figure combined with all earlier times. This combination of periods increased the expected value of all cells to above 3. The chi-square values for the tests that the relative frequencies of citation of *Eenie Meenie, One Potato,* and *Onery Twoery* can be predicted by the overall frequency of citations in Abrahams and Rankin's (1980) dictionary are 5.57 (not significant), 27.82, and 54.84, respectively (all $df = 5$). This null hypothesis is equivalent to a horizontal straight line in Figure 10.1. Although *Eenie Meenie* demonstrates a clear increase in frequency over time, the expected frequency at the oldest time period, where the rhyme differs most from its expected value, was too low to contribute highly to the chi-square value. Although the chi-square test does not support the conclusions made in the text for *Eenie Meenie,* the qualitative data presented in the chapter do. In addition, clearly the three rhymes differ from one another: The chi-square value for the test that the relative frequencies of citation of the three rhymes are the same over time is 53.71 ($df = 10$).

17. The procedure used for classifying the 24 common rhymes was as follows. The percentage of citations accounted for by each rhyme was calculated for the period 1919 and earlier and for the period 1920 and later. This is equivalent to what was presented in Figure 10.1, except that here only two values, rather than the seven of Figure 10.1, were calculated for each rhyme: one value combining all dates prior to 1920 and one combining the last three 20-year periods of Figure 10.1. The 1920 date was chosen from Figure 10.1 because it produced

approximately equal numbers of citations in the two periods. The ratio of the bigger to the smaller of these percentage-of-citations-accounted-for values was taken. Values above 1.5 indicated an increase or a decrease in popularity, depending on whether the early or the late period had more citations, and values between 1.0 and 1.5 indicated no clear change in popularity. The 1.5 value was chosen for the criterion because it was a round value that had no borderline cases (there were no ratios between 1.32 and 1.76) and because it provided similar numbers of rhymes in each category (8, 6, and 10 in the increase, decrease, and no-change categories, respectively).

18. A second random sample of rare rhymes was selected as a check and it followed the same trends as the first, but the magnitude of the correlations were much smaller. Thus the finding of systematic changes in properties over time in rare rhymes must be considered as tentative. However, if generalizations are to be made not to all counting-out rhymes in a collection but to the everyday use of the tradition, then the sample of 24 common rhymes accounts for almost all the usage.

CHAPTER 11

North Carolina Ballads

Balladry belongs to the none too literate . . . people who know it by heart
where it can weather and season properly. Ballads lead their life in the mouths
and ears of men by hear-say like bluebirds and flickers in the nest of hollow
trees.

Frost, 1953, p. xii

And here the very Prince of Poets, old Homer, *if we may trust ancient Records,
was nothing more than a blind* Ballad-singer, *who writ Songs of the Siege of*
Troy, *and the Adventures of* Ulysses; *and playing Tunes upon his Harp, sung
from Door to Door, till at his Death somebody thought it fit to collect all his
Ballads, and by a little connecting 'em, gave us the* Iliad *and* Odysses, *which
since that Time have been so much admired.*

A Collection of Old Ballads, 1723, Vol. 1, pp. iii–iv

The ballad and heroic epic have little in common save that each tells a story.

Gerould, 1957, p. 103

Following a brief general description of oral-tradition ballads, the history of ballads
is outlined. In the next section, the forms of organization, or constraints, of the genre
are provided in detail. The third main section is an analysis of three cases in which an
event gave rise to a new ballad. These newly generated ballads provide a strong test
of the role of constraints outlined because, by definition, their formation cannot
depend on rote recall of an existing ballad. In the last main section, laboratory and
field studies with expert and novice singers are described. These studies test the
basic ideas developed here in a more rigorous fashion than is possible with historical
evidence, thereby providing converging evidence for the observational work.[1]

Much has been written about ballads (Richmond, 1989). Here the viewpoint is
that of a cognitive psychologist. What can be measured or counted is emphasized,
even though more often exists. The process of recall is emphasized even though
most of the data are the products of long past recalls by anonymous singers.

Ballads and Their History

Definition by Description and Example

Counting-out rhymes were defined by the unique purpose they served. The oral tradition of ballads is a more difficult genre to define because it shares with other genres many of its functions and structural features. Nonetheless, oral-tradition ballads, hereafter simply called ballads, are a genre in English and in other languages. In his introduction to an annotated bibliography of over 1,600 entries on ballad scholarship, Richmond (1989) lists the properties of a ballad:

> It is usually anonymous, it concentrates on a single episode, it begins *in medias res,* it is dramatic in its narrative structure, and it is impersonal (objective) in its telling. Moreover, it is always stanzaic, either seven- or eight-stress rhymed couplets or quatrains rhyming *a,b,c,b,* and generally alternates light and heavy stresses in each line. In addition, repetition of words, phrases, and stanzas is common, not only in individual ballads but also in the genre as a whole. . . . It is, in other words, the kind of thing collected and/or edited by Child, Grundtvig, and Meier. . . . (pp. xx–xxi)

Whiting (1955) provides a similar description:

> "A ballad is a song that tells a story.". . . It is plain in diction and imagery, it tells an elemental story of universal appeal, it concentrates on a single incident, it is sparing of explanatory details and background, it often begins *in medias res,* it employs abrupt transitions, it makes free use of dialogue and calculated repetition, its emphasis is on action rather than reflection, it is associated with a tune which is often more stable that its text, and it tells its tale impersonally without author's asides or editorial comment. . . . Of course, it could be argued, has been indeed, that to attempt to define a ballad is otiose as well as embarrassing, and that the individual need only be advised to read ballads and judge for himself. (p. vii)

Quiller-Couch (1927), writing in an earlier period of literary criticism, stresses the difference between literary and oral-tradition ballads. Along with Whiting and Richmond, Quiller-Couch (1927) argues for the power of examples:

> Let me apply a test which I have applied elsewhere. If any known man ever steeped himself in balladry, that man was Sir Walter Scott, and once or twice, in *Proud Maisie* and *Brignall Banks* he came near to distil the essence. If any man, taking the Ballad for his model, has ever sublimated its feeling and language in a poem "seraphically free / From taint of personality," that man was Coleridge, and that poem *The Ancient Mariner.* If any writer today alive can be called a ballad-writer of genius, it is the author of *Danny Deever* and *East and West.* But suppose a bundle of most carefully selected ballads by Scott, Coleridge, Kipling, bound up in a volume with such things as *Clerk Saunders, Cospatrick, Robin Hood and the Monk,*—you feel (do you not?)—you know—they would intrude almost, though not quite, as obviously as would a ballad of Rossetti's or one from Morris's *Defence of Guinevere.* (p. 35)

Following Richmond's, Whiting's, and Quiller-Couch's suggestion, an example of a ballad, *Lord Thomas and Fair Annet* (Child 73), still current in North Carolina, is presented. Because the ballad was first recorded prior to 1690 (Child, 1885, pt. 3, p. 180), it has a documented history of over 300 years. Figure 11.1 is an early-

Figure 11.1. An illustration of the last verses of *Lord Thomas and Fair Annet*. (From *A Collection of Old Ballads*, 1723)

eighteenth-century illustration of *Lord Thomas*. The variant of *Lord Thomas and Fair Annet* given here (Brown, 19M) was reported by a Durham woman as having been sung between 1812 and 1820. It appears in *The Frank C. Brown Collection of North Carolina Folklore* (Belden & Hudson, 1952, Vol. 2, pp. 77–79), along with the comment that "of all the old ballads, this probably stands next to 'Barbara Allen' in popular favor" (p. 69).

How stable are such ballads? Table 11.1 provides versions of the two most graphic stanzas of *Lord Thomas* dating from 1723 to 1989. As with the counting-out rhymes, variants with stanzas different from these exist at all time periods.[2] Nonetheless, the small amount of change in the particular variants chosen is striking. The rest of the chapter examines this stability.

1 Lord Thomas, Lord Thomas he was a brave man;
  He courted the king's high dame.
  She had but one own fair daughter—
  Fair Eleanor was her name.

2 "O mother, O mother, come riddle to me,
  And riddle us both as one,
  And say shall I marry the fair Eleanor
  Or bring the brown girl home?"

3 "The brown girl she hath both house and lands,
  Fair Eleanor she hath none.
  So I would advise you with all of my mind
  To bring the brown girl home."

4 He clad himself in velvet fine,
  His waiters all in white;
  And every town that they passed through
  They took him to be some knight.

5 He rode and he rode till he came to the castle;
  He made the knocker to ring.
  There was none so ready as the fair Eleanor
  To rise and let him in.

6 "What news, what news, Lord Thomas?" she cried,
  "What news do you bring to me?"
  "I come to invite you to my wedding.
  Tomorrow it is to be."

7 "Bad news, bad news, Lord Thomas," she cried,
  "Bad news do you bring to me.
  I thought to have been myself your bride
  And you bridegroom to me."

8 "O mother, O mother, come riddle to me,
  And riddle us both as one,
  And say shall I go to Lord Thomas's wedding
  Or tarry alone at home?"

9 "There are many that are our friends, daughter,
  But thousands are our foes.
  So I would advise you with all of my mind
  To Lord Thomas's wedding don't go!"

10 "There are many that are our friends, mother,
  Though thousands be our foes.
  So, betide me life, betide me death,
  To Lord Thomas's wedding I'll go."

11 She clad herself in satin fine,
  Her maidens all in green,
  And every town that she passed through
  They took her to be some queen.

12 She rode and she rode till she came to the hall;
   She made the knocker to ring.
   There was none so ready as Lord Thomas himself
   To rise and let her in.

13 He took her by her lily-white hand,
   He led her through the hall,
   He led her into an upper room
   Where sat the ladies all.

14 "Is this your bride, Lord Thomas?" she cried,
   "Methinks she looks wondrous brown,
   When you might have had so fair a lady
   As ever the sun shone on!"

15 "Oh, speak no ill," Lord Thomas said,
   "Oh, speak no ill of she;
   For I do love your little finger more
   Than I do her whole body."

16 The brown girl she had a little pen-knife,
   And it was keen as a dart;
   And between the short ribs and the long
   She pierced fair Eleanor's heart.

17 "Oh, you are blind, Lord Thomas," she cried,
   "Or can't you very well see?
   Oh, don't you see my young heart's blood
   Come trickling down to my knee?"

18 Lord Thomas he had a sword by his side,
   And it was sharp and small;
   And with it he cut off the brown girl's head
   And he flung it against the wall.

19 "Oh, dig my grave, oh, dig my grave,
   Oh dig it wide and deep.
   Bury fair Eleanor in my arms,
   The brown girl at my feet."

20 He placed the hilt upon the ground,
   The point against his heart.
   Did ever three lovers meet together
   So very soon to part?

A Brief History of Ballads

Old World Origins

An oral tradition of ballad singing exists now and has existed for a long time. Exactly when, where, and how long ago ballad singing began cannot be resolved, but the written record and speculations that have been made about its interpretation

Table 11.1 Two Verses of *Lord Thomas and Fair Annet* from the 1720s to the 1980s

London, 1723 (A Collection of Old Ballads, 1723, 35; Child 73 Db)

This brown Bride had a little Penknife,	Lord Thomas he had a Sword by his Side,
That was both long and sharp,	As he walk'd about the Hall
And betwixt the short Ribs and the long,	He cut off his Brides' Head from her Shoulders,
Prick'd fair Ellinor to the Heart.	And threw it against the Wall.

Widow McCormick, Drumbarton, Scotland, 1825 (Child 73 De)

She took up a little pen-knife,	He took up a little small sword,
That was baith sharp and small,	That hung low by his knee,
She struck Fair Helen fornents the heart,	And he cut off the brown girl's head,
And down the blood did fall.	And dashed it against the wall.

Mrs. R. D. Blacknall, Durham, NC, ca. 1812–1820 (Belden & Hudson, 1952, Vol. 2, 19M)

The brown girl she had a little pen-knife,	Lord Thomas he had a sword by his side,
And it was keen as a dart;	And it was sharp and small;
And between the short ribs and the long	And with it he cut off the brown girl's head
She pierced fair Eleanor's heart.	And he flung it against the wall.

Mrs. Julie Boone, Yancy County, NC, 1918 (Sharp MSS. 4683/3260; Bronson, 1962, 142)

The brown girl having a knife in her hand	Lord Thomas having his sword by his side,
Which were both keen and sharp,	It was both keen and sharp,
Between the long ribs and the short	He cut the brown girl's head clean off
She pierced fair Ellender's heart.	And clave her body apart.

Mrs. J. E. Schell, Banner Elk, NC, 1933 (Bronson, 1962; Matteson & Henry, 1936)

The brown girl having a sword in her hand,	He took the sword from the brown girl's hand,
It being both keen and sharp,	And led her from the hall.
She thrust it into Fair Eleanor's side,	He cut her head right off from the shoulders,
Which entered into her heart.	And kicked it against the wall.

Eleazar Tillett and Martha Etheridge, Wanchese, NC, 1941 (Warner, 1984, 140)

The brown girl having a little pen knife,	He took the brown girl by the hand,
The blade was keen and sharp,	He led her through the hall,
Right between fair Ellen's ribs	Took out his sword, cut off her head,
She pierced her to the heart.	And threw it against the wall.

Sheila Barnhill, Morris Hill, NC, 1988 (collected by Wanda T. Wallace)

The brown girl had a little pen knife,	He took the brown girl by the hand,
It was both keen and sharp,	He led her across the hall,
Betwixed the long rib and the short,	He pulled out his sword and cut off her head,
She pierced fair Ellender's heart.	And he kicked it against the wall.

Bobby McMillon, Lenoir, NC, 1989 (collected by Wanda T. Wallace)

Well, the brown girl she had a little pen knife,	He taken the brown girl by the hand,
The blade were wonderful sharp,	And he led her from the hall,
Betwixt the long ribs and the short,	And with his sword cut off her head,
She pierc-ed fair Ellender's heart.	And he kicked it against the wall.

can be reviewed. The basic problem is that oral traditions need not leave any written trace. Thus the absence of a written record can mean that no tradition existed, that the tradition was not recorded, or that the record was lost. For instance, in Chapter 10, the existence of a widespread, active oral tradition of counting-out rhymes was demonstrated for a span of over a century, but not for two. From this, it could not be decided whether counting-out rhymes were a relatively recent development or one that dates back to the beginnings of language. An old engraving of children in a circle counting out or an ancient Greek reference to the practice would leave many scholars unconvinced of a continuous, as opposed to a reinvented, tradition. What can be firmly established for ballads is that at the time North Carolina was first settled, there existed in the Old World an active English-language oral tradition of ballad singing, one that some scholars say was near its peak, and that ballads much like those sung there have been sung in North Carolina continuously from about that time.

In order to provide a sample of the range of opinion, the views of two ballad scholars are presented. Fowler (1968) provides an argument for the most recent possible origin of ballads given a careful review of the manuscript evidence. In contrast, Kittredge (1904), using the same records, argues for an earlier origin.

Fowler (1968) makes two conservative assumptions in arriving at the most recent possible dates for the ballads: (1) "that a given ballad took the particular shape it has about the same time it was written down" (p. 5), and (2) that a ballad-like piece in a manuscript may not have been a ballad in that it may have been recited, but not sung.[3] By examining changes in style in medieval songs and literature, both within and outside the ballad form, Fowler comes to the conclusion that ballads originated when the decreasing status of the minstrel caused the professional, literate, minstrel tradition to mix with a balladless, folk, oral tradition. This began in the fifteenth century, but did not result in the full ballad style until later, peaking when "the resulting intensity of narrative symmetry, the growing reservoir of commonplaces, and the remarkable developments of style . . . made the eighteenth century a major creative period in the history of balladry" (p. 19).

Kittredge (1904) uses the same data, but different assumptions, to come to the conclusion that "there is no difficulty in proving beyond a reasonable doubt that there were ballads in plenty from the dawn of English history" (p. xiv). That there is only one ballad "completely popular in metre, in phraseology, and in what we call atmosphere" (p. xiv) from the thirteenth century, none before, and none after for a period of 200 years merely shows that ballads were an oral tradition that was not recorded. Similarly, although the *Geste of Robin Hood* was first recorded around 1500, its language is much older, and Robin Hood ballads were mentioned in *Piers Plowman*, placing them before 1377. Of course, from Fowler's point of view, it need not be the case that the thirteenth-century ballad or the reference in *Piers Plowman* was really to ballads as we know them. One of Kittredge's anecdotes, however, is especially convincing. Bishop Percy obtained a manuscript from about 1650 that is the basis of much of what we know about early ballads and that contains a version of *The Maid and the Palmer*. The next recording of the ballad was from Sir Walter Scott's memory and was included in an 1880 collection. Kittredge reports that Scott was ignorant of the recorded 1650s version. If the 1650 manuscript was destroyed— and Kittredge reports it was being used as kindling when Bishop Percy obtained it— the ballad's earliest dating would be two centuries later than it now is.

Kittredge makes two other points that should be noted. The first is that just because a literate piece predates the first recorded ballad version of a story does not mean that the literate piece is the source of the ballad; the literate piece could have as easily come from an older unrecorded ballad, or both could have come from another source. The probability that the ballad and the literate version of the story would be found in written form, assuming that both were present at some date, needs to considered. The second point is that ballads closely related in content and style to those considered here existed and have been studied in European languages other than English. For example, Child (1885, pt. 3) traces the history of Norse ballads that "have the story of 'Lord Thomas and Fair Annet' [the ballad used earlier as an example], coming very close in details" (p. 180), and Hodgart (1962, pp. 88–95) traces both the Scandinavian and French versions of the ballad (see Gerould, 1957, pp. 23–25, for an alternative view). Similarly, Nygard's (1958) scholarly and exhaustive study of *Lady Isabel and the Elf-Knight* (Child 4), a ballad still popular in the North Carolina tradition, compares variants from throughout Europe. He notes manuscripts by 1570 from Denmark, Germany, and Spain, and by 1665 from Iceland. The ballad story and many details persist over centuries and over changes in language and culture. Although such data cannot speak directly to the age of the British ballads, it makes their origin less likely to be a strictly British phenomenon.

Under either Fowler's or Kittredge's extreme estimates, there was time for an oral tradition to develop fully and be shaped by transmission through human memory before it was carried to the New World.

North Carolina Ballads

Ballads in North America, in general, and North Carolina, in particular, are of either British or North American origin. Both kinds of ballads are sung by the same singers and thus have most of the same attributes. Nonetheless, differences exist between the two (Laws, 1964). Ballads of British origin are much as they were in the Old World, with minor adaptations to the new culture and geography. They are more likely than North American ballads to contain suspense, class distinctions, pageantry, and supernatural agents, and they usually have a greater geographic distribution and popularity. North American ballads are more likely to have an explicit moral, to omit descriptions of sex or shocking details even when they are central to the story, to be about physical labor, and, because they are more recent, to have their content more easily traced to an actual event or a single source. The differences are not mysterious. Many of the differences were already present within the corpus of British ballads at the time and in the areas from which migration to North America occurred (McCarthy, 1991). In addition, differences in the extent of supernatural agents (Nygard, 1958), geographic distribution, and popularity may be more a factor of the age of the ballad than the continent of origin.

Because ballads that started in the South of the United States have a wider distribution than ballads that started in other regions, Laws (1964) concluded that the South had a more active tradition and served as a point of distribution. Patterns of migration make it reasonable to assume that early immigrants who sang British ballads settled in North Carolina and surrounding states before moving to other parts of the country. British and older North American ballads traveled with them. North American ballads often started from literate, if not literary, sources and were often circulated initially in print or phonograph record before entering the oral tradition. A thriving commercial newspaper and phonograph ballad tradition existed in parallel to the oral tradition, much as the broadside and oral ballad traditions existed in parallel in the Old World. Laws (1964) concludes that "in general, however, American ballads have been distributed by individual singers performing non-professionally before small audiences in homogeneous communities and within families in the form of private singing" (p. 52).

In spite of Laws's assurances, there remains the serious question of the influence of broadsides, newspapers, and phonograph records on the transmission of ballads. For the purposes of this book, this is not a question about authentic ballads or literary origins but one about the role of memory. If the stability and change found are due to external memory aids, then little about human memory can be found from studying such stability. There is certainly some influence of writing, printing, and the phonograph, but how much?

In the Old World, in addition to the oral tradition of ballads, there existed in English a printed broadside tradition (Pinto & Rodway, 1957) and printed songbooks in other languages (Holzapfel, 1982). Broadsides were printed from at least the sixteenth to the early twentieth centuries, but mostly in times before newspapers were common. Most of these broadsides were quickly written pieces or occasionally the works of skilled literary poets and are easily distinguished from the oral-tradition ballads. Some were closer in style to oral-tradition ballads, and true oral-tradition ballads were sometimes printed, thereby appearing in the broadside tradition. The degree of interplay between the oral and written ballads and the impact of written versions on the stability of oral ballads are not clear (Andersen, 1982), but the existence of easily available written version of oral ballads tempers the conclusions that can be drawn about the role of memory. For instance, it can be argued that the repeated printings of early broadsides of *Lord Thomas and Fair Annet,* not oral transmission, are responsible for some (Andersen, 1982; Beard, 1955) or most (Hodgart, 1962, pp. 104–108) of the stability shown in Table 11.1.[4] Nonetheless, for the ballads in the Old World, the broadside and oral traditions were, for the most part, different genres. Ballads in one genre are easily separated from ballads in the other, so it is doubtful that the constraints to be noted here were greatly influenced by the broadsides, though stability probably was.

The case of the modern ballads could be much worse because the phonograph could preserve not only the words, but also the tune, but here we are on firmer ground because we have living singers who can be asked how they learned ballads and what use they make of writing, recorded music, and the home tape recorder. The singers who Wallace used as her primary informants learned orally from other singers and made little use of external memory aids. For many ballads in North Carolina, there was probably a period early in their history when they were spread by phonograph or printed record, but this does not seem to be of major importance in the oral tradition even at the time such ballad recordings were popular. For instance, *The Wreck of the Old 97,* which is examined later, probably sold as many records as any ballad. In the traditional ballads Wallace collected, "Steve" is going to "Spencer" when he loses his "air brakes," which agrees with what we know of the actual event. In contrast, in the most popular phonograph version, "Pete" is going to "Center" when he loses his "average" (Wallace & Rubin, 1988b). Moreover, the phonograph records of the day could hold only about five stanzas, so that only five stanzas that summarized the ballad could be affected even though the ballad might have been much longer.

Properties of Ballads

Quantitative measures, while often not as subtle as the qualitative analyses of literary critics, are useful in describing the extent to which various regularities exist. Such regularities are documented in detail because they provide one description of the forms of constraints that ballad singers follow. Although the details of this description may not ultimately be the ones best suited to a model of how ballads are remembered and sung, the description provides an indication of the variety and extent of such constraints.

All quantitative estimates provided are based on the 29 ballads that were collected seven or more times in forming *The Frank C. Brown Collection of North Carolina Folklore* volume on ballads (Belden & Hudson, 1952, Vol. 2). For each ballad, the first complete variant, accompanied by a transcript of its music (if such a variant existed), was included in the analysis.[5] The version of *Lord Thomas and Fair Annet* presented earlier is one of these ballads.

The Brown collection represents a cross section of folklore collected in North Carolina in the period between World War I and World War II. It provides a sample of the tradition in which the expert North Carolina singers who took part in the analyses presented later in the chapter developed. It is also a well-executed, minimally edited collection, with archives of the original transcriptions and recordings still available. Limiting the sample to the most frequently recorded ballads was an attempt to capture the tradition as it was most often heard.

Verse structure, meter, music, the correspondence between meter and music, and poetics are outlined to provide a quantitative description of the local tradition for which other results are presented. Ballad scholars have noted many of these patterns in a qualitative fashion (e.g., Child, 1882–1898; Gerould, 1957; Hodgart, 1962; Kittredge, 1904; Laws, 1964; McCarthy, 1990; Sharp, 1908).

Verse Structure

The stanza is a basic unit of the ballads. The boundaries of each stanza are clear because both the poetic structure and the music repeat each stanza. As noted later in the chapter, the short length of the stanza and the fact that each stanza must complete an idea heavily determine the thematic structure. The judgment of the Brown collection's editors was used as a knowledgeable determination of the internal structure of stanzas in what is an orally transmitted tradition—that is, a tradition in which the singers do not record verse structure using typographic conventions. In fact, when Wallace (personal communication) asked singers if they had ever written a ballad, those who had often used a paragraph rather than a verse style.

Like the Old World ballads, those in the Brown collection have a four-line structure; 21 of the 29 ballads have four-line stanzas. Of the 8 ballads that do not have four-line stanzas in the variant chosen, all have an underlying four-line structure and all but 1 have four-line stanzas in another variant.[6]

Choruses, or refrains, are more likely to occur in the ballads of more recent origin.[7] Although 11 of the 29 ballads in the Brown collection sample are in Child's (1882—1898) collection, none of the 6 with full choruses are.[8]

Meter

A judge indicated the meter of each ballad. Although more subjective, this method seemed more likely to capture the subtleties present in the ballads than the more mechanical method of assigning stress by the part of speech and the dictionary stress pattern, as used with the counting-out rhymes in Chapter 10. The two methods agreed on the stresses of 80% of the words. Of the 29 ballads, 25 are predominantly iambic (an unstressed followed by a stressed syllable), 2 are trochaic (a stressed followed by an unstressed syllable), 1 is anapestic (an unstressed, unstressed, and stressed syllable), and 1 varies (Wallace & Rubin, 1991).

The number of stresses per line is also fairly regular. The most common pattern for the counting-out rhymes and much of children's song (Burling, 1966) is four lines of four stresses each, with some lines having their last stress falling on a musical rest rather than on a word. That is, chanting a 4, 3, 4, 3 stress counting-out rhyme takes as long as a 4, 4, 4, 4 one. The notation of scansion does not note this, but the notation of music does. Another way of saying this is that there is a longer pause between the last word of the second line and the first word of the third line for the 4, 3, 4, 3 stress pattern than for the 4, 4, 4, 4 stress pattern. The same general pattern holds for ballads, though there are exceptions, with the first four lines of each stanza having either four stresses or a 4, 3, 4, 3 stress pattern. In particular, of the first and third lines, 75% have four stresses and 13% have three stresses. In contrast, of the second and fourth lines, 34% have four stresses and 61% have three stresses. The music for the three-stress lines usually marks with a rest the place where the fourth stress would have been.

The 4, 4, 4, 4 (long meter) and 4, 3, 4, 3 (common meter) beat structures, with a rest after the third beat of the three-beat lines, dominate both the counting-out rhymes and the ballads. Both traditions consist of mostly one-syllable words, so this structure translates to approximately four lines of 7 to 10 words each. The four-line-per-stanza structure is the typical way to present ballads and captures many of the poetic regularities. A less conventional typographic convention, but often a superior metrical alternative, is to present each stanza as a couplet, combining, from the four-line structure, line 1 with line 2 and line 3 with line 4. Based on musical considerations, Bronson (1944/1961) argues that this is the only structure for *The False Knight upon the Road* (Child 3). Based on meter, Stewart (1925) argues that it is the dominant structure for the tradition as a whole, and that a stress pattern more subtle than the iambic is present, a pattern that could be sustained in an oral tradition only if it were sung.

A long-meter ballad stanza—that is, a stanza with four beats per line when written in traditional four-line form—when considered as a couplet, becomes

$$\smile\;\acute{}\;\smile\;\acute{}\;\smile\;\acute{}\;\smile\;\acute{}\;\big|\;\smile\;\acute{}\;\smile\;\acute{}\;\smile\;\acute{}\;\smile\;\acute{}$$
$$\smile\;\acute{}\;\smile\;\acute{}\;\smile\;\acute{}\;\smile\;\acute{}\;\big|\;\smile\;\acute{}\;\smile\;\acute{}\;\smile\;\acute{}\;\smile\;\acute{}$$

where ⌣ represents an unstressed syllable, ‐ represents a stressed syllable, and | a break, or caesura. A common-meter ballad stanza—that is, a stanza with a 4, 3, 4, 3 structure when written in four lines—becomes

$$\smile\;\acute{}\;\smile\;\acute{}\;\smile\;\acute{}\;\smile\;\acute{}\;\big|\;\smile\;\acute{}\;\smile\;\acute{}\;\smile\;\acute{}$$
$$\smile\;\acute{}\;\smile\;\acute{}\;\smile\;\acute{}\;\smile\;\acute{}\;\big|\;\smile\;\acute{}\;\smile\;\acute{}\;\smile\;\acute{}$$

Stewart notes that two levels of stress are discernible—primary (´) and secondary (`)—and that they occur in a regular alternating pattern. The long meter becomes

$$\smile\;\acute{}\;\smile\;\grave{}\;\smile\;\acute{}\;\smile\;\grave{}\;\big|\;\smile\;\acute{}\;\smile\;\grave{}\;\smile\;\acute{}\;\smile\;\grave{}$$
$$\smile\;\acute{}\;\smile\;\grave{}\;\smile\;\acute{}\;\smile\;\grave{}\;\big|\;\smile\;\acute{}\;\smile\;\grave{}\;\smile\;\acute{}\;\smile\;\grave{}$$

The common meter becomes

$$\smile\;\acute{}\;\smile\;\grave{}\;\smile\;\acute{}\;\smile\;\grave{}\;\big|\;\smile\;\acute{}\;\smile\;\grave{}\;\smile\;\acute{}$$
$$\smile\;\acute{}\;\smile\;\grave{}\;\smile\;\acute{}\;\smile\;\grave{}\;\big|\;\smile\;\acute{}\;\smile\;\grave{}\;\smile\;\acute{}$$

The addition of a secondary level of stress changes the meter from 14 or 16 iambic feet per stanza to 7 or 8 dipodic feet. That is, the repeating pattern is no longer ⌣ ´, but rather ⌣ ´ ⌣ `, a pattern noted apparently independently by Gerould (1957) and Leech (1969) and stressed by Hodgart (1962).

The dipodic meter is presented here in detail because it is a complex constraint that severely limits both word choice and word order. Words must fit an unstressed–primary-stress–unstressed–secondary-stress pattern, which is considerably more difficult than an unstressed–stressed pattern. Moreover, the use of such a structure strongly suggest musical support and thereby makes it more likely that a ballad with dipodic rhythm was originally composed with music.

Stewart provides many arguments for this change from iambic to dipodic foot, but only two are presented here. The stronger argument is that the accented syllables of nouns, main (as opposed to auxiliary) verbs, adverbs, and adjectives tend to fall on the primary rather than the secondary stresses of the dipodic pattern. That is, as with the counting-out rhymes, the match between the stress assigned to the syllables of words in isolation by the dictionary and the stress assigned to those syllables by the underlying meter can be compared as a way of testing the validity of the underlying meter.

The second line of evidence for the dipodic structure comes from an analysis of end rhyme. In terms of the four-line presentation of ballads, the most common rhyme scheme is that the last words of lines 2 and 4 rhyme. This means that the last words of the two dipodic couplet lines rhyme. In musical and metrical terms, the long meter can be viewed as the basic underlying meter, with the common meter as a derivative produced by omitting the last two syllables. Evidence for this view is that the place in which these two syllables would normally occur is marked by a rest in music or a pause in meter (see Burling, 1966, for a similar point using counting-out rhymes). In terms of rhyme, this omission moves the rhyming word from a second-ary to a primary stress, if a dipodic meter is assumed, but has no effect on an iambic meter. This can be seen clearly by contrasting the long and common meter displayed in dipodic and iambic terms. Note in the lines that follow that the last syllable is always stressed in the iambic lines, but that it changes from a secondary to a primary stress in the dipodic lines as one switches from long to common meter:

Long iambic	⌣ ´ ⌣ ´ ⌣ ´ ⌣ ´ | ⌣ ´ ⌣ ´ ⌣ ´ ⌣ ´
Long dipodic	⌣ ´ ⌣ ˋ ⌣ ´ ⌣ ˋ | ⌣ ´ ⌣ ˋ ⌣ ´ ⌣ ˋ
Common iambic	⌣ ´ ⌣ ´ ⌣ ´ ⌣ ´ | ⌣ ´ ⌣ ´ ⌣ ´
Common dipodic	⌣ ´ ⌣ ˋ ⌣ ´ ⌣ ˋ | ⌣ ´ ⌣ ˋ ⌣ ´

For a sample of Child's ballads, Stewart found that 36% of the rhymes fall on dictionary-defined, accented syllables for long meter, whereas 72% of the rhymes fall on dictionary-defined, accented syllables for common meter. It therefore appears that the underlying dipodic meter tends to make the last syllable of lines unaccented in long meter, even when these word should be highly stressed to draw attention to the end rhyme.[9]

The Correspondence Between Meter and Music

The study of the music of ballads has been neglected relative to the study of the ballads as poem (Richmond, 1989, p. xxvi). As those who study the music are quick to note (e.g., Bronson, 1944/1961, 1962), this leads to a dangerously incomplete knowledge of oral transmission. This chapter will do little to remedy this discrep-ancy.[10] Music affects all aspects of the text, but here only one aspect will be noted: the match between musical and metrical stress. The tune and text should reinforce each other; both should stress the same place. In order to test this hypothesis, for the first stanza of each song with a printed musical score, the percentage of stressed syllables from the metrical feet that fall on the accented notes was calculated (Wal-lace & Rubin, 1991).[11]

There is good agreement between the stresses in the text and the stresses in the music. For the sample of 29 popular ballads, 83% of stressed syllables fall on the accented notes of the musical score. Some of the disagreements between text and musical stresses would disappear in singing because, as Hodgart (1962) states, "the rhythms of folksong do not always correspond to speech rhythms" (p. 57). For instance, using Hodgart's examples from *Patrick Spens,* when a disyllabic word ends a line, the "wrenched" accent regularly goes to the last syllable of the line and *the best sai´ lor* becomes *the best sai-lor´* and *dear ma´ ster* becomes *dear ma-ster´* . That is, certain instances that were counted as mismatches follow standard patterns of their genre and are not mismatches in any real sense. Nonetheless, for the Brown collection, most disagreements between text and musical stresses occur in one of two time signatures where the simple algorithm used to determine the accented note was inappropriate.[12] Thus the quantitative agreement between text and tune is high, and the actual agreement would have been even higher if more subtle measures of the placement of poetic and musical stress had been used.

Word Choice and Poetics

The number of repeating, rhyming, and alliterating words within each line was counted. Standard typography lines, not Stewart's (1925) couplets, were used. As with the counting-out rhymes in Chapter 10, the first occurrence of a word was not counted, producing a conservative measure. For instance, if a word occurs three times in a line, it would count as two repetitions, and a pair of rhyming words would add one word to the rhyme count.[13] Poetics links occur for about 15% of the words within a line. On average, 3% of the words in a line rhyme with one other word in that line; 9% of the words alliterate with one other word; and 3% repeat within the line. If stanzas were used instead of lines, as was the case with counting-out rhymes this figure would have been somewhat higher, but not as high as it was for counting-out rhymes, where 87% of the words in the sample of common rhymes repeated, rhymed, alliterated, or shared assonance with another word in the rhyme.

Nonetheless, line-internal poetics are important. McCarthy (1990, pp. 146–147) provides examples of variation on the theme of reading a letter that preserves an *l* alliteration while varying the words used. Within one collection of variants of *Johnie Scot* (Child 99), he finds "*l*ong *l*etter," "first *l*ine of the *l*etter," "first *l*ine that Johnie *l*ooked on," "first *l*ang *l*ine that he *l*ooked to," and "Johnie *l*ooked the *l*etter upon." Such variation suggests that within the tradition, alliteration exists independently of the words used to express it. The alliteration makes it more likely that a long letter will have a line looked at rather than a short page read, but it allows for variation on whether the letter or the line is long. Experimental support for this argument is provided later in the chapter.

The end-rhyme pattern was identified by the pattern contained in more than half the stanzas for each song, where end rhyme was defined as exact rhyme, not near-rhyme or assonance. In 55% of the popular ballads, lines 2 and 4 rhyme, in 10% just lines 1 and 2 rhyme, and in another 14% both lines 1 and 2 and lines 3 and 4 rhyme. Thus 79% of the ballads have some pattern of consistent end rhyme. Including both near rhyme and assonance would have made the percentages higher, since the rhymes used are often not exact (Zwicky, 1976), as would have counting repeating words as part of the rhyme pattern. In the majority of ballads, lines 2 and 4 rhyme, supporting the underlying couplet structure of most ballads, but in nearly one-quarter of the ballads, lines 1 and 2 rhyme, showing that the four-line structure is not without merit (also see Hodgart, 1962, pp. 57–59).

A few rhyme sounds account for a large proportion of the rhymes used in the sample of 29 popular ballads. Five rhymes ending in vowels account for 34% of the lines with end rhymes (words rhyming with *bee* account for 9.2%;[14] *bay*, 8.2%; *bow*, 6.0%; *by*, 6.0%; and *boo*, 4.9%). The next most frequent 3 end-rhyme sounds bring the cumulative total to 45% (*bin*, 3.8%; *beer*, 3.3 %; and *Bart*, 3.3 %), and 3 more, for a total of 11 different end-rhyme sounds, are needed to account for half the end-rhyme occurrences (*bite*, 2.2%; *boar*, 1.6 %; and *ball*, 1.6%). The limited rhyme-sound set, and the limited vocabulary of rhyming words that it implies, provides constraint on word choice in addition to the end rhyme itself (Buchan, 1972, p. 152).[15]

For the sample of 29 popular ballads, 81% of the words are one syllable long, 17% are two syllables long, and only 2% are three or more syllables long. These values

Table 11.2 Percentage of Words with One, Two, Three, or More Syllables

Source	Number of Syllables			
	1	2	3	4+
Sample of 29 popular ballads	81	17	2	0
Literary ballads				
Coleridge, *The Ancient Mariner*	85	13	2	0
Kipling, *Danny Deever, East and West*	80	19	1	0
Scott, five imitations of ancient ballads	77	20	3	0
Average of the literary ballads	81	17	2	0
Literary prose				
Coleridge, *The Friend*	69	19	10	2
Kipling, *The Phantom 'Rickshaw*	71	18	8	3
Scott, *Ivanhoe*	66	21	9	5
Average of the literary prose	68	19	9	3
Homeric epics (O'Neill, 1942, p. 155)				
Iliad	30	34	20	16
Odyssey	29	34	21	15

are in line with the literate ballads chosen by Quiller-Couch as being most like oral-tradition ballads, but they differ drastically from prose written by the same authors and from Homeric epic, as shown in Table 11.2.[16] The reason for this favoring of single-syllable words is not clear, but at least two factors seem likely. The first is that the most often used words in English are one syllable long. For instance, the most frequent 57 words, which together account for over 40% of written English, are all single-syllable words (Rubin, 1974). This surely plays a role, especially in an oral folk tradition, but it cannot account for the differences between the literary ballads and prose. The second factor, which contrasts the literary and oral-tradition ballads to the literary prose, is that single-syllable words are easier to fit into the metrical patterns of English verse (Rosenberg, 1988, p. 147). Whatever the causes, however, the mnemonic implication of this observation is clear: only a small subset of the words in the English language are used in ballads; when a word is needed, a word of one syllable will usually do, sometimes a word of two syllables, but rarely one that is longer. This constraint, like the others, lessens the memory load.

Word Choice and Commonplaces

Word choice is limited not only in terms of length, but also in terms of the particular words used. Many oral traditions contain formulas: often repeated phrases that fit a given metrical and meaning requirement. In ballads, they are called *commonplaces*. In the example of *Lord Thomas and Fair Annet* given at the beginning of the chapter, the heroine is *fair* and her hand is *lily-white,* and the grave is both *wide and deep,* with *deep* ending the line so that it provides a near-rhyme for *feet.* If two horses are traveling together, the first is most likely to be a milk-white steed and the second a dappled bay. Longer sequences, or *motifs,* also often occur. Among the best known are the two stanzas with the rose-and-briar motif from *Barbara Allen* (Brown 27F), which follows. It appears with minor modifications in *Lord Lovel,* in variants of the

Lord Thomas and Fair Annet ballad given earlier, and, as Andersen (1985, pp. 275–283) and Gerould (1957, p. 152) note, elsewhere throughout the tradition.

> They buried him in one church yard
> And Barbara in another.
> From his there sprang a red rose,
> And from hers there sprang a brier.
>
> They grew, they grew to the steeple top
> Till they could grow no higher;
> They tied themselves in a true love knot,
> The wild rose and the brier.
>   (Belden & Hudson, 1952, Vol. 2, p. 117)

Similarly, a variant of the ballad *Child Maurice* (Child 83B) collected in Scotland in 1825 contains the following two stanzas, which are similar to stanzas in *Lord Thomas and Fair Annet:*

> O' when he came to Lord Bernard's castle,
> He tinkled at the ring;
> Who was as ready as Lord Bernard himself
> To let this little boy in?
>
> Lord Bernard he had a little small sword,
> Hung low down by his knee;
> He cut the head off Child Noryce,
> And put the body on a tree.

The ballad *Child Maurice* does not appear in the Brown collection of North Carolina ballads, so it is doubtful that the singer who recorded the variant of *Lord Thomas and Fair Annet* given earlier knew these stanzas as being common to the two ballads. However, at one time, British singers probably did.

Approximately 5% of the lines in the sample of 29 popular ballads used here repeat in another ballad in the set, with only minor variation (Wallace & Rubin, 1991). If the entire corpus of 314 ballads in the Brown collection were used, the number would obviously be higher.

Andersen (1985) notes that by appearing in similar contexts in many ballads, these repeating commonplaces acquire nonliteral meaning for those familiar with the genre, setting the tone for the ballad and foreshadowing events. Meanings accrued by use in similar contexts are also found for formulas in epic by Foley (1991, 1992). Four of the 27 commonplaces Andersen examined across the Anglo-Scottish corpus are in *Lord Thomas and Fair Annet.*

The lines *He clad himself in velvet fine, / His waiters all in white,* in stanzas 4 and 11, always indicates that a change in scene is coming. When a woman dresses, as in stanza 11, it is usually to regain a lost love who is about to wed another, as it is here and in six other ballads noted by Andersen. Moreover, as occurs here, the woman usually succeeds. Thus the commonplace of dressing foreshadows much of what follows (Andersen, 1985, pp. 249–253).

[H]e came to the castle; / He made the knocker to ring, from stanzas 5 and 12, and from *Child Maurice,* is a standard transition. What follows is usually a lover's visit, the beginning of a violent confrontation, or a usually failed attempt to resolve a conflict (Andersen, 1985, pp. 221–232).

What news, what news, from stanza 6, is the sign of a dramatic turning point. The news is almost always bad, involving violence, and the remaining stanzas are a reaction to the conflict presented. The news signals impending confrontation, impending imprisonment, or death. Thus the request for news is far from neutral and indicates that a major change in events is unfolding (Andersen, 1985, pp. 201–208).

He took her by her lily-white hand, from stanza 13, is usually a rape or seduction formula, and in many cases, including this one, can be a prelude to death. When the line is followed by *He led her through the hall,* as it is here and in nine other ballads noted by Andersen, the sexual act is minimized and it is usually a prelude to marriage. Thus this simple, concrete act is a way of indicating to those familiar with the genre that Annet has been chosen over the brown girl by Lord Thomas and that her death may be near (Andersen, 1985, pp. 161–174).

Repetition of lines also occurs within single ballads. Returning to the example of *Lord Thomas and Fair Annet,* the following stanza is repeated with changes. The first occurrence's alternatives are shown in brackets, and the second occurrence's alternatives are shown in parentheses:

> "O mother, O mother, come riddle to me,
> And riddle us both as one,
> And say shall I [marry the fair Eleanor] (go to Lord Thomas's wedding)
> Or [bring the brown girl] (tarry alone at) home?"

The next three stanzas also repeat, with some changes:

> [He] (She) clad [himself] (herself) in [velvet] (satin) fine,
> [His waiters] (Her maidens) all in [white] (green);
> And every town that [they] (she) passed through
> They took [him] (her) to be come [knight] (queen).

> [He] (She) rode and [he] (she) rode till [he] (she) came to the [castle] (hall);
> [He] (She) made the knocker to ring.
> There was none so ready as [the fair Eleanor] (Lord Thomas himself)
> To rise and let [him] (her) in.

> "[What] (Bad) news, [what] (bad) news, Lord Thomas[?](,)" she cried,
> "[What] (Bad) news do you bring to me[?"](.)
> "I . . ."

In addition, the two stanzas beginning *There are many that are our friends* are near repetitions. Finally, the two stanzas shown in Table 11.1 to demonstrate stability over time, as well as other lines, have a marked parallel, though not at the level of the exact words.

In the sample of 29 popular ballads, 24% of the lines, excluding choruses, repeat within their ballad, with only minor variation (Wallace & Rubin, 1991). Thus about half the lines appear more than once in a single ballad. The repetition reduces the number of novel lines produced, adds structure, and provides repeated exposure for these lines.

Theme

The repetition of lines not only affects word selection, but also is a bridge to the overall organization of the ballad. Consider the *O mother* stanza just given. In the stanzas following its first occurrence, bad advice is given by a mother and followed, whereas in the stanzas following its second occurrence, good advice is given by a mother and ignored. Both sequences combine to produce the tragedy. Thus this repeated stanza serves to organize most of the ballad. Although it is repeated only once, this stanza is an example of incremental repetition—that is, repetition in which minor modifications are made to the same basic stanza throughout part or all of a ballad.

In another variant of the same ballad (Child 73B, 1885, pt. 3, p. 184), the equivalent stanza is part of a three-stanza sequence in which the hero visits some-one in the first stanza, asks who he should marry in the second, and is given an answer in the third. This sequence of three stanzas repeats three times for the hero's father, mother, and sister and repeats once more when "Fair Annie" asks her father whether she should go to the wedding. Thus a dozen stanzas are organized around this incremental repetition. The organizational device of incre-mental repetition can also be seen in the set of 29 popular North Carolina ballads. In *The Gallows Tree* (Brown 30c; Child 95), the man about to be hanged, in separate stanzas, sees his father, mother, sister, and sweetheart coming. Each of these four stanzas is followed by a stanza in which the person coming is asked if he or she has brought gold, and another stanza in which the person answers, accounting for all dozen stanzas of the variant. Similarly, in *Frankie Baker* (Brown 251a), Frankie spends one stanza each looking for Albert down the Broadway, in a gin house, a barroom, and a pool room. In each of these sequences, the incremental repetition organizes a large part of the ballad while increasing tension and sus-pense.

Question-and-answer or action-and-reaction sequences can be viewed as minimal incremental repetitions or as common organizational forms in their own right. Much of what has been offered as examples of repetition consists of such questions and answers, and *The Gallows Tree* contains such pairings in each of its incremental repetitions.

Annular or ring structure or composition is common in ballads, epic, and other oral traditions (e.g., Andersen, 1982; Gaisser, 1969; Niles, 1983, pp. 152–162; Stanley, 1993). Progress through a piece can be viewed as a skewer traveling in a straight line through an onion, piercing the skin, each layer, and the center before continuing through the same layers in reverse order until the skin is reached again at the opposite side. Each layer entered provides the expectation of a layer to be encountered again. Individual layers can contain incremental repetition or other forms of organization, making the ring structure a flexible frame for a ballad. In computer terms, it is a push-down stack: first in, last out. Lord (1991b) argues that although this pattern can be transformed into a technique of literary rhetoric, it is a natural way for an illiterate poet to compose orally. Momentary con-tinuity of thought is maintained by picking up the most recently dropped theme. In Havelock's (1971) words, ring structures "are not patterns, . . . but echoes" (p. 52).

For one variant of *Johnie Scot* (Child 99G) analyzed by McCarthy (1990, pp. 57–68), the layers to the center, which correspond to stanzas or groups of stanzas, might be

(a) Johnie seemingly dishonors England and its princess
  (b) The king of England reveals his low regard for the princess
    (c) The king plans treachery for Johnie
      (d) Johnie lets the king know he is coming
        (e) Johnie sees the princess and realizes the treachery
      (d) Johnie confronts the king
    (c) Johnie overcomes the king's treachery
  (b) Johnie proves his high regard for the princess
(a) Johnie proclaims honor for Scotland and the princess

Thus each action to the center implies a parallel action from the center to the end, providing an elegant symmetry in combination with the story's progression. Moreover, the characters involved and the use of dialogue can follow the same pattern, reinforcing it. In terms of characters, for both occurrences of each layer, (a) is about Johnie and the princess, (b) is mainly about the princess, and (c) and (d) are about Johnie and the king. Using N for narrative and D for a stanza containing any direct dialogue, the 23 stanzas of the variant can be listed in the fairly symmetrical pattern: $N\ DD\ NDDD\ NNNN\ D\ DDDD\ NNND\ DD\ N$, where spaces indicate a change in scene and the layers of the ring.

Buchan (1983) gives the following ring structure for a variant of *Hugh Spencer's Feats in France* (Child 158):

(a) Mission given
  (b) Obstacle shown
    (c) Test announced
      (d) Test prepared for
    (c) Test overcome
  (b) Obstacle overcome
(a) Mission completed

The characters, though more complex than those in *Johnie Scot,* follow the ring structure, as might be expected from the plot, though the pattern of narrative and dialogue is not quite as clear (e.g., *NNN DDD DDD DDD NND ND ND ND DDD*).

Such ring structures provide a strong aid to memory. They are, however, difficult to apply in a simple, mechanical fashion to ballads because they require a sophisticated interpretation of the ballad. Although this makes the ring structure difficult to use in a detailed quantitative fashion suitable for an experimental psychology journal, the evidence presented is clear enough to convince most skeptics that ring structure is a good description of many ballads.

As an example, consider the variant of *Lord Thomas and Fair Annet* given earlier in the chapter. It has 20 stanzas. One possible ring structure is

	Stanza
(a) Lord Thomas and Fair Eleanor praised	1
(b) Problem of the place of two woman given	2
(c) Lord Thomas gets advice and acts on a solution	3–5
(d) Eleanor questions Thomas and acts unwisely	6–13
(d) Eleanor questions Thomas; dies from unwise acts	14–17
(c) Lord Thomas takes new action for a new solution	18
(b) Problem of place of two woman resolved	19
(a) Lord Thomas and Fair Eleanor mourned	20

An alternative ring structure is

	Stanza
(a) Lord Thomas and Fair Eleanor praised	1
(b) Lord Thomas questions and acts on a solution	2–5
(c) Fair Eleanor questions and acts on a solution	6–13
(d) Fair Eleanor insults the brown girl verbally	14
(e) Lord Thomas tries to mediate	15
(d) The brown girl insults Fair Eleanor physically	16
(c) Death brings a new solution	17
(b) Death brings a new solution	18–19
(a) Lord Thomas and Fair Eleanor mourned	20

The character structure for the first ring structure is (a) Lord Thomas and Fair Eleanor, (b) Lord Thomas, (c) Lord Thomas, and (d) Fair Eleanor and Lord Thomas in the first instance and Fair Eleanor and the brown girl in the second. The character structure for the second ring structure is (a) Lord Thomas and Fair Eleanor, (b) Lord Thomas, (c) Fair Eleanor, (d) Fair Eleanor in the first instance and the brown girl in the second, and (e) Lord Thomas. Either ring structure has some merit (and the reader might do better), so the ambiguity of which is better does not argue against the value of considering ring structures as constraints in some ballad, nor does the alternative representation based on incremental repetition based on the *O mother* stanza given at the beginning of this section.

To reinforce this point, consider Andersen's (1982) analysis, which I read after constructing the previous two ring structures. As opposed to a strict ring structure, Andersen favors a ring containing repetition in linear as opposed to mirror-image order; in particular, he bases much of the structure on the repetitions following the *O mother* stanzas.[17] Andersen's structure is

	Stanza
(a) Introduction	1
(b) Appeal 1: Lord Thomas taking mother's advice	2–3
(c) Journey 1: Lord Thomas goes to Eleanor	4–5
(d) News	6–7
(b) Appeal 2: Eleanor defying mother's advice	8–10
(c) Journey 2: Eleanor goes to Lord Thomas	11–12
(d) Reaction to news and counter-action	14–18
(a) Conclusion	20

Question-and-answer sequences, incremental repetition, and ring structure are ways to organize stanzas. They are all based on the stanza as an independent unit. For this approach, ballads are seen as a collection of stanzas organized into scenes, often by question-and-answer sequences or incremental repetitions. For longer ballads, the scenes can be grouped into acts, often using the same devices. The scenes or acts are then the layers of the ring structure, or larger units for an incremental repetition. These devices allow the local sequential process of recall in oral tradition to produce global structures and symmetry.

The ring and other organizational structures are based on the stanza as the unit of composition. Ballad scholars have noted this composition in stanza units. For instance, Hodgart (1962) states that ballads "present the narrative not as a continuous sequence of events but as a series of rapid flashes'' (p. 28), comparing each flash to a different scene in a film. Gerould (1957) makes the point in a similar way: ''The events burst out in a series of flashes, each very sharp and each revealing one further step in the action'' (p. 89). Later, he is explicit as to the reason:

> The peculiarities of ballad structure, as they appear throughout most parts of Europe, are explicable if we remember that the stories are moulded to fit a recurrent melody. Their compression, their centralization, . . . and, above all, the swiftly moving action, are precisely the qualities that would arrive, almost inevitably, from the practice of singing stories to brief tunes. (pp. 211–212)

A melody repeating every stanza produces a unit that can be moved, omitted, and put into an organization. Less than a whole stanza would not fit the repeating melody.

Having considered some of the special properties of ballad themes, we need to consider one of the general issues raised in Chapter 2. One claim of the story grammar reviewed in Chapter 2 is that all stories have explicit settings—a claim that is counter to what students of oral traditions (e.g., Ong, 1982) and ballads (e.g., Whiting, 1955, p. vii) have noted. The settings in many oral traditions are usually assumed or implied by the story and characters. In order to show that ballads do not consistently have explicit settings, a clear, easy to apply definition was needed. The following is a modification of a definition that Barbara Houston devised as part of her master's thesis work. Assume that the setting will occur as the first line or lines of the ballad. First, look for explicit setting markers. These would include the classic fairy-tale beginning *Once upon a time,* which introduces a whole world, or, in ballads, beginnings with the explicit introduction of a person (*There was a lady, a lady gay,* Brown 25C), a place (*In Scarlet town where I was born,* Brown 27A), or a time (*It was on one Monday morning about one o'clock,* Brown 287D). If any of these is present, there is a setting. If not, the second step is to examine the verb. If the first verb is a verb of state, there is a setting; if the first verb is a verb of action, there is no setting. Thus the three examples just listed that have an explicit setting statement also contained the verb *to be,* but the verb *to be* can also be the only cue (*Frankie was a good girl,* Brown 251A; *John Henry was a steel-driving man,* Brown 270A). Other examples use other state verbs (e.g., *stood,* Brown 21C, or *used to dwell,* Brown 81A). In contrast, the examples with no setting use verbs of action (*Hangman, Hangman, slack your rope,* Brown 30C).

A third step can be used to check that the system is working. It consists of trying to determine whether new information is being given or is assumed (Clark & Haviland, 1977). New information that is to be part of the setting will be introduced with the indefinite articles *a, an,* or *one* (*Lord Thomas, Lord Thomas he was a brave man,* Brown 19M), whereas old information for which a setting is already assumed will be introduced with the definite article *the* (*Sweet William rode up to the Old Man's gate,* Brown 3B) or with a pronoun without a prior referent (*He followed her upstairs and down,* Brown 2B). In the popular-ballad set, this third rule is always redundant with either the first and the second rule. For instance, ballads Brown 25C, 287D, 251A, 270, and 19M all have indefinite articles and all have settings under the first and second rules, whereas 2B and 3B have definite articles but have no settings under the first and second rules.

Applying these rules to the 29 popular ballads results in 17 ballads with settings and 12 without. There may be a trend toward an increase in the use of settings over time. Of the 11 ballads in the popular ballad set that are also in Child, only 4 have settings, whereas 13 of the 18 ballads not found in Child do.[18]

Imagery

Like works in other oral traditions, ballads are high in imagery. As summarized in the sections on history and on theme, ballad scholars have long noted that ballads consist of rapidly advancing action, with little discussion of thought, feelings, and abstract concepts. Morals and lessons are left for the hearer to add in the British tradition, though they often occupy a stanza or two in ballads of American origin (Laws, 1964). Similarly, if one attempts to divide ballads into *states* or *events* using Mandler and Johnson's (1977) story grammar, which was discussed in Chapter 2, there are few states (Houston, 1986).

As reviewed in Chapter 3, imagery can be divided into spatial and descriptive components on the basis of behavior and underlying neurology. Here a first attempt was made to examine the distinction in ballads. Five undergraduate judges were asked to place each line of each of the 29 popular ballads into one of the following three categories:

1. Spatial: the tracking of the location of people and objects in the visual scene. The line could provide a vivid image, but it had to specify either location or motion that produces a change in location (e.g., *He rode and he rode till he came to the castle*).
2. Descriptive: a description of the people and/or objects in a scene without regard to location or motion (e.g., *He clad himself in velvet fine*).
3. Abstract: a nonvisual line that does not describe a mental picture.

Dialogue was scored for the contents of what was said. Thus, *She told him to go to her father's stable* was scored as if it were *he went to her father's stable*. There was fair agreement among the judges, who received only a brief written instruction sheet and the ballads.[19] On the average, 28% of the lines are spatial, 52% are descriptive, and 20% are abstract.

Although more lines are descriptive than spatial by this definition, it should be noted that much of the description is stereotyped, consisting of commonplaces. Although some of the lines judged as spatial also consist of commonplaces, they contain the action that carries the story. In Gerould's (1957) words:

> Since these are tales of action, in which there is little effort to build up characters or setting in detail, we are satisfied with conventionalized descriptions like yellow hair and bodies "as white as milk" or "nut-brown" . . . but there is no elaboration of these things even in the longer ballads. . . . Description is stylized. (p. 116)

In addition, the spatial organization appears to coincide with the verse structure, with a new stanza coinciding with a change to a new location, scene, or view (Hodgart, 1962, pp. 27–31).

The descriptive lines, however, are far from mere fillers used to complete the metrical form of the ballad or to add specificity to concrete scenes. As noted in the discussion of Andersen's (1985) analyses of commonplaces, the details often come to have added meaning or symbolism within the ballad genre; for example, a woman's brilliant dress indicates that she will win back her lover. Making a similar point, Rogers (1980), combining the Hispanic and European ballad traditions, finds that details of descriptions set the tone and expectations of ballads. As examples, she notes that hunting foreshadows love or death, whereas games foreshadow love leading to death. And McCarthy (1990) notes that, at least for the singer he studied, a wedding consistently foreshadows a funeral, as it does in *Lord Thomas and Fair Annet*. Thus the stereotyped descriptive details take on added functions (see Foley, 1991, for a similar point in epic).

Combining Constraints

Some of the constraints outlined, such as the dipodic meter, occur infrequently outside ballads. Others, like four-line stanzas with the second and fourth lines rhyming, are more widespread. Finally, constraints like the one that a story should have one main character in each role, not two or nine, which plays an important part in the next section, may be just as common in most narrative forms as it is in ballads. The constellation of constraints outlined here, however, is unique to ballads. To the extent that definition is possible, the constraints taken together provide one. As the rest of the chapter demonstrates, the combined constraints converge to leave a limited set of solutions. In this way, they are powerful aids for cuing memory, for reconstruction, and even for generating a new ballad.

The particular set of multiple constraints used in a genre does increase stability and provides the genre with its own distinctive style. However, compromises must be made to fit all of the constraints simultaneously. Consider the combination of rhythm, music, theme, and imagery in ballads. Ballads are composed in stanzas of 14 to 16 stressed syllables. The melody repeats each stanza, making this rhythmic constraint especially hard to alter. Each stanza also expresses a complete idea and usually occurs in a different location from at least one of the two stanzas adjacent to it. That is, the lack of necessary enjambement for individual lines found in Homeric epic is found in ballads for stanzas. This has the advantage of having rhythm and theme reinforce each other and of allowing stanzas to be added or deleted in order to change the length of a singing without disrupting the rhythm, the music, and, with proper selection, the story line. Many of the properties of ballads noted by literary critics and listed at the beginning of the chapter can be seen as outcomes of satisfying this particular set of constraints. Expressing a complete idea in 14 to 16 stressed syllables leaves little room for explanatory details, background, explicit mention of the characters' motives, or editorial comments. Often the "he said" or "she said" that would appear in a prose format is missing from the dialogue. In epic, a line can be added where needed to fill in such details, but in ballads the only option is to add a whole stanza. This is rarely done, helping to give ballads their lauded characteristics of being fast-moving and impersonally told, but it also produces abrupt transitions and ambiguities. Such ambiguities can be heard differently by different singers and, if resolved differently in their retellings, can lead to change.

New Ballads as a Test of the Constraints

The formation of new ballads provides an especially telling way to study the effects of constraints. When an existing ballad is sung, the constraints outlined could operate to help stabilize the ballad, but theoretically, it is also possible that the singer simply reproduces the song, with no appreciation of the constraints of the genre. When a new ballad is created, however, no existing variant exists to be reproduced. The singer must use genre-specific rules, known consciously or not, and/or use general abilities not particular to the genre with a remembered store of examples from the genre in order to make a new ballad that is consistent with the genre (Rubin & Kontis, 1983; Rubin, Stolzfus, & Wall, 1991; Ward, 1994). Moreover, when an actual, complex event is transformed into a ballad, options within the genre, such as the particular rhyme sound and melody, need to be chosen and a few of the many possible details need to be selected, so a glimpse into these processes is available.

Three examples of ballad formation are examined. The first, which started outside the North Carolina ballad tradition, concerns the murder of Pearl Bryan (Cohen, 1973). The second and third, *The Wreck of the Old 97* (Cohen, 1981; Wallace & Rubin, 1988b) and *The Wreck of the Football Special* (Wallace, 1992), are about events that occurred in or near North Carolina.

The examples presented here are rare cases, though the genre convergence of new ballads noted here has been observed elsewhere in the tradition (Andersen & Pettitt, 1985). The examples are not intended to argue that ballads are normally created anew each time they are sung. They are intended to demonstrate the singers' considerable knowledge of the genre, knowledge that singers can make use of to aid their recalls, using the processes outlined in earlier chapters. For example, knowledge demonstrated in the generation of a new ballad can be used in the process of recalling an existing ballad: to aid cuing; to consciously decide on the best alternative or to unconsciously find one alternative more familiar; to anticipate what word is next on the basis of such properties of the genre as narrative structure, rhythm, and poetics, even though the word usually sung has not yet come to mind; to take advantage of the limitations imposed by multiple constraints; and to re-create when something cannot be recalled or has to be altered because of an earlier change in the ballad or the conditions of performance.

Poor Pearl

The murder of Pearl Bryan is an especially clear example because the actual event and the resulting ballads are discrepant in interesting ways and become more discrepant as time passes.

The event is as follows. In 1896, the headless body of Pearl Bryan was found. She was 5 months pregnant. Two men, Jackson and Walling, were arrested, tried, and convicted of the murder and were hanged on the same gallows. From evidence presented at the trial, Bryan became pregnant either with Jackson or with a cousin of hers who was not directly involved in the murder, but who knew one of the murderers. The head was never found. The headless body, the two murderers, the double hanging, her affair with her cousin, and the still missing head are highly distinctive and easy to image details that could make a ballad more memorable. However, they do not fit the thematic pattern of the genre.

Drawing in part from Laws's (1964) division of American ballad types, Cohen (1973) notes that the events could fit into either of two existing patterns of ballads: the murdered-girl pattern or the criminal-brought-to-justice pattern. The first includes the wooing of an innocent, trusting young woman by an artful man; the luring of the woman to a lonely spot; the murder of the woman, who offers little resistance; the abandonment of the body; occasionally regret by the lover-murderer; and a warning to women (as in the widely recorded traditional ballad *Pretty Polly*). If there were any mourning, it would be by the woman's family. The second pattern includes the youth, upbringing, or past deeds of the criminal; the crime and events leading to it; the pursuit, capture, trial, and execution of the criminal; his family's sorrow; and a warning to men (as in the widely recorded traditional ballad *Tom Dulla*). The actual murder has enough details to fill both patterns, but the traditional ballad must follow one or the other; it is either the victim's story or the murderer's. In this case, it is the victim's.

The discrepancy between the murdered-girl pattern and the actual event works against a simple translation of the event to song. In the ballad pattern, there is usually one lover-murderer, not two. The murderer is the victim's only lover; she has not had other lovers. The body is left, but not mutilated. Cohen carefully traces the resolution of these discrepancies over time. The murder spawned six discernible ballads, each with variants. The most popular one accounts for 65 of the 135 total variants. Cohen found historical trends among these 65 variants that here permit a quantitative analysis. Walling, the nonlover-murderer, is mentioned in 29% of the ballads prior to 1928, in 14% of the ballads between 1928 and 1938, and in none after 1938, leaving only one murderer. For the same three time periods, the body is headless in 46%, 28%, and 0% of the ballads. With time, the murdered-girl pattern of a single lover who quickly leaves the body (often behind in a shallow grave or a river) triumphs over the facts.

A less gruesome example can been seen in the psychology laboratory, where undergraduates read stories containing well-practiced scripts (e.g., ordering food in a restaurant) that combined atypical details from the scripts (e.g., Jack put a pen in his pocket) and typical details (e.g., Jack sat down at a table). As noted in Chapter 2, compared with recalls made during the same session, recalls a week later were more likely to leave out atypical details that did occur and to include typical details that did not occur (Graesser, Woll, Kowalski, & Smith, 1980; Smith & Graesser, 1981). Within a single person, this fits well with the analyses provided in Chapter 7; if two things are known equally well at one time, then the one learned earlier is forgotten more slowly. A similar effect may be working through many people in the ballad tradition. The mechanism for this schema-like behavior could be any of those outlined in Chapter 2, including the storage of numerous instances coupled with random decay of particular details over time (Hintzman, 1986).

The pattern of basic actions and characters is the most interesting aspect of *Poor Pearl* because they come to conform to the ballad constraints over many retellings. That is, they demonstrate genre convergence. In contrast, the word choice and poetics are fairly stable throughout the history of the ballad, following from the start-ballad constraints, which restrict word choice and reduce the memory load. The particular words chosen follow the language and poetics of ballads. In ballads, the murdered woman is usually ''sweet.'' Here her name is Pearl, and, for the sake of alliteration of the *p* and repetition of the *r,* she is ''poor.''

It is not just ballads that have these constraints. Cohen argues effectively that many, but not all, of the constraints are part of the larger culture and are reflected in the newspapers of the time. For instance, in the press, Bryan started out as a lower-class woman of the town, but became a young, trusting girl as soon as the coroner discovered that she was pregnant. Unlike the ballad tradition, the press presented both the murdered-girl pattern and the criminal-brought-to-justice pattern, but kept them in separate stories. The newspapers shared with the ballads not only the basic character types and plot structures, but also the alliterative epithets ''poor Pearl'' and ''dreadful deed.'' These practices may not have diminished. An extension student enrolled at my university was accused of posing as an heir to the Rothschild fortune. In the headlines, he became the ''bogus baron.''

Like the commonplaces, the basic poetic structure of the ballad appears stable. In fitting the story to song and meter, different solutions were used in different variants, but the most common appears to be a four-line stanza with lines 2 and 4 rhyming.

Thus a real event was transformed into a ballad that followed the basic poetic constraints of the genre. A few of the many details were selected for presentation in the ballad, with most discarded. Over time, even these details changed to make the ballad more like other murdered-girl ballads in the tradition.

The Wreck of the Old 97

The events of the wreck of the Southern Railway's Number 97 in 1903 were a much better fit to the pattern of existing train-wreck ballads than were the events of the murder of Pearl Bryan to the pattern of existing murdered-girl ballads, so there was little need for a ballad about the wreck to change over time in a systematic way. Nevertheless, the ballad is of special interest because lawsuits over the copyright of a variant that appeared on a Victor Talking Machine Company recording provided a history of variants 30 years after the incident. Moreover, because the ballad is still popular in North Carolina, it can be obtained from traditional singers, as discussed later in this chapter (Wallace & Rubin, 1988b).

Number 97 was apparently going too fast when it jumped the track right before a trestle 75 to 100 feet above the creek in which the train landed (Belden & Hudson, 1952; Cohen, 1981; Wallace & Rubin, 1988b). Details including the names of stations, the route taken, the number of the train, and the name of the engineer became part of the ballad. As Wallace (1992) notes, ship and train wrecks are either about the death of one main character or about the death of many, often nameless, people. *The Wreck of the Old 97* is about one person, the engineer, and only his name and death are explicitly mentioned, though eight others died in the wreck.

Several distinct variants were known 30 years later, though by that time they all had overlapping stanzas. Aspects of two older ballads, *The Ship That Never Returned* and *Parted Lovers,* were used in one or another of the distinct variants. All the variants follow the basic patterns reviewed earlier. For instance, stanzas are four lines long, with rhymes at the end of lines 2 and 4. Several variants end in a stanza giving a moral, as is common in American, but not British, ballads (Laws, 1964). Using variant A from the Brown collection, which was the basis for experiments to be reported later, there are 79% single-syllable words, 20% two-syllable words, and 1% three-syllable words. If proper names are excluded, these values become 85%, 15%, and 0%, respectively.

Thus a newsworthy event was transformed into a ballad that remains in the oral tradition nearly a century later.

The Wreck of the Football Special

In order to examine the birth of a ballad as it occurred, Wallace (1992) asked traditional singers to generate a ballad given a newspaper article describing a train wreck. In this way, Wallace could evaluate the knowledge and ability that known singers have about the genre. In addition, because she knew exactly what information was available to the singer, she could evaluate what was selected and what was omitted in forming the ballads.

As a warmup and an assessment of knowledge, traditional singers were asked to sing a few favorite ballads and then all the wreck ballads that they knew. Following this, singers were handed a copy of an article describing the wreck of the Football Special from the November 25, 1915, *Charlotte Observer* and asked to compose a ballad from it. Of the 11 traditional singers interviewed, 3 chose not to attempt the task; the 8 who did all succeeded.

Three of the traditional singers began singing immediately after they finished reading the newspaper article. The remaining five wrote down a version before singing it. The average time taken to read the article and to compose and sing the ballad was 12 minutes; the average length was 15 lines. One of the singers parodied an existing ballad in generating a new one. The remaining seven each generated a ballad that was not identical to or a parody of any of the ballads they had sung during the warmup period or during another session (or in any obvious fashion to any other ballad known to Wallace). That is, these seven singers all used a melody and stanzas that appeared novel; their generated ballads were new ballads, not just copies or conglomerations of stanzas from other ballads.

The eight generated ballads followed the constraints outlined earlier in the chapter. Four had a four-line stanza, and three had an eight-line stanza; none had a chorus. All were iambic, five were common meter, and one was long meter. Five rhymed lines 2 and 4; one rhymed lines 2 and 4 and lines 1 and 3; one rhymed lines 3 and 4, the singer commenting that he could not get the rhyme correct; and the singer who parodied a ballad used no rhyme, probably because the parodied ballad had no rhyme. There were 75% single-syllable words, 23% two-syllable words, and 2% three-or-more-syllable words.

The article mentioned the death of two passengers; in fact, the headline, which was included in the copy given to the singers, read "Squire Severs and Ned Hall Killed in Wreck." However, in wreck ballads, either one person dies or many die; the ballad is either about one hero or about the loss of life. The situation is parallel to that of the two murderers in *Poor Pearl* and to that of the nine deaths in *The Wreck of the Old 97* in that the existing ballad pattern and the facts do not fit the conventions of the genre. One singer did not explicitly mention that anyone died, leaving seven singers remaining for comparison. Of these, two followed the facts and sung ballads in which two people died; five followed the ballad constraints, with three singing that one person had died and two singing that many had.

The article was divided into 100 facts (e.g., date, time, location, and the names of the passengers injured and killed). On the average, only 6 of these 100 facts appeared in each ballad, producing ballads in which only the essentials were preserved. Another way to document this lack of specific details is that almost 60% of the lines produced could have occurred in a ballad about another train wreck, containing no information specific to the newspaper article. Thus much of the text of the generated ballads followed a general pattern, including just enough facts that fit the existing ballad pattern to keep the song unique. Similar results occurred in *Poor Pearl* and *The Wreck of the Old 97,* though for *Poor Pearl* it took decades, rather than minutes, for the ballad pattern to conquer reality.

Six months to a year after generating a ballad, six of the eight singers were asked to recall their ballad. None of the singers could recall any of the stanzas they had generated. They were then asked to select their stanza from among a set of four stanzas that included one of theirs and three others from different singers. They chose their stanzas 66% of the time, well above the chance level of one in four but also well below perfect. Comments of the singers indicated that many correct choices were conscious guesses based on what particular rhymes, words, or other properties the singer would or would not use, rather than on a sense of recognition. One singer even generated a new ballad from the newspaper article that differed from his first, while still following the ballad constraints and some of the particular stylistic choices he had made earlier. Thus the generated ballads did not seem to be worthy of memory, lacking the repeated practice, fine-tuning, and authoritative weight of traditional ballads.

Constraints Followed, Edges Worn Smooth

The section "Properties of Ballads" demonstrated that many constraints exist in the ballads. This section has shown that traditional singers use these constraints. In recalling an old ballad, singers either could be sensitive to the constraints or could try to act as rote memorizers (to the extant that any person can), treating each ballad as an entity unto itself. In generating a new ballad, there is no old ballad to remember and success requires a knowledge of the genre as a whole. As discussed in Chapter 2, singers either could have an implicit or explicit set of rules, or rules of thumb, that they follow, or could have access to many instances from which they forge a new ballad, or a combination of the two. In any case, they need a sense of a good portion of the genre; they could not produce the kind of ballads reviewed here by using knowledge of only one existing ballad (Rubin & Kontis, 1983; Rubin et al., 1991).

Generation of new ballads is a rare occurrence; recall of old ballads is not. The study of new ballads clarifies both the stability and the variation observed in the genre. Ballads are stable because once a ballad is begun, its generation or recall is restricted to the words and phrases that can support all the demands of the multiple constraints. Ballads vary from telling to telling because new alternatives can be generated within the constraints when needed or desired. Where more than one solution exists to the multiple constraints, more than one solution can and will be produced when a ballad is sung repeatedly.

Field and Laboratory Studies

The forms of organization, or constraints, present in ballads have been outlined, and their effect on the generation of new ballads has been demonstrated. From observation we know that (1) the changes that occur over long time periods preserve the constraints, rather than the exact words, (2) the changes that occur from singer to singer at one time period preserve the constraints, and (3) singers can generate new ballads that follow existing constraints. In this section, it will be demonstrated that the variations that regularly occur when the same singer repeats the same song occur where constraints are minimal. Direct tests of the effects of the constraints on the transmission of existing ballads within the tradition, however, are limited by the number of available traditional singers who can be tested and by the kinds of tests that one could or would perform with those singers. Therefore, controlled experiments using novices are used to extend these results and provide converging evidence.

Studies with Expert Singers

Changes Within One Singer over Four Ballads
Wallace (Wallace & Rubin, 1988a) recorded the same four ballads about ship wrecks from a traditional ballad singer, Bobby McMillon, during two sessions held 5 months apart. As would be expected from the view argued here, changes occurred within the constraints noted earlier in the chapter. At the level of verse structure, there were 10 cases of a verse being included in one session and not in the other. These verses were mostly descriptive and did not contain information central to the story progression. That is, the story flowed in a logical progression with or without these verses. In addition, for one ballad, two verses changed from a four-line to a six-line structure. For the six-line version, lines 5 and 6 repeat the words and melody of lines 3 and 4.

At the level of exact words recalled, there were 29 word substitutions preserving meaning; 4 changes in prepositions, pronouns, or articles that had only a slight effect on the meaning, and 2 changes in verb tense. There were 7 cases of words present in one version, but absent in the other. These cases, which had little effect on the meaning, were *a, and, as she, just, only, said,* and *sweet.* There were also four pairs of lines that differed in a way that changed the meaning. For these, the first session's alternatives are shown in brackets and the second session's alternatives are shown in parentheses.

There was another ship [and it sailed upon the sea] (in the North Amerikee)
And it went by the name of the Turkish Revelee

She had not sailed far over the [deep] (main)
[Till a large ship she chanced to meet]
(She spied three ships a sailing from Spain)

Her boat [against the rock she run] (she run against the rock)
[Crying alas I am undone]
(I thought my soul her heart is broke)

Go and dig my grave [don't cry don't weep] (both wide and deep)
Place [marble] (a stone) at my head and feet

Thus at the level of individual words and word order, there were few changes, and the changes that did occur tended to preserve the meaning. Even in the four cases in which the meaning clearly did change, the effect on the ballad story was not great. Moreover, most of the changes came from one of the four ballads sung, making it possible that Bobby McMillon knew and kept separate two versions of this ballad, singing a different version in each session.

Examination of the four cases in which the meaning did change shows a preservation of poetics as well as of the general story. For instance, the end rhyme and number of syllables tend to be preserved even though the exact words used to produce them differ. Buchan (1972, pp. 155–160) demonstrates the stability, or "tenacity," of rhymes in the same ballad, across different singers, concluding that "the rhyming sounds are likely to be more stable than individual words which, in turn, are likely to be more stable than the minor incidents, a scale of priority that has some significance for the study of story variation" (p. 158). A more detailed examination of rhyme and alliteration confirms this impression. Only 12 word changes occurred in the 121 rhymes and alliterations in the four ballads, and 10 of these 12 changes resulted in a new rhyme or alliteration, with only two changes resulting in a loss of rhyme or alliteration.

Changes Within Five Singers over One Ballad

Wallace (Wallace & Rubin, 1988b) tested five traditional North Carolina ballad singers in two sessions averaging 6 months apart on *The Wreck of the Old 97*. One of these singers was Bobby McMillon, so his data on this ballad are included in both this and the previous analysis. At the level of verse structure, there were two cases of one verse being present in one but not in the other singing of the ballad. All singers used the standard four-line common meter for the ballad, except for one singer, who in the first session added two extra lines to the first of six verses and one extra line to the fourth verse, repeating the melody of other lines to make the tune fit. At the level of individual words, 34 words were changed out of a total of 34 verses sung, and word order was inverted twice. In addition, there were the following 11 cases of a word or words being present in one singing but not in the other: *all, and, he, going down grade making, said, said, then, was, well, well they,* and *when his.* Most of these changes have little effect on the meaning and are unstressed words that can be slipped into the singing without greatly disrupting the music.

The melody was transcribed for the two singings of *The Wreck of the Old 97*. One singer made a change in the melody of the second line of each verse. The notes sung on the quarter note, with the just mentioned exception, did not change, though eighth and sixteenth notes did. Quarter notes are emphasized by ballad scholars (Bayard, 1950; Bronson, 1969). They also would be the notes where guitar strums would occur if the singers had been playing, introducing the possible motoric constraint of finger memory. Also, one note of a repeated note was occasionally sung one step higher or lower. The number of beats per line did not change, though there were minor changes in the rhythm, often in order to fit the words sung—for instance, with two eighth notes changing to a dotted eighth plus a sixteenth note, or an eighth note changing to two sixteenth notes. Changes that occurred between sessions also occurred among verses within the same session.

In summary, the changes observed within the singing of the same ballad by expert traditional singers followed the general pattern of the constraints outlined.

Recall and Constraints

Constraints Can Make Lines More Memorable
In order to examine whether the constraints outlined would make an existing ballad easier to learn, 27 Duke undergraduates listened to a tape-recording of *The Wreck of the Old 97* 10 times, waited 10 minutes, and then wrote down as much as they could of the ballad (Wallace and Rubin, 1988b). Each of the 20 lines in the five-verse version was scored for the percentage of words recalled completely. In this intentional learning situation with numerous repetitions and an imminent recall test, ratings by other undergraduates of how important each line was to the overall image of the story, the number of causal connections the line had (Trabasso & Sperry, 1985), and the percentage of syllables fitting the underlying metrical pattern all predicted the recall measure.[20]

Poetics Affect Recall Locally
As expected from the theory proposed in Chapter 8, even under these artificial conditions, the percentages of words that rhymed, alliterated, or assonated with other words in the line had nonsignificant correlations with the overall level of recall. Poetic ties internal to lines did not increase the overall accuracy of a line's recall, either here or.in other studies (Hyman & Rubin, 1990), but they did have an effect on the recall of the poetically linked words.

To demonstrate this, 24 words in *The Wreck of the Old 97* were changed to eliminate most cases of rhyme, alliteration, or assonance in words adjacent to or one word away from each other. The numbers of syllables, stress patterns, and meanings of the original words were preserved. Consistent with the previous experiment and the theory proposed in Chapter 8, there was no statistically reliable difference between the 60% level of overall recall of the 27 undergraduates who recalled the original ballad and the 55% level of the 27 who recalled the altered version; but there was a 2 to 1 difference of 51% versus 24% for the verbatim scoring of the 24 words that were changed.[21]

The nature of the errors clarifies the role of poetics. Table 11.3 presents the 27 recalls of one alliterative phrase, *rough road,* and its nonalliterative substitution,

Table 11.3 Recalls to the Phrases *Rough Road* and *Tough Road*

| Recalls with | Original Phrase | | | |
	Rough road		*Tough road*	
Rough	Rough road	16	Rough road	1
	Road is rough	1	Real rough road	1
	Road is . . . rough	1		
Tough			Tough road	2
			Road is tough	1
			Tough haul	1
Other	Hard road	1	Hard road	4
	Long haul	1	Hard way	1
	Long line	1	Hard track	1
	Long road	1	Long line	1
	Long track	1	Long road	2
			Long trip	1
			Long way	4
			Treacherous and steep trail	1
			Treacherous run	1
Omitted		4		5

tough road. Of the 27 undergraduates who heard *rough road,* 16 recalled it verbatim and 2 more recalled the alliterating words in a different order. In comparison, of the 27 undergraduates who heard *tough road,* 2 recalled it verbatim and 1 recalled *tough road* in a different order. No one who heard *rough road* erred by recalling *tough road,* but 1 person who heard *tough road* erred and recalled *rough road,* and another person overcompensated with the alliterative triple *real rough road.* In addition, alliteration appeared in other responses. Two undergraduates recalled *line* instead of *road,* and both modified it with *long.* One undergraduate recalled *trail,* modifying it with *treacherous and steep.*

In summary, for the 24 poetically linked words, there was lower recall when the poetics were removed and a greater variety in the words recalled to express the same basic idea. That is, the poetics tend to stabilize the exact wording. Moreover, on rare occasions, even the undergraduates, who were not experts in the tradition, recovered the original wording when they heard a less poetic alternative.

To test this finding further, a sample larger than one ballad was used to find a set of especially clear examples. Eight verses from eight different ballads in the Brown collection were found. Each had an end-rhyme pattern, adjacent alliterating words, or an end-rhyme pattern in which one of the rhyming words alliterated with the preceding word, and for which a synonym that preserved the meaning, meter, and tone could be substituted while removing the rhyme and/or alliteration.

Sixteen verses were produced: the eight original and the eight altered ones. Twenty-four undergraduates heard four original and four alternative verses sung three times to traditional tunes, and another 24 undergraduates heard the complementary eight verses sung three times.

After 30 seconds, the undergraduates wrote their recalls. Again, there was no statistically reliable difference in the overall level of recall for original or altered verses (74% to 71%, respectively), but there was a large difference (67% versus 47%, respectively) when the key words were scored.[22] For the original verse, the poetics were preserved an additional 8% of the time when the exact wording was not recalled and for the alternative versions the recall recovered the poetics, either with the word in the original version or another word, 7% of the time.

Consistent with the theory proposed in Chapter 8, poetics did not have an effect on the overall amount recalled. This is because the poetic devices of rhyme, alliteration, and assonance act locally. Until the first member of a pair of words with a repeated sound pattern is sung, it plays no role in cuing the second member. Once the first member of the pair is sung, poetics can and did have a large effect locally in determining the probability of recall of the poetically related words, as well as their exact wording and possible substitutions.

Music Aids Recall
Music aids recall. For instance, as reviewed in Chapter 8, Rubin (1977) had undergraduates recall the national anthem with the correct music, no music, or incorrect music and found that correct music increased recall and incorrect music decreased it. Similarly, Wallace (personal communication, December 1987) reports that the singers say that they use the melody to cue the ballad as a whole.

To examine the effect of music more carefully, Wallace (1994) had undergraduates listen to three verses of a ballad either sung or spoken five times. They wrote their recalls after the first, second, and fifth presentations of the ballad and after a delay of 20 minutes. The music aided recall in all cases. However, when the experiment was repeated using one instead of three verses, the spoken presentation resulted in better recall. Thus it appears that music is an aid in multiverse ballads in part because the music repeats, whereas the words change. For experts familiar with the genre, music might help even after one verse, but nonetheless, repetition of the melody or rhythm of each verse should serve to increase the ease of learning and memorability of the song. In art music, for which memory is replaced by notation, both the words and the music can change throughout a song; but in oral traditions, the music is more likely to provide a stable, repeating framework to aid recall.

Wallace then compared the three-verse ballad read rhythmically and accompanied by a metronome to the sung version. Recall was better after the sung version for all learning trials tested and for the delayed recall, indicating that music aids recall more than just rhythm, but leaving open the question of how.

Experimental Control
In order to examine the effects of individual constraints in some detail, undergraduate novices rather than traditional experts were tested. The results obtained would surely be altered if experts in the genre were tested. However, what was really being tested was the idea that the constraints outlined would affect recall in various ways (Mook, 1989), and that at this level, retaining traditional materials while switching to testing undergraduates is a reasonable compromise.

Imagery, causal connections, and metrical fit help determine the ease of learning lines, whereas line-internal poetics stabilize the verbatim recall of just the words involved. Music aids recall, but not when each verse is learned to a different melody. Experiments like these, when combined both with laboratory results using a range of materials and with naturalistic observations and experiments using ballads, provide converging evidence that the explanations guiding the research are valid.

Learning a Genre

As outlined in Chapter 7, knowing how to sing in a genre is a learned skill. As noted in Chapter 6, there are no detailed studies observing how a person learns to become a traditional ballad singer. Nonetheless, it is clear that there is no formal training, with the possible exception of having songs sung to the novice more often than they might be sung otherwise. In order to examine the beginnings of expertise, 14 undergraduates who were well versed in the songs and literature of their culture, but who knew no traditional ballads, learned five ballads (Rubin, Wallace, & Houston, 1993). For seven of these undergraduates, the first ballad was the variant of *Lord Thomas and Fair Annet* used throughout this chapter and the last ballad was *The House Carpenter* (Brown 40A; Child 243). For the other seven undergraduates, the order was reversed. Thus when performance is averaged over all 14 undergraduates, there are no differences in the ballads learned, and differences in recall between the first and last ballads can be attributed to the effects of the intermediate learning.

Before providing the results of this study, a few details are necessary.[23] During the first week a practice story was learned, and during each of the next 5 weeks a ballad was learned. The five traditional ballads were chosen from the popular-ballad set of Wallace and Rubin (1991) because they all had a similar story line. To provide ballads of approximately equal length, the 10 verses that best told the story were selected from each ballad. A tape was made by two professional singers familiar with the ballad tradition. During each learning session, the undergraduates heard their ballad for that session once through headphones, recalled as much as they could in writing, heard the ballad repeated four more times, and attempted a second recall. The undergraduates were instructed to try to recall the story or ballad as accurately as they could, leaving blanks where they knew they had omitted information. The second recall of each of the five sessions served to increase the undergraduates' practice, but their recalls were too close to perfect to show much change. On average, the undergraduates listened to each ballad for 18 minutes and recalled the ballad for another 18 minutes.

The basic recall results are shown in Figure 11.2. Undergraduates were able to improve their ability to acquire new information within a genre over the course of learning the five ballads. Compared with their recall of the first ballad, their recall of the fifth ballad contained about one and a half times as many of the original words. When scored for gist instead of exact words, similar results were obtained. Moreover, undergraduates gained information about the major constraints of the genre. The recall of their fifth ballad contained about twice as many of the end rhymes as the recall of their first ballad and contained about three times as much of the line structure.

After the recalls were completed, the beginning experts were given 20 minutes to make up a new ballad that a critic would find difficult to pick out as new if it were part of the set of five ballads learned. This task is directly comparable to the

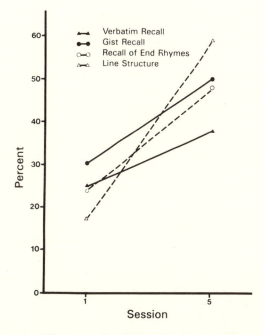

Figure 11.2. Increase in ability to recall ballads and their constraints with practice.

generation of new ballads discussed earlier, except that here, beginning experts are tested. Thus, as in *The Wreck of the Football Special,* there is a chance to see what regularities can be used in a new ballad. After a short break, the beginning experts were given 20 minutes to record the rules, generalizations, or properties of the five ballads learned, including comments on both the content and the structure.

A list of 30 characteristics common to the genre and the five learning ballads was made and adapted so that it would be easy to tell if a rule was present in the generated ballads and explicitly stated rules. The beginning experts generated, in 20 minutes, ballads about two-thirds as long as the ballads they had learned. These generated ballads used over half the 30 characteristics listed. The beginning experts also explicitly stated about one-quarter of these constraints. Table 11.4 lists 20 of the characteristics that were present in all five of the learning ballads, with the percentage of beginning experts who used them in the generation and explicit-rule tasks. As can be seen, the characteristics cover a wide range of constraints, including many outlined in this chapter. Moreover, as can be seen from examining the table, there was no statistical relationship between the constraints used and the constraints stated, even though the two tasks occurred one right after the other. Characteristics that are easy to use are not always easy to state, and characteristics that are easy to state are not always easy to use. For instance, all beginning experts avoided using a setting, but none mentioned this as a rule, whereas more beginning experts mentioned consistent rhythm than produced one. Thus after very little active exposure, the beginning experts could produce many aspects of a new ballad, often following rules that they did not state.

Table 11.4 Percentage of Use of Selected Constraints

Description of the Constraint	Generated	Rule
Content		
The main character or characters die	69	92
Explicit travel of main character(s)	85	15
Marriage proposed	54	15
Description of death, burial, blood, wounds	38	0
A moral lesson is obvious	30	38
Form		
No setting	100	0
First verse sets up plot of story	77	30
For most verses, each verse an event	38	23
Central action is dramatic and fast paced	38	8
Action tied to two or three main characters	38	8
Dialogue present	92	54
Word choice		
Most nouns concrete, not abstract	77	0
Archaic or uncommon words or usage	77	30
The word *and* begins at least one line	77	0
Very few words longer than two syllables	69	0
Poetics		
Four lines per verse	85	69
Alliteration	85	0
Lines 1 and 3 usually longer than lines 2 and 4	46	38
Last words of lines 2 and 4 usually rhyme	69	77
Consistent rhythm	38	62

Next, the beginning experts were asked to fill in the blanks in ballads from which every fifth word had been removed. They filled in more blanks using the correct number of syllables than did undergraduate novices who had not learned any ballads.

After this, 10 ballads were selected from the same popular-ballad set from which the learning ballads had been drawn, and each ballad was reduced to 10 verses. For each verse in each ballad, an alternative verse was formed. Each alternative was intended to change only one feature of the ballad, such as breaking the end rhyme, rhythm, or alliteration by substituting a synonym or inverting word order; negating the meaning of a line by introducing *no, not,* or an antonym; introducing a vocabulary word that would not appear in a traditional ballad; or reordering the lines.

Undergraduates were presented with 10 sheets of paper, each containing a complete ballad in a column on the left and the same ballad in a column on the right. Half the original verses were on each side. The undergraduates' task was to choose the "original" version of each verse. In all, 100 counterbalanced orders were produced, and 100 novice undergraduates drawn from introductory psychology courses completed them. From these 100 orders, 14 were selected randomly for the beginning experts. The beginning experts were better able than the novices to choose the original version of a verse from ballads they had learned and from different ballads with a similar theme. Such a choice would be of practical importance to a singer who had to decide which variant among many to retain and transmit.

Of special interest is that undergraduates were able to benefit from many characteristics of the ballads simultaneously. As argued here, multiple constraints play an important role in ballads and other oral traditions: each constraint helps in its own particular way, but also combines with other constraints to limit the alternatives in a powerful fashion. In all the tasks performed, the beginning experts showed the use of every constraint measured.

Learning five ballads for less than an hour each does not make an expert, but the beginning experts appeared to be well on their way to learning the genre.

Conclusions

Ballads, like epic, are a complex tradition. The constraints outlined here can be shown to have effects on stability across singers over decades, on stability within singers over months, in the generation of new ballads, and in the recall and singing of old ballads. Even novices hearing a handful of ballads become sensitive to the constraints.

The basic view taken here is shared, often with a few distinctions, by most ballad scholars. What has been added from psychology is a set of concepts, mechanisms, and methods to make these ideas more specific, more testable, and often, through the magic of quantification, considerably duller. Detailed answers have not been provided, but general forms of answers have been offered, and perhaps some questions have been formulated in a more productive way. The quest has led to useful information about ballads and about memory. For instance, there has been a debate in the ballad literature as to whether ballads are products of memorization or of re-creation (e.g., Friedman, 1961, 1983; Jones, 1961). The approach taken here is to try to develop an idea of how ballads are actually produced. Using this approach, it becomes apparent that memorization never takes place without the benefit of the constraints available to the memorizer and that re-creation, or even creation, cannot take place in a genre without attention to the constraints of that genre. If all the constraints are considered, and not just the theme or story line, memorization using constraints and re-creation within constraints produce much more similar results than those scholars debating memorization versus re-creation would have assumed. The lesson is not just for the humanists. The debate parallels one between reconstructive and reproductive memory (e.g., Hasher & Griffin, 1978; Rubin et al., 1991) that exists in psychology in part because meaning was considered as the only important constraint.

Two major obstacles stand in the way of progress toward a more rigorous, more predictive theory of ballad transmission and form. The first is the difficulty of establishing the set of possible alternatives for any word, phrase, or line of a ballad. In order to predict what changes will occur in a ballad under specific conditions we must know what changes possibly could occur that would maintain the constraints and what changes could occur if some constraints were relaxed. The second problem is the difficulty of adapting the more quantitative, less subjective methods of psychology to the subtle, adaptable, but more subjective approach of most ballad scholars. The ring composition of Bronson (1944/1961) and McCarthy (1990) or the rhythms of Stewart (1925) are hard to capture in an objective enough fashion to combine easily with the findings of experimental psychology, except in the general way done here. The need still exists to combine what is known about human memory and what is known about ballad transmission in a detailed manner, but care must be taken not to lose what cannot be put in the synthesis. As Fowler (1968) reminds us, "Of making many books there is no end, and much study is a weariness of the flesh. Ballads were meant to be sung" (p. 332).

Notes

1. The major credit for the addition of the data from North Carolina is not mine. Professor Wanda T. Wallace, who grew up within the North Carolina ballad tradition, located the traditional singers, collected and analyzed the data, refined and extended our framework to accommodate what she knew and learned about ballads, and was responsible for writing the reports of which she was the first author (e.g., Wallace & Rubin, 1988a, 1988b, 1991). Unlike our jointly authored papers, however, the opinions expressed in this chapter, insofar as they deviate from our joint work, are my own.

2. For analyses of other variations in this ballad, see Beard (1955), Harris (1955), and Miller (1937).

3. Stewart's (1925) analysis of ballad meter, discussed later in the chapter, could be used examine this possibility because he claims that the dominant ballad meter often produces lines that require music for their support.

4. Hodgart (1962) argues that the popularity in print of *Lord Thomas and Fair Annet* led to its stability and popularity in oral traditions. Although the broadsides must have contributed somewhat to the stability, it is more likely that the overall popularity of a ballad affects both its popularity in print and its popularity in the oral tradition, with neither being the cause of the other. In addition, independent of printed sources, one would expect that popularity would increase stability in oral traditions both through increased repetition within a single singer and through the likelihood of a singer's hearing the same ballad from different sources.

5. Additional analyses of this set and of other sets, as well as details of the procedures used, appear in Wallace and Rubin (1991).

6. Of these eight non-four-line variants, five have five-line stanzas, two have two-line stanzas, and one has an eight-line stanza. The five-line stanzas all have a refrain either in the form of repeating the fourth line as the fifth line or in the form of a fifth line that is the same for all stanzas. Often a word in the repeated line is changed as the story progresses, or the last word in the line is sung three times in the fourth line and once in the fifth. For example, lines 4 and 5 in the first stanza of Brown's ballad 2B (Child 4) are *No tongue for to tell him nay nay nay, / No tongue for to tell him nay*. One of the two-line-stanza ballads has lines that are twice as long as those of the other ballads and the other ballad has a three-line chorus, with the first two lines of the chorus being near-repetitions, making it like the five-line stanzas. The eight-line stanza has the general structure of two four-line stanzas; for instance, the last words of lines 2 and 4 rhyme with one sound, whereas those of lines 6 and 8 rhyme with another sound.

7. As mentioned in note 6, the 5 ballads with five-line stanzas have a refrain-like structure. In addition, 6 of the 29 ballads have full choruses; 4 four-line-stanza ballads have a four-line chorus; the eight-line-stanza ballad has an eight-line chorus; and 1 of the ballads with a two-line stanza has a three-line chorus.

8. Fisher's exact test, $p < .05$.

9. Dipodic meter implies 16 syllables per couplet line for long meter and 14 for common meter. Ballads have a freer form (Leech, 1969, p. 118). For instance, the first eight couplet lines (i.e., four stanzas) of the variant of *Lord Thomas and Fair Annet* given earlier in the chapter have 18, 15, 18, 17, 16, 17, 14, and 16 syllables. The extra syllables are unstressed, leaving the number of stressed syllables per line unchanged. If the ballad were scanned in the traditional way, these extra unstressed syllables would result in a variety of *trisyllabic feet,* such as the anapest or dactyl. After an extensive analysis of Child's ballads, Stewart (1925) concludes that such "trisyllabic substitution" does not alter the overall dipodic form. For example, for Child's version D of *Lord Thomas and Fair Annet,* Stewart calculates that 47% of the dipodic half-feet (i.e., the iambic feet) are trisyllabic but that the ballad is highly dipodic.

The trisyllabic feet, however, do make the application of Stewart's system more difficult in that specific training and conventions need to be added to what otherwise would be the relatively easy and objective dictionary assignment of stress to words taken in isolation and syllable-counting assignment of stress to words taken in context. For instance, when Duke University undergraduates and graduate students in English scan the sample of North Carolina ballads, the results are not as clearly dipodic as Stewart's, even for ballads that are variants of the ones Stewart reported. However, when told about the dipodic structure, the students could scan many of the ballads as more dipodic.

10. The lack of integration or even notation of music is not restricted to ballads. For instance, there is little on the role of music in South Slavic epic and other South Slavic traditions, though what there is is notable (Bartok, 1954; Bartok & Lord, 1951). For a brief analysis of the role of music in ballads, see Boswell and Reaver (1962, chap. 22, "Tune–text Fit in Folksong"). For an analysis of the stability of the tune family that includes *Lord Thomas and Fair Annet,* see Bronson (1951). Wallace and Rubin (1991) contains further analyses of the ballad set used in this chapter.

11. Only the first stanza was used because only the first stanza was printed with the musical score; therefore, it is the only stanza for which the correspondence of music and words is known. The stressed syllables from the metrical feet were marked without knowledge or exposure to any of the ballads' musical scores, and thus form an independent measure of the stress that occurs in the text alone. The first and middle notes of a musical measure are the most accented notes in the measure and have been used in describing ballad melodies (e.g., Bronson, 1969). By first and middle notes are meant, for example, the first and third quarter note in a 4/4 time signature or the first and fourth eighth note in a 6/8 time signature.

12. First, in a 3/4 time signature, the stresses fell on the first and third quarter notes rather than on the first and middle notes of each measure, as they would in 4/4 time. In this case, the mechanical rule of using the middle note often resulted in choosing a note that a musician would not choose as accented. Second, some songs have twice as many stresses per measure as others; thus instead of two metrical stresses per musical measure, there were four. Such cases usually occur in a 2/4 time signature in which all notes were eighth or sixteenth notes rather than quarter notes.

13. If a word repeated, the repetition was not counted as a rhyme or alliteration. The pronunciation used by the North Carolinians was considered. For example, in North Carolina, *pin* and *pen* are indistinguishable in sound. If these two words occurred in the same line, they would constitute one repetition even though the meaning is different. Where the accent of the singer was noted by the spelling in the text, this was also considered. Plurals or possessives of a word were not counted as repetitions of the singular form. Hyphenated words were counted as two words when both halves constituted separate words. This step was undertaken to minimize deviations in the printed text. Imperfect rhymes were not counted, though, as

mentioned in Chapter 4, they are present in oral traditions, including ballads (Buchan, 1972, p. 153; Zwicky, 1976). The measures were completed by one judge and checked by another. Assonance was not included as a formal measure because the changes in vowel sound with dialect made this an especially difficult decision to make from the text. An estimate of assonance, corresponding to the other measures, would be 9%.

14. The long-*e* rhyme is the most common in other collections of ballads (e.g., Buchan, 1972, p. 152; McCarthy, 1990, p. 75), as well as in the counting-out rhymes (Kelly & Rubin, 1988).

15. Rhyme sounds can be spelled in different ways. For instance, words rhyming with *me* can end in *e, ea, ee, ey, ie,* and *y*. Using the same orthography to express the rhyme sound can be an indication of literate composition in which the text cues similar-appearing words or even of the orally composed poems of literate poets if the rhyming words are close enough to each other (Kelly & Rubin, 1988; Seidenberg & Tanenhaus, 1979). Thus rhymes from the oral tradition of counting-out rhymes that are performed by nonliterate children match in spelling 22% of the time compared with 24% by chance. Comparable rhymes from the formal verse of literate adults taken from *Bartlett's Familiar Quotations* match 44% of the time compared with 32% by chance (Kelly & Rubin, 1988). That is, the children show no preference for orthographically matching rhymes, but the literate authors do.

The most common end-rhyme scheme of the ballads are rhymes separated by one line (e.g., *a b c b*), and the most common rhyme sounds rhyme with *me (E)*, *my (I)*, *mow (O)*, and *may (A)*. All instances of these rhymes were noted in the Brown collection ballads (Belden & Hudson, 1952, Vol. 2); however, because almost all the words found that rhymed with *may* were spelled with an *ay* ending, these were excluded. Rhymes that used the same word for both members of the pair were also excluded. Ballads with an *a a a a* or an *a b c b b* end-rhyme pattern were excluded to ensure that all rhymes would be separated by approximately the same number of syllables and not reinforced by nearby rhymes. A search using the same restrictions was made for the work of three literary poets in order to provide a comparison group. The first 200 poems from the collected works of Robert Burns (Kinsley, 1969), the first 500 poems from the collected works of Emily Dickinson (Johnson, 1960), and the first 200 poems from the collected works of James Whitcomb Riley (1937) were used. These were chosen because of their high frequency of the rhyme sounds common in the ballads. Because the singers in the Brown collection did not usually do their own transcriptions and because the orthography used by the editors was not consistent, words without standard spellings, such as *merry-o,* were removed from the rhyme set or changed to a standard spelling (e.g., *grey* to *gray*) using a computer spelling checking program. This was not done for the literary poets because it was assumed that they set their own orthography.

Using this procedure, 551 rhyming pairs were found in the ballads (411 *E,* 66 *I,* and 74 *O*) and 378 rhyming pairs were found in the literary poems (220 *E,* 70 *I,* and 88 *O;* 113 from Burns, 136 from Dickinson, and 129 from Riley).

An estimate of how often orthographic matches would occur by chance was made by listing the first member of the rhyming pair in one column and the second member in an adjacent column, and then randomizing the order of the second column and counting the number of matches. This was done five times to obtain a stable estimate (Kelly & Rubin, 1988).

There was little evidence of an orthographic effect in the ballad set. Here 35% of the pairs used the same rhyme spelling compared with 32% by chance ($z = 1.41$, $p = .16$), though there was a statistically significant difference for the literary poems (34% versus 28%, $z = 2.10$, $p < .05$). The degree of orthographic matching of rhyme sounds, however, was not uniform across the three poets. Randomizing the rhymes for each poet separately, 40% of the 113 rhyme pairs from Burns's poems had the same spelling, whereas 30% would be expected by chance ($z = 2.30$, $p < .05$), a strongly positive result in the direction expected. In contrast, 46% of the 129 rhyme pairs from Riley's poems had the same spelling, whereas 43% would be expected by chance ($z = 0.53$, $p = .60$), yielding no statistically significant difference between what was observed and what was expected by chance. In contrast, 17% of the 136 rhyme pairs from Dickinson's poems had the same spelling, whereas 32% would be expected by chance ($z = 3.56$, $p < .001$). This is the largest difference observed, and it is in the direction opposite to that expected. That is, Dickinson matches the spelling of her rhymes much less than would be expected by chance.

To investigate this difference further, a second series of five randomizations was performed, but this time the randomization was done only within each ballad or poem. In this way, different themes, styles, and vocabularies that might affect the orthography were not mixed. However, if orthographic matches were primed visually for literary poets, they could easily extend over a whole page of text. Thus the effect of interest could be controlled out of the analysis by using this measure, and this is what appears to have happened. Within-poem randomization requires more than one rhyme pair per ballad or poem, removing all rhyme pairs that were the only one from their poem and reducing the number of rhyme pairs to 362 for the ballads and 173 for the literary poems. For this analysis, there was no orthographic effect. The ballads had 39% orthographic matches and 39% by chance. The literary poems had 36% orthographic matches and 36% by chance.

If randomization is done within poems only, the sample sizes for the individual poets become smaller, reducing the power of the statistical test, but again, the orthographic effect is reduced or eliminated: 35% of the 63 rhyme pairs from Burns's poems had the same spelling, whereas 34% would be expected by chance ($z = 0.11$, $p = .92$); 49% of the 77 rhyme pairs from Riley's poems had the same spelling, whereas 47% would be expected by chance ($z = 0.37$, $p = .71$); and 12% of the 33 rhyme pairs from Dickinson's poems had the same spelling, whereas 26% would be expected by chance ($z = 1.82$, $p = .07$). Again, Dickinson shows the largest difference of the three poets, and again, it is in the direction opposite to that expected.

As in the results with counting-out rhymes, there was no effect of orthography on the oral-tradition ballads, but unlike the counting-out rhymes, there was also no simple effect of orthography on the literary poems. Thus there is evidence that ballads do not make use of orthography in selecting rhymes, but it is not clear that all literary poets do make use of orthography. The evidence is consistent with the ballads being oral, but it is also consistent with other interpretations. Further work with a wider sample of literary poets is needed before the lack of orthographic matches in the ballads can be taken as evidence for their oral origins.

There are several possible differences between this work and that with the counting-out rhymes that could lead to the difference in the orthographic matches in the literary sample. First is the differences among the sample of poets already noted. Second is that the control sample for the counting-out rhymes used adjacent rhyming lines, which should have stronger orthographic priming (Seidenberg & Tanenhaus, 1979), but with poems composed with the aid of writing, it is not clear how important this factor is because the rhyme structure can be noted without reading through the intermediate lines. Third is the possibility that the highly skilled, literate poets sampled chose the "best" word for each rhyme, leaving them little freedom to match orthography on their final edited version, even if the first word that came to mind was an orthographic match. For oral traditions, the same general argument could also be made, with editing being done through retelling.

16. For the literary ballads and prose counts, the first 1,000 words in a piece or sample of work were used. For Coleridge's *Ancient Mariner,* the first 1,000 words were used. All of *Danny Deever* and enough of *The Ballad of East and West* to total 1,000 words were used for Kipling's ballads. For Scott, the first 200 words of five ballads listed as "imitations of the ancient ballads" were used. The five ballads were *Glenfinlas, The Eve of St. John, Cadyow*

Castle, The Gray Brother, and *War-song of the Royal Edinburgh Light Dragoons.* For the three prose passages the first 1,000 words were used.

17. Andersen (1982) analyzed a broadside from the late seventeenth century (Child 73Da), which had no stanzas corresponding to stanzas 13 and 15 of the variant used here and had an additional stanza between stanzas 16 and 17 of the variant used here. The 18 overlapping stanzas were converted to the stanza numbering system used in this chapter.

18. Fisher's exact test, $p = .06$.

19. Cronbach's alphas calculated over the 29 ballads were above .7 for all three scales.

20. All r's $> .40$.

21. $F(1,52) = 24.81$.

22. Wallace and Rubin unpublished research. $F(1,47) = 15.30$.

23. Further details are available in Rubin et al. (1993).

CHAPTER 12

Discussion

Poor Galton would believe almost anything that allowed measurement and maintained an air of mystery.

Crovitz, 1970, p. 35

What Has Been Learned?

The goals of this book have been to learn about human memory by studying the transmission of oral traditions and to learn about oral traditions by applying what is known about human memory. It is time for an evaluation. I can make this evaluation only as a cognitive psychologist. Evaluations from other perspectives and contributions to other fields must be left to others.

At a general level, the standard methods of cognitive psychology proved useful. Quantitative measures, descriptive and inferential statistics, and the logic and use of the experimental method all functioned well, though there were times when I felt I could not quantify or manipulate some subtlety that nonetheless appeared real. The collection of observations, constructs, and theories that make up cognitive psychology also functioned well, though again, there were times when they were either too crude or unable to be applied with confidence outside their own paradigms. Nonetheless, considering the time that has been spent prior to this study analyzing epic poetry and ballads, the contributions and possible future contributions of applying cognitive psychology are impressive. Perhaps the best way to evaluate the project in some detail is to ask what cognitive psychology has added to our understanding of the three genres considered in Chapters 9, 10, and 11, and what modifications had to be made to existing theory in cognitive psychology.

Additions to the Study of Oral Traditions

By choosing the stability of oral traditions as the phenomenon of study and by approaching three genres as a cognitive psychologist, several things became clear that were not always easy to see from the perspective of scholars grounded in one tradition. The search for descriptions and explanations in terms of the postulated mechanisms of human memory proved useful. One view and set of mechanisms was applied to all three genres, varying only in the nature of the constraints used. The theory of serial recall for oral traditions, as discussed in the next section, gives a good account of the existing data. Borrowing in part from the parallel distributed processing approach to cognition, each genre was viewed as a unique set of multiple constraints. Each song is a solution to those constraints. Borrowing from information theory, the choices of solutions to the multiple constraints are choices made among existing alternatives. Where more freedom exists, there is more variety in recall. One surprise was how little choice is left in the three genres of oral tradition studied once all the constraints are considered. Verbatim or near-verbatim recall is easier if the choice of words that fit all constraints is limited. In counting-out rhymes, most words are tightly constrained and do not vary unless the whole line they are in is also changed, but the words that can vary do. In ballads and epic, there is less constraint and more variability, though in all genres the overall constraints are enough to prevent drift beyond local variation.

Formula and formulaic diction have been central to the study of oral traditions, in large part because Homeric epic was central in the development of the field. Here cues to memory, and in particular multiple cues acting together, are put in the central role and formulas become one possible solution to multiple-constraint satisfaction. This is probably the largest adjustment made to existing views in the humanities.

In oral traditions in which the same specific constraint-satisfaction problems repeat, the same solutions to them should also repeat. Through use, the solutions will become part of the vocabulary of the genre. This will often produce relatively fixed formulas, the degree of productivity of the formulas depending on the nature of the constraint-satisfaction problem. As noted in Chapter 5, phrase-length units are a common level of composition in oral traditions, so formulas of this length may appear even in genres that have formulas of other lengths.

The switch to constraints as a local cause and formulas as a symptom makes differences among the genres more understandable. It is not surprising that counting-out rhymes have no formulas. The set of pieces known by users of this tradition is small, and the pieces are short. There is therefore no need for a device to meet repeatedly the same combined metrical and meaning constraints. It is also not surprising to find ballad formulas that are not as strict metrically as epic formulas and to find longer sequences, called *motifs,* that often help to fill a stanza instead of the more usual half-line of epic formulas. In ballad composition, there is no strict quantity or other counting of syllables. Unstressed syllables can be added without violating the meter. The music of the ballad repeats each stanza, not each line, as in the epic on which formulas were first based, and in general, the stanza is the unit of composition for the ballad. Because each stanza transmits a large portion of the story told by the ballad, some formulas tend to appear at set places in the plot and come to have the added function of foreshadowing major actions, as described by Andersen (1985). Each genre has its own way of increasing its multiple constraints, so that choices will be limited enough and cuing will be narrow enough to achieve stability. Formulas of some form often result.

From this multiple-constraint perspective, Homeric epic was an unfortunate first choice for the development of the theory of oral composition. Homeric formulas, at least Homeric noun–epithet formulas, are an elegant solution for a genre with a strict and complex metrical constraint paired with a meaning constraint but no other constraints. This combination does not appear in counting-out rhymes, ballads, or even in South Slavic epic, where there are poetic constraints in addition to meter. The highly economic systems of formulas should not have been expected in these and other genres. But because they seemed so systematic in Homeric epic, they often were expected.

Epic is the most widely studied of the three genres considered and one in which no living singers were available for this study, which may be why the least could be added to its existing scholarship. For Homeric epic, scripts were investigated, which had been done by Homeric scholars using their own terms. The minor addition here was that of methodology. All instances of a script, rather than just the major instances, were examined. The patterns that occur for the major scenes occur as well for the minor ones, making it more likely that they were used productively as memory cues. In addition, the comparative method, which explicitly searched for multiple constraints, makes it clearer why Homeric epic has more elegant and economic formulaic systems than the other genres considered in this book and by scholars studying other genres.

Counting-out rhymes is the least well studied of the three genres considered and one in which many living singers are available for study, which may be why the most could be added to its existing scholarship. Folklorists have done careful collecting and definition of this genre, but little analysis. Given the cognitive psychology approach taken here, there was much to do, and the genre was ideally suited to the questions being asked. The genre was defined by its function of choosing a person to do a task, so the observation that both common and rare rhymes shared many properties was not confounded with the definition of the genre, as it would have been with the other two genres studied. That is, because a ballad can be defined as a story told in song, finding that all ballads are sung is not evidence of a coherent genre in the way that finding that counting-out rhymes share poetic properties is. In addition, there was little question that the main mode of transmission is oral. Although the genre is used mainly by children, both the rhythm and the sound pattern of the poetic devices of the genre were sophisticated; not having to satisfy much in the way of meaning or imagery constraints seems to have allowed the sound constraints to become well developed.

The basic result obtained from examining several samples of the two most common rhymes is that the rhymes remain extremely stable, and the changes that did occur did not violate the constraints of the genre or piece. Even when social forces required a word of one rhyme to change, the substitute finally settled on was the one that maximized the structure of the piece. This productivity in selecting a substitute word, as well as analyses of changes within the repeated tellings of one person, argue that the constraints, and not just verbatim memory, are being followed in recall. Finally, changes in the rhymes were analyzed over their recorded history of more than a century. Individual rhymes show little or no systematic change, though the popularity of individual rhymes has changed.

Some analyses performed could have been done without the benefit of cognitive psychology, but not all. However, it was the search to understand the mechanisms of transmission that led to all the analyses. It was difficult to make predictions from the theory proposed here, in large part because all possible alternatives to the words in the existing rhymes could not be listed. Nonetheless, the results obtained were consistent with it. Because the rhymes were stable, a high degree of constraint was expected and found; but variation was found where the constraints allowed for it.

The research on ballads was the most extensive. Again, the constraints of the genre, especially the importance of the stanza, controlled the multiple-constraint solutions obtained. Again, the variations in songs found were consistent within the constraints of the genre. With ballads, however, the long-term stability could not be credited entirely to human memory, so the empirical work concentrated on more recent samples from North Carolina and from laboratory and field experiments intended to simulate changes in the tradition and to test aspects of the theory proposed. Cognitive psychology again added the use of quantitative method and experiments. Although much of the analysis must seem pedantic to a literary critic, quantifying the basic properties of the genre and finding how they are similar to and how they differ from those of the other genres accentuate the notion that genres that provide stability in oral transmission can be formed in many different ways.

The basic properties or constraints of the ballad genre were established by reading the existing literature and, where possible, adding quantitative measures. The formation of new ballads was investigated. In these cases, existing ballads were not recalled or slightly modified, so the application of more general constraints could be more easily observed. As with the counting-out rhymes and with Lord's (1960) observations on South Slavic epic, multiple versions of the same ballad from the same singer were compared. In the new ballads and in the variation observed within a single ballad on repeated singing, variation was within the constraints outlined. In the case of a new ballad whose history was described by Cohen (1973), the ballad slowly drifted from a somewhat accurate but selective version of the murder it described to a description that contains no information discrepant with that usually contained in murder ballads. Laboratory experiments were used to test some of the isolated claims of the proposed theory, including the way in which students first learn the genre. All these studies were consistent with the theory in a general way.

Additions to the Study of Cognitive Psychology

Cognitive psychology increased our understanding of oral traditions, but there were cases where there was need for the revision of cognitive psychology, at least in its generally accepted form. Cognitive psychology is a diverse and active field, so the changes suggested here are not novel; nonetheless, they are changes to received wisdom in the field. The changes came, for the most part, from applying ideas to new domains. That is, the changes were necessitated by trying to apply principles to new situations.

Cognitive psychology tends to view organizational structures of memory as activated all at once in their entirety. Thus the hierarchical meaning of a story is available all at once. In contrast, in oral traditions, the overall meaning and poetics of a song are not always known; only the local meaning and poetics can be accessed at any one time, and then a running start is often needed. The idea of an overall structure accessed in its entirety is consistent with early applications of linguistic ideas from transformational grammars in which the sentence is a unit with a structure that is revealed at one time. Psycholinguists argue that processing of sentences has to occur in real time as the sentences are produced or heard, and theories that provide only a structure for completed sentences have to be augmented (Gernsbacher, 1990; Marslen-Wilson & Tyler, 1980; Rubin, 1976c; Wanner, 1988). Applying text structures to oral traditions led to a similar argument. The theory of serial recall developed here is an outcome of this; what is already recalled cues what will be recalled next. Some representations, such as scripts and some measures based on causal chains, work well in this serial mode, whereas others, like story grammars, do not without modification. In general, for activities that take place over extended periods of time, more consideration of the sequential nature of the processing is helpful.

Another general tendency of cognitive psychology is to put emphasis on abstract meaning, or gist, as opposed to the form or sound pattern of stimuli. Again, there has been argument that this is not correct, but the tendency is strong. Here patterns of sound were as important as and often more important than patterns of meaning in determining what would be recalled. People take advantage of whatever forms of organization they can find in performing tasks, and in oral traditions patterns of sound are often the clearest form of organization.

The structures for meaning devised by psychologists often have been based on a limited database that needs to be expanded. For instance, because ballads are classically defined as stories told in song, story grammars were expected to describe ballads well. Upon examination, it became obvious that existing story grammars are unable to describe ballad structure, but that a more restrictive, genre-specific grammar is possible and is also less subject to many of the criticisms leveled against story grammars. For example, although standard story grammars claim that all stories have a setting, ballads and other genres often do not have one. Moreover, psychologists have not sufficiently considered the abstractness of the domain for which to write story grammars or other theories of narrative structure. Should it be all stories, genres of stories, or subgenres? Here it is argued that the level of genres is preferable, but no matter where the evidence finally leads, the search is a fruitful theoretical question.

Perhaps the greatest change would be in the way psychologists think about combining various forms of organization. In the laboratory, factors are varied orthogonally. For every level of one variable there is an equal number of levels of all other variables. The combination of factors in oral traditions and in other real-world problems is more complex. Knowing about two factors individually often tells nothing about how they work together. As discussed in Chapter 5, psychologists do not have an efficient general way of combining constraints. The general solutions of systems theory and information theory are often difficult to apply. For a particular problem, a particular solution must be found. Here serial recall is used as the best available way of integrating various factors, but it does not by itself indicate how the individual combinations will work. For this, a great deal of theoretical and empirical investigation is needed.

The Process of Recall in Oral Traditions

By way of a theoretical review, a summary of the process of recall for oral traditions is given. The process is based on observations and theory from cognitive psychology and from oral traditions.

Recall of a song from an oral tradition, like all oral communication, is sequential. This observation suggests that the effects exerted by the various forms of constraint noted in this book also occur sequentially as a song is sung. That is, although theories and descriptions of the global structure of a song have uses, in order to be integrated into the process of recall outlined here, such theories and descriptions need to specify what constraints are active at each point in the singing. This approach is stressed because usually the meaning of a song is appreciated as it is sung, but its overall meaning is hard to summarize, and even local meanings are hard to access, except while the relevant part of the text is being sung. Similarly, the particular poetic constraints of a song usually cannot be accessed except while singing the line or stanza containing them.

Not only the song, but also the genre to which the song belongs, are important sources of constraints that become active as the song is sung. The genre establishes the expected constraints, or forms of organization, common to all songs in the genre. It fixes the general patterns, leaving only the specifics of the song to be selected. The term *genre* in oral tradition is analogous to the term *schema* in cognitive psychology. The specific variant of the song is an instantiation of the schema. Lord's (1960) concept of *multiformity* is the set of instantiations that can fit one schema or part of a schema. The genre provides general cues for recall and limits the available recalls to those that fit its pattern.

The general constraints of the genre and what has been sung cue what is to be sung. For efficient singing, enough cues must be present to discriminate what needs to be sung from all else in memory. The cues do not have to discriminate exactly what was sung before, but they must be sufficient to keep the recall within the structure of the genre and, if the tradition demands, close enough to other variants to produce a judgment that it is the same song. The process of sequential cuing is more like Lord's (1960) view of oral composition than it is the accurate verbatim memory of a computer or file cabinet. The same processes that are used for remembering can be used for composition, or creating a new song. The difference is in the degree to which the song produced is a match for a song sung earlier or in the degree to which the song relies on the memory of a particular song as opposed to the set of all songs in the genre.

Multiple cues make recall easier. Multiple cues help discriminate items in memory and, like the constraints common to the whole genre, show less loss of effectiveness with time. Interference theory and later theories of memory view cue overload as a major cause of forgetting; when a cue leads to many items, cue–item discrimination is low. Cue underload is a property of oral traditions and accounts for much of its stability. Each item to be sung is discriminated from others in memory by many different kinds of cues. Having several cues for one item often produces situations where cues that could cue many possible items in memory combine to discriminate one item. For instance, in counting-out rhymes, a combination of rhythm, rhyme, alliteration, and assonance limits choices and provides cues to keep lines extremely stable. Similarly, in the laboratory, multiple cues are much more effective than single cues (Bahrick, 1969, 1970; Mantyla, 1986; Mantyla & Nilsson, 1988; Solso & Biersdorff, 1975). A weak rhyme and a weak meaning cue can even combine to discriminate a word from all words in memory without any learning trials for that word (Rubin & Wallace, 1989).

The different forms of constraint—such as theme, associative meaning, spatial and object imagery, rhythm, and poetic devices—each have different time courses and other properties, making the contribution of each form of constraint especially effective in certain situations. This makes the set of multiple constraints more flexible. In addition, many of the multiple constraints reinforce one another. For example, the rhythm makes the rhyme clearer, and rhyme often marks the end of the line, making the rhythm clearer.

Several classes of constraints were discussed in the book, the major ones being theme, imagery, and patterns of sound, though others were mentioned, especially in Chapter 5. Cognitive psychologists have conceived of thematic or narrative structure in many different ways. Schema theory is the historical root of the way narrative structure has been discussed, and its basic tenets were extended to all forms of structure. For thematic structure in particular, two formalisms were discussed in some detail: scripts and story grammars. The first lends itself most easily to sequential processing. Both could be adapted to capture some aspects of thematic constraints in oral traditions, but they would work more easy and capture the most structure if they were written specifically for each genre. A network representation was also considered as a way of including narrative structure in an associative framework. Although it was argued that distinctions among classes of internal representation could not be decided from behavior, the network was offered as the easiest way to organize many of the results of experiments.

Imagery is among the oldest documented and most powerful mnemonic aids. Here it was used to introduce the idea that different forms of representation can have different neural bases. An examination of such neural considerations led to imagery being not only separated from theme, but also divided into two different systems: *object* (or descriptive) imagery and *spatial* imagery. Oral traditions make extensive use of both kinds of imagery. Following Havelock's (1978) observations, it was noted that oral traditions focus on concrete actions, not abstract ideas. That is, they consist of easy-to-describe and -image events. They are also highly spatial. In epic, the scene moves to a new location after a few actions. In ballads, a change in location occurs every stanza or two. The different locations, even when not well described, offer loci similar to those used in the classical method of loci. Images take longer to form and use than does associative meaning. This time difference suggests that images need to function for longer periods of the song than does associative meaning, which makes images especially suitable for scene-length intervals. Images also tend to lose exact wording and specific order information within a scene, though the sequencing of spatial imagery is a good device for ordering scenes. Other forms of constraint, however, are available to make up for these deficiencies.

The poetic devices of rhyme, alliteration, and assonance cue more broadly than does meaning, allowing alternative solutions to be found when a previous solution is no longer appropriate. They suffer less loss of effectiveness with time under some conditions and work as cues in short time intervals in which imagery and meaning cannot function effectively. Combined with meaning and imagery, rhyme, alliteration, and assonance are powerful cues to discriminate single words from all others in memory.

Rhythm, though not central in many recent theories of cognitive psychology, is central in oral traditions. Rhythm, like the other constraints mentioned, is a basic aspect of everyday speech that is accentuated in oral traditions. In oral traditions, it is the one constraint that is known in detail for all parts of a song once the song is begun. The theme, imagery, and exact rhyme scheme develop and change from line to line as the song is sung, but the meter for the first line or stanza is the meter for the whole piece. Rhythm plays many roles in organizing a song, including providing temporal coordination and specially marked times for the other constraints, temporal coordination among different individuals, and nested units at various levels of a rhythmic hierarchy that can be omitted or moved as wholes. It also requires singers to perform at a set pace and to fill all available rhythmic units.

The theory uses the ancient narrative–imagery–rhyme–rhythm division of Western civilization that organizes the academic literature. But these divisions correspond well with the more recent studies of behavior and neuroanatomy. People are not good at the verbatim memory of language. To improve their performance, it is as if abilities developed for other purposes were put to work. From perception, especially visual perception, and from the need to remember and manipulate what was seen were drawn the already developed abilities of spatial and descriptive imagery. From everyday language was drawn the developed ability to use narrative structure. Also, from language and its capacity to use concord morphology to make sounds repeat for grammatical purposes was drawn the sensitivity to rhyme and alliteration. Rhythmic organization from language and other behaviors provided sensitivity to meter. Combined and used with exaggerated material, these existing abilities could provide the missing ability of verbatim recall.

The ultimate test of the theory put forth here would have been to predict and then observe changes in an existing oral tradition. Although the theory is consistent with observed changes, predicting and observing new changes is difficult. The details of how the various constraints fit together in real time as the song is sung are beyond what can be given now, either for oral traditions or for specific genres. The basic data on the time course and actions of the various constraints are lacking at the detailed level that would be needed for accurate prediction. The set of alternative choices for words and phrases in the language is not available, even if the processes were better understood. That is, the set of all possible alternatives, not just those that occur in oral traditions, would need to be known to predict the changes. Moreover, for the three genres studied, most of the data were from existing collections. Thus on-line, real-time singing was usually not observed or manipulated, limiting the use of the proposed serial model of recall.

A general framework that is natural for the model was difficult to find, though recent advances in computer modeling are impressive. For instance, one way to put these observations together would be a network model of memory, as used in

Chapters 2 and 7. Network models, however, tend to have problems with sequential predictions, and it could be difficult to implement different properties for different constraints. A production system in which rules go into effect in given contexts could solve these problems, but the multiply constrained, complex situations might lead to a very large number of complex rules. A model combining several architectures may be needed. Thus unless one retreats from real oral traditions to laboratory experiments using artificial small worlds in which the complete set of possible alternatives is known, predictions of exact changes are not technically feasible.

The inability of cognitive psychology and cognitive science to predict exactly what words will change in a song is in many ways similar to the inability of physics to predict accurately tomorrow's weather, though the cynic might say that it is more like the inability of economics to predict next year's foreign exchange rates. Oral traditions are more orderly than the wind and less subject to changes from unpredictable events than world economics, so we should be able to do better, but the problem should not be underestimated. This book attempts to provide the best answer now available to the question of how oral traditions remain stable. It makes sense of what has been observed and can predict the types of changes that are likely and unlikely to occur, though it fails to predict exactly what those changes will be.

Regardless of how the process of recall is viewed, it is clear that the singer's knowledge of the genre, of individual songs, and of the constraints that function in them is gained without formal teaching. Exposure to variants of songs is the main learning device. At most, the novice will get the benefit of a repeated singing of the same song. From this exposure and from practice singing, the singer develops the skills needed to perform. These skills, like the cuing just reviewed, need not involve conscious explicit knowledge, but the ability to provide the correct response in a context. The internal representation of the constraints learned can be conceived of as collections of instances, associative networks, or even systems of rules; but again, decisions among these theoretical structures are difficult or impossible to make.

The expertise developed is maintained through singing, often at spaced intervals. This overlearning, practice, and spacing ensure long-term retention. In addition, in an active tradition, the singer is likely to hear many versions of a song and many songs from the genre, allowing selection among variants to be made and aspects of songs that do not quite fit the expected patterns to be altered.

CHAPTER 13

Epilogue:
A Note on the Future

The gradual diffusion of writing into human affairs can serve as a historical analogue for the seepage of artificial intelligence into human exchanges. Writing did not simply replace the linguistic activities that people carried out before there was writing; its major impact was to make new kinds of activity possible and to give a new shape to old kinds. It enlarged and differentiated economic, legal, political, and aesthetic activities, and it made history possible. . . . The question that can be put to artificial intelligence is whether it is merely an extension of printing or a readjustment in the human enterprise that began when writing entered into human affairs. . . . Will writing's full impact lie in its being a preparation for mechanical thinking?

Sokolowski, 1988, pp. 49–50

Mathematics and most other fields of knowledge have depended on the tools of making marks on paper. How the human cognitive performances of the future will depend on the use of electronic records and manipulation is impossible to know. But surely it would be nice if its evolution were guided by systematic psychological knowledge of the characteristics of the humans who use them.

Landauer, 1989, p. 129

Much of modern culture, science, and technology would not have been developed without the thought and memory aid of writing. Consider learning or teaching the basics of physics, chemistry, biology, or mathematics without a pencil or blackboard. Worse still, imagine trying to discover the principles involved in these or other subjects from a mass of data that had to be stored and manipulated using only human memory. Or, as a college professor, consider how and what you would teach, and how and on what you would do your research, if neither you nor your students, predecessors, or colleagues could record either in writing or in electronic form any ideas: that is, if all you could teach or learn had to be stored in your memory, in that of a professional mnemonist (Neusner, 1977), or in some cultural artifact such as a building or machine. You would hardly teach or do research as narrowly as is now common, and you probably would spend much more effort repeating your thoughts and trying to make your knowledge more memorable and easy to access. In particular, consider a college curriculum. What would be taught? Would rhetoric be reinstated? What about schoolwide daily convocations used to repeat important information? How would one add recent events, such as the conflict in what was Yugoslavia, to history? An epic added to a larger cycle might be a good solution. Even more debate would go into what is "the canon," because not much could be in it unless we divided into separate schools of thought.

This book showed some of these same effects in the organization of oral traditions. As discussed in Chapters 2 and 3, to the extent that the three genres considered contain meaning, that meaning is carried by specific, concrete, imageable actions set in narrative, not by abstract statements about universal truths (Havelock, 1978, 1986; Ong, 1982). In addition, many other aspects of the oral traditions also reflect the restrictions imposed by the requirement that all knowledge be kept in memory (Rubin, 1981). The singers do not try to be novel or creative, but try to reproduce the correct, true story, and the songs themselves are constrained to make them well suited for their niche in human memory.

The limitations in the thought portrayed in the oral traditions of ballads and counting-out rhymes underestimate the total impact of orality on thought. This is because these oral traditions exist in a literate society. Oral traditions are what the modern literate society chooses to let remain oral, not the total body of verbal knowledge that they would have to be in a truly oral culture. Singers of oral traditions in literate cultures have been exposed to language and concepts that do not exist in oral cultures. For instance, even though singers of an oral tradition in a literate culture must rely on their memory to judge whether two songs are exactly the same, their concept of "exactly the same" is conditioned by their literacy or that of their culture (Hunter, 1984, 1985).

Consider the changes that computers are introducing as thought and memory aids and as general cognitive prostheses for communication. I wrote this book on a word processor. With the push of a button, I could check and correct the spelling of a word or could ask for a synonym to be substituted for a word that did not have just the right meaning. I could move whole sections of text around in the manuscript, look for every place I used a term to ensure that I have been consistent, produce the index, automatically search through thousands of references for those on a certain topic or by a certain author, do statistical analyses, ask the University Library in Cambridge to search for books about epic poetry among all the books copyrighted in the United Kingdom in the past 10 years, send parts of the manuscript in minutes to colleagues around the world who are connected to various electronic educational and research networks, and even print out the manuscript in good-quality type. All this could be done without getting out of my chair and without touching anything but the computer keyboard. But all this is only a trivial extension of what I could have done with just pencils, paper, a pair of scissors, paste, a dictionary, a thesaurus, stamps, envelopes, additional clerical help, trips to the library, and much time.

How would this book have changed if my computer had allowed me to argue with it; had allowed me to draw, store, and manipulate images as a form of external imagery similar to the internal imagery discussed in Chapter 3; had allowed me to manipulate the sound of songs; or had allowed me to use the developing technology of expert systems to look for patterns in the oral traditions that musicologists or linguists would have looked for? None of these hypothetical functions are far from what is available or what is being promised for the future. More vexing is the question of how this book would have changed if my computer had allowed me to do things I would no more dream of asking a machine to do than would a Homer or an Avdo Medjedović.

The change from the pencil- and print-aided thought of literacy to computer-aided thought may be greater than the change from orality to literacy. Moreover, the change to computer-aided thought may be taking place much more rapidly than the centuries it took Western cultures to adapt to writing (Clanchy 1979; Ong, 1967). The study of oral traditions and their change in the face of the technology of writing is the past that is prologue.

In this final chapter, I consider three broad topics. The first section examines the question of how writing affects thought and memory by separating the effects into those that change the way people think and those that change the environment in which people think. In doing this, it is necessary to examine changes in thinking, which turn out to be specific, task-related changes in skills, not global shifts in thought. The second section examines how external representations change individuals' behavior on well-defined tasks in psychology experiments, as well as how they change whole fields of study. In these changes, external representations function primarily as tools, not as agents of change in the people using the tools. Oral traditions are reviewed as an example of what the lack of external representations produces. With this as background, the third section offers speculation about future changes. To start, a historical review puts the computer in the context of earlier technological changes in external representations. Next, findings from the book are used to note the strengths and weaknesses of human cognition that will affect the development of cognitive prostheses. Finally, there is a synthesis of all the factors.

Effects of Writing on Thought and Memory

Speculation on the effects of writing on thought and memory have continued at least since Plato (fourth century B.C.E./1973, fourth century B.C.E./1987). To add to the debates, it is necessary to clarify two issues. The first is the locus of the effect, which for the most part will be outside the individual. The second is the definition of thinking, which needs to be considered as a collection of specific skills rather than a global ability.

Changes in the Head Versus Changes in the World

A technological invention can bring with it many changes in the world. Writing is often confounded with formal schooling, a more technologically complex and bureaucratic society, and many forms of external aids to thought and memory such as pencil and paper, blackboards, note pads, books, tables of figures, and labeled line drawings. Moreover, writing is applied in varying degrees to different areas in cultures, yielding a range of effects (Clanchy, 1979; Coleman, 1981; Goody, 1987; Graff, 1979; McKitterick, 1990; Street, 1984). Because the cluster has profound effects does not mean that writing taken by itself does, or that writing is the cause of the changes (Street, 1984).

In asking how the invention of writing affects humankind, it is necessary not to confound the whole cluster of changes with changes within people. Predictions about what will happen with future changes in technology, or understanding the effects that writing had during some period in history (e.g., Bauml, 1980; Coleman, 1981; Green, 1990), require separating the complex of factors into its components. For instance, the change to computers will not be associated with large changes in formal schooling or increased urbanization, as the change to writing was, so the effects of these factors will be absent. In contrast, the computer will provide a host of new external aids to thought and memory, and these must be considered. In speculation about the future, the various separate effects need to be combined, but each effect has to be set for the new situation. Grouping all the effects of writing together does not allow such an analysis.

Consider a different example. When the automobile and all the changes in roads, design of cities, loss of horse-drawn transportation, and other factors are considered, the changes are immense. Where we live and work, who we see, and what we eat are all affected in profound ways. Little is left untouched. The answer to the practical question about the total effects of a technology is clear, but there is often an implied, more specific question about the nature of humankind. Are we as individuals or as members of groups really different, or is it that the technological world has changed? When these artifacts and the automobile itself are removed, what changes remain within us? It appears that we are different, but the changes are more subtle. We judge distances and read maps differently. Our leg muscles are less developed, but our eye–hand coordination is better developed. Our bodies contain a bit more lead, but our feet have fewer callouses. The differences are real, but they are only a subset of those that could be attributed to the whole complex of changes caused by the automobile.

Does writing change the way people think and remember? If writing and all the changes it brings and the cognitive prostheses it affords are considered, the answer is clearly yes. The effects of the cognitive prostheses will be considered later in the chapter, but for now, since it is doubtful that the automobile would have been invented if writing did not exist, the changes would dwarf those mentioned for the automobile. But are we different, or is the difference in the world we inhabit? Again, there are going to be real differences, but they will be a subset of those caused by writing and its ramifications. The thought experiment needed to answer this question shows the difficulties in knowing what the changes will be.

Imagine identical twins (or two samples of individuals randomly selected from the same population). One twin is raised with writing; the other, without. Both are given the same battery of tests that do not include reading or writing. Neither twin has access to writing materials. Do they differ in the way they think? The problem is that how the twins are raised determines the question asked. If one twin is raised in a highly literate culture and the other is raised in a culture that has no conception of writing, it is not the effects of writing alone that are measured, but the internal changes caused by writing and all its accompaniments. If less extreme environments are used, some of the power of writing will be underestimated. For instance, informing the twin without writing skills that writing exists may change his or her attitude toward language, whereas not providing the twin with writing skills with an environment that uses writing, in the full range of technologies that it can foster, may limit the effects of writing. Such cultural effects are profound and complex (Rogoff, 1990; Tomasello, Kruger, & Ratner, 1993). Twins will not suffice; many clones are needed. There is, however, a good existing study (Scribner & Cole, 1981) that will be discussed shortly.

Much of the debate on the effects of writing occurs because different researchers include different aspects of the complex of changes that go with writing in their analyses. Claims for great changes caused by writing are based on the cluster of effects, including formal schooling, that occur with writing (Goody & Watt, 1963; Greenfield, 1972; Luria, 1976; Olson, 1977, 1986; Ong, 1982), whereas claims for smaller changes (Scribner & Cole, 1981; Street, 1984) do not. For example, consider the classic work by Luria (1976). Luria asked people from Uzbekistan and Kirghizia questions in the 1930s, when familiarity with writing was not widespread in the region. Some people lacked any experience with writing. Others had been to school briefly for short courses and others for 2 to 3 years. All people were interviewed individually and probed with many questions, including the following two. One was a question about logical inference: "In the Far North, where there is snow, all bears are white. Novaya Zemlya is in the Far North. What color are bears there?" (p. 107). The second was about categorization. People were shown a picture containing a hammer, saw, log, and hatchet and asked to select the similar things. People who could not write could not answer the questions in the way expected by a literate culture. Not having been in Novaya Zemlya in the Far North, they did not see the bear. Even after being told that a hammer, saw, and hatchet were tools, they responded with answers such as "There is little use for them without a log."

Writing changed the way these people thought. But was it really the writing? Answering questions about hypothetical situations like the two examples just given is playing a game learned at school. A totally oral education in a formal school might have produced the same results. Formal education in classrooms with a professional teacher and contrived questions, however, usually occurs only with writing.

Thinking as Specific Skills Versus Thinking as a General Ability

In the automobile example, the changes noted for the automobile and all its cultural and environmental effects were global, but the changes noted in the person when the environmental changes were removed were specific. The same is true of existing analyses of the effects of writing. Those favoring massive changes talk in global terms; those favoring smaller effects examine particular literacy skills and their particular effects. For a psychologist, the question of whether writing affects how we think is difficult because the phrase "how we think" is left undefined and unmeasurable. Moreover, as was reviewed on the section on expertise in Chapter 7, changes in ability with experience tend to be specific. A chess master has improved perception and memory for the location of chess pieces, but not improved perception, memory, or thought in general (Chase & Simon, 1973). The skills can be very specific. The chess master's memory for the name and position of chess pieces taken from a game is impressive, but not for the same pieces arranged randomly on the board. A person trained to recall long strings of digits does not improve on strings of letters (Chase & Ericsson, 1981). Cognitive expertise produces a set of skills for a particular task, not a general change in consciousness. There is no reason to expect expertise in writing to produce the general changes in thought and memory that have been claimed for it, no matter how large the general effects caused by the cognitive tools and other changes that occur with writing. Luria used a collection of specific tasks to measure the types of skills usually learned in schools. Conclusions about these tasks, though confounding schooling, writing, and surrounding culture, are reasonable. General conclusions that divide people into primitive and sophisticated thinkers are not. Tannen (1988) warns that "it is a short step from 'This is oral and that literate' to 'You're oral and I'm literate'" (p. 41), and Bauml (1980) views "literacy and illiteracy as determinants of different types of communication, rather than as personal attributes" (p. 264).

The best study to have separated the effects of culture, writing, and schooling and to have shown the specific as opposed to the general effects of writing on the individual once the environmental support of writing is minimized is the extensive work of Scribner and Cole (1981), who took advantage of a situation in Liberia. There the Vai people had their own syllabary form of writing for their native Vai language. The script contains about 200 characters and was taught without formal schooling. In addition, there were formal Western schools, conducted in English, and there were Koranic schools for Arabic, which stressed oral repetition and memorization. Thus in one place, there were three languages and three types of script, each with its own way of being taught. Moreover, each language was used for a different purpose. Vai was the native tongue used for traditional social exchange and business. English was used for modern economic transactions and government. Arabic was used for religion. People could know the languages independent of whether they could write them, and in the case of Arabic, some people could read the language without knowing what it meant. In addition, people could live in more or less rural conditions. This unusual situation provided Scribner and Cole with a natural laboratory to study the effects of writing, but one not so different from medieval Europe, with separate literacies in Latin and the vernaculars (Bauml, 1980).

By administering a large battery of tests to many people, Scribner and Cole could separate the effects of different kinds of living conditions, schooling, and writing skills. Formal schooling in English had the most impact on the tests used, but it did not affect performance on all tests and was often less important than other factors. English-language schooling was most important in a host of what Scribner and Cole (1981) call "expository talk in contrived situations" (p. 244), which included explanations of sorting tasks, of grammatical rules, of game instructions, and of logic. The effects of English-language schooling on the ability to talk about tasks were often strong even when performance on the tasks being talked about did not differ. Formal schooling also had effects on story recall, list recall, sorting, and logic problems. Formal schooling did not have much effect on grouping objects by class membership; urban experience did. The two tasks mentioned from Luria's study were expository talk in contrived situations, one involving logic and the other involving grouping by class membership; thus formal schooling (and possibly the less rural experience of the collective), rather than writing, may have been the major factors in his work.

Knowing how to write Vai or Arabic script helped in tasks that were specifically based on skills used with those scripts. For instance, whereas knowledge both of English and of Vai script helped in integrating words read slowly into sentences, only knowledge of Vai script, which records syllables as separate units but does not separate words or phonemes, helped in integrating syllables read slowly into sentences. Similarly, knowledge of Arabic script improved recall in an incremental memory task that modeled the type of serial learning used with the Koran. There was no general change associated with literacy once it was unconfounded from formal schooling and rural versus urban living, only specific script-related changes. Formal schooling did have a general effect when the criterion of a general effect was the types of tasks tested in formal schooling.

This detailed analysis of the work of Scribner and Cole results in different conclusions than those of Luria, Havelock, and others who would claim a large, general change in thought processes with literacy, but it does not dispute their basic observations. Rather, it separates the factors and measures that were previously confounded.

Work like Scribner and Cole's is hard to replicate, both because of the effort involved and because situations like the one in Liberia are rare. Nonetheless, similar findings occur in the Cree of northern Canada, who also have syllabic script (Berry & Bennett, 1989). In addition, parallel to the finding that the Vai syllabic script helps with tasks involving syllables, experience with a phonemic alphabet allows people to perform tasks involving phonemes (Morais, Bertelson, Cary, & Alegria, 1986), whereas familiarity with Chinese characters does not (Read, Yun-Fei, Hong-Yin, & Bao-Qing, 1986). Studies that combine the effects of learning to write and formal schooling, however, are more common and produce results consistent with Scribner and Cole's (e.g., Greenfield, 1972; Luria, 1976).

In making predictions about the future (or in trying to understand another culture or historical period), the effects of writing itself and the complex of institutions and external thought and memory aids that accompany writing need to be separated because the complex that occurs at one time will not occur again, and it is this complex that has the largest effects.

Effects of External Representations on Thought and Memory

Up to this point, individuals have been tested without allowing them to make use of the skills of writing that are under debate. This makes sense if we want to separate the changes within individuals, but to understand the full force of writing, we must observe people allowed to make use of writing. The effects are large.

Observations from Psychology

Although cognitive psychology often makes representations internal, there is an advantage to external representations. With the possible exception of highly trained experts, external representations are easier to manipulate than internal ones. Thus one can learn to do mental arithmetic and abacus manipulations (Hunter, 1979) or play mental chess, but it is doubtful that an individual could learn this from scratch without first having an external representation and even more doubtful that it could be invented in the first place. By varying the tasks and external representations given to people, we can begin to understand how such representations can aid thought and memory (Bauer & Johnson-Laird, 1993; Day, 1988; Schonpflug, 1986).

Consider the following experiment by Bower, Clark, Lesgold, and Winzenz (1969). Undergraduates were asked to learn 112 words. Approximately one-quarter of the words were presented on each of four cards. The cards were each shown for about 1 minute. After all four cards were presented, the undergraduates were given as much time as they required to recall all the words they could in any order. The procedure was repeated four times. The words were drawn from four categories to have a hierarchical organization, with nodes in the hierarchy being included among the words. For one group of subjects, this structure was made explicit by the layout of the words on the card. Figure 13.1(a) shows what the card would look like for the category of minerals. For another group, the same 112 words and the same hierarchical layout were used for the four cards, but the words were assigned randomly to the positions on the cards, so that neither the hierarchical nor the category structure was emphasized. Figure 13.1(b) shows how one of these cards might appear. Over the four trials, the undergraduates recalled 65%, 95%, 100%, and 100% of the words correctly when they were presented in the organized fashion, but only 18%, 35%, 47%, and 63% correct in the random fashion. One trial with the organized presentation was as good as four trials with the random presentation. Further experiments showed that the effects held for associated words that were not a true hierarchy (e.g., *bread, mouse,* and *yellow* listed under the node *cheese*), that the effect was present but reduced for recognition, and that guessing from the category heading made a minimal contribution. Presenting the words externally in a clearly organized fashion greatly increased the amount recalled and did so in part by providing a recall strategy for the undergraduates, which they could use when no external cues remained.[1]

The way in which material is presented affects not only its recall, but also how efficiently it can be manipulated (Day, 1988). Oral traditions adopt a style of presentation that facilitates memory, but hinders many forms of reasoning. Consider the following game (Norman, 1988, p. 126). The two players take turns choosing a digit from among the digits 1 to 9. Each digit can be chosen only once in the game. The first player to get a sum of exactly 15 with any three of the chosen digits wins. The game seems like an intellectual challenge, but it is the equivalent of tic-tac-toe. To see this, all that needs be done is to present the nine digits in the following array:

$$
\begin{array}{ccc}
8 & 1 & 6 \\
3 & 5 & 7 \\
4 & 9 & 2
\end{array}
$$

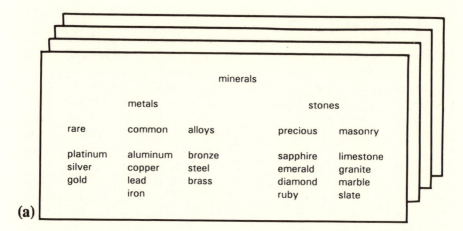

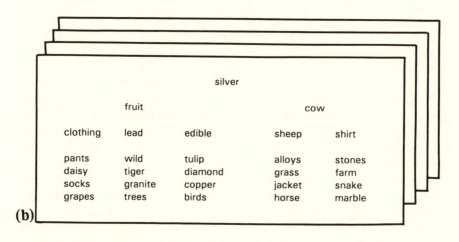

Figure 13.1. Bower, Clark, Lesgold, and Winzenz (1969) presented undergraduates with four cards with words organized (a) hierarchically or (b) randomly.

When an X or O is placed, a digit is chosen without replacement. If three digits are chosen that total exactly 15, three marks have been put in a straight line.

In the extreme case, changes in the way problems are seen are insights. In the mutilated-checkerboard problem, two squares in diagonally opposite corners of a standard 8 × 8 checkerboard are removed, leaving 64 − 2, or 62, squares. The problem is either to provide a solution in which 31 dominoes, each two squares large, exactly cover the mutilated checkerboard or to prove that such a solution is impossible. The problem is difficult, but it is much easier once it is noticed that each domino can cover exactly one white and one black square, but never two squares of the same color; that is, it is easier once the board is seen as pairs of domino-size, oppositely colored squares and each domino as painted half-white and half-black. The two missing diagonal corners are either both black or both white. The 31 dominoes can cover exactly 31 black and 31 white squares, but either 32 black and 30 white squares or 30 white and 32 black squares need to be covered. The solution is that the problem cannot be solved. Hints that helped undergraduates change their representation of the board as 31 pairs of squares instead of 62 individual squares changed the nature of their problem solving and dramatically sped their arrival at the correct solution, a solution that was often experienced as an insight (Kaplan & Simon, 1990). Thus changes in representation, or notation, can be seen as a model for scientific discovery.

The three examples given make a point besides the one that external representations aid thought and memory. All three examples make use of our visual imagery and perceptual system. Some things are easier to see; others are easier to hear. For the three examples just given, our ability to see relationships was aided by vision. Semantic organization became spatial organization, sums became straight lines, and patterns of squares became patterns of rectangles. Other problems are better handled by audition. For instance, small differences in the rate of firing of a neuron are easier to hear when the amplified output of the neuron is connected to a loudspeaker than they are to see when the output is directed to a light. Similarly, it is much easier to judge whether two sounds are the same phoneme by ear than by any visual representation yet devised. Oral traditions use only the auditory mode, writing uses the visual mode, and computers can use both. Presentation in any sense can arouse imagery in other senses, but the full use of the perceptual systems of each sense is made easier by an external representation in that sense, especially one designed to make particular acts of thought and memory easier. External representations aid thought and memory in part by using the various perceptual abilities of each sense.

Observations from Oral Traditions

Oral traditions maximize memorability so that information can be stored without external memory aids for long periods of time. The cost of maximizing mnemonic efficiency, however, is in not maximizing for other purposes. Thus information stored in an oral tradition is hard to use in many contexts. The three main causes are (1) the lack of an external representation, (2) the linear order of songs, and (3) the restrictions on word and syntax choice. Examination of these limitations provides another measure of the power of external representations.

Oral traditions transmit information without external thought and memory aids. The lack of an external representation adds a concurrent memory load to any task that uses information from an oral tradition. Because information cannot be written and manipulated externally, there is a memory demand on ongoing processing. The mind that is manipulating information is also maintaining the information and performing the intermediate steps necessary in the manipulation.

Oral traditions are songs or stories that progress in a linear order, and this is not always optimal. They cannot be scanned, as an external visual representation can. Information is recalled starting at the beginning of a song or the beginning of a major division. It is recalled line by line, verse by verse (Chapter 8). Thus oral traditions allow easy access of information in only a linear, sequential fashion. Oral traditions are a good source of knowledge for series of events. But they are not a good source for information that has to be recalled in different orders or have its order manipulated. Oral traditions share this limitation to a limited extent with normal printed text, but the use of tables of contents, indexes, and knowledge of the spatial arrangement of the text on a page (Rothkopf, 1971) help to alleviate the problem. Moreover, following from the theory in Chapter 8, the serial-recall process is one of cuing that goes on with little conscious control. Thus the singer may not know the contents of a line until the line is sung. If a summary of the important ideas of a piece is needed, it may have to be sung and listened to first. Knowledge kept in an oral tradition thus can often be accessed only through a complete performance.

Even within the linear order, word choice and syntax are limited. Words in oral traditions have several properties selected for ease of recall. As noted in Chapter 3, words are high in imagery. Thus abstract concepts cannot easily be directly presented, but must be drawn from concrete examples. As Havelock (1978) documents, concepts such as justice were presented by concrete example in Greek literature until it changed from oral to written form. Similarly, rhythmic constraints limit most English oral traditions to a mix of one- and two-syllable words, though not the Homeric epic. In this way, many words, especially rarer words with specific meanings that tend to be longer (Brown, 1958), are excluded from oral traditions. Moreover, the rhythmic constraint also limits the syntax that can be used. Changing the word order often violates the rhythmic structure, so the order chosen may need to be less than optimal for the meaning desired. Thus Havelock (1986) notes that the Greek word for *justice* is a five-syllable word in Plato's *Republic,* whereas in Homer it is a two-syllable word that never occurs "in the kind of syntax assigned to the longer form" (p. 3).

The restrictions of individual constraints including those reviewed are limiting, but it is the combination of constraints that provides most of the benefit for memory (Chapter 5) and that causes the most trouble for other uses. The multiple constraints of imagery, rhythm, meaning, rhyme, and alliteration all combine to limit word choice. Words cannot be chosen for their exact sense or implication, but must fill a host of restrictions of which meaning is not the most pressing. It is no accident that in the oral tradition of Homeric epic, Lattimore (1951, p. 40) notes that Aphrodite is given the epithet *laughing* when she is in tears because the rhythm requires it (for other examples, see Bowra, 1962b; Combellack, 1965; Lattimore, 1951). Epithets can be avoided, but if they are used, the choices are highly constrained. They are developed to satisfy recurring patterns of multiple constraints and thus may not fit any one meaning context optimally. Noting that the meaning of such epithets refers to the characters in general, not to the specific situation, does not alter this observation.

The lack of external representations, which leads to a linear order and limited verbal vocabulary, removes from oral traditions the flexibility of alternative forms of external representation that facilitated solutions to the tic-tac-toe and mutilated-checkerboard problems. External representation of text is a help to thought. Drawings and pictures (Arnheim, 1969), matrices, graphs, outlines, and other external representations allow people to do much that would be difficult or impossible if only oral traditions were available. Yet oral traditions are of great use. For all their limitations, in an oral culture or in a written culture in contexts where external memory aids are unavailable, oral traditions provide a solution to the problem of information storage and transmission. Even where external memory aids are possible, oral traditions provide an enjoyable (i.e., motivating) way to learn information that is linear and concrete. Such information makes up much of life (Schank & Abelson, 1977).

External representations remove many of these constraints. There is much greater freedom in choosing the visual form of the representation to use because it does not need to be kept memorable; because it does not need to be accessed serially, as sound does; and because many forms of visual representation are available. The history of producing written documents, from rolls containing only script to printed volumes like this one, with figures, table of contents, and indexes, follows the break from a strict linear order and a restricted form of representation (Saenger, 1982). Computers can continue this trend, allowing not only visual but also auditory information to be presented, and not only greater freedom in the order of access of information, but also the ability to have variable orders of presentation that can be determined at the time of access, as in hypertext (Bolter, 1991). Earlier chapters have shown how the need to be memorable has restricted the form of oral traditions. Rather than review these findings in more detail with the aim of supporting the claim that the computer will provide even more freedom, one counterintuitive finding will be reviewed to demonstrate that changes in technology can often produce an effect opposite to what is expected. This cautionary note is needed in a discussion that pretends to predict the future.

Hunter (1984, 1985) defines *lengthy verbatim recall* as "recall with complete word-for-word fidelity of a sequence of 50 words of longer" (1985, p. 207), 50 being an arbitrary round number coming from the value of L in Roman numerals. Lengthy verbatim recall is the kind of behavior that might be expected of people without writing and the kind of behavior that one might expect to disappear with the ability to write. That is, following Plato (fourth century B.C.E./1973) writing might be expected to weaken our ability to remember text verbatim. Hunter argues just the opposite. He claims that lengthy verbatim recall is absent from primary oral cultures—that is, cultures without writing. The person who performs the feat need not be able to read, but there must be a written record for comparison or the feat cannot be done. Hunter searched the literature for cases of lengthy verbatim recall, and found that they occurred only where there is writing and where individuals have an interest in or need for verbatim recall. Thus actors learning scripts, people interested in literature, or people motivated to learn a sacred religious text are candidates for such a performance. As seen in Chapter 9, singers in an oral tradition may claim such an ability, but have no way of knowing whether they succeed. Their recall is word-for-word accurate as far as they can tell from the limits of their memories. Changes that occur as new technologies develop may be just as surprising.

Observations from Law, Religion, Music, and Mathematics

The observations from psychology and from oral traditions stress the importance of external representations, but even these can leave an impression that underestimates the profound changes that writing has made. Therefore, a few observations on its effect on modern culture are warranted. Havelock (1978) traces the concept of justice as it developed over the course of the introduction of writing into ancient Greece. He notes that in the oral tradition of epic there appears no abstract concept of justice, but rather concrete examples of justice. The effects of writing on law are profound. Enter the office of a lawyer in many countries, and the walls are covered with books that record the written precedents on which future decisions will be based. Law was not always this way (Clanchy, 1979), but it is now hard to imagine a system of law in which such written records do not exist and the precedents and past agreements are kept in human memory.

Harder still is imagining religion without writing, especially in the form of a sacred text. Buddhism, Christianity, Islam, Judaism, and many other religions each have a sacred text that is their ultimate authority. Without writing, these sacred texts could not exist and the religions would change radically. Writing has other, more subtle effects throughout religion (Ong, 1967), but pondering the role of the sacred text and the effects of its absence are difficult enough.

Notation has many of the same effects on music that it has on literature (Treitler, 1974, 1981). For instance, without notation there are greater limits on the size of the repertoire, pieces must be easy to remember or to re-create, and credit for authorship is not as prevalent (Rubin, 1981). That is, notation allows art music, as opposed to folk music, to exist. Imagine a Mozart put into a culture without notation. He could write one major work a week for a decade, each complex and each different, but at the end there would be nothing left but the memory of brilliant performances. No one could remember that much to reproduce it, except perhaps Mozart, and then we would have no way of checking on him. With advances in recording technology, the need for notation as a memory aid disappears and music can simply be recorded. This change in technology means that people can play by ear without knowing any notation and still have large repertoires of music that do not require a highly constrained genre to limit the memory load and provide memory cues. The notation, however, may allow the viewer to see relationships that the listener cannot easily hear.

The changes in mathematics are at least as great as those in literature (Crump, 1990; Rotman, 1988). Consider dividing DCCXCVIII by LVII, using only Roman numerals. We do not have procedures to calculate the answer of XIV. In contrast, we do have procedures for using Arabic numerals to divide 798 by 57 and get 14. Hidden in the change from Roman to Arabic numerals is a system in which there is an explicit 0 and columns, with each column a factor of 10 greater than the column to its right (Ullman, 1932/1969). The symbols of mathematics offer a range of notations to make problems easier to solve, as do various graphic techniques. The ancient Greeks produced a geometry with a proof structure similar to that of the syllogisms they also developed, but the notation they had was not as conducive to algebra.

Speculations About the Future

A History of Writing

In order to provide some cautionary notes about future developments, a brief history of the technology of writing is included, which emphasizes the slow rate at which change occurred and argues with some existing views (for fuller expositions and bibliographies, see Bolter, 1991; Derrida, 1976; Gelb, 1963; Goody, 1987; Harris, 1986, and his annotated bibliography; Sampson, 1985).

After reviewing evidence about human origins that argues that humans and apes separated from their common ancestral line about 6 million years ago, Simons (1989) notes,

> Studies of later early modern *H. sapiens* show that much of what we hold "near and dear" about ourselves—our very anatomical proportions, our ability to create art and symbols, sophisticated tool manufacture, and construction of house and home may have appeared only a few tens of thousand years ago. (p. 1349)

This was the time when different localities began to show different art forms and tools—that is, different cultures (Diamond, 1991). Thus drawings that could have been used as external thought and memory aids are as old as "our very anatomical proportions." From among these drawings and all that followed, various forms of writing can be defined. Caution must be used, however, especially in a field where definitions and viewpoints often decide the answer to theoretical questions (Harris, 1986).

If to write is described as "to communicate relatively specific ideas by means of permanent, visible marks" (Sampson, 1985, p. 26), then the cave drawings might have been writing, as are the symbols on traffic signs and automobile dashboards, the labels giving washing instructions for clothes, and the icons used on computer screens. These forms of writing are termed *semasiographic* in that they are not given in terms of the sounds of any one language. The other main division of writing, and the one that is often colloquially meant by the word *writing,* is *glottographic.* Glottographic systems make spoken language visible. Glottographic systems, but not all semasiographic systems, have a linear order to reflect the temporal order of speech. The written phrase "do not iron" corresponds more closely to an English than to a French spoken utterance in a way that a picture of an iron with a line through it does not. Both kinds of writing have advantages now and in the future technologies of computers. For instance, mathematical notation and music notation are certainly as sophisticated as our alphabet, and they are semasiographic. Although glottographic writing will be the focus of this and most other histories of writing, semasiographic writing holds the potential of representations that differ dramatically from everyday language and that will probably be the most relevant in the "computer revolution."

The most striking aspect of the development of glottographic writing is the difficulty with which it occurred. Inventions were rare, and adapting borrowed systems to new uses were slow. In fact, Gelb (1963), in his classic work, could provide a respectable argument for the monogenesis of glottographic writing, including Chinese script, worldwide, though he had to define away some scripts, including those in the New World, as "limited systems" (p. 51). Nonetheless, a reasonable conclusion is that all the glottographic scripts that have left a record developed from at most a handful of independent inventions, with borrowing and imitation accounting for the rest. A stronger claim can be made for the subset of glottographic systems that are based on phonemes. The invention of a phonemic script appears to have occurred only once in the history of humankind. Because the development of the phonemic system, which includes our alphabet, plays an important role in claims about technological development and its effect on thought, it will be dealt with in more detail.

Sumerian is the oldest glottographic system for which we have records. It first took form before 3000 B.C.E. (i.e., more than 5,000 years ago). If 30,000 years ago is taken as the time of the development of different cultures and complex drawings, then glottographic writing was present for the most recent sixth of that period. At the root of a confound that continues to modern time, its use coincides with what appears to be the emergence of the earliest cities. In this context, Sumerian was first used for accounting and administrative purposes. The pointed stylus used for producing iconic drawings on wet clay changed to a blunt stylus pressed into the clay. The shape of the letters was simplified with the new technique, producing cuneiform. Sumerian was known throughout the region and may have provided the idea for other scripts, including hieroglyphics. Over time, a limited syllabic system was added to the original word-based system, in part to include proper names. Other groups with different languages adapted the script and thereby carried this development further. In particular, the Akkadians, who conquered the Sumerians, adapted the script to their more inflected language. The Akkadians also kept the older Sumerian language for some record keeping, producing the first known use of a dead language.

In small changes, Sumerian went from a set of fairly easy to interpret, iconic, drawn signs, to a system in which the relation between the meaning and the sign appeared more arbitrary (cuneiform), and finally to a syllabic system in which the graphs represented sounds rather than meanings. Similar changes can be seen in hieroglyphics.

The next step to our alphabet is the change from a syllabic to a phonemic system. Before 1000 B.C.E., Semitic scripts appeared in an area in contact with both Egypt and the lands once ruled by Sumeria. These Scripts, then, are about one-tenth as old as cave-complex drawings and one-half as old as Sumerian glottographic scripts. The Hebrew names for the first four letters of the Semitic script are aleph, bet, gimel, and dalet. These became the first four letters of the Greek script: alpha, beta, gamma, and delta; and the first four letters of modern English: *a, b, c,* and *d.* The /g/ sound went to a /c/ in Etruscan and was maintained by the Romans and remains in our alphabet (Sampson, 1985, pp. 108–109). The Semitic alphabet was written from right to left. The Greeks first wrote in the pattern in which an ox would plow a field, alternating lines from right to left with lines from left to right. On the left-to-right lines, they used the mirror image of the letters. Eventually, the Greeks standardized on the left-to-right form that we use today, so that the Greek and Roman characters are closer to the mirror image of the Semitic ones.

Some Semitic graphs have no obvious source, but others can be traced to ones used in hieroglyphics. For instance, the hieroglyphic graph that looked like the rippled surface of water had an /n/ sound because the Egyptian word for water began with that sound. The Hebrew word for water began with an /m/ sound, so this graph was taken over to have an /m/ sound—hence the rippled-water appearance of the letter *m* (Sampson, 1985, p.78; Ullman, 1932/1969, p. 14). In the Semitic languages of the time there were no words beginning with vowels, and in the script there were no vowels.

The absence of vowels was not a major problem for the Semitic languages, in which the root meaning is determined by the consonants, with the vowels marking the syntactic function of the root meaning, such as tense or number. In fact, modern Arabic and Hebrew are still written without vowels, except for beginners and other special uses (Shimron, 1993). The consonants were the less variable parts of the words, and so were the parts notated (Gelb, 1963). This was not so for Greek, and several Semitic graphs that had no use for Greek were put to use as vowels, coming close to the alphabet we use today. This change was probably made by Phoenician traders, who used the Semitic script and knew both the Phoenician and Greek languages. The change could have been as simple as extending the principle of using the initial sounds of words for letters from a language that had no words beginning with vowels to one that did (Sampson, 1985; Ullman, 1932/1969). Thus the alphabet that in various forms was the script for ancient Ugaritic, Phoenician, Palestinian, Aramaic, Hebrew, Syriac, Arabic, South Arabic, and Ethiopic (Gelb, 1963, p. 137), with the addition of vowels by the Greeks for some languages, has been adapted to different phonetic needs and serves modern Arabic, Cyrillic, German, Greek, Hebrew, and Roman scripts (Ong, 1967; Sampson, 1985).

This view is not universally accepted (Gelb, 1963; Lloyd-Jones, 1992). Gelb considers the Semitic scripts as syllabaries because they do not explicitly notate vowels. Thus he takes each consonant as a degenerate graph for all syllables in the language consisting of that consonant followed by any vowel, rather than taking each consonant as a phoneme with vowels filled in by context instead of being notated. In either case, the Greeks made an addition by notating something that was left out, but in Gelb's version they made a giant leap that separates Europe from Asia and Africa. This leap is needed by Havelock's theory (1978, 1982, 1986).

Greek civilization made great advances at the time their alphabet was devised. Havelock credits these advances to the alphabet. Thus it needs to be qualitatively different from all that went before, or else people using the earlier scripts would have made the discoveries the Greeks did. Within the otherwise identical context of ancient Greece, having the Greek script was qualitatively different from not having it, and so massive intellectual changes did occur. The alphabet was necessary for these changes, including the recording of Homer (Powell, 1991), but was not suffi-cient. There are other differences between the cultures with similar scripts besides notating vowels, and some of these differences also contributed to the Golden Age of Greece (Goody, 1987; Goody & Watt, 1963). In part, as Havelock notes, having vowels made the alphabet easier to learn, and thus a larger percentage of people used it. This no doubt was important, but we need to note that even true syllable-based systems can produce widespread literacy (e.g., Berry & Bennett, 1989).

Including vowels allowed writing to capture more of what occurred in speech. Standardized punctuation, which appeared much later with printing, allowed even more to be specified, but it must be remembered that much was and still is not notated. Like a musical score or any other form of notation or representation of sound, writing is incomplete. For instance, we still do not notate intonation patterns; thus a skilled actor could read even this dull paragraph and produce many meanings. Adding vowels was an important step, especially for the Greek language, but it was only a step.

We cannot stop here, with the alphabet of this book as the height of sophistication in transcribing speech sounds. There is one later invention. If moving from words to syllables to phonemes is progress then the next step forward is from phonemes to features, another step that apparently occurred only once. In the fifteenth century, King Sejong of Korea had a group of scholars devise a script for his country to replace the Chinese characters that were then being used (Sampson, 1985, pp. 120–144). They devised the 28 graphs of Han'gul, each a phoneme, of which modern Korean uses 24. The graphs for the consonants each have a component that in stylized graphics shows one of five place of articulations. A second component shows one of six manners of articulation. Vowels have their own two-component feature definition. Thus the Korean script uses a system much less arbitrary than our own and one much closer to what modern linguists use to describe phonemes. Moreover, the Korean script maintains a more consistent emphasis on sound than does ours, grouping together graphs that form syllables rather than grouping graphs that form words (Tzeng & Wang, 1983).

Up to this point, the term *writing* has been used. Now it is time to consider technologies more complex than putting marks on one isolated scrap of material (Bolter, 1991). The oldest existing writing is on stone and clay, and the oldest libraries are collections of these tablets. Papyrus allows for surface areas larger than clay tablets. The Greeks borrowed this technology, producing scrolls 8 meters long, with the writing occurring in columns perpendicular to the length of the scroll. In the Middle Ages, rolls, as opposed to scrolls, were used. They had one long column running with, as opposed to perpendicular to, the length of the roll and provided even less spatial distinctiveness. In these methods, the writing was much more linear than that of this book. As with oral traditions, it was easiest to start at the beginning and proceed in a fixed order. Moving from one place to another in a long scroll or roll was not easy. Moreover, the conventions of having pages, putting spaces between words and chapters, and numbering columns were not yet developed, making finding one specific piece of information within the scroll difficult.

The manuscript book, or codex, had many advantages over the roll. Pages were defined, though not initially numbered. Moving to various parts of the text was simplified. From the second century to the Middle Ages, many of the techniques present in this book evolved. Punctuation became more standardized; spaces appeared between words; page numbers, tables of contents, headings for sections, entries filed by alphabetical order, and indexes appeared (Clanchy, 1979, pp. 144–145; Rouse & Rouse, 1982); blank borders developed that provided margins for discourse in which scribes entered commentary that might become part of a later hand-copied codex. Unlike the scroll or roll, the page defined a rectangular space that could be seen and remembered at one time (Rothkopf, 1971). Location on the page could then serve as a cue to reading and to the organization of the page, unlike the current computer displays of text, which "scroll" and disappear off the top of the screen, as they would in a long medieval roll. Printing further standardized the layout of pages, punctuation, and other changes that made reading easier. It made a major improvement in the technology that had large effects on the use of writing (Eisenstein, 1979).

Green (1990) notes parallels in the changes from oral traditions to written manuscripts and from manuscripts to printed books. Writing liberated the bard from learning a large corpus, whereas printing liberated the scribe from endlessly copying the corpus. Writing increased the chance of survival of a piece by making one copy outside of memory, whereas printing increased the chances of survival of a piece by making many copies. Writing limited the changes that occur in repeated remembering, whereas printing limited the changes that occur in repeated copying.

But even with printing, progress was slow. The Chinese used movable type for their logographic characters, each of which was a word. Movable type was adapted for other scripts, but continued to use movable words. The small change of making type for individual letters was the breakthrough that made movable type practical. Like other small changes, it appears to have occurred only once (Ong, 1967, p. 49).

Besides the main, relatively permanent methods of recording text, there were other methods. Note taking was done on wax tablets even as late as the Middle Ages (Bolter, 1991, p. 39), though rolls made of scraps of writing material were also used (Bauml & Rouse, 1983).

Like the history of scripts, the history of changes in layout shows slow progress with few inventions. Old devices were put to new uses. Both the history of script and the history of books developed very slowly. Major advances were invented only once or at most a few times in the history of ideas, and then copied and slowly adapted. This history is important because we are at the edge of a new technology, and we seem just as conservative in adapting it to make up for the limits in our cognitive abilities. Even the icons of the most advanced computer systems have pictures of old-fashioned scissors, paste, paintbrushes, and file cabinets to indicate their modern functions. The revolution being allowed by the CD-ROM is being marketed as providing a library of much the same type as the Sumerians had, just easier to store. The computer can do more.

Present Skills, Present Needs

In the change from oral traditions to writing (1) serial, spoken presentation changed to spatial, visual presentation; (2) representations developed for ease of memory changed to a set of more flexible representations developed for ease of performing various tasks; and (3) information that was embodied only at the time of performance changed to more permanent information. The new technology will (1) allow both serial-spoken and spatial-visual information to be presented as desired, (2) further increase the flexibility and range of material presented, and (3) increase the ease with which permanently stored information can be embodied in new ways as needed at specific times. If cognitive prostheses are to be built from such a technology, we should consider not only the abilities of that technology and what has happened when other technologies developed in the past, but also the strengths and weaknesses of the human cognitive system that the technology will augment (for earlier formulations of cognitive prostheses from different perspectives, see Bush, 1945; Engelbart, 1963).

The brief, tentative list of cognitive strengths and weaknesses that follows was compiled from studies reviewed in this book, from observations of the abilities used by oral traditions, and from general findings in cognitive psychology. Others would make a different list. Human cognition has impressive abilities: to perform perceptual and perceptual–motor tasks, including pattern recognition, which here have been evident in spatial and visual imagery; to use language, including the ability to notice and use patterns of meaning (especially narrative) and patterns of sound, including rhythm, rhyme, and alliteration; and to develop expertise in various skills, including the knowledge of a genre. Human cognition is weaker in its ability: to remember accurately and without distortion; to keep many things in consciousness at once (Baddeley, 1986); and to remember much of what is in its memory without cuing.

Our existing writing technologies and other memory aids (Herrmann & Petro, 1990) take advantage of some of these strengths and alleviate some of these weaknesses, but more is possible. Hypertext, complex cuing systems, and externalized images are a sample of three cognitive prostheses that expand on ones we have had.

First, consider hypertext (Beck & Spicer, 1988; Bolter, 1991; Egan, Remde, Landauer, Lochbaum, & Gomez, 1989; Wright, 1989). Hypertext allows the user to access material in any order and in auditory and graphic form, as well as in text. Thus if this book were produced in hypertext, the reader could access topics from the index in any order, ask to hear the music or see a performance of a particular piece mentioned, or retrieve the dictionary or encyclopedia entry of words in the text. The reader could view all sections dealing with rhythm at one time or all sections dealing with ballads at one time, so that the author's decision on where to discuss the rhythm of ballads could be overridden. Thus the relaxing of the restriction of linear order—from oral transmission to scrolls to books—is continued.

Given this freedom, hypertext tries to make use of people's well-developed spatial sense in that the spatial metaphors of space, paths, and navigation are used to discuss accessing information. People do not want to get lost in hypertext. They need to find information and escape back out of the program. Narrative organization also can be used where appropriate. As with all forms of external memory aids, including writing, people's weakness with verbatim recall is overcome.

From the studies discussed in Chapter 7, cuing is a reasonable second prosthesis to consider—both the cuing of the user by the machine and the cuing of the machine by the user. Fixed tables of contents and index entries are easy to include. Cuing by combining terms with Boolean operators, such as *and* and *or,* is currently available, even on most library search systems, providing the benefits of multiple constraints observed in Chapter 5. However, as discussed in Chapter 7, much of the cuing that people use is associative and is not always done consciously. Cuing based on general associations, as discussed in Chapters 2 and 7, often succeeds in retrieving additional information from human memory. Systems using such cuing would provide many advantages (Egan et al., 1989).

A main use of imagery is to build mental models (Johnson-Laird, 1983; Rumelhart & Norman, 1986), and this provides the third example of a possible cognitive prosthesis. Books contain static illustrations, but the computer could allow illustrations that move. This would allow analog models to be constructed and tested without taxing cognitive processes, as imagery does. Specific quantifiable relations and information could be included with a precision exceeding that of mental imagery. Thus if a physics student wanted to understand what would happen in a particular problem—involving pulleys with suspended weights, say, or ladders leaning against walls—the appropriate laws of physics and problem details could be given to the machine and the resulting action watched. A flexible system of this kind could allow a range of "what if" problems to be turned into models that could be viewed instead of being reduced to equations, taking advantage of the strengths of the visual system in a way that equations do not.

The outline of cognitive strengths and weaknesses and the three possible cognitive prostheses given here are a sample of the kinds of considerations that need to be made in adapting the computer technology to human needs. They are not the only ones. For example, Bolter (1991) describes systems that let architects walk through and see from different perspectives a yet to be constructed building based on its plans, as well as systems that allow fictional works to be interactive, being constructed by the reader's choices that affect the basic plot or more subtly that change perspective by altering which character is the narrator. Given the history of slow advances in earlier cognitive prostheses, considerable creativity and effort will be needed if a technology is be developed and adopted rapidly.

What Can We Expect from Computers?

The previous pages remind us of writing's many functions in contemporary society and that it is an aid to thought and memory. When we learn to write, we learn a new skill, or form of expertise, just as if we learned to sing a genre of oral traditions, learned chess, or learned to drive a car. Although one could argue that writing dramatically changes thinking, a more fruitful view might be that, with writing, a culture increases the mental prostheses available to its members. It has added to the collection of tools that can solve thought problems.

This increase in the types of tools, as documented, has been extremely slow, but the power of the tools is rapidly expanding. There is not a large conceptual jump from semasiographic to glottographic script, from syllabaries to phonetic alphabets, or from manuscripts to type, though each change took a long time. However, the increase in the power of these tools is large. Our cultural resources have changed, so we can perform cognitive tasks in different ways, and we can solve problems that we were once incapable of solving. It is not clear, however, that there is a change that extends beyond this area of expertise any more than there is with learning to sing, to play chess, or to drive. Any greater flexibility or apparent increase in intelligence with writing compared with the other skills may be little more than differences in the tools used. The same should hold for computer-aided thought and memory.

From what we know, an outline of the effects of future changes can be assembled. Thought and memory will change little with new computer devices, but specific new skills will be learned that will have small effects when taken in isolation. There will be changes in education and other cultural institutions, which must be studied carefully because they will have larger effects. If, for instance, children learn to work through interactions with machines more than through interactions with teachers and peers, there could be large changes in society. Most important will be the power and use of the tools themselves. These will have the major effect. Examination of the specific changes as they unfold, and of specific cognitive strengths and weaknesses, rather than general statements about thought and memory, are what we need to foretell the shape of things to come.

Note

1. I owe the use of this example to Michael Watkins.

REFERENCES

Aaronson, D., & Scarborough, H. S. (1977). Performance theories for sentence coding: Some quantitative models. *Journal of Verbal Learning and Verbal Behavior, 16,* 277–303.

Abbott, V., Black, J. B., & Smith, E. E. (1985). The representation of scripts in memory. *Journal of Memory and Language, 24,* 179–199.

Abrahams, R. D., & Rankin, L. (Eds.). (1980). *Counting-out rhymes: A dictionary.* Austin: University of Texas Press.

Ackerman, P. L. (1987). Individual differences in skill learning: An integration of psychometric and information processing perspectives. *Psychological Bulletin, 102,* 3–27.

Adams, J. L. (1974). *Conceptual blockbusting: A guide to better ideas.* San Francisco: Freeman.

Alba, J. W., & Hasher, L. (1983). Is memory schematic? *Psychological Bulletin, 93,* 203–231.

Albrecht, J. E., & O'Brien, E. J. (1991). Effects of centrality on retrieval of text-based concepts. *Journal of Experimental Psychology: Learning, Memory, and Cognition, 17,* 932–939.

Alessi, S. M., Anderson, T. H., & Goetz, E. T. (1979). An investigation of lookbacks during studying. *Discourse Processes, 2,* 197–212.

Alexanderson, B. (1970). Homeric formulae for ships. *Eranos: Acta Philologica Suecana a Vilelmo Lundstrom Condita, 68,* 1–46.

Allen, R., & Reber, A. S. (1980). Very long term memory for tacit knowledge. *Cognition, 8,* 175–185.

Allport, G. W., & Postman, L. (1947). *The psychology of rumor.* New York: Holt.

Andersen, F. G. (1982). From tradition to print: Ballads on broadsides. In F. G. Andersen, O. Holzapel, & T. Pettitt (Eds.), *The ballad as narrative* (pp. 39–58). Odense, Denmark: Odense University Press.

Andersen, F. G. (1985). *Commonplace and creativity: The role of formulaic diction in Anglo-Scottish traditional balladry.* Odense, Denmark: Odense University Press.

Andersen, F. G., & Pettitt, T. (1985). The murder of Maria Marten: The birth of a ballad. In C. L. Edwards & K. B. Manley (Eds.), *Narrative folksong: New directions; Essays in appreciation of W. Edson Richmond* (pp. 132–178). Boulder, CO: Westview Press.

Anderson, J. R., & Schooler, L. J. (1991). Reflections of the environment in memory. *Psychological Science, 2,* 396–408.

Anderson, R. C., Pichert, J. W., Goetz, E. T., Schallert, D. L., Stevens, K. V., & Trollip, S. R. (1976). Instantiation of general terms. *Journal of Verbal Learning and Verbal Behavior, 15,* 667–679.

Anderson, R. C., & Watts, G. H. (1971). Response competition in the forgetting of paired associates. *Journal of Verbal Learning and Verbal Behavior, 10,* 29–34.

Anderson, R. E. (1976). Short-term retention of the where and when of pictures and words. *Journal of Experimental Psychology: General, 105,* 378–402.

Arend, W. (1933). *Die typischen Szenen bei Homer. Problemata: Forschungen zur klassischen Philologie* (Vol. 7). Berlin: Weidmann.

Armstrong, J. I. (1958). The arming motif in the *Iliad. American Journal of Philology, 79,* 337–354.

Arnheim, R. (1969). *Visual thinking.* Berkeley: University of California Press.

Atkinson, R. C. (1972). Optimizing the learning of a second–language vocabulary. *Journal of Experimental Psychology, 96,* 124–129.

Austin, N. (1975). *Archery at the dark of the moon: Poetic problems in Homer's Odyssey.* Berkeley: University of California Press.

Baddeley, A. D. (1976). *The psychology of memory.* New York: Basic Books.

Baddeley, A. D. (1986). *Working memory.* Oxford: Oxford University Press.

Baddeley, A. D. (1990). *Human memory: Theory and practice.* Boston: Allyn and Bacon.

Bahrick, H. P. (1965). The ebb of retention. *Psychological Review, 72,* 60–73.

Bahrick, H. P. (1969). Measurement of memory by prompted recall. *Journal of Experimental Psychology, 79,* 213–219.

Bahrick, H. P. (1970). Two-phase model for prompted recall. *Psychological Review, 77,* 215–222.

Bahrick, H. P. (1974). The anatomy of free recall. *Memory & Cognition, 2,* 484–490.

Bahrick, H. P. (1979). Maintenance of knowledge: Questions about memory we forgot to ask. *Journal of Experimental Psychology: General, 108,* 296–308.

Bahrick, H. P. (1983). The cognitive map of a city: Fifty years of learning and memory. In G. H. Bower (Ed.), *The psychology of learning and motivation* (Vol. 17, pp. 125–163). New York: Academic Press.

Bahrick, H. P. (1984). Semantic memory content in permastore: Fifty years of memory for Spanish learned in school. *Journal of Experimental Psychology: General, 113,* 1–27.

Bahrick, H. P., Bahrick, L. E., Bahrick, A. S., & Bahrick, P. E. (1993). Maintenance of foreign language vocabulary and the spacing effect. *Psychological Science, 4,* 316–321.

Bahrick, H. P., Bahrick, P. O., & Wittlinger, R. P. (1975). Fifty years of memory for names and faces: A cross–sectional approach. *Journal of Experimental Psychology: General, 104,* 54–75.

Bahrick, H. P., & Phelps, E. (1987). Retention of Spanish vocabulary over 8 years. *Journal of Experimental Psychology: Learning, Memory, and Cognition, 13,* 334–349.

Bakker, E. J. (1988). *Linguistics and formulas in Homer.* Amsterdam: Benjamins.

Bakker, E. J. (1990). Homeric discourse and enjambement: A cognitive approach. *Transactions of the American Philological Association, 120,* 1–21.

Bakker, E. J. (1992). *Beyond the formula: Involvement, visualization and "presence" in Homeric poetry.* Unpublished manuscript.

Bakker, E. J. (1993a). Activation and preservation: The interdependence of text and performance in an oral tradition. *Oral Tradition, 8,* 5–20.

Bakker, E. J. (1993b). Discourse and performance: Involvement, visualization and "presence" in Homeric poetry. *Classical Antiquity, 12,* 1–29.

Bakker, E. J., & Fabbricotti, F. (1991). Peripheral and nuclear semantics in Homeric diction: The case of dative expressions for 'spear'. *Mnemosyne, 44,* 63–84.

Barsalou, L. W. (1983). Ad hoc categories. *Memory & Cognition, 11,* 211–227.

Barsalou, L. W. (1987). The instability of graded structure: Implications for the nature of concepts. In U. Neisser (Ed.), *Concepts and conceptual development: Ecological and intellectual factors in categorization* (pp. 101–140). New York: Cambridge University Press.

Barsalou, L. W. (1990). On the indistinguishability of exemplar memory and abstraction in category representation. In T. K. Srull & R. S. Wyer, Jr. (Eds.), *Advances in social cognition: Vol. 3. Content and process specificity in the effects of prior experiences* (pp. 61–88). Hillsdale, NJ: Erlbaum.

Barsalou, L. W., & Sewell, D. R. (1985). Contrasting the representation of scripts and categories. *Journal of Memory and Language, 24,* 646–665.

Bartlett, F. C. (1920a). Psychology in relation to the popular. *Folklore, 30,* 264–295.

Bartlett, F. C. (1920b). Some experiments on the reproduction of folk-stories. *Folklore, 31,* 30–47.

Bartlett, F. C. (1932). *Remembering: A study in experimental and social psychology.* London: Cambridge University Press.

Bartok, B. (1954). Music and notes to the music. In M. Parry & A. B. Lord (Eds.), *Serbo-croatian heroic songs: Vol. 1. Novi Pazar: English translations* (pp. 437–468). Cambridge, MA: Harvard University Press.

Bartok, B., & Lord, A. B. (1951). *Serbo-Croatian folk songs.* New York: Columbia University Press.

Basden, D. R., Basden, B. H., & Galloway, B. C. (1977). Inhibition with part-list cuing: Some tests of the item strength hypothesis. *Journal of Experimental Psychology: Human Learning and Memory, 3,* 100–108.

Basgoz, I. (1975). The tale-singer and his audience. In D. Ben–Amos & K. S. Goldstein (Eds.), *Folklore: Performance and communication.* Paris: Mouton.

Bates, E., Masling, M., & Kintsch, W. (1978). Recognition memory for aspects of dialogue. *Journal of Experimental Psychology: Human Learning and Memory, 4,* 187–197.

Bauer, M. I., & Johnson-Laird, P. N. (1993). How diagrams can improve reasoning. *Psychological Science, 4,* 372–378.

Bauml, F. H. (1980). Varieties and consequences of medieval literacy and illiteracy. *Speculum, 55,* 237–265.

Bauml, F. H. (1984–1985). Medieval texts and two theories of oral-formulaic composition: A proposal for a third theory. *New Literary History, 16,* 31–49.

Bauml, F. H. (1987). The theory of oral-formulaic composition and the written medieval text. In J. M. Foley (Ed.), *Comparative research on oral traditions: A memorial for Milman Parry* (pp. 29–45). Columbus, OH: Slavica.

Bauml, F. H., & Rouse, R. H. (1983). Roll and codex: A new manuscript fragment of Reinmar von Zweter. *Beitrage zur Geschichte der deutschen Sprache und Literatur, 105,* 192–231, 317–330.

Bayard, S. P. (1950). Prolegomena to a study of the principal melodic families of British-American folk song. *Journal of American Folklore, 63,* 1–44.

Beard, A. (1955). "Lord Thomas" in America. *Southern Folklore Quarterly, 19,* 257–261.

Beck, J. R., & Spicer, D. Z. (1988, February). Hypermedia in academia. *Academic Computing,* pp. 22–25, 49, 50.

Bede (1969). *Bede's ecclesiastical history of the English people* (B. Colgrave & R. A. G. Mynors, Eds. and Trans.). Oxford: Clarendon Press. (Original work, 731)

Begg, I. (1972). Recall of meaningful phrases. *Journal of Verbal Learning and Verbal Behavior, 11,* 431–439.

Begg, I., & Sikich, D. (1984). Imagery and contextual organization. *Memory & Cognition, 12,* 52–59.

Belden, H. M., & Hudson, A. P. (Eds.). (1952). *The Frank C. Brown collection of North Carolina folklore* (Vols. 2, 3). Durham, NC: Duke University Press.

Bell, B. E., & Loftus, E. F. (1989). Trivial persuasion in the courtroom: The power of (a few) minor details. *Journal of Personality and Social Psychology, 56,* 669–679.

Bellezza, F. S. (1983). The spatial-arrangement mnemonic. *Journal of Educational Psychology, 75,* 830–837.

Bellezza, F. S., & Bower, G. H. (1982). Remembering script-based text. *Poetics, 11,* 1–23.

Bellezza, F. S., & Buck, D. K. (1988). Expert knowledge as mnemonic cues. *Applied Cognitive Psychology, 2,* 147–162.

Berry, D. C., & Broadbent, D. E. (1984). On the relationship between task performance and associated verbalizable knowledge. *Quarterly Journal of Experimental Psychology, 36A,* 209–231.

Berry, J. W., & Bennett, J. A. (1989). Syllabic literacy and cognitive performance among the Cree. *International Journal of Psychology, 24,* 429–450.

Bettelheim, B. (1976). *The uses of enchantment: The meaning and importance of fairy tales.* New York: Knopf.

Bickerton, D. (1982). An Afro–Creole origin for eena meena mina mo. *American Speech, 57,* 225–228.

Bikerman, E. (1952). La chaine de la tradition pharesian. *Revue Biblique, 59,* 44–54.

Binchy, D. A. (1971). An archaic legal poem. *Celtica, 9,* 152–168.

Bird, C. P., & Campbell, P. L. (1982). Orienting tasks and release from proactive inhibition. *American Journal of Psychology, 95,* 251–265.

Bisiach, E., & Luzzatti, C. (1978). Unilateral neglect of representational space. *Cortex, 14,* 129–133.

Bjork, R. A., & Bjork, E. L. (1992). A new theory of disuse and an old theory of stimulus fluctuation. In A. Healy, S. Kosslyn, & R. Shiffrin (Eds.), *From learning processes to cognitive processes: Essays in honor of William K. Estes* (Vol. 2, pp. 35–67). Hillsdale, NJ: Erlbaum.

Black, J. B., & Bern, H. (1981). Causal coherence and memory for events in narratives. *Journal of Verbal Learning and Verbal Behavior, 20,* 267–275.

Block, N. (Ed.). (1981). *Imagery.* Cambridge, MA: MIT Press

Boas, F. (1925). Stylistic aspects of primitive literature. *Journal of American Folk-Lore, 38,* 329–339.

Bock, J. K. (1986). Syntactic persistence in language production. *Cognitive Psychology, 18,* 355–387.

Bock, K. (1989). Closed-class immanence in sentence production. *Cognition, 31,* 163–186.

Bock, K., & Loebell, H. (1990). Framing sentences. *Cognition, 35,* 1–39.

Bolter, J. D. (1991). *Writing space: The computer, hypertext, and the history of writing.* Hillsdale, NJ: Erlbaum.

Bolton, H. C. (1888). *The counting-out rhymes of children: Their antiquity, origin, and wide distribution.* London: Elliot Stock.

Boltz, M. (1991). Some structural determinants of melody recall. *Memory & Cognition, 19,* 239–251.

Boltz, M., & Jones, M. R. (1986). Does rule recursion make melodies easier to reproduce? If not, what does? *Cognitive Psychology, 18,* 389–431.

Boomsliter, P. C., Creel, W., & Hastings, G. S., Jr. (1973). Perception and English poetic meter. *Publications of the Modern Language Association of America, 88,* 200–208.

Boswell, G. W., & Reaver, J. R. (1962). *Fundamentals of folk literature.* Oosterhout, Netherlands: Anthropological Publications.

Bousfield, W. A. (1953). The occurrence of clustering in the recall of randomly arranged associates. *Journal of General Psychology, 49,* 229–240.

Bousfield, W. A., & Sedgewick, C. H. W. (1944). An analysis of sequences of restricted associative responses. *Journal of General Psychology, 30,* 149–165.

Bousfield, W. A., & Wicklund, D. A. (1969). Rhyme as a determinant of clustering. *Psychonomic Science, 16,* 183–184.

Bower, G. H. (1970a). Analysis of a mnemonic device. *American Scientist, 58,* 496–510.

Bower, G. H. (1970b). Imagery as a relational organizer in associative learning. *Journal of Verbal Learning and Verbal Behavior, 9,* 529–533.

Bower, G. H. (1974). Selective facilitation and interference in retention of prose. *Journal of Educational Psychology, 66,* 1–8.

Bower, G. H., Black, J. B., & Turner, T. J. (1979). Scripts in memory for text. *Cognitive Psychology, 11,* 117–220.

Bower, G. H., & Bolton, L. S. (1969). Why are rhymes easier to learn? *Journal of Experimental Psychology, 82,* 453–461.

Bower, G. H., Clark, M. C., Lesgold, A.M., & Winzenz, D. (1969). Hierarchical retrieval schemes in recall of categorized word lists. *Journal of Verbal Learning and Verbal Behavior, 8,* 323–343.

Bower, G. H., & Hilgard, E. R. (1981). *Theories of Learning* (5th ed.). Englewood Cliffs, NJ: Prentice-Hall.

Bower, G. H., & Morrow, D. G. (1990). Mental models in narrative comprehension. *Science, 247,* 44–48.

Bower, G. H., & Springston, F. (1970). Pauses as recoding points in letter series. *Journal of Experimental Psychology, 83,* 421–430.

Bower, G. H., & Winzenz, D. (1969). Group structure, coding, and memory for digit series. *Journal of Experimental Psychology Monographs, 80*(2, Pt. 2), 1–17.

Bowra, C. M. (1952). *Heroic poetry.* London: Macmillan.

Bowra, M. (1962a). Metre. In A. J. B. Wace & F. H. Stubbings (Eds.), *A companion to Homer* (pp. 19–25). London: Macmillan.

Bowra, M. (1962b). Style. In A. J. B. Wace & F. H. Stubbings (Eds.), *A companion to Homer* (pp. 26–37). London: Macmillan.

Bransford, J. D., & Franks, J. J. (1971). The abstraction of linguistic ideas. *Cognitive Psychology, 2,* 331–350.

Brewer, W. F. (1980). Literary theory, rhetoric and stylistics: Implications for psychology. In R. J. Spiro, B. C. Bruce, & W. F. Brewer (Eds.), *Theoretical issues in reading comprehension* (pp. 221–239). Hillsdale, NJ: Erlbaum.

Brewer, W. F. (1985). The story schema: Universal and culture–specific properties. In D. R. Olson, N. Torrance, & A. Hildyard (Eds.), *Literacy, language, and learning: The nature and consequences of reading and writing* (pp. 167–194). Cambridge: Cambridge University Press.

Brewer, W. F. (1986). What is autobiographical memory? In D. C. Rubin (Ed.), *Autobiographical memory* (pp. 25–49). Cambridge: Cambridge University Press.

Brewer, W. F., & Hay, A. E. (1984). Reconstructive recall of linguistic style. *Journal of Verbal Learning and Verbal Behavior, 23,* 237–249.

Brewer, W. F., & Lichtenstein, E. H. (1981). Event schemas, story schemas, and story grammars. In J. Long & A. Baddeley (Eds.), *Attention and performance IX* (pp. 363–379). Hillsdale, NJ: Erlbaum.

Brewer, W. F., & Lichtenstein, E. H. (1982). Stories are to entertain: A structural-affect theory of stories. *Journal of Pragmatics, 6,* 473–486.

Brewer, W. F., & Nakamura, G. V. (1984). The nature and function of schemas. In R. S. Wyer, Jr., & T. K. Skrull (Eds.), *Handbook of social cognition* (Vol. 1, pp. 119–160). Hillsdale, NJ: Erlbaum.

Brewer, W. F., & Tenpenny, P. L. (1993). *The role of schemata in the recall and recognition of episodic information.* Unpublished manuscript.

Britton, B. K., & Gulgoz, S. (1991). Using Kintsch's computational model to improve instructional text: Effects of repairing inference calls on recall and cognitive structures. *Journal of Educational Psychology, 83,* 329–345.

Broadbent, D. E., FitzGerald, P., & Broadbent, M. H. P. (1986). Implicit and explicit knowledge in control of complex systems. *British Journal of Psychology, 77,* 33–50.

Bronson, B. H. (1944). The interdependence of ballad tunes and text. *California Folklore Quarterly, 3,* 185–207. (Reprinted in M. Leach & T. Coffin [Eds.], *The critics and the ballad* [pp. 77–102]. Carbondale: Southern Illinois University Press, 1961)

Bronson, B. H. (1951). Melodic stability in oral transmission. *International Folk Music Journal, 3,* 50–55.

Bronson, B. H. (1962). *The traditional tunes of the Child ballads: With their texts, according to the extant records of Great Britain and America* (Vol. 2). Princeton, NJ: Princeton University Press.

Bronson, B. H. (1969). *The ballad as song.* Berkeley: University of California Press.

Brown, A. L., & Day, J. D. (1983). Macrorules for summarizing texts: The development of expertise. *Journal of Verbal Learning and Verbal Behavior, 22,* 1–14.

Brown, A. S., & Knight, K. K. (1990). Letter cues as retrieval aids in semantic memory. *American Journal of Psychology, 103,* 101–113.

Brown, J. J., & Reingen, P. H. (1987). Social ties and word-of-mouth referral behavior. *Journal of Consumer Research, 14,* 350–362.

Brown, R. (1958). *Words and things: An introduction to language.* New York: Free Press.

Brown, R. (1973). *A first language: The early stages.* Cambridge, MA: Harvard University Press.

Brown, R. (1979). *The three moonrakers: An inquiry into the communication potentials of different media.* Unpublished manuscript.

Brown, R. (1986). *Social psychology: The second edition.* New York: Free Press.

Brown, R. (1989). Roger Brown. In G. Lindzey (Ed.), *A history of psychology in autobiography* (Vol. 8, pp. 36–60). Stanford, CA: Stanford University Press.

Brown, R., & McNeill, D. (1966). The "tip of the tongue" phenomenon. *Journal of Verbal Learning and Verbal Behavior, 5,* 325–337.

Bruce, D., & Bahrick, H. P. (1992). Perceptions of past research. *American Psychologist, 47,* 319–328.

Bruner, J. (1986). *Actual minds, possible worlds.* Cambridge, MA: Harvard University Press.

Bruner, J. (1990). *Acts of meaning.* Cambridge, MA: Harvard University Press.

Bruner, J. S., & O'Dowd, D. (1958). A note on the informativeness of parts of words. *Language and Speech, 1,* 98–101.

Buchan, D. (1972). *Ballad and the folk.* London: Routledge & Kegan Paul.

Buchan, D. (1983). Ballad tradition and Hugh Spencer. In J. Porter (Ed.), *The ballad image: Essays presented to Bertrand Harris Bronson* (pp. 173–191). Los Angeles: Center for the Study of Comparative Folklore and Mythology, University of California.

Buggie, S. E. (1974). *Imagery and relational variety in associative learning.* Unpublished doctoral dissertation, University of Oregon, Eugene.

Burling, R. (1966). The metrics of children's verse: A cross–linguistic study. *American Anthropologist, 68,* 1418–1441.

Bush, V. (1945, July). As we may think. *Atlantic Monthly,* pp. 101–108.

Bynum, D. E. (1968). Themes of the young hero in Serbocroatian oral epic tradition. *Publications of the Modern Language Association of America, 83,* 1296–1303.

Campbell, J. (1949). *The hero with a thousand faces.* Princeton, NJ: Princeton University Press.

Caplan, D. (1988). The biological basis for language In F. J. Newmeyer (Ed.), *Linguistics:*

The Cambridge survey: Vol. 3. Language: Psychological and biological aspects (pp. 237–255). Cambridge: Cambridge University Press.

Cermak, L. S., & Youtz, C. P. (1976). Retention of phonemic and semantic features of words. *Memory & Cognition, 4,* 172–175.

Chafe, W. L. (1982). Integration and involvement in speaking, writing and oral literature. In D. Tannen (Ed.), *Spoken and written language: Exploring orality and literacy* (pp. 35–53). Norwood, NJ: Ablex.

Chafe, W. (1990). Some things that narratives tell us about the mind. In B. K. Britton & A. D. Pellegrini (Eds.), *Narrative thought and narrative language* (pp. 79–98). Hillsdale NJ: Erlbaum.

Chafe, W., & Danielowicz, J. (1987). Properties of spoken and written language. In R. Horowitz & S. J. Samuels (Eds.), *Comprehending oral and written language* (pp. 83–113). New York: Academic Press.

Chafe, W., & Tannen, D. (1987). The relation between written and spoken language. *Annual Review of Anthropology, 16,* 383–407.

Chang, P., & Hammond, G. R. (1987). Mutual interactions between speech and finger movements. *Journal of Motor Behavior, 19,* 265–274.

Chase, W. G., & Ericsson, K. A. (1981). Skilled memory. In J. R. Anderson (Ed.), *Cognitive skills and their acquisition* (pp. 141–189). Hillsdale, NJ: Erlbaum.

Chase, W. G., & Simon, H. A. (1973). Perception in chess. *Cognitive Psychology, 4,* 55–81.

Chi, M. T. H., Feltovich, P. J., & Glaser, R. (1981). Categorization and representation of physics problems by experts and novices. *Cognitive Science, 5,* 121–152.

Child, F. J. (1882–1898). *The English and Scottish popular ballads* (Pts. 1–10). Boston: Houghton Mifflin.

Chomsky, N. (1965). *Aspects of the theory of syntax.* Cambridge, MA: MIT Press.

Chomsky, N., & Halle, M. (1968). *The sound pattern of English.* New York: Harper & Row.

Christian, J., Bickley, W., Tarka, M., & Clayton, K. (1978). Measures of free recall of 900 English nouns: Correlations with imagery, concreteness, meaningfulness, and frequency. *Memory & Cognition, 6,* 379–390.

Christie, J. M., & Just, M. A. (1976). Remembering the location and content of sentences in a prose passage. *Journal of Educational Psychology, 68,* 702–710.

Clanchy, M. T. (1979). *From memory to written record: England, 1066–1307.* Cambridge, MA: Harvard University Press.

Clark, H. H., & Haviland, S. E. (1977). Comprehension and the given-new contract. In R. O. Freedle (Ed.), *Discourse production and comprehension* (pp. 1–40). Norwood, NJ: Ablex.

Cofer, C. N. (1941). A comparison of logical and verbatim learning of prose passages of different lengths. *American Journal of Psychology, 54,* 1–20.

Cohen, A. B. (1973). *Poor Pearl, poor girl: The murdered-girl stereotype in ballad and newspaper.* Austin: University of Texas Press.

Cohen, N. (1981). *The long steel rail: The railroad in American folksong.* Urbana: University of Illinois Press.

Coleman, J. (1981). *Medieval readers and writers: 1350–1400.* New York: Columbia University Press.

A collection of old ballads: Corrected from the best and most ancient copies extant (Vol. 1). (1723). London: Printed for F. Roberts.

Collins, B. E., & Raven, B. H. (1969). Group structure: Attraction, coalitions, communication, and power. In G. Lindzey and E. Aronson (Eds.), *The handbook of social psychology* (2nd ed.): *Vol. 4. Group psychology and phenomena of interaction* (pp. 102–204). Reading, MA: Addison-Wesley.

Combellack, F. M. (1965). Some formularly illogicalities in Homer. *Transactions and Proceedings of the American Philological Association, 96,* 41–56.

Condon, W. S. (1982). Cultural microrhythms. In M. Davis (Ed.), *Interaction rhythms* (pp. 53–77). New York: Human Sciences Press.

Condon, W. S., & Sander, L. W. (1974). Neonate movement is synchronized with adult speech: Interactional participation and language acquisition. *Science, 183,* 99–101.

Cooper, L. A., & Shepard, R. N. (1973). Chronometric studies of the rotation of mental images. In W. G. Chase (Ed.), *Visual information processing.* New York: Academic Press.

Cooper, L. A., & Shepard, R. N. (1975). Mental transformations in the identification of left and right hands. *Journal of Experimental Psychology: Human Perception and Performance, 1,* 48–56.

Cooper, W. E., & Paccia-Cooper, J. (1980). *Syntax and speech.* Cambridge, MA: Harvard University Press.

Cornoldi, C., & De Beni, R. (1991). Memory for discourse: Loci mnemonics and the oral presentation effect. *Applied Cognitive Psychology, 5,* 511–518.

Craik, F. I. M., & Lockhart, R. S. (1972). Levels of processing: A framework for memory research. *Journal of Verbal Learning and Verbal Behavior, 11,* 671–684.

Cronbach, L. J. (1951). Coefficient alpha and the internal structure of tests. *Psychometrika, 16,* 297–334.

Crovitz, H. F. (1970). *Galton's walk: Methods for the analysis of thinking, intelligence, and creativity.* New York: Harper & Row.

Crovitz, H. F., Schiffman, H., & Apter, A. (1991). Galton's number. *Bulletin of the Psychonomic Society, 29,* 331–332.

Crowder, R. G. (1976). *Principles of learning and memory.* Hillsdale, NJ: Erlbaum.

Crowder, R. G., Serafine, M. L., & Repp, B. (1990). Physical interaction and association by contiguity in memory for the words and melodies of songs. *Memory & Cognition, 18,* 469–476.

Crump, T. (1990). *The anthropology of numbers.* Cambridge: Cambridge University Press.

Cuddy, L. J., & Jacoby, L. L. (1982). When forgetting helps memory: An analysis of repetition effects. *Journal of Verbal Learning and Verbal Behavior, 21,* 451–467.

Cutler, A., & Carter, D. M. (1987). The predominance of strong initial syllables in the English vocabulary. *Computer Speech and Language, 2,* 133–142.

Cutler, A., & Norris, D. G. (1988). The role of strong syllables in segmentation for lexical access. *Journal of Experimental Psychology: Human Perception and Performance, 14,* 113–121

Cutler, A., & Swinney, D. A. (1987). Prosody and the development of comprehension. *Journal of Child Language, 14,* 145–167.

D'Amato, M. F., & Diamond, M. (1979). Role of rules in paired-associate learning. *Psychological Reports, 44,* 618–650.

Darnton, R. (1984, February 2). The meaning of Mother Goose. *New York Review of Books,* pp. 41–47.

Davison, J. A. (1962). The transmission of the text. In A. J. B. Wace & F. H. Stubbings (Eds.), *A companion to Homer* (pp. 215–233). London: Macmillan.

Day, R. S. (1988). Alternative representations. In G. H. Bower (Ed.), *The psychology of learning and motivation* (Vol. 22, pp. 261–305). San Diego, CA: Academic Press.

Dee-Lucas, D., & Larkin, J. H. (1988). Novice rules for assessing importance in scientific texts. *Journal of Memory and Language, 27,* 288–308.

Deese, J. (1965). *The structure of associations in language and thought.* Baltimore: Johns Hopkins University Press.

Degh, L., & Vazsonyi, A. (1975). The hypothesis of multi-conduit transmission in folklore. In D. Ben-Amos & K. S. Goldstein (Eds.), *Folklore: Performance and communication* (pp. 207–252). Paris: Mouton.

Dell, G. S., & Reich, P. A. (1981). Stages in sentence production: An analysis of speech error data. *Journal of Verbal Learning and Verbal Behavior, 20,* 611–629.

Dempster, F. N. (1988). The spacing effect: A case study in the failure to apply the results of psychological research. *American Psychologist, 43,* 627–634.

Derrida, J. (1976). *Of grammatology* (G. C. Spivak, Trans.). Baltimore: Johns Hopkins University Press.

Deutsch, D. (Ed.). (1982). *The psychology of music.* New York: Academic Press.

Devisch, R. (1993). *Weaving the threads of life: The Khita gyn-eco-logical healing cult among the Yaka.* Chicago: University of Chicago Press.

Diamond, J. (1991). *The rise and fall of the third chimpanzee.* London: Radius

Dowling, W. J., & Harwood, D. L. (1986). *Music cognition.* Orlando, FL: Academic Press.

Dowling, W. J., Lung, K. M.-T., & Herrbold, S. (1987). Aiming attention in pitch and time in the perception of interleaved melodies. *Perception & Psychophysics, 41,* 642–656.

Dresher, E. B., & Lahiri, A. (1991). The Germanic foot: Metrical coherence in Old English. *Linguistic Inquiry, 22,* 251–286.

Dukat, Z. (1991). Enjambement as a criterion for orality in Homeric and South Slavic epic poetry. *Oral Tradition, 6,* 303–315.

Dunlosky, J., & Nelson, T. O. (1992). Importance of the kind of cue for judgments of learning (JOL) and the delayed-JOL effect. *Memory & Cognition, 20,* 374–380.

Earhard, M. (1967). Cued recall and free recall as a function of the number of items per cue. *Journal of Verbal Learning and Verbal Behavior, 6,* 257–263.

Ebbinghaus, H. (1964). *Memory: A contribution to experimental psychology* (H. A. Ruger & C. E. Bussenius, Trans.). New York: Dover. (Original work published 1885)

Edwards, M. W. (1966). Some features of Homeric craftsmanship. *Transactions and Proceedings of the American Philological Association, 97,* 116–179.

Edwards, M. W. (1986). Homer and oral tradition: The formula, Part I. *Oral Tradition, 1,* 171–230.

Edwards, M. W. (1992). Homer and oral tradition: The type-scene. *Oral Tradition, 7,* 284–330.

Egan, D. E., Remde, J. R., Landauer, T. K., Lochbaum, C. C., & Gomez, L. M. (1989). Acquiring information in books and SuperBooks. *Machine-Mediated Learning, 3,* 259–277.

Eich, J. M. (1982). A composite holographic associative recall model. *Psychological Review, 89,* 627–661.

Einstein, G. O., & McDaniel, M. A. (1987). Distinctiveness and the mnemonic benefits of bizarre imagery. In M. A. McDaniel & M. Pressley (Eds.), *Imagery and related mnemonic processes: Theories, individual differences, and applications* (pp. 78–102). New York: Springer-Verlag.

Einstein, G. O., McDaniel, M. A., & Lackey, S. (1989). Bizarre imagery, interference, and distinctiveness. *Journal of Experimental Psychology: Learning, Memory, and Cognition, 15,* 137–146.

Einstein, G. O., McDaniel, M. A., Owen, P. D., & Coté, N. C. (1990). Encoding and recall of texts: The importance of material appropriate processing. *Journal of Memory and Language, 29,* 566–581.

Eisenstein, E. L. (1979). *The printing press as an agent of change: Communication and cultural transformations in early-modern Europe* (Vols. 1, 2). Cambridge: Cambridge University Press.

Engelbart, D. C. (1963). A conceptual framework for the augmentation of man's intellect. In

P. W. Howerton & D. C. Weeks (Eds.), *Vistas in information handling: Vol. 1. The augmentation of man's intellect by machine* (pp. 1–29). Washington, DC: Spartan Books.

Engle, R. W., & Bukstel, L. (1978). Memory processes among bridge players of differing expertise. *American Journal of Psychology, 91,* 673–689.

Ericsson, K. A. (1985). Memory skill. *Canadian Journal of Psychology, 39,* 188–231.

Farah, M. J. (1988). Is visual imagery really visual? Overlooked evidence from neuropsychology. *Psychological Review, 95,* 307–317.

Farah, M. J., Hammond, K. M., Levine, D. N., & Calvanio, R. (1988). Visual and spatial mental imagery: Dissociable systems of representation. *Cognitive Psychology, 20,* 439–462.

Farah, M. J., Weisberg, L. L., Monheit, M., & Peronnet, F. (1989). Brain activity underlying mental imagery: Event-related potentials during mental image generation. *Journal of Cognitive Neuroscience, 4,* 302–316.

Fenik, B. (1968). *Typical battle scenes in the Iliad: Studies in the narrative technique of Homeric battle descriptions* (Hermes Einzelschrift No. 21). Weisbaden, Germany: Steiner.

Fillenbaum, S., & Rapoport, A. (1971). *Structures in the subjective lexicon.* New York: Academic Press.

Fillmore, C. J. (1968). The case for case. In E. Bach & R. T. Harms (Eds.), *Universals in linguistic theory* (pp. 1–90). New York: Holt, Rinehart and Winston.

Fine, G. A. (1979). Folklore diffusion through interactive social networks: Conduits in a preadolescent community. *New York Folklore, 5,* 87–126.

Finke, R. A. (1985). Theories relating mental imagery to perception. *Psychological Bulletin, 98,* 236–259.

Finke, R. A., & Kosslyn, S. M. (1980). Mental imagery acuity in the peripheral visual field. *Journal of Experimental Psychology: Human Perception and Performance, 6,* 126–139.

Finnegan, R. (1977). *Oral poetry: Its nature, significance, and social context.* Cambridge: Cambridge University Press.

Fish, S. E. (1970). Literature in the reader: Affective stylistics. *New Literary History, 2,* 123–162.

Fisher, R. P., & Craik, F. I. M. (1977). Interaction between encoding and retrieval operations in cued recall. *Journal of Experimental Psychology: Human Learning and Memory, 3,* 701–711.

Fivush, R. (1991). The social construction of personal narratives. *Merrill-Palmer Quarterly, 37,* 59–81.

Fodor, J. A. (1983). *The modularity of the mind: An essay on faculty psychology.* Cambridge, MA: MIT Press.

Fodor, J. A., Bever, T. G., & Garrett, M. F. (1974). *The psychology of language: An introduction to psycholinguistics and generative grammar.* New York: McGraw-Hill.

Foley, J. M. (1976). Formula and theme in old English poetry. In B. A. Stolz & R. S. Shannon III (Eds.), *Oral literature and the formula* (pp. 207–232). Ann Arbor: Center for the Coordination of Ancient and Modern Studies, University of Michigan.

Foley, J. M. (1985). *Oral-formulaic theory and research: An introduction and annotated bibliography.* New York: Garland.

Foley, J. M. (1988). *The theory of oral composition: History and methodology.* Bloomington: Indiana University Press.

Foley, J. M. (1990). *Traditional oral epic: The Odyssey, Beowulf, and the Serbo-Croatian return song.* Berkeley: University of California Press.

Foley, J. M. (1991). *Immanent art: From structure to meaning in traditional oral epic.* Bloomington: Indiana University Press.

Foley, J. M. (1992). Word-power, performance, and tradition. *Journal of American Folklore, 105,* 276–301.

Fowler, D. C. (1968). *A literary history of the popular ballad.* Durham, NC: Duke University Press.

Franks, N. R. (1989). Army ants: A collective intelligence. *American Scientist, 77,* 139–145.

Frick, R. W. (1989). Explanations of grouping in immediate ordered recall. *Memory & Cognition, 17,* 551–562.

Friedman, A. B. (1961). The formulaic improvisation theory of ballad tradition: A counter-statement. *Journal of American Folklore, 74,* 113–115.

Friedman, A. B. (1983). The oral-formulaic theory of balladry—a re-rebuttal. In J. Porter (Ed.), *The ballad image: Essays presented to Bertrand Harris Bronson* (pp. 215–240). Los Angeles: Center for the Study of Comparative Folklore and Mythology, University of California.

Friendly, M. L. (1977). In search of the M-gram: The structure of organization in free recall. *Cognitive Psychology, 9,* 188–149.

Friendly, M. (1979). Methods for finding graphic representations of associative memory structures. In C. R. Puff (Ed.), *Memory organization and structure* (pp. 85–129). New York: Academic Press.

Fries, C. C. (1952). *The structure of English.* New York: Harcourt, Brace & World.

Frost, R. (1953). The hear-say ballad. In H. H. Flanders & M. Olney (Eds.), *Ballads migrant in New England* (pp. xii–xiii). New York: Farrar, Straus, and Young.

Fry, D. K. (1967). Old English formulas and systems. *English Studies, 48,* 193–204.

Fry, D. K. (1975). Caedmon as a formulaic poet. In J. J. Duggan (Ed.), *Oral literature: Seven essays* (pp. 41–61). Edinburgh: Scottish Academic Press.

Fry, D. K. (1980). *The memory of Caedmon.* Unpublished manuscript, State University of New York at Stony Brook.

Gaisser, J. H. (1969). A structural analysis of the digressions in the *Iliad* and the *Odyssey.* *Harvard Studies in Classical Philology, 73,* 1–43.

Galambos, J. A., & Rips, L. J. (1982). Memory for routines. *Journal of Verbal Learning and Verbal Behavior, 21,* 260–281.

Galton, F. (1879). Psychometric experiments. *Brain, 2,* 149–162.

Galton, F. (1883). *Inquiries into the human faculty and its development.* London: Macmillan.

Gardiner, J. M., Craik, F. I. M., & Birtwistle, J. (1972). Retrieval cues and release from proactive inhibition. *Journal of Verbal Learning and Verbal Behavior, 11,* 778–783.

Gardner, H. (1982). *Art, mind, and brain.* New York: Basic Books.

Garner, W. R. (1978). Aspects of a stimulus: Features, dimensions, and configurations. In E. Rosch & B. Lloyd (Eds.), *Cognition and categorization* (pp. 99–133). Hillsdale, NJ: Erlbaum.

Garnham, A. (1983). What's wrong with story grammars? *Cognition, 15,* 145–154.

Garro, L. C. (1982). *Imagery's role in cognition: Integrating imagery theory with an individual differences approach.* Unpublished doctoral dissertation, Duke University, Durham, NC.

Garrod, S., & Trabasso, T. (1973). A dual-memory information processing interpretation of sentence comprehension. *Journal of Verbal Learning and Verbal Behavior, 12,* 155–167.

Gates, A. I. (1917). Recitation as a factor in memorizing. *Archives of Psychology, 6,* No. 40.

Geers, A. E. (1978). Intonation contour and syntactic structure as predictors of apparent segmentation. *Journal of Experimental Psychology: Human Perception and Perfor-mance, 4,* 273–283.

Geiselman, R. E., & Crawley, J. M. (1983). Incidental processing of speaker characteristics: Voice as connotative information. *Journal of Verbal Learning and Verbal Behavior, 22,* 15–23.

Gelb, I. J. (1963). *A study of writing* (rev. ed.). Chicago: University of Chicago Press.

Georges, R. A. (1969). Toward an understanding of storytelling events. *Journal of American Folklore, 82,* 313–328.

Gernsbacher, M. A. (1990). *Language comprehension as structure building.* Hillsdale, NJ: Erlbaum.

Gerould, G. H. (1957). *The ballad of tradition.* New York: Oxford University Press.

Gerrig, R. J. (1989). Suspense in the absence of uncertainty. *Journal of Memory and Language, 28,* 633–648.

Gerritsen, W. P. (1976). Corrections and indications for oral delivery in the Middle Dutch Lancelot manuscript. In *Neerlandica Manuscripta: Essays presented to G. I. Lieftinck* (Vol. 3, pp. 39–59). Amsterdam: A. L. van Gendt.

Gilbert, T. F. (1957). Overlearning and the retention of meaningful prose. *Journal of General Psychology, 56,* 281–289.

Glaser, R., & Chi, M. T. H. (1988). Overview. In M. T. H. Chi, R. Glaser, & M. J. Farr (Eds.), *The nature of expertise* (pp. xv–xxi). Hillsdale, NJ: Erlbaum.

Gleitman, L. R., Gleitman, H., Landau, B., & Wanner, E. (1988). Where learning begins: Initial representations for language learning. In F. J. Newmeyer (Ed.), *Linguistics: The Cambridge survey: Vol. 3. Language: Psychological and biological aspects* (pp. 150–193). Cambridge: Cambridge University Press.

Gleitman, L. R., & Wanner, E. (1982). Language acquisition: The state of the art. In E. Wanner & L. R. Gleitman (Eds.), *Language acquisition: The state of the art* (pp. 3–48). Cambridge: Cambridge University Press.

Glenberg, A. M., & Jona, M. (1991). Temporal coding in rhythm tasks revealed by modality effects. *Memory & Cognition, 19,* 514–522.

Glenberg, A. M., & Lehman, T. S. (1980). Spacing repetitions over 1 week. *Memory & Cognition, 8,* 528–538.

Glenberg, A. M., & Swanson, N. G. (1986). A temporal distinctiveness theory of recency and modality effects. *Journal of Experimental Psychology: Learning, Memory, and Cognition, 12,* 3–15.

Glenn, C. G. (1978). The role of episodic structure and of story length in children's recall of simple stories. *Journal of Verbal Learning and Verbal Behavior, 17,* 229–247.

Goldenberg, G., Podreka, I., Steiner, M., & Willmes, K. (1987). Patterns of regional cerebral blood flow related to memorizing of high and low imagery words—an emission computer tomography study. *Neuropsychologia, 25,* 473–485.

Goldstein, K. S. (1967). Experimental folklore: Laboratory vs. field. In D. K. Wileus (Ed.), *Folklore international: Essays in traditional literature, beliefs and custom in honor of Wayland Debs Hand* (pp. 71–82). Hatsboro, PA: Folklore Associates.

Goody, J. (1987). *The interface between the written and the oral.* Cambridge: Cambridge University Press.

Goody, J., & Watt, I. (1963). The consequences of literacy. *Comparative Studies in Society and History, 5,* 304–245.

Grabe, M. D. (1979). Reader imposed structure and prose retention. *Contemporary Educational Psychology, 4,* 162–171.

Graesser, A. C. (1978). How to catch a fish: The memory and representation of common procedures. *Discourse Processes, 1,* 72–89.

Graesser, A. C., Gordon, S. E., & Sawyer, J. D. (1979). Recognition memory for typical and atypical actions in scripted activities: Tests of a script pointer + tag hypothesis. *Journal of Verbal Learning and Verbal Behavior, 18,* 319–332.

Graesser, A. C., Lang, K. L., & Roberts, R. M. (1991). Question answering in the context of stories. *Journal of Experimental Psychology: General, 120,* 254–277.

Graesser, A. C., Woll, S. B., Kolwalski. D. J., & Smith, D. A. (1980). Memory for typical and atypical actions in scripted activities. *Journal of Experimental Psychology: Human Learning and Memory, 6,* 503–515.

Graf, P., & Mandler, G. (1984). Activation makes words more accessible, but not necessarily more retrievable. *Journal of Verbal Learning and Verbal Behavior, 23,* 553–568.

Graff, H. J. (1979). *The literacy myth: Literacy and social structure in the nineteenth-century city.* New York: Academic Press.

Green, B. F. (1956). A method of scalagram analysis using summary statistics. *Psychometrika, 21,* 79–88.

Green, D. H. (1990). Orality and reading: The state of research in medieval studies. *Speculum, 65,* 267–280.

Greene, R. L. (1989). Spacing effects in memory: Evidence for a two-process account. *Journal of Experimental Psychology: Learning, Memory, and Cognition, 15,* 371–377.

Greenfield, P. M. (1972). Oral or written language: The consequences for cognitive development in Africa, the United States and England. *Language and Speech, 15,* 169–178.

Grendon, F. (1909). The Anglo-Saxon charms. *Journal of American Folklore, 22,* 105–237.

Grosjean, F., Grosjean, L., & Lane, H. (1979). The patterns of silence: Performance structures in sentence production. *Cognitive Psychology, 11,* 58–81.

Grossberg, S. (1980). How does the brain build a cognitive code? *Psychological Review, 87,* 1–51.

Grossberg, S. (1988). *Neural networks and natural intelligence.* Cambridge, MA: MIT Press.

Gruenewald, P. J., & Lockhead, G. R. (1980). The free recall of category examples. *Journal of Experimental Psychology: Human Learning and Memory, 6,* 225–240.

Gruneberg, M. M. (1978). The feeling of knowing, memory blocks and memory aids. In M. M. Gruneberg & P. Morris (Eds.), *Aspects of memory* (pp. 186–209). London: Methuen.

Guinee, L. N., & Payne, K. B. (1988). Rhyme-like repetitions in songs of humpback whales. *Ethology, 79,* 295–306.

Gumenik, W. E. (1979). The advantage of specific terms over general terms as cues for sentence recall: Instantiation or retrieval? *Memory & Cognition, 7,* 240–244.

Haberlandt, K. (1980). Story grammar and reading time of story constituents. *Poetics, 9,* 99–118.

Halpern, B. K., & Foley, J. M. (1978). The power of the word: Healing charms as an oral genre. *Journal of American Folklore, 91,* 903–924.

Hamm, V. P., & Hasher, L. (1992). Age and the availability of inferences. *Psychology and Aging, 7,* 56–64.

Handel, S. (1989). *Listening: An introduction to the perception of auditory events.* Cambridge, MA: MIT Press.

Harlow, H. F. (1949). The formation of learning sets. *Psychological Review, 56,* 51–65.

Harris, R. (1955). "Lord Thomas and Fair Ellinor": A preliminary study of the ballad. *Midwest Folklore, 5,* 79–94.

Harris, R. (1986). *The origin of writing.* London: Duckworth.

Hasher, L., & Griffin, M. (1978). Reconstructive and reproductive processes in memory. *Journal of Experimental Psychology: Human Learning and Memory, 4,* 318–330.

Hasher, L., & Zacks, R. T. (1979). Automatic and effortful processes in memory. *Journal of Experimental Psychology: General, 108,* 356–388.

Havelock, E. A. (1963). *Preface to Plato.* Cambridge, MA: Harvard University Press.

Havelock, E. A. (1971). *Prologue to Greek literacy.* Cincinnati: University of Cincinnati Press.

Havelock, E. A. (1978). *The Greek concept of justice: From its shadow in Homer to its substance in Plato.* Cambridge, MA: Harvard University Press.

Havelock, E. A. (1982). *The literate revolution in Greece and its cultural consequences.* Princeton, NJ: Princeton University Press.

Havelock, E. A. (1986). *The muse learns to write: Reflections on orality and literacy from antiquity to the present.* New Haven, CT: Yale University Press.

Hawkes, T. (1977). *Structuralism and semiotics.* Berkeley: University of California Press.

Hayes, B. (1984). The phonology of rhythm in English. *Linguistic Inquiry, 15,* 33–74.

Hayes, B. (1988). Metrics and phonological theory. In F. J. Newmeyer (Ed.), *Linguistics: The Cambridge survey: Vol. 2. Linguistic theory: Extensions and implications* (pp. 220–249). Cambridge: Cambridge University Press.

Hayes, D. S., Chemelski, B. E., & Palmer, M. (1982). Nursery rhymes and prose passages: Preschoolers' liking and short-term retention of story events. *Developmental Psychology, 18,* 49–56.

Haymes, E. R. (1973). *A bibliography of studies relating to Parry's and Lord's oral theory.* Cambridge, MA: Harvard University Press.

Healy, A. F. (1977). Pattern coding of spatial order information in short-term memory. *Journal of Verbal Learning and Verbal Behavior, 16,* 419–437.

Held, R. (1968). Dissociation of visual functions by deprivation and rearrangement. *Psychologische Forschung, 31,* 338–348.

Helson, H. (1964). *Adaptation-level theory: An experimental and systematic approach to behavior.* New York: Harper & Row.

Herrmann, D. J., & Petro, S. J. (1990). Commercial memory aids. *Applied Cognitive Psychology, 4,* 439–450.

Herskovits, A. (1986). *Language and spatial cognition: An interdisciplinary study of the prepositions in English.* Cambridge: Cambridge University Press.

Higbie, C. (1990). *Measure and music: Enjambement and sentence structure in the Iliad.* Oxford: Clarendon Press.

Hillinger, M. L. (1980). Priming effects with phonemically similar words: The encoding-bias hypothesis reconsidered. *Memory & Cognition, 8,* 115–123.

Hintzman, D. L. (1968). Explorations with a discrimination net model for paired-associate learning. *Journal of Mathematical Psychology, 5,* 123–162.

Hintzman, D. L. (1974). Theoretical implications of the spacing effect. In R. L. Solso (Ed.), *Theories in cognitive psychology: The Loyola symposium* (pp. 77–99). Potomac, MD: Erlbaum.

Hintzman, D. L. (1986). "Schema abstraction" in a multiple-trace memory model. *Psychological Review, 93,* 411–428.

Hintzman, D. L. (1990). Human learning and memory: Connections and dissociations. *Annual Review of Psychology, 41,* 109–139.

Hintzman, D. L. (1991). Why are formal models useful in psychology? In W. E. Hockley & S. Lewandowsky (Eds.), *Relating theory and data: Essays on human memory in honor of Bennet B. Murdock* (pp. 39–56). Hillsdale, NJ: Erlbaum.

Hintzman, D. L. (1993). Twenty-five years of learning and memory: Was the cognitive revolution a mistake? In D. E. Meyer & S. Kornblum (Eds.), *Attention and perfor-*

mance XIV: Synergies in experimental psychology, artificial intelligence, and cognitive neuroscience (pp. 359–391). Cambridge, MA: MIT Press.

Hockett, C. F. (1963). The problem of universals in language. In J. H. Greenberg (Ed.), *Universals of language* (pp. 1–29). Cambridge, MA: MIT Press.

Hodgart, M. J. C. (1962). *The ballads.* New York: Norton.

Holding, D. H. (1985). *The psychology of chess skill.* Hillsdale, NJ: Erlbaum.

Holmes, V. M., & Langford, J. (1976). Comprehension and recall of abstract and concrete sentences. *Journal of Verbal Learning and Verbal Behavior, 15,* 559–566.

Holoka, J. P. (1976). The oral formula and Anglo-Saxon elegy: Some misgivings. *Neophilologus, 60,* 570–576.

Holzapfel, O. (1982). "Winterrosen" ("Winter Roses"): A German narrative love song from the songbook of Ambras (1582). In F. G. Andersen, O. Holzapfel, & T. Pettitt (Eds.), *The ballad as narrative* (pp. 103–110). Odense, Denmark: Odense University Press.

Horbury, D. F., & Guttentag, R. E. (1992). *The effects of restricting hand gesture production on lexical retrieval and free recall.* Unpublished manuscript, Bennett College, Greensboro, NC.

Horowitz, L. M., Chilian, P. C., & Dunnigan, K. P. (1969). Word fragments and their redintegrative powers. *Journal of Experimental Psychology, 80,* 392–394.

Horowitz, L. M., & Manelis, L. (1972). Toward a theory of redintegrative memory: Adjective–noun phrases. In G. H. Bower (Ed.), *The psychology of learning and motivation: Advances in research and theory* (Vol. 6, pp. 193–224). New York: Academic Press.

Horowitz, L. M., White, M. A., & Atwood, D. W. (1968). Word fragments as aids to recall: The organization of a word. *Journal of Experimental Psychology, 76,* 219–226.

Houston, B. C. (1986). *Schema: Organizing principles for human memory.* Unpublished master's thesis, Duke University, Durham, NC.

Humphrey, G. (1933). *The nature of learning in its relation to the living system.* London: Kegan Paul, Trench, Tubner.

Hunt, R. R., & Einstein, G. O. (1981). Relational and item-specific information in memory. *Journal of Verbal Learning and Verbal Behavior, 20,* 497–514.

Hunt, R. R., & McDaniel, M. A. (1993). The enigma of organization and distinctiveness. *Journal of Memory and Language, 32,* 421–445.

Hunt, R. R., & Mitchell, D. B. (1982). Independent effects of semantic and nonsemantic distinctiveness. *Journal of Experimental Psychology: Learning, Memory and Cognition, 8,* 81–87.

Hunter, I. M. L. (1979). Memory in everyday life. In M. M. Gruneberg & P. E. Morris (Eds.), *Applied problems in memory* (pp. 1–24). New York: Academic Press.

Hunter, I. M. L. (1984). Lengthy verbatim recall (LVR) and the mythical gift of tape-recorder memory. In K. M. J. Lagerspetz & P. Niemi (Eds.), *Psychology in the 1990's* (pp. 425–440). Amsterdam: North Holland.

Hunter, I. M. L. (1985). Lengthy verbatim recall: The role of text. In A. Ellis (Ed.), *Progress in the psychology of language* (Vol. 1, pp. 207–235). Hillsdale, NJ: Erlbaum.

Hunter, I. M. L. (1990). Exceptional memory performers: The motivational background. In M. J. A. Howe (Ed.), *Encouraging the development of exceptional skills and talents* (pp. 131–148). Leicester: British Psychological Society.

Hyman, I. E., Jr., & Rubin, D. C. (1990). Memorabeatlia: A naturalistic study of long-term memory. *Memory & Cognition, 18,* 205–214.

Hymes, D. (1976–1977). Discovering oral performance and measured verse in American Indian narrative. *New Literary History, 8,* 431–457.

Ingle, D. (1967). Two visual mechanisms underlying the behavior of fish. *Psychologische Forschung, 31,* 44–51.

Inhoff, A. W., & Bisiacchi, P. (1990). Unimanual tapping during concurrent articulation: Examining the role of cortical structures in the execution of programmed movement sequences. *Brain and Cognition, 13,* 59–76.

Jackendoff, R. (1987). The status of thematic relations in linguistic theory. *Linguistic Inquiry, 18,* 369–411.

Jacobs, M. (1959). *The content and style of an oral literature: Clackamas Chinook myths and tales.* Chicago: University of Chicago Press.

Jacoby, L. L., & Brooks, L. R. (1984). Nonanalytic cognition: Memory, perception and concept learning. In G. Bower (Ed.), *The psychology of learning and motivation* (Vol. 18, pp. 1–47). Orlando, FL: Academic Press.

Jacoby, L. L., & Hollingshead, A. (1990). Toward a generate/recognize model of performance on direct and indirect tests of memory. *Journal of Memory and Language, 29,* 433–454.

Jakobson, R. (1952). Studies in comparative Slavic metrics. In S. Konovalov (Ed.), *Oxford Slavonic papers* (Vol. 3, pp. 21–66). Oxford: Oxford University Press.

Jakobson, R. (1960). Closing statement: Linguistics and poetics. In T. A. Sebeok (Ed.), *Style in language* (pp. 350–377). Cambridge, MA: MIT Press.

James, C. T. (1975). The role of semantic information in lexical decisions. *Journal of Experimental Psychology: Human Perception and Performance, 1,* 130–136.

James, W. (1890). *The principles of psychology* (Vols. 1, 2) New York: Holt.

Janko, R. (1992). *The Iliad: A commentary, Vol. 4: Books 13–16.* Cambridge: Cambridge University Press.

Johnson, G. J. (1991). A distinctiveness model of serial learning. *Psychological Review, 98,* 204–217.

Johnson, J. L., & Hayes, D. S. (1987). Preschool children's retention of rhyming and nonrhyming text: Paraphrase and rote recitation measures. *Journal of Applied Developmental Psychology, 8,* 317–327.

Johnson, M. K., & Hasher, L. (1987). Human learning and memory. *Annual Review of Psychology, 38,* 631–668.

Johnson, M. K., & Raye, C. L. (1981). Reality monitoring. *Psychological Review, 88,* 67–85.

Johnson, R. E. (1970). Recall of prose as a function of the structural importance of the linguistic units. *Journal of Verbal Learning and Verbal Behavior, 9,* 12–20.

Johnson, R. E. (1982). Retrieval cues and the remembering of prose: A review. In A. Flammer & W. Kintsch (Eds.), *Discourse processing* (pp. 219–238). Amsterdam: North Holland.

Johnson, T. H. (Ed.). (1960). *The complete poems of Emily Dickinson.* Boston: Little, Brown.

Johnson-Laird, P. N. (1983). *Mental models: Towards a cognitive science of language, inference, and consciousness.* Cambridge, MA: Harvard University Press.

Jones, G. V. (1976). A fragmentation hypothesis of memory: Cued recall of pictures and of sequential position. *Journal of Experimental Psychology: General, 105,* 227–293.

Jones, G. V. (1983). Structure of the recall process. *Philosophical Transactions of the Royal Society of London* (Series B), *302,* 373–385.

Jones, G. V. (1987). Independence and exclusivity among psychological processes: Implications for the structure of recall. *Psychological Review, 94,* 229–235.

Jones, J. H. (1961). Commonplace and memorization in the oral tradition of the English and Scottish popular ballads. *Journal of American Folklore, 74,* 97–112.

Jones, M. R. (1987). Dynamic pattern structure in music: Recent theory and research. *Perception & Psychophysics, 41*, 621–634.

Jones, M. R., & Boltz, M. (1989). Dynamic attending and responses to time. *Psychological Review, 96*, 459–491.

Jones, M. R., Kidd, G., & Wetzel, R. (1981). Evidence for rhythmic attention. *Journal of Experimental Psychology: Human Perception and Performance, 7*, 1059–1073.

Jorgensen, C. C., & Kintsch, W. (1973). The role of imagery in the evaluation of sentences. *Cognitive Psychology, 4*, 110–116.

Joseph, R. (1988). The right cerebral hemisphere: Emotion, music, visual-spatial skills, body-image, dreams, and awareness. *Journal of Clinical Psychology, 44*, 630–673.

Jost, A. (1897). Die Assoziationsfestigkeit in ihrer Abhängigkeit von der Verteilung der Wiederholungen. *Zeitschrift für Psychologie und Physiologie der Sinnesorgane, 14*, 436–472.

Jusczyk, P. W. (1977). Rhymes and reasons: Some aspects of the child's appreciation of poetic form. *Developmental Psychology, 13*, 599–607.

Jusczyk, P. W., Cutler, A., & Redanz, N. J. (1993). Infant's preference for the predominant stress patterns of English words. *Child Development, 64*, 675–687.

Just, M. A., & Brownell, H. H. (1974). Retrieval of concrete and abstract prose descriptions from memory. *Canadian Journal of Psychology, 28*, 339–350.

Just, M. A., & Carpenter, P. A. (1987). *The psychology of reading and language comprehension*. Boston: Allyn and Bacon.

Just, M. A., & Carpenter, P. A. (1992). A capacity theory of comprehension: Individual differences in working memory. *Psychological Review, 99*, 122–149.

Kalat, J. W. (1985). *Difference between rumor and legend*. Unpublished manuscript, North Carolina State University, Raleigh.

Kapferer, B. (1991). *A celebration of demons: Exorcism and the aesthetics of healing in Sri Lanka* (2nd ed.). Providence, RI: Berg.

Kaplan, C. A., & Simon, H. A. (1990). In search of insight. *Cognitive Psychology, 22*, 374–419.

Karmiloff-Smith, A., & Inhelder, B. (1974–1975). If you want to get ahead, get a theory. *Cognition, 3*, 195–212.

Kausler, D. H. (1974). *The psychology of verbal learning and memory*. New York: Academic Press.

Keenan, J. M., MacWhinney, B., & Mayhew, D. (1977). Pragmatics in memory: A study in natural conversation. *Journal of Verbal Learning and Verbal Behavior, 16*, 549–560.

Kelly, M. H., & Bock, J. K. (1988). Stress in time. *Journal of Experimental Psychology: Human Perception and Performance, 14*, 389–403.

Kelly, M. H., & Rubin, D. C. (1988). Natural rhythmic patterns in English verse: Evidence from child counting-out rhymes. *Journal of Memory and Language, 27*, 718–740.

Kenny, D. A., & Rubin, D. C. (1977). Estimating chance reproducibility in Guttman scaling. *Social Science Research, 6*, 188–196.

Keppel, G. (1964). Facilitation in short- and long-term retention of paired associates following distributed practice in learning. *Journal of Verbal Learning and Verbal Behavior, 3*, 91–111.

Keppel, G., Postman, L., & Zavortink, B. (1968). Studies of learning to learn: VIII. The influence of massive amounts of training upon the learning and retention of paired-associate lists. *Journal of Verbal Learning and Verbal Behavior, 7*, 790–796.

Kersenboom, S. C. (1991). The traditional repertoire of the Tiruttani Temple Dancers. In J. Leslie (Ed.), *Roles and rituals for Hindu women* (pp. 131–147). London: Pinter.

Keyser, S. J. (1969). The linguistic basis of English prosody. In D. A. Reibel & S. A. Schane (Eds.), *Modern studies in English: Readings in transformational grammar* (pp. 380–394). Englewood Cliffs, NJ: Prentice-Hall.

Kieras, D. (1978). Beyond pictures and words: Alternative information-processing models for imagery effects in verbal memory. *Psychological Bulletin, 85,* 532–554.

King, D. R. W., & Anderson, J. R. (1976). Long-term memory search: An intersecting activation process. *Journal of Verbal Learning and Verbal Behavior, 15,* 587–605.

Kinsley, J. (Ed.). (1969). *Burns: Poems and songs.* London: Oxford University Press.

Kintsch, W. (1970). *Learning, memory and conceptual processes.* New York: Wiley.

Kintsch, W. (1988). The role of knowledge in discourse comprehension: A construction-integration model. *Psychological Review, 95,* 163–182.

Kintsch, W. (1994). Kognitionspsychologische Modelle des Textverstehens: Literarische Texte. In K. Reusser & M. Reusser-Weyenth (Eds.), *Verstehen* (pp. 39–54). Bern: Huber.

Kintsch, W., & Bates, E. (1977). Recognition memory for statements from a classroom lecture. *Human Learning and Memory, 3,* 150–159.

Kintsch, W., & Greene, E. (1978). The role of culture-specific schemata in the comprehension and recall of stories. *Discourse Processes, 1,* 1–13.

Kintsch, W., & van Dijk, T. A. (1978). Toward a model of text comprehension. *Psychological Review, 85,* 363–394.

Kiparsky, P. (1975). Stress, syntax, and meter. *Language, 51,* 576–616.

Kiparsky, P. (1976). Oral poetry: Some linguistic and typological considerations. In B. A. Stolz & R. S. Shannon III (Eds.), *Oral literature and the formula* (pp. 73–125). Ann Arbor: Center for the Coordination of Ancient and Modern Studies, University of Michigan.

Kiparsky, P. (1977). The rhythmic structure of English verse. *Linguistic Inquiry, 8,* 189–247.

Kipling, R. (1923). *Land and sea tales for scouts and guides.* London: Macmillan.

Kirk, G. S. (1962). *The songs of Homer.* Cambridge: Cambridge University Press.

Kirk, G. S. (1976). *Homer and the oral tradition.* Cambridge: Cambridge University Press.

Kittrege, G. L. (1904). Introduction. In H. C. Sargent & G. L. Kittredge (Eds.), *English and Scottish popular ballads edited from the collection of Francis James Child* (pp. xi–xxxi). Boston: Houghton Mifflin.

Klahr, D., Chase, W. G., & Lovelace, E. A. (1983). Structure and process in alphabetic retrieval. *Journal of Experimental Psychology: Learning Memory, and Cognition, 9,* 462–477.

Klatzky, R. L., Pellegrino, J. W., McCloskey, B. P., & Doherty, S. (1989). Can you squeeze a tomato? The role of motor representations in semantic sensiblity judgments. *Journal of Memory and Language, 28,* 56–77.

Klee, H., & Eysenck, M. W. (1973). Comprehension of abstract and concrete sentences. *Journal of Verbal Learning and Verbal Behavior, 12,* 522–529.

Kohler, W. (1974). *Gestalt psychology.* New York: Liveright.

Kolers, P. A., & Roediger, H. L., III (1984). Procedures of mind. *Journal of Verbal Learning and Verbal Behavior, 23,* 425–449.

Kosslyn, S. M. (1983). *Ghosts in the mind's machine: Creating and using images in the brain.* New York: Norton.

Kosslyn, S. M., Pinker, S., Smith, G., & Shwartz, S. P. (1979). On the de-mystification of mental imagery. *Behavioral and Brain Sciences, 2,* 535–581.

Kreitler, H., & Kreitler, S. (1972). *Psychology of the arts.* Durham, NC: Duke University Press.

Krueger, W. C. F. (1929). The effect of overlearning on retention. *Journal of Experimental Psychology, 12,* 71–78.

Krumhansl, C. L., & Keil, F. C. (1982). Acquisition of the hierarchy of tonal functions in music. *Memory & Cognition, 10,* 243–251.

Kubovy, M. (1977). Response availability and the apparent spontaneity of numerical choices. *Journal of Experimental Psychology: Human Perception and Performance, 3,* 359–364.

Lakoff, G. P. (1972). Structural complexity in fairy tales. *Study of Man, 1,* 128–190.

Lakoff, G., & Johnson, M. (1980). *Metaphors we live by.* Chicago: University of Chicago Press.

Landauer, T. K. (1989). Some bad and some good reasons for studying memory and cognition in the wild. In L. W. Poon, D. C. Rubin, & B. A. Wilson (Eds.), *Everyday cognition in adult and late life* (pp. 116–125). Cambridge: Cambridge University Press.

Landauer, T. K., & Ainslie, K. I. (1975). Exams and use as preservatives of course-acquired knowledge. *Journal of Educational Research, 69,* 99–104.

Langer, E. J. (1983). *The psychology of control.* Beverly Hills, CA: Sage.

Langhorne, J., & Langhorne, W. (1879). *Plutarch's lives.* London: Routledge.

Lanz, H. (1931). *The physical basis of rime: An essay on the aesthetics of sound.* Stanford, CA: Stanford University Press.

Larsen, S. F. (1988). Remembering without experiencing: Memory for reported events. In U. Neisser & E. Winograd (Eds.), *Remembering reconsidered: Ecological and traditional approaches to the study of memory* (pp. 326–355). Cambridge: Cambridge University Press.

Lashley, K. S. (1951). The problem of serial order in behavior. In L. A. Jeffress (Ed.), *Cerebral mechanisms in behavior* (pp. 112–136). New York: Wiley.

Lashley, K. S., & Wade, M. (1946). The Pavlovian theory of generalization. *Psychological Review, 53,* 72–87.

Lattimore, R. (1951). Introduction. In R. Lattimore (Trans.), *The Iliad of Homer* (pp. 11–55). Chicago: University of Chicago Press.

Lattimore, R. (1965). *The Odyssey of Homer: A modern translation.* New York: Harper & Row.

Laughery, K. R., & Spector, A. (1972). The roles of recoding and rhythm in memory organization. *Journal of Experimental Psychology, 94,* 41–48.

Laws, G. M., Jr. (1964). *Native American balladry: A descriptive study and a bibliographical syllabus.* Philadelphia: American Folklore Society.

Leech, G. N. (1969). *A linguistic guide to English poetry.* London: Longmans.

Lenneberg, E. H. (1967). *Biological foundations of language.* New York: Wiley.

Levelt, W. J. M., & Kelter, S. (1982). Surface form and memory in question answering. *Cognitive Psychology, 14,* 78–106.

Levine, D. N., Warach, J., & Farah, M. (1985). Two visual systems in mental imagery: Dissociation of "what" and "where" in imagery disorders due to bilateral posterior cerebral lesions. *Neurology, 35,* 1010–1018.

Lewandowsky, S., & Murdock, B. B., Jr. (1989). Memory for serial order. *Psychological Review, 96,* 25–57.

Liberman, M., & Prince, A. (1977). On stress and linguistic rhythm. *Linguistic Inquiry, 8,* 249–336.

Lima, S. D. (1993). Word-initial letter sequences and reading. *Current Directions in Psychological Science, 2,* 139–142.

Lindauer, M. S. (1974). *The psychological study of literature: Limitations, possibilities, and accomplishments.* Chicago: Nelson-Hall.

Lingoes, J. C. (1973). *The Guttman–Lingoes nonmetric program series*. Ann Arbor, MI: Mathesis Press.

Livingstone, M., & Hubel, D. (1988). Segregation of form, color, movement, and depth: Anatomy, physiology, and perception. *Science, 240,* 740–749.

Lloyd-Jones, H. (1992, March 5). Becoming Homer. *New York Review of Books,* pp. 52–57.

Lockhead, G. R. (1972). Processing dimensional stimuli: A note. *Psychological Review, 79,* 410–479.

Lockhead, G. R. (1992). On identifying things: A case for context. In B. Burns (Ed.), *Percepts, concepts and categories* (pp. 109–143). Amsterdam: Elsevier.

Lockhead, G. R., & Evans, N. J. (1979). Emmert's imaginal law. *Bulletin of the Psychonomic Society, 13,* 114–116.

Lord, A. B. (1956). Avdo Mededović, guslar. *Journal of American Folklore, 69,* 54–89.

Lord, A. B. (1960). *The singer of tales*. Cambridge, MA: Harvard University Press.

Lord, A. B. (1976). The traditional song. In B. A. Stolz & R. S. Shannon III (Eds.), *Oral literature and the formula* (pp. 1–29). Ann Arbor: Center for the Coordination of Ancient and Modern Studies, University of Michigan.

Lord, A. B. (1986). Perspectives on recent work on the oral traditional formula. *Oral Tradition, 1,* 467–503.

Lord, A. B. (1991a). *Epic singers and oral tradition*. Ithaca, NY: Cornell University Press.

Lord, A. B. (1991b). Ring composition in *Maldon;* or, a possible case of chiasmus in a late Anglo-Saxon poem. In J. Harris (Ed.), *The ballad and oral literature* (pp. 233–242). Cambridge, MA: Harvard University Press.

Lord, A. B., & Bynum, D. E. (Eds.). (1974). *Serbo-Croatian heroic songs: Vol. 3. The wedding song of Smailagic Meho by Avdo Mededović*. Cambridge, MA: Harvard University Press.

Lorenz, C., & Neisser, U. (1985). Factors of imagery and event recall. *Memory & Cognition, 13,* 494–500.

Lupker, S. J., & Williams, B. A. (1989). Rhyme priming of pictures and words: A lexical activation account. *Journal of Experimental Psychology: Learning, Memory, and Cognition, 15,* 1033–1046.

Luria, A. R. (1968). *The mind of a mnemonist*. New York: Basic Books.

Luria, A. R. (1976). *Cognitive development: Its cultural and social foundations*. Cambridge, MA: Harvard University Press.

MacDonald, D. A. (1978). A visual memory. *Scottish Studies, 22,* 1–26.

Magoun, F. P., Jr. (1955). Bede's story of Caedman: The case history of an Anglo-Saxon oral singer. *Speculum, 30,* 49–63.

Mandler, G. (1967). Organization and memory. In K. W. Spence & J. T. Spence (Ed.), *The psychology of learning and motivation: Advances in research and theory* (pp. 327–372). New York: Academic Press.

Mandler, G. (1969). Input variables and output strategies in free recall of categorized lists. *American Journal of Psychology, 82,* 531–539.

Mandler, J. M. (1978). A code in the node: The use of a story schema in retrieval. *Discourse Processes, 1,* 14–35.

Mandler, J. M. (1984). *Stories, scripts, and scenes: Aspects of schema theory*. Hillsdale, NJ: Erlbaum.

Mandler, J. M., & Johnson, N. S. (1977). Remembrance of things parsed: Story structure and recall. *Cognitive Psychology, 9,* 111–151.

Mantyla, T. (1986). Optimizing cue effectiveness: Recall of 500 and 600 incidentally learned words. *Journal of Experimental Psychology: Learning, Memory, and Cognition, 12,* 66–71.

Mantyla, T., & Nilsson, L. G. (1988). Cue distinctiveness and forgetting: Effectiveness of self-generated retrieval cues in delayed recall. *Journal of Experimental Psychology: Learning, Memory, and Cognition, 14,* 502–509.

Marschark, M. (1985). Imagery and organization in the recall of prose. *Journal of Verbal Learning and Verbal Behavior, 24,* 734–745.

Marschark, M. E. (1979). The syntax and semantics of comprehension. In G. D. Prideaux (Ed.), *Perspectives in experimental linguistics* (pp. 52–72). Amsterdam: Benjamins.

Marschark, M., & Hunt, R. R. (1989). A reexamination of the role of imagery in learning and memory. *Journal of Experimental Psychology: Learning, Memory, and Cognition, 15,* 710–720.

Marschark, M., & Paivio, A. (1977). Integrative processing of concrete and abstract sentences. *Journal of Verbal Learning and Verbal Behavior, 16,* 217–231.

Marschark, M., Richman, C. L., Yuille, J. C., & Hunt, R. R. (1987). The role of imagery in memory: On shared and distinctive information. *Psychological Bulletin, 102,* 28–41.

Marslen-Wilson, W., & Tyler, L. K. (1980). The temporal structure of spoken language understanding. *Cognition, 8,* 1–71.

Massaro, D. W., & Friedman, D. (1990). Models of integration given multiple sources of information. *Psychological Review, 97,* 225–252.

Matteson, M., & Henry, M. E. (1936). *Beech Mountain folk-songs and ballads.* New York: Schirmer.

McBurney, D. H. (1983). *Experimental psychology.* Belmont, CA: Wadsworth.

McCarthy, W. B. (1990). *The ballad matrix: Personality, milieu, and the oral tradition.* Bloomington: Indiana University Press.

McCarthy, W. B. (1991). The Americanization of Scottish ballads: Counterevidence from the southwest of Scotland. In J. Harris (Ed.), *The ballad and oral literature* (pp. 97–108). Cambridge, MA: Harvard University Press.

McClelland, J. L., & Rumelhart, D. E. (1985). Distributed memory and the representation of general and specific information. *Journal of Experimental Psychology: General, 114,* 159–188.

McClelland, J. L., Rumelhart, D. E., & Hinton, G. E. (1986). The appeal of parallel distributed processing. In D. E. Rumelhart, J. L. McClelland, & PDP Research Group (Eds.), *Parallel distributed processing: Explorations in the microstructure of cognition: Vol. 1. Foundations* (pp. 3–44). Cambridge, MA: MIT Press.

McCloskey, M. (1991). Networks and theories: The place of connectionism in cognitive science. *Psychological Science, 2,* 387–395.

McCloskey, M., & Cohen, N. J. (1989). Catastrophic interference in connectionist networks: The sequential learning problem. In G. H. Bower (Ed.), *The psychology of learning and motivation* (Vol. 24, pp. 109–165). San Diego, CA: Academic Press.

McDaniel, M. A., & Einstein, G. O. (1986). Bizarre imagery as an effective memory aid: The importance of distinctiveness. *Journal of Experimental Psychology: Learning, Memory, and Cognition, 12,* 54–65.

McDaniel, M. A., Hines, R. J., Waddill, P. J., & Einstein, G. O. (1994). What makes folk tales unique: Content familiarity, causal structure, scripts, or superstructures? *Journal of Experimental Psychology: Learning, Memory, & Cognition, 20,* 169–184.

McEvoy, C. L., & Nelson, D. L. (1980). *The University of South Florida rhyme category norms.* Unpublished manuscript, University of South Florida, Tampa.

McEvoy, C. L., & Nelson, D. L. (1982). Category name and instance norms for 106 categories of various sizes. *American Journal of Psychology, 95,* 581–634.

McEvoy, C. L., & Nelson, D. L. (1990). Selective access in cued recall: The roles of retrieval cues and domains of encoding. *Memory & Cognition, 18,* 15–22.

McGeoch, J. A. (1932). Forgetting and the law of disuse. *Psychological Review, 39,* 352–370.

McGeoch, J. A. (1942). *The psychology of human learning.* New York: Longmans, Green.

McGovern, J. B. (1964). Extinction of associations in four transfer paradigms. *Psychological Monographs: General and Applied, 78* (16, No. 593).

McKitterick, R. (Ed.). (1990). *The uses of literacy in early mediaeval Europe.* Cambridge: Cambridge University Press.

McNeill, D. (1987). *Psycholinguistics: A new approach.* New York: Harper & Row.

McNeill, D. (1992). *Hand and mind.* Chicago: University of Chicago Press.

Medin, D. L., & Ross, B. H. (1989). The specific character of abstract thought: Categorization, problem solving, and induction. In R. J. Sternberg (Ed.), *Advances in the psychology of human intelligence* (Vol. 5, pp. 189–223). Hillsdale, NJ: Erlbaum.

Melton, A. W., & Irwin, J. M. (1940). The influence of degree of interpolated learning on retroactive inhibition and the overt transfer of specific responses. *American Journal of Psychology, 53,* 173–203.

Mensink, G. J., & Raaijmakers, J. G. W. (1988). A model for interference and forgetting. *Psychological Review, 95,* 434–455.

Meyer, B. J. F. (1977). What is remembered from prose: A function of passage structure. In R. O. Freedle (Ed.), *Discourse production and comprehension* (pp. 307–333). Norwood, NJ: Ablex.

Meyer, B. L. (1980). *The psychoanalytic concept of adolescence and the pattern of the initiatory hero in Serbocroatian folktales and modern American fantasy.* Unpublished undergraduate honor's thesis, Harvard College, Cambridge, MA.

Meyer, D. E., & Schvaneveldt, R. W. (1975). Meaning, memory structure, and mental processes. In C. N. Cofer (Ed.), *The structure of human memory* (pp. 54–89). San Francisco: Freeman.

Meyer, D. E., Schvaneveldt, R. W., & Ruddy, M. G. (1974). Functions of graphemic and phonemic codes in visual word-recognition. *Memory & Cognition, 2,* 309–321.

Meyer, D. E., Schvaneveldt, R. W., & Ruddy, M. G. (1975). Loci of contextual effects on visual word recognition. In P. M. A. Rabbitt & S. Dornic (Eds.), *Attention and performance V* (pp. 98–118). London: Academic Press.

Miller, D. G. (1987). Towards a new model of formulaic composition. In J. M. Foley (Ed.), *Comparative research on oral traditions: A memorial for Milman Parry* (pp. 351–393). Columbus, OH: Slavica.

Miller, E. S. (1937). Nonsense and new sense in "Lord Thomas." *Southern Folklore Quarterly, 1,* 25–37.

Minchin, E. (1992). Scripts and themes: Cognitive research and the Homeric epic. *Classical Antiquity, 11,* 229–241.

Moeser, S. D. (1974). Memory for meaning and wording in concrete and abstract sentences. *Journal of Verbal Learning and Verbal Behavior, 13,* 682–697.

Monroe, W. S. (1904). Counting-out rhymes of children. *American Anthropologist, 6,* 46–50.

Monty, R. A., Geller, S. E., Savage, R. E., & Perlmutter, L. C. (1979). The freedom to choose is not always so choice. *Journal of Experimental Psychology: Human Learning and Memory, 5,* 170–178.

Mook, D. G. (1989). The myth of external validity. In L. W. Poon, D. C. Rubin, & B. A. Wilson (Eds.), *Everyday cognition in adulthood and late life* (pp. 25–43). Cambridge: Cambridge University Press.

Morais, J., Bertelson, P., Cary, L., & Alegria, J. (1986). Literacy training and speech segmentation. *Cognition, 24,* 45–64.

Morgan, J. L., Meier, R. P., & Newport, E. L. (1987). Structural packaging in the input to language learning: Contributions of prosodic and morphological marking of phrases to the acquisition of language. *Cognitive Psychology, 19,* 498–550.

Morrel-Samuels, P. M., & Krauss, R. M. (1992). Word familiarity predicts temporal asynchrony of hand gestures and speech. *Journal of Experimental Psychology: Learning, Memory, and Cognition, 18,* 615–622.

Morris, C. D., Bransford, J. D., & Franks, J. J. (1977). Levels of processing versus transfer appropriate processing. *Journal of Verbal Learning and Verbal Behavior, 16,* 519–533.

Morrow, D. G. (1985). Prepositions and verb aspect in narrative understanding. *Journal of Memory and Language, 24,* 390–404.

Morrow, D. G., Bower, G. H., & Greenspan, S. L. (1989). Updating situation models during narrative comprehension. *Journal of Memory and Language, 28,* 292–312.

Morrow, D. G., Greenspan, S. L., & Bower, G. H. (1987). Accessibility and situation models in narrative comprehension. *Journal of Memory and Language, 26,* 165–187.

Moulton, J., & Robinson, G. M. (1981). *The organization of language.* Cambridge: Cambridge University Press.

Moyer, R. S. (1973). Comparing objects in memory: Evidence suggesting an internal psychophysics. *Perception & Psychophysics, 13,* 180–184.

Murdock, B. B., Jr. (1960). The distinctiveness of stimuli. *Psychological Review, 67,* 16–31.

Myers, J. L., O'Brien, E. J., Balota, D. A., & Toyofuku, M. L. (1984). Memory search without interference: The role of integration. *Cognitive Psychology, 16,* 217–242.

Nagler, M. H. (1967). Towards a generative view of the oral formula. *Transactions and Proceedings of the American Philological Association, 98,* 269–311.

Nagy, G. (1974). *Comparative studies in Greek and Indic meter.* Cambridge, MA: Harvard University Press.

Nagy, G. (1976). Formula and meter. In B. A. Stolz & R. S. Shannon III (Eds.), *Oral literature and the formula* (pp. 239–272). Ann Arbor: Center for the Coordination of Ancient and Modern Studies, University of Michigan.

Nairne, J. S. (1990). Similarity and long-term memory for order. *Journal of Memory and Language, 29,* 733–746.

Nairne, J. S., & Neumann, C. (1993). Enhancing effects of similarity on long-term memory for order. *Journal of Experimental Psychology: Learning, Memory, and Cognition, 19,* 329–337.

Neath, I., & Crowder, R. G. (1990). Schedules of presentation and temporal distinctiveness in human memory. *Journal of Experimental Psychology: Learning, Memory, and Cognition, 16,* 316–327.

Neisser, U. (1967). *Cognitive psychology.* New York: Appleton-Century-Crofts.

Neisser, U. (1976). *Cognition and reality: Principles and implications of cognitive psychology.* San Francisco: Freeman

Neisser, U. (1978). Memory: What are the important questions? In M. M. Gruneberg, P. E. Morris, & R. N. Sykes (Eds.), *Practical aspects of memory* (pp. 1–24). London: Academic Press.

Neisser, U. (1981). John Dean's memory: A case study. *Cognition, 9,* 1–22.

Neisser, U. (1982). *Memory observed.* San Francisco: Freeman.

Neisser, U. (1983). Toward a skillful psychology. In D. Rogers & J. A. Sloboda (Eds.), *The acquisition of symbolic skills* (pp. 1–17). New York: Plenum.

Neisser, U. (1987). A sense of where you are: Functions of the spatial module. In P. Ellen & C. Thinus-Blanc (Eds.), *Cognitive and spatial orientation in animal and man: Vol. 2. Neurophysiology and developmental aspects* (pp. 293–310). Dodrecht: Nijhoff.

Neisser, U. (1988). Domains of memory. In P. R. Soloman, G. R. Goethals, C. M. Kelley, & B. R. Stephens (Eds.), *Memory: Interdisciplinary approaches* (pp. 67–83). New York: Springer-Verlag.

Nelson, D. G. K., Hirsh-Pasek, K., Jusczyk, P. W., & Cassidy, K.W. (1989). How the prosodic cues in motherese might assist language learning. *Journal of Child Language, 16,* 55–68.

Nelson, D. L. (1981). Many are called but few are chosen: The influence of context on the effects of category size. In G. H. Bower (Ed.), *The psychology of learning and motivation* (Vol. 15, pp. 129–162). New York: Academic Press.

Nelson, D. L., & Borden, R. C. (1977). Encoding and retrieval effects of dual semantic-sensory cues. *Memory & Cognition, 5,* 457–461.

Nelson, D. L., & Garland, R. M. (1969). Amount and locus of stimulus–response overlap in paired-associate accquisition. *Journal of Experimental Psychology, 82,* 297–300.

Nelson, D. L., & McEvoy, C. L. (1979a). Effects of retention interval and modality on sensory and semantic trace information. *Memory & Cognition, 7,* 257–262.

Nelson, D. L., & McEvoy, C. L. (1979b). Encoding context and set size. *Journal of Experimental Psychology: Human Learning and Memory, 5,* 292–314.

Nelson, D. L., McEvoy, C. L., & Casanueva, D. M. (1982). Category size and free recall. *American Journal of Psychology, 95,* 235–249.

Nelson, D. L., & Rowe, F. A. (1969). Information theory and stimulus encoding in paired-associate acquisition: Ordinal position of formal similarity. *Journal of Experimental Psychology, 79,* 342–346.

Nelson, D. L., Schreiber, T. A., & McEvoy, C. L. (1992). Processing implicit and explicit representations. *Psychological Review, 99,* 322–348.

Nelson, D. L., Wheeler, J. W., Jr., Borden, R. C., & Brooks, D. H. (1974). Levels of processing and cuing: Sensory versus meaning features. *Journal of Experimental Psychology, 103,* 971–977.

Nelson, K. (1988). The ontogeny of memory for real events. In U. Neisser & E. Winograd (Eds.), *Remembering reconsidered: Ecological and traditional approaches to the study of memory* (pp. 244–276). Cambridge: Cambridge University Press.

Nelson, K. (1993). The psychological and social origins of autobiographical memory. *Psychological Science, 4,* 7–14.

Neusner, J. (1977). Form and meaning in Mishnah. *Journal of the American Academy of Religion, 45,* 27–54.

Newell, A. (1973). You can't play 20 questions with nature and win: Projective comments on the papers of this symposium. In W. G. Chase (Ed.), *Visual information processing* (pp. 283–308). New York: Academic Press.

Newell, W. W. (1903). *Games and songs of American children.* New York: Harper.

Newton, R. P. (1975). Trochaic and iambic. *Language and Style, 8,* 127–156.

Nielsen, K. (1992). *Cognitive constraints and situational factors affecting speech and writing.* Unpublished doctoral dissertation, Duke University, Durham, NC.

Nigrin, A. (1993). *Neural networks for pattern recognition.* Cambridge, MA: MIT Press.

Niles, J. D. (1983). *Beowulf: The poem and its tradition.* Cambridge, MA: Harvard University Press.

Noice, H. (1991). The role of explanations and plan recognition in the learning of theatrical scripts. *Cognitive Psychology, 15,* 425–460.

Noice, H. (1992). Elaborative memory strategies of professional actors. *Applied Cognitive Psychology, 6,* 417–427.

Noice, H. (1993). Effects of rote versus gist strategy on the verbatim retention of theatrical scripts. *Applied Cognitive Psychology, 7,* 75–84.

Norman, D. A. (1988). *The psychology of everyday things*. New York: Basic Books.

Notopoulos, J. A. (1949). Parataxis in Homer: A new approach to Homeric literary criticism. *Transactions of the American Philological Association, 80*, 1–23.

Nyberg, L., Nilsson, L. G., & Backman, L. (1992). Recall of actions, sentences, and nouns: Influences of adult age and passage of time. *Acta Psychologica, 79*, 245–254.

Nygard, H. O. (1958). *The ballad of Heer Halewijn: Its forms and variations in Western Europe: A study of the history and nature of a ballad tradition*. Knoxville: University of Tennessee Press.

O'Connell, D. C., Turner, E. A., & Onuska, L. A. (1968). Intonation, grammatical structure, and contextual association in immediate recall. *Journal of Verbal Learning and Verbal Behavior, 7*, 110–116.

O'Neill, E. G., Jr. (1942). The localization of metrical word-types in the Greek hexameter. *Yale Classical Studies, 8*, 105–177.

Oliver, W. L., & Ericsson, K. A. (1986). Repertory actors' memory for their parts. In *Proceedings of the Eighth Annual Conference of the Cognitive Science Society* (pp. 399–406). Hillsdale, NJ: Erlbaum.

Olrik, A. (1965). Epic laws of folk narrative. In A. Dundes (Ed.), *The study of folklore* (pp. 129–141). Englewood Cliffs, NJ: Prentice-Hall. (Original work published 1909)

Olson, D. R. (1977). From utterances to text: The bias of language in speech and writing. *Harvard Educational Review, 47*, 257–281.

Olson, D. R. (1986). The cognitive consequences of literacy. *Canadian Psychology/ Psychologie Canadienne, 27*, 109–121.

Ong, W. J. (1967). *The presence of the word: Some prolegomena for cultural and religious history*. New Haven, CT: Yale University Press.

Ong, W. J. (1982). *Orality and literacy: The technologizing of the word*. London: Methuen.

Opie, I., & Opie, P. (1951). *The Oxford dictionary of nursery rhymes*. London: Oxford University Press.

Opie, I., & Opie, P. (1959). *The lore and language of schoolchildren*. Oxford: Clarendon Press.

Opie, I., & Opie, P. (1969). *Children's games in street and playground*. Oxford: Clarendon Press.

Opland, J. (1988). Lord of the singers. *Oral Tradition, 3*, 353–367.

Opland, J. (1992). The making of a Xhosa oral poem. In J. M. Foley (Ed.), *De gustibus: Essays for Alain Renoir* (pp. 411–440). New York: Garland.

Osborne, H. F. (1902). Rapid memorizing, "winging a part," as a lost faculty. *Psychological Review, 9*, 183–184.

Ozier, M. (1978). Access to the memory trace through orthographic and categoric information. *Journal of Experimental Psychology: Human Learning and Memory, 4*, 469–485.

Paivio, A. (1968). A factor-analytic study of word attributes and verbal learning. *Journal of Verbal Learning and Verbal Behavior, 7*, 41–49.

Paivio, A. (1969). Mental imagery in associative learning and memory. *Psychological Review, 76*, 241–263.

Paivio, A. (1971). *Imagery and verbal processes*. New York: Holt, Rinehart and Winston.

Paivio, A. (1975a). Imagery and synchronic thinking. *Canadian Psychological Review, 16*, 147–163.

Paivio, A. (1975b). Perceptual comparisons through the mind's eye. *Memory & Cognition, 3*, 635–647.

Paivio, A. (1976). Imagery in recall and recognition. In J. Brown (Ed.), *Recall and recognition* (pp. 103–129). London: Wiley.

Paivio, A. (1983a). The empirical case for dual coding. In J. C. Yuille (Ed.), *Imagery, memory, and cognition: Essays in honor of Allan Paivio* (pp. 307–332). Hillsdale, NJ: Erlbaum.

Paivio, A. (1983b). The mind's eye in arts and science. *Poetics, 12,* 1–18.

Paivio, A. (1986). *Mental representations: A dual coding approach.* New York: Oxford University Press.

Paivio, A. (1991). Dual coding theory: Retrospect and current status. *Canadian Journal of Psychology, 45,* 255–287.

Paivio, A., & Csapo, K. (1969). Concrete image and verbal memory codes. *Journal of Experimental Psychology, 80,* 279–285.

Paivio, A., & te Linde, J. (1982). Imagery, memory, and the brain. *Canadian Journal of Psychology, 36,* 243–272.

Palmer, C., & Kelly, M. H. (1992). Linguistic prosody and musical meter in song. *Journal of Memory and Language, 31,* 525–542.

Park, D. C., Smith, A. D., & Cavanaugh, J. C. (1990). Metamemories of memory researchers. *Memory & Cognition, 18,* 321–327.

Parry, M. (1929). The distinctive character of enjambement in Homeric verse. *Transactions and Proceedings of the American Philological Association, 40,* 200–220.

Parry, M. (1930). Studies in the epic technique of oral verse-making: I. Homer and the Homeric style. *Harvard Studies in Classical Philology, 41,* 73–147.

Parry, M. (1934). The traces of the digamma in Ionic and Lesbian Greek. *Language, 10,* 130–144.

Parry, M. (1971a). Homeric formulae and Homeric metre. In A. Parry (Ed. & Trans.), *The making of Homeric verse: The collected papers of Milman Parry* (pp. 191–239). Oxford: Oxford University Press. (Original work published 1928).

Parry, M. (1971b). The traditional epithet in Homer. In A. Parry (Ed. & Trans.), *The making of Homeric verse: The collected papers of Milman Parry* (pp. 1–190). Oxford: Oxford University Press. (Original work published 1928).

Parry, M., & Lord, A. B. (Eds.). (1954). *Serbocroation heroic songs: Vol. 1. Novi Pazar: English translations.* Cambridge, MA: Harvard University Press.

Payne, R. B., Payne, L. L., & Doehlert, S. M. (1988). Biological and cultural success of song memes in indigo buntings. *Ecology, 69,* 104–117.

Peretz, I., & Morais, J. (1988). Determinants of laterality for music: Towards an information processing account. In K. Hugdahl (Ed.), *Handbook of dichotic listening: Theory, methods and research* (pp. 323–358). New York: Wiley.

Perkins, N. L. (1914). The value of distributed repetitions in rote learning. *British Journal of Psychology, 7,* 253–261.

Perlmutter, C. E., & Monty, R. A. (1977). The importance of perceived control: Fact or fantasy? *American Scientist, 65,* 759–765.

Perlmutter, L. C., Monty, R. A., & Kimble, G. A. (1971). Effect of choice on paired-associate learning. *Journal of Experimental Psychology, 91,* 47–53.

Peronnet, F., & Farah, M. J. (1989). Mental rotation: An event-related potential study with a validated mental rotation task. *Brain and Cognition, 8,* 279–288.

Perrig, W., & Kintsch, W. (1985). Propositional and situational representations of text. *Journal of Memory and Language, 24,* 503–518.

Pezdek, K., & Royer, J. M. (1974). The role of comprehension in learning concrete and abstract sentences. *Journal of Verbal Learning and Verbal Behavior, 13,* 551–558

Piaget, J. (1965). *The moral judgment of the child* (M. Gabain, Trans.). New York: Free Press.

Pichert, J. W., & Anderson, R. C. (1977). Taking different perspectives on a story. *Journal of Educational Psychology, 69,* 309–315.

Pillemer, D. B. (1992). Remembering personal circumstances: A functional analysis. In E. Winograd & U. Neisser (Eds.), *Affect and accuracy in recall: Studies of "flash-bulb" memories* (pp. 236–264). Cambridge: Cambridge University Press.

Pinto, V. De S., & Rodway, A. E. (1957). *The common muse: An anthology of popular British ballad poetry, XVth–XXth century.* London: Chatto & Windus.

Plato (1973). *Phaedrus and letters VII and VIII* (W. Hamilton, Trans.). London: Penguin Books. (Original work, fourth century B.C.E.)

Plato (1987). *The Republic* (rev. ed.) (D. Lee, Trans.). London: Penguin Books. (Original work, fourth century B.C.E.)

Pohl, W. (1973). Dissociation of spatial discrimination deficits following frontal and parietal lesions in monkeys. *Journal of Comparative and Physiological Psychology, 82,* 227–239.

Porter, D. B. (1991). Computer games and cognitive processes: Two tasks, two modes, too much. *British Journal of Psychology, 82,* 343–357.

Porter, H. N. (1951). The early Greek hexameter. *Yale Classical Studies, 12,* 3–63.

Posner, M. I., & Keele, S. W. (1968). On the genesis of abstract ideas. *Journal of Experimental Psychology, 77,* 353–363.

Posner, M. I., & Petersen, S. E. (1990). The attention system of the human brain. *Annual Review of Neuroscience, 13,* 25–25.

Posner, M. I., Petersen, S. E., Fox, P. T., & Raichle, M. E. (1988). Localization of cognitive operations in the human brain. *Science, 240,* 1627–1631.

Postman, L. (1972). A pragmatic view of organization theory. In E. Tulving & W. Donaldson (Eds.), *Organization of memory* (pp. 3–48). New York: Academic Press.

Postman, L., & Stark, K. (1969). Role of response availability in transfer and interference. *Journal of Experimental Psychology, 79,* 168–177.

Potter, C. F. (1949). Eeny, meeny, miney, mo. In M. Leach (Ed.), *Funk and Wagnalls standard dictionary of folklore, mythology, and legend* (Vol. 1, pp. 339–340). New York: Funk and Wagnalls.

Powell, B. B. (1991). *Homer and the origin of the Greek alphabet.* Cambridge: Cambridge University Press.

Propp, V. (1968). *Morphology of the folktale* (2nd ed.) (L. Scott, Trans.). Austin: University of Texas Press. (Original work published 1928)

Quiller-Couch, A. (1927). *Studies in literature: First series.* Cambridge: Cambridge University Press.

Read, C., Yun-Fei, Z., Hong-Yin, N., & Bao-Qing, D. (1986). The ability to manipulate speech sounds depends on knowing alphabetic writing. *Cognition, 24,* 31–44.

Reece, S. (1993). *The stranger's welcome: Oral theory and the aesthetics of the Homeric hospitality scene.* Ann Arbor: University of Michigan Press.

Reisberg, D. (Ed.). (1992). *Auditory imagery.* Hillsdale, NJ: Erlbaum.

Rescorla, R. A., & Cunnignham, C. L. (1979). Spatial contiguity facilitates Pavlovian second-order conditioning. *Journal of Experimental Psychology: Animal Behavior Processes, 5,* 152–161.

Restlé, F. (1972). Serial patterns: The role of phrasing. *Journal of Experimental Psychology, 92,* 385–390.

Richardson, A. (1969). *Mental imagery.* New York: Springer.

Richardson, J. T. E. (1980). *Mental imagery and human memory.* London: Macmillan.

Richardson-Klavehn, A., & Bjork, R. A. (1988). Measures of memory. *Annual Review of Psychology, 39,* 475–543.

Richmond, W. E. (1989). *Ballad scholarship: An annotated bibliography*. New York: Garland.

Rieu, E. V. (Trans.) (1950). *Homer: The Iliad*. Harmondsworth: Penguin Books.

Riley, J. W. (1937). *The complete poetical works of James Whitcomb Riley*. Indianapolis: Bobbs-Merrill.

Robinson, G. M. (1977). Rhythmic organization in speech processing. *Journal of Experimental Psychology: Human Perception and Performance, 3*, 83–91.

Roediger, H. L. (1990). Implicit memory: Retention without remembering. *American Psychologist, 45*, 1043–1056.

Roediger, H. L., Stellon, C. C., & Tulving, E. (1977). Inhibition from part-list cues and rate of recall. *Journal of Experimental Psychology: Human Learning and Memory, 3*, 174–188.

Rogers, E. R. (1980). *The perilous hunt: Symbols in Hispanic and European balladry*. Lexington: University Press of Kentucky.

Rogoff, B. (1990). *Apprenticeship in thinking: Cognitive development in social context*. New York: Oxford University Press.

Roland, P. E., & Friberg, L. (1985). Localization of cortical areas activated by thinking. *Journal of Neurophysiology, 53*, 1219–1243.

Rollins, M. (1989). *Mental imagery: On the limits of cognitive science*. New Haven, CT: Yale University Press.

Rosch, E. (1975). Cognitive representations of semantic categories. *Journal of Experimental Psychology: General, 104*, 192–233.

Rosenberg, B. A. (1970). The formulaic quality of spontaneous sermons. *Journal of American Folklore, 83*, 3–20.

Rosenberg, B. A. (1988). *Can these bones live? The art of the American folk preacher* (rev. ed.). Urbana: University of Illinois Press.

Rothkopf, E. Z. (1971). Incidental memory for location of information in text. *Journal of Verbal Learning and Verbal Behavior, 10*, 608–613.

Rothkopf, E. Z., Fisher, D. G., & Billington, M. J. (1982). Effects of spatial context during acquisition on the recall of attributive information. *Journal of Experimental Psychology: Learning, Memory, and Cognition, 8*, 126–138.

Rotman, B. (1988). Toward a semiotics of mathematics. *Semiotica, 72*, 1–35.

Rouse, R. H., & Rouse, M. A. (1982). *Statim invenire:* Schools, preachers, and new attitudes to the page. In R. L. Benson & G. Constable (Eds.), *Renaissance and renewal in the twelfth century* (pp. 201–225). Cambridge, MA: Harvard University Press.

Rubin, D. C. (1974). The subjective estimation of relative syllable frequency. *Perception & Psychophysics, 16*, 193–196.

Rubin, D. C. (1975). Within word structure in the tip-of-the-tongue phenomenon. *Journal of Verbal Learning and Verbal Behavior, 14*, 392–397.

Rubin, D. C. (1976a). Applying psychometric methods in linguistic research: Some recent advances. *Linguistics, 168*, 63–66.

Rubin, D. C. (1976b). Frequency of occurrence as a psychophysical continuum: Weber's fraction, Ekman's fraction, range effects, and the phigamma hypothesis. *Perception & Psychophysics, 20*, 327–330.

Rubin, D. C. (1976c). The effectiveness of context before, after and around a missing word. *Perception & Psychophysics, 19*, 214–216.

Rubin, D. C. (1977). Very long-term memory for prose and verse. *Journal of Verbal Learning and Verbal Behavior, 16*, 611–621.

Rubin, D. C. (1978). A unit analysis of prose memory. *Journal of Verbal Learning and Verbal Behavior, 17*, 599–620.

Rubin, D. C. (1980). 51 properties of 125 words. *Journal of Verbal Learning and Verbal Behavior, 19,* 736–755.

Rubin, D. C. (1981). Cognitive processes and oral traditions. In D. Heartz & B. Wade (Eds.), *International Musicological Society: Report of the Twelfth Congress, Berkeley.* Kassell, Germany: Barenreiter-Verlag.

Rubin, D. C. (1982). On the retention function for autobiographical memory. *Journal of Verbal Learning and Verbal Behavior, 21,* 21–38.

Rubin, D. C. (1983). Associative asymmetry, availability, and retrieval. *Memory & Cognition, 11,* 83–92.

Rubin, D. C. (1985). Memorability as a measure of processing: A unit analysis of prose and list learning. *Journal of Experimental Psychology: General, 114,* 213–238.

Rubin, D. C. (Ed.). (1986). *Autobiographical memory.* Cambridge: Cambridge University Press.

Rubin, D. C. (1988a). Go for the skill. In U. Neisser & E. Winograd (Eds.), *Remembering reconsidered: Ecological and traditional approaches to the study of memory* (pp. 374–382). Cambridge: Cambridge University Press.

Rubin, D. C. (1988b). Learning poetic language. In F. S. Kessel (Ed.), *The development of language and language researchers: Essays in honor of Roger Brown* (pp. 339–351). Hillsdale, NJ: Erlbaum.

Rubin, D. C. (1989). Issues of regularity and control: Confessions of a regularity freak. In L. W. Poon, D. C. Rubin, & B. A. Wilson (Eds.), *Everyday cognition in adult and later life* (pp. 84–103). Cambridge: Cambridge University Press.

Rubin, D. C. (1990). Directed graphs as memory representations: The case of rhyme. In R. W. Schvaneveldt (Ed.), *Pathfinder associative networks: Studies in knowledge organization* (pp. 121–133). Norwood, NJ: Ablex.

Rubin, D. C., & Corbett, S. (1982). Adaptation-level theory and the free recall of mixed-frequency lists. *Bulletin of the Psychonomic Society, 20,* 27–29.

Rubin, D. C., & Friendly, M. (1986). Predicting which words get recalled: Measures of free recall, availability, goodness, emotionality, and pronunciability for 925 nouns. *Memory & Cognition, 14,* 79–94.

Rubin, D. C., & Kontis, T. C. (1983). A schema for common cents. *Memory & Cognition, 11,* 335–341.

Rubin, D. C., & Olson, M. J. (1980). Recall of semantic domains. *Memory & Cognition, 8,* 354–366.

Rubin, D. C., Stoltzfus, E. R., & Wall, K. L. (1991). The abstraction of form in semantic categories. *Memory & Cognition, 19,* 1–7.

Rubin, D. C., & Wallace, W. T. (1989). Rhyme and reason: Analyses of dual cues. *Journal of Experimental Psychology: Learning, Memory, and Cognition, 15,* 698–709.

Rubin, D. C., Wallace, W. T., & Houston, B. C. (1993). The beginnings of expertise for ballads. *Cognitive Science, 17,* 435–462.

Ruch, T. C. (1928). Factors influencing the relative economy of massed and distributed practice in learning. *Psychological Review, 35,* 19–45.

Rumelhart, D. E. (1975). Notes on a schema for stories. In D. G. Bobrow & A. M. Collins (Eds.), *Representation and understanding: Studies in cognitive science* (pp. 211–236). New York: Academic Press.

Rumelhart, D. E., McClelland, J. L., & PDP Research Group. (Eds.). (1986). *Parallel distributed processing: Explorations in the microstructure of cognition: Vol 1. Foundations.* Cambridge, MA: MIT Press.

Rumelhart, D. E., & Norman, D. A. (1986). Representation in memory. In R. C. Atkinson, R. J. Herrnstein, G. Lindzey, & R. D. Luce (Eds.), *Steven's handbook of experimen-*

tal psychology: Second edition: Vol. 2. Learning and cognition (pp. 511–587). New York: Wiley.

Rumelhart, D. E., Smolensky, P., McClelland, J. L., & Hinton, G. E. (1986). Schemata and sequential thought processes in PDP models. In J. L. McClelland, D. E. Rumelhart, & PDP Research Group (Eds.), *Parallel distributed processing: Explorations in the microstructure of cognition: Vol. 2. Psychological and biological models* (pp. 7–57). Cambridge, MA: MIT Press.

Russo, J. A. (1963). A closer look at Homeric formulas. *Transactions and Proceedings of the American Philological Association, 94,* 235–247.

Russo, J. A. (1976). Is "oral" or "aural" composition the cause of Homer's formulaic style? In B. A. Stolz & R. S. Shannon III (Eds.), *Oral literature and the formula* (pp. 31–71). Ann Arbor: Center for the Coordination of Ancient and Modern Studies, University of Michigan.

Ryan, J. (1969a). Grouping and short-term memory: Different means and patterns of grouping. *Quarterly Journal of Experimental Psychology, 21,* 137–147.

Ryan, J. (1969b). Temporal grouping, rehearsal and short-term memory. *Quarterly Journal of Experimental Psychology, 21,* 148–155.

Sachs, J. S. (1967). Recognition memory for syntactic and semantic aspects of connected discourse. *Perception & Psychophysics, 2,* 437–442.

Saenger, P. (1982). Silent reading: Its impact on late medieval script and society. *Viator, 13,* 367–414.

Salasoo, A., & Pisoni, D. B. (1985). Interaction of knowledge sources in spoken word identification. *Journal of Memory and Language, 24,* 210–231.

Sale, W. M. (1989). The Trojans, statistics, and Milman Parry. *Greek, Roman, and Byzantine Studies, 30,* 341–410.

Saltz, E. (1988). The role of motoric enactment (M-processing) in memory for words and sentences. In M. M. Gruneberg, P. E. Morris, & R. N. Sykes (Eds.), *Practical aspects of memory: Current research and issues: Vol 1. Memory in everyday life* (pp. 408–414). Chichester: Wiley.

Saltz, E., & Donnenwerth-Nolan, S. (1981). Does motoric imagery facilitate memory for sentences? A selective interference test. *Journal of Verbal Learning and Verbal Behavior, 20,* 332–332.

Sampson, G. (1985). *Writing systems.* Stanford, CA: Stanford University Press.

Samson, S., & Zatorre, R. J. (1991). Recognition memory for text and melody of songs after unilateral temporal lobe lesion: Evidence for dual encoding. *Journal of Experimental Psychology: Learning, Memory, and Cognition, 17,* 793–804.

Schacter, D. L. (1987). Implicit memory: History and current status. *Journal of Experimental Psychology: Learning, Memory, and Cognition, 13,* 501–518.

Schank, R. C., & Abelson, R. P. (1977). *Scripts, plans, goals and understanding: An inquiry into human knowledge structures.* Hillsdale, NJ: Erlbaum.

Schiffrin, D. (1987). *Discourse markers.* Cambridge: Cambridge University Press.

Schneider, G. E. (1967). Contrasting visuomotor functions of tectum and cortex in the golden hamster. *Psychologische Forschung, 31,* 52–62.

Schober, M. F., & Clark, H. H. (1989). Understanding by addressees and overhearers. *Cognitive Psychology, 21,* 211–232.

Schoenfeld, A. H., & Herrmann, D. J. (1982). Problem perception and knowledge structure in expert and novice mathematical problem solvers. *Journal of Experimental Psychology: Learning, Memory, and Cognition, 8,* 484–494.

Schonpflug, W. (1986). The trade-off between internal and external information storage. *Journal of Memory and Language, 25,* 657–675.

Schultz, K. A., Schmitt, F. A., Logue, P. E., & Rubin, D. C. (1986). Unit analysis of prose memory in clinical and elderly populations. *Developmental Neuropsychology, 2*, 77–87.

Schvaneveldt, R. W. (Ed.). (1990). *Pathfinder associative networks: Studies in knowledge organization*. Norwood, NJ: Ablex.

Schwanenflugel, P. J., Akin, C., & Luh, W. M. (1992). Context availability and the recall of abstract and concrete words. *Memory & Cognition, 20*, 96–104.

Schwanenflugel, P. J., & LaCount, K. L. (1988). Semantic relatedness and the scope of facilitation for upcoming words in sentences. *Journal of Experimental Psychology: Learning, Memory, and Cognition, 14*, 344–354.

Schwanenflugel, P. J., & Shoben, E. J. (1983). Differential context effects in the comprehension of abstract and concrete verbal material. *Journal of Experimental Psychology: Learning, Memory, and Cognition, 9*, 82–102.

Schwanenflugel, P. J., & Shoben, E. J. (1985). The influence of sentence constraint on the scope of facilitation for upcoming words. *Journal of Memory and Language, 24*, 232–252.

Scollon, R. (1982). The rhythmic integration of ordinary talk. In D. Tannen (Ed.), *Analyzing discourse: Text and talk* (pp. 335–349). Washington, DC: Georgetown University Press.

Scribner, S., & Cole, M. (1981). *The psychology of literacy*. Cambridge, MA: Harvard University Press.

Seamon, J. G. (1972). Imagery codes and human information retrieval. *Journal of Experimental Psychology, 96*, 468–470.

Seeley, T. D. (1989). The honey bee colony as a superorganism. *American Scientist, 77*, 546–553.

Seidenberg, M. S., & Tanenhaus, M. K. (1979). Orthographic effects on rhyme monitoring. *Journal of Experimental Psychology: Human Learning and Memory, 5*, 546–554.

Serafine, M. L. (1983). Cognition in music. *Cognition, 14*, 119–183.

Serafine, M. L., Crowder, R. G., & Repp, B. H. (1984). Integration of melody and text in memory for songs. *Cognition, 16*, 285–303.

Serafine, M. L., Davidson, J., Crowder, R. G., & Repp, B. H. (1986). On the nature of melody–text integration in memory for songs. *Journal of Memory and Language, 25*, 123–135.

Shannon, C. E., & Weaver, W. (1949). *The mathematical theory of communication*. Urbana: University of Illinois Press.

Sharp, C. J. (1908). *English folk-song: Some conclusions*. London: Simpkin.

Shaw, M. E. (1964). Communication networks. In L. Berkowitz (Ed.), *Advances in experimental social psychology* (Vol. 1, pp. 111–147). New York: Academic Press.

Sheingold, K., & Foundas, A. (1978). Rhymes for some reasons: Effect of rhyme on children's memory for detail and sequence in simple narratives. *Psychological Reports, 43*, 1231–1234.

Shepard, R. N. (1978). The mental image. *American Psychologist, 33*, 125–137.

Shepard, R. N., & Metzler, J. (1971). Mental rotation of three-dimensional objects. *Science, 171*, 701–703.

Shimron, J. (1993). The role of vowels in reading: A review of studies of English and Hebrew. *Psychological Bulletin, 114*, 52–67.

Shive, D. (1987). *Naming Achilles*. New York: Oxford University Press.

Sifakis, G. M. (1992). Homeric survivals in the mediaeval and modern Greek folksong tradition? *Greece & Rome, 39*, 139–154.

Simon, H. A. (1962). The architecture of complexity. *Proceedings of the American Philosophical Society, 106*, 467–482. (Reprinted in H. A. Simon, *The Sciences of the artificial* [2nd ed.]. Cambridge, MA: MIT Press, 1981)

Simons, E. L. (1989). Human origins. *Science, 245*, 1343–1350.

Singer, M. (1980). The role of case-filling inferences in the coherence of brief passages. *Discourse Processes, 3*, 185–201.

Singley, M. K., & Anderson, J. R. (1989). *The transfer of cognitive skill*. Cambridge, MA: Harvard University Press.

Sinnott, J. D. (1989). General systems theory: A rationale for the study of everyday memory. In L. W. Poon, D. C. Rubin, & B. A. Wilson (Eds.), *Everyday cognition in adult and later life* (pp. 59–70). Cambridge: Cambridge University Press.

Skinner, B. F. (1939). The alliteration in Shakespeare's sonnets: A study in literary behavior. *Psychological Record, 3*, 186–192.

Skinner, B. F. (1942). A quantitative estimate of certain types of sound-patterning in poetry. *American Journal of Psychology, 30*, 64–79.

Skinner, B. F. (1974). *About behaviorism*. New York: Knopf.

Slamecka, N. J. (1966). Differentiation versus unlearning of verbal associations. *Journal of Experimental Psychology, 71*, 822–828.

Slamecka, N. J. (1968). An examination of trace storage in free recall. *Journal of Experimental Psychology, 76*, 504–513.

Slamecka, N. J. (1969). Testing for associative storage in free recall. *Journal of Experimental Psychology, 81*, 557–560.

Slamecka, N. J., & McElree, B. (1983). Normal forgetting of verbal lists as a function of their degree of learning. *Journal of Experimental Psychology: Learning, Memory, and Cognition, 9*, 384–397.

Sloboda, J. A. (1977). Phrase units as determinants of visual processing in music reading. *British Journal of Psychology, 68*, 117–124.

Sloboda, J. A. (1985). *The musical mind: The cognitive psychology of music*. Oxford: Clarendon Press.

Smith, B. H. (1968). *Poetic closure: A study of how poems end*. Chicago: University of Chicago Press.

Smith, B. H. (1978). *On the margins of discourse: The relation of literature to language*. Chicago: University of Chicago Press.

Smith, B. H. (1985). *Contingencies of value: Alternative perspectives for critical theory*. Cambridge, MA: Harvard University Press.

Smith, D. A., & Graesser, A. C. (1981). Memory for actions in scripted activities as a function of typicality, retention interval, and retrieval tasks. *Memory & Cognition, 9*, 550–559.

Smith, J. D. (1977). The singer or the song? A reassessment of Lord's "Oral Theory." *Man, 12*, 141–153.

Smith, M. U. (1990). Knowledge structures and the nature of expertise in classical genetics. *Cognition and Instruction, 7*, 287–302.

Smith, S. M., & Rothkopf, E. Z. (1984). Contextual enrichment and distribution of practice in the classroom. *Cognition and Instruction, 1*, 341–358.

Snodgrass, J. G., Burns, P. M., & Pirone, G. V. (1978). Pictures and words and space and time: In search of the elusive interaction. *Journal of Experimental Psychology: General, 107*, 206–230.

Sokolowski, R. (1988, Winter). Natural and artificial intelligence. *Deadalus*, pp. 45–64.

Solso, R. L., & Biersdorff, K. K. (1975). Recall under conditions of cumulative cues. *Journal of General Psychology, 93*, 233–246.

St. John, M. F. (1992). The story gestalt: A model of knowledge-intensive processes in text comprehension. *Cognitive Science, 16,* 271–306.

Staddon, J. E. R. (1981). On a possible relation between cultural transmission and genetical evolution. In P. P. G. Bateson & P. H. Klopfer (Eds.), *Advantages of diversity* (Vol. 4, pp. 135–145). New York: Plenum.

Stadler, M. A. (1993). Implicit serial learning: Questions inspired by Hebb (1961). *Memory & Cognition, 21,* 819–827.

Stanford, W. B. (1969). Euphonic reasons for the choice of Homeric formulae? *Hermathena, 58,* 15–17.

Stanley, K. (1993). *The shield of Homer: Narrative structure in the Iliad.* Princeton, NJ: Princeton University Press.

Staszewski, J. J. (1990). Exceptional memory: The influence of practice and knowledge on the development of elaborative encoding strategies. In W. Schneider & F. E. Weinert (Eds.), *Interactions among aptitudes, strategies, and knowledge in cognitive performance* (pp. 252–285). New York: Springer-Verlag.

Stewart, G. R., Jr. (1925). The meter of the popular ballad. *Publications of the Modern Language Association of America, 40,* 933–962.

Stine, E. A. L., & Wingfield, A. (1990). The assessment of qualitative age differences in discourse processing. In T. M. Hess (Ed.), *Aging and cognition: Knowledge organization and utilization* (pp. 33–92). Amsterdam: North-Holland.

Stoltzfus, E. R. (1992). *Aging and breadth of availability during language processing.* Unpublished doctoral dissertation, Duke University, Durham, NC.

Stoltzfus, E. R., Hasher, L., & Zacks, R. (1992, November). *Semantic priming during language processing: Several failures to replicate.* Paper presented at the annual meeting of the Psychonomic Society, St. Louis.

Street, B. V. (1984). *Literacy in theory and practice.* Cambridge: Cambridge University Press.

Stuss, D. T., Sarazin, F. F., Leech, E. E., & Picton, T. W. (1983). Event-related potentials during naming and mental rotation. *Electroencephalography and Clinical Neurophysiology, 56,* 133–146.

Suci, G. J. (1967). The validity of pause as an index of units in language. *Journal of Verbal Learning and Verbal Behavior, 6,* 26–32.

Sutton-Smith, B. (1953). *The historical and psychological significance of the unorganized games of New Zealand primary school children.* Unpublished doctoral dissertation, University of New Zealand, Wellington.

Sutton-Smith, B. (1959). *The games of New Zealand children.* Berkeley: University of California Press.

Sutton-Smith, B., & Rosenberg, B. G. (1961). Sixty years of historical change in the game preference of American children. *Journal of American Folklore, 74,* 17–46.

Tabossi, P. (1988). Effects of context on the immediate interpretation of unambiguous nouns. *Journal of Experimental Psychology: Learning, Memory, and Cognition, 14,* 153–162.

Takezawa, K. (1981). Rhythm rule in metrical theory. *Linguistic Analysis, 8,* 1–14.

Tanenhaus, M. K., & Carlson, G. N. (1989). Lexical structure and language comprehension. In W. Marslen-Wilson (Ed.), *Lexical representation and process* (pp. 529–561). Cambridge, MA: MIT Press.

Tannen, D. (Ed.). (1982). *Spoken and written language: Exploring orality and literacy.* Norwood, NJ: Ablex.

Tannen, D. (1987). Repetition in conversation as spontaneous formulaicity. *Text, 7,* 215–243.

Tannen, D. (1988). The commingling of orality and literacy in giving a paper at a scholarly conference. *American Speech, 63*, 34–43.

Tannen, D. (1989). *Talking voices: Repetition, dialogue, and imagery in conversational discourse*. New York: Cambridge University Press.

Taylor, H. A., & Tversky, B. (1992). Spatial mental models derived from survey and route descriptions. *Journal of Memory and Language, 31*, 261–292.

Taylor, I. K., & Taylor, M. M. (1965). Another look at phonetic symbolism. *Psychological Bulletin, 64*, 413–427.

Thelen, E. (1981). Rhythmic behavior in infancy: An ethological perspective. *Developmental Psychology, 17*, 237–257.

Thompson, C. P., Wenger, S. K., & Bartling, C. A. (1978). How recall facilitates subsequent recall: A reappraisal. *Journal of Experimental Psychology: Human Learning and Memory, 4*, 210–221.

Thorndyke, P. W. (1977). Cognitive structures in comprehension and memory of narrative discourse. *Cognitive Psychology, 9*, 77–110.

Thorndyke, P. W., & Hayes-Roth, B. (1979). The use of schemata in the acquisition and transfer of knowledge. *Cognitive Psychology, 11*, 82–106.

Thorndyke, P. W., & Yekovich, F. R. (1980). A critique of schema-based theories of human story memory. *Poetics, 9*, 23–49.

Tippett, L. J. (1992). The generation of visual images: A review of neuropsychological research and theory. *Psychological Bulletin, 112*, 415–432.

Tomasello, M., Kruger, A. C., & Ratner, H. H. (1993). Cultural learning. *Behavioral and Brain Sciences, 16*, 495–552.

Trabasso, T., & Sperry, L. L. (1985). Causal relatedness and importance of story events. *Journal of Memory and Language, 24*, 595–611.

Trabasso, T., & van den Broek, P. (1985). Causal thinking and the representation of narrative events. *Journal of Memory and Language, 24*, 612–630.

Treitler, L. (1974). Homer and Gregory: The transmission of epic poetry and plainchant. *Music Quarterly, 60*, 333–372.

Treitler, L. (1981). Oral, written, and literate processes in the transmission of medieval music. *Speculum, 56*, 471–491.

Trevarthen, C. B. (1968). Two mechanisms of vision in primates. *Psychologische Forschung, 31*, 299–337.

Tulving, E. (1962). Subjective organization in free recall of "unrelated" words. *Psychological Review, 9*, 344–354.

Tulving, E. (1985). How many memory systems are there? *American Psychologist, 40*, 385–398.

Tulving, E., & Psotka, J. (1971). Retroactive inhibition in free recall: Inaccessibility of information available in the memory store. *Journal of Experimental Psychology, 87*, 1–8.

Tulving, E., & Schacter, D. L. (1990). Priming and human memory systems. *Science, 247*, 301–306.

Tulving, E., & Thomson, D. M. (1973). Encoding specificity and retrieval processes in episodic memory. *Psychological Review, 80*, 352–373.

Turner, F. (1985). *Natural classicism: Essays on literature and science*. New York: Paragon House.

Turvey, M. T., Brick, P., & Osborn, J. (1970). Proactive interference in short–term memory as a function of prior-item retention interval. *Quarterly Journal of Experimental Psychology, 22*, 142–147.

Tye, M. (1991). *The imagery debate*. Cambridge, MA: MIT Press.

Tzeng, O. J. L., & Wang, W. S.-Y. (1983). The first two r's. *American Scientist, 71,* 238–243.

Ullman, B. L. (1969). *Ancient writing and its influence.* Cambridge, MA: MIT Press. (Original work published 1932)

Underwood, B. J. (1957). Interference and forgetting. *Psychological Review, 64,* 49–59.

Underwood, B. J. (1961). Ten years of massed practice on distributed practice. *Psychological Review, 68,* 229–247.

Underwood, B. J. (1964). Degree of learning and the measurement of forgetting. *Journal of Verbal Learning and Verbal Behavior, 3,* 112–129.

Underwood, B. J. (1965). False recognition produced by implicit verbal responses. *Journal of Experimental Psychology, 70,* 122–129.

Underwood, B. J. (1966). *Experimental psychology* (2nd ed.). New York: Appleton-Century-Crofts.

Underwood, B. J. (1969). Attributes of memory. *Psychological Review, 76,* 559–573.

Underwood, B. J., & Ekstrand, B. R. (1966). An analysis of some shortcomings in the interference theory of forgetting. *Psychological Review, 73,* 540–549.

Ungerleider, L. G., & Mishkin, M. (1982). Two cortical visual systems. In D. J. Ingle, M. A. Goodale, & R. J. W. Mansfield (Eds.), *Analysis of visual behavior* (pp. 549–586). Cambridge, MA: MIT Press.

van den Broek, P. (1990). The causal inference maker: Towards a process model of inference generation in text comprehension. In D. A. Balota, G. B. Flores d'Arcais, & K. Rayner (Eds.), *Comprehension processes in reading* (pp. 423–445). Hillside, NJ: Erlbaum.

van den Broek, P. (1994). Comprehension and memory of narrative texts: Inferences and coherence. In M. A. Gernsbacher (Ed.), *Handbook of psycholinguistics* (pp. 539–588). San Diego, CA: Academic Press.

Van Peer, W. (1988). Counting out: Form and function of children's counting-out rhymes. In M. MacLure, T. Phillips, & A. Wilkinson (Eds.), *Oracy matters: The development of talking and listening in education* (pp. 174–181). Milton Keynes, England: Open University Press.

Vikis-Freibergs, V. (1984). Creativity and tradition in oral folklore or the balance of innovation and repetition in the oral poets art. In W. R. Crozier & A. J. Chapman (Eds.), *Cognitive processes in the perception of art* (pp. 325–343). Amsterdam: Elsevier.

Visser, E. (1988). Formulae or single words? Towards a new theory on Homeric verse-making. *Würzburger Jahrbücher für die Altertumswissenschaft, Neue Folge, 14,* 21–37.

von Bertalanffy, L. (1968). *Organismic psychology and systems theory.* Worcester, MA: Clark University Press.

von Sydow, C. W. (1965). Folktale studies and philology: Some points of view. In A. Dundes (Ed.), *The study of folklore* (pp. 219–242). Englewood Cliffs, NJ: Prentice-Hall. (Original work published 1948)

Wallace, W. T. (1992). *The generation of a new ballad: Evidence of characteristic knowledge.* Unpublished manuscript, Duke University, Durham, NC.

Wallace, W. T. (1994). Memory for music: Effect of melody on recall of text. *Journal of Experimental Psychology: Learning, Memory, and Cognition, 20,* 1471–1485.

Wallace, W. T., & Rubin, D. C. (1988a). Memory of a ballad singer. In M. M. Gruenberg, P. E. Morris, & R. N. Sykes (Eds.), *Practical aspects of memory: Current research and issues: Vol. 1. Memory in everyday life* (pp. 257–262). Chichester: Wiley.

Wallace, W. T., & Rubin, D. C. (1988b). "The wreck of the old 97": A real event remembered in song. In U. Neisser & E. Winograd (Eds.), *Remembering reconsidered:*

Ecological and traditional approaches to the study of memory (pp. 283–310). Cambridge: Cambridge University Press.

Wallace, W. T., & Rubin, D. C. (1991). Characteristics and constraints in ballads and their effects on memory. *Discourse Processes, 14*, 181–202.

Wanner, E. (1968). *On remembering, forgetting and understanding sentences.* The Hague: Mouton.

Wanner, E. (1988). The parser's architecture. In F. S. Kessel (Ed.), *The development of language and language researchers: Essays in honor of Roger Brown* (pp. 79–96). Hillsdale, NJ: Erlbaum.

Ward, T. B. (1994). Structured imagination: The role of category structure in exemplar generation. *Cognitive Psychology, 27*, 1–40.

Warner, A. (1984). *Traditional American folk songs from the Anne and Frank Warner collection.* Syracuse, NY: Syracuse University Press.

Warr, P. B. (1964). The relative importance of proactive inhibition and degree of learning in retention of paired associate items. *British Journal of Psychology, 55*, 19–30.

Watkins, C. (1963). Indo-European metrics and archaic Irish verse. *Celtica, 6*, 194–249.

Watkins, M. J. (1979). Engrams as cuegrams and forgetting as cue overload: A cueing approach to the structure of memory. In C. R. Puff (Ed.), *Memory organization and structure* (pp. 347–372). New York: Academic Press.

Watkins, M. J. (1990). Mediationism and the obfuscation of memory. *American Psychologist, 45*, 328–335.

Watkins, O. C., & Watkins, M. J. (1975). Buildup of proactive inhibition as cue-overload effect. *Journal of Experimental Psychology: Human Learning and Memory, 104*, 442–452.

Watson, M. E. (1994). *Object and spatial subsystems in mental imagery: Behavioral investigations.* Unpublished doctoral dissertation, Duke University, Durham, NC.

Weiner, B. (1966). Effects of motivation on the availability and retrieval of memory traces. *Psychological Bulletin, 65*, 24–37.

Weir, R. H. (1962). *Language in the crib.* The Hague: Mouton.

Wesling, D. (1980). *The chances of rhyme: Device and modernity.* Berkeley: University of California Press.

White, N. I. (Gen. Ed.). (1952). *The Frank C. Brown collection of North Carolina folklore* (Vols. 1–7). Durham, NC: Duke University Press.

Whitehurst, G. J., Ironsmith, M., & Goldfein, M. (1974). Selective imitation of the passive construction through modeling. *Journal of Experimental Child Psychology, 17*, 288–302.

Whiting, B. J. (1955). *Traditional British ballads.* New York: Appleton-Century-Crofts.

Wickens, D. D. (1970). Encoding categories of words: An empirical approach to meaning. *Psychological Review, 77*, 1–15.

Wijers, A. A., Otten, L. J., Feenstra, S., Mulder, G., & Mulder, L. J. M. (1989). Brain potentials during selective attention, memory search, and mental rotation. *Psychophysiology, 26*, 452–466.

Wilkins, W. (1988). *Syntax and semantics: Vol. 21. Thematic relations.* San Diego, CA: Academic Press.

Williams, J. M. G., & Dritschel, B. H. (1988). Emotional disturbance and the specificity of autobiographical memory. *Cognition and Emotion, 2*, 221–234.

Wills, G. (1992). *Lincoln at Gettysburg: The words that remade America.* New York: Simon and Schuster.

Wilson, S. G., Rinck, M., McNamara, T. P., Bower, G. H., & Morrow, D. G. (1993).

Mental models and narrative comprehension: Some qualifications. *Journal of Memory and Language, 32,* 141–154.

Winner, E. (1982). *Invented worlds: The psychology of the arts.* Cambridge, MA: Harvard University Press.

Winograd, E., & Church, V. E. (1988). Role of spatial location in learning face–name associations. *Memory & Cognition, 16,* 1–7.

Winograd, E., & Neisser, U. (Eds.). (1992). *Affect and accuracy in recall: Studies of "flashbulb" memories.* Cambridge: Cambridge University Press.

Wixted, J. T., & Ebbesen, E. B. (1991). On the form of forgetting. *Psychological Science, 2,* 409–415.

Woodworth, R. S. (1938). *Experimental psychology.* New York: Holt.

Wright, P. (1989). Interface alternatives for hypertext. *Hypermedia, 1,* 146–166.

Yates, F. A. (1966). *The art of memory.* Chicago: University of Chicago Press.

Zajonc, R. B. (1968). Attitudinal effects of mere exposure. *Journal of Personality and Social Psychology Monograph Supplement, 9,* 1–27.

Zatorre, R. J. (1985). Discrimination and recognition of tonal melodies after unilateral cerebral excisions. *Neuropsychologia, 23,* 31–41.

Zechmeister, E. B., & McKillip, J. (1972). Recall of place on the page. *Journal of Educational Psychology, 63,* 446–453.

Zeki, S. (1993). *A vision of the brain.* Oxford: Blackwell Scientific.

Zimmer, H. D. (1991). Memory after motoric encoding in a generation-recognition model. *Psychological Research, 53,* 226–231.

Ziven, G. (1976). Developmental aspects of rhythm in self-regulation. In K. F. Riegel & J. A. Meacham (Eds.), *The developing individual in a changing world* (Vol. 1, pp. 161–171). The Hague: Mouton.

Zwicky, A. M. (1976). Well, this rock and roll has got to stop. Junior's head is as hard as a rock. In S. S. Mufwene, C. A. Walker, & S. B. Steever (Eds.), *Papers from the Twelfth Regional Meeting, Chicago Linguistic Society* (pp. 676–697). Chicago: Chicago Linguistic Society.

Zwicky, A. M. (1986). Linguistics and the study of folk poetry. In P. C. Bjarkman and V. Raskin (Eds.), *The real-world linguist: Linguistic applications in the 1980s* (pp. 57–73). Norwood, NJ: Ablex.

AUTHOR INDEX

SUBJECT INDEX